Windows Vista™
Inside Out

Ed Bott
Carl Siechert
Craig Stinson

Published by
Microsoft Press
A Division of Microsoft Corporation
One Microsoft Way
Redmond, Washington 98052-6399
Copyright © 2007 by Microsoft Corporation

Library of Congress Control Number: 2006938200

Printed and bound in the United States of America.

1 2 3 4 5 6 7 8 9   QWT   2 1 0 9 8 7

Distributed in Canada by H.B. Fenn and Company Ltd.

A CIP catalogue record for this book is available from the British Library.

Microsoft Press books are available through booksellers and distributors worldwide. For further information about international editions, contact your local Microsoft Corporation office or contact Microsoft Press International directly at fax (425) 936-7329. Visit our Web site at www.microsoft.com/mspress. Send comments to mspinput@microsoft.com.

Acquisitions Editor: Juliana Aldous Atkinson
Project Editor: Sandra Haynes
Editorial Production Services: Custom Editorial Productions, Inc.
Body Part No. X12-48756

Dedicated to the memory of Charles Bott (1932-2006) and Ruth Siechert (1919–2006), and to our families, for their unceasing love and support.

— Ed Bott, Carl Siechert, and Craig Stinson

Contents at a Glance

Part IV System Maintenance and Management

Part V Advanced System Management

Part VI Appendices

Table of Contents

What do you think of this book? We want to hear from you!

Microsoft is interested in hearing your feedback so we can continually improve our books and learning resources for you. To participate in a brief online survey, please visit:

www.microsoft.com/learning/booksurvey/

Part III Digital Media

Part IV System Maintenance and Management

Appendices

What do you think of this book? We want to hear from you!

Microsoft is interested in hearing your feedback so we can continually improve our books and learning resources for you. To participate in a brief online survey, please visit:

www.microsoft.com/learning/booksurvey/

Acknowledgments

We began work on this project more than three years ago. Given that much time, you'd think we'd be more self reliant, but we could not have finished it without the help of many people.

We met and exchanged e-mail messages with dozens of developers and technical professionals at Microsoft. We extend special thanks to Julie Nowicki, Charlie Owen, Rob Franco, Sriram Subramanian, Kam Vedbrat, James Finnigan, and the prolific community of Microsoft bloggers, who answered questions and provided technical guidance for us. Thanks go also to the engineers who analyzed our bug reports and helped make sure those bugs didn't end up in the code we're running today.

Our partners and collaborators at Microsoft Press have earned our admiration and gratitude through every step of this long journey: Juliana Aldous, product planner; Sandra Haynes, content development manager; Lynn Finnel, project editor; and, of course, our unflappable publisher, Lucinda Rowley. Working with Microsoft Press, Asa Noriega spearheaded development of the companion CD.

The production team worked miracles under extremely tight deadlines to turn our words and figures into printed pages. Our sincere thanks and appreciation to our always cheerful project editor, Megan Smith-Creed.

Technical editor Ben Smith read every manuscript page and offered valuable input. Our colleague Steve Suehring pitched in to help with some much-needed updates on three chapters. Thanks, gentlemen.

As always, we relied on the guidance and support of Claudette Moore and Ann Jaroncyk of Moore Literary Agency. And we were lucky to have the support of friends and family, especially our long-suffering spouses Judy Bott, Jan Siechert, and Jean Stinson, who have been asking for three years, "When are you going to finish that book?" We can now proudly say, it's finished.

Thank you, one and all.

Ed Bott, Carl Siechert, Craig Stinson

December 2006

Conventions and Features Used in This Book

This book uses special text and design conventions to make it easier for you to find the information you need.

Text Conventions

Convention	Meaning
Abbreviated commands for navigating the Ribbon	For your convenience, this book uses abbreviated commands. For example, "Click Home, Insert, Insert Cells" means that you should click the Home tab on the Ribbon, then click the Insert button, and finally click the Insert Cells command.
Boldface type	**Boldface** type is used to indicate text that you type.
Initial Capital Letters	The first letters of the names of tabs, dialog boxes, dialog box elements, and commands are capitalized. Example: the Save As dialog box.
Italicized type	*Italicized* type is used to indicate new terms.
Plus sign (+) in text	Keyboard shortcuts are indicated by a plus sign (+) separating two key names. For example, Ctrl+Alt+Delete means that you press the Ctrl, Alt, and Delete keys at the same time.

Design Conventions

INSIDE OUT

These are the book's signature tips. In these tips, you'll get the straight scoop on what's going on with the software—inside information about why a feature works the way it does. You'll also find handy workarounds to deal with software problems.

Sidebars

Sidebars provide helpful hints, timesaving tricks, or alternative procedures related to the task being discussed.

TROUBLESHOOTING

Look for these sidebars to find solutions to common problems you might encounter. Troubleshooting sidebars appear next to related information in the chapters.

Cross-references point you to other locations in the book that offer additional information about the topic being discussed.

CAUTION

Cautions identify potential problems that you should look out for when you're completing a task or problems that you must address before you can complete a task.

Note

Notes offer additional information related to the task being discussed.

About the CD

The companion CD that ships with this book contains many tools and resources to help you get the most out of your Inside Out book.

What's on the CD

Your Inside Out CD includes the following:

- Downloadable gadgets and other tools to help you customize Windows Vista
- Microsoft resources to help keep your computer up-to-date and protected
- Insights direct from the product team on the official Windows Vista blog
- Links to product demos, expert's blogs, user communities, and product support
- **Additional eBooks** In this section you'll find the entire electronic version of this book along with the following fully searchable eBooks:
  - Microsoft Computer Dictionary, Fifth Edition
  - First Look 2007 Microsoft Office System (Katherine Murray, 2006)
- Sample chapter and poster from *Look Both Ways: Help Protect Your Family on the Internet* (Linda Criddle, 2007)
- Windows Vista Product Guide

System Requirements

The following are the minimum system requirements necessary to run the CD:

- Microsoft Windows Vista, Windows XP with Service Pack (SP) 2, Windows Server 2003 with SP1, or newer operating system
- 500 megahertz (MHz) processor or higher
- 2 gigabyte (GB) storage space (a portion of this disk space will be freed after installation if the original download package is removed from the hard drive)
- 256 megabytes (MB) RAM
- CD-ROM or DVD-ROM drive
- 1024×768 or higher resolution monitor
- Microsoft Windows or Windows Vista–compatible sound card and speakers
- Microsoft Internet Explorer 6 or newer
- Microsoft Mouse or compatible pointing device

> **Note**
> An Internet connection is necessary to access the hyperlinks on the companion CD. Connect time charges may apply.

Support Information

Every effort has been made to ensure the accuracy of the contents of the book and of this CD. As corrections or changes are collected, they will be added to a Microsoft Knowledge Base article. Microsoft Press provides support for books and companion CDs at the following Web site:

http://www.microsoft.com/learning/support/books/

If you have comments, questions, or ideas regarding the book or this CD, or questions that are not answered by visiting the site above, please send them via e-mail to:

mspinput@microsoft.com

You can also click the Feedback or CD Support links on the Welcome page. Please note that Microsoft software product support is not offered through the above addresses.

If your question is about the software, and not about the content of this book, please visit the Microsoft Help and Support page or the Microsoft Knowledge Base at:

http://support.microsoft.com

In the United States, Microsoft software product support issues not covered by the Microsoft Knowledge Base are addressed by Microsoft Product Support Services. Location-specific software support options are available from:

http://support.microsoft.com/gp/selfoverview/

Microsoft Press provides corrections for books through the World Wide Web at *http://www.microsoft.com/mspress/support/*. To connect directly to the Microsoft Press Knowledge Base and enter a query regarding a question or issue that you may have, go to *http://www.microsoft.com/mspress/support/search.htm*.

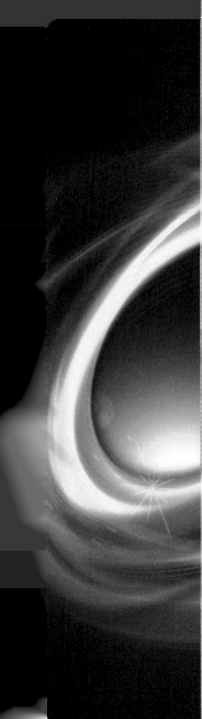

PART I
Setup and Startup

CHAPTER 1

What's New in Windows Vista

Home Basic ●
Home Premium ●
Business ●
Enterprise ●
Ultimate ●

Technically, Windows Vista is just the latest in a long line of business-class operating systems that started with Windows NT more than a decade ago. Practically, the changes in this new member of the Windows family are equal parts evolution and revolution.

In some ways, that's not surprising. The gap between Windows XP and Windows Vista spanned more than five years. In operating system terms, that's two generations. So it's not surprising that Windows Vista incorporates a broad swath of platform pieces and infrastructure, including sweeping changes to networking and security, support for new classes of hardware, new capabilities for creating and playing digital media, and a distinctive new interface.

In this chapter, we briefly introduce the new and notable features and capabilities in Windows Vista.

What's in Your Edition?

Because Windows Vista has been sliced, diced, and packaged into at least five distinct editions, it's possible that some of the features and capabilities we describe in this book will be unavailable on your computer. At the beginning of each chapter, we've included two elements to help you sort out where your edition fits in. A sidebar box like this one, typically placed on the opening page, summarizes the differences in each edition, as they relate to the content of that chapter. The banner along the top of each chapter's opening page lists the five mainstream editions with a graphic representation of how each edition measures up with the features in that chapter. A filled-in circle (●) means all features are available in your edition; a half-filled circle (◐) means some features are missing outright or are only partially implemented; an empty circle (○) means the features and capabilities in that chapter are completely unavailable with the designated edition.

Introducing the Windows Vista Family

Windows Vista is available in four retail versions and one corporate edition, all available worldwide, along with a handful of specialized versions tailored to specific markets. Although at first glance that might seem like too many choices, there's actually a solid rationale behind the mix of products. Here's a brief introduction to each member of the Windows Vista family (for a more detailed look at what features are included with each edition, see Appendix A, "Windows Vista Editions at a Glance.")

- **Windows Vista Home Basic** This entry-level edition, the successor to Windows XP Home Edition, includes the core elements of the new Windows Vista interface, notably Internet Explorer 7, Windows Media Player 11, Windows Movie Maker, and Windows Mail. It's perfectly suited for simple e-mail and web browsing, and it runs most programs written for Windows Vista. It rips and burns CDs (but not DVDs), and it works well on a simple home or small business network. Using Windows Vista Home Basic, you're limited to either the Windows Vista Standard interface or the Windows Vista Basic interface.

- **Windows Vista Home Premium** As the name suggests, this edition includes all the features found in Windows Vista Home Basic, plus the noteworthy addition of the Windows Vista Aero user experience and Windows Media Center features. (For all practical purposes, this is the successor to Windows XP Media Center Edition.) It also adds support for Tablet PC features (assuming you have compatible hardware), a more robust Backup program, the ability to create and edit DVDs, and support for high-definition content in Windows Movie Maker.

- **Windows Vista Business** Like its predecessor, Windows XP Professional, this edition is designed for use in the workplace. Using Windows Vista Business, you can connect to a corporate domain, create image-based backups, encrypt files, host a Remote Desktop session, take full advantage of Tablet PC features, and use roaming user profiles—to name just a few of its many business-oriented features. Although this edition offers basic multimedia capabilities, such as the ability to play video clips and music CDs, it doesn't include Windows DVD Maker, or Windows Media Center.

- **Windows Vista Enterprise** This edition is not for sale through retail channels and is available only to corporate and institutional customers through Volume Licensing programs. It's essentially identical to Windows Vista Business, with the addition of Windows BitLocker drive encryption, support for multiple languages in the Windows user interface, and additional licenses that allow you to run up to four additional copies of Windows Vista using Virtual PC 2007.

- **Windows Vista Ultimate** The most expansive (and expensive) retail edition of Windows Vista combines all the features found in the other editions. Thus, it includes Media Center features, just like Windows Vista Home Premium, and support for multiple physical CPUs and the Volume Shadow Service, just like Windows Vista Business. It also includes access to a suite of premium products and services called Ultimate Extras.

If you decide that you need a more potent Windows Vista version than the one you're currently running, you can take advantage of a new feature called Anytime Upgrade to purchase an upgrade license. The process uses your existing installation media to perform an in-place upgrade that preserves data and settings.

> **Note**
>
> Did we say there are five editions of Windows Vista? We left out a few. For openers, you can double the entire list by counting the 32-bit and 64-bit versions of each one separately. In addition, you'll find Windows Vista editions in South Korea and the European Community that have had key features removed in response to antitrust actions; in both locales, for example, Microsoft makes Windows available for sale in editions that don't include Windows Media Player. Finally, in emerging markets only, you can purchase Windows Vista Starter Edition preinstalled on new hardware. This variation of Windows Vista is limited in its feature set and capabilities and sells at a dramatically lower price than its full-featured siblings.

For a detailed inventory of what features and capabilities are available in each Windows Vista edition, see Appendix A, "Windows Vista Editions at a Glance."

The Windows Vista Interface: Up Close and Personalized

When you first start Windows Vista, you're greeted with the Welcome Center, which contains information about your current configuration, shortcuts to common tasks, and offers from Microsoft. Clicking the Show More Details link leads to the System dialog box, shown in Figure 1-1, which includes a more detailed look at system information, shortcuts to system configuration tools, and a performance rating called the Windows Experience Index.

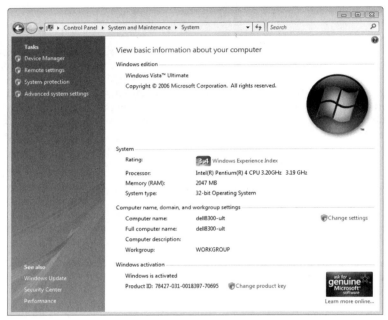

Figure 1-1 The System Control Panel provides a detailed look at current configuration and performance details. Click the Windows Experience Index link to break down the overall performance rating by component.

If you've grown accustomed to the Windows XP interface, prepare to make a few adjustments. Most of the basic elements are still present but have been redesigned for Windows Vista. The word *Start*, for instance, no longer appears on the Start menu, and the All Programs menu now slides smoothly up and down instead of flying out to the right. Buttons on the taskbar have a more rounded appearance, with soft color gradients. The new Sidebar allows you to customize your display with gadgets—a clock, calendar, stock ticker, search boxes, and so on—that can remain within the sidebar itself or can be torn off to float on the desktop. Figure 1-2 shows a typical desktop display.

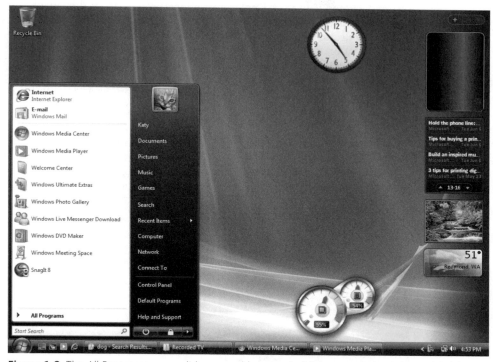

Figure 1-2 The All Programs menu slides smoothly instead of flying out to the right, and Sidebar gadgets add information and entertainment to the desktop.

The Control Panel has been extensively redesigned in Windows Vista to use a series of well-organized, task-oriented pages instead of bare categories. The Personalization page, for instance, puts display settings, window colors, the desktop background, screen savers, sounds, and more in a single location.

The appearance of those interface elements varies as well. If you have a premium or business version of Windows Vista and a sufficiently muscular display adapter, you get the Aero User Experience (Aero is actually an acronym for Authentic, Energetic, Reflective, and Open). The added visuals include translucent window frames, smooth animations, live thumbnail previews that appear when you hover the mouse pointer over taskbar buttons, and a new Flip 3D task switcher (Windows logo key+Tab) that cycles through open windows in a three-dimensional stack.

For more details about customizing the Windows user interface, see Chapter 3, "Personalizing Windows Vista."

Searching, Sharing, and Other File Management Tasks

The redesigned Windows Explorer provides a much richer display of information about files and folders. It also changes just about every organizational element from its predecessor. By default, Explorer windows have no menus, and a Favorite Links list is pinned to a Navigation Pane along the left side, above the tree-style Folders list. To navigate through a folder hierarchy, you use a "breadcrumb bar" at the top of the window, and the display of files can be filtered or arranged in stacks using values in each field. The contents pane shows live thumbnails, where appropriate, and an optional preview pane allows you to look more closely at image files, Microsoft Office documents, and e-mail messages without leaving the Explorer window.

A robust, well-integrated search capability is built into Windows Vista. By default, all locations containing data files are indexed, as are e-mail messages, music tracks, and ratings or tags you apply to digital photos and videos. For simple searches, you can type directly into the Search bar in the top right corner of an Explorer window. For more complex searches, use the Advanced Search pane. Figure 1-3 shows the results of a search, using the Medium Icons view.

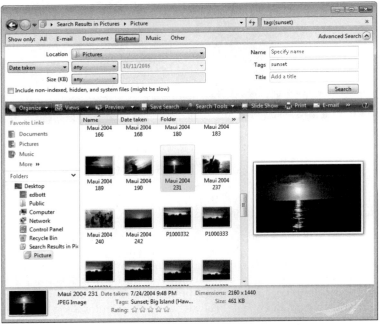

Figure 1-3 The Preview pane (right) shows a larger view of the selected file. The Details Pane (bottom) includes user-generated metadata in the Tags and Rating fields.

To learn more about file management and desktop search capabilities, see Chapter 7, "Finding and Organizing Files and Information."

Windows Vista Security at a Glance

Improved security is on display just about anywhere you go in Windows Vista. The basics of the security model are unchanged from Windows XP: as an administrator, you create individual user accounts whose assigned permissions control access to various parts of the operating system, the file system, and network resources. But specific implementations of security features are dramatically changed.

The most visible change is User Account Control, a new feature that requires explicit permission from a local administrator before Windows will accept changes to protected system settings. When you initiate any action that requires administrative permissions—as indicated by a small shield overlaying a program icon or Control Panel shortcut—the display fades, and a consent dialog box appears in the context of the Secure Desktop. If you're logged on using an account in the Administrators group, you see a dialog box like the one shown in Figure 1-4. If you log on with a standard user account, you have to enter the password for an administrative account before you can continue.

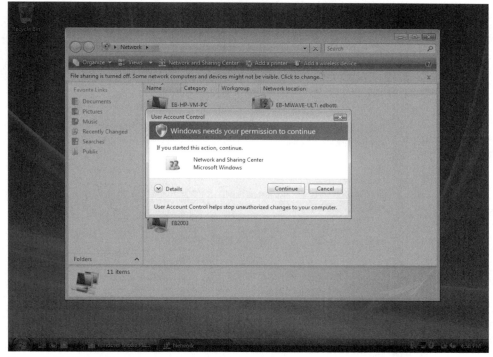

Figure 1-4 When a User Account Control dialog box appears, it takes complete focus. You must choose Continue or Cancel to return to the normal desktop display.

A key change in the security architecture of Windows Vista is how it deals with programs that insist on trying to write data to protected system folders and machine-wide keys in the registry. Allowing these changes has the potential to compromise system security; blocking them prevents the program from working properly.

The clever solution? The system redirects those files and registry changes to per-user keys that appear to the originating program as if they were located in the original protected location. This process, called virtualization, is done behind the scenes, and in most cases the person using the program is unaware that anything is out of the ordinary.

Internet Explorer 7, the default browser in Windows Vista, uses a similar feature to virtualize user data and browser add-ons. By using Internet Explorer in Protected Mode (the default setting), you're insulated from a rogue add-on that tries to take over system-level functions. Even if a naïve or careless user approves the installation of a piece of spyware or a browser helper object that spawns unsolicited pop-ups, the damage is strictly contained and can be cleaned up in short order.

Speaking of spyware...Windows Defender, originally introduced as an add-on product for Windows XP, is integrated into every Windows Vista edition and enabled as part of a default installation. As Figure 1-5 shows, it includes a wide-ranging set of features designed to identify installed and running software and to protect the operating system from unwanted changes.

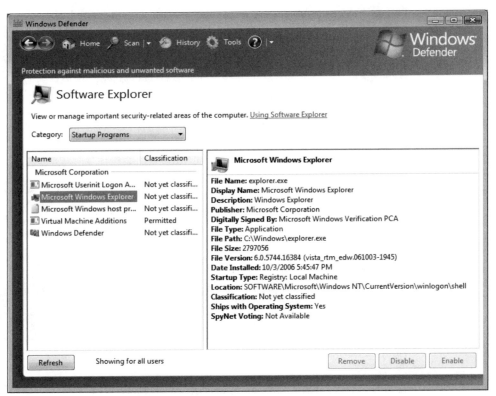

Figure 1-5 The Software Explorer module in Windows Defender provides detailed information about installed and running programs.

Some security settings need to be applied globally; others are more appropriate when tailored to the specific needs of an individual user. If you've created accounts for children using a computer running any home edition of Windows Vista, you can use the new Parental Controls interface to restrict the hours during which they can use the computer and to enforce rules about programs they're allowed to run and websites they're permitted to visit.

Our coverage of Windows Vista security starts with the must-read contents of Chapter 10, "Security Essentials," and continues with Chapter 31, "Advanced Security Management."

Digital Media Essentials

Virtually every tool for creating, organizing, editing, and playing back digital media files has been improved in Windows Vista. No matter which Windows Vista edition you use, you get Windows Media Player 11 (shown in Figure 1-6), which handles playback of audio CDs and video files, ripping and burning of audio CDs, access to online music and movie stores, and a rich set of tools for searching and categorizing your media library.

Figure 1-6 Windows Media Player 11 displays music by artist or genre (shown here) in stacks that show the number of tracks and total playing time.

For digital photos, all editions of Windows Vista include Windows Photo Gallery, which organizes photos in common image file formats. The Photo Gallery software includes basic editing tools to allow cropping, red-eye removal, and adjustments to color and exposure, but its most valuable feature of all is the ability it gives you to "tag" photos with keywords that are stored directly in supported image files. These tags and your ratings (on a scale of 1 to 5 stars) are fully searchable, which allows you to search for favorite photos, as in the example in Figure 1-7, and save a collection as a movie, a slide show, or a DVD.

Figure 1-7 Windows Photo Gallery stores these keyword tags directly in digital image files, allowing you to quickly retrieve a set of related photos.

Finally, Windows Movie Maker allows you to create movies by stitching together clips of your own footage from a digital video camera, still images, recorded TV shows, and other sources. After the movie project is complete, you can export it to Windows DVD Maker to burn the finished work onto a DVD that will play back on another PC or in any consumer DVD player.

And if you're not afraid to move Windows into the living room, you can take advantage of Windows Media Center. This feature, with its remote control–friendly 10-foot interface, includes all the software (you might need extra hardware too) to record broadcast, cable, or satellite TV and manage a library of digital music and photos on a big screen.

For an overview of the capabilities of Windows Vista to handle music, photos, videos, and DVDs, see Chapter 15, "Digital Media Essentials." For instructions on how to master Windows Media Center, see Chapter 19, "Using Windows Media Center."

New Ways to Network

The new Network And Sharing Center is emblematic of the collective changes in Windows Vista. It's the center for most network-related tasks, with a clean, well-organized, easy-to-follow interface. And it's almost certain to be disorienting at first, because its organization is so radically different from its predecessor in Windows XP. Figure 1-8 shows the basic organization of Network And Sharing Center, with a simple graphical representation of your network connection (clicking a link produces a more detailed map of all discoverable network resources). A set of file sharing and discovery options appear below the network map, with shortcuts to common configuration tasks along the left side.

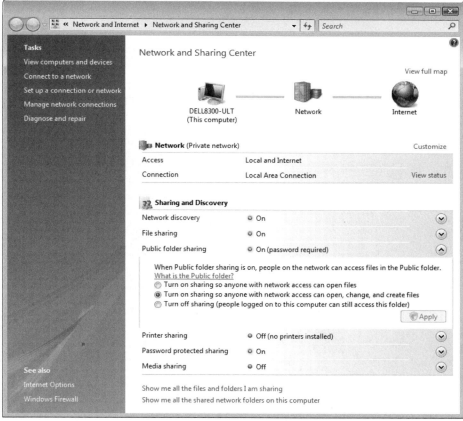

Figure 1-8 Network And Sharing Center is a hub for common network-related activities. Expand any of the sharing choices on the right to see its full range of options

Some of the most basic building blocks for Windows networking are fundamentally changed in Windows Vista. To master networking, you'll need to know how IPv6 and IPv4 cooperate with one another, for example, and how the Link-Layer Topology Discovery subsystem works.

Windows Vista also reworks the system for sharing files and folders. In the Network and Sharing Center, you can specify different levels of security for sharing; on individual files and folders stored on NTFS volumes, you can specify which accounts and groups, if any, are allowed to access those files.

Wireless networking in Windows has been steadily improving in both ease of setup and reliability since the launch of Windows XP in 2001. The wireless connection capabilities of Windows Vista, available in all editions, are remarkably easy to use, and the default configuration for new networks provides generally effective security when connecting to a public network.

Our coverage of Windows Vista networking begins in Chapter 12, "Setting Up a Small Network."

Inside Internet Explorer 7

Internet Explorer 7 represents a major overhaul of the venerable web browser that's been part of Windows for more than a decade. There are plenty of changes under the hood, but the change you're most likely to notice first is the addition of tabbed browsing. You can open new webpages on separate tabs with the same browser window, rearrange tabs by dragging them left and right, and press Ctrl+Q (or click the Quick Tabs button at the left of the tab row) to switch into Quick Tabs mode, as in Figure 1-9.

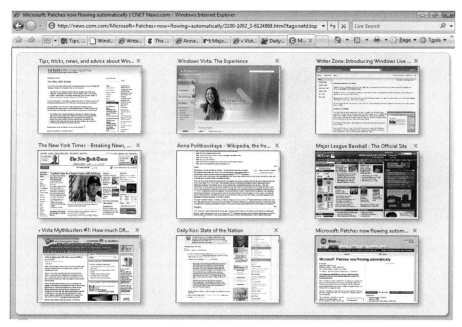

Figure 1-9 Quick Tabs view in Internet Explorer 7 allows you to see all open tabs in live previews; click a thumbnail to switch to that webpage, or click an X to close the page.

The interface for IE7 is sleeker than its predecessor, with the main menu hidden by default and the standard toolbar and common options collapsed to a small row of buttons to the right of the tab bar. A customizable search box in the upper right corner sends terms you type here to your default search engine.

IE7 also includes support for web feeds that use the RSS format. When you subscribe to a feed for a blog or news site, the Common Feed List engine checks for new content periodically and downloads it into the feed store, where you can view new posts in the browser window.

We mentioned the Protected Mode feature earlier, in our discussion of Windows Vista's breakthrough security technologies. Another security feature is the built-in Phishing Filter, which checks websites as they're loaded. The anti-phishing technology is designed to detect suspicious behavior commonly used by sites that impersonate legitimate banking and commerce sites to steal financial information or logon credentials from unsuspecting victims. When the Phishing Filter finds a positive match, it blocks access to the page and displays a blood-red warning page instead. For suspicious web pages, a yellow warning appears.

For more details about Internet Explorer, start with Chapter 6, "Using Internet Explorer 7."

Mail and Collaboration

With all editions of Windows Vista, you get a collection of contact tools that work reasonably well together. The one you're most likely to use is Windows Mail, the successor to Outlook Express. Don't let the name fool you—Windows Mail also works with NNTP newsgroups.

Clicking Windows Calendar from the Accessories group on the All Programs menu opens a bare-bones appointment and to-do list manager. Clicking Windows Contacts opens the Contacts folder, where information about individual contacts is stored in individual files that can be opened and edited in a small viewer program. The Contacts folder serves as the Address Book for Windows Mail and Windows Calendar, but you can use it with other programs as well.

Windows Meeting Space is a new collaboration tool that allows you to share documents, programs, and your desktop with other people over a local network or the internet. For more information about Mail, Contacts, Calendar, and Meeting Space, see Chapter 8, "E-Mail, Collaboration, and Personal Productivity."

Performance and Reliability

Increased reliability and snappier performance were among the design goals for Windows Vista. To see for yourself how well the results turned out, open the new Reliability and Performance Monitor (Figure 1-10 on the next page), which displays detailed information about system resource usage and allows you to collect mountains of data for in-depth analysis. The Reliability Monitor provides a day-by-day display of system events that can be tremendously useful in pinpointing the source of performance and stability problems.

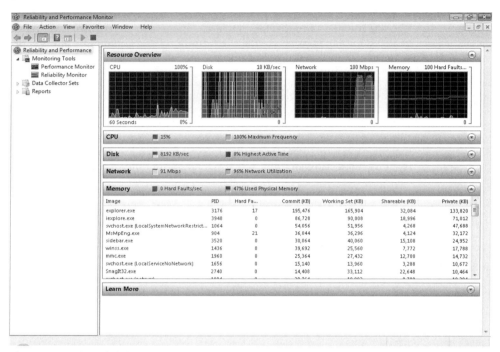

Figure 1-10 The Reliability and Performance Monitor provides a real-time display of resource usage, which can be saved for more detailed analysis.

All editions of Windows Vista include a capable Backup program that's much easier to use than its Windows XP counterpart. Business versions include the CompletePC Backup feature.

The System Restore feature is spiffed up but essentially unchanged from its Windows XP incarnation. But the Volume Snapshot Service that powers System Restore has been pressed into double duty with the prosaically named but amazingly useful Previous Versions feature. Maybe a better name would be Universal Undo: The Volume Snapshot Service keeps track of changes automatically as you work with data files. If you need to undo a change or recover an earlier version of any data file on a protected drive, click Properties on the shortcut menu, select an entry from the list on the Previous Versions tab, and click Restore.

To learn more about how to tune up Windows Vista, see Chapter 21, "Tuning Up and Monitoring Performance and Reliability." For more on using System Restore to bring a crashed PC back to life, see Chapter 23, "Recovering After a Computer Crash."

And Much, Much More...

In this brief introductory chapter, we've barely scratched the surface of what's new and what's changed in this version of Windows. We didn't get a chance to mention the addictive games, or the performance improvements you get when you plug a USB flash drive into a PC and turn on ReadyBoost, or the new audio subsystem with its rich support for surround sound systems, or the improved power management options, or support for Tablet PCs, or ...

Well, maybe we should just begin.

CHAPTER 2

Installing and Configuring Windows Vista

Home Basic ⚫
Home Premium ⚫
Business ⚫
Enterprise ⚫
Ultimate ⚫

$\mathbf{S}$ome Windows users never have to deal with the Windows Setup program. If you buy a new computer with Windows Vista already installed, you may be able to use it forever without having to do anything more than minor maintenance.

For upgraders, hobbyists, and inveterate tinkerers, however, the Windows Vista Setup program is inescapable. Knowing how to upgrade properly or perform a clean install can spell the difference between a smooth-running system and a box of troubles. If you mastered this subject in previous versions, prepare to unlearn everything you knew. The image-based installation process in Windows Vista is faster and much more reliable than its predecessor, especially when it comes to upgrades.

In this chapter, we'll explain the subtleties and intricacies of the Windows Setup program, explore the workings of the Windows Easy Transfer utility, and show you how to set up a computer with multiple versions of Windows.

> ### What's in Your Edition?
> All the features we discuss in this section are available in all editions of Windows Vista.

Before You Start...

Many programs originally written for earlier versions of Windows (including Windows XP) won't run properly under Windows Vista. Likewise, some hardware devices use drivers that aren't compatible with Windows Vista. The worst possible time to find out about either type of compatibility problem is right after you complete a fresh installation of Windows Vista, when you try to use a favorite program or device.

To spare yourself unnecessary headaches, if the computer on which you plan to install Windows Vista is currently running a 32-bit version of Windows XP (with Service Pack 2) or another edition of Windows Vista that you are planning to upgrade, download and run the free Windows Vista Upgrade Advisor first. This tool, available from *http://www.vista-io.com/0201*, scans installed programs and devices and produces a report identifying any potential issues you're likely to confront as part of an upgrade.

The purpose of the Upgrade Advisor is to identify hardware and software issues that may interfere with your ability to install Windows Vista or programs that may not run properly after the upgrade is complete. Figure 2-1 shows a typical Upgrade Advisor report. Scroll through the entire list to identify any urgent warnings or compatibility issues that require your immediate attention. If this tool identifies any potential problems with drivers or installed software, we recommend that you resolve those issues before continuing.

Figure 2-1 Read this upgrade report carefully before continuing with Setup. In some cases, you might need to uninstall programs or find new drivers before going any further.

INSIDE OUT **Use dynamic updates**

When you upgrade over an existing Windows version, Setup offers to check for dynamic updates. If you have an active internet connection, be sure to take advantage of this option. Dynamic updates can include service packs, updated drivers for hardware detected on your system, and upgrade packs for programs you're currently running. Rolling these updates into Windows Setup increases the likelihood that your installed applications and devices will work with Windows Vista and ensures that you don't have to install a bunch of updates immediately after you run Windows Vista for the first time.

Know Your Hardware

Microsoft has defined two sets of hardware requirements for Windows Vista. These requirements form the basis of marketing programs that allow manufacturers to use the corresponding logo on computers they sell and in the advertising for those computers. The Windows Vista Capable logo indicates that a computer meets the minimum standards to run Windows Vista. The Windows Vista Premium Ready logo identifies a system that meets or exceeds the requirements to run a premium edition of Windows Vista, including the Aero user experience. The specifics of the two designations are listed in Table 2-1.

Table 2-1. Windows Vista Hardware Requirements

Component	Windows Vista Capable	Windows Vista Premium Ready
Processor (CPU)	A modern processor (at least 800 MHz)	1 GHz 32-bit (x86) or 64-bit (x64) processor
Memory	512 MB	1 GB
Graphics processor	DirectX 9 capable, SVGA (800 x 600 resolution)	Support for DirectX 9 graphics with a WDDM driver, 128 MB of graphics memory (minimum), Pixel Shader 2.0, and 32 bits per pixel
Hard disk	20 GB (15 GB free space)	40 GB (15 GB free space)
Optical media	CD-ROM drive	DVD-ROM drive
Audio	Not required	Audio output capability

You'll also need a mouse or other pointing device, a keyboard, and internet access.

Chapter 2

INSIDE OUT   **Find the hardware bottlenecks**

Defining an acceptable level of performance is strictly a matter of personal preference. Some tasks, such as rendering 3D graphics or encoding video files, are CPU-intensive and will benefit greatly from the most muscular processor you can afford. For most everyday activities, including web browsing, sending and receiving e-mail, and creating standard business documents, the speed of the CPU is less critical. A fast hard disk with ample free space and at least 1GB of memory will do much more to keep multiple applications running smoothly. If you use large, memory-intensive programs such as Adobe Photoshop, don't settle for less than 2 GB of RAM.

Note

If you intend to install a 64-bit version of Windows Vista, you'll need to confirm that digitally signed drivers are available for all devices you intend to install. This compatibility bar is far more stringent than with 32-bit versions, where you can choose to install unsigned drivers originally developed for earlier Windows versions. In 64-bit versions of Windows Vista, those drivers will not load.

Avoiding Software Compatibility Problems

When upgrading, be especially vigilant with utility software that works at the system level. If you use a system utility that was originally written for a previous Windows version, it's prudent to assume that it won't work properly with Windows Vista. Always look for upgraded versions that are certified to be compatible with Windows Vista before continuing with setup.

Which classes of software are most likely to cause problems with an upgrade or a clean installation of Windows Vista?

- Antivirus software
- Software firewalls and other security programs
- CD- and DVD-burning programs
- Disk partitioning utilities and other low-level system maintenance programs

As a precaution, you should consider disabling antivirus software and other system utilities that might interfere with setup. After setup is complete, review the settings for all such programs to ensure that they're working properly. Windows Vista automatically disables third-party firewall programs during setup, for example, and enables the

Windows Vista Firewall; after setup is complete, you'll need to adjust the settings for your security software.

If the Upgrade Advisor identifies any programs as incompatible with Windows Vista, we strongly recommend that you uninstall those programs before continuing with the upgrade.

Backing Up Data and Settings

If you're planning an upgrade, don't underestimate Murphy's Law. Use a reliable back-up program or Windows Easy Transfer (described in "Transferring Files and Settings From Another Computer," later in this chapter.) to make a safe copy of important data files before continuing with the upgrade.

> **Note**
>
> If you use the Windows XP Backup program on your old computer (or on your current computer if you plan to upgrade) to save data files to a network drive or another disk, be aware that the Backup program in Windows Vista uses a different, incompatible for-mat and cannot open or restore files backed up using that earlier format. At the time we wrote this chapter, Microsoft was working on a utility to import Windows XP backup files; for details, open the Backup Status And Configuration dialog box and click the How Do I Restore Files From Backups Made Using A Previous Version Of Windows? link.

If you own a software utility that can create an image copy of your existing system volume, this is an excellent strategy. Some hard disk upgrade packages sold at retail include this sort of tool; Norton Ghost (*http://www.vista-io.com/0202*) and Acronis TrueImage (*http://www.vista-io.com/0203*) are highly regarded examples of third-party imaging tools. A disk image stored on an external hard disk is excellent protection against data disasters.

Setting Up Windows Vista

As we mentioned briefly at the beginning of this chapter, the Setup program in Win-dows Vista is unlike that found in any previous Windows version. The re-engineered process is specifically designed to go very quickly, with an absolute minimum of atten-tion required from you. In this section, we'll explain the ins and outs of the most com-mon scenarios you'll confront when installing or upgrading Windows Vista on a single PC. We assume that you have a bootable DVD containing a full copy of Windows Vista, suitable for use in a clean install or upgrade. (If you have only a CD drive and no DVD drive, you can contact Microsoft and ask for the five-CD package; see the product docu-mentation for details on acquiring alternative media.)

> **Note**
>
> Windows Vista is sold in a variety of packages, and not all are covered in the scenarios we discuss here. For a discussion of the different types of licenses and installation media available to you, see "Activating And Validating Windows Vista," later in this chapter.

As part of the setup process, you need to make a series of relatively simple but important decisions:

- **Which Windows Vista edition do you want to install?** This will normally be the version you purchased; however, retail copies of the Windows Vista DVD contain program code for all four Windows editions available through the retail channel—Home Basic, Home Premium, Business, and Ultimate. As we explain later in this section, you can install and run any of these editions for up to 30 days without entering a product key or activating your copy of Windows Vista.

- **Do you want to perform a clean install or an upgrade?** A clean install starts from scratch; you need to reinstall your programs and re-create or transfer settings from another system. An upgrade retains installed programs and settings, at the risk of some compatibility issues.

- **Which disk partition do you want to use?** The Windows Vista installation program includes disk management tools that you can use to create, delete, format, and extend (but not shrink) partitions on hard disks installed in your computer. Knowing how these tools work can save you a significant amount of time when setting up Windows.

- **Do you want to install Windows Vista alongside another operating system?** The Windows Vista startup process is radically different from that found in previous Windows versions. If you want to set up a dual-boot (or multiboot) system, you'll need to understand how different startup files work so you can manage your startup options effectively.

Performing a Clean Install

The simplest setup scenario of all is installing Windows Vista in a newly created partition on a system that does not currently have any version of Windows installed (or, as an alternative, wiping out a partition that contains an existing version of Windows and completely replacing it with a clean install of Windows Vista). The safest way to embark on a clean install is to boot from the Windows Vista DVD. Insert the Windows DVD and restart your computer. Watch for a boot prompt; typically, you need to press a key to boot from the DVD. After the setup process begins, you can follow the instructions as outlined in this section.

INSIDE OUT   **Working around DVD issues**

For a bootable CD or DVD to work properly, you must set the boot order in the BIOS so that the drive appears ahead of the hard disk drive and any other bootable media; we recommend setting the DVD drive as the first boot device, followed by the hard disk, floppy disk, and any other bootable devices, in whichever order you prefer. The boot options available for every computer are different, as is the technique for accessing the BIOS setup program. During boot, watch for a message that tells you which key to press for setup. If you're lucky, the BIOS setup program on your computer includes a Boot tab where you can specify the order of boot devices; if this option isn't immediately apparent, look for a page called Advanced CMOS Settings or something similar.

What if your computer lacks the capability to boot from a DVD drive? This problem is most likely to affect you if you're trying to install Windows Vista on a notebook computer that doesn't include an integrated DVD drive and that does not support booting from an external (USB or FireWire) drive, or if the DVD drive in an existing system is damaged. Try one of these alternatives to work around the problem (you might need access to another computer with a functioning DVD drive and a network connection to complete either or both of these steps):

- Copy the DVD files to a folder on your hard disk and run Setup from that location.
- Use a full-featured DVD burning program such as Nero 7 (*http://www.nero.com*), Roxio Easy Media Creator, or Roxio RecordNow (*http://www.roxio.com*) to copy the Windows Vista DVD to an ISO image file. Then install an ISO image mounting program such as IsoBuster (*http://www.isobuster.com*) or DaemonTools (*http://www. daemon-tools.cc*) and point it at the ISO file you created. The mounted image file appears as a DVD drive in the Computer window, and you can run Setup from that virtual drive.

Either of the above options allow you to upgrade the current Windows installation or to install a clean copy on a separate volume or on the same volume, alongside the current copy of Windows. This option does not allow you to delete the current partition on which Windows is installed and install a clean copy in that location.

Chapter 2

When you boot from the Windows DVD, your first stop is the Install Windows screen shown in Figure 2-2. Choose your language preferences and click Next.

Figure 2-2 The language preferences available here should match the version you purchased. Options for a Western European version will be different from those in this U.S. version.

On the following screen, click Install Now.

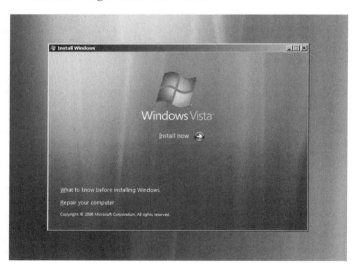

On the following screen, you're prompted to enter your product key. You can enter the product key included with your purchased copy, or you can bypass this screen and install Windows without entering a product key. (For more details on these options, see

"Activating and Validating Windows Vista," later in this chapter.) After you complete this step and accept the license agreement, you'll reach the screen shown here.

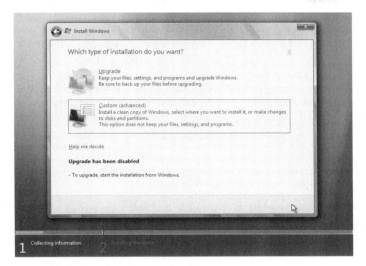

Because you booted from the DVD, the Upgrade option is disabled. Click the Custom (Advanced) option to continue with a clean install. The Where Do You Want To Install Windows? screen, shown in Figure 2-3, lists all physical disks, partitions, and unallocated space.

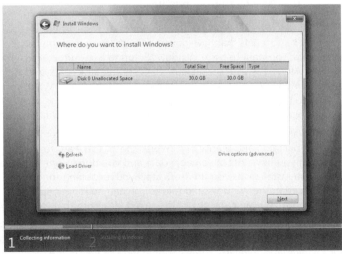

Figure 2-3 In this simple scenario, with a single physical disk that does not contain any partitions, you can click Next to create a partition and install Windows using the entire physical drive.

TROUBLESHOOTING

Setup doesn't detect your hard disk

The Windows Vista DVD includes drivers for most commonly used IDE and SATA disk controllers. However, this coverage is not complete. If Setup does not recognize your disk controller, you'll be prompted to provide a driver when you reach the Where Do You Want To Install Windows? screen. For 32-bit (x86) versions of Windows Vista, you should be able to supply a driver that is compatible with Windows XP, Windows Server 2003, or Windows Vista on a floppy disk, on a USB flash drive, or on a CD or DVD. For the latter option, remove the Windows Vista DVD and insert the disk containing the storage driver; after the driver loads successfully, remove the disk and reinsert the Windows DVD.

If you want to make adjustments to existing disk partitions, click Drive Options (Advanced) to accomplish any of the following tasks:

- **Select an existing partition or unallocated space on which to install Windows Vista.** Setup is simple if you already created and formatted an empty partition in preparation for setting up Windows, or if you plan to install Windows Vista on an existing partition that currently contains data or programs but no operating system, or if you want to use unallocated space on an existing disk without disturbing the existing partition scheme. Select the partition or unallocated space and click Next.

INSIDE OUT   It's okay to share a partition

Thanks to the radically revised Setup program in Windows Vista, Windows users can safely discard one of the basic tenets that have governed installation decisions since the beginning of the Windows era. You want to point Windows Setup to a partition on which Windows is already installed? As long as you have at least 15 GB of free disk space and you don't plan to use the copy of Windows on that partition anymore, go right ahead. When you choose to do a clean install in this configuration, Windows Vista Setup moves the old Windows, Program Files, and Documents and Settings folders to a folder named Windows.old.

Why would you want to do this? Let's say you currently have a system that has a single disk with a single partition and plenty of free disk space. You want to start fresh with a clean install, but you have lots of valuable data and you don't want to lose any of it. Performing a clean install gives you the fresh start you're looking for, and your data files are safely ensconced in the Windows.old folder. You can no longer start up your old Windows installation, but you can copy any of the saved files from that folder to your new user profile whenever you're ready.

Why is this option acceptable now? In previous Windows versions, the operation of the Setup program invariably involved some commingling of files in the old and new Windows installations. Those unwanted system files and leftovers from previously installed programs defeated the purpose of doing a clean install. But the image-based Windows Vista setup makes a clean break, allowing you to quarantine the old files and do a truly clean installation of your new operating system.

- **Delete an existing partition.**   Select a partition and then click Delete. This option is useful if you want to do a clean install on a drive that currently contains an earlier version of Windows. Because this operation deletes data irretrievably, you must respond to at least two "Are you sure?" confirmation requests. After deleting the partition, you can create a new one and select it as the destination for your Windows Vista installation. Be sure to back up any data files before choosing this option.

- **Create a new partition from unallocated space.**   Select a block of unallocated space on a new drive or on an existing drive after deleting partitions and click New to set up a partition in that space. By default, Setup offers to use all unallocated space on the current disk. You can specify a smaller partition size if you want to subdivide the disk into multiple drives. If you have a 300-GB drive, for example, as in Figure 2-4, you might choose to create a small partition on which to install Windows and use the remaining space to create a second volume with its own drive letter on which to store data files such as music, pictures, documents, and recorded TV.

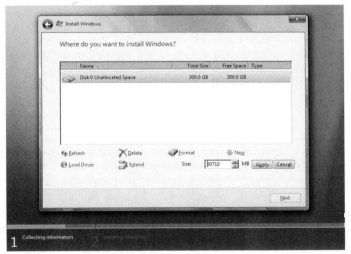

Figure 2-4 Use the disk management tools in this phase of the Windows Vista Setup program to subdivide an empty disk into multiple partitions for more efficient data storage.

- **Extend an existing partition using unallocated space.** If you want to upgrade an existing copy of Windows and you're not happy with your existing partition scheme, you can use the Extend option to add unallocated space to any partition. If you originally set up a 60-GB notebook hard drive with a 10-GB partition for Windows XP and set aside the remaining 50 GB for data files, you'll be unable to upgrade to Windows Vista because your system drive doesn't meet the requirement of at least 15 GB of free space. The solution? Back up your data files to an external drive, delete the data partition, select the partition you want to make larger, and click Extend. Choose the total size of the extended partition in the Size box (the default is to use all available unallocated space) and click Apply.

Alert observers will no doubt notice that one option is missing from that list. Unfortunately, the Setup program does not allow you to shrink an existing disk partition to create unallocated space on which to install a fresh copy of Windows Vista. The option to shrink a volume is available from the Disk Management console after Windows Vista is installed, but if you want to accomplish this disk before or during Setup, you'll need to use third-party disk-management tools.

TROUBLESHOOTING

During setup, some peripherals don't work properly

Check your system BIOS. An outdated BIOS can cause problems with disk partitioning, power management, peripheral configuration, and other crucial low-level functions. To find out whether an update is available, check with the manufacturer of your computer or its motherboard. Identifying the BIOS and tracking down the appropriate source for updates isn't always easy; you'll find detailed information at the indispensable (and thoroughly independent) Wim's BIOS (*http://www.wimsbios.com*).

After you select the disk location where you want to install Windows Vista, Setup finishes automatically, with no further input required from you. The Installing Windows screen provides a progress bar to indicate how close to completion you are. After Setup concludes, you need to fill in some basic information before you can log on for the first time:

1. **Choose a user name and picture.** The user account you create here is a member of the Administrators group. Although you're not required to assign a password to this account, we strongly recommend you do so.

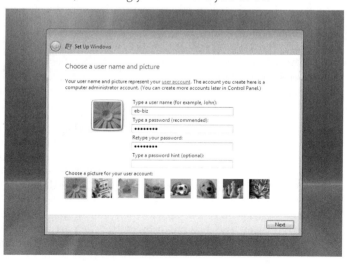

2. **Type a computer name and choose a desktop background.** Setup suggests
    a default name by tacking the "-PC" suffix to the user name you created in the
    previous step. You're free to suggest a more descriptive name if you prefer.

> **Note**
>
> The selections for user picture and desktop background represent a relatively small sub-
> set of the options available. Most people will want to explore the more complete range
> of options after logging on for the first time.

3. **Select Automatic Update settings.** For most people, the first option, Use Recommended Settings, is the correct one.

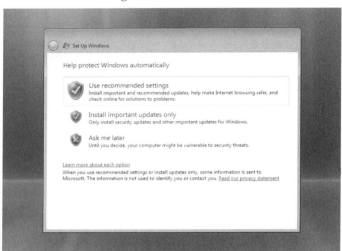

4. **Review your date and time settings.** After selecting your time zone, check the date and time carefully. Incorrect values in either of these settings can cause complications later.

5. **Select a network location.** This setting determines basic network security, including firewall settings and sharing options. On most home or small business networks connected to the internet through a router, you can safely select the Home or Work option. Click Public if you are directly connected to a cable or DSL modem or if you connect to the internet by means of a dial-up modem.

After completing the final step in this process, click Start to proceed to a logon screen.

Upgrading a Previous Windows Version

To perform an in-place upgrade of your existing copy of Windows, you must be running a 32-bit version of Windows XP with Service Pack 2 installed. In addition, the drive on which Windows is currently installed must be formatted as NTFS and not FAT32. Finally, you must have enough free disk space to accommodate the new installation of Windows Vista—typically, 11-15 GB. The exact upgrade paths available are listed in Table 2-2.

Table 2-2. Supported Paths for In-Place Upgrades

If your current operating system is...	You may upgrade to...
Windows XP Home	Windows Vista Home Basic, Home Premium, Business, Ultimate
Windows XP Media Center Edition	Windows Vista Home Premium, Ultimate
Windows XP Professional	Windows Vista Business, Ultimate
Windows XP Tablet PC	Windows Vista Business, Ultimate

If you want to install a 64-bit edition of Windows Vista, no upgrade options are available. In addition, if you want to replace your existing copy of Windows XP with a Windows Vista edition that is not listed in the supported paths in Table 2-2, you'll need to perform a clean install and use the Windows Easy Transfer utility to migrate your files and settings from the old computer to the new one.

To begin an in-place upgrade, start your existing copy of Windows XP and insert the Windows Vista DVD. Run Setup from the AutoPlay dialog box or, if AutoPlay is disabled, enter d:\setup.exe (substituting the letter of your DVD drive for *d:*) at any command prompt, including the Run dialog box. In the Install Windows dialog box, click Install Now to begin.

The upgrade process involves significantly fewer steps than a clean install. After Setup begins, you see the dialog box shown in Figure 2-5. If you have a working internet connection, we strongly recommend that you accept the default option to download the latest updates for installation.

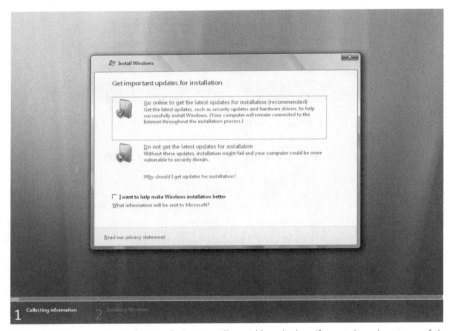

Figure 2-5 For an upgrade installation, you'll avoid headaches if you take advantage of the option to download security updates and new drivers as part of setup.

Next, you're prompted to enter the product key and accept a license. (For details on your options, see "Entering a Product Key," later in this chapter.) After these steps, you reach the dialog box shown here. Click Upgrade to begin Setup.

Before beginning the actual upgrade, Setup runs a brief compatibility test analogous to the Windows Vista Upgrade Advisor. If this test detects any potential software or hardware compatibility issues, you will see a Compatibility Report dialog box listing the issues and recommending steps to resolve them. You can interrupt Setup at this point to uninstall a program or driver; or, if you're satisfied that the issue won't affect your upgrade, click Next to continue.

An upgrade from Windows XP takes significantly more time than a clean install. In fact, the upgrade actually gathers settings and drivers from your existing installation; moves your existing Windows, Program Files, and Documents and Settings folders to a new folder; performs a clean install of Windows Vista using a prebuilt image file; migrates the settings and drivers it gathered in the first step to the new copy of Windows Vista; moves user data to the correct locations in the newly created user profiles; and finally restarts Windows Vista. All of this happens without requiring any intervention on your part. During the upgrade, Setup creates the following temporary hidden folders in the root of your system drive:

- **$WINDOWS.~BT** This folder contains the minimal copy of Windows Vista that manages the actual work of setting up the new operating system and migrating files and settings.

- **$UPGRADE.~OS** Setup gathers settings for the operating system and stores them in this temporary folder to be applied to Windows Vista after installation is complete.

- **$WINDOWS.~LS**   This folder contains the large image file (in Windows Image format) and temporary files used during the upgrade.

- **$INPLACE.~TR**   User- and machine-specific settings are temporarily stored here after being gathered during the first stage of the upgrade.

- **$WINDOWS.~Q**   This folder contains the original Windows installation.

If Setup fails for any reason, it automatically rolls back the installation, removing the newly installed image and restoring the original Windows installation from its saved location. After a successful upgrade, most of these temporary folders are deleted. The $INPLACE.~TR and $WINDOWS.~Q folders are preserved, to allow you to recover files and settings that were not properly migrated.

INSIDE OUT   Clean up after an upgrade

After you complete the upgrade and are satisfied that all your data files are intact and all settings were properly migrated, you can clean up the bits and pieces the upgrade process leaves behind. The quickest and safest way to accomplish this goal is to use the Disk Cleanup utility. Select the Files Discarded By Windows Upgrade option and click OK. If you've installed Windows Vista on the same partition as an existing copy of Windows, use the Previous Installation(s) Of Windows option, which removes the Windows.old folder and its contents. For more details on how to use this option, see "Cleaning Up with Disk Cleanup," in Chapter 20.

Upgrading from Another Windows Vista Edition

The basic procedure for upgrading from one edition of Windows Vista to another is similar to that involved in upgrading from Windows XP. If you have a Windows Vista DVD and a new product key, you can run Setup using the same procedure we outlined in the previous section, choosing the Upgrade option from the Which Type Of Installation Do You Want? screen. Not every Windows Vista–to–Windows Vista upgrade scenario is supported. From Home Basic, you can upgrade to Home Premium or Ultimate only. From either Business or Home Premium, you can upgrade to Ultimate. You can't perform an in-place upgrade from Home Basic to Business, and the only way to replace Home Premium with Business (or vice-versa) is to purchase a new license, do a clean install, and transfer your files and settings using Windows Easy Transfer.

If you're already running a Windows Vista edition that supports one of the upgrade scenarios listed above, you can take advantage of a new feature that allows you to purchase upgrade rights without having to pay for a full copy of your new edition. This feature, called Windows Anytime Upgrade, is available only on editions that can be upgraded; it's not available on any computer running Windows Vista Ultimate. You'll find links to this feature under Extras and Upgrades folder on the All Programs menu, or you can access it from the top section of the Welcome Center or by clicking the Upgrade Windows Vista link at the top of the System dialog box in Control Panel.

Starting Windows Anytime Upgrade takes you to a page that lists the upgrade options available for your edition. When you select an upgrade path, you end up at the screen shown in Figure 2-6.

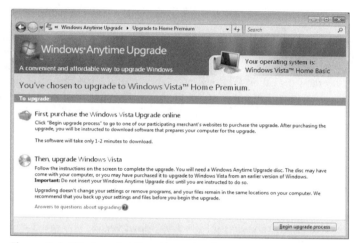

Figure 2-6 Windows Anytime Upgrade allows you to choose a more powerful edition of Windows Vista without having to pay for a completely new license.

To perform an Anytime Upgrade, you start by purchasing the upgrade license from an online vendor. After completing the transaction, you download a product key for the new edition. That key allows you to complete the upgrade using your existing Windows Vista installation media. If you can't locate your original installation media, you can have a Windows Vista DVD mailed to you as part of the upgrade process, paying shipping and handling for the replacement media,

Installing Windows Vista on a Computer with Other Windows Versions

If your computer already has a 32-bit version of Windows installed *and* you have at least two disk partitions defined, you can install a clean copy of Windows Vista without disturbing your existing Windows installation. At boot time, you choose your Windows version from a startup menu. Although this is typically called a dual-boot system, it's more accurate to call it a multiboot configuration, because you can install multiple copies of Windows.

INSIDE OUT Control which drive letter your boot volume uses

Which drive letter will your clean installation of Windows Vista use? That depends on how you install it. If you currently have a working copy of any Windows version on drive C and you install a clean copy of Windows, drive letters are assigned using the following logic:

- If you begin the installation process by booting from the Windows Vista media and choose a partition other than the one containing your current copy of Windows, the new installation uses the drive letter C when you start up. The volume that contains the other Windows installation uses the next available drive letter. When you choose the previous Windows installation from the startup menu, it uses the drive letter C, and your new Windows Vista installation is assigned the next available drive letter. In this configuration, you can be certain that your current operating system is always on the C drive, but drive letters assigned to volumes you use for data may shift in unexpected ways.

- If you begin the installation process by running Setup from within your current version of Windows and use the Custom (Advanced) option to perform a clean install on a partition other than the one currently in use, the new installation uses the next available drive letter. The volumes containing each installation have the same drive letters regardless of which Windows version you select at startup.

There's no inherent reason to prefer either of these options over the other. If you prefer the consistency of knowing that all system files and program files are on the C drive, you'll probably want to choose the first option. If you would rather use drive letters to keep track of which Windows version is running at any given time, you'll prefer the second option. But either configuration should work reliably with any combination of software, hardware, and settings.

Having the capability to choose your operating system at startup is handy if you have a program or device that simply won't work under Windows Vista. When you need to use the legacy program or device, you can boot into your other Windows version without too much fuss. This capability is also useful for software developers, who need to be able to test how their programs work under different operating systems.

For experienced Windows users, installing a second copy of Windows Vista in its own partition can also be helpful as a way to experiment with a potentially problematic program or device driver without compromising a working system. After you finish setting up the second, clean version of Windows Vista, you'll see an additional entry on the startup menu that corresponds to your new installation. (The newly installed version is the default menu choice; it runs automatically if 30 seconds pass and you don't make a choice.) Experiment with the program or driver and see how well it works. If, after testing thoroughly, you're satisfied that the program is safe to use, you can add it to the Windows Vista installation you use every day.

Understanding the Windows Vista Startup Process

If you've worked with multiboot systems in previous Windows versions, including Windows XP, you'll need to understand how fundamental changes in the Windows Vista boot loader change the way you manage multiple operating systems. For the purposes of running Windows Vista, the old Ntldr and Boot.ini files are no longer used (although they are called on in a secondary role when you use Windows XP, Windows 2000, or Windows Server 2003 in a multiboot configuration with Windows Vista).

The startup process in Windows Vista begins when your computer performs its power-on self test (POST), which is followed by the POST for each adapter card that has a BIOS, such as advanced storage adapters and video cards. The system BIOS then reads the master boot record (MBR)—the first physical sector on the hard disk defined as the boot device—and transfers control to the code in the MBR, which is created by Windows Vista Setup. This is where Windows takes over the startup process. Here's what happens next:

1. The MBR reads the boot sector—the first sector of the active partition—which contains code that starts the Windows Boot Manager program, Bootmgr.exe.

2. The Windows Boot Manager reads the contents of the Boot Configuration Data store, which contains configuration information about all operating systems installed on the computer. It uses this data to build and display the boot menu.

3. When you make a selection from the boot menu, you trigger one of the following actions:

   ○ If you select an instance of Windows Vista, the Windows Boot Manager starts the OS loader, Winload.exe, from the %SystemRoot%\System32 folder for that installation.

   ○ If you choose the option to resume Windows Vista from hibernation, the Boot Manager loads Winresume.exe and restores your previous environment.

   ○ If you choose the Earlier Version Of Windows option from the boot menu, the Boot Manager locates the volume containing that installation, loads its Windows NT-style Legacy OS loader (Ntldr .exe), and if necessary, displays a new startup menu drawn from the Boot.ini file on that volume.

Windows Vista starts by loading its core files, Ntoskrnl.exe and Hal.dll, reading settings from the registry, and loading drivers. That's followed by the Windows Session Manager (Smss.exe), which starts the Windows Start-Up Application (Wininit.exe), which in turn starts the Local Security Authority (Lsass.exe) and Services (Services.exe) processes, after which you're ready to log on.

Understanding the boot process can help you to pinpoint problems that occur during startup. For more information, see "Using Advanced Boot Options," in Chapter 24.

Chapter 2

INSIDE OUT Use virtual machines instead of hassling with multiboot menus

You can create truly elaborate multiboot configurations using more than a decade's worth of Windows versions. But unless you're running a hardware testing lab, there's no good reason to do that. The much simpler, smoother alternative is to use virtualization software to run multiple versions of Windows on virtual hardware that faithfully recreates the operating environment. During the course of researching and writing this book, we installed Windows Vista in virtual machines to capture details of several crucial tasks and processes that can't easily be documented on physical hardware, and we saved many hours compared to how long those tasks would have taken had we set up and restored physical hardware. Microsoft's Virtual PC 2007 (*http://www.vista-io.com/0206*) runs on all editions of Windows Vista, and Virtual Server 2005 R2 (*http://www.vista-io.com/0205*) offers the same capabilities in a package designed to run on Windows Server 2003. VMWare (*http://www.vmware.com*) also offers excellent virtualization software for use on desktop Windows machines and servers. Using any of these solutions, you can install even the most ancient Windows version. Backing up a machine's configuration and restoring it is as simple as copying a file. Legally, you'll need a license for every operating system you install in a virtual machine. If you have a license to use Windows for evaluation purposes, this option is a life-saver.

To add Windows Vista to a system where an existing version of Windows is already installed, first make sure that you have an available partition (or unformatted disk space) separate from the partition that contains the system files for your current Windows version.

The target partition can be a separate partition on the same physical disk, or it can be on a different hard disk. If your system contains a single disk with a single partition used as drive C, you cannot create a multiboot system unless you add a new disk or use software tools to shrink the existing partition and create a new partition from the free space. (The Windows Vista Disk Management console, Diskmgmt.msc, includes this capability; to shrink partitions on a system running an older Windows version, you'll need third-party software.) The new partition does not need to be empty; however, it should not contain system files for another Windows installation. Run Setup, choose the Custom (Advanced) option, and select the disk and partition you want to use for the new installation.

The Setup program automatically handles details of adding the newly installed operating system to the Boot Configuration Data store.

And how do you edit and configure the Boot Configuration Data store? Surprisingly, the only official tool is a command-line utility called Bcdedit. Bcdedit isn't an interactive program; instead, you perform tasks by appending switches and parameters to the Bcdedit command line. To display the complete syntax for this tool, open an elevated Command Prompt window (using the Run As Administrator option) and enter the command **Bcdedit -?**

For everyday use, most Bcdedit options are esoteric and unnecessary. In fact, the only option that we remember using more than once during the entire development cycle for Windows Vista was the command to change the text for each entry in the boot menu. By default, Setup adds the generic entry "Microsoft Windows Vista" for each installation. If you set up a dual-boot system using Windows Vista Home Premium and Windows Vista Business, you'll be unable to tell which is which, because the menu text will be the same for each. To make the menu more informative, follow these steps:

1. Start your computer and choose either entry from the boot menu. After startup completes, make a note of which installation is running.

2. Click Start, type **cmd** in the Search box, and press Ctrl+Shift+Enter. Click Continue in the User Account Control box to open an elevated Command Prompt window.

3. Type the following command: **bcdedit /set description** "*Menu description goes here*" (substitute your own description for the placeholder text, and be sure to include the quotation marks). Press Enter.

4. Restart your computer and note that the menu description you just entered now appears on the menu. Select the other menu option.

5. Repeat steps 2 and 3, again adding a menu description to replace the generic text and distinguish this installation from the other one.

A few startup options are still available from the Startup And Recovery dialog box (open the System option in Control Panel, click the Advanced System Settings link in the Tasks pane, and click the Settings button under the Startup and Recovery heading). As shown on the next page, you can choose which installation is the default operating system (this is where descriptive menu choices come in handy) and how long you want to display the list of operating systems. The default is 30 seconds; we typically set this value to no more than 10 seconds (you can choose any number between 1 and 99). To set the boot menu so that the default operating system starts automatically, clear the check box at the left, or enter 0. These options write data directly to the Boot Configuration Data store.

Chapter 2

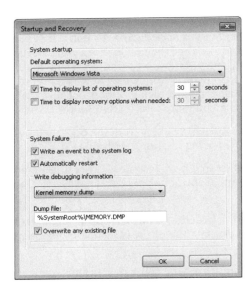

The syntax of the Bcdedit command is daunting, to say the least. It's also something you're unlikely to use often enough to memorize. Those facts are enough to strongly recommend using a graphical editor for the BCD store instead. VistaBoot Pro (*http://www.vista-io.com/0207*) gets consistently high marks and includes the capability to repair the Vista boot loader or uninstall it and return to booting from the Legacy OS Boot Loader (Ntldr.exe)

TROUBLESHOOTING

You installed a different Windows version and Windows Vista is no longer on the boot menu

Each time you install a version of Windows, it rewrites the MBR to call its own boot loader. If you install Windows Vista as a second operating system on a PC where Windows XP is already installed, the Windows Vista boot menu incorporates the options from the older boot menu. But if you install a fresh copy of Windows XP on a system that is already running Windows Vista, you'll overwrite the MBR with one that doesn't recognize the Windows Vista Boot Loader. To repair the damage, open a Command Prompt window in the older operating system and run the following command from the Windows Vista DVD, substituting the letter of your drive for *<d>* here.

<*d*>:\Boot\ Bootsect.exe –NT60 All

When you restart, you should see the Windows Vista menu. To restore the menu entry for your earlier version of Windows, open an elevated Command Prompt and enter this command:

Bcdedit –create {ntldr} –d *"Menu description goes here"*

Substitute your own description for the placeholder text. The next time you start your computer, the menus should appear as you intended.

How do you remove Windows Vista from a dual-boot installation and restore the Windows XP boot loader? Enter the following command at a command prompt:

<d>:\Boot\Bootsect.exe –NT52 All

You can now delete all system files from the volume containing the Windows Vista installation you no longer plan to use. For even more effective removal, use the Disk Management console in Windows XP to reformat the drive and start fresh.

Activating and Validating Windows Vista

Windows Vista includes a group of antipiracy and antitampering features that Microsoft collectively refers to as the Software Protection Platform (SPP). The basic requirements are similar to those used with Windows XP, with a few extra twists. The technological mechanisms in SPP are, in essence, enforcement mechanisms for the Windows Vista license agreement, which you agree to during the process of installing the operating system. We're not lawyers, so we won't presume to interpret this license agreement. We do recommend that you read the license agreement, which contains considerably less legalese than its predecessors. In this section, we explain how the technological mechanisms in SPP affect your use of Windows Vista.

Entering a Product Key

Whether you perform a clean installation or upgrade an existing Windows installation, you'll see the following dialog box early in the setup process.

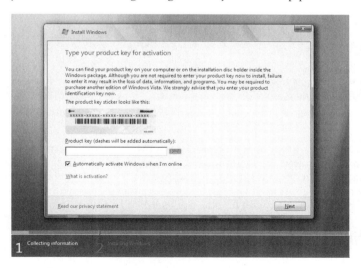

As with previous Windows versions, the product key is a 25-character alphanumeric value that uniquely identifies your licensed copy of Windows. But there are two noteworthy differences between this step and the equivalent process used in Windows XP:

- **Your product key identifies your edition of Windows Vista.** The Windows Vista DVD you purchase from a retail outlet contains four editions of Windows Vista: Home Basic, Home Premium, Business, and Ultimate. The product key unlocks the edition you purchased. When you enter a valid product key in this box and click Next, Setup installs the edition that matches that key.

- **You don't have to enter a product key to install Windows Vista.** If you leave the Product Key box blank and click Next, the Setup program asks you if you want to enter a product key. Click No, and you're greeted with the dialog box shown in Figure 2-7.

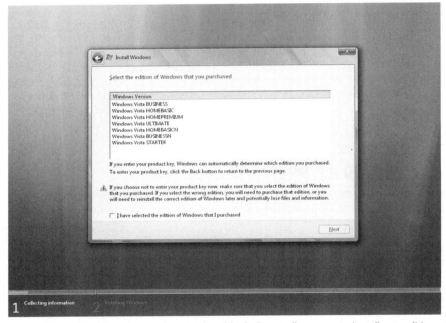

Figure 2-7 If you leave the Product Key box blank, Setup allows you to install any edition of Windows Vista and use it for up to 30 days.

You can select any edition of Windows Vista in this list, finish Setup, and use the installed copy of Windows Vista without restriction for 30 days. Before the end of that 30-day grace period, you must enter a valid product key and activate your copy, as described in the next section. If you fail to complete these steps, your copy of Windows shifts into reduced functionality mode, as described later in this section.

Activating a Retail Copy of Windows

Just as with Windows XP, you must *activate* your installation of a retail copy of Windows Vista within 30 days, either by connecting to a Microsoft activation server over the internet, or by making a toll-free call to an interactive telephone activation system.

The activation mechanism is designed to enforce license restrictions by preventing the most common form of software piracy: casual copying. Typically, a Windows Vista license entitles you to install the operating system software on a single computer. If you use the same product key to install Windows Vista on a second (or third or fourth) system, you'll be unable to activate the software automatically.

On the Setup screen where you enter your product key, the Automatically Activate Windows When I'm Online box is selected by default. If you leave this option selected, Windows will contact the activation servers three days after installation and complete the activation process for you. At any time, you can check your system's activation status by looking at the Windows Activation section at the bottom of the System dialog box. (Click Start, right-click Computer, and click Properties.) This dialog box displays the number of days left in the grace period and includes links where you can manually activate or change your product key.

If the 30-day grace period expires and you have not successfully activated, you'll see the dialog box shown in Figure 2-8. Click Activate Windows Online Now to begin the internet activation process. If you left the Product Key box blank when installing Windows Vista, you'll be prompted to enter a valid product key before you can complete activation.

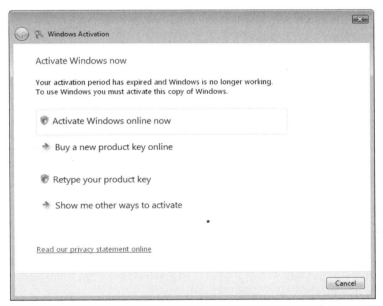

Figure 2-8 If you fail to activate Windows Vista within 30 days after installation, you're greeted with this dialog box, which must be dealt with before you can continue using Windows.

Under most circumstances, activation over the internet takes no more than a few seconds. If you need to use the telephone, the process takes longer, because you have to enter a 50-digit identification key (either by using the phone's dial pad or by speaking to a customer service representative) and then input the 42-digit confirmation ID supplied in response, as shown in Figure 2-9.

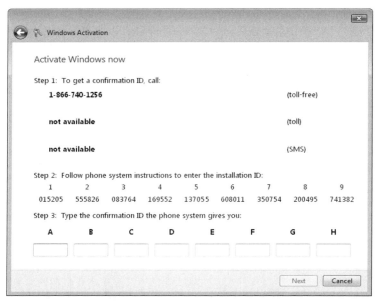

Figure 2-9 Activating a copy of Windows over the phone is considerably more complex than doing it over the internet.

INSIDE OUT **Don't rush to activate**

When you install a retail copy of Windows Vista, Windows Vista normally waits three days before automatically activating the product. We recommend that you clear the Automatically Activate Windows When I'm Online box when entering your product key. This option gives you a full 30 days to verify that Windows Vista works properly on your hardware and that you won't be required to replace any hardware or the entire computer. After you're confident that Windows Vista is completely compatible with your hardware, you can open the System dialog box and choose the manual activation option.

The activation process is completely anonymous and does not require that you divulge any personal information. If you choose to register your copy of Windows Vista, this is a completely separate (and optional) task.

You're allowed to reinstall Windows Vista an unlimited number of times on the same hardware. During the activation process, Windows Vista transmits a hashed file that serves as a "fingerprint" of key components in your system. When you attempt to activate Windows Vista using the same product key you used previously, the activation server calculates a new fingerprint and compares the value against the one stored in its database. If you're reinstalling Windows Vista on the original hardware, the finger-prints will match and activation will be automatic.

Just as with earlier Windows versions, the activation process is designed to prevent attempts to "clone" an activated copy of Windows and install it on another computer. What happens if you upgrade the hardware in your computer? When you activate your copy of Windows Vista, a copy of the hardware fingerprint is stored on your hard disk and checked each time you start your computer. If you make substantial changes to your system hardware, you may be required to reactivate your copy of Windows. Because the activation mechanism assumes (mistakenly) that you've tried to install your copy of Windows on a second computer, internet activation will not work. In this case, you'll be required to speak to a support representative and manually enter a new activation code. For Windows XP, Microsoft published a detailed description of the algorithm it used to determine whether hardware changes were significant enough to require reactivation. For Windows Vista, Microsoft has chosen not to publish those details but has hinted that if you replace either your motherboard or your hard drive, you'll be required to reactivate your copy of Windows.

INSIDE OUT   Recover your product key

When you install a retail copy of Windows, the product key gets filed away, usually never to be seen again. But you might need to retrieve the product key at some point. If you have Windows Vista installed on multiple computers in your home or office, for example, you might lose track of which product key goes with which computer, resulting in confusion and hassle if you need to reinstall Windows Vista, or if you retire a computer and want to transfer its copy of Windows to a new computer. To find out which product key is in use on a given computer, we recommend a wonderful freeware utility called Keyfinder (*http://www.vista-io.com/0204*). This application displays the product keys that were used to install any version of Windows or Microsoft Office on a computer.

Activation Requirements for OEM Copies

If you purchase a new computer from an Original Equipment Manufacturer (OEM) with Windows Vista already installed on it, the licensing procedures are different, as are the rules for activation. To make matters more confusing, not all OEMs are created equal; instead, they're divided into two classes:

- Large system builders (Microsoft refers to these firms as "named" or "multi-national" OEMs or, informally, as "royalty OEMs") are allowed to install and preactivate Windows using a technology called System Locked Preinstallation (SLP). The preinstalled copy of Windows (including the recovery CD) contains configuration files that look for specific information in the system BIOS. As long as the BIOS matches, no activation is required. When you purchase a new computer from one of these large companies, a sticker containing a unique product key is affixed to the PC's case, but that key isn't used to activate Windows initially. Instead, the OEM uses a single master key to activate large numbers of computers. If you need to reinstall Windows, you can use the recovery disk provided by the manufacturer and you won't be asked for a product key at all, nor is activation required—as long as you start your computer using the SLP CD on the same computer (or one with the same motherboard/BIOS combination).

- Smaller firms that build PCs can also preinstall Windows Vista. These OEM copies are called System Builder copies, and they do require activation. The rules of the System Builder program require that the PC manufacturer preinstall Windows using specific tools so that you accept a license agreement and activate the software when you first turn on the PC. In addition, they are required to supply the purchaser with the Windows Vista media (typically a DVD) and affix a product key sticker to the PC's case. If you need to reinstall Windows on this computer, you must enter the product key and go through activation again.

The license agreement for a retail copy of Windows Vista allows you to transfer it to another computer, provided that you completely remove it from the computer on which it was previously installed. An OEM copy, by contrast, is tied to the computer on which it was originally installed. You may reinstall an OEM copy of Windows Vista an unlimited number of times on the same computer. However, you are prohibited by the license agreement from transferring that copy of Windows to another computer.

Product Activation and Corporate Licensing

Businesses that purchase licenses in bulk through a Microsoft Volume Licensing (VL) program receive VL media and product keys that require activation under a different set of rules than those that apply to retail or OEM copies. Under the terms of a volume license agreement, each computer with a copy of Windows Vista must have a valid license and must be activated. Under new activation procedures for Windows Vista, businesses can purchase product keys that allow multiple activations, or they can use Key Management servers to activate computers within their organization.

For more details on volume licensing programs for Windows and other Microsoft software, check the Microsoft Volume Licensing home page at *http://www.microsoft.com/ licensing*.

Dealing with Product Validation

After you successfully activate your copy of Windows Vista, you're still subject to periodic anti-piracy checks from Microsoft. This process, called *validation*, verifies that your copy of Windows Vista has not been tampered with to bypass activation. It also allows Microsoft to undo the activation process for a computer when it determines after the fact that the product key was stolen or used in violation of a volume licensing agreement.

Validation takes two forms: an internal tool that constantly checks licensing and activation files to determine that they haven't been tampered with; and an online tool that restricts access to some downloads and updates.

If your system fails validation, some key features no longer work, including the Windows Vista Aero interface, ReadyBoost, and Windows Defender. Updates to Windows are also unavailable, with the exception of critical security updates delivered via Automatic Updates.

In Microsoft's parlance, a system that has failed a validation check is no longer "genuine," and messages to that effect appear on the desktop and when you attempt to access features that have been restricted. After the initial validation failure, you have 30 days to reactivate and revalidate. When that grace period expires, Windows shifts into a "reduced functionality mode," in which your ability to use Windows is severely limited. There is no Start menu, desktop icons are hidden, and the desktop background is solid black. You can use Internet Explorer for one hour, at which time the system logs you out with no warning.

If this sounds like an unpleasant experience, you're right. Dialog boxes that appear when you shift into reduced functionality mode allow you to activate Windows or purchase a product key online; if you feel that the validation or activation failure is in error, you should contact Microsoft as soon as possible after seeing the initial warning message rather than waiting for the 30-day grace period to expire.

Transferring Files and Settings from Another Computer

If you upgrade an existing computer to Windows Vista, all of your data and most of your programs should survive the journey intact. But what do you do with your data and settings if you purchase a new computer, or if you decide to do a clean install on your existing system? With Windows Vista, you can use a utility called Windows Easy Transfer to handle most of the grunt work.

With the help of this utility, the direct successor to Windows XP's Files And Settings Transfer Wizard, you can migrate settings and files from your old computer to the new one (or from your old installation of Windows Vista to a new, clean one). Although the wizard has its limitations, it's highly flexible and offers an impressive number of customization options. You can use it to transfer files and settings from Windows XP or any edition of Windows Vista except Starter Edition; it also allows you to transfer files (but not settings) from a computer running Windows 2000.

> **Note**
> You can transfer files and settings from a 32-bit version of Windows to a 64-bit version, but the transfer won't work in reverse. You can't use this utility to copy files or settings from a 64-bit Windows version to a 32-bit version.

Windows Easy Transfer is simple and straightforward in operation, but describing it is another story. It would take a whiteboard the size of a billboard to map out all the possible paths you can follow when using this utility. So rather than describe every step, we'll list the broad outlines and count on you to find your way through the maze.

> **Note**
>
> If you want to transfer programs as well as files from your old PC to a new one, Microsoft plans to offer a utility called the Windows Easy Transfer Companion. The software is based on technology acquired when Microsoft purchased Apptimum Inc., the developer of the Alohabob PC Relocator program. At the time we wrote this book, Windows Easy Transfer Companion was scheduled to enter beta testing in early 2007.

Making a Connection

To accomplish the transfer, you need to establish a data connection between the old and new computer. You can use any of these four methods:

- **Easy Transfer Cable** This custom cable, available for purchase from Microsoft, allows high-speed transfers over a direct connection between USB 2.0 ports on both computers. You cannot use a standard USB cable for this task.

- **Network** You can connect two computers over a local area network and transfer settings directly from the old computer to the new one. A Fast Ethernet or Gigabit Ethernet connection is by far your best choice, especially if you want to transfer a large number of data files.

- **Writable CDs or DVDs** Using this method has the advantage of creating a backup copy that you can store. Pay particular attention to the transfer size, as calculated by the wizard; this value determines how many disks will be required for the transfer

- **Removable media, including USB flash drives and external hard disks** If a direct connection isn't practical or possible (if you're planning to wipe out an existing partition so that you can do a clean install on the same computer, for example), you can save the wizard's output to a compressed file and then restore it after you finish setup. If you're using a USB flash drive that's smaller than the total amount of date to be transferred, you can fill it up on the old computer, transfer its contents to the new computer, then return to the old computer and repeat the process. Do this as many times as is necessary to complete the transfer.

If you're replacing your old computer with a new one running Windows Vista, your best bet is to connect the two computers over a local area network (or using an Easy Transfer cable) and then run Windows Easy Transfer. This technique is not only the fastest way to get your new computer up and running, it's also the best way to avoid losing data. Because your existing data files remain intact on the old computer, you can recover easily if the wizard inadvertently leaves behind a crucial data file. If neither of these options is available, you can use external storage devices or media—an external USB or FireWire hard drive, or dual-layer DVDs, for example—to physically carry the data between the two computers.

1. Start the Windows Easy Transfer utility on both computers.

    ○   On the old computer, you can use the Windows Vista DVD (run Setup.exe and click Transfer Files And Settings From Another Computer on the opening screen). If the installation disc isn't available, run the wizard on the new computer first and follow the prompts to copy the program files to a USB flash drive, to a writable CD or DVD, or to an external hard disk. If the old computer is running Windows Vista, this step isn't necessary. If you've connected the computers using an Easy Transfer cable, this step is handled automatically.

    ○   On the new computer, click the Start button and then choose All Programs, Accessories, System Tools, Windows Easy Transfer. (You can also type **Windows Easy Transfer** in the Search box on the Start menu or type **migwiz** at any command prompt, including the Run dialog box.) Click Next at the opening page.

2. On the new computer, click Start a New Transfer. Follow the prompts to choose how you want to transfer the data between computers.

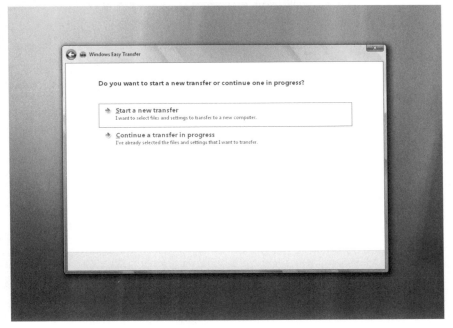

   3. Click My New Computer.

   1. Follow the next few prompts to specify that Windows Easy Transfer is already running on the old computer. If you're using a network connection, you'll be prompted to open Windows Firewall settings if necessary. You'll also need to obtain an eight-digit alphanumeric key (click No, I Need a Key, as shown on the next page); this security precaution prevents Windows Easy Transfer from being used to steal data surreptitiously.

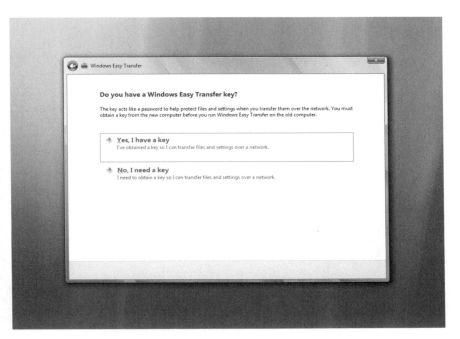

2. Write down the eight-digit key displayed on the screen and return to the old computer.

3. Follow the wizard's prompts, choosing the New Transfer operation, and specify that you plan to use the network to transfer files. When you reach the Do You Have a Windows Easy Transfer Key screen, click Yes, I Have a Key. On the following page enter the key from the other computer.

4. When Windows confirms that you've successfully made a connection, return to the old computer and choose which files to transfer.

Choosing What To Transfer

When you reach the What Do You Want To Transfer To Your New Computer stage, you have the three choices shown on the next page.

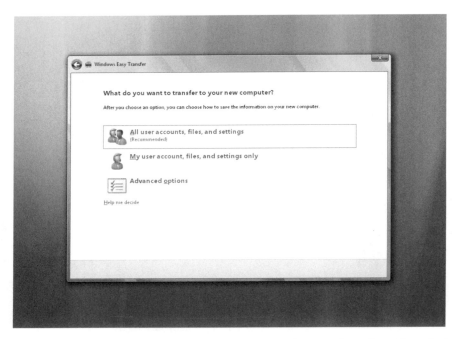

The top two options offer simple, no-nonsense results: Windows Easy Transfer locates everything in your user profile or grabs all files and settings for all defined user profiles. By default, the default settings migrate the following items:

- **Files and folders** From folders that are typically used for data files—My Documents, My Pictures, and Shared Documents, in Windows XP—all files are migrated automatically, regardless of extension. You can specify additional folders that you want the wizard to copy to the new computer.

- **Digital media files** Music files, playlists, album art, pictures in standard formats, and video files are transferred, regardless of their location.

- **E-mail and contacts** The wizard collects mail account settings, messages, and address books from Microsoft Outlook Express, Windows Mail, and Microsoft Outlook. It does not keep track of individual identities in Outlook Express; all mail for all identities is merged during the transfer.

- **User-specific settings** This category includes visual settings, such as your current color scheme, desktop background, and screen saver; folder and taskbar options; accessibility options; phone, modem, and dial-up networking connections; and network printers and drives.

- **Internet settings and Favorites** The wizard copies the contents of your Favorites folder and cookies to the new computer. It does not, however, retain user names, passwords, and other details saved by Microsoft Internet Explorer's Auto-Complete feature.

- **Application settings**   The wizard does not migrate program files; instead, it copies the settings and preference files to the correct location on the new computer and uses those preferences when you install the program on the new computer. Registry settings and preference files for a long list of programs are copied automatically. Naturally, this list is heavy on Microsoft programs—all versions of Microsoft Office from Office 2000 through 2007, Microsoft Works 8.0, MSN Messenger, Windows Live Messenger, and Windows Movie Maker 2.1. But it also includes the following list of third-party products:

  - Ad-aware 6 Professional
  - Adobe Creative Suite 2
  - Adobe ImageReady CS
  - Adobe Photoshop CS and CS 9
  - Adobe Acrobat Reader 4.0 and 5.0 and Reader 6.0 and 7.0
  - AOL Instant Messenger 5.9
  - Corel Paintshop Pro 9
  - CuteFTP 6 and 7 Professional
  - Eudora 5 or 6
  - ICQ 2003
  - Ipswitch WS_FTP Professional
  - iTunes 6
  - Lotus Notes
  - Lotus SmartSuite
  - Mozilla Firefox 1.5
  - MusicMatch Jukebox
  - Odigo 4
  - Quicken Home and Business
  - QuickTime Player
  - RealPlayer Basic
  - SpyBot Search & Destroy 1.4
  - Winamp
  - Windows Media Player
  - WinZip
  - WordPerfect Office 11, 12 and X3
  - Yahoo! Messenger

Chapter 2

INSIDE OUT See the full list of migrated programs

Is your favorite program on the list of programs whose settings are migrated by the Files And Settings Transfer Wizard? You can view the full list by opening an XML file called Migapp.xml, which is stored in the Support\Migwiz folder on the Windows Vista DVD. (After installation, this and other setting files are available in %SystemRoot%\System32\ Migwiz.) Entries here define the registry settings and user files that are migrated for each program.

You'll notice that some of the applications listed in Migapp.xml do not appear to be the latest versions. For example, iTunes 7 was released around the same time as Windows Vista, as was Mozilla Firefox 2.0. It's possible that Microsoft will provide downloadable updates for these configuration files. And in many cases, the registry settings for newer versions are the same as for older ones, making it possible for the wizard to perform the transfer successfully despite the incorrect version information.

If you select Advanced Options from the What Do You Want To Transfer To Your New Computer? page of the wizard, it's possible to customize the options you choose here. (You can reach the exact same dialog box even if you chose one of the first two options in this dialog box. Just click the Customize button at the bottom of the Review Selected Files and Settings dialog box.)

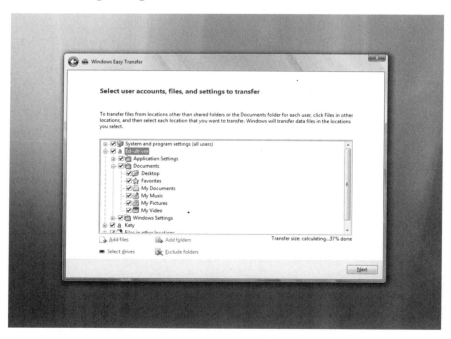

From top to bottom, the items in this tree include system and program settings for all users, documents and settings in each selected profile, and files in other locations. By default, every available application setting, Windows setting, and shared document location is selected. You can remove settings from this list, add or remove individual files or entire drives, or designate folders to be on include and exclude lists. Why exclude a drive or folder? If you have particularly large collections of some types of data files, such as digital music or videos, you might want to copy those files directly, using an external hard disk.

- **Add Files**   Choose this option if you want to be certain that you migrate a specific file from a specific location without also transferring other files in that folder. You can add an unlimited number of files to this list.

- **Select Drives**   A simple browse box displays a list of all drives that Windows can detect. Select or clear the checkboxes to include or exclude files and folders from those drives.

- **Add Folders**   Use this option if you store data in a location other than the default system folders and you want the wizard to migrate all files and subfolders from that folder, regardless of their extension. You can add an unlimited number of folders to this list.

- **Exclude Folders**   If you mistakenly add a folder to the list above, select it here to remove it again. This option is useful if you want to migrate files from an external drive or a separate data volume but want to avoid copying files in some locations.

Restoring Files and Settings on Your New Computer

If you use a network or cable connection to transfer files between two computers with Windows Easy Transfer, you control both ends of the process. After you enter the correct security keys on each end, establish a connection, and specify which files and settings you want to copy to your new PC, click Transfer. When the operation is complete, you'll see a detailed status report on the new computer indicating which files and settings were transferred.

If you've saved the files and settings to a USB flash drive, an external hard disk, a shared network drive, or a stack of writable CDs or DVDs, run Windows Easy Transfer on the new computer, choose the Continue A Transfer in Progress option, and click No, I've Copied Files And Settings to a CD, DVD, or Other Removable Media. Choose the location, enter a password (if you set one when saving the data), and click Next.

If the user names on the old and new computers are different, you'll be prompted to choose matching pairs of accounts, as shown here. You can choose from existing accounts or type in a new name to create an account on the fly.

Chapter 2

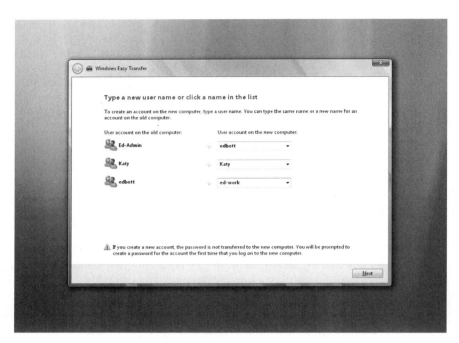

After completing the match-up, click Next, and then click Transfer to complete the operation.

Configuring System Recovery Options

System Restore made its first shaky appearance in the late, unlamented Windows Me. It was vastly improved in Windows XP, and in Windows Vista it takes on whole new responsibilities. As in previous Windows versions, the System Restore feature takes periodic snapshots of system files and configuration details, allowing you to undo changes and roll back a system configuration to a time when it was known to work correctly. In Windows Vista, the service responsible for the System Restore function expands to include regular volume snapshots that include data files. The effect of this expansion is to create real-time backups of individual data files, allowing you to recover from unwanted edits or unexpected deletions by restoring a previous version of a file.

System Restore in Windows Vista offers far fewer opportunities for customization. In this section, we explain how System Restore works and what it backs up, how to turn it on or off for a given disk, and how to create a manual restore point at a time when you're not trying to solve a problem. If you're looking for step-by-step instructions on how to use System Restore to recover from a crash, see "Rolling Back to a Stable State with System Restore," in Chapter 23.

To access the full set of System Restore options, open System in Control Panel and click the System Protection link in the Tasks pane. The resulting dialog box is shown in Figure 2-10.

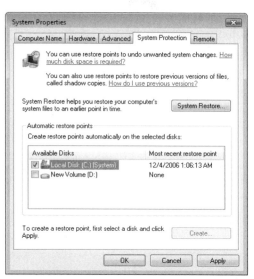

Figure 2-10 By default, System Restore monitors changes to the System drive. If you enable automatic restore points for a drive, Windows sets aside up to 15 percent of that drive's space for storage of restore points.

Using this dialog box, you can enable automatic monitoring for any local drive. By design, System Restore keeps tabs only on the system drive on your system. If you've set aside one or more drives exclusively for data, you might want to enable the creation of automatic restore points on those drives, which has the effect of creating shadow copies of files you change or delete on that drive. This step is especially important if you've relocated one or more profile folders to drives other than the one on which Windows is installed. To enable or disable the creation of automatic restore points for a drive, open the System Properties dialog box and select or clear the checkbox next to that drive letter on the System Protection tab.

You can also use this dialog box to manually create a restore point for any drive currently being monitored. Normally, automatic restore points are created once daily and before major system events, such as the installation of a program or a device driver. System Restore points are also created by Windows Vista Backup (both file backups and Complete PC Backups). To manually create a restore point, click the Create button at the bottom of the System Protection tab of the System Properties dialog box

By default, Windows uses up to 15 percent of a drive's available space to save restore points. (The minimum space required is 300 MB.) In Windows XP, the amount of space set aside for System Restore was configurable on the System Restore tab of the System Properties dialog box; this option is no longer offered in Windows Vista. You can, however, reduce this value if you want to pare back the amount of space used by System Restore. To do so, open Registry Editor (Regedit.exe) and navigate to the key HKLM\SOFTWARE\Microsoft\WindowsNT\CurrentVersion\SystemRestore\Cfg. In the right-hand pane, double-click the DiskPercent value and adjust it from the default setting of

15 to a number you find more reasonable. Note that this percentage applies to all monitored drives and cannot be configured individually.

To see how much space System Restore is currently using, open a Command Prompt window and issue the following command:

Vssadmin list shadowstorage

> **Note**
>
> The default location for System Restore data is *d*:\System Volume Information, where *d* is the letter of each drive. Each restore point is stored in its own subfolder, under a name that includes a unique 32-character alphanumeric identifier called a GUID. This location cannot be changed. On an NTFS drive, these files are not accessible to users, even those in the Administrators group; the default NTFS permissions grant access only to the System account.

If you've set up a dual-boot system with Windows XP and Windows Vista on the same system, you should be aware of one unfortunate side effect caused by this configuration. When you boot into Windows XP, the system wipes out all restore points created by Windows Vista. This unfortunate state of affairs is caused because Windows XP doesn't recognize the format of the newer restore points; assuming they're corrupt, it deletes them and creates new ones

> **CAUTION**
>
> System Restore is a powerful tool, and you shouldn't disable it without a good reason. If you're extremely low on disk space and a hard disk upgrade is impractical or impossible (as on some notebook computers), you might choose to do so. Otherwise, let it run.

INSIDE OUT   Customize System Restore intervals

System Restore settings and preferences are stored in the registry, in the key HKLM\SOFTWARE\Microsoft\WindowsNT\CurrentVersion\SystemRestore. Most of the values found here can be adjusted safely and easily using the System Protection tab of the System Properties dialog box. However, some settings can only be adjusted by editing the values stored in this registry key.

Normally, System Restore automatically creates restore points every 24 hours. To adjust this interval, change the value RPGlobalInterval from its default setting of 86,400 seconds (24 hours).. Cut this figure in half, to 43,200, if you want to save restore points twice a day; triple it, to 259,200, if you want restore points created every three days.

By default, System Restore is set to delete restore points after roughly 136 years—or 4,294,967,295 seconds, to be more precise. The practical effect of this setting (which was a mere 90 days in Windows XP) is to delete System Restore points only when space is absolutely required. If you prefer to adjust this interval, change the value of RPLifeInterval; a setting of 7,776,000 seconds is equivalent to 90 days). A value of 2,592,000 seconds is equal to 30 days.

Finishing Your Windows Vista Installation

Technically, Windows Vista setup is complete when you reach the desktop and see the Welcome Center for the first time. In the real world, there's still a short checklist of system settings you'll want (or need) to go through soon. Most of the items on the following list are one-time tasks that you'll set and forget. It doesn't include performance tweaks or maintenance tasks that you perform occasionally, nor does it include personalization settings you might want to change over time. What all of these settings have in common is that they are per-machine settings, not per-user settings.

To learn how to adjust personal settings for your user account, see Chapter 3, "Personalizing Windows Vista."

Adjust Basic Display Settings

Your screen resolution determines how many pixels are available for Windows to use when displaying on-screen objects. Objects on the screen appear larger at lower resolutions and smaller when you switch to a higher resolution. The Display Settings dialog box, available from Control Panel's Personalization menu, shows the full range of supported resolutions for your video adapter and display (as determined by Plug and Play). In Figure 2-11, for example, you can slide the Resolution to any of eight settings, ranging from 800 x 600 at the Low end of the scale to 1280 x 1024 at the High end.

Figure 2-11 If you've connected multiple monitors, you can adjust display settings independently for each one. Click the monitor icon to select settings for that display.

On analog monitors, you can adjust the display to any resolution and get acceptable results. On flat-panel LCD displays, you'll get best results by setting this value to match the display's native resolution, which corresponds to the number of pixels on the display. If your video memory is limited, you may need to choose a lower color depth to enable higher resolutions.

For instructions on how to adjust other display-related settings, including the DPI Scaling option that improves readability at high resolutions, see "Making Text Easier to Read," in Chapter 3.

Check Your Security Settings

The Windows Security Center should be familiar, at least conceptually, to anyone who's previously used Windows XP. In Windows Vista, this dialog box is available from the top of the Security page in Control Panel and covers the territory shown in Figure 2-12.

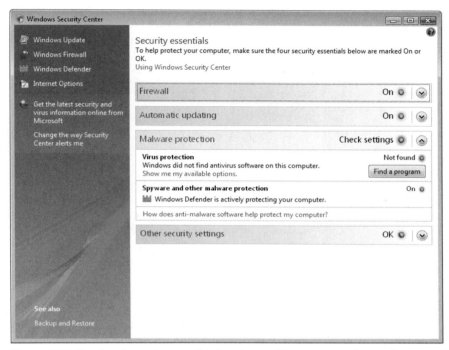

Figure 2-12 If you've chosen to use a third-party security program, make sure it reports its status accurately to Security Center.

A default installation of Windows Vista includes solutions that turn every item on the Security Center list green, indicating an OK level of protection—with one exception. Under the Malware Protection heading, you'll see an amber icon next to Virus Protection, indicating that this level of protection requires additional software.

If you've chosen to use a different program in place of any of the Windows default security features, you should check here after installing the other program to ensure that it's correctly reporting its coverage to Security Center.

> For details on how to customize Security Center, including instructions for disabling its notifications, see "Monitoring Security in Windows Vista," in Chapter 10.

Connect to the Internet and Your Local Network

The Network and Sharing Center, shown in Figure 2-13, provides one-stop access to all networking settings. Windows Vista doesn't include a wizard to adjust these settings; you'll need to check them manually here, or adjust each one as the need for network features arises. If you want to share files among computers on a home or small business network, check the settings for Network Discovery and File Sharing. Both should be on for sharing to work properly.

Chapter 2

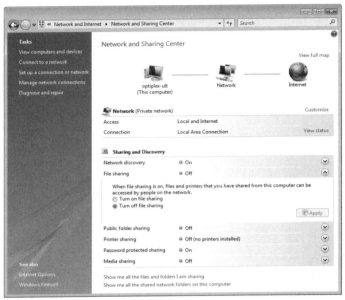

Figure 2-13 In a default installation, File Sharing is disabled but Network Discovery is enabled. That means other network users will be able to see your computer but won't be able to access files stored on it.

Finish Hardware Setup

The DVD containing the initial release of Windows Vista includes more than 19,500 drivers, and on the day that Windows Vista was first available on retail shelves another 10,000 signed drivers were available from Windows Update. By the time you read this, that number will no doubt have increased again. Considering that many of those drivers work with multiple devices, the chances are good that most if not all of your hardware will work immediately after you finish Windows Setup. (That's guaranteed to be true if you purchase a new PC with Windows Vista already installed; in that case, the manufacturer typically installs drivers for all devices in the system.)

To verify that every installed device is working as it should, open Device Manager (type Device Manager in the Search box on the Start menu or in Control Panel and click the icon in the results list). Look in the list of installed devices, shown in Figure 2-14, for any warning icons that indicate a device was detected but no driver was installed.

Figure 2-14 The yellow exclamation point over the USB 2.0 Gigabit Adapter device means you'll have to manually locate and install a driver for this device.

If you have any USB or IEEE 1394 (FireWire) devices, such as printers, external hard drives, cameras, or scanners, connect them now and confirm they work correctly. If you downloaded any updated drivers before setting up Windows Vista, this is the time to install them. In many cases, a visit to Windows Update will locate the correct driver for a device.

For a complete discussion of Device Manager and drivers, see Chapter 5, "Setting Up and Troubleshooting Hardware."

Add or Remove Windows Features

The Windows Vista edition you purchase determines its basic feature set, and a standard installation makes all those features available without asking you (or allowing you, for that matter) to pick and choose. In addition to these core features, a small set of advanced and specialized features is available as well. To review this list and enable or disable any of the features on it, open the Programs menu in Control Panel and click Turn Windows Features On Or Off (under the Programs And Features heading).

Compared to previous Windows versions, the number of available options is extremely limited. The Windows Features dialog box, shown in Figure 2-15 on the next page, indicates which features are available for your edition. A check mark means the feature is currently enabled, and a blank box means the feature is disabled. If you see a filled box, the feature is partially enabled; click the plus sign to the left of the entry to see more details about it.

Chapter 2

Figure 2-15 Some of the features in this list are familiar, but most involve esoteric networking options. Click any item in the list to see descriptive help text for that option.

Set Power and Sleep Settings

By default, Windows Vista applies the Balanced power scheme, one of three predefined options, to all systems. These settings might not match your preference, especially if you want to have your system accessible from the network and available for in-person access without having to resume from hibernation. To change power schemes, open the Power Options dialog box (available from the System And Maintenance or Hardware And Sound menu in Control Panel) and choose one of the three options shown in Figure 2-16.

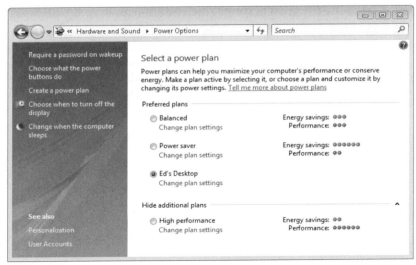

Figure 2-16 Use the Create A Power Plan link in the Tasks pane to add to the list of ready-made power schemes. Click Change Plan Settings to adjust individual options for your new plan.

The deeper you dig into Power Options, the more likely you are to discover a wealth of useful settings there, especially on notebook computers, where you can make adjustments that are different based on whether a system is running on batteries or on AC power.

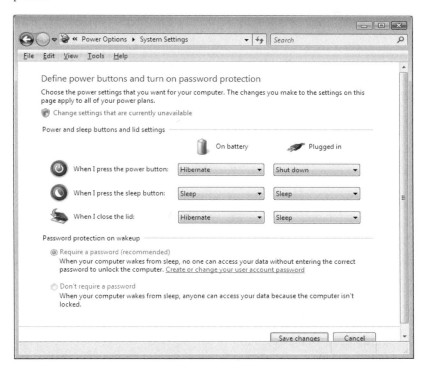

Configure Remote Access Options

All Windows Vista editions support Remote Assistance, and by default all Windows Vista installations allow Remote Assistance connections with proper authentication. Business, Ultimate, and Enterprise editions support incoming Remote Desktop connections as well, a powerful option that allows you to log on to any Windows Vista system from across a network. By default, Remote Desktop connections are disabled. To change these settings, open System in Control Panel, click Remote Settings, and adjust the options shown under the Remote Desktop heading. In Figure 2-17 on the next page, for example, we've allowed incoming connections only from computers where users log on using Network Level Authentication in Windows Vista.

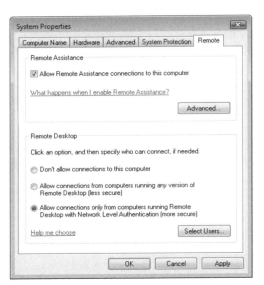

Figure 2-17 Allowing incoming Remote Desktop connections only from users who can authenticate using Network Level Authentication with a strong password provides excellent security.

For more details on how to use Remote Assistance, see "Connecting to Another PC with Windows Remote Assistance," in Chapter 9.

Set Up Additional User Accounts

If you anticipate that your computer will be used by more than one person, set up accounts for each additional user now. Creating standard accounts for users, as we've done in Figure 2-18, ensures that they won't be fooled into accepting malware and will be unable to install unsigned device drivers that can cause system instability. They'll also be blocked from deleting essential system files.

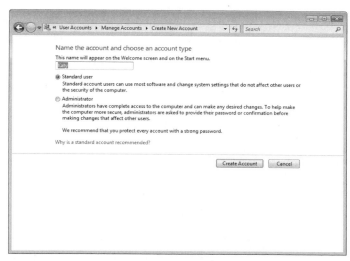

Figure 2-18 Set up ordinary user accounts using the Standard User account option.

For more details on how to create and manage user accounts in Windows Vista, see "Working with User Accounts," in Chapter 11.

Create a Backup Image

When you've finished with Setup and tweaked basic system settings to match your preferences, it's a perfect time to back up your system by creating a system image. This option is available as part of the built-in Complete PC Backup feature in Business, Ultimate, and Enterprise editions. You'll need third-party software such as Norton Ghost to handle this task in Home Basic and Home Premium edition. Figure 2-19 on the next page shows a Complete PC Backup about to be created.

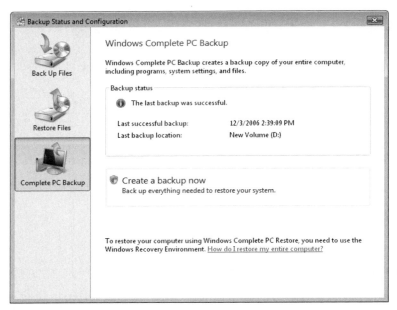

Figure 2-19 The Complete PC Backup feature (available only in Business, Ultimate, and Enterprise editions) allows you to create a snapshot of a working system that can be restored in minutes.

Personalizing Windows Vista

One of the subtle changes that Microsoft made in moving from Windows XP to Windows Vista was to include the word *Personalize* prominently in the user interface of the new operating system. Certainly earlier versions of Windows could be tailored, customized, modified to suit a user's needs and preferences—in a word, *personalized*. But the P word itself was missing. Now, when you right-click your desktop, the shortcut menu that pops up features an icon-festooned *Personalize* command. *Personalize Windows* is also one of the fourteen "Get Started with Windows" tasks that appear in the new operating system's Welcome Center.

So the message is clear: It's your operating system; make it reflect your tastes, your needs, your style. Make it work for you. More than any previous version of Windows, Windows Vista provides myriad tools for doing just that—tools that we will survey in this chapter.

What's in Your Edition?

The Aero interface, described in the section "Customizing the Aero Interface," is not available in Windows Vista Home Basic Edition. All other features described in this chapter are available in all editions.

Customizing the Aero User Interface

The Windows Vista setup program performs various performance tests as one of the last steps in the installation process, and if your graphics hardware meets certain requirements, it enables the full Aero user interface on your system. In a nutshell, the graphics requirements for Aero are:

- A Windows Vista Display Driver Model (WDDM) (Aero does not run on devices with Windows XP drivers)

- A DirectX 9–class graphics processing unit (GPU) that supports Pixel Shader 2.0 in hardware, with 32 bits per pixel

- Graphics throughput of at least 1800 MB per second at resolutions equivalent to 1280 × 1024 (or at the native resolution of a mobile computer's built-in display)

- At least 1 GB of random access memory (RAM)

> **Note**
>
> The complete Aero "experience" also requires Windows Vista Home Premium, Business, Ultimate, or Enterprise.

The most prominent features of the full Aero interface are as follows:

- Transparent window frames

- Live previews of icons on the taskbar (hover your mouse over a taskbar icon and see a miniature representation of the contents of the window that will open if you click)

- Live previews of the windows that you can switch to by pressing Alt+Tab

- "Flip 3D"—a feature that shows all open windows (and the desktop) as a three-dimensional stack when you press the Windows logo key+Tab

- Smoother window dragging, without "tearing" artifacts

- Interactive window controls (close buttons that glow on hover, for example)

- Animated window closings and openings

If your system meets the performance criteria for Aero, then when you right-click the desktop, choose Personalize, and click Window Color And Appearance, you will see a dialog box comparable to the one shown in Figure 3-1.

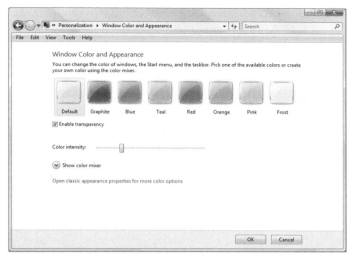

Figure 3-1 On Aero-capable systems, the Windows Color And Appearance dialog box lets you change the display characteristics of window frames and the taskbar.

Note

If you're running Windows Vista Home Basic on a system that has the requisite graphics muscle for Aero, you will see a dialog box similar to Figure 3-1, but without the Enable Transparency check box.

The eight color options in this dialog box have their most pronounced effect on window frames. You'll also notice some effect on your taskbar and Start menu, particularly with the brighter colors (red and orange, for example) and at higher Color Intensity levels. If none of the eight choices meets your needs exactly, you can click Show Color Mixer and dial in your own blend of Hue, Saturation, and Brightness:

Besides letting you choose colors, the Window Color And Appearance dialog box enables you to adjust the transparency of your window frames. Dragging the Color Intensity slider to the right makes window frames darker and less transparent. If you want lighter colors but don't fancy transparency at all, you can clear the Enable Transparency check box. You might find this "Aero sans trans" approach convenient at times if you need to generate pictures of windows for presentation purposes and don't want the pictures to include distracting "behind the scenes" material.

INSIDE OUT Keep the glass, squelch the animation

What if you like transparency but don't care for the animated opening and closing of windows? You can try opening Control Panel, clicking System And Maintenance, clicking Performance Information And Tools, then clicking Adjust Visual Effects (in the task pane at the left). Clearing Animate Windows When Minimizing And Maximizing, in the Performance Options dialog box, will turn off these animated transitions. On our test systems, this resulted in unnatural, jerky display behavior. Your mileage might differ, however; if you dislike animation, it's worth a try.

Turning Aero Off

Even if you're not wild about transparency and animation, there's plenty to like about Aero. Smoother window dragging, the preview icons on the taskbar, and the improved task-switching features (Alt+Tab and Windows logo key+Tab) are well worth the price admission—for most users. Nevertheless, admission is not entirely free; the Aero interface uses more graphics memory than the non-Aero interface—especially because achieving smoother window movement, without tearing artifacts, requires Aero to store the contents of all open windows in video memory, not just the windows that are currently visible.

If Aero slows you down or annoys you for any other reason, you can turn it off. In the Window Color And Appearance dialog box (see Figure 3-1), click Open Classic Appearance Properties For More Color Options. This will take you to the Appearance Settings dialog box, shown in Figure 3-2. (If you change your mind, revisit the Appearance Settings dialog box and choose Windows Aero.)

Figure 3-2 To turn the Aero interface off, choose a color scheme other than Windows Aero.

Choosing anything in the Color Scheme list, other than Windows Aero, turns the Aero interface off. For a solid, if stolid, user interface that retains the new look and feel of Windows Vista without taxing your graphics subsystem, choose Windows Vista Basic.

If you are running the Home Premium, Ultimate, Business, or Enterprise edition of Windows Vista on a system without Aero capability, right-clicking the desktop, choosing Personalize, and clicking Window Color And Appearance will take you directly to the Appearance Settings dialog box shown in Figure 3-2, rather than the Window Color And Appearance dialog box shown in Figure 3-1. (Your Color Scheme list will look a little different, because it won't include the Windows Aero option.)

Adopting the Retro (Windows 2000) Look

If what you crave is the latest operating-system feature set on a Windows 2000–style desktop, Windows Vista will accommodate you. In fact, the Color Scheme list shown in Figure 3-2 includes two options—Windows Standard and Windows Classic—that will recreate the look and feel of earlier days. If you're really into right angles, check out these color schemes. (There's not a lot of difference between the two.)

Chapter 3

In addition to squaring off the window frames and taskbar buttons, the Windows Standard and Windows Classic color schemes replace the relatively compact Windows Vista-style Start menu with one that uses fly-out submenus, like this:

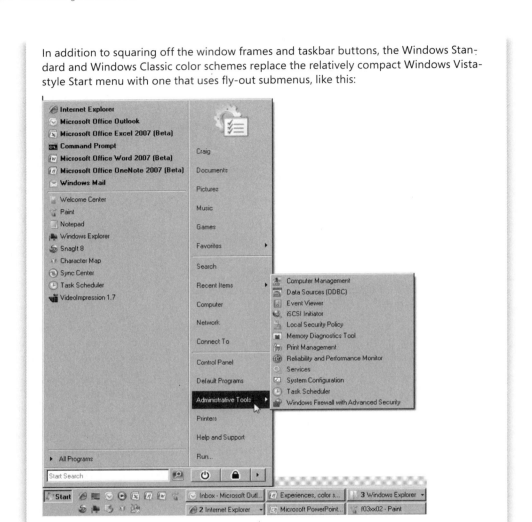

Modifying the Predefined Color Schemes

Each of the predefined color schemes is a group of settings that specifies fonts and sizes of certain interface elements, as well as colors. You can tweak these predefined schemes by clicking Advanced in the Appearance Settings dialog box (see Figure 3-2). Doing so produces the Advanced Appearance dialog box, shown in Figure 3-3.

Figure 3-3 The Advanced Appearance dialog box lets you further customize the built-in color schemes.

In the sample window of the Advanced Appearance dialog box, click the screen element you want to change. Then use the lists and buttons at the bottom of the dialog box to make your color, font, and size selections. For title bars, you can specify two colors; Windows creates a gradient from Color 1 (at the left end of the title bar) to Color 2 (at the right end). The Item list includes some items that don't appear in the sample window, so you might want to review it in its entirety before you move on.

INSIDE OUT   Be careful with the Advanced Appearance dialog box

The Advanced Appearance dialog box itself has a distinctly "unadvanced" appearance. The squared-off windows in its sample area betray its ancient heritage, and the text below the sample window gives fair warning. The dialog box is really designed for customizing the Windows Classic and Windows Standard color schemes. You can use it to modify the Windows Aero and Windows Vista Basic color schemes, but you might not get exactly the results you're looking for, and you won't find Undo or Default buttons anywhere. Experiment carefully and keep your own mental cookie trail. If you want to be absolutely sure you can find your way out of the pool, create a restore point before you dive in. (See "Configuring System Protection Options," in Chapter 20.)

The Color button for each item opens a selection of standard colors. If you don't see the one you're looking for, click the Other button. Windows then displays a Color dialog box, as shown in Figure 3-4. Should you fail to find exactly the color you want in the Basic Colors palette, you can define your own custom colors. Change the color that appears in the Color|Solid box, either by adjusting the positions of the hue/saturation crosshair and the luminosity arrow or by specifying numeric values. When you have found the color you want, click Add To Custom Colors. If you want to replace an existing custom color, select it before you specify your new color.

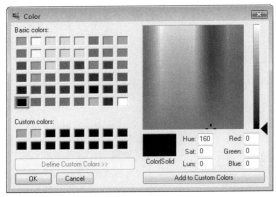

Figure 3-4 If you know a color's RGB specification, you can enter the values directly in the Red, Green, and Blue boxes.

Making Text Easier to Read

If you scroll through the Item list in the Advanced Appearance dialog box (see Figure 3-3) you'll find several text elements that you can customize. In earlier versions of Windows, users who wanted larger text sometimes bumped up the point size for one or more of these elements. Scaling up this way was problematic, though, because not all elements of the Windows user interface could be scaled successfully. Dialog box text in particular was a problem, so that users sometimes found themselves looking at large title bars and scroll bars, large menu text, but small dialog-box text. Windows Vista offers a better way.

If you like to work at high screen resolutions but you find yourself straining to read the text, you can try the following:

- Look for scaling ("zoom") commands in the text-centered programs you use. Many programs, including most modern word processors, include these scaling features. Scaling text up to a readable size this way is a good solution for particular programs but doesn't change the size of icon text, system menus (such as the Start menu), or system dialog boxes.

- Use the Advanced Appearance dialog box to adjust the size of particular user-interface text elements. This method is still available but is not ideal.

- Use the Adjust Font Size (DPI) command—the "better way" offered by Windows Vista. (DPI stands for *dots per inch*.)

To get to the Adjust Font Size (DPI) command, right-click the desktop and choose Personalize from the shortcut menu. You'll find the command in the task pane at the left side of the window. (Alternatively, type **dpiscaling** in the Start menu's Search box and press Enter.) You'll need to pass a UAC prompt when you choose this command. Figure 3-5 shows the DPI Scaling dialog box.

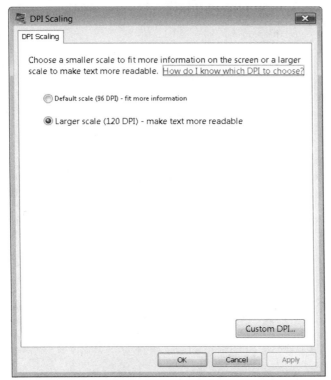

Figure 3-5 Adjusting the DPI scaling from the default 96 to a higher level allows you to have readable text at higher screen resolutions.

> **Note**
>
> A change in DPI scaling affects all accounts at a particular computer, not just the account that makes the change.

The dialog box makes it look like your only choices are 96 DPI (the default) or 120 DPI, which increases text size to about 125 percent of default. In fact you can set the DPI scaling factor to any position you like. Click Custom DPI to get to the dialog box shown in Figure 3-6 on the next page.

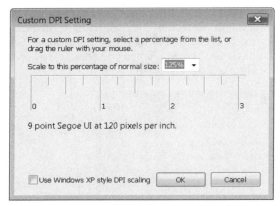

Figure 3-6 You can drag the ruler to adjust the scaling factor, or type directly into the Scale To This Percentage Of Normal Size box.

To change the scaling factor, drag any part of the ruler. Alternatively, you can either se-lect a value in the Scale To This Percentage Of Normal Size list or type directly into this box. What scaling factor is right? It depends on many things—the size and resolution of your screen, the programs you use, your eyes, and your preferences. You will likely need to try more than one combination of screen resolution and scaling factor to get your system exactly the way that works best for you.

> **Note**
>
> Changing the DPI scaling also changes the size of your desktop icons. To change icon size more dramatically, right-click the desktop and choose View. At the top of the sub-menu that appears, you'll find three commands—Large Icons, Medium Icons, and Clas-sic Icons. Medium is the default. Large is *really* large, and "Classic" is a euphemism for teensy. Take your pick.

If your system does not meet the hardware requirements for Aero, or if you are running Windows Vista Home Basic, the Use Windows XP Style DPI Scaling check box will be selected and unavailable. Windows will do its best to scale all text elements, both in the operating system's user interface and in your applications, using methods that do not involve desktop composition.

On the other hand, if you are using the full Aero interface, try clearing this check box if it's currently selected. Windows Vista will then use desktop composition in scaling your text.

(*Desktop composition* is the technology that enables Windows Vista, when running un-der the Aero interface, to achieve smooth window movement, thumbnail previews of taskbar buttons, transparent window frames, Flip 3D, and so on. With desktop composition on, applications write to video card memory buffers instead of directly to the screen, and the Desktop Window Manager component of Windows Vista arranges the video surfaces in the appropriate order and presents the results to the screen.)

Changes that you make in the DPI Scaling dialog box require a system restart to take effect. After you reboot, test some text-centered applications to see if you like the result. If you don't, return to the DPI Scaling dialog box and try another setting.

TROUBLESHOOTING

Some programs produce fuzzy text

If you're running Aero and have applied a nondefault font scaling factor, it is possible that some of your older programs will produce fuzzy text. Newer "DPI-Aware" programs get information about the current scaling factor from the operating system and adjust themselves accordingly. Older applications that were not designed with DPI scaling in mind assume they are running under the default scale of 96 DPI, and the operating system scales them. A side effect of this is that fonts and icons can sometimes appear fuzzy. If you find a particular program's display unsatisfactory, find the executable file for that program in Windows Explorer. (With most programs, you can right-click the entry in the Start menu and choose Open File Location on the shortcut menu.) Right-click the icon for the executable, choose Properties from the shortcut menu, and click the Compatibility tab. In the Settings section, select Disable Display Scaling On High DPI Settings.

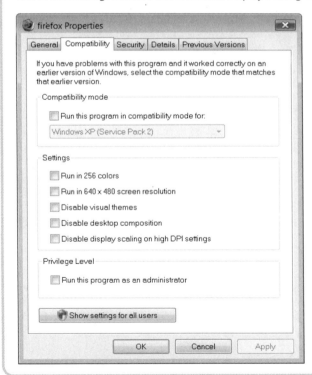

Chapter 3

Using Font Smoothing to Make Text Easier on the Eyes

ClearType is a "font-smoothing" technology patented by Microsoft and optimized for LCD (flat panel) displays. Font-smoothing rounds the corners of characters, eliminating jagged edges and easing eye strain. ClearType is turned on by default on all systems, regardless of display type, but if you're using a cathode-ray tube (CRT) display instead of an LCD display, you might want to try using Standard font-smoothing instead of ClearType. Microsoft believes that ClearType improves readability on both CRT and LCD displays, but if you're a CRT user you should probably compare the two font-smoothing methods to see which one works better for you. (You can also turn font-smoothing off altogether, of course, but it's hard to imagine any benefit from doing so.)

To check or change your font-smoothing settings, right-click the desktop, choose Personalize from the shortcut menu, click Effects in the Appearance Settings dialog box (see Figure 3-2). As Figure 3-7 shows, you can switch from one smoothing method to the other by opening the Use The Following Method To Smooth Edges Of Screen Fonts list.

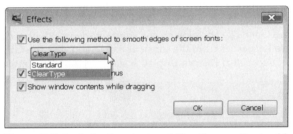

Figure 3-7 Both the Standard and ClearType methods of font smoothing can improve screen readability, but ClearType, the default, is optimized for LCD displays.

Windows Vista includes seven new fonts that are optimized for ClearType. The names of six of these—Constantia, Cambria, Corbel, Calibri, Candara, and Consolas—begin with the letter *c*—just to help *c*ement the *c*onnection with ClearType. If you're particularly prone to eye fatigue, you might want to consider favoring these fonts in documents you create. (Constantia and Cambria are serif fonts, considered particularly suitable for longer documents and reports. The other four are sans serif fonts, good for headlines and advertising.) The seventh ClearType-optimized font, Segoe UI, is the typeface used for text elements throughout the Windows Vista user interface. (The operating system also includes a ClearType-optimized font called Meiryo that's designed to improve the readability of horizontally arrayed Asian languages.)

For information about how ClearType works, visit Microsoft's ClearType site, at *http://www.vista-io.com/0301*. Microsoft also offers a valuable ClearType "tuner" that lets you optimize the way ClearType works on your system. You'll find the tuner at *http://www.vista-io.com/0302*. Additional information is available in the Knowledge Base; see article 306527, "How To use ClearType to Enhance Screen Fonts in Windows XP."

Customizing the Desktop Background

You can perk up any desktop with a background image. You can center an image on the desktop, stretch an image to fill, or repeat any image as many times as necessary to fill the space. Your background can be supplied by a graphics file in any of several common formats: bitmap (.bmp or .dib extension), Graphics Interchange Format (.gif), Joint Photographic Experts Group (.jpg or.jpeg), or Portable Network Graphics (.png).

> **Note**
>
> Unlike Windows XP, Windows Vista does not support the use of HTML files as desktop backgrounds.

To select a background, right-click the desktop, choose Personalize from the shortcut menu, and then click Desktop Background. The Picture Location in the Choose A Desktop Background dialog box (see Figure 3-8) provides a selection of useful categories. The Windows Wallpapers category itself is divided into several image categories. You might want to maximize the dialog box to get a better look at the offerings.

Figure 3-8 If you get tired of the wallpaper selections that come with Windows, you can always use your own pictures instead.

Chapter 3

If you don't find what you need, click Browse. The Open dialog box that appears will be focused at %Windir%\Web\Wallpaper—the folder that Windows Vista uses for its own offerings. But, of course, you can navigate to any folder on your system. Folders to which you navigate via the Browse button will subsequently appear in the Picture Location list, making it easy for you to go back and grab a different image from the same folder.

After you have chosen an image for your desktop background, select one of the three options at the bottom of the dialog box to let Windows know how you want the image positioned. The option at the left stretches the selected picture to fill the screen. This is most likely to be useful with JPEG images that have the same aspect ratio as your screen. Stretching bitmaps or images in a different aspect ratio is likely to produce unwelcome distortions. The center option tiles the selected image, and the option on the right centers it.

Here are some other ways to change the wallpaper:

- Right-click a JPEG or GIF file in Windows Explorer or Windows Photo Gallery and choose Set As Desktop Background. This centers the selected image.

- Right-click any image in Internet Explorer and choose Set As Background, This displays the selected image using the current sizing setting—full screen, tiled, or centered.

- Open any image file in Paint and choose one of the following command's from Paint's File menu: Set As Background (Tiled), Set As Background (Centered), or Set As Background (Stretched).

Choosing a Screen Saver

Screen savers don't save screens (in long-gone days when screens were invariably CRTs and in many offices displayed the same application at all hours of the working day, having an image move about during idle times probably did extend the service life of some displays), and they certainly don't save energy. But they're fun to watch. Windows Vista includes a few new ones and eliminates some that were part of Windows XP. To see the current offerings, right-click the desktop, choose Personalize from the shortcut menu, and then click Screen Saver.

> **Note**
>
> If you use a multi-monitor setup, the screen savers supplied with Windows Vista, unfortunately, "save" only the primary screen. The other(s) go blank when the screen saver goes into action.

As Figure 3-9 shows, the Screen Saver Settings dialog box includes a handy On Resume, Display Logon Screen check box. This box is selected by default. If you work in an environment where privacy is not a big concern, you can save yourself some hassle by clearing this check box.

Figure 3-9 Clearing the On Resume, Display Logon Screen in the Screen Saver Settings dialog box can save you the trouble of logging in every time you return to your desk.

Changing the Way Events Are Mapped to Sounds

Perhaps you've had this experience: You arrive a moment or two late for a meeting or class, discreetly turn on your computer at the end of the table or back of the room, and then cringe as your speakers trumpet your arrival. True, the Windows Startup sound is less raucous in Windows Vista than it was in Windows XP. But it's still a recognizable item, apt to cause annoyance in libraries, classrooms, concert halls, and other hushed venues. You can't substitute your own tune, but you can turn the startup sound off.

To turn the Windows Startup sound off, right-click the desktop, choose Personalize from the shortcut menu, and then click Sounds. In the Sound dialog box (see Figure 3-10), clear Play Windows Startup Sound.

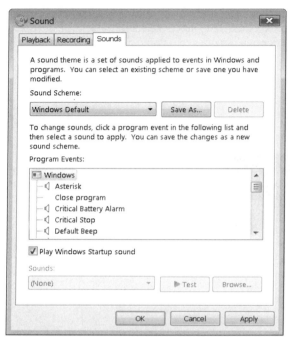

Figure 3-10 You can make sound decisions on the Sounds tab of the Sound dialog box.

In the same dialog box, you can customize the sounds that Windows plays in response to other system and application events. To see what sounds are currently mapped to events, scroll through the Program Events list. If an event has a sound associated with it, its name appears in the Sounds list, and you can click Test to hear it. To switch to a different sound, scroll through the Sounds list or click Browse. The list displays .wav files in %Windir%\Media, but any .wav file is eligible. To silence an event, select (None), the item at the top of the Sounds list.

INSIDE OUT

If you like event sounds in general but occasionally need complete silence from your computer, choose No Sounds in the Sound Scheme list when you want the machine to shut up. (Be sure to clear Play Windows Startup Sound as well.) When sound is welcome again, you can return to the Windows Default scheme—or to any other scheme you have set up. Switching to the No Sounds scheme won't render your system mute (you'll still be able to play music when you want to hear it), but it will turn off the announcement of incoming mail and other events.

If you rearrange the mapping of sounds to events, consider saving the new arrangement as a sound scheme. (Click Save As and supply a name.) That way you can experiment further and still return to the saved configuration.

The other two tabs in Sound dialog box provide hardware-specific configuration options for your speakers and microphone.

Customizing Mouse Pointers

As you have undoubtedly noticed, Windows Vista has dispensed with the time-dishonored hourglass mouse pointer. That might be a welcome development, particularly if you've logged a lot of hours with earlier versions of Windows. On the other hand, if you think an hourglass depicts the passage of time more unambiguously than a rolling doughnut, you can easily bring back the old shape. You can customize the entire array of pointer shapes your system uses by right-clicking the desktop, choosing Personalize, and then choosing Mouse Pointers. On the Pointers tab of the Mouse Properties dialog box, you can select a pointer type in the Customize box, and then click Browse to select an alternative pointer shape. (The Browse button takes you to %Windir%\Cursors and displays files with the extensions .cur and .ani. The latter are animated cursors.)

Just as Windows Vista encapsulates an entire assortment of color choices as a color scheme and a collection of sound choices as a sound scheme, it wraps up a gamut of pointer shapes as a mouse-pointer scheme. The system comes with a generous assortment of predefined schemes, making it easy for you to switch from one set of pointers to another as needs or whims suggest. Figure 3-11 shows the list.

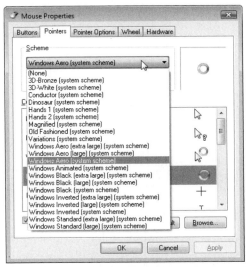

Figure 3-11 Some of the predefined mouse-pointer schemes are better suited for challenging light conditions than the default (Windows Aero) scheme.

Chapter 3

If you sometimes use your portable computer in lighting conditions that make it hard for you to find the pointer, consider switching to one of the large or extra large schemes. If nothing else, those will give your eyeballs a larger target to pursue.

For something perhaps more novel than large or animated pointers, try one of the inverted schemes. These make your mouse pointer appear to pass behind the text on your screen, rather than in front of it. (It's an acquired taste.)

If you're inclined to roll your own mouse scheme (by using the Browse button to assign cursor files to pointer types), be sure to use the Save As command and give your work a name. That way you'll be able to switch away from it and back to it again at will.

It's worth taking a minute or two to explore the remaining tabs on the Mouse Properties dialog box. Some of the more useful options there are Button Configuration (on the Buttons tab), which lets you swap the roles of the left and right mouse buttons; Display Pointer Trails, in the Visibility section of the Pointer Options tab (this one makes the mouse cursor even easier to find in lousy lighting conditions); and Select A Pointer Speed, in the Motion section of the Pointer Options tab. This last option governs the rate at which the pointer travels in response to mouse movement. If you have switched to a high DPI setting (see "Making Text Easier to Read") and a higher-resolution display, you might also need to increase the pointer speed to accommodate the increased number of pixels on your screen.

Saving Your Settings as a Theme

A *theme* in Windows Vista is a scheme of schemes, an *über* configuration that combines and names the various personalization settings that you have made elsewhere. Themes can incorporate the following:

- Color and appearance choices
- Color schemes
- Settings that you have made in the Advanced Appearance dialog box
- Screen saver
- Sound schemes
- Mouse pointer schemes

Note that these are all settings that pertain to your own profile; that is, they're specific to your user account. Settings that apply to all users at your computer, such as DPI scaling and screen resolution, are not included in the current theme.

If you've got all the visual and aural aspects of your profile set up just the way you want them, and you want to be able to experiment further but still return to the current settings, it's time to visit the Theme Settings dialog box (right-click the desktop, choose Personalize, and then choose Theme.). As Figure 3-12 shows, the dialog box will probably show *Modified Theme* as the current theme. That's because you (presumably) have made changes to whatever theme was previously in effect. To make those changes reusable, click Save As and supply a name. Windows will save a .theme file in your Documents folder (by default).

Figure 3-12 Clicking Save As in the Theme Settings dialog box lets you name the current constellation of visual and sound settings so that you can reinstate them after further changes.

Configuring Screen Resolution

Changing screen resolution changes the number of pixels that Windows displays on your screen. Increasing the resolution—say from 1024 × 768 to 1600 × 1200 lets you see more action on your display—more windows, more text, larger graphics, and so on—with various tradeoffs. Text at a given point size will appear smaller at higher resolutions. A mouse at a given pointer speed will require more arm and wrist motion to traverse a high-resolution screen than a low-resolution one. And higher resolutions use more video memory. In short, the right resolution for you depends on your hardware, your preferences, and visual acuity.

To change screen resolution, right-click the desktop, choose Personalize, and then choose Display Settings. Figure 3-13 shows the Display Settings dialog box. To change resolution, drag the Resolution slider to the left or right. Windows will apply the new settings, then ask you to confirm.

Chapter 3

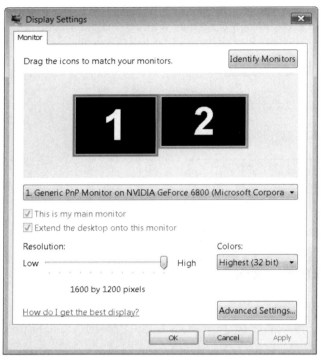

Figure 3-13 In the Display Settings dialog box you can change screen resolution and color depth.

Configuring a Multi-Monitor Display

Extending your desktop across two or more monitors can be a great way to increase your productivity. You can do your main work on one screen and keep auxiliary information, e-mail, or even Windows Media Player open and visible on the second. Or if you work with large spreadsheets or database tables, you can spread them across multiple screens so that you can see more data without having to set your resolution to stratospheric levels.

If your display adapter supports two monitors (these days, most do), the Display Settings dialog box will show two boxes, labeled 1 and 2, whether or not you have a second monitor connected. Assuming you do have two monitors, you can click these boxes to configure them independently. If adjusting the settings for monitor 1 appears to be affecting what you consider to be monitor 2, click the Identify Monitors button. Windows will display large white numerals on your screen temporarily to let you know which screen is which. If it happens that screen 2 is on the left of screen 1, you can drag the boxes in the Display Settings dialog box so that they match the physical layout of your monitors.

Assuming you want to add screen space to your visual layout, be sure to select Extend The Desktop Onto This Monitor when you click on the number 2 box. If you prefer to have your second monitor function as a duplicate display (for example, to make a presentation easier for a group of clients to see), leave this check box clear.

Configuring Desktop Icons

A freshly, cleanly installed Windows Vista desktop (as opposed to one generated by an upgrade installation) includes a single lonely icon—Recycle Bin. If you want other system icons, right-click the desktop, choose Personalize, and click Change Desktop Icons (in the task pane at the left). The Desktop Icons Settings dialog box, shown in Figure 3-14, provides check boxes for five system folders—Computer, the root folder of your own profile (User's Files), Network, Recycle Bin, and Control Panel.

Figure 3-14 You can choose to display or hide any of these five system icons.

If you're really into customization, you can change any of the five icons that appear in the large box in the center. Note that the Control Panel icon will not appear in this center box, even if you select its check box; customizing the Control Panel icon, like changing the Windows startup sound, is not permitted.

To change an icon, select it in the center box and click Change Icon. You'll find an interesting assortment of alternative icons in the file %SystemRoot%\System32\Imageres.dll (be sure to use the horizontal scroll bar to see them all). If none of those suit you, try browsing to %SystemRoot%\System32\Shell32.dll.

Chapter 3

> **Note**
>
> If you're interested in creating your own icons, you'll find an excellent description of the process in the MSDN Library at *http://www.vista-io.com/0303*

INSIDE OUT Customize icon spacing

If you're really into desktop icons, you might find it worthwhile to move the ones you have closer together—so you'll have room for more or to keep the current collection from completely overrunning the desktop. The most effective way we've found to do that is by adjusting the Icon size in the Advanced Appearance dialog box. (Right-click the desktop, choose Personalize, choose Window Color And Appearance. If you don't see the Appearance Settings dialog box, click Open Classic Appearance Properties For More Color Options. In the Appearance Settings dialog box, click Advanced.) The Icon size setting, curiously enough, does not change the size of icons. It does change their spacing, however. Reducing the value from the default 32 to 16 (the minimum) produces a compact icon display without sacrificing readability.

After you've populated your desktop with icons, you might want to control their arrangement. If you right-click the desktop, you'll find two commands at the top of the shortcut menu that will help in this endeavor. To make your icons rearrange themselves when you delete one of their brethren, choose View, and then choose Auto Arrange. To ensure that each icon keeps a respectable distance from each of its neighbors (and that the whole gang stays together at the left side of your screen), choose View, and then choose Align To Grid. And if your icons occasionally get in the way (for example, if you want to take an unimpeded look at the current desktop background image), choose View, and then choose Show Desktop Icons. (Return to this command when you want the icons back.)

To change the sort order of your desktop icons, right-click the desktop and choose Sort By. You can sort on any of four attributes: Name, Size, Type, or Date Modified. Sorting a second time on any of these attributes changes the sort order from ascending to descending (or vice versa).

Sorting by name has the advantage of putting your own icons in an alphabetical sequence. It scatters the system-folder icons (Computer, your profile folder, Network, and so on) amidst the non-system types. If you want the system folders to appear at the head of the list, sort by either Type or Date Modified. (The latter option works because you presumably don't modify the system folders.)

Sorting by type puts your shortcut icons together, separating them from any actual documents or programs you happen to have on the desktop. But it won't arrange the shortcuts alphabetically. If that's a problem, you can always turn Auto Arrange off and drag icons into whatever arrangement pleases you.

Chapter 3

TROUBLESHOOTING

When you delete a desktop item, it also disappears from other users' desktops

The items that appear on your desktop (aside from the system-folder icons) come from two sources: your own desktop folder, which is ordinarily %UserProfile%\Desktop (unless you have relocated it), and the public desktop folder, %Public%\Desktop. Items in the latter folder appear on the desktop of everyone who uses your computer. Ordinarily, items that you place on the desktop yourself are stored as part of your profile—in your own Desktop folder. But the setup routines for some programs add a shortcut to the public desktop folder. When you delete a desktop item that's stored in the public folder, the deletion affects all accounts, not just your own. Windows gives no indication that your change might affect others, nor is there any visual clue to an item's actual storage location. Before you delete an item from your desktop, you might want to confirm its location. Right-click its icon and choose Properties. On the General tab, see whether the Location field shows Public or your own user name.

To delete a public-desktop item without affecting others, you'll need to copy it to the Desktop folder in each user's profile before you delete it. Under the default access controls, you will also need administrative privileges to plant a copy in someone else's profile.

Adding or Moving Start Menu Items to the Desktop

If you want to be able to launch a program by double-clicking an icon on the desktop, and you already have an item on the Start menu for that program, you can create the desktop icon by dragging the Start menu item and dropping it on the desktop. Windows creates a new shortcut on the desktop when you do this. If you want the item on the desktop and not on the Start menu, create the desktop shortcut as just described. Then right-click the item on the Start menu and choose Delete. Windows will warn you that your deletion will remove a shortcut, not the program itself—but that, of course, is just what you want.

You can use the same technique to create desktop icons for the system folders that appear on the right side of your Start menu—Documents, Pictures, and so on. With some of these items, you can choose a Show On Desktop command from the shortcut menu that appears when you right-click. But whether or not that command is there, you can simply drag to the desktop to create a shortcut there.

Using and Customizing Windows Sidebar

One of the most conspicuous new features in Windows Vista is Windows Sidebar, a repository for mini-programs (called *gadgets*) that can amuse, inform, and distract you all day long. By default, Windows Sidebar inhabits the right edge of your primary monitor, but you can move it to the left or to a secondary monitor. You can make it rise above all other windows at all times (so it can *really* inform or distract), you can make it start automatically when Windows starts (that's its default behavior), and you can close and open it at will. Most important, you can easily add or remove gadgets whenever you feel the need for something new on your computer screen. The gadget gallery that comes with Windows includes just under a dozen offerings but has a handy link to a much larger online gallery.

INSIDE OUT

Gadgets don't have to stay anchored to the sidebar pane. You can drag them out to the desktop. Many respond to this action by enlarging themselves and making their features more visible and useful.

If Windows Sidebar is not currently open on your screen, you can open it by clicking the Start button and typing Sidebar in the Start menu's Search box. Then click Windows Sidebar when it appears at the top of the menu. (You might also find a Windows Sidebar icon in your notification area. Clicking that should open the sidebar if it's not currently open.)

To add a gadget to your gallery, right-click anywhere in the sidebar and choose Add Gadgets. That will summon the gadget gallery:

For clues about what a gadget might do, select it and click Show Details. To install a gadget, you can either just drag it to the sidebar or right-click it and choose Install. After you have installed a gadget, you'll probably want to prod it with your mouse (try both buttons, and click on various parts) to see what tricks it knows and what options it offers. Each gadget is different, but they're all designed to make their features discoverable.

To remove a gadget, right-click it and choose Close Gadget.

To get to the online gadget site, click Get More Gadgets Online, in the bottom right corner of the gadget gallery. If you download a gadget from this site, it will take up residence in the gallery, so you can easily close it and reopen it whenever you want. The search box in the gadget gallery is also a list. By opening the list, you can filter the gallery to show recently installed gadgets or gadgets from particular publishers.

INSIDE OUT

If you don't choose to make Windows Sidebar appear on top of all windows at all times, you can bring it to the foreground at any time by pressing Windows logo+Spacebar. This will make all your gadgets visible (even those that you have liberated from the confines of the sidebar).

To customize Windows Sidebar (other than by adding or removing gadgets), right-click any part of the sidebar other than on a gadget, and choose Properties. Figure 3-15 on the next page shows the Windows Sidebar Properties dialog box. The options are few and simple.

Chapter 3

Figure 3-15 The Windows Sidebar Properties dialog box presents a straightforward set of display options.

To close Windows Sidebar and hide all your gadgetry, first drag any gadgets that lie outside the sidebar back into the sidebar. (Those you don't corral will remain visible after you close the sidebar.) Then right-click Windows Sidebar and choose Close Sidebar.

INSIDE OUT

If you're having trouble dragging a gadget, place your mouse just to the right of the gadget's upper right corner. A small panel of three controls will appear. The top control closes the gadget, the middle one opens the gadget's options dialog box, and the bottom one provides a handle by means of which you can drag.

Personalizing the Start Menu

It all begins (and ends) with the Start menu, which provides access to nearly everything you need to do in Windows. Windows Vista offers two versions of the Start menu, as shown in Figure 3-16 and 3-17, on the next page.

Figure 3-16 The default Start menu provides a place to "pin" your most frequently needed programs, displays recently used programs below that, and offers access to crucial system folders on the right.

Figure 3-17 The classic Start menu, a recreation of the Windows 2000 Start menu, is more compact but less easily customized. It also lacks a Search box.

Like the default Start menu in Windows XP, the Windows Vista Start menu is a two-column affair, the left side of which is reserved for the programs you use most often or that you have used most recently. Rather than displaying other programs on the right side, however (as the Windows XP Start menu does), Windows Vista devotes the right side of the menu to various important system folders, such as your Documents and Pictures folders, Search, and Control Panel.

The classic Start menu recreates the look and feel of Windows 2000. Its main virtue is that it takes up very little room on the desktop. Among its drawbacks: It is less easily customized than the default Start menu, and it typically requires numerous cascading submenus to display its wares.

The single most important difference between the two menus, however, is that the default menu includes a Search box (at the bottom on the left, directly below All Programs). You can get to anything on the menu, no matter how deeply nested it might be, by typing a few characters into this box. In Figure 3-16, for example, Microsoft Office Publisher 2007 does not appear on the left side of the menu, because we haven't pinned it to the top of the menu or used it recently. Navigating to this program's menu entry would require a couple of clicks and a bit of scrolling (one click to open All Programs, another to open Microsoft Office). As Figure 3-18 shows, two characters in the Search box are enough to bring Microsoft Office Publisher 2007 to the Programs area of the Search results, at the top of the Start menu.

Provided you're not completely averse to typing, the Search box pretty much eliminates the hassle of finding items that are buried several folders deep within the menu structure. (As you'll see, there are ways to make deeply nested items more mouse-accessible as well—in case typing is not your idea of pleasure.)

INSIDE OUT

The Run command, shown on the right side of Figure 3-18, is not a default component of the Start menu—and is nearly obviated by the Search box. If you still find yourself reaching for it occasionally (as we do), you can add it to the menu via the Customize Start Menu dialog box.

Figure 3-18 Typing "pu" into the Search box is sufficient to bring Microsoft Office Publisher 2007 to the top of the Start menu.

To switch from one style of Start menu to the other, as well as to perform a variety of other customizing tasks, right-click the Start button, choose Properties, and click the Start Menu tab. Figure 3-19 on the next page shows the Start Menu tab of the Taskbar And Start Menu Properties dialog box.

Chapter 3

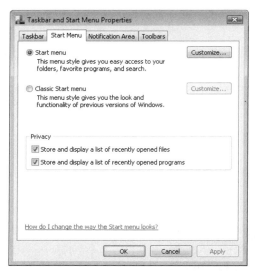

Figure 3-19 Options and check boxes on the Start Menu tab of the Taskbar And Start Menu Properties dialog box let you switch between default and classic menu styles and erase evidence of what you've been doing at your computer.

The option buttons in the top part of this dialog box let you switch between the two Start menu styles. The Privacy check boxes are available in case you need to suppress the evidence of what you've been doing at the Start menu.

INSIDE OUT

The picture that appears at the top of the right side of the Start menu is the one associated with your user account (the one that also appears on the Welcome screen). If you're not happy with it, click it. That will take you to the User Accounts section of Control Panel, where you can specify a different picture.

Controlling the Content of the Start Menu

Quite apart from the what appears on the left side of the Start menu (see "Making Your Programs More Accessible," in this chapter, for information about customizing that aspect of the menu), you have a lot of choices about what shows up on the right side. To see those choices, click Customize on the Start Menu tab of the Taskbar And Start Menu Properties dialog box (see Figure 3-19). This action takes you to the Customize Start Menu dialog box. Figure 3-20 illustrates some of the options available there.

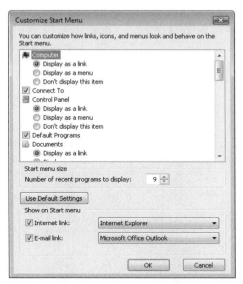

Figure 3-20 On the Customize Start Menu dialog box, you can make decisions about what appears on the right side of your Start menu.

> **Note**
> Several of the choices that you can make in the Customize Start Menu dialog box have more to do with the behavior of the Start menu than its content. You should take a stroll through this dialog box, even if you're entirely happy with the content defaults.

Choosing Link, Menu, or No Show

Several of the items in the Customize Start Menu list offer you the choice of Display As A Link, Display As A Menu, and Don't Display This Item. The items you can customize in this manner include:

- Computer
- Control Panel
- Documents
- Games
- Music
- Personal Folder

The defaults in all cases is Display As Link, which helps keep submenus from sprawling across your desktop. The reason you might prefer to retain these default settings, in addition to avoiding sprawl, is that clicking a link opens the item in question in Windows Explorer, where you have display options that can help you sort through the folder contents. If you click a Computer link, for example, you might see something like the following:

You might find the alternative, an uncategorized submenu, harder to navigate.

INSIDE OUT

You can have it both ways. If you opt for submenus, you can still open items in Windows Explorer. Just right-click and choose Open.

Displaying the Run Command

The Run command, a perennial favorite of computer enthusiasts, is no longer a standard Start menu feature. You can make sure it's still part of *your* Start menu by selecting the Run Command check box in the Customize Start Menu dialog box.

You might find you can live comfortably without the Run command. When you're tempted to type a program name in the Run dialog box, try typing it in the Start menu Search box instead (it's a mouse-click closer). The Search feature won't always get you where you want to go (it's no good when you need a command-line switch, for example), but it's more versatile than you might expect. Typically, you can run an executable by simply typing its name in the Search box and pressing Enter, just as you would in the Run dialog. On the other hand, the Run dialog box remembers command strings that you have entered before, and the Search box has nothing to replace that.

INSIDE OUT

Whether or not your Start menu includes it, you can always get to the Run command by pressing Windows logo key+R.

Controlling Where the Search Box Searches

Several options let you customize the behavior of the Start menu Search box. Specifically you can opt to omit any or all of the following from Start menu searches:

- Communications (e-mail and contact information)

- Favorites and history

- Files

- Programs

Because indexed searching in Windows Vista is fast, you might think it would be pointless to restrict Start menu searches in any way. Reasons to consider doing so include the following:

- The Start menu search options affect only the results that appear in the Start menu. Even if you have a particular search domain turned off in the Start menu, you can still find what you need in the full Search window. (If you turn off Start menu searching for favorites and history, you will have to go to your browser to find what you need.)

- The number of items that a Start menu search can return is limited by the size of the Start menu. If you usually employ the Start menu Search box to look for a particular kind of item—e-mail messages, for example—you might find it useful to turn off the other types of searches in the Start menu. That would give the Start menu room to display more of the result type that you typically are looking for.

For more about searching from the Start menu, see "Using the Start Menu Search Box," in Chapter 7.

Making Your Programs Easy to Find on the Start Menu

Three areas of the Start menu make it easy to run the programs and open the documents you need most. Those areas (illustrated in Figure 3-21 on the next page) are:

- **Pinned programs** The area in the upper-left corner of the Start menu, above the horizontal line, is reserved for the programs you want to be accessible at all times. Once you have "pinned" an item to this part of the Start menu, it stays there (unless you subsequently remove it).

- **Recently used programs** Windows populates the area directly below the pinned programs with programs that you have used recently.

- **Recent Items** The Recent Items item, on the right side of the Start menu, produces a submenu of the 15 documents you have most recently opened. If you choose an item from this list, Windows reopens the document in the application with which the document is associated.

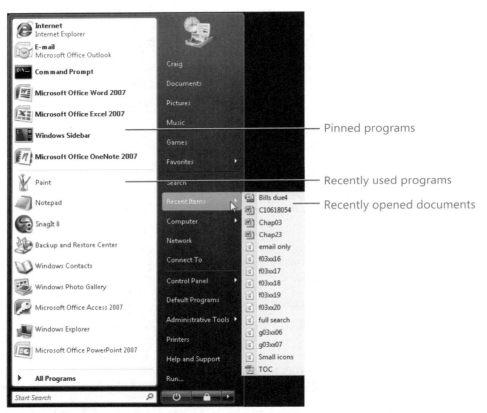

Figure 3-21 Three areas of the Start menu make it easy to get to programs and documents that you need frequently or have used recently.

Adding and Removing Pinned Programs

All you need to do to add a program to the pinned programs area of the Start menu is right-click it wherever you see it (elsewhere on the Start menu, for example) and choose Pin To Start Menu. The Item will take up residence at the bottom of the pinned programs area. If you'd like to give it a more prominent location, drag it upward.

> **Note**
>
> If no shortcut menu appears when you right-click an item, and you can't drag the item to the pinned programs area, go back to the Customize Start Menu dialog box (see Figure 3-20). In the list of options, select Enable Context Menus And Dragging And Dropping.

To remove an item from the pinned programs area, right-click it and choose Unpin From Start Menu.

Controlling the Number of Recently Used Programs

The list of recently used programs—the items that appear below the pinned programs on the left side of the Start menu—is controlled by Windows. The list includes only shortcuts to .exe files; other executable files you open (such as .msc files) do not appear. In addition, the following items are excluded by default (for more information, see Knowledge Base article 282066, "Frequently Used Programs Not Automatically Added to the Start Menu"):

- Programs listed in the AddRemoveApps value of the registry key HKLM\Software\Microsoft\Windows\CurrentVersion\Explorer\FileAssociation. By default, the following items are excluded: Setup.exe, Install.exe, Isuninst.exe, Unwise.exe, Unwise32.exe, St5unst.exe, Rundll32.exe, Msoobe.exe, and Lnkstub.exe. By modifying this registry value, you can tailor the exclusion list to suit your needs.

- Items whose shortcut names include any of the following text: Documentation, Help, Install, More Info, Readme, Read Me Read First, Setup, Support, What's New, Remove. This list of exclusion strings is specified in the AddRemoveNames value of HKLM\Software\Microsoft\Windows\CurrentVersion\Explorer\FileAssociation.

To specify the number of programs that appear on the most frequently used programs list, right-click the Start button, choose Properties, and click Customize on the Start Menu tab of the Taskbar And Start Menu Properties dialog box. In the Customize Start Menu dialog box (see Figure 3-20), enter the value you desire in the Number Of Recent Programs To Display control. You can specify any number from 0 (if you hate the feature) through 30 (if you have a large screen, high resolution, and lots of different programs).

Chapter 3

INSIDE OUT

To make more programs accessible via the pinned programs area and the recently used programs list, scroll to the bottom of the list of options in the Customize Start Menu dialog box (see Figure 3-20). Clear the last item in the list, Use Large Icons. Windows uses large icons by default, on the presumption that you have few programs and like large mouse targets. Most users who use more than a handful of applications will find the small icon setting more practical.

If you really hate having recently used programs appear on the Start menu, rather than set the maximum number to 0, simply right-click the Start button, choose Properties, and then clear Store And Display A List Of Recently Opened Programs. (Windows also clears the Run command history when you do this.) If you like the feature most of the time but want to cover your tracks on occasion, simply clear this check box, click OK (or Apply), then return to the Taskbar And Start Menu Properties dialog box and reselect the check box. The first action cleans the slate. The second reinstates the feature—starting with *tabula rasa*.

Managing the Recent Items Menu

The Recent Items menu, on the right side of the Start menu, contains shortcuts to 15 of your most recently used documents. To reopen one of these documents, simply click its name.

You can prune items from this menu the same way you remove items anywhere else— right-click and choose Delete. Notice that when you remove an item from Recent Items, 15 items remain. That's because the Recent Items menu reflects the contents of the folder %UserProfile%\Recent. Windows keeps shortcuts to all recently used documents there but displays only the most recent 15 of the lot.

Note that you can't add items to the Recent Items menu by making direct additions to %UserProfile%\Recent. For the purposes of building this menu, Windows simply ignores anything in the Recent folder that it didn't put there itself.

To clear everything from the Recent Items menu, right-click the Start button and choose Properties from the shortcut menu. On the Start Menu tab of the Taskbar And Start Menu Properties dialog box, clear Store And Display A List Of Recently Opened Programs. Windows clears out the menu (as well as the %UserProfile%\Recent folder) when you do this.

To cover your tracks ad hoc, clear the Store And Display A List Of Recently Opened Programs check box, and then click OK or Apply. After the menu has been wiped clean, you can go back and reselect the check box, and Windows will build the list anew.

Working with Start Menu Folders in Windows Explorer

The Start menu is generated by the contents of two folders:

- A personal folder, located at %AppData%\Microsoft\Windows\Start Menu

- An "all users" folder, located at %ProgramData%\Microsoft\Windows\Start Menu

Fortunately, you don't have to memorize these paths to look into the Start Menu folders. To open the personal folder, right-click the Start button and choose Open from the shortcut menu. To open the "all users" folder, right-click the Start button and choose Open All Users.

As you might expect, items stored in the personal folder appear only on your own Start menu. Items stored in the "all users" folder appear on the Start menu of everyone who has an account at your computer.

Each of these folders includes a subfolder named Programs. The items that appear on the Start menu when you open All Programs (the item just above the Search box, on the left side of the Start menu) are the items stored in these two Programs subfolders. By adding shortcuts or folders to (or deleting them from) either of these two Programs subfolders, you can manipulate the contents of the Start menu. Note the following, however:

- Making changes to any part of the "all users" Start menu requires administrative privileges.

- You can't use Windows Explorer to change the top level of the left side of the Start menu or any part of the right side of the Start menu. You can only manipulate the portion of the menu that appears when you open All Programs.

If you install so many programs that the layout of your All Programs menu becomes unwieldy, you might want to create inclusive program categories in the Programs subfolder of your personal Start Menu folder. You could create one for Work, another for Play, a third for Utilities, and so on, and then drag existing folders into these "super" folders, to simplify the appearance of the menu.

Setting the Internet and E-Mail Links at the Top of the Start Menu

Windows ordinarily reserves the top two spaces in the pinned programs section of the Start menu for your default internet browser and default e-mail program. You can change what appears here or get rid of either or both. To customize this part of the Start menu, right-click the Start button and choose Properties from the shortcut menu. On the Start Menu tab of the Taskbar And Start Menu Properties dialog box, click Customize. Near the bottom of the Customize Start Menu dialog box, you'll find check boxes labeled Internet Link and E-Mail Link. Clear either of these to remove the associated item.

Chapter 3

To change the program that appears in either slot, use the lists at the right. For example, if you decide to switch from using Windows Mail as your customary e-mail client to Windows Live Mail, you could install Windows Live Mail near the top of the Start menu by opening the drop-down list next to E-Mail Link and choosing Windows Live Mail.

Launching Programs with the Quick Launch Toolbar

If you like to launch programs by clicking icons (instead of menu items), but you don't like having to minimize all your windows to do it, check out the Quick Launch toolbar. It's a terrific compromise between the Start menu and a set of desktop icons.

The Quick Launch toolbar, like the desktop itself, is a place to put shortcuts that launch programs, open documents, or open folders. The icons on the toolbar are smaller than desktop icons, of course, but they're visible whenever the toolbar is visible.

INSIDE OUT

The first ten shortcuts on the Quick Launch toolbar are accessible by keyboard as well as mouse. Press Windows logo key+1 for the first, Windows logo key+2 for the second, and so on (using 0 for the tenth). If you use certain shortcuts more often than others, you'll probably want to move them to the left to lower their keyboard access numbers. (To move a Quick Launch icon, unlock the taskbar, and then drag.)

The Windows Vista setup program installs the Quick Launch toolbar by default and populates it with a Show Desktop shortcut and a Switch Between Windows shortcut. Clicking the former minimizes all open windows at once (or reopens them if you click a second time). Clicking the second activates Windows Flip 3D, if your system is running the Aero interface. (If it's not, clicking Switch Between Windows is equivalent to pressing Alt+Tab.)

If you don't see the Quick Launch toolbar, right-click any unoccupied spot on the taskbar, choose Toolbars from the shortcut menu, and choose Quick Launch. A check mark next to Quick Launch confirms that the toolbar is deployed.

Windows Vista makes it exceedingly easy to add programs to the Quick Launch toolbar. Simply right-click the program's name in the Start menu (or in Windows Explorer) or an existing desktop icon, and choose Add To Quick Launch. To remove an item from the Quick Launch toolbar, right-click it and choose Delete.

You can add non-program shortcuts (shortcuts for folders or documents, for example) to the Quick Launch toolbar by dragging them from the desktop or Windows Explorer. (If they don't already exist on the desktop or in a Windows Explorer folder, you'll need to create them there first. For details, see "Creating and Customizing Program Shortcuts," in Chapter 4.)

Customizing the Taskbar

The taskbar houses the Start button, the notification area, and a button for each running program. You can use these task buttons to switch from one running program to another. You can also click a task button to minimize an open window or to reopen a minimized window. The taskbar can also hold one or more toolbars. (Typically, it hosts the Quick Launch toolbar, described in the previous section. You can also put additional toolbars there as well; see "Adding Toolbars to the Taskbar," in this chapter.)

Changing the Taskbar's Size and Appearance

The default height of the taskbar is enough to display one taskbar button. You can enlarge it—and given the typical size and resolution of computer displays these days, enlarging it is often a great idea. Before you can change the taskbar's dimensions, you need to unlock it. Right-click an unoccupied area of the taskbar, and if a check mark appears next to the Lock The Taskbar command, choose the command to clear the check mark. Then position the mouse along the upper border of the taskbar. When the mouse pointer becomes a two-headed arrow, drag toward the center of the screen to expand the taskbar.

Controlling Taskbar Grouping

Windows Vista, like Windows XP, preserves space on the taskbar by grouping similar items when the taskbar fills up. For example, if you have seven folders open in Windows Explorer, the taskbar buttons for those seven are grouped into a single button, and a number on the button indicates how many items are included in the group. Clicking the button displays a list of windows, as shown in Figure 3-22.

Figure 3-22 Click one of the taskbar button's list of items to select its window.

In addition to reducing taskbar congestion, grouping offers some other benefits that aren't immediately apparent. The menu that appears when you right-click the group button provides several useful commands. With a single click, you can:

- Display all windows in the group (choose Show Windows Stacked or Show Windows Side By Side)

- Close all windows in the group

Taskbar grouping is enabled by default. If you don't prefer it, right-click the Start button, choose Properties, and click the Taskbar pane in the Taskbar And Start Menu

Properties dialog box. Then clear the Group Similar Taskbar Buttons checkbox, as shown in Figure 3-23.

Figure 3-23 If taskbar button grouping doesn't appeal to you, clear this check box.

INSIDE OUT Customize taskbar grouping

By default, taskbar grouping comes into play only when the taskbar fills up. Even if you have multiple windows from the same application open, if there's room for a separate button for each window, that's what you get.

You might prefer to have all similar windows grouped together all the time. To do that, you'll need to edit the registry. Use Registry Editor to open HKCU\Software\Microsoft\ Windows\CurrentVersion\Explorer\Advanced. Create a new DWORD value named TaskbarGroupSize.

This setting controls how many windows are allowed before Windows starts grouping them under a single taskbar button. A setting of 2 groups related items as soon as you open a second window, even if there's plenty of room on the taskbar; 3 enables grouping as soon as you have three or more similar windows; and so on. If you prefer to prevent taskbar grouping unless your taskbar gets *really* crowded, use a higher setting (say, 5). You must log off and then back on before this setting takes effect.

Getting the Taskbar Out of Your Way

By default, the taskbar remains visible even when you're working in a maximized program. If that's inconvenient for any reason, you can tell it to get out of the way. The Taskbar And Start Menu Properties dialog box, shown in Figure 3-23, offers two options to control this behavior.

- **Keep The Taskbar On Top Of Other Windows** Clearing this check box means that you'll be able to see the taskbar at all times *except* when a window is maximized or placed over the taskbar.

- **Auto-Hide The Taskbar** With this option selected, the taskbar retreats into the edge of the desktop. To display the taskbar, move the mouse pointer to the edge of the desktop where the taskbar is "hidden."

> **Note**
> Regardless of how you set options in the Taskbar And Start Menu Properties dialog box, you can make the taskbar visible at any time by pressing the Windows logo key or Ctrl+Esc.

Moving the Taskbar

The taskbar docks by default at the bottom of the screen (the primary screen, if you have more than one), but you can move it to any other edge, including any edge of a secondary screen. (If you move to an edge that's already occupied by the Sidebar, the Sidebar steps aside.)

To move the taskbar, unlock it (right-click an unoccupied spot and choose Lock The Taskbar—unless no check appears beside that command, which means that taskbar is already unlocked). Then drag any unoccupied part of the taskbar in the direction you want to go. (Don't drag the inside edge of the taskbar; doing that changes the taskbar's size, not its position.)

Be aware that with the taskbar docked against either side or the top of the screen, the Start menu descends from the Start button when you click that button (or press the Windows logo key or Ctrl+Esc). If your customary destination in the Start menu is the Search box, you might find it disconcerting not to have the Search box right next to the Start button.

Controlling the Display of Icons in the Notification Area

The notification area (also sometimes called the system tray or the status area) can become crowded with tiny icons—many of which don't "notify" you of anything. A variety of programs use the notification area to provide program-starting icons. But many of those programs seldom need to be started; they continue to do their job without any intervention from you. To deal with notification-area congestion, Windows Vista, by default, keeps a few icons visible at all times but hides most of the icons that you aren't actually using. Icons that aren't currently visible are only a click away; click the arrow at the left end of the notification area to display the hidden items.

You can personalize this behavior on the Notification Area tab of the Taskbar And Start Menu Properties dialog box (shown in Figure 3-24). To get there, right-click the Start button, choose Properties, and click the Notification Area tab.

Figure 3-24 Windows keeps four notification area icons visible at all times, unless you modify the System Icons options here.

If you want to see all your notification area icons at all times, clear Hide Inactive Icons. If you like the default icon-hiding behavior in general but disagree with the system's choices about which icons it should always display, start by clearing the check box for any of the four items in this dialog box (Clock, Volume, Network, and Power) that you don't need to see all the time. Then click Customize for additional options.

The Customize Notification Icons dialog box, shown in Figure 3-25, lists all notification area icons that are currently open and all that have been open in the past. Next to each item is a drop-down list with three choices: Hide When Inactive, Hide, and Show. You can use these options to make the notification area behave exactly as you want it to.

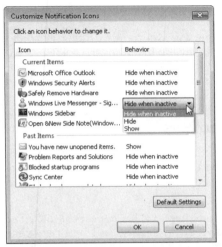

Figure 3-25 You determine which icons you want to be visible and which ones you want to be accessible only when you expand the notification area.

Using Additional Toolbars

The Quick Launch toolbar, discussed earlier in this chapter (see "Launching Programs with the Quick Launch Toolbar," in this chapter), is only one of several toolbars available in Windows Vista. Others you can choose to install include:

- **Address** The Address toolbar provides a place where you can enter an internet address or the name and path of a program, document, or folder. When you press Enter or click the Go button, Windows takes you to the internet address, starts the program, opens the document, or displays the folder in a Windows Explorer window. The Address toolbar is functionally equivalent to the Start menu's Run command or the Address bar in Windows Explorer or Internet Explorer.

- **Links** The Links toolbar provides a set of shortcuts to selected internet sites. It is equivalent to the Links toolbar in Internet Explorer.

- **Desktop** The Desktop toolbar provides copies of all the icons currently displayed on your desktop.

Additional application-specific toolbars might also be available on your system. Windows Media Player, for example, can minimize itself into a taskbar-docked toolbar, allowing easy access to player controls.

> **Note**
> Unlike Windows XP, Windows Vista insists that most toolbars be docked to the taskbar.

Installing and Removing Toolbars

To install a new toolbar or remove one you're currently using, right-click any unoccupied part of the taskbar or any existing toolbar. Choose Toolbars from the shortcut menu that appears, and then choose from the ensuing submenu. A check mark beside a toolbar's name means that it is already displayed on the taskbar. Clicking a checked toolbar name removes that toolbar.

Sizing and Positioning Toolbars

Before you can change a toolbar's size or position on the taskbar, the taskbar itself must be unlocked. To do that, right-click an unoccupied area of the taskbar and, if a check mark appears next to the Lock The Taskbar command, click the command to clear the check mark.

When the taskbar is not locked, a dotted vertical bar appears at the left edge of every toolbar. (If the taskbar is displayed vertically against the left or right edge of the desktop, the bar is horizontal and appears at the top of the toolbar.) This is the toolbar's handle. To reposition a toolbar within the taskbar, drag the handle.

INSIDE OUT   **Create a cascading menu of your folders and files**

When set up in a certain way, the Desktop toolbar can provide a cascading menu of all the folder and files on your system. Follow these steps to set up this handy feature:

1. Add the Desktop toolbar to the taskbar, and be sure its toolbar title is displayed.

2. Reduce the Desktop toolbar's size by dragging its handle (and the handles of surrounding toolbars, if necessary) until it displays only the toolbar title and a double arrow.

Now when you click the toolbar's double arrow, a menu of desktop items appears. Desktop items that contain other folders and files (such as Computer, Documents, and Network) cascade to show their contents when you point at them.

Creating a New Toolbar

Any folder on your system can become a toolbar. This includes Windows system folders as Control Panel. To create a new toolbar, right-click an existing toolbar or a spot on the taskbar, choose Toolbars, and then choose New Toolbar. In the next dialog box, navigate to a folder and click OK.

The folder's name becomes the name of the new toolbar, and each item within the folder becomes a tool.

Setting Default Programs, File Type Associations, and AutoPlay Options

Most of the programs you use in Windows are associated with particular file types and protocols. These associations are what enable you, for example, to double-click a Windows Media Audio (.wma) file in Windows Explorer and have your favorite audio program play the file; or click an internet hyperlink in a document or e-mail message and have your favorite web browser take you to the appropriate website. The Windows Setup program establishes many of these associations for you when the operating system is installed. The Setup programs for various applications also create associations with the file types those programs can use. (Sometimes such programs, when installed, change existing file-type associations; generally, but not invariably, they ask for your permission before doing this.)

But regardless of how the associations between programs and file types and protocols are currently set, Windows makes it easy for you to see and modify the settings. You can inspect and alter current defaults by clicking Default Programs, on the right side of the Start menu, or opening Control Panel, clicking Programs, and then clicking Default Programs. Either way, you arrive at the section of Control Panel shown in Figure 3-26.

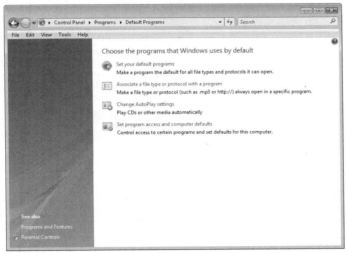

Figure 3-26 The designers of Windows Vista considered this aspect of Control Panel so important that they gave it its own Start menu entry.

Setting Default Programs

The first item on this menu, Set Your Default Programs, approaches the issue of associations from the standpoint of particular vital applications. You undoubtedly have a good many other applications in addition to these (and you might not have all of these), but the programs listed here are all capable of handling multiple file types and protocols, and this list gives you a way to assign programs to *all* the items they can handle—should you choose to do that. (You can also assign programs to a subset of their possible associations.)

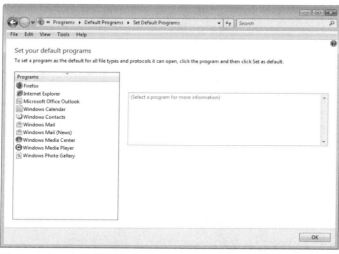

Figure 3-27 The Set Your Default Programs dialog box lets you approach associations from the standpoint of certain vital applications—such as your web browser(s) and e-mail client(s).

To illustrate how this works, we'll select Firefox in the dialog box shown in Figure 3-27. As Figure 3-28 shows, the dialog box responds by indicating that Firefox currently is the default program for three of the file types or protocols it is capable of handling.

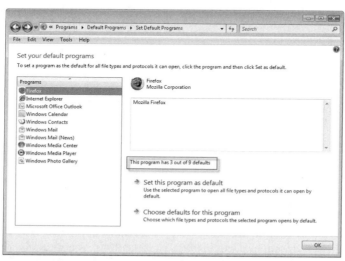

Figure 3-28 In this example, Mozilla Firefox is set as the default handler for three of the nine protocols it is capable of handling.

To see which defaults Firefox currently "owns" (and modify particular ones if we want), we click Choose Defaults For This Program. The dialog box then lists file extensions and protocols that are possibilities for Firefox (see Figure 3-29).

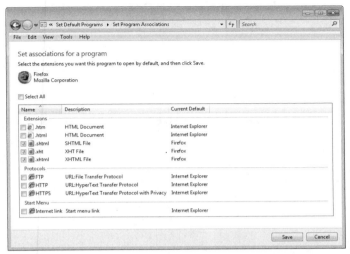

Figure 3-29 Firefox "owns" the SHTML File, XHT File, and XHTML File associations; the rest belong to Internet Explorer.

If we wanted to make Firefox the default program for other extensions or protocols, we could select the check boxes associated with these protocols, and then click Save. To make Firefox the default for everything, we could select all the check boxes or, more simply, return to the dialog box shown in Figure 3-28 and click Set This Program As Default.

Changing File Type Associations

The second item on the menu shown in Figure 3-26 approaches the matter of file-to-program associations from the perspective of the file type. Figure 3-30 on the next page shows a list of file types comparable to what you would see if you clicked this menu item.

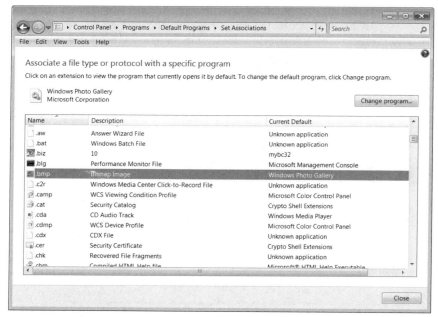

Figure 3-30 The list of file extensions shown in this dialog box lets you change the program or programs associated with individual file types.

The file-type list is alphabetized by extension. For each extension, the list shows a description of the file and the program that is currently set as the default application for that file type. So, for example, in Figure 3-30, we see that the extension .bmp represents Bitmap Image files, and that Windows Photo Gallery is the program currently associated with such files. In other words, double-clicking a .bmp file in Windows Explorer, as things now stand, will open that file in Windows Photo Gallery.

To change the default, click Change Program. As Figure 3-31 shows, the Open With dialog box that appears has a section called Recommended Programs and a section called Other Programs. The Recommended Programs section includes the current default (Windows Photo Gallery) and other programs that are registered as being capable of opening files of the current type (bitmap images, in this case). The dialog box also includes an Always Use The Selected Program To Open This Kind Of File check box, which is grayed out and unavailable. The reason the check box is unavailable is that Windows assumes that because you have arrived in the Open With dialog box by way of the Default Programs command (on the Start menu or in Control Panel), the only business you have here is to change the program that's always used to open the selected file type. (As we'll see in a moment, there's another way to get to this dialog box.)

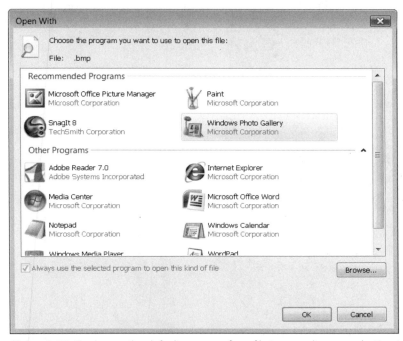

Figure 3-31 To change the default program for a file type, make your selection in the Recommended Programs section of this dialog box, and then click OK.

The Other Programs section of this dialog box will at first appear unpopulated. To make its contents visible, click the little arrow at the end of the dividing line between the Recommended Programs section and the Other Programs section. (We've already done that in Figure 3-31.)

Be careful. The programs listed in Other Programs are simply commonplace applications installed on your system. They are almost guaranteed to be bad choices for the selected file type. If you select one of these and click OK, it will become the default program for the current file type, no matter how unsuitable it might be. You can fix that easily enough, by returning to the Open With dialog box. But, as Figure 3-32 shows, the spurned program will make a nuisance of itself by remaining in the Recommended Programs dialog box. (For information about getting it out of there, see the Troubleshooting sidebar on the next page.)

Chapter 3

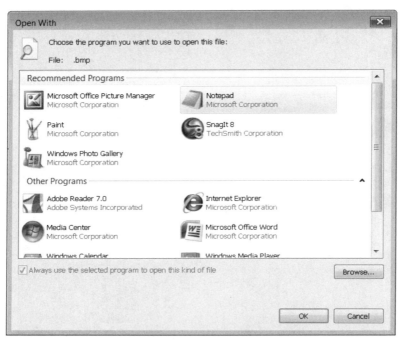

Figure 3-32 Because we chose Notepad in the Other Programs section of the dialog box, Notepad now appears in the Recommended Programs section.

Changing the Default Application from Windows Explorer

If you right-click a file in Windows Explorer and choose Open With from the shortcut menu, the programs that appears in the submenu are those that appear in the file type's Recommended Programs list, as shown in Figure 3-31. In Figure 3-33, for example, we've right-clicked a .bmp file in Windows Explorer and chosen Open With, and we're presented with Microsoft Office Picture Manager, Paint, Snagit 8, and Windows Photo Gallery, the same four programs that appear in the Recommended Programs section of Figure 3-31.

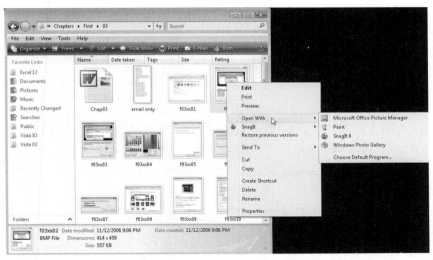

Figure 3-33 The options that appear when you right-click a file in Windows Explorer and choose Open With are those that appear in the file type's Recommended Programs list in Control Panel.

Notice that the programs are listed alphabetically, and the menu does not indicate which one is the current default. The assumption is that if you've gone to the trouble of choosing Open With, it's because you want, this time, to open the file in a nondefault program.

You can use this Open With menu either to open the selected file one time in a nondefault application or to change the default. To do the latter, click Choose Default Program from the menu shown in Figure 3-33. The Open With dialog box that appears will be just like the one shown in Figure 3-31, with one major exception: the Always Use The Selected Program To Open This Kind Of File check box will be available. Note that it will be available *and selected*. If you don't want to make a change to the default (if you're just looking around or curious about what might show up in the Other Programs section of the dialog box), be sure to clear the check box before you select a program and click OK. (If you do unintentionally reset the default, you can always return to this Open With dialog box and fix the problem.)

TROUBLESHOOTING

You need to remove a program from the Recommended Programs section of the Open With dialog box

The contents of the Recommended Programs list are determined by the registry key HKCU\Software\Microsoft\Windows\CurrentVersion\Explorer\FileExts*filetype* \OpenWithList (where *filetype* is the extension of the file type in question). So, for example, in the case shown in Figure 3-32, the ...\.bmp\OpenWithList key includes five values, one of which is Notepad.exe. Deleting the unwanted item in the OpenWithList key removes it from the Recommended Programs list.

Setting Program Access and Computer Defaults

The dialog box that appears when you choose Default Programs on the Start menu and click Set Program Access And Computer Defaults (see Figure 3-34) became a fixture of Windows at the time of Windows XP Service Pack 1. It was introduced to the operating system as a settlement condition in an antitrust suit brought by the United States Department of Justice against Microsoft. It is designed to give Windows users the option to remove access to a number of Microsoft programs that were previously tightly integrated into Windows. This list of "middleware" components includes the following:

- **Web Browser**   The Microsoft default program is Internet Explorer.

- **E-mail Program**   Unless you specify otherwise, Windows uses Windows Mail for this function.

- **Media Player**   In Windows Vista, Windows Media Player is the default utility for playing sounds, video, and media files.

- **Instant Messaging Program**   Now that Windows Messenger is no longer bundled with the operating system, there is no current default messaging program.

- **Virtual Machine for Java**   In the past, Microsoft included its own Java VM. Although it's no longer available from Microsoft, you can continue to use it if it's installed on your computer.

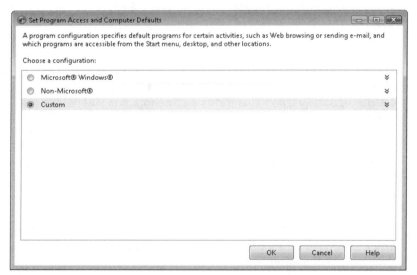

Figure 3-34 You can use this dialog box to remove certain Microsoft programs from menus in Windows.

In the Set Program Access And Computer Defaults dialog box, the default selection on all newly installed systems is Custom. This essentially means that you are willing to make your own decisions about what Microsoft middleware programs are visible and accessible on your system. This works for most users. If you want to remove the evidence of Internet Explorer, Windows Mail, Windows Media Player, or Windows Media Center, click the arrow next to Non-Microsoft and make your choices in the expanded dialog box. If you change your mind and want the Microsoft tools back, return to the dialog box and click Microsoft Windows or Custom.

Setting AutoPlay Options

AutoPlay is the feature that enables Windows to take appropriate action when you insert a CD or DVD into a drive. The operating system detects the kind of disc you have inserted—an audio disc, a program, or a DVD movie, for example—and takes the action that you have requested for that type of media. If you have not already made a decision about what the operating system should do, an AutoPlay dialog box appears when the disc is detected, and Windows presents a list of possible actions (including in some cases an option to do nothing at all). A check box in this dialog box lets you specify that the action you're currently choosing is should be the default for all discs of the current type. Figure 3-35 shows an example of the AutoPlay dialog box.

Figure 3-35 The AutoPlay dialog box that appears when you first insert an optical disc of a given type lets you tell Windows how to process the disc—either this time or every time.

If you have used the AutoPlay dialog box shown in Figure 3-35 to set a default action for a particular kind of optical media, and you subsequently change your mind and want a different default, open the Start menu, choose Default Programs, and then choose Change AutoPlay Settings. The dialog box that appears, shown in Figure 3-36 on the next page provides a drop-down list of possible actions for each media type. You can make your selection from this list and then click Save.

INSIDE OUT

To have *no* default action for a given optical media type, choose Ask Me Every Time.

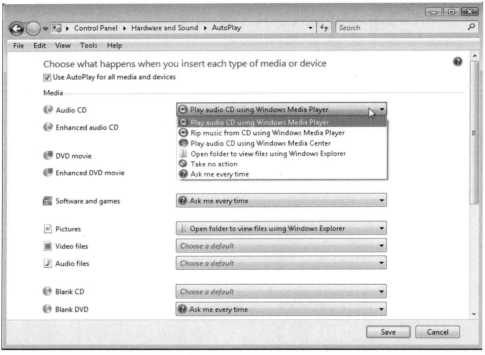

Figure 3-36 For each optical media type, Windows lets you choose from a list of appropriate default possibilities.

CHAPTER 4

Home Basic ○
Home Premium ○
Business ●
Enterprise ●
Ultimate ●

Adding, Removing, and Managing Programs

Y ou don't need a wizard or a Control Panel applet to install a new piece of software in Windows Vista. As a matter of fact, if you go looking for such a wizard, you'll come up empty. The Control Panel item called Add Or Remove Programs, familiar to most users of Windows XP, has made a graceful exit. Apparently, Microsoft realized that, while Windows XP users often turned to Add Or Remove Programs to uninstall software, it wasn't necessary to use Control Panel to perform an installation. Setting up a new program from a CD is typically a straightforward matter of inserting a disc and following the instructions that appear courtesy of your CD drive's AutoPlay settings. Setting up a program that you download is usually a matter of clicking Run or Open after the download has finished. In neither scenario do you need a wizard to hold your hand.

That's the theory, at any rate. In practice, there may be hurdles to surmount or hoops to jump through when it comes to installing programs. Potential complications can arise from two sources:

- User Account Control (UAC)

- Compatibility issues

The first of these is usually no more than a minor annoyance. The second can be more vexatious, but it usually only arises with programs designed for an earlier generation of operating system.

In this chapter, we'll survey the hoops and hurdles and everything else having to do with the addition, removal, updating, and management of applications in Windows Vista.

What's in Your Edition?

The Group Policy Editor, discussed in "Managing Startup Programs," later in this chapter, is not available in Windows Vista Home Basic or Windows Vista Home Premium. Everything else in this chapter applies equally to all editions.

Dealing with User Account Control (UAC)

Occasional exceptions aside, the rule in Windows Vista is: To install a program, you need administrative credentials. Software installers—the programs that install programs—typically create files in system folders (subfolders of %ProgramFiles%) and keys in protected registry locations, and these are actions that require elevated privileges.

Installing the program files and registry keys in protected locations protects your programs (hence, you) from tampering by malicious parties, but it means that you need to deal with User Account Control prompts to complete the process. If you install a program while running under an administrative account, a UAC prompt will request your consent for the actions the installer is about to undertake. If you install while running under a standard account, you will be asked to supply the name and password of an administrative user.

For more information about User Account Control, see "Preventing Unsafe Actions with User Account Control," in Chapter 10.

Windows Vista employs "installer detection" technology to determine when you have launched an installation process. This technology enables the operating system to request credentials at the time the process is launched, rather than waiting until the installer actually attempts to write to a protected location.

The system presumes that any process with a filename containing particular keywords (such as *install*, *setup*, or *update*) or any process whose data includes particular keywords or byte sequences, is going to need elevated privileges to complete its work, and so the UAC prompt appears as soon as the installer process begins. After you have satisfied the UAC mechanism, the process runs in the security context of TrustedInstaller, a system-generated account that has access to the appropriate secure locations.

TROUBLESHOOTING

No UAC prompt appears, and the install fails

If installer-detection technology fails to detect your installer, and if your installer tries to write to a protected area (in file storage or the registry), your setup will fail—typically with an error message like this:

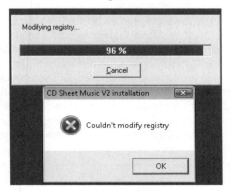

To solve this problem, first do whatever is necessary to back out of the failed installation (click OK, Exit, Cancel, or whatever else seems appropriate). Then try to find the executable file for the installer. It will *not* be named Setup or Install (because if it were, it would not have evaded the detector), but it will be an .exe file. When you find it, right-click it in Windows Explorer and choose Run As Administrator. Supply your administrative credentials, and let the installer run.

The same technology that detects an installation process also recognizes when you're about to update or remove a program. So you can expect to see UAC prompts for these activities as well.

Rules have exceptions, of course. The following kinds of programs are not flagged by installer-detection technology:

- 64-bit executables

- Programs that have a "RequestedExecutionLevel" embedded in their application manifests.

Moreover, it is possible, although uncommon, for a program to install itself in an unprotected, "per-user" location. For example, SyncToy 1.4 for Windows Vista, a PowerToy program available free at *http://www.vista-io.com/0401*, installs itself in %LocalAppData%\SyncToy, a location in the profile of the person installing the application. The setup program also avoids detection by installer-detection technology, making SyncToy a rare case—a program that you can install without administrative credentials. (For an interesting description of the how, if not the why, of creating a per-user installer, see "How Do I Build a Standard User Package," in the blog post at *http://www.vista-io.com/0402*.)

Chapter 4

TROUBLESHOOTING

The setup process hangs on reboot

If you launch a setup program as a standard user and supply the name and password of an administrative account, and if the setup program requires a system reboot to complete, you might not be able to complete the installation unless you log back in (after the reboot) as that administrative user, rather than under your own standard-user account. Installer routines that include a reboot typically record post-reboot instructions in the registry key HKLM\Software\Microsoft\Windows\CurrentVersion\RunOnce. The value of the RunOnce key is, as the key name suggests, run one time—and then discarded. The hitch is that RunOnce values are executed only when an administrator logs on. If you log on as a standard user, the RunOnce instructions are ignored, and your setup process may appear to hang. The solution is to log off and log back on as an administrator. To forestall problems of this kind, you might want to adopt the practice of elevating your own account to administrative status, using the Manage Accounts section of Control Panel, before you begin installing applications. Afterward, if you're more comfortable running as a standard user, you can return to Control Panel and demote yourself.

Turn off Start menu notifications

After you install a program, Windows announces additions to the Start menu by highlighting the changes on the menu itself. It's reasonably intelligent about this; it doesn't highlight additions that aren't programs (shortcuts to documents, for example), it removes the highlight for items that you ignore for at least a week, and it doesn't highlight anything that you install within an hour of installing Windows itself. Nevertheless, some users would rather it didn't highlight any Start-menu changes. If you're in that camp, right-click the Start button and choose Properties. On the Start Menu tab of the Taskbar And Start Menu Properties dialog box, click Customize. Then, in the Customize Start Menu dialog box, clear Highlight Newly Installed Programs.

Dealing with Compatibility Issues

Most recent application programs should install and run without problems in Windows Vista. Certain older ones might not. Windows Vista attempts to recognize potential compatibility problems *before* you install. Immediately after running a program's installer and satisfying the UAC sentry, you might, for example, see a message like the one shown in Figure 4-1.

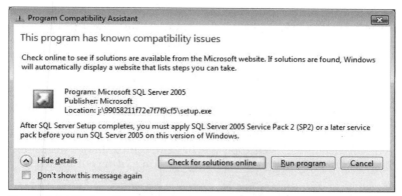

Figure 4-1 Windows flags some potential compatibility problems and recommends solutions before you install.

In this example, Windows has not only recognized a potential compatibility issue prior to installing your program, but also given you some cause for optimism that you might achieve a successful installation by following the directions in the message box. In other cases where a known compatibility issue is detected, the outlook might seem a little less bright:

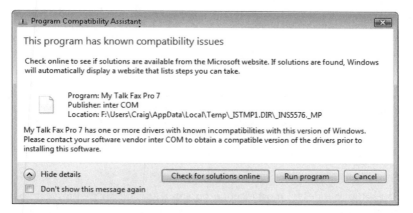

You should click Check For Solutions Online in any case, however. As time passes, you can expect more and more information to be available about compatibility issues affecting particular legacy programs, so the online link might actually solve your problem. (You can also expect independent software vendors to provide updates for Windows Vista, so the advice to contact your software vendor is also definitely worth heeding.) If you're sure that no help is available online or from your vendor, and you want to try installing the software despite the potential compatibility problem, click Run Program.

In other cases, you might see a more serious-looking message with a red X in the title bar instead of a yellow information symbol. Here again, you have nothing to lose by clicking Check For Solutions Online, but you can be pretty sure the solution is going

Chapter 4

to involve purchasing a newer version of your software. A message like this appears when Windows regards the program you want to install as a threat to its own (that is, your system's) stability. No manner of compatibility tweak is going to get you past this defense.

If an installation routine runs but fails for any reason to complete successfully (even if you simply cancel out of the setup process), you will see a Program Compatibility Assistant message, comparable to the one shown in Figure 4-2. If the Assistant is mistaken and you really have successfully installed your program, click This Program Installed Correctly. Otherwise, click Reinstall Using Recommended Settings. The Program Compatibility Assistant will then apply one or more compatibility tweaks (unfortunately, without telling you what it's doing) and try again to run your installer.

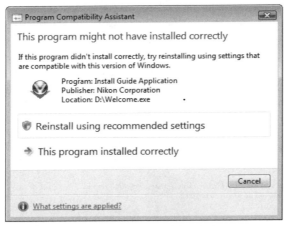

Figure 4-2 The Program Compatibility Assistant appears when an installation program does not reach a successful conclusion.

Set a restore point

The setup routines for most recent programs automatically create a restore point before making any changes to your system. A restore point is a snapshot of your current system state. If an installation destabilizes your system, you can use System Restore to return to the snapshot state. (For more information about using System Restore, see, "Configuring System Recovery Options," Chapter 2, and "Making Repairs with the Windows Recovery Environment," Chapter 23.) The installers for some older programs do not create restore points, unfortunately, and it is precisely these older programs that present the most potential hazard. If you're about to install a program that's not of recent vintage (say, one written for Windows 9x), it's not a bad idea to create a restore point manually before you begin. (Open System And Maintenance in Control Panel, click System, then click System Protection in the Tasks pane. Bring along your administrative credentials.)

In some cases, a program written for an earlier version of Windows might install successfully but still not run well. In such situations, the Program Compatibility Wizard is your friend. The wizard lets you take measures designed to convince your program that it's running in the environment for which it was designed.

To run the Program Compatibility Wizard, open Programs in Control Panel. Then, under Programs And Features, click Use An Older Program With This Version Of Windows. Then follow the step-by-step instructions.

As an alternative to using the Program Compatibility Wizard, you can modify the properties of the program's shortcut. Open the Start menu, find the program you want to adjust, right-click its Start-menu entry, and choose Properties from the shortcut menu. Then click the Compatibility tab. Figure 4-3 shows an example of what you'll see.

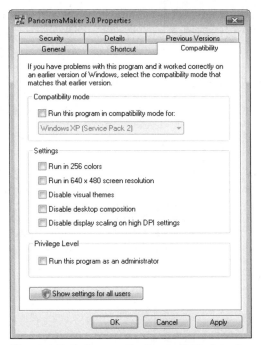

Figure 4-3 Options on the Compatibility tab of a program shortcut's properties dialog box might enable some older programs to run in Windows Vista.

Select the Run This Program In Compatibility Mode For check box, and choose one of the six available operating systems: Windows 95, Windows 98 / Windows Me, Windows NT 4.0 (Service Pack 5), Windows 2000, or Windows XP (Service Pack 2). Use the Settings options to deal with programs that experience video problems when run at higher resolutions and color depths.

Chapter 4

Configuring MS-DOS Programs

To control the behavior of MS-DOS-based programs, you use a properties dialog box whose design hasn't changed much since Windows 95. Custom property settings for each program are stored in a shortcut file called a *program information file (PIF)*.

Set global PIF options

Is the default MS-DOS environment not right? You can adjust the default settings that apply to all MS-DOS programs by editing the settings stored in %SystemRoot%_default.pif. When you double-click the icon for an MS-DOS-based program and Windows can't find a matching PIF, it uses the settings recorded here. Likewise, when you create a new PIF, it starts with these default settings. If you want an MS-DOS batch file to run each time any MS-DOS program starts up, save the file as %SystemRoot%_default.bat.

You can create multiple shortcuts (PIFs) for a single MS-DOS program, each with its own custom settings, such as a default data file or working directory. When you right-click the icon for an MS-DOS executable file and make any changes to its properties, Windows saves your changes in the same folder, creating or updating a file with the same name as the executable file and the extension .pif. You can change the name of the shortcut file or move it to another folder.

The PIF format is binary and can't be edited except through the properties dialog box. Right-click the icon for the MS-DOS program's executable file to display this dialog box, which adds four tabs containing options that are exclusively available to MS-DOS programs. Using the Misc tab, shown in Figure 4-4, for instance, you can disable Windows shortcut keys that conflict with shortcuts in the MS-DOS program. Options on other tabs allow you to adjust the amount of memory allocated to a program, specify the program's initial display mode (full-screen or windows), and change the icon associated with the program—among other things.

Figure 4-4 The Font, Memory, Screen, and Misc tabs in this dialog box control settings that are exclusive to MS-DOS programs.

Running some MS-DOS programs properly might require that you change the system configuration used by the MS-DOS virtual machine. Two files, Autoexec.nt and Config.nt, serve this function in Windows Vista. These two files play a role similar to that of Autoexec.bat and Config.sys in MS-DOS and Windows 9X, with several important differences:

- Autoexec.nt and Config.nt are located by default in the %SystemRoot%\System32 folder. (The corresponding files on an MS-DOS or Windows 9X machine are in the root folder of drive C.)

- In Windows Vista, you can create custom versions of Autoexec.nt and Config.nt for specific applications. To associate your custom configuration files with a specific application, copy the default files to a separate location and edit them as needed. Next, open the properties dialog box for the MS-DOS program, click the Advanced button on the Program tab, and then enter the correct locations as shown below. (Note that this dialog box includes a Compatible Timer Hardware Emulation check box. This option imposes a performance penalty, so you should select it only if your application won't run with the box cleared.)

- Commands you enter in these two files affect only the MS-DOS subsystem. Many commands, such as Buffers and Break, are ignored, although they can be entered for compatibility purposes when an MS-DOS program insists that they be present.

Installing Programs on 64-bit Versions of Windows

If you're running an x64 version of Windows, you'll notice the following differences when it comes to program installation:

- 16-bit Windows applications will not install.

- 64-bit programs will be installed, by default, in subfolders of the Program Files folder (%ProgramFiles%), but 32-bit programs will land in subfolders of a separate program-file folder called Program Files (x86).

- While most programs designed for a 32-bit environment will run with full functionality in the x64 version of Windows, some might not, and certain of those might be courteous enough to notify you in advance:

Creating and Customizing Program Shortcuts

During setup, nearly all Windows programs create shortcuts on the Start menu. Many also create (or at least offer to create) shortcuts on your desktop and your Quick Launch toolbar. You can tailor these shortcuts to your advantage by right-clicking them and choosing Properties from the menu that appears (which is, incidentally, also called a shortcut menu). You can also create and customize shortcuts to particular documents and folders.

Here are some useful things you can do:

- **Create a shortcut to a document you're currently working with** To make a frequently needed document more accessible, display the document in Windows Explorer. Then, to create a Start-menu item that will open this document (in the program with which the document's file type is associated), drag the document to the Start button. When the menu opens, release the mouse button. To put a shortcut on your Quick Launch toolbar, drag the document there; when you see the tip Copy To Quick Launch, release the mouse button. To create a desktop shortcut, hold down the right mouse button and the drag the document to the desktop. (Don't do this with the left button, because that will actually move the document instead of creating a shortcut.) When the tip Move To Desktop appears, release the mouse button and choose Create Shortcuts Here from the menu that appears:

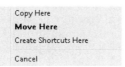

- **Create a shortcut to a folder that you need frequently** You can create a shortcut to a folder the same way you would create a shortcut to a document. Use Windows Explorer to display the parent folder that contains the folder you're interested in. Then drag the folder from that window.

- **Create shortcuts to deeply nested Control Panel applets and other administrative tools** Tired of clicking Control Panel headings and subheadings to get to the item you need? Go there in the usual way, and then drag the icon at the left side of Control Panel's address bar to your desktop. In most cases, the system will reward you with a handy shortcut.

- **Specify startup options** Many programs allow command-line arguments that alter the program's startup location or behavior. For example, Snagit 8, the program used to capture most of the illustrations in this book, includes an optional /h command switch that hides the program's window at startup. You can use shortcuts to simplify the use of such startup options. Generally speaking, the easiest way to accomplish this is to copy and then modify an existing shortcut—such as one on the start menu or desktop. Right-click the copy, click the Shortcut tab, and then modify the command string that appears on the Target line.

- **Make a program run with elevated privileges** You can run a program as an administrator by right-clicking its shortcut and choosing Run As Administrator. If you need to do this most of the time for a particular program—for example, if you regularly run Command Prompt with elevated privileges—consider customizing the program's shortcut so that it runs by default as administrator. Right-click the program's shortcut and choose Properties. On the Shortcut tab of the properties dialog box, click Advanced. In the Advanced Properties dialog box, select Run As Administrator:

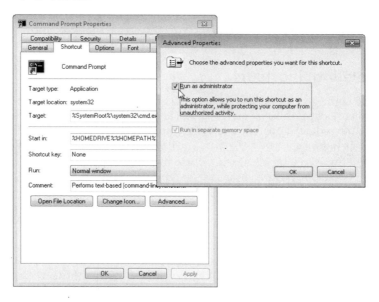

> **Note**
>
> If you run in a non-administrative (standard) account but occasionally need to use administrative tools—such as Registry Editor or one of the Microsoft Management Console (MMC) snap-ins—you can save yourself some hassle by creating Run As Administrator shortcuts for these tools. Various of the MMC snap-ins (as well as Registry Editor) fail to prompt for administrative credentials when you launch them from a standard account. Instead, they simply block you when you try to do anything useful in them. To avoid frustration create shortcuts in advance, with the Run As Administrator check box selected.

Creating New Shortcuts from Scratch

The easiest ways to create a new shortcut are:

- Copy an existing shortcut and modify the copy
- Right-drag an object to the place where you want the shortcut, then choose Create Shortcuts Here (in some cases, you can drag with the left mouse button, but right-dragging always works)
- Right-click an object in Windows Explorer and choose Create Shortcut (to create a shortcut in the same location as the object; subsequently you can move or copy the new shortcut)

If you'd like to work a bit harder, you can right-click the desktop (or another location in Windows Explorer), choose New, and then choose Shortcut. The Create Shortcut wizard will prompt first for the location of the item, then for the name of the shortcut. What the wizard calls "location" is the command string that the shortcut should execute. Because that command string is apt to be long, a Browse button is provided.

Deleting Shortcuts

One of the great things about shortcuts is that you can throw them out when they're no longer needed. In fact, you really *should* toss them, because not doing that is what leads to cluttered desktops. (You might also want to look at desktop shortcuts created by installer routines. If you not actually using them, consider them candidates for the green barrel.)

To remove a shortcut from the top level of the Start menu (the menu that appears on the left when you click the Start button), right-click it and choose Remove From This List.

Deleting a shortcut does not remove the program, document, or folder to which the shortcut is linked. (For information about removing programs, see "Uninstalling Programs," later in this chapter.) If you're in any doubt about whether the object you're about to delete is a shortcut or an object—a document or program—that you will regret deleting, look for the arrow on the lower-left corner of the icon. Shortcuts have these; objects do not. (Start-menu shortcuts are an exception. They don't have arrows.)

Managing Startup Programs

Setting up a program to run automatically when you start Windows is easy. If the program's installer doesn't offer to do this for you (many do) and you want the program to run every time you begin a Windows session, create a shortcut for the program in the Startup folder of your Start menu. Here's one good way to do it:

1. Right-click the Start button and choose Open.

2. In the Windows Explorer window that appears, open the Programs folder, and then open the Startup folder.

3. On the Start menu, find the item that you want to launch automatically when you start Windows.

4. Drag the item to the Startup folder.

TROUBLESHOOTING

You can't create a shortcut in the Startup folder

If you see a message like this:

you're in the All Users Startup folder instead of your own Startup folder. The All Users folder holds shortcuts for everyone with an account at your computer. Program installers (running under the TrustedInstaller account) can create shortcuts there, but you cannot (without changing the access control entries associated with that folder). To get to your own Startup folder, be sure that you choose Open, not Open All Users, when you right-click the Start button.

Controlling Startup Programs with Windows Defender

The problem that many users have with startup programs is not creating them (that's easy, and in many cases it happens more or less automatically), but getting rid of them. Having too many startup programs not only makes your system take a longer time to start, it also has the potential to waste memory. If you don't require a program at start-up, it's a good idea to get it out of your startup path.

Unfortunately, tracking down programs that start automatically isn't as easy as you might think. A program can be configured to run at startup in many ways, not just by having a shortcut in a Startup folder. To wit:

- **Run key (machine)** Programs listed in the registry's HKLM\Software\Microsoft\Windows\CurrentVersion\Run key are available at startup to all users.

- **Run key (User)** Programs listed in the HKCU\Software\Microsoft\Windows\CurrentVersion\Run key run when the current user logs on. A similar subkey, HKCU\Software\Microsoft\Windows NT\CurrentVersion\Windows\Run, may also be used.

- **Load value** Programs listed in the Load value of the registry key HKCU\Software\Microsoft\Windows NT\CurrentVersion\Windows run when any user logs on.

- **Scheduled tasks** The Windows task scheduler (see "Using the Windows Vista Task Scheduler," Chapter 30) can specify tasks that run at startup. In addition, an administrator can set up tasks for your computer to run at startup tasks for your computer to run at startup that are listed only on the administrator's system, not your own.

- **Win.ini** Programs written for 16-bit Windows versions may add commands to the Load= and Run= lines in the [Windows] section of this startup file, which located in %SystemRoot%. The Win.ini file is a legacy of the Windows 3.1 era.

- **RunOnce and RunOnceEx keys** This group of registry keys identifies programs that run once and only once at startup. These keys may be assigned to a specific user account or to the machine.

  - HKLM\Software\Microsoft\Windows\CurrentVersion\RunOnce
  - HKLM\Software\Microsoft\Windows\CurrentVersion\RunOnceEx
  - HKCU\Software\Microsoft\Windows\CurrentVersion\RunOnce
  - HKCU\Software\Microsoft\Windows\CurrentVersion\RunOnceEx

- **RunServices and RunServicesOnce keys** As the names suggest, these rarely used keys can control automatic startup of services. They may be assigned to a specific user account or to a computer.

- **Winlogon key** The Winlogon key controls actions that occur when you log on to a computer running Windows Vista. Most of these actions are under the control of the operating system, but you can also add custom actions here. The HKLM\Software\Microsoft\Windows NT\CurrentVersion\Winlogon\Userinit and HKLM\Software\Microsoft\Windows NT\CurrentVersion\Winlogon\Shell subkeys can automatically launch programs.

- **Group Policy** The Group Policy console includes two policies called Run These Programs At User Logon that specify a list of programs to be run whenever any user logs on.

- **Policies\Explorer\Run keys** Using policies to specify startup programs, as described in the previous paragraph, creates corresponding values in either of two registry keys: HKLM\Software\Microsoft\Windows\CurrentVersion\Policies\Explorer\Run or HKCU\Software\Microsoft\Windows\CurrentVersion\Policies\Explorer\Run.

- **BootExecute value** By default, the multi-string BootExecute value of the registry key HKLM\System\CurrentControlSet\Control\Session Manager is set to *autocheck autochk **. This value causes Windows, at startup, to check the file-system integrity of your hard disks if your system has been shut down abnormally. It is possible for other programs or processes to add themselves to this registry value. (Note: Microsoft warns against deleting the default BootExecute value. For information about what to do if your system hangs while Autocheck is running, see Microsoft Knowledge Base article 151376, "How to Disable Autochk If It Stops Responding During Reboot.")

- **Shell service objects** Windows loads a number of helper dynamic-link libraries (DLLs) to add capabilities to the Windows shell.

- **Logon scripts** Logon scripts, which run automatically at startup, can open other programs. Logon scripts are specified in Group Policy in Computer Configuration\Windows Settings\Scripts (Startup/Shutdown) and User Configuration\Windows Settings\Scripts (Logon/Logoff).

Veterans of Windows XP might be familiar with System Configuration Utility (Msconfig.exe), a tool that allows you to see most of the programs that run at startup and disable particular ones if you choose to do so. Windows Vista retains System Configuration Utility but also offers a startup program listing in Windows Defender, the anti-spyware utility included with the operating system. Neither list includes startup programs established by policy or scheduled tasks. But the Windows Defender list is a bit easier to read and offers more details about each startup program.

To see the list of startup programs in Windows Defender, open Control Panel. Then, under Programs, click Change Startup Programs. Initially, the list shows only those tasks that run in your own user account. To see startup programs that run in other accounts as well, click Show For All Users.

The default organization of the list that appears on the left side of the Windows Defender Software Explorer (see Figure 4-5 on the following page) is By Publisher. You can group items by Startup Type, if you prefer. To do this, right-click any part of the list and choose Startup Type. In Figure 4-5, the list is organized by Startup Type, and you can see that this system includes one item in the user profile Startup folder, two more in the All Users Startup folder, two Current User (HKCU) registry items, and eight items in the Local Machine (HKLM) section of the registry. Included in the information on the right side of the window is the exact registry key responsible for each of the Current User and Local Machine registry items.

Chapter 4

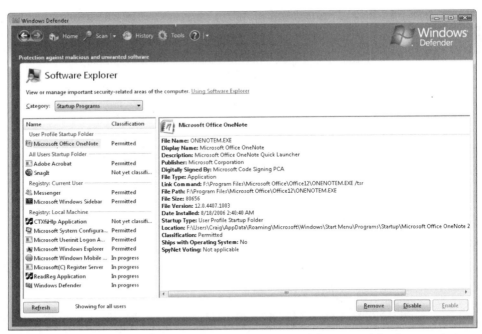

Figure 4-5 Windows Defender is primarily an antispyware tool, but it can defend you against unwanted startup programs as well.

The reason that Windows Defender includes a list of startup programs, of course, is that it's important to know about any startup programs that manage to arrive without your knowledge or consent. It's also important to know about those to which you do consent, because they can clog up your system if you're not actually using them.

To determine whether an item is needed or not, you can select the item and click Disable. Then restart your system. After verifying that your system works properly without the program starting automatically, you can use the Remove button to remove it. Before you lop off a startup item, however, check to see if that item is configured by means of a Startup folder on the Start menu. If it is, you might prefer to move it from the Startup folder to another Start menu location, rather than using Windows Defender. Using Windows Defender to remove a Startup folder item doesn't delete the program, but it does erase the shortcut—and you might want to use that shortcut in some other part of the Start menu or elsewhere.

TROUBLESHOOTING

A startup program doesn't start

If a startup program requires elevated (administrative) credentials, Windows Defender will prevent it from starting when you log on to your system. You should see a message in your notification area advising you that one or more items has been blocked. Click that message to see what's been blocked and (optionally) to run the blocked program or programs.

For more information about Windows Defender, see "Stopping Spyware with Windows Defender," Chapter 10.

Using Policies to Control Startup Applications

The Group Policy console (Gpedit.msc) includes three policies that affect startup applications (and documents):

- Run These Programs At User Logon
- Do Not Process The Run Once List
- Do Not Process The Legacy Run List

Each of these policies appears in two places in Group Policy:

- Computer Configuration\Administrative Templates\System\Logon
- User Configuration\Administrative Templates\System\Logon

Changes at either node affect all users of the current computer. If startup programs are specified for the Run These Programs At User Logon policy in both nodes, all such programs are run at startup—the Computer Configuration programs first, followed by the User Configuration programs. If policy settings at the two nodes conflict, the Computer Configuration settings take priority. To view or modify any of these policy settings, run Gpedit.msc (you'll need administrative credentials). Note that the Group Policy console is not available in Windows Vista Home Basic or Windows Vista Home Premium.

Run These Programs At User Logon

This policy lets you specify a list of startup applications. To implement the policy, in the details pane of the Group Policy console, double-click Run These Programs At User Logon. Then select Enabled, click Show, and click Add. In the Add Item dialog box, type the name of an executable, or a document associated with an executable. If necessary, specify the complete path of the item, so that Windows can find it at startup.

Do Not Process The Run Once List

Enabling this policy prevents Windows from processing the contents of HKLM \Software\Microsoft\Windows\CurrentVersion\RunOnce. Windows includes the policy as a security measure. If you're concerned that a virus or Trojan horse might use the RunOnce key to launch some malicious code on your system, enable the policy. Be aware, though, that many legitimate programs rely on this key to complete their setup routines.

Do Not Process The Legacy Run List

What Group Policy calls the "legacy run list" is the list of programs launched at startup via the registry keys HKLM\Software\Microsoft\Windows\CurrentVersion\Run and HKCU\Software\Microsoft\Windows\CurrentVersion\Run. Like the policy described in the previous paragraph, this one appears to be included as a security measure. If you're concerned about the possibility that a rogue application might infiltrate your system via one of these registry keys, enable the policy. Be aware, though, that many legitimate programs rely on one of these registry keys for startup launch. If you decide to enable the policy, you will need to find another way to launch such programs.

Managing Running Programs and Processes with Windows Task Manager

Windows Task Manager is a tool that serves two essential purposes. You can use it to track aspects of your system's performance, and you can use it to see what programs and processes are running and terminate items when the normal shutdown methods aren't working.

For information about using Windows Task Manager to monitor system performance, see "Monitoring Performance in Real Time," Chapter 21.

The easiest way to run Windows Task Manager is by means of its keyboard shortcut, Ctrl+Shift+Escape. Figure 4-6 shows the Applications tab and Processes tab of Windows Task Manager.

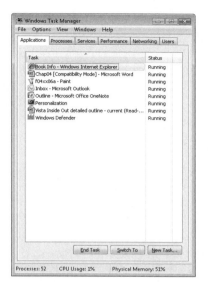
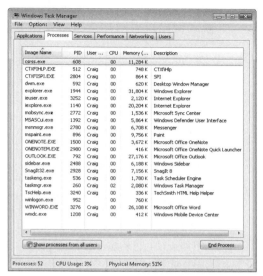

Figure 4-6 Windows Task Manager is useful for terminating recalcitrant applications and processes, as well as for monitoring system performance.

In Windows Task Manager, the Applications tab lists all running programs that have corresponding taskbar buttons. The entries you see here are approximately the same as the ones presented by the Windows Alt+Tab task switcher. Each entry in the Task column consists of descriptive text and not a program now, as is found on the Processes tab. This text is identical to the text displayed in the program's title bar.

The Applications tab also includes a Status column. Most of the time, the entries in this list will read *Running*. If an application hangs or freezes for any reason, you will see the words *Not Responding* in this column instead. In that case, you can attempt to shut down the misbehaving program by selecting its entry and clicking End Task. Don't be too quick on the trigger, however; Not Responding doesn't necessarily mean that an application is irredeemably lost. If the program is using every bit of resources to handle a different task, it might simply be too busy to communicate with Windows Task Manager. Before you decide to end the program, give it a chance to finish whatever it's doing. How long should you wait? That depends on the task. If the operation involves a large data file (performing a global search and replace in a large Microsoft Access database, for instance), it's appropriate to wait several minutes, especially if you can hear the hard disk chattering or see the disk activity light flickering. But if the task in question normally completes in a few seconds, you needn't wait more than a minute.

The items listed on the Applications tab represent only a portion of the total number of programs and services running on a Windows computer at any given time. To see the entire list of running processes and gain access to a broader selection of tools for managing them, click the Processes tab.

Note

To find out what process is associated with a given application, right-click the application on the Applications tab, and choose Go To Process from the shortcut menu.

Initially, the Processes tab lists programs and services that are directly accessible to the user. To see everything, including processes running under system accounts, click Show Processes From All Users.

For each process, Windows Task Manager includes the following information by default: Image Name (the name of the process), user name (which user started the process), CPU (the percentage of the CPU's capacity that the process is currently using), Memory (Private Working Set) (the amount of memory the process requires to perform its regular functions), and Description, a text field identifying the process.

If you need to shut down a process, select it and click End Process.

Be smart about shutdowns

When you shut down an application by clicking the End Task button on the Applications tab, the effect is the same as if you had chosen to shut down the program using its menus or by right-clicking its taskbar button and choosing Close. If the program can respond to the shutdown request, it should prompt you for confirmation or give you a chance to save open files, if necessary. By contrast, the End Process button on the Processes tab zaps a process immediately and irrevocably, closing any open files without giving you a chance to save them. Whenever possible, you should try the End Task option first and reserve the drastic End Process option for situations in which you have no alternative.

INSIDE OUT   Assign a Program to a Specific Processor

If you have a dual-core or multi-processor system, you can assign a process to a specific processor—but only after the process is already running. To do this, right-click the process on the Processes tab and choose Set Affinity. In the dialog box that appears:

select the process you want to use. (If all CPUs are selected, Windows sets the process affinity as it sees fit.)

Running a Program as an Administrator or Another User

As mentioned earlier in this chapter, you can run a program as an administrator by right-clicking any shortcut for the program (in the Start menu or elsewhere), choosing Run As Administrator, and satisfying the UAC prompt with either consent or credentials. Here are two additional ways to do it:

- Start a Command Prompt session as Administrator (by right-clicking a shortcut for Cmd.exe and choosing Run As Administrator). Then, from the Command Prompt, type the executable for whatever program you want to run as administrator. To run Registry Editor, for example, type **regedit**. Because you've already passed UAC inspection for the Command Prompt session, and because whatever you run from Command Prompt is a child process of Command Prompt, you don't have to deal with any further UAC prompts. This method is excellent for situations where you need to run a sequence of programs as an administrator. Keep one admin-level Command Prompt open and run your programs from the command line.

- Type the name of the program you want to run in the Start menu's search box. Then press Ctrl+Shift+Enter.

To run a program under a different user account, you can use the Runas command. Runas no longer appears on the shortcut menus for programs, as it did in Windows XP. But you can still use it from the Command Prompt or a shortcut. The syntax is:

```
runas /user:username cmd
```

Chapter 4

After you issue the command or activate the shortcut, you'll be prompted to enter the password for the specified user account. For security reasons, you cannot save the password with the shortcut. Note that the Runas command does not work with Microsoft Management Console (MMC) shortcuts.

Uninstalling Programs

To remove an installed Windows program, open Control Panel and click Uninstall A Program (you'll find that under the heading Programs). The list of uninstallable programs that appears does not include usage information (as it did in Windows XP, although the information there was seldom accurate), but it does list the size of each program. Click the program you want to remove, or select it and click Uninstall/ Change. A UAC prompt will appear.

Here are some basic facts you should know about uninstalling programs:

- Windows Vista warns you if you attempt to remove a program while other users are logged on. For safety's sake, you should always completely log off any other user accounts before attempting to remove a program.

- Many uninstall programs leave a few traces of the programs behind, either inadvertently or by design. For instance, programs that create data files typically do not remove custom user settings and data files as part of the uninstall process.

- You can remove programs from Control Panel only if they were originally installed with a Windows-compatible setup program. Some older programs and utilities work by copying their files to a folder. In this case, you uninstall the program by manually removing its files and shortcuts.

- In some cases, a poorly written uninstall routine may leave a phantom entry behind in the list of installed programs, even after it has successfully removed all traces of the program itself. To remove an item from the list in this case, remove entries manually, using Registry Editor. Detailed instructions are available in Knowledge Base article 314481, "How to Manually Remove Programs from the Add or Remove Programs Tool."

CHAPTER 5

Setting Up and Troubleshooting Hardware

Home Basic ●
Home Premium ●
Business ●
Enterprise ●
Ultimate ●

It's probably only a slight exaggeration to say that no two computers are alike. Motherboards, disks and controllers, video and network adapters, and peripherals of all shapes and sizes combine to create a nearly infinite number of possible computer configurations.

Windows Vista supports a long list of computer peripherals. For supported hardware upgrades, Windows detects the device automatically and installs the correct driver software so that you can use the device and its full array of features. As we note in this chapter, however, the compatibility bar has been raised for some classes of older devices, and for 64-bit versions of Windows Vista the list of compatible devices is even more exclusive.

If Windows has a problem with a device, you have your choice of troubleshooting tools. Device Manager, available as part of the Computer Management console and as a stand-alone snap-in for Microsoft Management Console, is the primary tool for gathering information about installed devices and drivers and adjusting their configuration details.

What's in Your Edition?

You'll encounter no differences in working with hardware devices when you switch between computers running different editions of Windows Vista. The procedures for installing devices, working with device drivers, and troubleshooting hardware problems are the same in all editions.

A Crash Course in Device Drivers

Before Windows can work with any piece of hardware, it requires a compatible, properly configured device driver. *Drivers* are compact control programs that hook directly into Windows and handle the essential tasks of communicating your instructions to a hardware device and then relaying data back to you. After you set up a hardware device, its driver loads automatically and runs as part of the operating system, without requiring any further intervention on your part.

Windows Vista includes a library of drivers—for internal components like sound cards, storage controllers, and display adapters as well as external add-ons such as printers, keyboards, scanners, mice and other pointing devices, digital cameras, and removable storage devices. This core library is copied during Windows Vista Setup to a protected system folder, %SystemRoot%\System32\DriverStore. (Driver files and associated components are stored in the FileRepository subfolder.) Anyone who logs on to the computer can read and execute files from this location. But only an installation program working with authorization from a member of the Administrators group can create or modify files and folders there.

You can add new drivers to the driver store in a variety of ways. Windows Update offers drivers when it detects that you're running a device that is compatible with that driver and is currently using an older version. (You can also search for the most recent driver via Windows Update when installing a new device.) In addition, installing a Windows service pack typically refreshes the driver store with new and updated drivers. All drivers that are copied here from Microsoft servers are certified to be fully compatible with Windows Vista and are digitally signed by Microsoft. As an administrator, you can add third-party drivers, signed or unsigned, to the driver store by specifically giving consent. All drivers added to the driver store in this fashion are saved in their own subfolder beneath the FileRepository folder, along with some supporting files created by Windows Vista, allowing them to be reinstalled if necessary. Any driver that has been added to the store, signed or unsigned, is considered to be trusted and can be installed without prompts or administrator credentials.

In Windows Vista, you do not have to be an administrator to install drivers; Windows checks the current driver installation policy to determine whether installation is permitted. When you install a new Plug and Play–compatible device, Windows checks the driver store first. If it finds a suitable driver, installation proceeds automatically. If no compatible driver is available, you're prompted to search for driver software.

By default, Windows Vista installs drivers from trusted publishers without prompts and never installs drivers from publishers that the user has chosen not to trust. (Domain administrators can override these settings using group policy.) When you attempt to install a signed third-party driver and have not previously designated the publisher as trusted or untrusted, you're presented with a consent dialog box like the one in Figure 5-1.

Figure 5-1 When you install a digitally signed driver, you're presented with this consent dialog box.

By contrast, if you point the driver installer to an unsigned file while running a 32-bit version of Windows Vista, you see the dialog box shown in Figure 5-2. You can cancel the installation and look for a signed file, or you can ignore the warning and continue.

Figure 5-2 On 32-bit versions of Windows Vista, administrators will see this warning message when attempting to install an unsigned driver.

To be properly installed in Windows Vista, a hardware driver must have a Setup Information file (with the extension .inf). This is a text file that contains detailed information about the device to be installed, including the names of its driver files, the locations where they are to be installed, any required registry settings, and version information. All devices with drivers in the DriverStore folder include Setup Information files in the %SystemRoot%\Inf folder.

The basic structure of a Setup Information file is similar to an old-fashioned Windows 3.x–style .ini file. Each piece of setup information appears on its own line under a bracketed section heading. Windows will not allow the driver package to be copied into the driver store unless these sections are present and filled in correctly. In particular, an

.inf file must contain valid [SourceDisksFiles] and [SourceDisksNames] sections. At the time the .inf file is copied into the driver store, Windows creates a folder for the driver files using the name of the .inf file with an eight-character hash appended to it. Inside that folder, Windows uses the data in the .inf file to create a Precompiled Setup Information file with the .pnf extension, which it uses for installation tasks.

Although the Setup Information file is a crucial part of the driver installation process, you don't work with it directly. Instead, this file supplies instructions that the operating system uses during Plug and Play detection, or when you use the Add Hardware Wizard or a Setup program to install a device.

> **Note**
>
> The syntax of Setup Information files is complex, and the intricacies of .inf files can trip up even experienced software developers. If you find that a driver setup routine isn't working properly, you might be tempted to try editing the Setup Information file to work around the hang-up. Trust us: That approach is almost certain to fail. In fact, by tinkering with .inf files, you run the risk of corrupting registry settings and crashing your system.

When Windows completes the installation of a driver package, it performs all the tasks specified by the Setup Information file and copies the driver files themselves to %SystemRoot%\System32\Drivers.

Is That Driver Signed?

As we noted earlier in this chapter, Windows Vista requires that all driver packages be trusted before they can be added to the driver store. Drivers pass an initial threshold of trust when they are digitally signed. But not all signatures are created equal. Here's a description of how Windows Vista handles different types of drivers:

- The highest level of trust is assigned to drivers that are signed by Microsoft's Windows Hardware Quality Lab (WHQL) through the Windows Logo Program. These so-called WHQL-signed drivers can be installed by any user, on any 32- or 64-bit version of Windows Vista, without any warnings or request for consent.

- Drivers can also be signed by third parties using Authenticode signatures, which use a certificate that is issued by a Certificate Authority whose certificate is stored in the Trusted Root Certification Authorities store. If an Administrator has added the publisher's certificate to the Trusted Publishers store, the driver can be installed with no prompts by any user.

- If a driver is signed by a publisher whose certificate is not in the Trusted Publishers store, it can be installed by an administrator only. Installation will fail silently for users who are not members of the Administrators group. An administrator can also choose to add this type of signed driver to the driver store, after which it can be installed by any user with no prompts.

- Drivers that are unsigned, or with a signature that is invalid or cannot be verified by a trusted Certificate Authority, or with a digital signature that has been altered, can be installed by an administrator on 32-bit (x86) versions of Windows Vista but cannot be installed on any 64-bit (X64) version of Windows Vista.

To make the issue of driver signing even more confusing, there are two additional levels of digital signing to consider. For most driver packages, the only file that must be digitally signed is the *catalog file,* which uses a .cat extension. It lists the files included with the driver package and provides hashed digest numbers that uniquely identify each file and confirm that it has not been tampered with. For drivers that start at boot-up on X64 versions of Windows Vista, the driver file itself must contain an embedded signature. In addition, any device that is used to play back media that uses the Protected Media Path (PMP), such as HD-DVD disks and other formats that use the Advanced Access Content System (AACS) specification, must have a driver that is signed using a PMP-PE certificate. You can verify the contents of a Security Catalog file by double-clicking it in Windows Explorer.

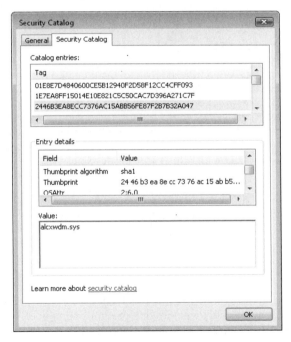

In general, you should prefer WHQL-signed drivers, which have undergone extensive compatibility testing using procedures established by Microsoft's hardware testing labs. It represents a strong assurance that the driver follows installation guidelines and that you can count on it not to cause your system to crash or become unstable. A digital signature from another trusted source doesn't confer the same assurance of reliability but does provide confidence that the driver hasn't been tampered with by other installation programs or by a virus or Trojan horse program.

Don't underestimate the negative consequences that can result from installing an unsigned driver that turns out to be faulty. Because hardware drivers access low-level functions in the operating system, a badly written driver is much more likely to cause STOP (blue screen) errors than a buggy program. Even a seemingly innocuous driver can result in sudden crashes that result in loss of data and prevent you from restarting your computer.

Sometimes you will have to make the difficult decision of whether to install an unsigned driver or give up the use of a piece of hardware. If the hardware device is essential and replacing it would be prohibitively expensive, and you're using a 32-bit version of Windows Vista, you might decide that the risk is worth it. In other cases, the choice is more difficult, as in the case when you have to choose between a signed driver that offers a minimal set of features and an unsigned alternative driver that allows you to take advantage of special features that are specific to your hardware.

INSIDE OUT   Give unsigned drivers a workout

If you decide to take a chance on an unsigned driver, your best strategy is to back up your data first, install the new driver, and then thoroughly test it right away, without introducing any additional software or drivers. (Windows automatically sets a System Restore point when you install an unsigned driver.) Run every application that's installed on your computer. Try to run a few CPU-intensive and disk-intensive tasks at the same time. Open and save files, especially big, complex ones. Try running disk utilities such as Chkdsk and Defrag. If the new driver is going to cause problems with the hardware and software you currently use, you want to find out immediately after installing it so you can roll back to your previous configuration with as little hassle as possible.

Previous versions of Windows allowed users to change the default settings and completely eliminate warnings about unsigned drivers. This option is not available in Windows Vista.

Finding the Right Driver File

If a signed, Windows Vista–compatible driver is not available for a given device, you might be able to use a driver originally written for a previous version of Windows. For the best chance of success, find a driver written for Microsoft Windows XP or Windows Server 2003. Many (but certainly not all) of these drivers will work properly in Windows Vista. Some drivers that were originally written for Windows 2000 might work under Windows Vista, but the odds are against it.

You'll have best luck with drivers that were signed by WHQL for Windows XP or Windows Server 2003. Under normal circumstances, these should install with no warnings.

Drivers originally written for Microsoft Windows 95/98/Me or Microsoft Windows NT are unlikely to work properly with Windows Vista, because the architectural differences between those operating systems and Windows Vista are just too great.

INSIDE OUT   Dig deep for drivers

It's not always clear from the labeling on the outside of a floppy disk or CD that the drivers it contains are for multiple Windows versions. Sometimes the structure of the disk itself can offer important clues. Look for a Windows Vista or Vista subdirectory, for example, and point the Add Hardware Wizard to that location when prompted. If a suitable .inf file is available, you may be able to complete the installation.

Viewing Driver Details

Knowing what hardware drivers are installed on your computer can make a huge difference when it comes to troubleshooting problems or configuring advanced features for a device. In every case, your starting point is Device Manager, a graphical utility that provides detailed information about all installed hardware, along with controls that you can use to configure devices, assign resources, and set advanced options. To open Device Manager, use any of the following techniques:

- From any command prompt, type **devmgmt.msc**.

- Right-click the Computer icon on the Start menu or the desktop, choose Manage, and then select Device Manager from the left pane of the Computer Management console, under System Tools.

- In Control Panel, open System and click the Device Manager link in the Tasks list in the left column.

As Figure 5-3 on the next page shows, Device Manager is organized as a hierarchical list that inventories every piece of hardware within or connected to your computer. The default view shows devices by type.

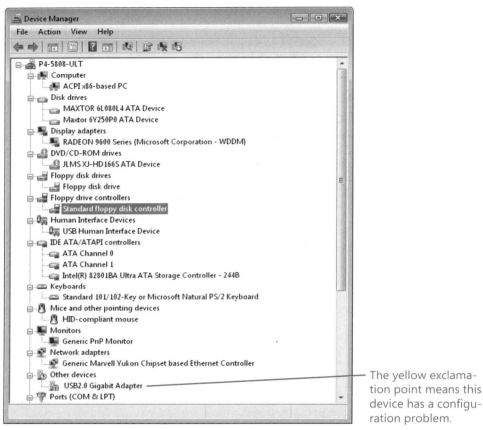

The yellow exclamation point means this device has a configuration problem.

Figure 5-3 Click the plus sign to the left of each category in Device Manager to see individual devices within that category.

INSIDE OUT   Change the Device Manager view

You can change the default view of Device Manager to organize entries in the list by resource or by connection. Use Device Manager's View menu to switch between any of the four built-in views. Resource views are especially useful when you're trying to track down problems caused by IRQ conflicts. Choosing either the Resources By Type view or the Resources By Connection view shows a list of all devices in which you can see how DMA, IO addresses, and IRQs are assigned. Another option on the View menu lets you show hidden devices.

To view information about a specific device, double-click its entry in Device Manager's list of installed devices. Each device has its own multitabbed properties dialog box. At a minimum, each device includes two tabs, General and Driver. The General tab lists basic facts about the device, including the device name, the name of its manufacturer, and its current status, as shown in Figure 5-4.

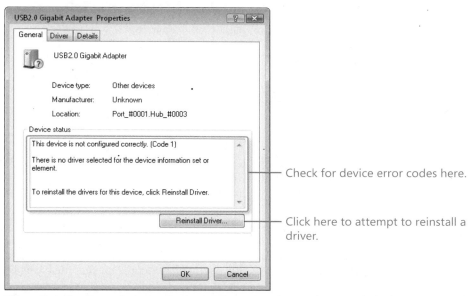

Check for device error codes here.

Click here to attempt to reinstall a driver.

Figure 5-4 The General tab supplies basic information about a device and whether it is currently functioning properly.

The Driver tab, shown in Figure 5-5 on the next page, lists version information about the currently installed driver for the selected device. Although the information shown here is sparse, it covers the essentials. You can tell at a glance who supplied the driver and whether it's digitally signed; you can also determine the date and version number of the driver, which is important when deciding whether you should download and install an available update.

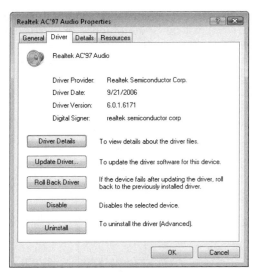

Figure 5-5 The Driver tab, which is available for every installed device, offers valuable information and tools for managing installed drivers.

To view additional information about an installed driver, click the Driver Details button. As you can see from Figure 5-6, the Driver File Details dialog box provides far more comprehensive information, including the names and locations of all associated files. Selecting any file name from this list displays details for that file in the lower portion of the dialog box.

Figure 5-6 This detailed view of an installed driver provides important information about each file the device uses. In this example, a number of files are not digitally signed.

In addition to this basic information, the properties dialog box for a given device can include any number of custom tabs. The Intel USB Controller shown in Figure 5-7, for example, includes the basic information on the General and Driver tabs and adds a custom tab that allows you to control bandwidth allotments to connected devices.

Figure 5-7 Any device that requires system resources includes the Resources tab in its Device Manager entry.

INSIDE OUT   **Take inventory of installed drivers**

If you want a more compact record of installed drivers in a format that you can review later, use the Driverquery command. Entering this command with no switches produces a simple list of installed devices and drivers. You can modify the output of the command with a variety of switches, and you can redirect the output of the command to a file so that you can load it in another program. For instance, you can use the /V switch to produce a detailed (verbose) listing, and add the /Fo switch with the Csv parameter to generate the output in a format suitable for use in Microsoft Excel:

```
driverquery /v /fo csv > drvlist.csv
```

Open Drvlist.csv in Excel to see a neatly formatted and highly detailed list of all your hardware. (For a full list of the switches available for the Driverquery command, add the /? switch or search for Driverquery in the Help And Support Center.)

Chapter 5

By design, the information displayed in Device Manager is dynamic. When you add, re-move, or reconfigure a device, the information stored here changes as well. In Windows XP, Device Manager included a Print command; this option is no longer available in Windows Vista. To save a record of the settings for your system, including details about installed devices, open Control Panel, click Performance Information And Tools (in the System And Maintenance category) and then click Advanced Tools. Click the Gener-ate A System Health Report option and wait about a minute until it finishes collecting data. The Devices section, under the Hardware Configuration category, includes all the information you would normally find under Device Manager. You can save the result-ing report as an HTML file (click Save As on the File menu) or click File, Print to send the full report to your default printer. The latter option, unfortunately, requires that you manually expand all the branches in the Devices category before printing.

Installing and Configuring a New Device

Since its introduction in Windows 95, Plug and Play technology has evolved tremen-dously. Early incarnations of this technology were notoriously unreliable, leading some users to dismiss the feature as "plug and pray." In recent years, however, hardware and software standards have converged to make most device configuration tasks completely automatic. With true Plug and Play devices, Windows Vista handles virtually all of the work of configuring computer hardware and attached devices. For Plug and Play to work properly, all the pieces of a computer system must be capable of working together to perform hardware configuration tasks, specifically:

- The system BIOS must be capable of responding to Plug and Play and power man-agement events. By definition, any system with an ACPI BIOS includes this capa-bility. Non-ACPI computers with a Plug and Play BIOS are capable of performing a subset of Plug and Play functions but will not be as capable as ACPI computers.

- The operating system must be capable of responding to Plug and Play events. Windows Vista (like Windows XP and Windows Server 2003) fully supports the Plug and Play standard.

- The device must be capable of identifying itself, listing its required resources (in-cluding drivers), and allowing software to configure it. The Microsoft "Designed for Windows" logo identifies hardware that meets all these requirements.

- The device driver must be capable of interacting with the operating system and responding to device notification and power management events. A Plug and Play driver can load automatically when Windows detects that a device has been plugged in, and it can suspend and resume properly along with the system.

In Windows Vista, Plug and Play support is optimized for USB, IEEE 1394 (FireWire), PCMCIA (PC Card), PCI, and PCI Express (PCIe) devices. By definition, any USB or PC-MCIA device is a Plug and Play device, as are virtually all PCI and PCIe devices. Devices that connect to a parallel or serial port may or may not be fully Plug and Play compat-ible. Legacy devices that use the ISA bus are by definition not capable of being managed by Plug and Play; for the most part, ISA devices are found only in computers manufactured before the year 2000, and it's unlikely that Windows Vista will run acceptably—if at all—on hardware of that vintage.

INSIDE OUT   Run setup software at the right time

In many cases, new hardware devices include a setup CD that contains driver files and utility software. The best time to run this CD is *before* plugging in the device. If the drivers are signed, the setup program copies the driver files and Setup Information (.inf) file to your driver store folder so that installation can proceed automatically when you plug in the device. Some newer advanced devices work in just the opposite fashion and will only install drivers if the device itself is physically installed. When in doubt, check the documentation.

Managing the Plug and Play Process

When you install a Plug and Play device for the first time, Windows reads the Plug and Play identification tag in the hardware's BIOS or firmware. It then compares that ID tag with a master list of corresponding tags drawn from all the Setup Information files in the %SystemRoot%\Inf folder. If it finds a signed driver with a matching tag, it installs the correct driver file (or files) and makes other necessary system modifications with no intervention required from you. Windows Vista displays the progress of Plug and Play operations in pop-up messages in the notification area. You might see a series of these notifications, culminating with the final message shown here.

When Windows detects a Plug and Play device (after you've plugged it into a USB port, for instance) but cannot locate a suitable signed device driver, it starts the Found New Hardware wizard.

Note

Any user can install a new device if a driver for that device is included in the driver store. To install any driver, signed or unsigned, when logged on as a member of the local Administrators group you must provide your consent in a UAC dialog box. If you're logged on using an account without administrative permissions, you'll be prompted to supply an administrator's credentials to install a signed driver but will be unable to install any unsigned drivers.

The basic workings of the Found New Hardware Wizard should be familiar to anyone who's ever installed a device in any version of Windows. As Figure 5-8 shows, the wizard's opening screen offers three choices.

Figure 5-8 Select the first option to begin the process of installing a new device driver after connecting a Plug and Play device.

Click Locate And Install Driver Software to search for a suitable driver. Windows searches all removable drives for a compatible driver. If the search is unsuccessful, you see the dialog box shown in Figure 5-9.

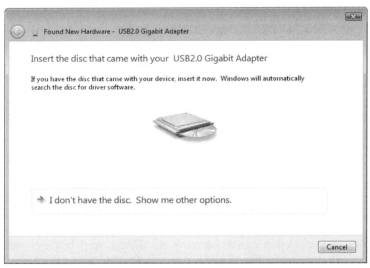

Figure 5-9 Windows displays this dialog box if it's unable to locate driver software on any removable media.

If your new device came with an installation CD containing Windows Vista–compatible drivers, place that disk in your CD or DVD drive and allow installation to continue. If you've previously downloaded a Windows Vista–compatible driver to your hard disk or to another form of removable media, click I Don't Have The Disk. Show Me Other Options. In the resulting dialog box, click Browse My Computer For Driver Software (Advanced), which leads to the dialog box shown in Figure 5-10.

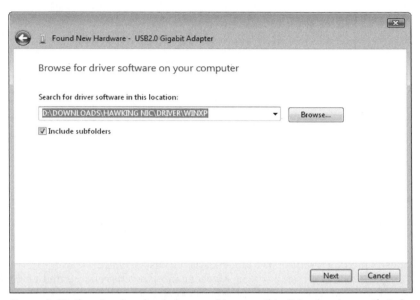

Figure 5-10 If you've downloaded a new driver, use this dialog box to specify its location.

Enter the full path of the folder that contains the downloaded driver and Setup Information file, or click Browse to point to this location. Click Next to search the specified location. Follow the prompts to complete the installation. Clear the Include Subfolders box if your downloaded driver package includes drivers for multiple Windows versions and you want to designate a specific version for installation. This option might be necessary if you can't find a Windows Vista driver and have to choose between drivers written for Windows XP and for Windows Server 2003.

Installing and Managing Printers and Print Queues

If you have a printer that plugs into a USB port, installation should be automatic, with Plug and Play kicking things off the first time you plug in the printer and power it up. You'll need to supply a driver (on disk or via download), if it's not already in the driver store.

Printers that physically attach through a non–Plug and Play connection, such as a parallel port, may require some extra setup work. If the printer driver package includes a setup program, run it first. Then open the Printers folder in Control Panel and click Add A Printer. In the Add Printer dialog box, click Add A Local Printer.

Chapter 5

To complete the setup process, you need to first specify the port to which the printer is attached. For most older printers that attach to a parallel port, the correct choice is LPT1.

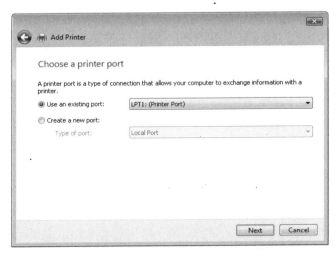

Click Next to select the correct driver. You can choose from a list of drivers available in the Windows Vista driver store (see Figure 5-11). This list should include any drivers you installed by running a setup program. If you have downloaded a printer driver that doesn't include a setup program, click Have Disk and browse to the correct location. If you don't have a driver, or if you suspect a more recent version might be available, click Windows Update to check Microsoft's collection of updated, signed drivers; after the update is complete, check the list again to see if your printer model is available.

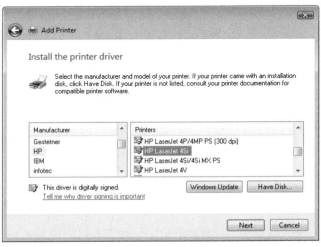

Figure 5-11 When installing a non-Plug and Play printer, use this dialog box to select the most up-to-date driver.

INSIDE OUT **Use a compatible driver**

If you can't find a driver that's specifically designed for your printer, you might be able to get away with another driver. Check the hardware documentation to find out whether the printer emulates a more popular model, such as a Hewlett-Packard LaserJet. If so, choose that printer driver, and then print some test documents after completing setup. You might lose access to some advanced features available with your model of printer, but this strategy should allow you to perform basic printing tasks.

The final step in the printer setup process is giving the printer a name. The default name typically includes the manufacturer's name and printer model; you can change this value to a more descriptive name now or later.

After completing printer setup, be sure to print a test page to verify that the driver was installed correctly. You can adjust additional settings for any installed printer (including changing the default printer) by using buttons on the taskbar in the Printers folder.

For instructions on how to make a local printer available for other users on a network and connect to shared printers, see "Sharing a Printer," in Chapter 13.

Setting Up Scanners

Scanners have always posed special challenges on installation and use, and Windows Vista raises a new set of issues. Many scanners include a specialized control program that allows you to take full advantage of hardware features and manage scanned images. A generic driver that works with some scanners is available; in Windows Vista Business, Ultimate, and Enterprise editions, this connects the scanner to the Windows Fax and Scan program.

The Scanners And Cameras option in Control Panel is necessary only if you have a legacy scanner whose driver is not installed properly during initial setup.

Managing Modems and Fax Devices

Virtually all modems use generic drivers supplied with Windows Vista. For specific hardware brands, installing a driver typically adds values to the registry that enable custom commands, such as those issued through AT commands. To adjust modem settings, open the properties dialog box for the device and look at the Advanced tab. Figure 5-12 shows the interface for adding custom AT commands.

Figure 5-12 Use this dialog box to add custom AT commands to a modem.

Making Connections with Portable and Mobile Devices

The lines are increasingly becoming blurred between SmartPhones, handheld computers, and music players. A SmartPhone with a Secure Digital memory card, for instance, can synchronize files with Windows Explorer, music with Windows Media Player, and contact information with Microsoft Office Outlook. The drivers installed by default may only enable some of this functionality, so be sure to check for custom drivers that unlock all features. To enable SmartPhone functionality, visit Windows Update and install the Windows Mobile Device Center software.

Configuring Legacy Devices

Windows XP included hundreds of drivers for legacy devices that don't support Plug and Play; the Windows Vista driver store includes a much smaller collection, mostly for older printers, modems, scanners, infrared ports, PCMCIA controllers, and other oddball devices that don't use Plug and Play connections. As you might suspect, Windows will not automatically set up such devices, and you're rolling the dice if you find one of these old but still worthwhile devices and try to install an old driver. But what if the device in question is valuable to you and can't be easily replaced by a newer, supported one? Then by all means give it a try. Download the most recent hardware drivers you can find (ideally for Windows XP or Windows Server 2003), and then use the Add Hardware Wizard to complete the hardware setup process. Follow these steps:

1. If you've found a downloadable driver package or a CD that came with the device, look for a Setup program and run it. This option places the driver files on your hard disk and simplifies later installation steps.

2. Connect the new hardware to your computer. In the case of an internal device such as an add-in card, turn off the computer, add the device, and then restart.

3. Open Device Manager, select any item in the list of installed devices, and then click Add Legacy Hardware on the Action menu.

4. Click Next to skip past the Welcome screen. On the next wizard screen, choose how you want to select the device to be installed.

    ○ For printers, network cards, modems, and other devices that can be detected mechanically, choose Search For And Install The Hardware Automatically (Recommended). After you click Next, the wizard quickly runs a detection module that searches for anything on its list of non–Plug and Play devices. If it finds the new device, it installs the driver automatically, and your work is finished. If the wizard doesn't find any new hardware, you'll be prompted to click Next and look manually.

    ○ If you have a driver on a disk, skip the detection process. Choose Install The Hardware That I Manually Select From A List (Advanced) and click Next.

5. From the Common Hardware Types list, select a hardware category (or the inclusive Show All Devices category) and click Next.

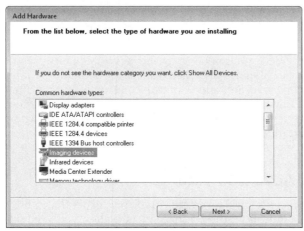

6. From the master list of available drivers, select the device manufacturer and the correct model. Click Next to continue. Follow the prompts to complete the wizard.

Changing Settings for an Installed Device

By default, Device Manager displays information about all currently installed and connected Plug and Play devices. To view devices that use non–Plug and Play drivers, as well as previously installed devices that are not currently connected, you need to tweak Device Manager slightly.

- To view non–Plug and Play devices, open Device Manager and choose Show Hidden Devices from the View menu. In the default Devices By Type view, the formerly hidden devices appear under the Non–Plug And Play Drivers branch.

- To view devices that were once installed but are no longer attached to the computer, open a Command Prompt window using the Run As Administrator option and enter the command **SET DEVMGR_SHOW_NONPRESENT_DEVICES=1**. Then, from the same command prompt, type **devmgmt.msc** to open Device Manager. Choose View, Show Hidden Devices. The new instance of Device Manager now shows "ghosted" entries for devices that were once present. This technique is especially useful for fixing problems caused by leftover drivers after replacing a network card or video card—just delete the ghosted device.

- To see advanced details about a device, open the properties dialog box for the device and look on the Details tab. The value shown under Device Instance Id is especially useful for tracking down devices that are detected incorrectly. The full details for a device ID shown here can be found in the registry, under HKLM \System\CurrentControlSet\Enum. Although we don't recommend idly deleting the found key, this information might provide enough information to figure out why a device isn't being identified properly.

Setting the DEVMGR environment variable described in this section affects only the instance of Device Manager launched from that Command Prompt window. If you want the change to be persistent, open Control Panel, open System, click Advanced System Settings, click Environment Variables on the Advanced tab, and define a new variable for this setting. If you add the variable to the User Variables section, the setting applies only to the current user; if you edit the System Variables section, the extra information is visible in Device Manager for all users of the current computer.

Adjusting Advanced Settings

Some devices include specialized tabs in the properties dialog box available from Device Manager. Controls on these additional tabs allow you to change advanced settings and properties for devices. For instance:

- Network cards and modems typically include a Power Management tab that allows you to control whether the device can force the computer to wake up from

Standby mode. This option is useful if you have fax capabilities enabled for a modem, or if you use the Remote Desktop feature over the internet on a machine that isn't always running at full power. On portable computers, you can also use this option to allow Windows to turn off a device to save power.

● The Volumes tab for a disk drive contains no information when you first display the properties dialog box for that device. Click the Populate button to read the volume information for the selected disk; you can then choose any of the listed volumes, as shown in Figure 5-13, and click the Properties button to check the disk for errors, run the Defrag utility, or perform other maintenance tasks. Although you can perform these same tasks by right-clicking a drive icon in the Computer window, this option may be useful in situations where you have multiple hard disks installed and you suspect that one of those disks is having mechanical problems. Using this option allows you to quickly see which physical disk a given volume is stored on.

Figure 5-13 After you click the Populate button, the Volumes tab lists volumes on the selected drive and gives you full access to troubleshooting and maintenance tools.

Chapter 5

● DVD drives offer an option to change the DVD region, which controls what disks can be played on that drive, as shown here.

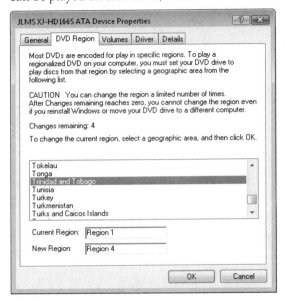

CAUTION

The DVD Region setting actually increments a counter on the physical drive itself, and that counter can be changed only a limited number of times. Be extremely careful with this setting, or you might end up losing the capability to play any regionally encoded DVDs in your collection.

- When working with network cards, you can often choose from a plethora of settings on an Advanced tab, as shown in this example. Randomly tinkering with these settings is almost always counterproductive; however, you may be able to solve specific performance or connectivity problems by adjusting settings as directed by the device manufacturer or a Microsoft Knowledge Base article.

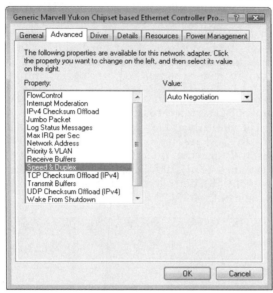

- Self-powered USB hubs (hubs that are connected to an AC power source) include a Power tab. Use the information on the Power tab to calculate the amount of power required by devices that draw power from the hub. If the total power requirement is more than the hub can supply, you might need a new hub.

INSIDE OUT   View devices over the network

You can use Device Manager to inspect settings on a remote computer. This option can be useful when troubleshooting from a distance. To view devices on another computer, open the Computer Management console (Compmgmt.msc), select the Computer Management icon at the top of the left pane, and choose Action, Connect To Another Computer. This feature allows you to view information but not change device settings. If you need to change device settings over a network, use Remote Assistance (described in "Connecting to Another PC with Windows Remote Assistance," Chapter 9) or a Remote Desktop connection.

Chapter 5

Viewing and Changing Resource Assignments

If you're a PC veteran, you probably remember struggling with MS-DOS and early versions of Windows to resolve device conflicts, most often when two or more pieces of hardware lay claim to the same IRQ. On modern computers with an ACPI BIOS, those sorts of conflicts are practically extinct. In the original design of the IBM Personal Computer, IRQs were in short supply, with a total of 15 available, many of those reserved by system devices, such as communications ports, keyboards, and disk controllers. With older Windows versions, problems could occur when adding a new device such as a sound card or network adapter. If the new device was hardwired to a specific IRQ that was already in use, or if there were no free IRQs, the device simply would not work.

On computers running Windows 2000, Windows XP, Windows Server 2003, or Windows Vista with a mix of PCI add-in cards, the operating system takes advantage of the ACPI features on the motherboard to share scarce IRQs among multiple devices. In Device Manager, you can check resource allocations at a glance by choosing Resources By Type or Resources By Connection from the View menu. In the example shown here, Windows Vista has assigned nearly 200 IRQs; IRQ 17 is being shared successfully by two PCI devices; a pair of USB Controllers, one built-in and the other on a PCI add-in card, are peacefully coexisting on IRQ 23.

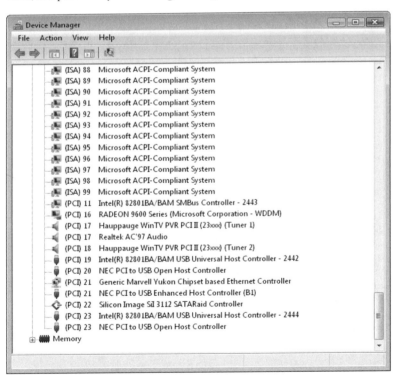

Under most circumstances, you cannot use Device Manager to change resource settings for a specific PCI or USB device. Resources are allocated automatically by the operating system at startup, and the controls to change resource settings are unavailable. Resource conflicts are most common with legacy devices that are not fully compatible with Plug and Play. In the rare event that you experience a resource conflict, you might be able to adjust resource settings manually from the Resources tab: Clear the Use Automatic Settings check box and cycle through different settings to see if any of the alternate configurations resolve the conflict.

If you suspect that a hardware problem is caused by a resource conflict, you can access an overview of resource usage by opening the System Information utility (Msinfo32.exe), which is found on the All Programs menu under Accessories, System Tools. Open Hardware Resources in the console pane and pay special attention to the Conflicts/Sharing entry, shown in Figure 5-14, and the Forced Hardware item. Don't be alarmed if you see a number of devices sharing a single IRQ; that's perfectly normal.

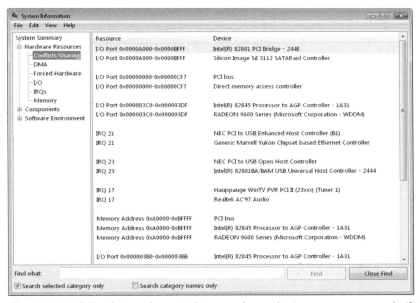

Figure 5-14 All the devices shown in this example are sharing resources properly. If two unrelated devices try to share a resource other than an IRQ, you may need to adjust device settings manually.

For more information about the System Information utility, see "Digging Deeper with Dedicated System Information Tools," in Appendix D.

For legacy devices whose resources can't be assigned by Windows, you'll need to adjust jumpers on the card or device, or use a software-based setup/configuration utility to change resource settings for that device.

TROUBLESHOOTING

Resource conflicts prevent a device from working

If two devices are in conflict for a system resource, try any of these strategies to resolve the problem:

1. With PCI devices, try swapping cards, two at a time, between PCI slots. On some motherboards, IRQs and other resources are assigned on a per-slot basis, and moving a card can free up the proper resources. Check the motherboard documentation to see which IRQs are assigned to each slot and experiment until you find an arrangement that works.

2. If the conflict is caused by a legacy (ISA) device, replace it with a Plug and Play–compatible PCI device.

3. Use jumpers or a software utility to change settings on a legacy device so that it reserves a different set of resources. You will need documentation from the manufacturer to accomplish this goal.

If you have problems with PCI devices, the device itself might not be to blame. When drivers and ACPI BIOS code interact improperly, conflicts can result. Check for an updated hardware driver (especially if the current driver is unsigned), and look for a BIOS update as well.

Managing Installed Drivers

If you're having a hardware problem that you suspect is caused by a device driver, your first stop should be Device Manager. Open the properties dialog box for the device, and use the following buttons on the Driver tab to perform maintenance tasks:

- **Update Driver**   This choice starts the Hardware Update Wizard.

- **Roll Back Driver**   This option uninstalls the most recently updated driver and "rolls back" your system configuration to the previously installed driver. Unlike System Restore, this option affects only the selected device. If you have never updated the selected driver, this option is unavailable.

- **Uninstall**   This button completely removes driver files and registry settings for the selected device. This option is available from Safe Mode if you need to remove a driver that is causing blue-screen (Stop) errors. You can also use this capability to remove a driver that you suspect was incorrectly installed and then reinstall the original driver or install an updated driver.

INSIDE OUT   Create a safety net before tinkering with drivers

When you install a new, unsigned hardware driver, Windows automatically attempts to create a new System Restore checkpoint. That doesn't mean it will be successful, especially if a problem with your System Restore settings has caused this utility to suspend operations temporarily. To make certain that you can roll back your changes if necessary, set a new System Restore checkpoint manually before making any kind of hardware configuration change. (For more details, see "Rolling Back to a Stable State with System Restore," in Chapter 23.)

Updating a Device Driver

Microsoft and third-party device manufacturers frequently issue upgrades to device drivers. In some cases, the updates enable new features; in other cases, the newer version swats a bug that might or might not affect you. New WHQL-signed drivers are sometimes (but not always) delivered through Windows Update. Other drivers are only available by downloading them from the device manufacturer's website.

If the new driver includes a setup program, run it first, so that the proper files are copied to your system. Then start the update process from Device Manager by selecting the entry for the device you want to upgrade and clicking the Update Driver button on the toolbar or the Update Driver option on the right-click shortcut menu. (You can also click Update Driver on the Driver tab of the properties dialog box for the device.) Click Search Automatically For Updated Driver Software if you want to look in local removable media and check Windows Update. Click Browse My Computer For Driver Software if you want to enter the location of a downloaded driver package or choose from a list of available drivers in the driver store.

INSIDE OUT   Make sure that update is really an update

How do you know whether a downloaded version is newer than the currently installed driver on your system? A good Readme file should provide this information and is the preferred option for determining version information. In the absence of documentation, file dates offer some clues, but they are not always reliable. A better indicator is to inspect the properties of the driver files themselves. After unzipping the downloaded driver files to a folder on a local or network drive, right-click any file with a .dll or .sys extension and choose Properties. On the Version tab, you should be able to find details about the specific driver version, which you can compare to the driver details shown in Device Manager.

Rolling Back to a Previous Driver Version

Unfortunately, updated drivers can sometimes cause new problems that are worse than the woes they were intended to fix. This is especially true if you're experimenting with unsigned drivers or beta versions of new drivers. If your troubleshooting leads you to suspect that a newly installed driver is the cause of recent crashes or system instability, consider removing that driver and rolling your system configuration back to the previously installed driver.

In Windows Vista, this process is essentially the same as in Windows XP. Open Device Manager and double-click the entry for the device you want to roll back. Then go to the Driver tab and click Roll Back Driver. The procedure that follows is straightforward and self-explanatory.

Uninstalling a Driver

There are at least three circumstances under which you might want to completely remove a device driver from your system:

- You're no longer using the device, and you want to prevent the previously installed drivers from loading or using any resources.

- You've determined that the drivers available for the device are not stable enough to use on your system.

- The currently installed driver is not working correctly, and you want to reinstall it from scratch.

To remove a driver permanently, open Device Manager and double-click the entry for the device in question. On the Driver tab, click Uninstall. Click OK when prompted to confirm that you want to remove the driver, and Windows removes files and registry settings completely.

INSIDE OUT **Manage Plug and Play drivers**

Removing and reinstalling the driver for a Plug and Play device requires a little extra effort. Because these drivers are loaded and unloaded dynamically, you can remove the driver only if the device in question is plugged in. Use the Uninstall button to remove the driver before unplugging the device. To reinstall the device driver without unplugging, open Device Manager and choose Action, Scan For Hardware Changes.

TROUBLESHOOTING

Your computer experiences sporadic blue screens, lockups, or other strange behavior

When your computer acts unpredictably, chances are good that a buggy device driver is at fault.

If you're experiencing unexplained computer problems, a powerful troubleshooting tool called Driver Verifier Manager (Verifier.exe) is a terrific way to identify flawed device drivers. Instead of your computer locking up at a most inopportune time with a misleading Blue Screen of Death (BSOD), Driver Verifier stops your computer predictably at startup with a BSOD that accurately explains the true problem. Although this doesn't sound like a huge improvement (your system still won't work, after all), Driver Verifier Manager performs a critical troubleshooting step: identifying the problem. You can then correct the problem by removing or replacing the offending driver. (If you're satisfied that the driver really is okay despite Driver Verifier Manager's warning, you can turn off Driver Verifier for all drivers or for a specific driver. Any driver that Driver Verifier chokes on should be regarded with suspicion, but some legitimate drivers bend the rules without causing problems.)

Driver Verifier works at startup to thoroughly exercise each driver. It performs many of the same tests that are run by WHQL as part of the certification and signing process, such as checking for the way the driver accesses memory.

Beware: If Driver Verifier Manager finds a nonconforming driver—even one that doesn't seem to be causing any problems—it will prevent your system from starting. Use Driver Verifier only if you're having problems. In other words, if it ain't broke ...

To begin working with Driver Verifier Manager, you must start it using credentials from an account in the Administrators group. Open a Command Prompt window using the Run As Administrator option, type **verifier** at the command line, and press Enter. In the Driver Verifier Manager dialog box, shown below, select Create Standard Settings. In the next dialog box, select the type of drivers you want to verify; unsigned drivers are a likely cause of problems, as are those created for an older version of Windows.

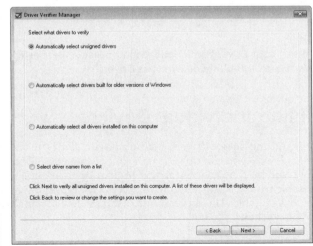

When you click Next, you get a list of all currently installed drivers that match the conditions you specified. Note that the list might contain a mix of hardware drivers and some file-system filter drivers, such as those used by antivirus programs, CD burning software, and other low-level system utilities.

At this point you have two choices:

- Go through the list and make a note of all drivers identified and then click Cancel. No changes are made to your system configuration; all you've done is gather a list of suspicious drivers, which you can then try to remove or disable manually.

- Click Finish to complete the wizard and restart your computer. Don't choose this option unless you're prepared to deal with the consequences, as explained in the remainder of this sidebar.

If your computer stops with a blue screen when you next log on, you've identified a problem driver. The error message includes the name of the offending driver and an error code. For information about the error codes, see Microsoft Knowledge Base article 229903, "Partial List of Possible Error Codes With Driver Verifier." (Although this article is specifically for Windows 2000, the information is valid for Windows XP and Windows Vista.) To resolve the problem, boot into Safe Mode (press F8 during startup) and disable or uninstall the problem driver. You'll then want to check with the device vendor to get a working driver that you can install.

To disable Driver Verifier so that it no longer performs verification checks at startup, run Driver Verifier Manager again and select Delete Existing Settings in the initial dialog box. Alternatively, at a command prompt, type **verifier /reset**. (If you haven't yet solved the driver problem, of course, you'll be stopped at a BSOD, unable to disable Driver Verifier. In that case, boot into Safe Mode and then disable Driver Verifier.)

You can configure Driver Verifier so that it checks only certain drivers. To do that, open Driver Verifier Manager, select Create Standard Settings, click Next, and select the last option, Select Driver Names From A List. This option lets you exempt a particular driver from Driver Verifier's scrutiny—such as one that Driver Verifier flags but you are certain is not the cause of your problem.

You can read more about Driver Verifier online in Knowledge Base article 244617, "How to Use Driver Verifier to Troubleshoot Windows Drivers."

Enabling and Disabling Individual Devices

Installing and uninstalling device drivers can be a hassle. If all you want to do is enable or disable a specific device, you can do so from Device Manager. Select the device and click the Disable button on the Device Manager toolbar or right-click the device name and then click Disable from the shortcut menu. If a device is already disabled, both of these options toggle to Enable. The drivers for a disabled device remain available, but Windows does not load them.

You might choose to disable the driver for a device if all of the following conditions are true: you use it infrequently (or never), the device cannot be physically removed, and you want to avoid having it use resources or cause stability problems. This might be the case with an infrared receiver or Bluetooth adapter on a notebook, for example. Enable the device when you want to use it, and keep it disabled the rest of the time.

> **Note**
>
> In previous Windows versions, including Windows XP, it was possible to define configurations called hardware profiles that could be chosen at startup. Each profile contained a list of installed devices that were enabled or disabled when that profile was selected. This feature is not available in Windows Vista. Will you miss it? Probably not. Hardware profiles are a relic of a bygone day, before Plug and Play, when portable computers were designed for use with docking stations containing add-in cards. Virtually all modern hardware devices, including docking stations, are capable of installing and uninstalling dynamically, making hardware profiles unnecessary.

Decoding Hardware Errors

When Windows encounters a problem with a device or its driver, it changes the icon in Device Manager and displays an error code on the General tab of the device's properties dialog box. Each code is identified by a number and a brief text description. Table 5-1 contains a partial list of error codes and suggested actions you should take to try to resolve them.

Table 5-1 Common Device Manager Error Codes

Error Code	Error Message	What To Do About It
1	This device is not configured correctly. (Code 1)	After downloading a compatible driver for the device, click the Update Driver button and follow the wizard's prompts to install the new driver.
3	The driver for this device might be corrupted, or your system may be running low on memory or other resources. (Code 3)	Check available memory and, if necessary, close some programs to free up RAM. If you have sufficient memory, try uninstalling and reinstalling the driver.
10	This device cannot start. (Code 10)	Device failed to start. Click the Update Driver button to install updated drivers if available. The Troubleshoot button may provide useful information as well.

Chapter 5

Error Code	Error Message	What To Do About It
12	This device cannot find enough free resources that it can use. If you want to use this device, you will need to disable one of the other devices on this system. (Code 12)	The device has been assigned one or more I/O ports, IRQs, or DMA channels used by another device. This error message can also appear if the BIOS is configured incorrectly (for example, if a USB controller doesn't get an IRQ from the BIOS). Check BIOS settings. Use the Resources tab to identify the conflicting device.
14	This device cannot work properly until you restart your computer. (Code 14)	The driver has probably been installed correctly, but will not be started until you reboot the system.
16	Windows cannot identify all the resources this device uses. (Code 16)	A legacy device is improperly configured. Use the Resources tab to fill in the missing details.
18	Reinstall the drivers for this device. (Code 18)	Click the Update Driver button to start the Update Hardware Wizard and reinstall the driver.
19	Your registry might be corrupted. (Code 19)	Incorrect or conflicting information is entered in the registry settings for this device. Try uninstalling and then reinstalling the driver. Try using System Restore to roll back the configuration to a point where the device worked properly.
21	Windows is removing this device. (Code 21)	The system will remove the device. Wait a few seconds, and then refresh the Device Manager view. If the device continues to display, restart the computer.
22	This device is disabled. (Code 22)	The device has been disabled using Device Manager. To enable it, click the Enable Device button.
24	This device is not present, is not working properly, or does not have all its drivers installed. (Code 24)	This is a catch-all error that can be caused by bad hardware or corrupt or incompatible drivers. This message also appears after you use the Remove Device option.
28	The drivers for this device are not installed. (Code 28)	After downloading a compatible driver for the device, click the Update Driver button and follow the wizard's prompts to install the new driver.
29	This device is disabled because the firmware of the device did not give it the required resources. (Code 29)	This is most commonly seen with SCSI adapters, third-party disk controllers, and other devices that supply their own BIOS. Check the documentation for the device to learn how to re-enable it.

Error Code	Error Message	What To Do About It
31	This device is not working properly because Windows cannot load the drivers required for this device. (Code 31)	Windows was unable to load the driver, probably because it is not compatible with Windows Vista. After downloading a compatible driver for the device, click the Update Driver button and follow the wizard's prompts to install the new driver.
32	A driver service for this device was not required, and has been disabled. (Code 32)	The driver has been disabled. The start type for this service is set to Disabled in the registry. If the driver really is required, change the start type in the BIOS, using the BIOS setup utility as defined in the documentation for the device. If the device previously worked properly, use System Restore to return to a working configuration.
33	Windows cannot determine which resources are required for this device. (Code 33)	This error typically indicates a misconfigured legacy device or a hardware failure. See the documentation for the device for more information.
34	Windows cannot determine the settings for this device. Consult the documentation that came with this device and use the Resource tab to set the configuration. (Code 34)	This legacy device requires a forced configuration. Change the hardware settings (using jumpers or a software utility), and then use Device Manager's Resources tab to set the forced configuration.
35	Your computer's system BIOS does not include enough information to properly configure and use this device. To use this device, contact your computer manufacturer to obtain a firmware or BIOS update. (Code 35)	This error is specific to multiprocessor systems. Check with the system manufacturer for a BIOS upgrade.
36	This device is requesting a PCI interrupt but is configured for an ISA interrupt (or vice versa). Please use the computer's system setup program to reconfigure the interrupt for this device. (Code 36)	IRQ translation failed. This error usually occurs on Advanced Power Management (APM) machines. Check BIOS settings to see if certain IRQs have been reserved incorrectly. Upgrade to an ACPI BIOS if possible.
37	Windows cannot initialize the device driver for this hardware. (Code 37)	After downloading a compatible driver for the device, click the Update Driver button and follow the wizard's prompts to install the new driver.

Chapter 5

Error Code	Error Message	What To Do About It
38	Windows cannot load the device driver for this hardware because a previous instance of the device driver is still in memory. (Code 38)	Restart the computer.
39	Windows cannot load the device driver for this hardware. The driver may be corrupted. (Code 39)	The driver is missing or corrupted, or is in conflict with another driver. Look for an updated driver or reinstall the current driver. If the device worked previously, use System Restore to roll back to a working configuration.
40	Windows cannot access this hardware because its service key information in the registry is missing or recorded incorrectly. (Code 40)	Information in the registry's service key for the driver is invalid. Reinstall the driver.
41	Windows successfully loaded the device driver for this hardware but cannot find the hardware device. (Code 41)	Windows loaded the driver but cannot find the device. This error occurs with legacy devices because Plug and Play cannot detect them. Use Device Manager to uninstall the driver and then use the Add Hardware Wizard to reinstall it.
42	Windows cannot load the device driver for this hardware because there is a duplicate device already running in the system. (Code 42)	Restart the computer.
43	Windows has stopped this device because it has reported problems. (Code 43)	A driver has reported a device failure. Uninstall and reinstall the device. If that doesn't work, contact the device manufacturer.
44	An application or service has shut down this hardware device. (Code 44)	The device has been halted by an application or service. Restart the computer.
47	Windows cannot use this hardware device because it has been prepared for "safe removal," but it has not been removed from the computer. (Code 47)	The device has been prepared for ejection from a PCMCIA slot, a USB port, or a docking station. Unplug the device and plug it in again, or restart the computer.

Error Code	Error Message	What To Do About It
48	The software for this device has been blocked from starting because it is known to have problems with Windows. Contact the hardware vendor for a new driver. (Code 48)	Contact the hardware vendor for a compatible driver.

CHAPTER 6

Using Internet Explorer 7

Home Basic ●
Home Premium ●
Business ●
Enterprise ●
Ultimate ●

Internet Explorer 7 is the first major upgrade to Microsoft's flagship web browser since 2001. After a long public testing period, it was officially released in October 2006 as an upgrade to Windows XP and Windows Server 2003. Windows Vista uses Internet Explorer 7 as its default web browser as well. Because the Windows Vista and Windows XP versions share a common user interface, many features are identical in the two versions. If you've used Internet Explorer 7 for Windows XP, you'll find that tabbed browsing, the Instant Search box, the built-in Phishing Filter, and web feed subscriptions work exactly the same in Windows Vista, as do all of the basics of browsing. (We cover all the above-mentioned features in this chapter.)

What Windows Vista adds to Internet Explorer 7 is a new level of security called Protected Mode, which builds on the foundation of User Account Control. In Windows Vista, the browser runs with sharply reduced rights and permissions. Any webpage that attempts to install software, communicate with other running programs, or run a script, hostile or otherwise, will find itself unable to alter system files or settings. The overall effect is to make Internet Explorer 7 significantly safer in everyday operation than any previous version.

What's in Your Edition?

Internet Explorer 7 is one of the core tools of Windows Vista, and its feature set is identical in every edition. You'll find some differences between editions when you dig deep into its security infrastructure. We cover those issues in more detail in Chapter 27, "Advanced Internet Explorer Security and Administration."

For more details on how Protected Mode works, see "Working With (and Around) Protected Mode," Chapter 27.

Choosing a Default Web Browser

If you have installed another web browser in addition to Internet Explorer, you can specify that you want to use that browser as your default program for opening web-based content instead of Internet Explorer. Setting a default browser associates it with the Internet icon at the top of the Start menu and also associates it with internet short-cuts, HTML files, and other files normally viewed in a browser.

For more details on how to choose which programs are available when you click Start, see "Personalizing the Start Menu," Chapter 3.

Most web browsers include an option you can click to set that program as the default for webpages. For Internet Explorer 7, this option is located at the top of the Programs tab in the Internet Options dialog box. If you install another web browser that sets it-self as default, you'll see a warning dialog box the next time you start Internet Explorer, offering to restore it as the default browser.

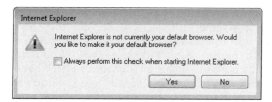

If you intended to make this change, you can disable the option by clearing the Always Perform This Check When Starting Internet Explorer check box and then clicking No. (This has the same effect as clearing the Tell Me If Internet Explorer Is Not the Default Web Browser option in the Internet Options dialog box.)

The Set Default Programs tool allows you to control which file types open in a particu-lar browser. Click Default Programs on the Start menu to open this dialog box, and then click Set Your Default Programs to open the dialog box shown in Figure 6-1.

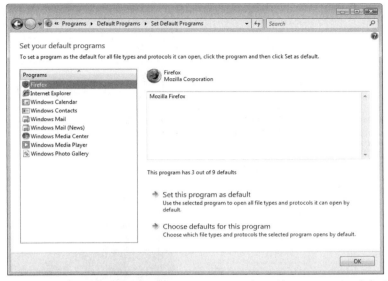

Figure 6-1 Use this dialog box to restore your preferred browser as the default choice for opening webpages or specific file types.

Using and Personalizing Internet Explorer

The basics of a web browser aren't difficult to understand. Point. Click. Search. Print. Save. If you've made it this far, we can safely assume you know your way around a browser window, and in this chapter we focus on what's new in Internet Explorer 7. Figure 6-2 on the next page shows a typical browser window, with some useful elements highlighted.

If this is the first time you've used Internet Explorer 7, you'll notice one major change in the interface immediately. Previous versions of Internet Explorer included a traditional menu and a toolbar, both of which occupied space at the top of the browser window. In Internet Explorer 7, the menu is hidden by default, and the toolbar has been made over completely, with most commonly used functions consolidated into a single compact Command bar located above the contents pane and to the right of the last open browser tab. Third-party programs can add buttons to the Command bar, and you can customize which buttons appear and their order, as we explain later in this section.

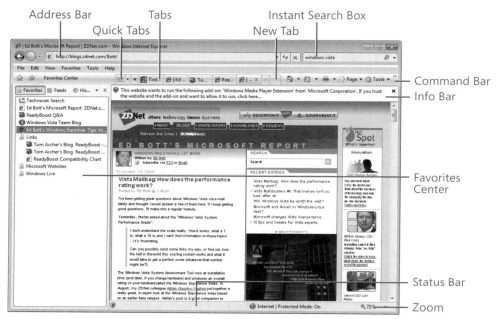

Figure 6-2 Internet Explorer hides the menu bar by default (we've tapped the Alt key to make it visible here) and scoots commonly used functions into the compact Command bar.

INSIDE OUT

Zoom in (or out) on pages and printouts

Two of the least noticed changes in the Internet Explorer interface are among the most welcome. For starters, look in the lower right corner of the browser window at the Change Zoom Level button. Normally, you view webpages at their actual size, using the default Zoom level of 100%. You can make the page—including text and graphics—larger or smaller by clicking this button or using the menu that flies out from the arrow on its right. Make a page larger to make tiny text easier to read; zoom out to read a page that was designed to be wider than your browser window. The same capabilities are available when you print a page. Click the arrow to the right of the Print button and click the Print Preview option on the Print menu. By default, the Shrink To Fit option is selected, which means you'll see fewer of those annoying printouts where the final page contains a single line of text. From the same menu at the top of the Print Preview screen, you can choose a percentage of scaling for the page or selection, blowing it up for extra readability or shrinking it for more efficient use of paper.

The other obvious change—at least after you open more than one page—is the addition of tabs to the browsing window. Here's how to work with tabs:

- To open a new, blank browser tab, press Ctrl+T or click New Tab, just to the right of the current tab.

- To open a link in a new tab without shifting focus from the current tab, right-click the link and choose Open In New Tab, or hold down Ctrl while clicking the link, or use the middle mouse button to click the link.

- To open a link in a new tab and shift focus to the newly opened tab, hold down Ctrl and Shift and click using the left or middle mouse button.

- To close the current tab, click the small X at the right side of its tab, or press Ctrl+W. To close any open tab, point to it and click the middle mouse button.

- To switch between tabs, press Ctrl+Tab (moves from left to right) or Ctrl+Shift+Tab (moves from right to left).

- To change the order of tabs, click and drag any tab to a new position. (Small black indicators mark where the relocated tab will go.)

- If more tabs are open than will fit in the browser window, double arrows appear to the left of the first tab and to the right of the last tab; click to scroll through the full selection.

- To see a visual display of all open tabs, like the one shown in Figure 6-3, click the Quick Tabs icon or press Ctrl+Q.

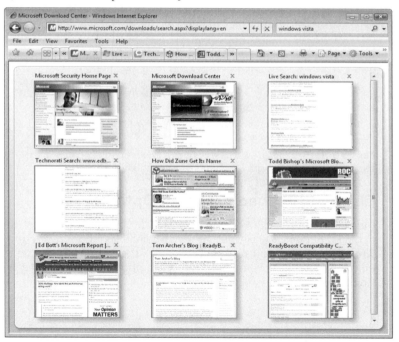

Figure 6-3 The Quick Tabs window displays thumbnails of all open tabs. Click to switch to a tab, or click the X in the tab's upper right corner to close that tab.

The Favorites Center replaces the old Explorer bars along the left side of the browser window. To open it, press Alt+C or click the gold star icon to the left of the row of browser tabs. The name of the Favorites Center is slightly misleading: in addition to Favorites, it displays the browser's history and allows you to navigate through RSS feeds to which you've subscribed using Internet Explorer 7. By default, the Favorites Center opens as a drop-down pane (as in the example in Figure 6-4) and disappears after you make a selection. Click any of the icons at the top of the pane to change the view. To lock the pane into place, click the Pin Favorites Center button.

Pin Favorites Center

Open Tab Group

Figure 6-4   The blue arrow to the right of a folder opens all pages in that folder in new tabs. Click the blue arrow to the right of a favorite to open that link in a new tab.

Changing Tabbed Browsing Options

Internet Explorer 7 allows you to customize a limited number of settings that affect the behavior of tabbed browsing. To see all available options, click Internet Options on the Tools menu (or in Control Panel) and click the Settings button under the Tabs section on the General tab. Figure 6-5 shows the options available in the Tabbed Browsing Settings dialog box.

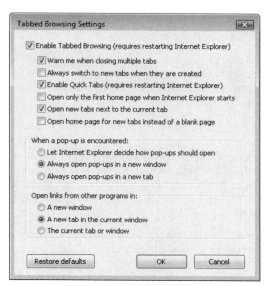

Figure 6-5 Use any of the options shown here to change the behavior of tabbed browsing—or disable it completely.

Most of the options shown here are self-explanatory. The most radical option, of course, is the check mark at the top of the dialog box, which allows you to completely disable tabbed browsing and configure Internet Explorer so every page opens in its own window. Two other options deserve special mention:

- **Open Only The First Home Page When Internet Explorer Starts** This option allows you to define multiple pages as your home page without slowing you down when you first open Internet Explorer. By selecting this option, you load only the top item in the Home Page list at startup but can open all the pages in that list later by clicking the Home Page icon on the Command bar.

- **Open New Tabs Next To The Current Tab** If you regularly keep a large number of tabs open, consider disabling this option, which is on by default. If you have 15 tabs open and you click to open a new tab in the background, you might have trouble finding the newly opened page in the list. With this option cleared, new tabs always appear at the right side of the tab row, and you can drag them into a different position if you prefer.

Changing Search Settings

Internet Explorer 7 provides two ways to search for information on the internet without actually visiting a website. The easiest alternative is to enter search terms in the Instant Search box in the top right corner of the browser window and click the Search button. You can also enter search terms directly in the Address bar and click Go. Internet Explorer attempts to parse whatever you type in the Address bar into a URL (an internet address). If it cannot do so, it hands your entry off to the default search provider. (In either case, you can press Enter to execute the search as well.)

Chapter 6

INSIDE OUT   **Learn the keyboard shortcuts**

Two search-specific keyboard shortcuts in Internet Explorer are well worth learning. Press Ctrl+E to position the insertion point in the Instant Search box and begin entering search terms. Press Alt+Enter to display the search results in a separate tab instead of replacing the contents of the current tab.

If you installed Windows Vista as an upgrade on a system using Internet Explorer 6, you're prompted to choose a default search provider when you first open Internet Explorer 7. With a clean install, the default search provider is set to Windows Live search. In either case, you can change the default search provider and add other search providers to the list of available search engines.

The drop-down arrow to the right of the Instant Search box allows you to send the current search terms to a site other than the default search provider.

To customize the list of available search providers, click Find More Providers. This leads to Microsoft's Add Search Provider's page, where you can choose from a long list of websites. Click a link to display the dialog box shown here and add the provider to the list. (A separate link leads to a Global Search Guides page with customized listings for other countries and languages.)

To remove a search provider from the list of options or to change the default provider, click the arrow to the right of the Instant Search box and click Change Search Defaults. The resulting dialog box, shown in Figure 6-6, lists all currently installed providers.

Figure 6-6 Use this dialog box to remove an installed search provider or change the default provider for Instant Search and Address bar searches.

INSIDE OUT   **Create a custom search provider**

If the site isn't listed at Microsoft's index of search providers, you can still add it to the Instant Search menu. First, check the site to see whether the site owner has customized the site to be aware of the Instant Search box in Internet Explorer 7. If the correct XML code has been added to the site, you'll see an orange glow on the Instant Search drop-down menu. When you click the down arrow you'll see two additional items: a new menu item (identified by an orange star to its left) and a fly-out Add Search Providers menu option.

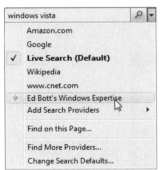

If you just want to search the current site, enter a search term and click the temporary menu option for that site. When you navigate away from the site, both menu items disappear. If you want the custom search option to be available any time, click Add Search Providers, click the provider name, and click OK in the Add Search Provider dialog box.

If the site owner hasn't made this easy option available, you can still add the site to the list of available search providers. Find the site search box and enter the term TEST (in all capital letters). Copy the URL for the search results page to the Clipboard. Next, click Find More Providers on the Instant Search menu and paste the URL you just copied into the Create Your Own form. Specify a name for the menu item and click Install.

Among the sites worth adding in this fashion are Microsoft's Knowledge Base (*http://support.microsoft.com/kb*), Acronymfinder.com, and Dictionary.com.

Changing Your Home Page

The first group of options on the General tab of the Internet Options dialog box allows you to define your home page for Internet Explorer. Click the Use Current button to define the current tab as home. Click Use Default to reset the home page to the setting that was established when your copy of Windows was installed (if you purchased Windows Vista with a new computer, this location was defined by the computer maker). Click Use Blank to open a single blank page (using the about:blank URI) when you start Internet Explorer.

Unlike its predecessor, Internet Explorer 7 allows you to define multiple home pages, each of which loads in its own tab when you open a new browser session. You can create a multi-tab home page manually, by entering the addresses for all pages (each on its own line) in the box at the top of the General tab of the Internet Options dialog box. A simpler technique is to open only the page or pages you want to use, click the arrow to the right of the Home Page button, and then click Add or Change Home Page from the drop-down menu. The resulting dialog box, shown in Figure 6-7, allows you to use the current tab as your only home page, add the current tab to your existing home page configuration, or use all currently open tabs as your new home page.

Figure 6-7 Be careful with the bottom option; if you add too many tabs to your home page list, you can adversely affect startup times for Internet Explorer.

To remove one or more pages from your current Home Page list, open the Home Page menu, click Remove, and select from the fly-out list of currently assigned pages.

Managing Toolbars

As we noted earlier, Internet Explorer's Command bar consolidates commonly used functions that used to be available on pull-down menus and the Standard toolbar. Third-party programs can add their own buttons to this list as well. Although you can add or remove buttons from this toolbar, change the order of toolbar buttons, order and resize the Command bar by sliding it to the right, you can't move the Command bar.

You can, however, change the location of other toolbars, including the Links toolbar and additional toolbars installed by third-party developers. After you have positioned your toolbars to your liking, you can take advantage of the program's toolbar-locking feature to prevent anyone (yourself included, of course) from accidentally upsetting your carefully wrought layout.

Before you can reposition any currently installed toolbars, you first have to unlock them: click Tools, then click Toolbars, and finally clear the checkmark to the left of the Lock The Toolbars option. When toolbars are unlocked, a dotted handle appears to the left of each toolbar, as shown in Figure 6-8.

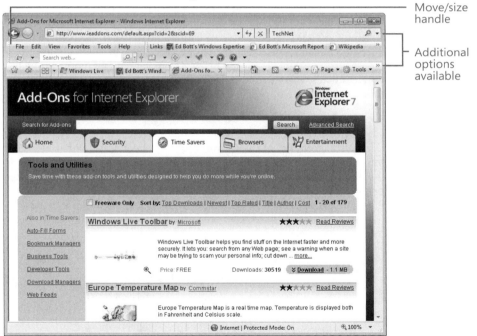

Move/size handle

Additional options available

Figure 6-8 When toolbars are unlocked, dotted handles appear to the left of each one. Click to move or resize any toolbar.

Chapter 6

Note that the menu bar is resizable and movable, just as other toolbars are. To change the position of any element, aim the mouse pointer just to the right of the sizing handle and click; when you see the Move pointer with its four arrows, you can drag the toolbar to any location between the Address bar and the row of open tabs. To show or hide any toolbar, click Tools, then click Toolbars, and finally select the name of the toolbar in the menu; a checkmark indicates that the toolbar is currently visible.

To make more efficient use of space, you can put two or more toolbars on a single line. If all buttons or menu choices on a toolbar don't fit in the space allotted to them, Internet Explorer displays a chevron to indicate that additional options are available. Click the chevron to display the remaining choices on a drop-down list.

INSIDE OUT Press F11 for full-screen display

To make the most efficient use of the browser window, press F11. This action puts Internet Explorer into a full-screen mode, in which only the Status bar is normally visible. While in full-screen mode, you can move the mouse pointer to the top of the screen to display the Address bar, the Instant Search box, the tabs row, and the Command bar. If you click in the Search box or the Address bar, these interface elements remain visible while you type. As soon as you move the mouse pointer away or click in the page itself, they slide away again. In full-screen mode, Internet Explorer is maximized, even if it was previously not maximized, and the Windows taskbar is covered. In other words, you get every available square millimeter of screen space for interacting with the webpages you visit. You can still display the taskbar by hovering your mouse at the bottom of the screen (if that's where you've chosen to put it), and you can return Internet Explorer to its normal display style by pressing F11 a second time.

To change the contents of the Command bar, select Tools, Customize Toolbar. To add a button, select it from the Available Toolbar Buttons list and click Add; to remove a currently visible button, select its entry in the Current Toolbar Buttons list and click Remove. Select any button and click Move Up or Move Down to change the button's order on the list. This option allows you to move the buttons you use most often to the left, where they're most likely to be visible even if a portion of the toolbar is truncated.

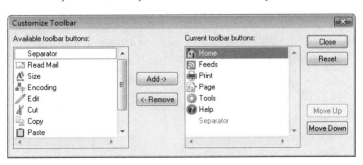

Other applications can add their own tools to the Command bar. You can add and remove such application-specific buttons via the Customize Toolbar dialog box, exactly as you would add or remove one of the built-in buttons.

The other toolbar built in to Internet Explorer is the Links toolbar, which is designed to hold shortcuts to your most favorite favorites—the websites you visit most often. Windows initially populates the Links toolbar with a Customize Links shortcut, which leads to a help page explaining how to add links to the toolbar. After making the Links toolbar visible, you can remove that link and any others you no longer want; right-click the link and choose Delete from the shortcut menu.

The simplest way to add a shortcut to the Links toolbar is to open the webpage, click the icon to the left of the URL in the Address bar, drag it to the Links toolbar, and drop it in the position you want the new shortcut to occupy. To make most efficient use of toolbar space, right-click the newly added item, choose Rename from the shortcut menu, and then type a short descriptive name.

The last step is optional, of course, but toolbar real estate is scarce, and you don't want to fill the space with a verbose shortcut name.

INSIDE OUT   Create a more useful Links toolbar

In Internet Explorer 7, the Links toolbar is hidden by default, and unlike in previous versions it isn't filled by default with Microsoft-related websites (those are now on the Favorites menu instead). But if all you do is add a handful of favorite links to the toolbar, you'll quickly fill it up. If you find the idea of easily accessible Favorites appealing, try adding subfolders to the Links toolbar. Each subfolder you add appears as a folder icon on the Links toolbar; clicking that icon displays the contents of the folder in a drop-down menu. A News folder, for instance, could contain shortcuts to your favorite news sites, any of which would be only two clicks away on the Links bar.

You can also position the Links bar on the same row as another toolbar and push it up against the right side of the browser window, so that only the toolbar name is visible. If you click the chevron at the right side of this customized Links toolbar, your entire Links list is visible as a drop-down menu.

Enabling and Disabling Add-ons

Browser add-ons can be a mixed blessing. On the plus side, browser helper objects and toolbars allow you to greatly extend the capabilities of Internet Explorer. The down side is that a poorly written (or deliberately hostile) add-on can have a deleterious impact on performance and security and, in extreme examples, can cause the browser to crash or become unstable. Like its predecessor, Internet Explorer 7 includes the capability to manage individual add-ons. We discuss this option in more detail in Chapter 27, "Advanced Internet Explorer Security and Administration."

For a complete discussion of how to manage toolbars and other add-ons, see "Installing, Removing, and Troubleshooting Add-ons," Chapter 27.

If you suspect that a balky add-on is causing you problems with Internet Explorer, you can start in a special No Add-ons mode to troubleshoot the problem. You'll find the Internet Explorer (No Add-ons) shortcut in the System Tools subfolder under Accessories on the All Programs menu. To start Internet Explorer manually in No Add-ons mode, open the Run dialog box or a Command Prompt window and enter the command **iexplore -extoff**.

Configuring Internet Explorer to Work with Other Programs

In previous versions, Internet Explorer maintained a list of six programs related to your use of the internet. The purpose of this list was to control what happens when you click links that lead to internet content other than webpages—mailto: links for e-mail addresses, for example, or news: links for newsgroup messages. In Internet Explorer 7, that list has been pared down to a single entry, which defines the program you want to use when you edit HTML files. This option is available on the Programs tab of the Internet Options dialog box, under the HTML Editing section.

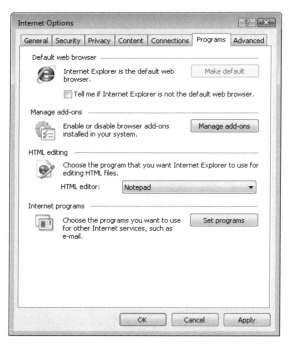

So what does the Set Programs button (under the Internet Programs category) do? It leads to the Default Programs option in Control Panel, where you can define programs for use throughout Windows, not just in Internet Explorer.

Resetting Internet Explorer to Its Default Settings

As every Windows user know from (sometimes painful) experience, too much customization can lead to problems, and troubleshooting is often a hit-or-miss process. Internet Explorer 7 lets you bypass the hassle and start over with a clean slate by resetting Internet Explorer to its default settings. This option has the following effects:

- Disables all toolbars, browser helper objects, and browser extensions

- Resets all ActiveX controls except those on the pre-approved list to their default (opt-in) settings

- Resets all security zones and the Phishing Filter to default settings

- Erases the browser history, the list of typed URLs, Windows Explorer's list of most recently used files, and the complete contents of the Temporary Internet Files folder

- Deletes all saved cookies and restores privacy options to their default settings

- Deletes all saved AutoComplete data, including data from web forms and stored passwords, and resets AutoComplete preferences to default settings

- Removes all defined exceptions on the Pop-up Blocker list, and restores the default Pop-Up Blocker settings

- Restores all customizations to their default settings, including your home page, custom search providers, tabbed browsing settings, colors, fonts, and text sizes

Resetting Internet Explorer options does not change your saved Favorites, feeds (except custom retrieval schedules), Content Advisor settings, or installed certificates. It also leaves your internet connection settings alone, including any proxy servers you've defined.

We don't recommend this radical option unless you're experiencing persistent browser problems and troubleshooting hasn't been successful. If that's the case, the solution is relatively straightforward. Start by closing all open Internet Explorer and Windows Explorer windows. Then, from Control Panel, open Internet Options, click the Advanced tab, and click Reset. You'll see the following stern warning.

Click Reset to make the changes. A dialog box informs you as each step completes. When the reset is complete, click Close and reopen Internet Explorer.

Managing Your Favorites

Internet Explorer maintains a repository of shortcuts to your favorite websites in the Favorites folder within your user profile. Any time you discover a site that you know you'll want to return to, you can add a shortcut to that site to the Favorites folder. To return to a favorite site, select it from the Favorites menu, from the Favorites Center, or from the Favorites submenu of your Start menu (if you set your Start menu to display Favorites).

We introduced the Favorites Center, which is new to Internet Explorer 7, at the beginning of this chapter. You can display your saved Favorites in the Favorites Center in any of the following ways:

- Click Tools, Toolbars, Favorites.

- Press Ctrl+Shift+I.

- Click the Favorites Center icon (the gold star to the left of the row of browser tabs).

Remember also that the Windows Vista Search index includes the contents of the Favorites folder and your browser's history. You can find individual items from the Favorites folder by typing search terms in the Search box on the Start menu; you can also open the Favorites folder in Windows Explorer; from that window, you can use the Search box to find any individual item.

Adding Pages to Your Favorites List

Internet Explorer makes it easy to add the currently displayed webpage (or an entire group of tabs) to your Favorites. Any of the following methods will work:

- Press Ctrl+D.

- Click the Add to Favorites button (just above the Favorites Center) and choose Add to Favorites.

- Pin the Favorites Center open; then drag the icon to the left of the URL in the Address bar and drop it into the Favorites bar. If you want the item to go inside an existing subfolder that isn't open, pause your mouse pointer over the folder icon. After a half second or so, the folder will open, and you can position the item appropriately within the subfolder. After you have added a favorite in this manner, you can edit its name by right-clicking it and choosing Rename from the shortcut menu.

- Right-click anywhere within the current page (but not on a link) and choose Add To Favorites from the shortcut menu.

If you press Ctrl+D, right-click, or use the Add a Favorite menu, the Add a Favorite dialog box (shown here) appears.

The contents of the Name box are drawn from the page title, as defined by the page designer. You can (and usually should) edit this name to make it as descriptive as possible—a small amount of effort when you create the favorite will pay off later when you're using the Search index to find that page.

The Create In box allows you to save the new favorite within the top level of the Favorites folder, choose an existing subfolder, or create a new subfolder. It's efficient to use subfolders to organize favorites (with each folder representing a category of your choosing). If you prefer to clean up after the fact, use the Organize Favorites command to put items into subfolders.

To finish creating the new favorite, click Add.

INSIDE OUT   Type a top-level favorite into the Address bar

If a favorite is stored in the root of your Favorites folder (not in a subfolder), you can type the name of the saved favorite directly in the Address bar to jump straight to the page it's associated with. Knowing how this feature works, you can use the top-level Favorites folder to create a collection of easy-to-access shortcuts. The secret is to name the favorites in this level using short, memorable text tags. For example, if you have *www.microsoft.com* assigned to a top-level favorite named MS, you can simply type **ms** and press Enter. Internet Explorer will execute the favorite shortcut, exactly as it would if you had selected it with the mouse. (If you type the name of a Favorites subfolder, the folder appears in Windows Explorer.) If you choose to use this technique, you'll have best results if you reserve the top-level Favorites folder for favorites with short, memorable names and put all others in subfolders.

Adding Groups of Pages to the Favorites List

Internet Explorer 7 allows you to save groups of pages to the Favorites list in a single operation. *Tab groups* are actually nothing more than subfolders in the Favorites list, and saving a tab group simply saves all open tabs into the folder you specify. If you have 12 tabs open, saving the tab group creates new shortcuts for all 12 pages. To save a subset of the currently open tabs, you either have to close those tabs you don't want to save, or save the entire group and then edit the new folder to remove the items you don't want.

To add all open tabs to the Favorites list, click the Add To Favorites button and then click Add Tab Group To Favorites. The resulting dialog box looks similar to the one for adding an individual favorite, with the following exceptions:

- Shortcuts to all open tabs are created and saved in a new subfolder using the name you specify in the Tab Group Name box.

- The Create In list allows you to choose the folder in which your new subfolder will be created.

- You can't edit any details about the individual favorites created in your new sub-folder. Each one is added using the default title as defined by the website designer.

- If the name you enter in the Tab Group Name already exists, all currently open tabs are added to the existing group.

To open all the tabs in a tab group in the current browser window, open Favorites Center, point to the folder name, and click the blue arrow to its right.

Editing Favorites

Each favorite you create is saved as an internet shortcut in the Favorites folder within your user profile. You can edit these shortcuts the same way you would edit any other kind of shortcut. Right-click the item you want to edit (on the Favorites menu, in the Favorites Center, or in the Favorites folder) and choose Properties from the shortcut menu. Figure 6-9 shows the properties dialog box for a saved favorite.

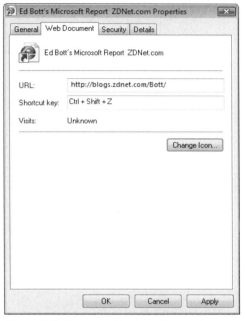

Figure 6-9 You can edit a favorite in various ways, including adding a keyboard shortcut to activate it.

You might want to edit a favorite item for the following reasons:

- To change the name of the favorite
- To change its URL
- To change its icon
- To assign it a keyboard shortcut
- To make it available offline or change its offline-update parameters

To change the name that appears in your Favorites menu, edit the text in the box at the top of the General tab. To change the URL, edit the URL box on the Web Document tab. To select a different icon for this shortcut, click Change Icon on the Web Document tab.

Favorites, which are internet shortcuts, can have keyboard shortcuts, just like file and folder shortcuts. Click in the Shortcut Key field and press a key combination that you want to use to open the specified page. The shortcut key you assign must consist of one character key (a letter, number, or symbol) plus at least two of the following three keys: Ctrl, Alt, and Shift. (If you press a character key only, Windows automatically adds Ctrl+Alt.) This same basic technique is used with program and document shortcuts as well.

Organizing Favorites

Internet Explorer provides a small dialog box, shown in Figure 6-10, that you can use to add subfolders to your Favorites tree, move items between folders, rename folders and shortcuts, and delete favorites or folders. To open this dialog box, click the Add To Favorites button and then click Organize Favorites.

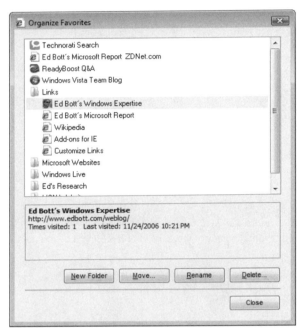

Figure 6-10 If you find the Organize Favorites dialog box confining, you can reorganize your favorites in Windows Explorer instead.

An easier way to organize your favorites is to use Windows Explorer. To get to the Favorites folder, click Start, click your user name at the top of the Start menu's right column, and then click Favorites in your profile folder.

Importing, Exporting, and Sharing Favorites

Got a batch of favorites you want to share? Because Favorites are nothing more than saved internet shortcuts, you can transfer any number of favorites by copying them to whatever storage medium you prefer: a network drive, writable CD, or flash drive, for example.

For a long list of favorites, a simpler alternative is Internet Explorer's Import/Export Wizard, which lets you save any branch of your Favorites folder tree (or the entire tree) as an HTML file (named Bookmark.htm, by default), suitable for e-mailing to a friend or co-worker, for maintaining as a backup of your Favorites folder, and for use as an alternative route to your favorite websites. To open the wizard, tap the Alt key, click File, and then click Import And Export. Follow the prompts to choose Export Favorites, select which portion of the Favorites folder you want to export, and provide a file name and location.

You can use the same command and the same wizard to merge a set of links in an HTML file into your own Favorites tree. In the first step of the wizard, choose Import Favorites. The wizard will prompt for a file name and for the branch of your current Favorites tree to which you want to import the new links.

Using Third-Party Tools to Manage Favorites

A number of free or inexpensive third-party products and web-based services are available to help you manage your favorites and expand on features in Internet Explorer. Among the features offered by these advanced bookmark managers are the following:

- The capability to share favorites between different computers

- The capability to share favorites with other people, either on a public website or privately

- The ability to annotate favorites

- Advanced sorting and searching capabilities

- The ability to check your favorites list periodically and flag those with unreachable URLs

If you're interested in a more powerful bookmark manager, we recommend either of the following options:

- **Del.icio.us** (*http://del.icio.us*) bills itself as a "social bookmarking" site. After you create an account on this free service, you can publish website addresses with titles, descriptions, and tags. Your collection can be marked as private or public and can have its own RSS feed. Toolbar buttons are available as add-ons for Internet Explorer, making it easy to quickly add a bookmark to your Del.icio.us collection.

- **Windows Live Favorites** (*http://favorites.live.com/*) is a free web-based service, operated by Microsoft. It integrates with the Windows Live Toolbar and allows you to synchronize your local Favorites with a server. The benefit is twofold: you never have to worry about backing up your Favorites folder, and if you install the service on each computer you use you can always be certain that your favorites are in sync.

Blocking Pop-Up Windows

Internet Explorer includes a feature that can eliminate most pop-up windows, sparing you the annoyance of unsolicited advertisements that appear in windows lying either over or under the websites you visit. Pop-up Blocker is turned on by default. To determine or change its status, choose Tools, Pop-up Blocker. If the feature is on, the Pop-up Blocker submenu displays a command to turn it off—and vice versa.

In its default configuration, Pop-up Blocker suppresses most new windows that are spawned directly by websites you visit. (Pop-up Blocker calls these "automatic pop-ups.") If you initiate an action that opens a new window (by clicking a link), Pop-up Blocker assumes you want the new window to open and does not interfere. You can configure the feature to be more or less permissive than it is by default. (See "Setting the Filter Level" below.)

Pop-up Blocker, by default, operates on sites in the Internet, Trusted Sites, and Restricted Sites security zones. It does not suppress the display of new windows generated by sites in the Local Intranet zone. Pop-up Blocker maintains an exception list of sites that you want it to ignore. If you regularly visit a site that generates new windows (such as an online shopping site that asks you to log on via a separate window), you can easily add that site to the exception list and prevent Pop-up Blocker from interfering with your transaction. (See "Allowing Pop-ups from Specific Sites," later in this section.)

INSIDE OUT   Bypass Pop-up Blocker temporarily

You might find it convenient to allow selected pop-up windows from a particular site, without changing settings so that all pop-ups from that site are permitted. To squelch the pop-up blocker temporarily, hold down the Ctrl and Alt keys simultaneously while clicking the link that spawns the pop-up. You can also give a temporary pass to a particular site by clicking the Information bar that appears at the top of the Internet Explorer window when a pop-up is suppressed. The first item on the menu that appears, Temporarily Allow Pop-ups, displays the window that was just suppressed and allows further pop-ups until you navigate away from that site's domain.

Setting the Filter Level

Pop-up Blocker offers three standard levels of vigilance—Low, Medium (the default setting), and High. The characteristics of these levels are as follows:

- **High** Pop-up Blocker tries to suppress all new windows, including those that result from your own actions. ActiveX controls might not work in this setting.

- **Medium** Pop-up Blocker allows new windows that result from links that you click. New windows that would otherwise appear as a result of data submitted on forms might be suppressed. If you discover this to be the case for a particular site, consider adding that site to the exception list. If it happens on several sites and that creates a problem, set the registry value UseTimerMethod to 1 (see "Creating a Custom Filter Level," next).

- **Low**   Pop-up Blocker tries to permit all new windows except those that arise automatically when you visit a website. Pop-up Blocker also turns a blind eye to all new windows arising on secure (HTTPS) sites.

To change from one standard filter level to another, choose Tools, Pop-up Blocker, Pop-up Blocker Settings. (Alternatively, you can click Settings on the Privacy tab of the Internet Options dialog box.) In the Pop-up Blocker Settings dialog box, shown in Figure 6-11, open the Filter Level drop-down list and select one of the three settings.

Figure 6-11   Use the Pop-up Blocker Settings dialog box to configure the Filter level, modify the list of exempted websites, and adjust notification options.

Creating a Custom Filter Level

Pop-up Blocker's filtering behavior is determined by five DWORD values of the registry key HKCU\Software\Microsoft\Internet Explorer\New Windows. Those values, each of which can be set to 0 (no) or 1 (yes), are as follows:

- **BlockControls**   This setting, newly added in Internet Explorer 7, controls pop-up windows generated by ActiveX controls. It is set to 1 in High level only.

- **BlockUserInit** This determines whether Pop-up Blocker suppresses windows arising from clicks on links within a website. In the High level, BlockUserInit is 1; in the other two levels, it is 0.

- **UseTimerMethod** Some pop-up windows appear not as a result of clicked links but of data submitted on web forms. With UseTimerMethod set to 1, such pop-ups are permitted; otherwise, they are suppressed. UseTimerMethod is set to 0 in the High and Medium levels.

- **UseHooks** This value, if set to 1, enables Internet Explorer to monitor messages sent to and from ActiveX controls by a website you visit. If UseHooks is set to 0, most ActiveX controls are suppressed as pop-ups. UseHooks is 0 only in the High level.

- **AllowHTTPS** This value, if set to 1, causes Pop-up Blocker to snooze when you visit a secure site. AllowHTTPS is set to 1 only in the Low level.

The five registry values and their standard settings are summarized in Table 6-1.

Table 6-1. Registry Keys That Control Pop-up Blocker Filtering Behavior

	Standard Filter Level Setting		
Registry Value	High	Medium	Low
AllowHTTPS	0	0	1
BlockControls	1	0	0
BlockUserInit	1	0	0
UseHooks	0	1	1
UseTimerMethod	0	0	1

You can create a custom filter level by using Registry Editor to change one or more of these values. If the four values do not conform to one of the three standard constellations shown in Table 6-1, the Filter Level drop-down list in the Pop-up Blocker Settings dialog box displays Custom.

Allowing Pop-ups from Specific Sites

Because some websites might not function properly if they aren't allowed to generate pop-ups, and because you might actually welcome pop-up advertising from particular sites, Internet Explorer's Pop-up Blocker can maintain an exception list of exempted URLs. These URLs are user-specific and are maintained as values in the registry key HKCU\Software\Microsoft\Internet Explorer\New Windows\Allow.

If Pop-up Blocker suppresses a pop-up from a site that you want to be on the exception list, click the Information bar at the top of the screen, and choose Allow Pop-ups From This Site. If you know in advance that you want to exempt a site, choose Tools, Pop-up Blocker, Pop-up Blocker Settings. In the Pop-up Blocker Settings dialog box, enter the address of the website you want to exempt, and then click Add.

Pop-up Blocker normally naps whenever you visit sites in the Local Intranet security zone, on the assumption that sites inside your own network are implicitly trustworthy. If you want to apply the blocker to this security zone, follow these steps:

1. Choose Tools, Internet Options, and click the Security tab.

2. Select the zone you want to adjust, and click Custom Level.

3. In the Miscellaneous section of the Settings list (it's near the bottom of the list), under the heading Use Pop-up Blocker, select Enable.

Configuring Notification Options

When Pop-up Blocker prevents a window from appearing, you are informed, by default, in the following ways:

- An Information bar appears.

- An icon appears in the status bar.

- A sound is played.

To suppress either the Information bar or the notification sound, choose Tools, Pop-up Blocker, Pop-up Blocker Settings. Then clear one or both of the check boxes in the Notifications and Filter Level section of the Pop-up Blocker Settings dialog box.

INSIDE OUT   Change the blocked pop-up sound

If you don't fancy the sound that Internet Explorer uses to announce a blocked pop-up, you can assign a different sound via the Change System Sounds option in the Hardware And Sound section of Control Panel. You'll find the event you need to configure—Blocked Pop-up Window—under the Windows Explorer heading. (Internet Explorer doesn't have its own heading in this dialog box.)

Using (or Refusing) AutoComplete

Internet Explorer's AutoComplete features can help reduce keystrokes (and keystroke errors) by remembering URLs you type, data you enter into web forms, logon names, and passwords. As you begin entering data in a field on a web form, AutoComplete consults its list of previous entries and proposes possible matches—thereby reducing the amount of typing you have to do. Likewise, when Internet Explorer detects matching user name and password fields on a webpage, it asks if you want to save the data as a matched pair. If you click Yes, the values you enter are encrypted and saved in the registry. Both types of data are stored in HKCU\Software\Microsoft\Internet Explorer\IntelliForms—forms in a subkey called Storage1, credentials in Storage2.

Not everyone welcomes this kind of assistance, though. Depending on your preferences and your level of caution, you might want to use all, none, or only some of the browser's AutoComplete services.

To enable or disable AutoComplete options that affect forms and password prompts, click Tools, Internet Options, click the Content tab, and then click the AutoComplete button. This dialog box (shown in Figure 6-12) provides control over all but one of the AutoComplete options. (The other option, called Inline AutoComplete, appears in a different dialog box. For more information, see "Using Inline AutoComplete," later in this section.) Here you can select any or all of the following check boxes:

- Web Addresses to enable auto-completion of data typed in the Address bar

- Forms to enable auto-completion of data that you type into webpages, such as the names and shipping addresses that you supply on e-commerce sites

- User Names And Passwords On Forms to have Internet Explorer remember logon credentials for various sites that you visit

CAUTION

If you select User Names And Passwords On Forms, Internet Explorer always prompts before collecting a new password. The password itself appears on screen as a string of asterisks and is encrypted for storage on your disk. A person reading over your shoulder or prowling your hard disk will therefore not be able to pick up your password when AutoComplete supplies it. However, anyone who has physical access to your computer when you are logged on to your user account could interact with websites for which you have AutoComplete user name and password data, effectively impersonating you. Unless you are sure that no one else will ever use your account, you might want to decline the browser's offer to remember logon credentials.

Figure 6-12 You can turn various AutoComplete options on or off individually.

If you want Internet Explorer to remember logon credentials for new sites that you visit, be sure to select Prompt Me To Save Passwords, as well as User Names And Passwords On Forms. If you clear this suboption, the AutoComplete feature will retain entries that it already has recorded but will not record any new ones.

Saving and Protecting Passwords and Other Sensitive Data

In the course of a year, you might visit literally hundreds of websites that ask you to log on with a user name and password. You might use credentials to access accounts at online merchants or banks, to access web-based services such as photo-sharing sites or bulletin boards, and to manage a website or blog. Keeping track of those passwords can be a hassle, especially if you maintain unique, hard-to-guess passwords for each one.

AutoComplete provides a convenient, reasonably secure way of caching these credentials so that they're available when you revisit a website. Here's how the process works:

The first time you visit a site that includes a logon form, you enter your user name and password and click the button that submits the credentials you entered to the site. Before processing the form, Internet Explorer displays a dialog box asking if you want to save the password.

- If you click Yes, your user name and password are encrypted, using your Windows logon credential and the website address as keys, and stored as binary data in a

Chapter 6

secure location within the registry (HKCU\Software\Microsoft\Internet Explorer\ IntelliForms\Storage2). The key name consists of a long string of characters that identifies the page URL; the key's data contains the encrypted credentials.

- If you click No, Windows records an entry in the same secure location in the registry as if you had clicked Yes, but the data field contains no user name or password, only instructions to ignore this site's logon form in the future.

The next time you open the page containing the logon form, Windows checks the registry to see if that URL is listed. If it contains a saved user name/password combination, the drop-down AutoComplete list appears as soon as you begin typing in the user name box, displaying saved entries that match your input. (Alternatively, you can double-click in the name box to display all saved user names.) If Windows finds the URL in the list with a notation that you previously clicked No when asked whether you wanted to save your password, it waits for you to enter the credentials and doesn't prompt you again.

How Secure Are Your Saved Passwords?

The natural human reaction when one hears that Windows stores user names and passwords for websites is skepticism. Where are the passwords stored? Can someone snooping on my PC find the list of saved passwords and read it? If I forget my password, can I find it in the list? How do I back up the saved passwords?

You can relax on the security front. User names and passwords are encrypted using Triple-DES format through the Data Protection Application Programming Interface (DPAPI)—the same system cryptographic engine that manages the Encrypting File System. The saved data is encrypted using your 512-bit account Master Key, and for security reasons you cannot view the encrypted data directly. Instead, Windows allows programs to query the store for specific data under tightly controlled conditions.

That's a big jump in security over the Windows XP implementation of this feature, which used the Protected Storage subsystem for encryption. The so-called PStore offers relatively weak encryption, as we discovered while researching *Windows XP Networking and Security Inside Out* a few years ago. It took us only minutes to find a handful of utilities designed to read and export the PStore's contents, and the ones we tested worked as advertised. We have yet to find any tool that can retrieve the DPAPI-encrypted store.

If you're visiting a high-security site such as a bank, it's highly likely that the site's designers created their logon forms using attributes that block AutoComplete. That prevents you from accidentally saving credit card details or your Social Security number in an AutoComplete cache.

The bad news about using strong encryption is it makes password recovery nearly impossible for you, too. We know of no way to back up or recover this information; for that, you'll need to use another tool. For all-purpose management of forms, passwords, and web logons, we highly recommend AI RoboForm. This program integrates tightly with Internet Explorer and other browsers, saving passwords, form data, credit card details, and other commonly used information and providing automatic logons when you access pages that require a password. You can encrypt your saved data with a strong password, back up your data to a USB key or network location, and easily move your settings from one PC to another. For details, visit *http://www.roboform.com*.

When it comes to entering passwords, AutoComplete can be both a help and a hazard. If you're prone to forgetting your passwords, AutoComplete can do your remembering for you and save you time and frustration. On the other hand, AutoComplete can also make it easier for someone else to log onto one of your private accounts.

If you'd rather do without AutoComplete for user names and passwords, open the Auto-Complete Settings dialog box (click the Settings button on the Content tab in the Internet Options dialog box) and clear User Names And Passwords On Forms. To erase all previously saved user names and passwords, click Clear Passwords.

If you like using AutoComplete for user names and passwords but want to forgo it for particularly sensitive accounts, click Clear Passwords (to get back to an initial state, before Internet Explorer began remembering any of your passwords), and then make sure that Prompt Me To Save Passwords is selected. As you use your various accounts, you will be prompted the first time you enter a password that Internet Explorer can (optionally) remember. Click Yes to record passwords for the accounts you're not concerned about and decline its offer to remember passwords for more critical sites.

INSIDE OUT   Force Internet Explorer to save a site password

With AutoComplete for User Names And Passwords turned on, Internet Explorer prompts before saving a new logon name and password. If you click No, your choice is recorded in the registry and Internet Explorer won't prompt you again for that site. So, what happens if you change your mind?

If you're willing jump through a few small hoops, you can replace the No entry for that site with a saved password. The task is complicated by the fact that the site in question is stored in the registry using an incomprehensible long string of characters, instead of an easily searchable name. Here's the technique we recommend:

1. Open Registry Editor (type **regedit** at a command prompt or in the Start menu Search box) and navigate to HKCU\Software\Microsoft\Internet Explorer\ IntelliForms\Storage2.

2. In the left (tree) pane, select the Storage2 key. Click File, Export, and save the key to a safe location, using a descriptive name like Saved Passwords.reg.

3. In the right pane, select all values and press Delete.

4. In Internet Explorer, navigate to the site whose password you want to save, fill in your credentials, and click the button to submit the form data. When Internet Explorer asks if it should remember your password, click Yes.

5. Return to Registry Editor and click File, Import. Select the file you saved in Step 2 and click Open to merge the saved data into the registry. This action restores your previously saved passwords, without wiping out the one you just created.

One more gotcha goes along with using AutoComplete to save passwords from web forms: each saved pair is tied to a specific web address. If the site designer changes the URL of the page containing the logon form, your saved credentials from the old page will not work. If you can access a page in two different ways—with and without using the www prefix, for instance, *http://example.com/logon* and *http://www.example.com /logon*—each address will be saved as a different entry in the database.

Not all web-based logons are stored in this location, by the way. If you connect to a site that uses HTTP Authentication, where you enter credentials in a separate logon dialog box rather than in a web form, your secret details are saved as a hidden, encrypted file in %AppData%\Microsoft\Credentials.

Clearing the AutoComplete History

You can delete individual snippets of saved form data and saved web logon credentials from the AutoComplete list if you can reach the page associated with that data. (If the page no longer exists, credentials remain saved but can't be accessed.) This capability is especially useful if you make occasional (or frequent) typing errors and fill various AutoComplete lists with useless, misspelled entries.

To delete a single saved value, go to the webpage associated with the saved data. Click in the box that contains the form field or logon name and press the Down Arrow key to select the stored item (you may need to press this key repeatedly if you have a number of items stored for that field). When you've selected the data you want to get rid of, press the Delete key. If you select a logon name that is associated with a password, Windows displays a dialog box asking if you want to also delete the stored password.

For more thorough housecleaning, you can wipe out all saved username/password pairs and start from scratch. If you're uncertain of exactly what secrets are being re-membered by AutoComplete entries, you can induce immediate amnesia by clicking Clear Forms or Clear Passwords in the AutoComplete Settings dialog box. Each of these buttons deletes a particular category of entries. As the text below the buttons indicates, to clear web address entries, you have to go elsewhere—to the General tab of the Inter-net Options dialog box. Clicking Clear History there covers your tracks on the History Explorer bar in addition to clearing AutoComplete entries, as we explain in "Clearing Personal Information," later in this chapter.

INSIDE OUT   Save keystrokes by pressing Ctrl+Enter

With or without AutoComplete, you can reduce labor in the Address Bar with a handy keyboard shortcut. Pressing Ctrl+Enter prepends http://www. and appends .com to what-ever you've already typed.

Using Inline AutoComplete

The AutoComplete entries collected by the options appear in drop-down lists as you type. To use an entry, you select it with your mouse or with arrow keys. Inline Auto-Complete works differently. With this feature turned off (the default setting), Internet Explorer attempts to guess where you want to go as you type in the Address Bar, using saved favorites and previously typed addresses to build a drop-down list of likely destinations. Type **m**, for example, and Inline AutoComplete might propose a list like this one:

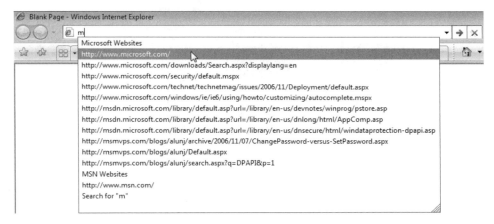

Use the down arrow to move to the correct entry and then press Enter.

With Inline AutoComplete enabled, the closest match from the drop-down list appears in the Address bar, with the portion after the character you just typed highlighted. You can use the End key or the arrow keys to move through the address and edit it manually. Most people want this option off; if you're an exception, click Tools, open the Internet Options dialog box, and then click the Advanced tab. In the Browsing section of the Settings list, select Use Inline AutoComplete.

Internet Explorer Security and Privacy Options

Thanks to Protected Mode browsing, most security options in Internet Explorer 7 for Windows Vista require only minimal configuration. (We provide many more details in Chapter 27, "Advanced Internet Explorer Security and Administration.") In this section, we briefly introduce the most common security options you can choose to customize.

Download Do's and Don'ts

The greatest risk from web-based file downloads is the possibility of being tricked into installing an unwanted ActiveX control or a program that performs nefarious functions.

In Windows Vista, you have multiple lines of defense against potentially dangerous downloads. The first barrier is the Information Bar, which appears at the top of the browser's contents pane if a website is trying to download an ActiveX control or an executable program.

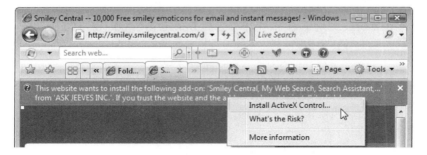

The most important characteristic of the Information Bar is that it doesn't require your attention. If you aren't interested in loading an ActiveX control (perhaps because you landed on the site by accident after mistyping a web address), you can ignore the Information Bar completely. If you do want to approve the activity it's warning you about, you need to click the Information Bar to display its menu and then choose the appropriate menu option. In all, you should always have at least two opportunities to decline an unwanted software installation, and users with standard accounts will be prohibited from installing any such programs without providing an administrator's password.

For more details about specific protections from unwanted downloads in Internet Explorer, see "Protecting Yourself from Unsafe and Unwanted Software," Chapter 27.

For an explanation of why and how User Account Control restricts software installation, see "Preventing Unsafe Actions with User Account Control," Chapter 10, and "Dealing with User Account Control (UAC)," Chapter 4.

Inspecting Website Certificates

Website certificates are the foundation of secure transactions on the Internet. When you visit a secure website in Internet Explorer, the padlock icon in the Address bar indicates that a digital certificate identifies the site; you can inspect the certificate's details by clicking the padlock icon and displaying the summary window shown on the next page.

To view more details about the certificate and its issuer, click the View Certificates link.

When the certificate is expired or invalid, or when the address assigned to the certificate doesn't match the domain that's presenting it, a warning message appears in the browser window. If you choose to continue, the Address bar turns bright red and a Certificate Error message appears there. Click the Error indicator to see a more detailed explanation of why you should be leery of the current site.

Note

Some certificate errors are benign and can be forgiven if you understand why they're occurring. Some web hosting companies use their own certificates to secure access to the control panels for managing domains hosted on their servers. If you try to access the administrative interface through your own domain, Internet Explorer will throw a security warning. The same may happen if a certificate is registered to one domain but a company applies it to another domain in the same family. If this happens frequently enough to be annoying, and you're confident in your ability to recognize a suspicious certificate when you see it, you can disable this check.

Internet Explorer 7 also supports a new form of certificate called the High Assurance certificate. When you visit a site secured by one of these certificates, the Address bar turns green, signifying that the site is certified to be legitimate. At the time we wrote this edition in late 2006, no mainstream websites had switched to this form of certificate.

Identifying Deceptive (Phishing) Websites

A signature feature of Internet Explorer is its capability to inspect websites and block access to or provide a warning about those that appear suspicious. These so-called phishing sites are designed by scammers to closely resemble online commerce and banking sites; the scammer's goal is to fool you into visiting the site (usually by enticing you to click a link in an e-mail message) and then fill in sensitive information such as your logon credentials, account numbers, and details about your identity.

When you first run Internet Explorer, it prompts you to turn on the phishing filter. You can enable or disable the phishing filter at any time by clicking Tools and then using the options on the Phishing Filter menu. These options allow you to manually check a website against Microsoft's servers, report a suspicious website to the online service that maintains the database of suspicious and known phishing sites, or turn automatic checking on or off. To disable the Phishing Filter completely, open the Internet Options dialog box, click the Advanced tab, and find the Phishing Filter group (near the bottom of the list, in the Security section).

The Phishing Filter does its detective work with the help of a whitelist, a set of rules, and a server-based blacklist that is continually updated. The initial check is heuristic, looking at the content of the page itself; if all the images are from a bank's website, but the submit button goes to an URL containing an IP address, red flags go up. When you encounter a suspicious site, you see a yellow banner warning you to look more closely and giving you the option to report the site to Microsoft; after a reported site is confirmed to be a phishing site, the server-side check blocks the page with the message shown in Figure 6-13.

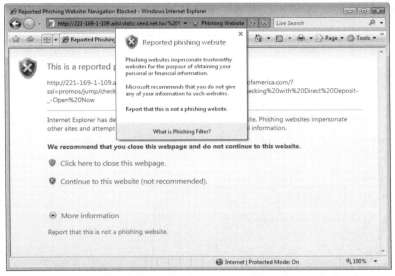

Figure 6-13 When the Phishing Filter is set to automatically check all websites, a "hit" leads to this page, with a bright red badge blocking access to the scam.

Managing Cookies

Cookies are tiny text files that can be stored on your computer by websites you visit and retrieved by those same sites when you return. The privacy threats of cookies have been greatly overblown through the years, but that doesn't mean they're completely innocent. Internet Explorer 7 offers a variety of tools to help you inspect, and manage cookies, either individually or as part of a group of privacy settings. For a much more detailed discussion of these tools and techniques, see "Managing Cookies," Chapter 27.

Clearing Personal Information

Internet Explorer keeps a copy of websites, images, and media you've viewed in your browser recently. It also maintains a list of websites you've visited, whether you arrived at the page by clicking a link or typing an address. This cached information, combined with cookies, saved form data, and saved passwords, can give another person who has access to your computer more information than you might want him to have.

To wipe away most of your online trail, click the Delete Browsing History option at the top of the Tools menu. This dialog box, shown in Figure 6-14 on the next page, allows you to clear any individual category of information. Click the Delete All button to erase all information in all categories.

Chapter 6

Figure 6-14 The options in the Delete Browsing History dialog box leave your Favorites and subscribed web feeds intact.

Finding, Reading, and Subscribing to RSS Feeds

When is a webpage not exactly a webpage? When it's a web *feed*. Feeds are delivered using the HTTP protocol, but they're put together programmatically, using Extensible Markup Language (XML) and the Really Simple Syndication (RSS) standard. A web feed is basically a well-structured list of items, each with a headline, a body, date and time stamps, and other standard details. The page is designed to be regenerated after new items are posted; the latest feed is downloaded at regular intervals and reconstituted at the receiver's end using any of what seems like a thousand RSS reading tools. Web feeds have become extraordinarily popular, as evidenced by the little RSS icons that dot just about every webpage you're likely to visit these days.

Web feeds allow you to avoid having to constantly check a news site or blog to find out if anything new has been posted. When you use Internet Explorer as a feed reader, you can subscribe to an RSS feed and allow the browser to download the feed on a schedule you set up. When a new post appears, the link for that site turns bold and clicking it shows the unread material in your browser window.

> **Note**
>
> In previous versions of Internet Explorer, you could click a Make This Page Available Offline option, which exposed a set of additional properties to allow automatic retrieval of webpages. This feature has been completely eliminated in Internet Explorer 7. If you want to read pages offline, web feeds are by far a better solution.

To get started with RSS feeds, click the orange RSS icon on any webpage (or look for a link with the label XML, RSS, or Atom, possibly followed by a version number). The Feed button on the Command Bar in Internet Explorer turns from its default gray to a bright orange when it detects the presence of a web feed on the page you're currently viewing. Click that button to display the feed (or choose from a menu of available feeds, if more than one is available)

When you open a feed in Internet Explorer, the browser applies a uniform style sheet to the page, and you see the feed's contents in the browser window, as shown in Figure 6-15.

Figure 6-15 Some RSS feeds contain only brief pointers to longer posts or media files, forcing you to click a link to read or play the associated post.

To add a new feed to the list in the Favorites Center and tell Internet Explorer to begin monitoring it, click the Subscribe To This Feed link. That action opens the dialog box shown here.

These settings, which are similar to those you enter when you create a web favorite, allow you to give the feed a descriptive name and, optionally, file it in a subfolder of the Feeds folder.

To view all feeds on your subscribed list, open the Feed list in Favorites Center. If Favorites Center is already open, press the Ctrl+J shortcut; if Favorites Center is hidden, press Ctrl+Shift+J. After you add a feed to your list of subscriptions, you can adjust its properties by right-clicking the feed name in the Favorites Center and choosing Properties. Figure 6-16 shows the properties available for you to change.

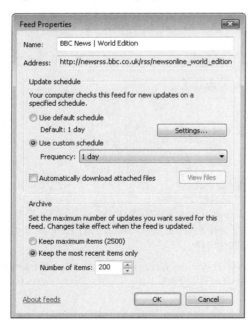

Figure 6-16 For a news-related web feed, you'll probably prefer to retrieve updates hourly rather than daily.

You can give the feed a new name (but you can't change its URL; to do that, you have to delete the feed and add a new subscription using the changed URL). You can choose a different value from the Use Custom Schedule drop-down list to change the retrieval schedule for the feed from its default of once per day to a custom schedule of your choosing. To change the default retrieval schedule, click Settings and adjust the options shown here.

INSIDE OUT   Update feeds on demand

Want to get the latest posts for a single feed? Bypass the regular schedule by pointing to the feed item in the Favorites Center and clicking the blue Refresh This Feed icon to its right. You can also right-click any item or folder and use the Refresh All option to force an immediate update for all subscribed feeds.

You can also control the number of items stored for each feed. By default, Internet Explorer begins throwing out old items for a given feed after the store for that feed fills up with 200 items. You can lower this number to as few as 1 or to its maximum of 2500. The feed store isn't indexed, so you can't use the Windows Search tools to find items in your downloaded feeds.

To read your subscribed feeds, open the Feeds list in Favorites Center and click any link (bold-faced links indicate that new, unread content is available). The latest updates to the feed you selected appear in the browser's contents pane, as shown in Figure 6-17 on the next page.

Figure 6-17 When you view a subscribed feed in the browser window, you can use the tools in the upper right corner to search, sort, and filter the selection.

INSIDE OUT   Import and export your feeds list

Internet Explorer's feed-reading capabilities are useful for light reading, but if you get hooked on RSS as a way to keep up with news and information, you'll want to switch to a more powerful platform. To make the switch, export your subscribed feeds as an Outline Processor Markup Language (OPML) file. Every mainstream feed-reading client, without exception, can process OPML lists. Tap the Alt key to expose Internet Explorer's menu bar, click File, and then click Import and Export. Follow the wizard's prompts and choose the Export Feeds option. Save the list as a file and import that file into your new feed reader. The process works in reverse as well. If you prefer the Internet Explorer approach, you can export a list of feeds from another program or Web-based service and import them using the Import/Export Wizard in Internet Explorer.

Using Internet Explorer as an FTP Client

You can use Internet Explorer to access repositories of files using File Transfer Protocol (FTP) sites as well as using HTTP to visit websites. To specify an FTP address, use the ftp:// prefix instead of http://. By default, Internet Explorer displays directory listings from FTP sites in a plain text view, using system fonts, as in the example in Figure 6-18. You can click the link to open any file saved in a browser-friendly format (text or HTML, for example) directly in the browser window. To save a file, right-click its hyperlink and choose Save Target As.

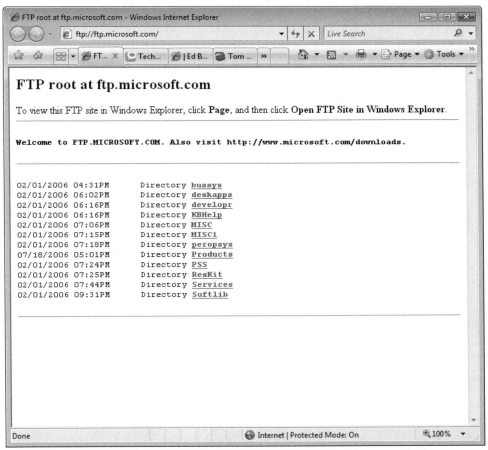

Figure 6-18 FTP listings in an Internet Explorer window use this bare-bones text format.

If you simply enter an FTP address or click an FTP link, Internet Explorer attempts to log you on with anonymous access, using no credentials. To use Internet Explorer to connect to an FTP server that requires a user name and password, you can include your logon information in the Address bar, like this:

`ftp://`*name:password*`@ftp.microsoft.com`

If you omit the password and enter only a user name followed by an @ sign and the FTP site address, Internet Explorer prompts you for credentials, using the dialog box shown here. You cannot save credentials in Internet Explorer.

Working with FTP sites in Internet Explorer is an awkward affair at best. For occasional anonymous access it will probably suffice, but for anything more than a quick download we recommend you work with an FTP site in folder view. Click Page and then click Open FTP Site in Windows Explorer. After approving a security prompt, you'll see the site's contents in a window like the one shown in Figure 6-19.

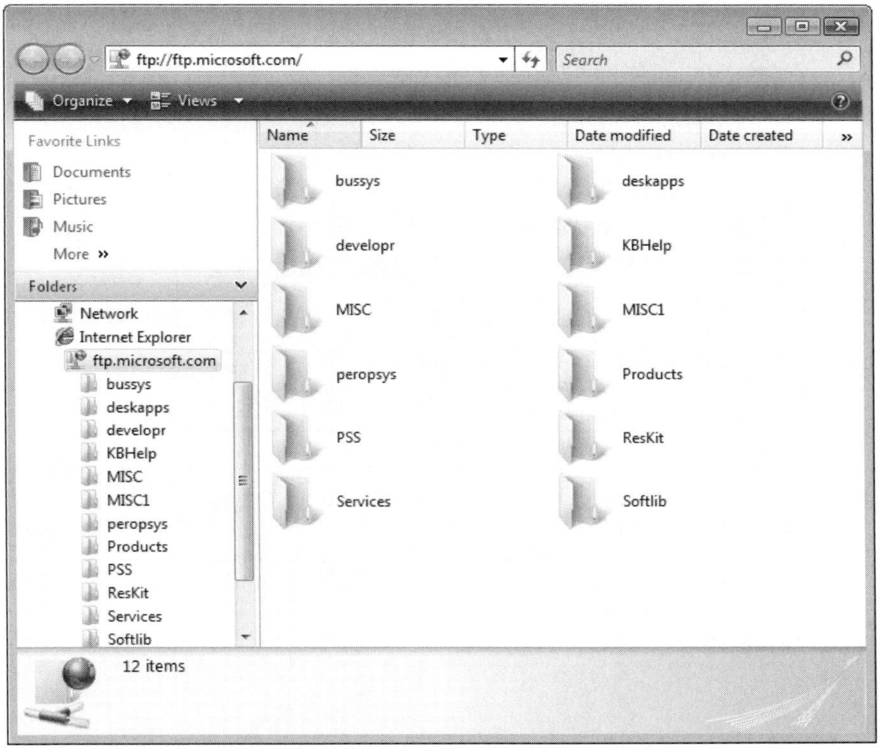

Figure 6-19 When you connect to an FTP site using Windows Explorer, you can manage files and folders directly. The site icon in the Navigation disappears when you close the window.

If the site requires you to enter credentials, press Alt to display the Windows Explorer menu, and then click File, Login As and provide your user name and password, using the dialog box shown here.

Using Windows Explorer for FTP site access provides basic functionality, including the capability to change file and folder permissions. (Right-click and choose Properties to adjust permissions.) If you prefer to use a third-party FTP client instead, you can disable FTP browsing in Windows Explorer. Open the Internet Options dialog box, click the Advanced tab, scroll to the Browsing section, and clear Enable FTP Folder View (Outside of Internet Explorer).

CHAPTER 7

Finding and Organizing Files and Information

Home Basic ◐
Home Premium ◐
Business ●
Enterprise ●
Ultimate ●

U nless you use your computer exclusively as a game machine or a media center, learning to manage your "stuff"—your documents, programs, and communications—is probably the single most critical computing skill you need to acquire. Because the continual growth in storage capacity encourages a corresponding increase in digital retentiveness, keeping track of stuff seems more crucial than ever. Fortunately, Windows Vista provides a terrific set of stuff-tracking tools.

Leading the way is a redesigned Windows Explorer, complete with live-icon previews of file contents (for applications and document types that support that), a Preview pane that lets you peek inside file contents without actually opening the files, and a Details pane that displays file properties and lets you add descriptive tags to files (again, for files that support the feature). The most important new element in the Windows Explorer landscape, though, is the Search box in the upper-right corner. Windows Explorer is now completely integrated with Search, so that you can find what you need where you need it (even within common dialog boxes).

Search itself, of course, is so much improved that comparisons with its predecessor in Windows XP are pointless. The dog is gone. (Say hello to the cheetah.)

In addition to the revamped Windows Explorer user interface and the fully functional search engine, Windows Vista also provides an easier-to-use backup program and—one of the unsung-hero feature of the entire operating-system update: *Previous Versions*. This unglamorous sounding novelty keeps daily iterations of your documents and folders (assuming System Protection is turned on), recording a change history at periodic intervals and allowing you to turn back the calendar if you delete a file or damage it beyond repair.

What's in Your Edition?

The Previous Versions feature described in this chapter is not available in Windows Vista Home Basic or Windows Vista Home Premium.

What's What in Windows Explorer

Figure 7-1 shows a folder containing two Microsoft Word documents and a subfolder. All of the several optional display elements are deployed in this example. The folder contents are shown in Large Icons view, one of several view options available in Windows Explorer.

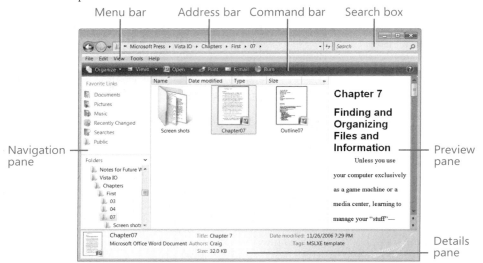

Figure 7-1 The new Windows Explorer includes these display elements, some of which are optional.

The important landmarks, optional and otherwise, are as follows:

- **Navigation pane** The optional Navigation pane, which appears at the left side of the Windows Explorer display, hosts a set of Favorite Links that provide instant access to particular folders. Windows provides some by default; you can add and subtract from this list as needed. The Navigation pane can also display the Folders list, a navigable outline of your folder structure.

- **Details pane** Running across the bottom of the window, the Details pane displays properties for the selected item. With many file types, you can add your own "tags" here, and you can use these tags in searches. Display of the Details pane is optional.

- **Preview pane** As its name suggests, the Preview pane lets you view the contents of a file without opening it. Its appearance and behavior vary, depending on what kind of file is selected. When a file containing text is selected (as in Figure 7-1), the Preview pane lets you read some or all of that text. Select an Excel workbook, and the Preview pane provides a navigable, read-only spreadsheet. Select a media item, and, as Figure 7-2 shows, you get a miniature player. The Preview pane is optional.

Figure 7-2 The Preview pane provides a miniature media player when music or video is selected.

- **Command bar** Unlike the other display elements described thus far, the Command bar is not optional; it's a permanent fixture. It's also not customizable. As you can see by comparing Figures 7-1 and 7-2, however, Windows Explorer varies the content of the Command bar so that it provides commands that are relevant to the selected item.

- **Menu bar** Lying directly above the Command bar is the optional menu bar—a relic from Windows XP. Most of its offerings are now duplicated in the Organize and Views commands (or, in some cases, on the shortcut menu that appears when you right-click in Windows Explorer). Nevertheless, some Windows XP veterans prefer to keep the menu bar visible because it takes up little space and leaves frequently needed functionality (such as the Folder Options dialog box) in familiar places. (In fact, the menu bar does include some commands that are not available elsewhere in Windows Explorer; see Figure 7-3.)

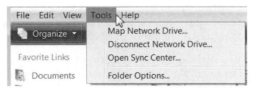

Figure 7-3 Most of the menu-bar commands are now available elsewhere; the first three on the Tools menu, however, are not.

INSIDE OUT

Another quick way to get to the Folder Options dialog box is to type **Folder** in the Start menu's Search box. Folder Options should pop to the top of the search results list, under the heading Programs.

If the menu bar isn't displayed, you can make it appear temporarily—long enough to open a menu and execute a command—by pressing Alt or F10.

- **Address bar** Like its counterpart in a web browser, the Address bar shows you where you are and helps you get where you want to go. (You can even type a URL here and launch your web browser, although that's hardly its principal function.) Because of its new "breadcrumb trail" feature, the Windows Vista Address bar is dramatically more useful than its forerunner in Windows XP.

INSIDE OUT

The Address bar no longer shows you the full path of the current folder in the traditional manner, with backslash characters separating folder names. If you need to see (or edit) the full path displayed that way, click anywhere to the right of the path in the Address bar or right-click the path and choose Edit As Address.

- **Search box** Typing in the Search box launches a search rooted at the current folder. It's a great tool for finding an item you're sure is located either in the current folder or a subfolder of the current folder.

Displaying or Hiding Optional Elements

The Navigation pane, Details pane, Preview pane, and menu bar are all optional. To display or hide any one of them, click Organize on the Command bar, and then click Layout. On the Layout submenu, all four commands are toggles. Only the Menu Bar command has a check mark to indicate its status, but a glance at your Windows Explorer window will tell you whether you're about to display or hide a given element.

You can change the size of a display element by dragging the line that divides that element from its neighbor. For example, to make the Preview pane larger, drag the vertical separator to the left.

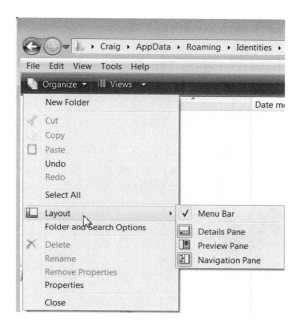

> **Note**
>
> Your decision to display or hide the Navigation pane or Details pane applies to all folders. You can display the Preview pane in particular folders without affecting other folders, however.

Choosing View Options

The Views menu in Windows Explorer now comes with a slider that lets you move smoothly between icon sizes. At medium sizes and above, the operating system displays thumbnails—previews of file or folder contents—if it finds something to display. In the illustration on the next page, for example, the folder named Stinson includes an image of Russell Stinson, so the image appears within the folder icon:

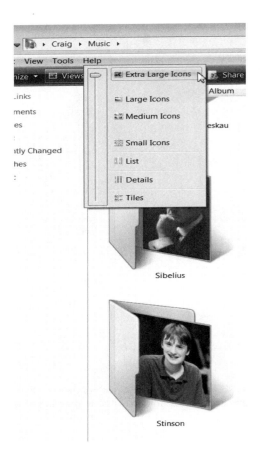

> **Note**
>
> You can turn the thumbnail display off if you find it distracting or if it slows your system down. To do so, choose Organize, Folder And Search Options. In the Folder Options dialog box, click View. Then, in the Advanced Settings list, select Always Show Icons, Never Thumbnails.

By default, your choice of viewing option applies only to the current folder; it is not inherited by subfolders. If you want all folders of a given type—all music folders, for example, or all documents folders—to have the same view, set up any one of those folders the way you want it. Then choose Organize, Folder And Search Options. In the Folder Options dialog box, shown in Figure 7-4, click Apply To Folders.

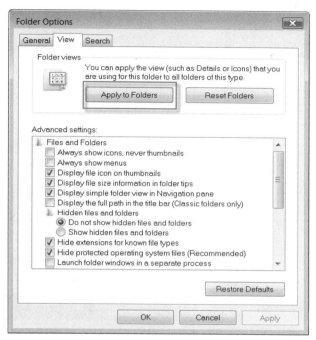

Figure 7-4 You can assign the same view settings to all folders of a given type by clicking Apply To Folders in the Folder Options dialog box.

> **Note**
>
> Not sure what folder "type" you're in? Right-click a blank space in the folder and choose Customize This Folder from the shortcut menu. On the Customize tab of the properties dialog box, the Use This Folder Type As A Template list will show the folder type that's currently in effect. (You can also use this list to change the folder to a different type.)

Sorting, Filtering, Stacking, and Grouping

In all views, Windows Explorer provides folders with headings that it considers appropriate for the content type. In the Documents folder shown in Figure 7-5 on the next page, for example, the default headings are Name, Date Modified, Type, Size, and Tags. You can add headings for other properties, delete existing ones, or change the order in which headings appear by right-clicking any heading (or right-clicking in the unoccupied space to the right of the headings) and choosing More. This action displays the Choose Details dialog box, which provides check boxes for all available headings.

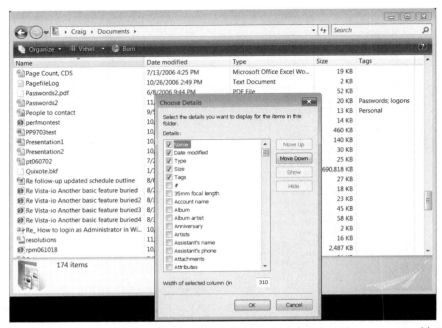

Figure 7-5 By right-clicking a heading in Details View and choosing More, you can add, remove, or rearrange headings.

Although the Choose Details dialog box includes Move Up and Move Down buttons, as well as a Width Of Selected Column field, you'll probably find it easier to make size and position adjustments directly, with the mouse. Drag a column heading to move it; drag a divider between columns to adjust a column's width.

To sort a folder in Details view, click the heading that you want to use as a sort key. For example, to sort by Date Modified, click the Date Modified heading. A second click on the same heading reverses the sort order.

INSIDE OUT

You can also sort a folder by right-clicking anywhere within it, choosing Sort By from the shortcut menu, and then choosing the column want to use as the sort key.

Filtering Folder Contents

Headings in any view can also be used to filter the contents of a folder. If you rest your mouse on a heading, a drop-down arrow appears at the right. Clicking the arrow reveals a set of filter check boxes appropriate for the heading. If you click a date heading (see Figure 7-6), for example, the filter options include common date groupings. You can also select the Filter By A Specific Date check box and use the calendar to specify that date.

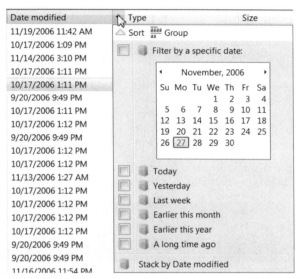

Figure 7-6 When you click the drop-down arrow next to a field heading, a set of filtering options, appropriate for the heading type, appears.

If you filter by Type, Windows Explorer gives you a check box for every file type represented in the current folder. If you filter by Size, you get a set of choices based on the file sizes that Windows deems appropriate, given current folder contents:

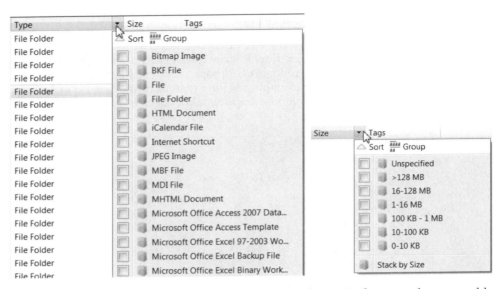

A filter can use multiple check boxes and multiple headings. So, for example, you could filter a picture folder based on several tags as well as a "date taken" value:

When a folder is filtered, check marks appear to the right of headings used for filtering (see the Date Taken and Size headings in the preceding illustration). The values on which you have filtered (for example, the specific tags) appear in the Address bar. In the preceding illustration for example, the Address bar shows "Jean,Miranda" (the two criteria we've used from the Tags column) and "A long time ago" (the Date Taken criterion).

Chapter 7

INSIDE OUT

The easiest way to clear a set of filtering criteria is to click to the left of the criteria on the Address bar. In the preceding illustration, for example, clicking Pictures in the Address bar returns the folder to its unfiltered state. You can also open a heading and clear individual check boxes, but that's a more laborious method—and the heading drop-down lists do not include an option to clear all filters. If you created the filtered view interactively, click the Back button to return to the unfiltered view.

When you select multiple check boxes in the same heading, Windows Explorer displays items that match any of the selected check boxes. The preceding illustration, for example, is filtered on two tags (Jean and Miranda), but only the first three pictures shown meet both criteria. Pictures that meet either criterion without the other, such as the fourth picture in the illustration, also pass the filter. When you select filtering check boxes from two or more separate headings, however, Windows Explorer displays only those items that satisfy the criteria applied to each heading (in Boolean terms, it uses the conjunction AND between the headings).

INSIDE OUT

Pressing Ctrl+N in Windows Explorer opens a new window on the same folder. Ctrl+W closes the current window. (These keyboard shortcuts function the same way in Internet Explorer.)

Filtering a folder puts you in the hands of the search engine, which is tightly integrated with Windows Explorer. In other words, filtering performs a search of the current folder based on the criteria you supply in the headings check boxes. At the bottom of the filtered folder, you will see a question and an invitation:

MIRANDA9   P1010480   P1010482

Did you find what you were searching for?
🔍 Search in Subfolders

If you did not find what you were looking for, you can click Search In Subfolders to extend the search.

Stacking Folder Contents

At the bottom of every list of filtering criteria is a Stack By command. You can also get to it by right-clicking in the folder, as shown here:

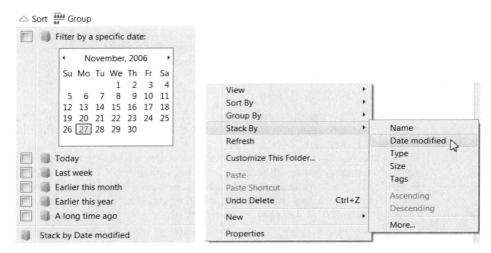

However you do it, stacking is equivalent to carrying out a batch of separate filtering operations, one for each of the available filtering criteria. Windows Explorer displays the outcome as a set of virtual folders, like the ones shown in Figure 7-7. (A *virtual folder*, denoted by a blue icon in Windows Explorer, is a collection of files and folders that typically do not correspond to a single disk-storage location. You can work with a virtual folder the same way you would work with an ordinary folder.)

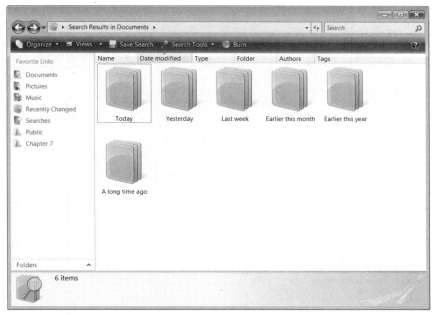

Figure 7-7 Stacking a folder produces a set of virtual folders, each one the equivalent of a separate filtering operation.

Note that the Address bar in Figure 7-7 starts with "Search Results." When you stack a folder, you're handing off your folder to the search engine. The only practical importance of that fact is that the next time you open the folder that you have stacked (for example, the next time you open the Start menu and click Documents), you'll need to re-create the stack. If you want to reuse a stacked folder, click Save Search and give the search-results folder a name. (For more about saving search results, see "Saving Search Results," later in this chapter.)

Grouping Folder Contents

If sorting, filtering, and stacking don't give you enough ways to organize or locate files, try grouping. Grouping generates a display comparable to the one shown in Figure 7-8 on the next page.

Click to expand or
collapse group

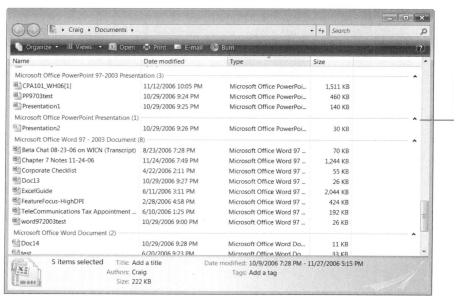

Figure 7-8 Grouping, like stacking, puts like with like, but leaves you in a standard Windows Explorer context instead of a Search Results folder.

When you group, Windows Explorer collects all the items that have some common property (in Figure 7-8, file type is the property), displaying each group under a heading that can be expanded or collapsed. Figure 7-9 shows the same grouped folder with most of its headings collapsed.

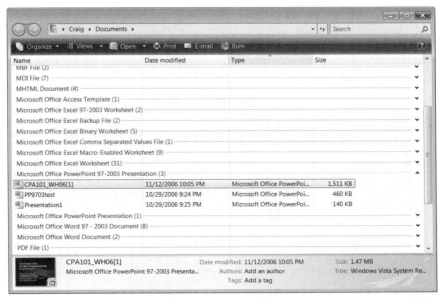

Figure 7-9 You can use the expand/collapse controls at the right side of a grouped folder to focus attention on particular items.

Because grouping, unlike stacking, leaves you in a standard Windows Explorer context instead of a Search Results folder, the grouped arrangement is stable; that is, the next time you open the folder, it will still be grouped.

INSIDE OUT

To return a grouped folder to its ungrouped state, don't bother opening headings (you won't find an Ungroup command there). Right-click in the folder, choose Group By in the shortcut menu, and choose (None) in the submenu that appears.

Navigating in Windows Explorer

Navigating in Windows Explorer is easier than it used to be, thanks to two innovations in Windows Vista: the breadcrumb trail and Favorite Links.

Navigating with the Breadcrumb Trail

As mentioned, Windows Explorer no longer displays conventional folder path specifications in the Address bar. The path is still there (although if it's long, it might be truncated on the left), but instead of using backslashes to separate folder names, Windows Explorer uses small arrows:

More important, every element in the Address bar—every folder name and each arrow—is not an inert piece of text but an active control. Thus you can step from the current folder directly to any folder above it in the path by clicking on a folder name. For example, in the illustration above, you could move directly from the Screen Shots folder to the Microsoft Press folder by clicking Microsoft Press.

The arrows meanwhile, as arrows so often do in Windows, open drop-down lists. Clicking the arrow to the right of Documents, for example, unfurls a drop-down list of subfolders of Documents:

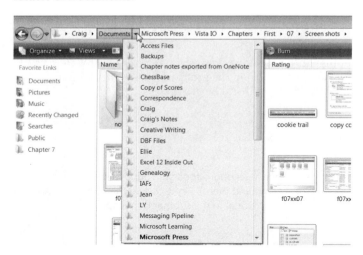

The folder that's in the current path (in this case, Microsoft Press) is displayed in a bold font. But all of the folders in the lists are targets available to your mouse. Thus, the breadcrumb trail not only lets you move from the current folder to its parent, grandparent, or great-grandparent, it also lets you visit uncles, aunts, nieces, nephews, cousins, and their assorted spouses. In short, you can wander the whole family tree.

INSIDE OUT
Create Shortcuts with Copy Address

If you right-click the Address bar, the shortcut menu that appears includes the unnecessary Edit Address command, which simply duplicates the effect of clicking in an unoccupied part of the Address bar. Along with that, however, come two ambiguously named but useful commands: Copy Address and Copy Address As Text.

Copy Address As Text creates a text string of the current path, which you can paste into any text-receiving application. Copy Address also puts the text of the current path on the Clipboard, allowing you to paste into a word processor or e-mail message, for example. But it does more. Copy Address lets you copy the entire contents of the current folder, or a shortcut to the current folder, into another location, such as the Desktop.

One of the handy things you can do with this obscure feature is create shortcuts to deeply buried "folders" that are not part of the file system, such as Control Panel applets. For example, to create a desktop shortcut to the Manage Network Connections folder in Control Panel, you could open Control Panel, click Network And Internet, and click Network And Sharing Center. Then you would click the Manage Network Connections link in the Network And Sharing Center task pane. At this point you would have a Windows Explorer folder with the path Control Panel\Network And Internet\Network Connections displayed in the Address bar. Right-click it, choose Copy Address, right-click the desktop, and choose Paste Shortcut.

Clicking the arrow to the left of the first crumb in the trail displays a list of root folders:

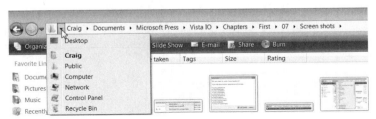

If you happen to be in a folder so deeply nested that the Address bar doesn't have room to show the entire path, you will see a chevron to the left of the first item, instead of an arrow. Clicking this will show the names of the parent folders that don't fit on the Address bar, and below those you will see root folders:

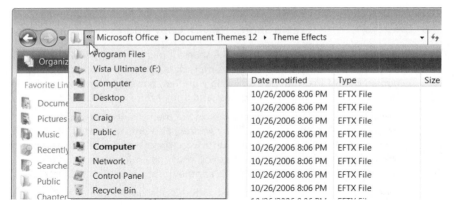

To the left of the Address bar itself, nestled between the Address bar and the Back and Forward buttons, you will find a Recent Items drop-down. This one acts like the History list in a web browser, showing you the folders you've recently visited and inviting you to return to familiar places:

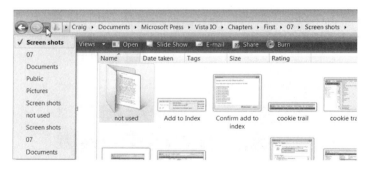

INSIDE OUT

If you hold down the Shift key while right-clicking a file, a Copy As Path command appears on the shortcut menu. This command puts the full path of the selected file, complete with enclosing quote marks, on the Clipboard, suitable for pasting into an e-mail message or other text application.

Navigating with Favorite Links

The Favorite Links list that appears in the top of the Navigation pane provides direct transport to folders that might or might not be located somewhere along the current path. Windows Explorer gives you a half-dozen of these by default:

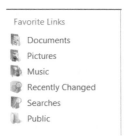

But you can amend the list any way you want. If you never need to visit the Music folder, for example, you can right-click it and choose Remove Link. If you continually need to return to the same folder (say, for a project that's hot), you can add a link to that folder. To do this, display the folder's parent in Windows Explorer, then drag the folder to the Navigation pane. Windows Explorer will display the following as you drag:

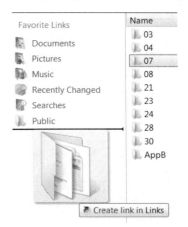

Release the mouse button, and you have a new link. Initially, your new link will have the same name as the folder you dragged, but you can right-click it and rename it.

All Windows Explorer folders (for a particular user profile) share the same Favorite Links list. The links are generated by a set of shortcuts stored in the Links folder within your user profile. You can manipulate these shortcuts in the Links folder, although there is seldom a need to do this; it's usually simpler to work with them in the Navigation pane.

One of the default links, Recently Changed, is a virtual folder—a creation of the search engine. This is an extremely useful item; clicking it generates a list of all the personal files (documents, pictures, music, movies, videos, notes, and journals) whose Date Modified property falls within the last 30 days. The list is sorted in descending order by Date Modified, so it's easy to relocate something you've been working with of late. (This is comparable to, but far more extensive than, the list that appears when you choose Recent Items on the Start menu; the latter option opens an actual folder, stored in your user profile at %Appdata%\Microsoft\Windows\Recent, which contains shortcuts to files and folders you've used lately.)

Navigating with the Folders List

Given the new navigational tools at your disposal, you might not need it. On the other hand, you might prefer it: The Folders list, familiar to Windows XP experts, is known as the Folders list in Windows Vista and isn't displayed by default. To open the Folders list, click Folders at the bottom of the Navigation pane. As Figure 7-10 shows, the Folders list initially shares quarters with Favorite links. You can adjust its size by dragging the horizontal bar above the word *Folders*. The Favorite Links list will display a More link if the Folders list starts crowding it out. If you don't want any traces at all of Favorite Links, you can drag the Folders list all the way up to the top of the Navigation pane.

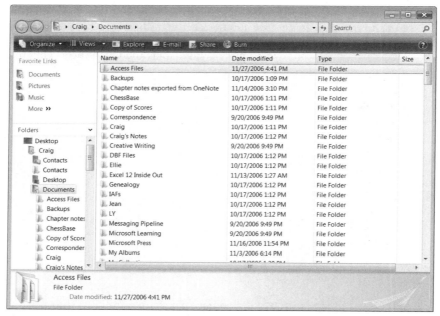

Figure 7-10 The Folders list is still available, although not displayed by default.

INSIDE OUT

To open a folder in a new window with the Folders list displayed, right-click it in Windows Explorer and choose Explore from the shortcut menu.

Navigating in the Common Dialog Boxes

If you're opening or saving files in a Windows program that uses the *common dialog boxes* (a set of dialog boxes provided by the Windows application programming interface to give applications a consistent appearance and behavior), you will find essentially the same navigation tools provided by Windows Explorer. Figure 7-11, for example, shows the Open dialog box used by Microsoft Office Excel 2007. Like a Windows Explorer folder, it includes a Navigation pane, a Command bar, an Address bar with breadcrumbs, a Search box, and column headings that can be used for sorting, filtering, stacking, and grouping. (Typically, the drop-down list to the right of the File Name box provides its own file-type filter.) It does not include the menu bar, even if you have chosen to display that feature in Windows Explorer.

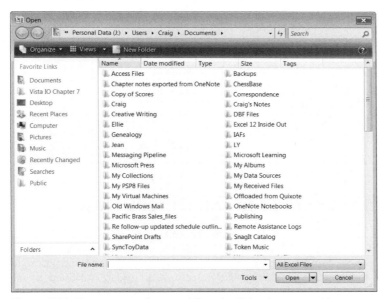

Figure 7-11 The common Open and Save As dialog boxes, used by most modern Windows applications, offer essentially the same set of navigational tools as Windows Explorer windows.

Initially, the common dialog boxes do not deploy the Details pane or Preview pane, but you can display them in the usual way—by choosing Organize, Layout. The Favorite Links list adds some links to the set of defaults shown initially in Windows Explorer. In Figure 7-11, for example, you can see that Excel has added a Desktop link (because many people store documents there).

An extremely handy link that appears in common dialog boxes is Recent Places. This one generates a list of shortcuts to folders that you have recently used for opening or saving files:

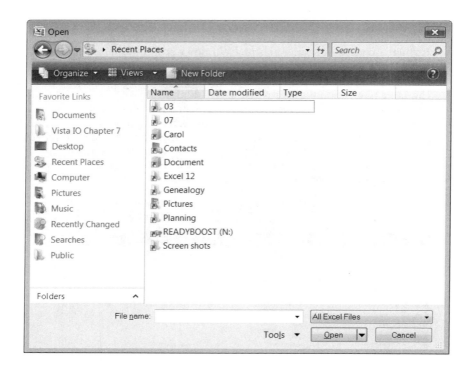

Working with Properties in the Details Pane

In its default size, the Details pane has room to display a small thumbnail of the selected file (if a thumbnail is available), plus a few properties. The number of properties shown depends on your screen resolution. In the following illustration, taken at 1024 x 768, we see only five properties—Title, Authors, Size, Date Modified, and Tags.

You can make more properties appear by enlarging the Details pane. Dragging the divider upwards, for example, changes the property display dramatically (it also brings the thumbnail closer to readability):

The properties that appear are of two types—read-only and read/write. Date properties (modified, created, accessed) are read-only, obviously. Authors, although initially filled out with the name of the user account under which the file was created, is an editable property.

Windows Explorer displays these properties, along with exhortations such as "Add a title," because properties are searchable. If you get in the habit of supplying a few, you'll be more likely to be able to find what you need later on.

Only the interface for reading and editing properties is completely new here. Properties have always been (and still are) accessible via the properties dialog box:

You can also fill out property dialog boxes in many applications. (In Excel 2007, for example, you can get to the properties dialog box by clicking the Microsoft Office button, choosing Prepare, then Properties.) The problem with properties dialog boxes is that few users bother to visit them. Now you don't have to (not for the most essential properties, at any rate; for ones that don't appear in the Details pane, you'll still need to use the old methods).

To enter or change a property in the Details pane, simply click and type. If you add two or more words or phrases to a field (such as Tags) that accepts multiple entries, use semicolons to separate them. A Save button will appear when you begin typing, as shown on the next page.

Click Save or just press Enter to record your new properties.

Properties, otherwise known as *metadata*, are saved within the file itself, rather than being stored in a "sidecar" file, alternate data streams, or a separate system "metabase." This means:

- You should be able to move files to other operating systems without losing their properties.

- You should be able to edit a file in an application other than the one in which it was created, without losing the file's properties (assuming the other application is reasonably well behaved).

- A file's properties are visible to anyone who has read access to the file.

Unfortunately, it also means that you can assign properties (or tags) only to those file types that can accommodate embedded metadata. Bitmapped images and graphics in PNG format cannot be tagged, for example; JPEG files can. Plain text and Rich Text Format files are untaggable; files saved in Microsoft Word formats can be tagged.

Managing User Profiles

A *user profile* contains all the settings and files for a user's work environment. In addition to personal documents and media, this includes the user's own registry settings, view settings used in applications, and such things as cookies and internet favorites.

What's What and Where in a User Profile

By default, each user who logs on to a computer has a local user profile, which is created when the user logs on for the first time. Local user profiles are stored in %Systemdrive%\Users. Each user's profile is stored in a subfolder where the user account name is the folder name (for example, C:\Users\Jean). The entire path for the current user's profile is stored in another commonly used environment variable, %UserProfile%.

Within a user's profile are a hierarchy of folders, as shown in Figure 7-12. The root of the profile (the folder that uses the same name as the current user account) contains Ntuser.dat, which is the user portion of the registry (in other words, the HKCU hive), and associated registry files. It also includes a number of hidden "junctions" (see, for example, NetHood, PrintHood, and SendTo in Figure 7-12) that provide compatibility with older applications that expect the Windows XP profile structure. The junctions are all identified with shortcut icons in Windows Explorer, although they are not conventional shortcuts. (For more about this, see "How Windows Vista Maintains Compatibility with Windows XP," later in this chapter.)

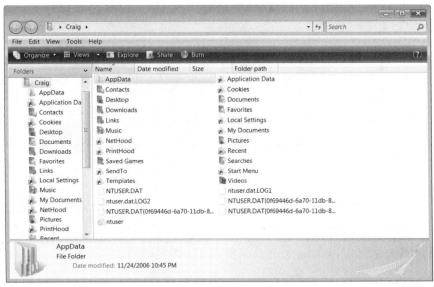

Figure 7-12 In addition to conventional document folders, a user profile includes a number of hidden registry files, a hidden AppData folder, and several junctions provided for compatibility with Windows XP.

Assuming you have not set Windows Explorer to display hidden and system folders, what you will see in %UserProfile% will look more like Figure 7-13 on the next page. The folder includes eleven subfolders, each intended to house a different category of personal information. Several of these—Documents, Favorites, Music, Pictures, and Videos—have counterparts in Windows XP, although Windows Vista has removed the personal pronouns and arranged the folders more logically. (My Pictures, My Music, and My Videos were subfolders of My Documents in Windows XP.) Others are new.

Figure 7-13 The unhidden portion of your profile consists of eleven subfolders of a folder named for your user account.

The complete subfolder organization of a profile folder, including both the visible and hidden items, is as follows:

- **AppData** This hidden folder contains application-specific data—customized dictionaries for a word processor, junk sender lists for an e-mail client, and so on. It's organized into three subfolders, named Local, LocalLow, and Roaming. The Roaming folder (which is also accessible via the environmental variable %AppData%) is for data that is made available to a roaming profile (a profile stored on a network server; the server makes the profile available to any network computer where the user logs on). The Local folder (which is also accessible via the system variable %LocalAppData%) is for data that should not roam. The LocalLow folder is used only for Internet Explorer Protected Mode data. System-generated subfolders within AppData\Local and AppData\Roaming are as follows:

  - **AppData\Local\Microsoft\Windows\History** This hidden folder contains the user's Internet Explorer browsing history.

  - **AppData\Local\Temp** This folder contains temporary files created by applications. The %Temp% variable points to AppData\Local\Temp.

  - **AppData\Local\Microsoft\Windows\Temporary Internet Files** This hidden folder contains the offline cache for Internet Explorer.

  - **AppData\Roaming\Microsoft\Windows\Cookies** This hidden folder contains Internet Explorer cookies.

  - **AppData\Roaming\Microsoft\Windows\Network Shortcuts** This folder contains shortcuts to network shares that appear in the Computer folder.

The folder is not hidden; you can add your own shortcuts here, although it is easier to right-click in Computer and choose Add A Network Location.

○ **AppData\Roaming\Microsoft\Windows\Printer Shortcuts** This seldom-used folder can contain shortcuts to items in the Control Panel\Hardware And Sound\Printers folder.

○ **AppData\Roaming\Microsoft\Windows\Recent Items** This folder contains shortcuts to recently used documents; the most recent 15 of these appear on the Start menu.

○ **AppData\Roaming\Microsoft\Windows\SendTo** This folder contains shortcuts to the folders and applications that appear on the Send To submenu. Send To is a command that appears on the shortcut menu when you right-click a file or folder in Windows Explorer (or on the desktop). The SendTo folder is not hidden. You can add your own items to the SendTo menu by creating shortcuts here.

○ **AppData\Roaming\Microsoft\Windows\Start Menu** This folder contains items that appear on the Start menu. (The Start menu also includes items stored in a Public counterpart to this folder, %ProgramData%\Microsoft\ Windows\Start Menu\Programs\Startup.)

○ **AppData\Roaming\Microsoft\Windows\Templates** This folder contains shortcuts to document templates. These templates are typically used by the New command in Windows Explorer (on the shortcut menu) and are referenced by the FileName value in the HKCR*class*\ShellNew key, where *class* refers to the extension and file type.

- **Application Data** This is a hidden junction that redirects data to %UserProfile%\ AppData\Roaming.

- **Contacts** This folder, whose nearest counterpart in Windows XP is the Windows Address Book application (Wab.exe), stores contact information used by Windows Mail and (potentially) other applications.

- **Cookies** This is a hidden junction that redirects data to %UserProfile%\App-Data\Roaming\Microsoft\Windows\Cookies.

- **Desktop** This folder contains items that appear on the user's desktop, including files and shortcuts. (A Public counterpart also contributes items to the desktop.)

- **Documents** This folder is the default location for storing user documents in most applications.

- **Downloads** This folder, which has no predecessor in Windows XP, is the default location for storing items downloaded from websites.

- **Favorites** This folder contains Internet Explorer favorites.

- **Links** This folder contains shortcuts that appear in the Favorite Links section of the Navigation pane in Windows Explorer. You can create shortcuts here, but it's easier to drag Windows Explorer items into the Navigation pane.

- **Local Settings** This is a hidden junction that redirects data to %UserProfile%\AppData\Local.

- **Music** This folder, called My Music in Windows XP (where it was a subfolder of My Documents) is the default location for ripped CD tracks.

- **My Documents** This is a hidden junction that redirects data to %UserProfile%\Documents.

- **NetHood** This is a hidden junction that redirects data to %UserProfile%\AppData\Roaming\Microsoft\Windows\Network Shortcuts.

- **Pictures** This folder, called My Pictures in Windows XP (where it was a subfolder of My Documents) is the default storage location for programs that transfer images from external devices (such as digital cameras).

- **PrintHood** This is a hidden junction that redirects data to %UserProfile%\AppData\Roaming\Microsoft\Windows\Printer Shortcuts.

- **Recent** This is a hidden junction that redirects data to %UserProfile%\AppData\Roaming\Microsoft\Windows\Recent.

- **Saved Games** This folder is the default storage location for game programs that can save a game in progress.

- **Searches** This folder stores saved search specifications, allowing you to reuse previous searches.

- **SendTo** This is a hidden junction that redirects data to %UserProfile%\AppData\Roaming\Microsoft\Windows\SendTo.

- **Start Menu** This is a hidden junction that redirects data to %UserProfile%\AppData\Roaming\Microsoft\Windows\Start Menu.

- **Templates** This is a hidden junction that redirects data to %UserProfile%\AppData\Roaming\Microsoft\Windows\Templates.

- **Videos** This folder, called My Videos in Windows XP (where it was a subfolder of My Documents) is the default location for programs that transfer video data from external devices.

INSIDE OUT **Mapped network shares are automatically added to the Send To menu**

You can customize the Send To menu by adding shortcuts to %UserProfile%\AppData\ Roaming\Microsoft\Windows\SendTo. Many users, for example, like to add a shortcut to Notepad.exe there, so that they can right-click a file and deliver it to a text-rendering application via the Send To command. Curiously, if you map a network share, you not only get to access that share with a drive letter, you also get an automatic addition to your Send To menu. To map a share, open Windows Explorer and display the menu bar. (Press Alt if you don't want to keep the menu bar visible after you finish this procedure.) Choose Tools, Map Network Drive. In the Map Network Drive dialog box, supply a drive letter and the UNC path to the network share:

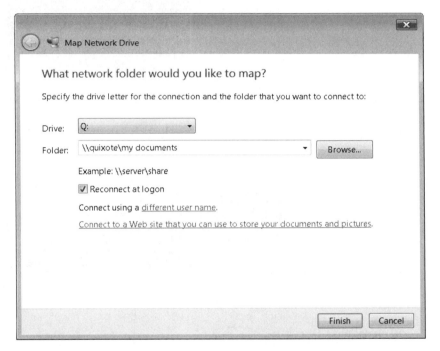

After you click Finish, the mapped drive will appear on your Send To menu:

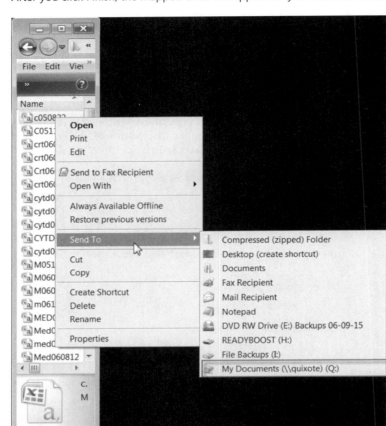

Common Profiles

Windows creates a local user profile for each user account, storing the profiles in account-named subfolders of %SystemDrive%\Users with folder names that match the account names. In addition to these user profiles, the operating system creates two others:

- **Public**   The Desktop and Start Menu folders of the Public profile are merged with those of the current user's profile to create the user's desktop and Start menu. Other folders in the Public profile are designed to hold documents, pictures, music, and other data that you want to share with other users. The Windows XP equivalent of the Public profile is called All Users, and this profile also served to store application data designed to be available to all users. In Windows Vista, this "all users" application data is stored in %SystemDrive%\ProgramData (which has its own system variable, %ProgramData%).

● **Default** When a user logs on to a computer for the first time (and his or her account is not set up to use a roaming profile or mandatory profile), Windows creates a new local profile by copying the contents of the Default profile to a new folder and giving it the user's name. Therefore, you can configure the Default profile the way you want new users' initial view of Windows to appear.

How Windows Vista Maintains Compatibility with Windows XP

Most applications that write to profile locations get those locations from the operating system as needed, rather than writing to absolute addresses. (Among other things, this allows applications to handle relocated folders.) A Windows XP program that's well-behaved will have no trouble accommodating the changed names and locations of profile folders in Windows Vista. On the other hand, a program that looks for Documents and Settings (the root of profile folders in Windows XP) as an absolute address could have a problem—were it not for the junctions (reparse points) that Windows Vista uses to redirect Windows XP folder names to the appropriate Windows Vista names.

You can see how these junctions are set up by running a Command Prompt session and typing **dir %userprofile%\ /ad**. The output from this command will look something like Figure 7-14.

Figure 7-14 Compatibility issues arising from the changes that Windows Vista made to profile folder names and locations are managed by junctions.

The reparse points in this directory list are identified by the label <JUNCTION>. The third column in the display lists the Windows XP folder name (SendTo, for example) followed, in brackets, by the redirect address (F:\Users\Craig\AppData\Roaming\Microsoft\Windows\SendTo). If you display the same folder (%UserProfile%) in Windows Explorer, with hidden and system files visible, the junctions will look like shortcuts and won't include any information about their targets. If you try to open one of these items, you'll be rebuffed:

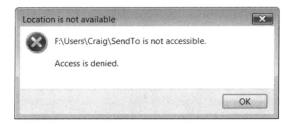

That's because in all of these junctions, the Everyone group has a Deny access control entry preventing users from listing folder contents (see Figure 7-15). This Deny ACE may seem drastic, but it's Windows Vista's way of telling you to keep your hands off the compatibility infrastructure.

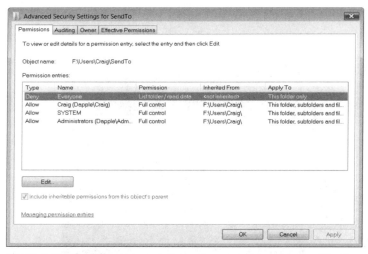

Figure 7-15 The Deny access control entry prevents members of the Everyone group (that's you) from displaying the contents of junction folders.

Chapter 7

CAUTION

The Deny ACE does not prevent you from deleting a junction, but you should never perform such a deletion unless you absolutely know what you are doing. Although a junction looks like an ordinary shortcut in Windows Explorer, it's not what it appears to be. Deleting a shortcut deletes a pointer, leaving the pointee unchanged. Deleting a junction has the same effect as deleting the location to which it points.

Compatibility and Virtualization

Many legacy applications write data (such as configuration information) to areas that are ordinarily inaccessible to standard accounts. This behavior presented few problems in Windows XP, because most users ran with administrative privileges. In Windows Vista, that is no longer the case. To avoid errors that would otherwise arise because users, even those with administrative accounts, are now expected to carry out most operations in a nonadministrative security context, Windows Vista redirects writes (and subsequent reads) to per-user virtualized locations.

So, for example, if an application, running in your security context, attempts to write to a location within %ProgramFiles%, the write will be redirected to a comparable location within %LocalAppData%\VirtualStore. When the application subsequently reads what it has written, the read request is redirected to the same virtualized location. As far as the application is concerned, everything is perfectly normal, and the operating system has prevented standard-user access to the %ProgramFiles% folder.

If you open a %ProgramFiles% folder in which a virtualized write has occurred, a Compatibility Files button will appear on the Command bar:

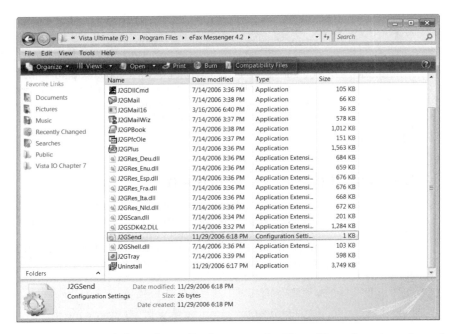

Clicking Compatibility Files will take you to the VirtualStore location where the data is actually written:

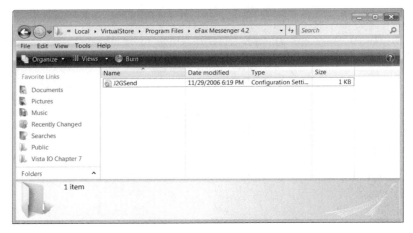

(Note that only the configuration settings file is virtualized; the other files in the %ProgramFiles% location were created by the program's setup routine, which ran under the TrustedInstaller account.)

If you try to edit the file at its apparent location (under %ProgramFiles%), you'll be told the file doesn't exist:

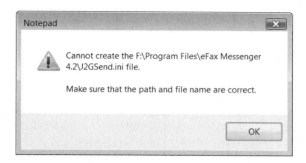

But when the program itself needs to read or update its configuration settings, Windows Vista will transparently redirect it to the VirtualStore location.

A similar form of virtualization protects sensitive areas of the registry. Programmatic access to HKLM\Software is redirected to HKLM\Software\Classes\VirtualStore.

Note the following about virtualization:

- Virtualization does not affect administrative access to files or registry keys.

- Virtualization does not affect 64-bit processes.

- Virtualized data does not move with roaming profiles.

- Virtualization is provided for the sake of compatibility with current legacy programs; Microsoft does not promise to include it with future versions of Windows.

Relocating Personal Data Folders

Although the organizational scheme that Windows Vista has adopted for your personal data folders—the eleven visible subfolders of %UserProfile% (see Figure 7-13 earlier in this chapter)—is much more rational than its predecessor in Windows XP, some users will want to relocate some or all of these folders. If your system volume doesn't have enough space for your video collection, for example, you might want to move the Videos folder to a disk or partition that has more room.

But even if space is plentiful on the system disk, a good argument can be made for putting all personal data folders on a volume other than %SystemDrive%. The gist of the argument is:

- Separating the operating system and program files from personal data makes it far easier to restore health in the event that your system files become corrupted or damaged by malware.

- Separating system and program files from personal data encourages the use of disk-imaging backup programs, such as the Complete PC Backup program included with Windows Vista. With personal files located on a separate volume, image backups of system drives are smaller and take less time to create.

- Separating system and program files from personal data makes it easier to upgrade to a new version of the operating system (or a different operating system).

For a cogent elaboration of these by ZDNet blogger George Ou, see *http://www.vista-io.com/0701*.

You can easily relocate any or all of your personal data folders as follows:

1. Click your account name at the top of the Start menu's right column to open the root folder of your profile (%UserProfile%), right-click a folder that you want to relocate, and choose Properties from the shortcut menu.

2. On the Location tab of the properties dialog box, enter the address that you want to relocate to. For example, to move this Documents folder from F:\Users\Jean\Documents to J:\Users\Jean\Documents, you could simply replace the F with a J at the beginning of the path:

3. Click OK. Windows will ask permission to create the target folder if it doesn't already exist. Click Yes. A Move Folder dialog box similar to this one will appear:

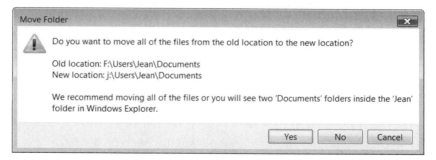

4. Unless you have some good reason not to move the existing files from the original location to the new one, click Yes.

It's really not a good idea *not* to click Yes in this dialog box. First, it's difficult to imagine why you would want some of your personal documents in a given category on one disk and the rest on another (if you want to segregate the existing material from whatever's coming in the future, make a subfolder in the new location instead of leaving the past behind). Second, because %UserProfile% is a system-generated folder, not an ordinary data folder that corresponds to a fixed disk location, leaving some files behind will give you two identically named subfolders in %UserProfile%. Figure 7-16 illustrates the effect. One of each of these identically named folder pairs represents the original location, and the other represents the new. But which is which?

Figure 7-16 Leaving files behind while relocating personal data folders can make you see double.

If you move any or all of your personal data folders, you must take one additional step following the move: You must add the new locations to the list of folders that the search engine indexes. The index includes the original profile locations by default, but it doesn't pay attention when you relocate. For information about how to do this, see "Adding Folders to the Index," later in this chapter.

Using and Configuring Search and Indexing

As we mentioned at the beginning of this chapter, Rover has retired and will not be missed. In his place, Windows Vista has provided a speedy indexed search facility that's accessible everywhere, mostly intuitive, and generally more than satisfactory. Perhaps more than any other new feature in Windows Vista, it has the potential to change the way you work—because it almost relieves you of the need to structure your folders and files sensibly. We don't recommend that you abandon organizational logic, but we urge you to learn the power of this new search tool.

Where to Search

You can search wherever you see a Search box. Specifically that means the following:

- From the Start menu
- From a Windows Explorer folder (including Control Panel and Computer)
- From a common dialog box
- From the Search folder

Searching from the Start Menu

The Start menu search box is designed to help you find programs on your Start menu, websites in your history or favorites, messages in your e-mail store, contact information (in Microsoft Outlook, for example, or in your Contacts folder), as well as files and folders in your file system. Results are categorized and limited to the space available in the left side of the Start menu. If you're not sure what an item returned by the search is, you can hover your mouse over it and read a tip. The tip might include media information, as in the example shown in Figure 7-17, or it might display the full path of a file or folder.

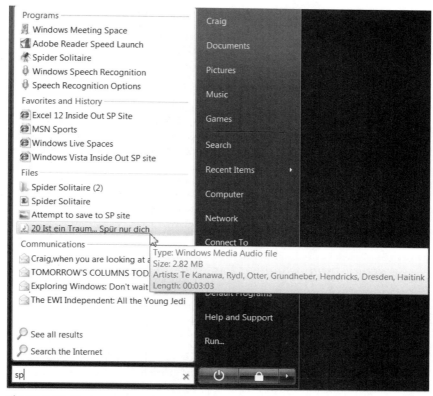

Figure 7-17 Start menu searches return categorized shortcuts to programs, files, websites, e-mail, and contact information.

The Start menu search box is a "word wheel"—which means that the search begins as soon as you start typing, and each new character you type refines the results. In Figure 7-17, for example, the two characters we've typed—*s* and *p*—are sufficient to return Windows Meeting *Sp*ace, *Sp*ider Solitaire, references to a SharePoint (*SP*) site and Windows Live *Sp*aces, plus an assortment of *sp*am.

Because the word wheel action is snappy and the Start menu search is optimized to find items on the Start menu, typing a few characters here can be a great alternative to hunting up a menu item manually. It's at least as quick and possibly quicker to run Spider Solitaire by typing *sp* and clicking in the Programs area of the search results than to open the Games folder and double-click an icon there. If the program you need is buried in the All Programs section of the Start menu, it's even more likely that you'll get to it quicker by searching.

If the item you're looking for doesn't appear in the search results, it's probably because the Start menu doesn't have room for it. In that event, you can click one of the two links that appear at the bottom of the search results. See All Results hands your search off to the Search folder, which can display as many hits as needed (and where you can refine or alter your search if necessary). Search The Internet takes you to your default internet search provider.

INSIDE OUT   You can search for programs that aren't on the Start menu

Searching from the Start menu search box can be a good way to run a program that isn't on the Start menu—such as Registry Editor or an .msc console. The Start menu's search will look for executables in system folders that are not ordinarily indexed. Because the search engine's word wheel feature works only with indexed locations, however, you'll need to type the full name before it will appear in the search results. You'll also need to identify the program by the name of its executable file, rather than its friendly title. Typing **Registry Editor** in the Search box will get you nothing (unless you happen to have a shortcut stored under that name). Typing **regedit** will summon the program.

Searching from Windows Explorer

Searching from a Windows Explorer folder yields an uncategorized list of items from that folder and its subfolders. It's a great way to find something when you know more or less where it is. For example, if you're looking for a music item but you're not sure how the subfolders of your Music folder are set up, don't even bother trying to figure the structure out; just type in the Search box.

Here again, the word wheel is your friend. Unless your fingers are as fleet as Rachmaninoff's, the odds are that any of his music you have will appear in the Search results long before you get to the last syllable of his name (see Figure 7-18). (What's more, if you try to type the whole thing and make a mistake somewhere along the line, you're likely to wind up with nothing.)

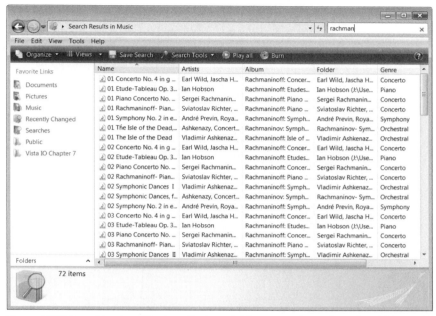

Figure 7-18 Searching in a Windows Explorer folder returns items from that folder and its subfolders, relieving you of the need to know how the subfolders are organized.

The behavior just described assumes default settings on the Search tab of the Folder Options dialog box, shown in Figure 7-19 on the next page. (To get there, choose Organize, Folder And Search Options in Windows Explorer). If your search scope does not extend to subfolders, be sure that Include Subfolders When Typing In The Search Box is selected. If you don't get word wheel behavior, be sure that Find Partial Matches is selected.

Figure 7-19 On the Search tab of the Folder Options dialog box, you can configure word wheel behavior, content search, and other important details.

The preceding also assumes that you're searching an indexed location, such as one of your personal data folders (these are indexed by default). If you need to search system files, which are not ordinarily indexed, you might want to consider adding them to the index. See "Adding Folders to the Index," later in this chapter.

A search in a Windows Explorer folder initially returns a maximum of 5,000 items. If your search generates more than 5,000 hits, the system will pause and display an Information bar, like the one shown in Figure 7-20. As the message indicates, you have two choices. You can refine your search or click the Information bar to see the rest of your results. Generally, if you've already got 5,000 items, seeing a few more isn't going to help you pinpoint the one you need, but if you want to see the whole lot, Windows will continue the search.

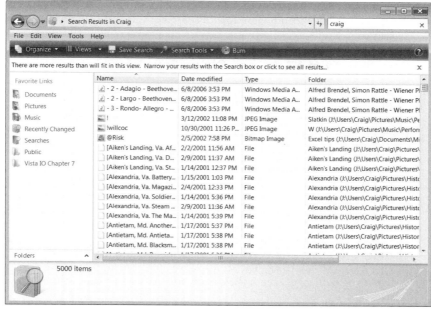

Figure 7-20 Windows will alert you if your search is so broad that it returns more than 5,000 items.

One way to refine the search is to add a second criterion, using the AND conjunction. For information about doing this, see "Using Multiple Criteria in the Search Box," later in this chapter.

If your search yields nothing, you'll see an Advanced Search link:

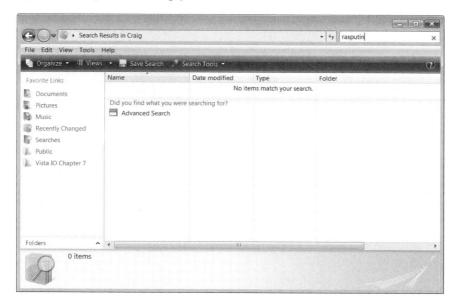

Clicking this link takes you to the Search folder, with the Search pane unfurled. Here you can click Advanced Search to add search criteria and change the scope of your search. For details, see "Using the Advanced Search pane," later in this chapter.

Searching from a Common Dialog Box

Like the Search box in Windows Explorer, the Search box in a common Open or Save As dialog box takes as its default scope the current folder and its subfolders. In most applications, the dialog box is already filtered for a particular file type, so that file type is the only one the search will consider.

Searching from a dialog box might not sound all that nifty at first. After all, if you're trying to open a file and you don't know exactly where it is, you can always hunt for it from a Windows Explorer folder, then double-click it when the search engine ferrets it out. But it can be quite useful if you're already in the dialog box and find yourself confronted with a superfluity of files. Figure 7-21, for example, shows the Open dialog box from Paint, focused on the Screen Shots folder for this chapter. At the moment there are more than 80 images in this folder, consisting of three groups—a set beginning with the characters *f07*, another group beginning with *g07*, and a third group of miscellaneous illogically named pictures. The simplest way to locate and open the last in the *f07* series is not to go scrolling through the dialog box but to type those three characters in the Search box.

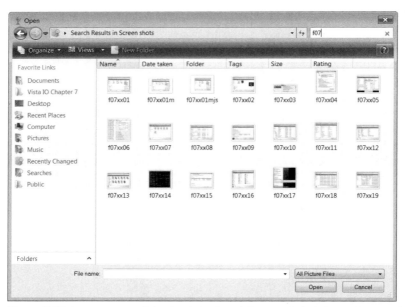

Figure 7-21 In a common dialog box, the Search box can help bring order to a chaotic folder.

Searching from the Search Folder

The Search folder is the place to begin if really have no idea where an item you want might be—or if you want a collection of items that are scattered in a variety of unrelated indexed folders. To get to the Search box, open the Start menu and choose Search.

The Search folder, shown in Figure 7-22, searches all indexed folders, by default. (It can certainly be set to a different search scope, but if you arrive at the folder by choosing Search on the Start menu, the scope will be set to Indexed Locations.) Near the top of the folder, below the Address bar, the Search pane contains filter buttons that constrain the results to six result categories: All, E-Mail, Document, Picture, Music, and Other. If you are looking for a specific kind of information—an e-mail message, for example—you can save the search engine a little trouble (and yourself a moment of time) by selecting that category before you begin searching. (The Other category in an indexed search produces miscellaneous items, such as folders, Microsoft OneNote notebooks, web feeds, videos, and scripts.) Alternatively, if you want everything, you can start with All—then use the categories to look at specific kinds of results after the search is complete.

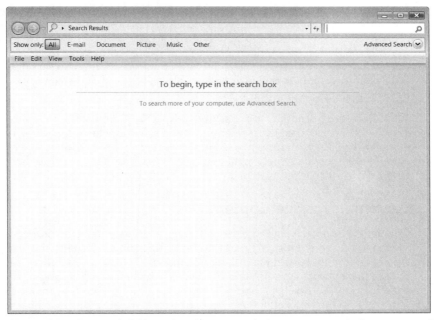

Figure 7-22 The Search folder is the place to search if you want a particular category of result, if you're not sure where in your folder system an item you want is located, or if you want to perform an advanced search.

To the right of the filter buttons is an Advanced Search button that enables you to launch more complex searches or searches of alternative locations (including unindexed folders). For more information, see "Using Advanced Search," later in this chapter.

INSIDE OUT

From anywhere in Windows, you can get to the Search folder by pressing Windows logo key+F. From Windows Explorer or the desktop, you can also get there by pressing F3. The two shortcuts are not the same, however. Windows logo key+F sets the search scope to its default, Indexed Locations. F3 sets the scope to whatever folder you were in when you pressed it (or to the desktop, if you started there).

After a search in Windows Explorer has completed, you can display the Search pane by clicking Search Tools on the Command bar, then clicking Search Pane. This is a good way to filter a large result set into a particular file category.

Saving a Search

After you have completed a search in Windows Explorer or the Search folder, you can manipulate the results using any of the techniques described earlier in this chapter (see "Sorting, Filtering, Stacking, and Grouping," earlier in this chapter). You can also use a Save Search button that appears on the Command bar to preserve the search specification for later reuse. The saved search is stored in %UserProfile%\Searches, and one of the default shortcuts in the Favorite Links list (at the top of the Navigation pane in Windows Explorer) provides quick transport to this folder.

When you save a search, you are saving its specification, not its current results. The search becomes a virtual subfolder of %UserProfile%\Searches, and the next time you reopen the folder, Windows re-executes the search. (If you're interested in the XML data that defines the search, right-click the saved search in your Searches folder, choose Open With, and choose Notepad.)

Searching for File Content

By default, the search engine indexes the contents, as well as the properties (name, author, size, and so on) for file types that typically include conventional text. Therefore, with such things as word processing documents, PDF files, Excel workbooks, and PowerPoint presentations, you should be able to locate items you're looking for on the basis of their contents as well as their properties—assuming, of course, that the items in question are stored in indexed folders. To search for some text within a file, enter it in the Search box, just as you would any other search criterion. Note the following:

- The search engine ignores capitalization.

- The search engine ordinarily ignores accents, umlauts, and other diacritical marks. If you need to be able to distinguish, say, Händel from Handel, type **Index** in the Start menu Search box. That should bring Indexing Options to the top of the search results. Open Indexing Options, click Advanced (you'll need administrative credentials), and then select Treat Similar Words With Diacritics As Different Words.

- To search for an exact phrase, enclose the phrase within quote marks. Otherwise you'll be searching for each word individually.

- To extend content search to folders that are not indexed, select Always Search File Names And Contents (Might Be Slow) on the Search tab of the Folder Options dialog box (see Figure 7-19 earlier in this chapter). Note the warning; searching the innards of unindexed files is likely to be exceedingly slow. (Use this option when you need it, and then disable it again for ordinary circumstances.)

Searching for Properties Other Than Name

You can search on the basis of any property recognized by the file system. To see the whole list of available properties, right-click any column heading in Windows Explorer and choose More from the shortcut menu. The Choose Details list that appears (see Figure 7-5 earlier in this chapter) enumerates the available properties.

Ordinarily when you enter a value in the Search box, Windows searches all possible properties for matches with that value. That often generates more search results than you want. You can limit the search to a particular property by typing the property name followed by a colon. For example, to find all documents of which Jean is the author, omitting documents from subfolders that include the name *Jean*, as well as documents that have *Jean* in their names, you would type **author:jean** in the Search box. (To eliminate documents authored by Jeanne, Jeannette, or Jeanelle, you could enclose *jean* in quote marks.)

When searching on the basis of dates, you can use long or short forms, as you please. For example, the search values

```
Date modified:6/15/06
```

and

```
Date modified:06/15/2006
```

are equivalent.

To search for dates before or after a particular date, use the less-than (<) and greater-than (>) operators. For example:

```
Date modified:>11/16/06
```

would search for dates falling later than November 16, 2006. Use the same two operators to specify file sizes below and above some value.

Searching by File Extension

To search for files with a particular extension, you can simply enter the extension in the Search box. You will get a more focused search by including an asterisk wildcard and a period, like this:

```
*.ext
```

If you omit the asterisk and period, you will get files that incorporate the extension in their contents as well as in their filenames—which might or might not be what you want.

Note that system folders, such as Program Files, Windows, and System32, are not included in the index, by default. If you want to search for program files, you will need to search outside the index. If you do this often, you'll probably want to add certain system folders to the index. (See "Searching Outside the Index" and "Adding Folders to the Index," later in this chapter.)

Using Multiple Criteria in the Search Box

You can use the Boolean operators AND, OR, and NOT to combine or negate criteria in the Search box. These operators need to be spelled in capital letters (or they will be treated as ordinary text). You can also use parentheses to group criteria. Table 7-1 provides some examples of combined criteria.

Table 7-1. Some examples of complex search values

This search value	Returns
Siechert AND Bott	Items in which any property equals Siechert and any property equals Bott
Siechert NOT Bott	Items in which a property equals Siechert and no property equals Bott
Tag:Tax AND Author:Doug	Items authored by Doug with a tag set to Tax
Tag:Tax AND Author:(Doug OR Craig) AND Date Modified:<1/1/07	Items authored by Doug or Craig, last modified before January 1, 2007, with a tag set to Tax

INSIDE OUT

When you use multiple criteria based on different properties, an OR conjunction is assumed unless you specify otherwise. The search value tag:Ed Author:Carl is equivalent to the search value tag:Ed OR Author:Carl.

Using Advanced Search

The Advanced Search pane, which you can display by clicking Advanced Search in the Search folder, offers a form that you can fill out to specify either a complex search or to specify a particular search scope (or both). Figure 7-23 illustrates the Advanced Search pane.

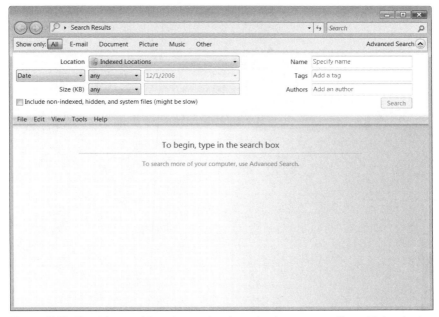

Figure 7-23 The Advanced Search pane is a form that lets you specify multiple criteria or control the search location.

Using Multiple Criteria in Advanced Search

The Advanced Search form makes it pretty straightforward to employ multiple criteria. Just fill out whatever boxes you need and click Search. The one crucial detail to remember is that multiple criteria are ORed, not ANDed. Any ANDs or NOTs that you need must be entered in the Search box, using the techniques described above (see "Using Multiple Criteria in the Search Box"). You'll also need to use the Search box if you want to base the hunt on a property not included on the form.

INSIDE OUT

To search the contents of all indexed files, use the Search box in the Search folder. Before you begin, click Advanced Search and make sure that the Location field is set to Indexed Locations.

Searching Nondefault Locations with Advanced Search

The Advanced Search form defaults to searching Indexed Locations (all of them). You can search elsewhere by opening the Location list. The list (see Figure 7-24) will include local and mapped hard drives and optical drives.

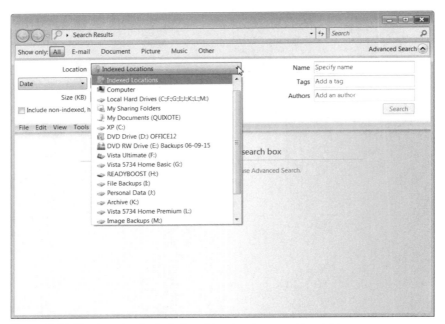

Figure 7-24 The Location list includes all local and mapped hard drives.

If you don't find what you want (for example, if you need to search a network drive that isn't mapped to a drive letter on your own system), scroll to the bottom of the list and click Choose Search Locations. The Choose Search Locations dialog box, shown in Figure 7-25, lets you specify multiple locations, both local and remote.

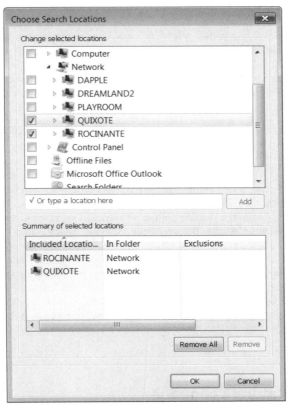

Figure 7-25 In the Choose Search Locations dialog box, you can specify one or more search locations, including network servers.

When you search an unindexed location, an Information Bar appears to warn you that the search is likely to be slow. You can click the Information Bar to add your current search target to the index. (See "Adding Folders to the Index," later in this chapter.) Be aware that just adding the folder to the index won't make the search any quicker until the system has had time to update the index.

Searching for Content in Unindexed Locations

After the search engine has finished performing a search on an unindexed location, it will display a link at the bottom of the search results, asking if you would like to continue your search into the contents of files in this location:

If you have time to wait, click Search In File Contents.

Searching for Hidden and System Files

The search engine ordinarily excludes system folders, even when you're searching unindexed locations. If you're hunting for a critical system file, that default will frustrate you. Click the Include Non-Indexed, Hidden, And System Files (Might Be Slow) check box to override it. To change the default, choose Organize, Folder And Search Options in Windows Explorer. On the Search tab of the Folder Options dialog box (see Figure 7-19 earlier in this chapter), select Include System Directories.

INSIDE OUT   Perform an indexed search of a remote folder

Windows Vista cannot index server shares, and searching a server without indexing can be excruciatingly slow. But if Windows Vista is running on the server and the folder you're interested is included in the remote computer's index, the search engine on your computer will query the remote index before beginning a file-by-file ("grep") search. If the server is not running Windows Vista, you can speed up a search of remote files by making them available offline. When you right-click the remote folder in Windows Explorer and choose Always Available Offline, Windows caches that folder on your system, and adds the cached copy to the index. As soon as the system has finished indexing your offline files, you'll be able to search them as quickly as you can search your local documents. (Note: offline files are not available in Windows Vista Home Basic or Windows Vista Home Premium.)

Searching with Natural Language

If you don't fancy Boolean formulations, try the natural-language approach to searching. With natural language enabled, the search engine promises to accept queries in plain English (see Figure 7-26). The system looks for key words (like "e-mail"), filters out prepositions (such as "from"), handles conjunctions without making you capitalize them, and assumes the rest of what you type consists of property values that it should try to match.

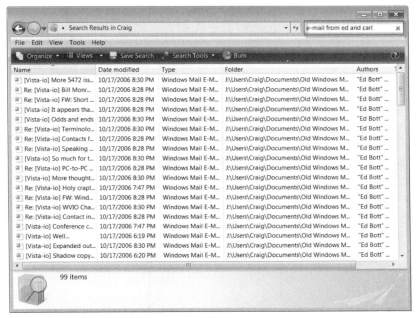

Figure 7-26 With natural language searching, you can forget about Boolean operators and express yourself in plain English.

To turn natural language searching on, choose Organize, Folder And Search Options in Windows Explorer. In the Folder Options dialog box, click the Search tab. On the Search tab (see Figure 7-19 earlier in this chapter), select Use Natural Language Search.

Administering the Search Engine and Index

Options for configuring the behavior of the search engine (as opposed to the content of the index) appear on the Search tab of the Folder Options dialog box, which is illustrated in Figure 7-19. Some of these options have been discussed elsewhere in this chapter. (See "Searching for File Content," "Searching for Hidden and System Files," and "Searching with Natural Language.") The Don't Use The Index When Searching The File System (Might Be Slow) check box is self-explanatory; it's hard to think of a reason to use it. The Include Compressed Files (.ZIP, .CAB) option enables the search engine to find files (but not their contents) stored within compressed archives.

The options for configuring the Index are accessible via the Indexing Options dialog box. You can find this in Control Panel, but it's usually quicker to type Index in the Start menu Search box. Indexing Options should appear at the top, under the heading Programs. Many of the choices offered by means of this dialog box will require that you pass a UAC prompt (in other words, you'll need administrative credentials).

Checking the Status of Your Index

As Figure 7-27 shows, the Indexing Options dialog box is the place to go if you want to confirm that your index is up to date. If the index is not up to date, you'll most likely be told that "Indexing speed is reduced due to user activity." Unfortunately, the system won't give you any details about whether the index is barely underway or nearly complete. If you haven't recently added any new folders to the index but have simply been changing a few files in the course of normal work, the index should stay close to complete (assuming you've ever had a complete index). If you've just added a bunch of new folders, you might have to wait a little longer before you have an up-to-date index.

Figure 7-27 The Indexing Options dialog box shows you how many items have been indexed and whether the index is up to date.

The Indexing Options dialog box is also your gateway to separate dialog boxes that let you rebuild a corrupted index, change the location where the index stores its data, add folders to the index, change how the index deals with particular file types, and so on.

Indexing Encrypted Files

The index ordinarily omits content indexing of encrypted files. If you need those files indexed, click Advanced in the Indexing Options dialog box (see Figure 7-27 above). On the Index Settings tab of the Advanced Options dialog box (shown in Figure 7-28), select Index Encrypted Files.

Figure 7-28 You can use this dialog box to rebuild an index that has stopped functioning.

Rebuilding an Index

It's not supposed to happen, but if your index stops working for any reason (for example, if searches that are ordinarily snappy start evoking memories of Rover), click Rebuild on the Index Settings tab of the Advanced Options dialog box. Then give your system time to recreate the index.

Moving the Index to a Faster Drive

By default, the index files live in subfolders of %ProgramData%\Microsoft\Search. If you install a faster hard disk on your computer, you can improve search performance by moving the index files to the new disk. Simply type a new location in the Current Location box (on the Index Settings tab of the Advanced Options dialog box; see Figure 7-28).

Changing the Way the Index Handles Particular File Types

On the File Types tab of the Advanced Options dialog box (see Figure 7-29) you will find a long list of file types. Those with selected check boxes are indexed; those with clear check boxes are not. If you need to add a file type to the index, select its check box.

Figure 7-29 The File Types list shows whether and how each file type is included in the index.

Each of the selected file types can be indexed in one of two manners—properties only or properties and contents. The option buttons below the list of file types show you which treatment is assigned to the currently selected file type. Windows Vista ordinarily looks at the contents of files only in file types that have human-readable text and for which a suitable filter is available. (The filter enables the indexer to parse the file; HTML, e-mail, and PDF files, for example, all require filters that are different from a plain-text filter.) If you don't need to search content in a file type that gets content indexing, you can save some processing overhead by selecting the file type and choosing Index Properties Only. If you need content indexing where none is currently provided, you can try switching a file from Properties Only to Index Properties And File Content. The search engine will apply a plain-text filter—which might or might not yield satisfactory results.

Adding Folders to the Index

To see what folders are currently indexed and add new ones (or remove current ones), click Modify in the Indexing Options dialog box. The Indexed Locations dialog box (see Figure 7-30) initially doesn't tell you much—except that it shows which items, other than ordinary file folders, are included in the index (Microsoft Office OneNote notebooks and offline files, for example).

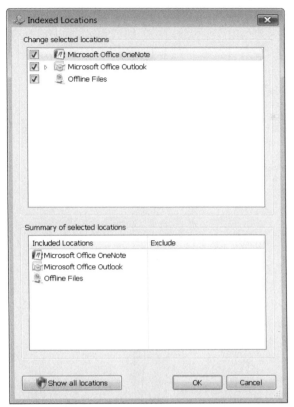

Figure 7-30 Some items other than ordinary file folders might be included in your index—data files from Microsoft Outlook, for example.

To see which folders are indexed, click Show all Locations. In the bottom portion of the ensuing dialog box (see Figure 7-31 on the next page), you'll find a summary of the index locations—the same summary that appears in the Indexing Options dialog box (see Figure 7-27). The top half of the dialog box is where the action is.

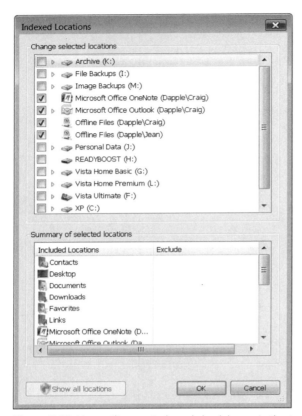

Figure 7-31 Use outline controls and check boxes in the top half of this dialog box to add or remove folders.

Selected check boxes indicate items that are indexed completely. Clear check boxes do not denote items that are completely unindexed. In Figure 7-31, for example, much of drive J (Personal Data) is in fact indexed, but you would have to click the outline control to see which subfolders are included and which are not. Once you get down to the appropriate level of detail, you can select check boxes for folders you want to add or clear them for folders you no longer need to index.

Restoring Files and Folders with Previous Versions

The Previous Versions feature in Windows Vista is a side benefit of the way the operating system now creates backup copies and restore points. With System Protection turned on (its default state), Windows creates a daily *restore point* that lets you roll your system back to an earlier state in the event that a new installation or some other event creates instability. (For more information, see "Configuring System Protection Options," Chapter 2.) Restore points are built from *shadow copies*, which are essentially change logs for files and folders. Shadow copies are also created by the Windows Backup program (for more details, see "Using the Windows Backup Program," Chapter 20). If you perform regular periodic backups, you have the Backup program's shadow copies as well as those created by System Protection.

You can use shadow copies to open, copy, or restore a document or folder as it stood at an earlier point in time. For example, if you have accidentally deleted files from a folder and you have a shadow copy from a time before you made the deletions, you can recover the deleted files by restoring the earlier version of the folder. (As an alternative to restoring the earlier version, you can create a copy of the folder, with the copy reflecting the earlier state.)

Note the following about shadow copies:

- Shadow copies have a limited shelf life. By default, the operating system reserves up to 15 percent of a disk's capacity for shadow copies. If the allotted space is filled, the earliest copies are replaced by the newest.

- Shadow copies record changes only. If you haven't changed a file, you won't have (or need) a shadow copy.

- Shadow copies in Windows Vista are completely erased if you boot your computer into a different operating system.

This last point bears reiteration: if you have set up your system to dual-boot with, say, Windows XP, starting up Windows XP wipes out your shadow copies in Windows Vista. That includes your restore points as well as your previous versions.

To see what previous versions are available for a file or folder, right-click the item in Windows Explorer and choose Restore Previous Versions. The Previous Versions tab of the object's properties dialog box (see Figure 7-32) will list the available shadow copies. Select the one you want, and then click Open (to view the file or folder), Copy (to create a copy of it without changing the original), or Restore (to overwrite the object in its current state with the selected copy).

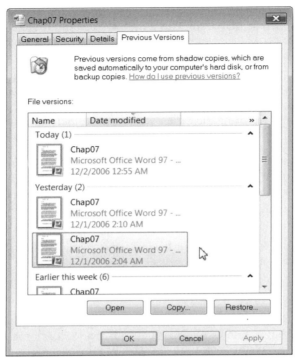

Figure 7-32 Shadow copies enable you to return a file or folder to a previous state.

> **Note**
> Previous versions are not available for system files or file's in an offline cache.

Recovering Files and Folders with the Recycle Bin

The Recycle Bin provides protection against accidental erasure of files. In most cases, when you delete one or more files or folders, the deleted items go to the Recycle Bin, not into the ether. If you change your mind, you can go to the bin and recover the thrown-out items. Eventually, when the bin fills up, Windows begins emptying it, permanently deleting the files that have been there the longest.

The following kinds of deletions do not go to the Recycle Bin:

- Files stored on removable disks
- Files stored on network drives
- Files deleted from compressed (zipped) folders

You can bypass the Recycle Bin yourself, permanently deleting an item, by holding down the Shift key while you press the Delete key. You might want to do this if you need to get rid of some very large files and you're sure you'll never want those files back. Skipping the Recycle Bin in this case will reclaim some disk space.

You can also turn off the Recycle Bin's services permanently. (For more details, see "Disabling the Recycle Bin," on the next page.)

Changing the Amount of Space Allocated to the Recycle Bin

To see and adjust the amount of space currently used by the Recycle Bin for each drive that it protects, right-click the Recycle Bin icon on your desktop and choose Properties from the shortcut menu. In the Recycle Bin Properties dialog box (shown in Figure 7-33), you can select a drive and enter a different value in the Custom Size box. Windows ordinarily allocates about 7.5 percent of a disk's space for recycling. (When the bin is full, the oldest items give way to the newest.) If you think that amount of space is excessive, enter a lower value.

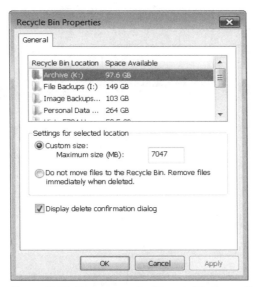

Figure 7-33 You can use the Recycle Bin Properties dialog box to alter the amount of space devoted to the bin—or to turn the feature off for selected drives.

> **Note**
>
> If you don't see a Recycle Bin icon on your desktop, right-click the desktop, choose Personalize, and then click Change Desktop Icons. In the Desktop Icon Settings dialog box, select Recycle Bin and click OK.

Disabling the Recycle Bin

If you'd rather do without the Recycle Bin for a particular drive, select the drive, then click Do Not Move Files To The Recycle Bin. Remove Files Immediately When Deleted. This action is equivalent to setting the maximum capacity to 0.

Suppressing Confirmation Prompts

Whether the Recycle Bin is enabled or disabled, Windows normally displays a confirmation prompt when you delete something. If that prompt annoys you, clear the Display Delete Confirmation Dialog check box.

Restoring Files and Folders

When you open the Recycle Bin, Windows displays the names of recently deleted items in an ordinary Windows Explorer window, as shown in Figure 7-34. In Details view, you can see when each item was deleted and which folder it was deleted from. You can use the column headings to sort the folder—for example, to display the items that have been in the bin the longest at the top with more recent arrivals below.

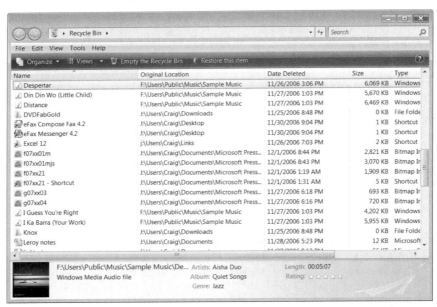

Figure 7-34 You can get useful information about deleted items by looking at the Recycle Bin's columns in Details view.

INSIDE OUT

Double-clicking Recycle Bin on the desktop lists deleted items from all drives. To focus on a particular drive, you can sort the Original Location column. Alternatively, you can open the Recycle Bin for a particular drive by opening that drive in Windows Explorer. On the View tab of the Folder Options dialog box, clear the Hide Protected Operating System Files (Recommended) check box, and answer the confirmation prompt. Now, a folder named $Recycle.Bin should appear. Open that folder, and then open the Recycle Bin subfolder. You can manipulate deleted items in this drive-specific Recycle Bin the same way you manipulate items in the general one.

Note that deleted folders are shown only as folders; you don't see the names of items contained within the folders. If you restore a deleted folder, however, Windows re-creates the folder and its contents.

The Restore This Item command (on the Command bar) puts the item back in the folder from which it was deleted. If that folder doesn't currently exist, Windows asks your permission to re-create it.

If you want, you can restore a file or folder to a different location. Select the item, choose Edit, Move To Folder, and then specify the new location. (If the menu bar isn't currently visible, you can right-click the item, choose Cut, and then paste it in the new location.) Or, simplest of all, you can drag the item out of the Recycle Bin and put it where you want it.

Purging the Recycle Bin

A deleted file sitting in your Recycle Bin takes up as much space as it did before it was deleted. If you're deleting files to free up space for new programs and documents, transferring them to the Recycle Bin won't help. You need to remove them permanently. The safest way to do this is to move the items to another storage medium—a different hard disk or a removable disk, for example.

If you're sure you'll never need a particular file again, however, you can delete it in the normal way, and then purge it from the Recycle Bin. Display the Recycle Bin, select the item, and then press Delete.

To empty the Recycle Bin entirely, right-click the Recycle Bin icon on your desktop and choose Empty Recycle Bin from the shortcut menu. Or display the Recycle Bin and click Empty The Recycle Bin in the Command bar.

Maximizing Storage Space with NTFS Compression and Compressed (Zipped) Folders

Even a huge hard disk eventually fills to capacity. To help you avoid running out of room, Windows Vista supports two forms of file compression: NTFS file compression and compressed (zipped) folders. Here are some essential points to note about these two compression methods:

- NTFS compression, available only on NTFS-formatted disks, achieves only modest compression but is extremely easy to use. After you have compressed a set of files and folders, files look and behave exactly as before. The only outwardly visible difference is that the names of your files are shown in blue. However, if you look at the properties dialog box for a compressed file, you'll see on the General tab that the Size On Disk value is (usually) considerably smaller than the Size value; with uncompressed files, the Size On Disk value is the same or slightly larger (because of the way disk space is allocated).

- Windows Explorer and your applications decompress NTFS-compressed files when you open them and recompress them when you save. This on-the-fly compression and decompression occurs so quickly that you shouldn't notice any performance effect.

- Files compressed via NTFS compression remain compressed only as long as they stay on NTFS disks. If you move a compressed file to a FAT32 device or e-mail it, the file is expanded to normal size, making it compatible with other machines and other viewers' software.

- NTFS compression is incompatible with NTFS encryption. A file can be compressed or encrypted (or neither), but not both.

- You can get more dramatic compression with zipped folders than with NTFS compression. Moreover, a zipped folder stays compressed, no matter where it is. Thus zipped folders are an ideal way to compress large files for e-mailing or uploading to internet sites.

- Because zipped folders use an industry-stand compression format, many of your associates will be able to work with your zipped folders, even if they don't use Windows.

- Windows Explorer compresses and decompresses files in zipped folders on the fly. But your applications do not. Therefore, you can open a zipped-folder file in its parent application by double-clicking it in Windows Explorer but not by using an application's Open command.

Implementing NTFS Compression

NTFS compression is implemented by means of a file attribute, much as read-only status is. To compress a file or folder using NTFS compression, follow these steps:

1. Right-click the file or folder (or selection of files or folders) in Windows Explorer and choose Properties from the shortcut menu.

2. On the General tab of the properties dialog box, click Advanced.

3. Select Compress Contents To Save Disk Space and then click OK in both dialog boxes.

Using Zipped Folders

To create a new archive using zipped folders, follow these steps:

1. In Windows Explorer, display the folder in which you want the new archive to reside.

2. Right-click any empty space in the folder.

3. From the shortcut menu, choose New, Compressed (Zipped) Folder.

4. Name the folder.

To add files and folders to your archive, simply copy or move them into the zipped folder.

You can also create an archive and copy one or more files or folders to it in one step by using the Send To command. To compress a single file or folder, follow these steps:

1. Right-click the file or folder.

2. From the shortcut menu, choose Send To, Compressed (Zipped) Folder.

Windows creates an archive with the same name as the selected object.

To compress a group of files or folders, follow these steps:

1. Select everything you want to compress.

2. Right-click one of the selected objects.

3. From the shortcut menu, choose Send To, Compressed (Zipped) Folder.

The new archive will have the same name as the object you right-clicked. You can then use the Rename command (or press F2) if that's not the name you want to use.

CHAPTER 8

Home Basic ○
Home Premium ○
Business ○
Enterprise ○
Ultimate ○

E-Mail, Collaboration, and Personal Productivity

Chances are you chose Windows Vista as your operating system for reasons other than the magnificence of its accessory programs. Nevertheless, there is ample reason to check out these "applets," particularly if you don't use a suite of full-featured office applications. And even if you do have a heavy-duty office suite on hand, you might find some of the Windows Vista accessories easier to use and ideal for particular tasks.

Windows Mail, for example, is not just an e-mail client but an excellent newsgroup reader. Windows Calendar is simpler to use than the calendar component of Microsoft Office, and its support for the iCalendar format makes it a great tool for sharing personal appointment and task data with family members. Windows Meeting Space, meanwhile, is handy for sharing program displays and desktops in a peer-to-peer setting.

We look at these three programs in this chapter, along with an important piece of communication infrastructure, the Contacts folder.

What's in Your Edition?

Users of Windows Vista Home Basic Edition do not have the ability to initiate a meeting in Windows Meeting Space (but they can join a meeting in progress or respond to a meeting invitation). The other features described in this chapter are available in all editions of Windows Vista.

Using Windows Mail

Windows Mail is the successor to Outlook Express, the e-mail client and newsgroup reader that was included with Windows XP and other earlier versions of Windows. If you've used Outlook Express, you'll notice a great deal that's familiar in Windows Mail. The most significant differences between Windows Mail and Outlook Express 6 (the version included with Windows XP) are as follows:

- Windows Mail stores messages individually, in human-readable .eml files. Outlook Express, in contrast, employed a system of binary (.dbx) files, storing all the messages for a given folder in a single .dbx file. The change promises to make

Windows Mail's message store less susceptible to corruption. It will also make it possible for you to retrieve particular messages from a backup folder, to read them in a text editor outside of Windows Mail if you choose, and so on.

- Windows Mail includes a search box that functions just like its counterpart in Windows Explorer, providing indexed content search for any particular folder. (The more elaborate Edit, Find command that enabled Outlook Express users to search across all folders remains in Windows Mail.)

- In place of the Windows Address Book application used by Outlook Express, Windows Mail and Windows Vista store contact information in a Windows Explorer folder, called Contacts. Like e-mail messages, contacts are stored in separate (.contact) files and are therefore less prone to corruption.

- Windows Mail, unlike Outlook Express, does *not* support Hotmail accounts.

- The identities feature in Outlook Express has been dropped in Windows Mail.

In changing the e-mail client's name from Outlook Express to Windows Mail, Microsoft has underscored the fact that this product is something quite distinct from Outlook, the personal information management component of Microsoft Office. Some users of earlier Windows versions were misled by the similarity of names to think that Outlook Express was simply a scaled down, "lite" version of Outlook. It was indeed smaller than Outlook, but it always included some features that Outlook lacked—most notably the ability to serve as a newsgroup reader.

Unfortunately, in eliminating one potential for name confusion, Microsoft has acquired an entirely new one. Hotmail, Microsoft's free HTTP e-mail service, has been renamed Windows Live Mail, and Microsoft has created a new e-mail client for Windows Live Mail called Windows Live Mail Desktop Client (it's a free download). So, if you choose Windows Mail for your POP3 e-mail accounts, IMAP accounts, or newsgroups, and you also rely on one or more Windows Live Mail (aka Hotmail) accounts, you might find yourself using two similarly named e-mail programs and needing to keep straight which is which.

Getting started with Windows Mail involves a few relatively painless steps: setting up your accounts, tailoring the program's visual presentation to taste, and making a few decisions in the Options dialog box.

Setting Up Accounts

The Internet Accounts dialog box (choose Tools, Accounts) is where you set up, review, edit, and delete accounts. Accounts are organized into three categories: Mail, News, and Directory Service (see Figure 8-1).

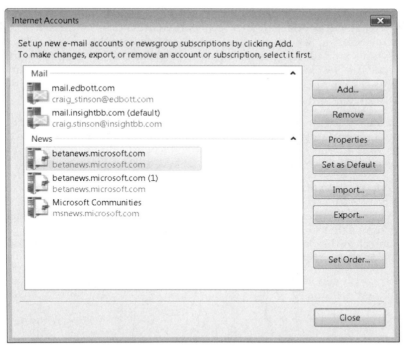

Figure 8-1 Windows Mail accommodates three kinds of accounts: Mail, News, and Directory Service.

Mail and news accounts are probably self-explanatory: They allow you to send and receive e-mail and newsgroup messages. Directory service accounts are different—and might better have been called connections than accounts. A directory service is a repository of information about people and businesses. When you don't know someone's e-mail address, you can try to find it by connecting to a directory service and performing a search. For more information about directory services, see "Creating a Directory Service Account," in this chapter.

Creating a Mail Account

If you start Windows Mail without already having established a mail account, the Internet Connection Wizard guides you through the steps necessary to create your first account. If you need to create an additional account, or if you declined to set one up at your first opportunity and are ready now to create your first account, choose Tools, Accounts. In the Internet Accounts dialog box, click Add, E-Mail Account. In the ensuing screen, you'll be asked to supply your display name. This screen gives you the chance to change the way your name is presented to recipients of your e-mail messages. For example, if your name is Ram Thirunavukkarasu, but you'd rather your recipients see your messages as coming from Ram (omitting the last name), you can make the necessary changes here. Type your name as you want others to see it, and then click Next.

The wizard's second page is called Internet E-Mail Address. Here you specify the address that will be added to your recipients' address books or Contacts folders if they exercise an Add Sender to Address Book command in their e-mail software. By default, this is also the address that your recipients will use if they click Reply to answer your e-mail. If you want replies to go to a different address, you'll need to edit the properties for your account after you've finished setting it up. (See the Inside Out sidebar "Finish Setting Up New Accounts," later in this chapter, for more details.)

On the wizard's E-Mail Server Names page, you'll need to supply server addresses for your inbound and outbound mail. If you're not sure what to enter on this screen, contact your internet service provider (ISP) or network administrator. Windows Mail supports two server protocols for inbound mail: POP3 and IMAP.

On the Internet Mail Logon page of the wizard, supply your logon information—the name of your account, as given to you by your ISP or other service provider, and your password. A Remember Password option on this screen is selected by default. If you're concerned that someone else might try to use your computer to access your e-mail account, clear the check box. You'll then be prompted for the password the first time you send or retrieve mail in each Windows Mail session.

After you've supplied the logon information, click Next, then Finish. You're ready to use your new account.

INSIDE OUT   Save your account information

If you don't ever want to be bothered to recreate an e-mail account, choose Tools, Accounts, select the account name, and then click Export. Windows Mail will save your account settings (including your password) in encrypted format in an .iaf file. If you ever need to re-establish the account—on this computer or another—you can import that .iaf file into Windows Mail. Be sure to store the .iaf file in a secure location.

Creating a News Account

Creating a newsgroup account is just like creating a mail account, except that you provide the address of an NNTP server instead of mail servers. Choose Tools, Accounts; click Add, Newsgroup Account; and then follow the wizard. On the first two pages, provide your display name (the name that other newsgroup users will see when you post or reply to messages) and your return e-mail address. On the third page, supply the server details. If your news server does not require you to log on (many do not), leave the My News Server Requires Me To Log On option unselected. Most internet service providers maintain an NNTP server for use by their subscribers. If you're setting up access to a private news server or if you subscribe to a commercial news server—that is, a news server that does require a logon—select this option, and then supply logon details on the ensuing page.

Creating a Directory Service Account

By default, Windows Mail provides access to your Active Directory (if you're working in an Active Directory environment) and several public Lightweight Directory Accesss Protocol (LDAP) servers. With these directory connections established, you can look for people or businesses on the internet (or in your Active Directory) by choosing Edit, Find, People. As Figure 8-2 shows, the Find People dialog box includes a drop-down list of available directory services (as well as your own Contact folder). If you have the server and logon information, you can make additional LDAP servers available by choosing Tools, Accounts, Add, Directory Service.

Figure 8-2 The Find People dialog box allows you to look for a contact in your Contacts folder, your Active Directory, and any of your established directory service accounts.

Editing Account Information

After you've used the Internet Connection Wizard to create an account, you can use the account's properties dialog box to modify any of the information you gave the wizard. To open an account's properties dialog box, choose Tools, Accounts, select the name of the account, and then click Properties.

INSIDE OUT   Finish setting up new accounts

You have no choice but to use the Internet Connection Wizard to set up a new mail account initially. However, if you're a sophisticated mail user, you should visit the properties dialog box for each mail account after completing the initial setup. Several options there are potentially useful:

- **Mail Account (General tab)** Use this option to change the name displayed in the Accounts dialog box. By default, the account name is the same as the mail server for SMTP/POP3 accounts. You might want to change it if you've created several versions of the same account with different properties for different uses.

- **Reply Address (General tab)** Enter an e-mail address here if you want to specify a return address other than the address from which you sent the original message. The address you enter will appear in the To line when your recipient uses the Reply option in his or her e-mail client. Use this option, for instance, of you send messages from a Windows Live Mail account while traveling because your regular SMTP server is unavailable but you want replies to be sent to the POP3 account you normally use for personal e-mail.

- **My Server Requires Authentication (Servers tab)** Select this option if you are connecting an SMTP server that requires an extra authentication step as an anti-spam measure. Many servers require that you log on to the POP3 server first (using your user name and password) before being allowed to send messages.

- **Leave A Copy Of Messages On Server (Advanced tab)** This option comes in handy if you're checking your work e-mail from a computer at home (or vice versa) but you want to maintain a complete archive of messages on the other computer. You can check for new messages at home; when you return to the office, your mail program will download those messages into your inbox.

Customizing the Look of Windows Mail

Figure 8-3 shows all of Windows Mail's optional visual elements. Everything in Windows Mail's presentation is optional, except for the menu bar and the message list. If the display feels crowded, you can eliminate elements that you don't need by selecting or deselecting options in the Windows Layout Properties dialog box (choose View, Layout).

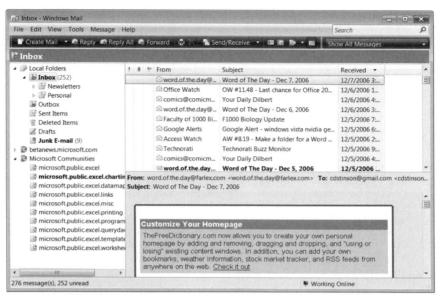

Figure 8-3 You can get rid of everything but the message list and the menu bar if you want a leaner look.

> **Note**
>
> Outlook Express veterans will probably notice the absence of a Contacts pane in Windows Mail. The Contacts pane, along with the Windows Address Book to which it was tethered, have been replaced by the Contacts folder in Windows Vista. To display the Contacts folder, press Ctrl+Shift+C, choose Tools, Contacts, or click the Contacts icon on the toolbar.

Previewing Messages

The preview pane displays the contents of the currently selected message. When you're scanning mail or newsgroup messages, you can save yourself a lot of time by scanning the first few lines of each message in the preview pane, rather than opening each message and reading it in its own window. If you choose to display the preview pane, you can position it either below the message list or alongside it. You can also choose whether or not to include the preview pane header. As you can see in Figure 8-3, the header doesn't offer any information that can't also be displayed in the column headings of the message list, so if you're short on visual space, you can economize by eliminating the preview pane header.

Navigating Folders

Windows Mail uses folders to organize messages. When you first run Windows Mail, the program creates one set of folders, called Local Folders, that are used for any POP3 and IMAP e-mail accounts. In addition, Windows Mail creates a separate set of folders for each of your newsgroup accounts. Figure 8-3, for example, shows three branches of folders in the folder list—Local Folders, betanews.microsoft.com, and Microsoft Communities.

The folder list provides familiar controls for navigating folders and subfolders. Nevertheless, you might choose to hide it and display the preview pane alongside, rather than below, the message list. This arrangement would let you peruse a larger message list. With the folder list suppressed, you would probably want to display the folder bar. Otherwise essentially useless, the folder bar acquires a handy drop-down arrow when the folder list is suppressed. Click the arrow, and your entire folder structure unfolds, allowing easy navigation.

For any even more economical layout, you can hide the folder list *and* the folder bar. When you want to move to a different folder, press Ctrl+Y. The Go To Folder dialog box appears, as shown in Figure 8-4, allowing you to navigate to any folder.

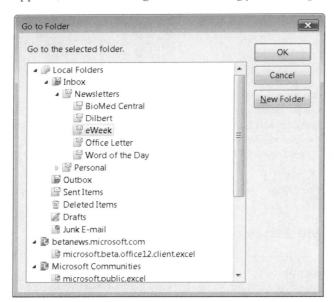

Figure 8-4 If you prefer not to display the folders list alongside your messages, you can navigate by pressing Ctrl+Y to summon this dialog box.

With the folder list out of your display layout, you can also use the Go To Folder dialog to create new folders at any level in your folder structure. The principal disadvantage of suppressing the folder list display is that eliminates the possibility of using drag and drop to move messages from one folder to another. You can still relocate a messages, of course, by right-clicking it in the message list and choosing Move To Folder, but it's somewhat less convenient to work that way.

Setting Basic Options

The Options dialog box (choose Tools, Options) offers a great many choices, some of which you should make right away, others of which you can defer or ignore.

Checking for Mail at Regular Intervals

By default, Windows Mail checks every 30 minutes to see whether you have new mail. You can change that interval (or disable automatic checking) on the General tab of the Options dialog box. Whether or not you fetch mail on a schedule, you can send and receive at any time by pressing Ctrl+M. This keyboard shortcut checks all your e-mail accounts, unless you have disabled automatic e-mail checking for a particular account (choose Tools, Accounts, select the account you want to check manually, click the Properties button, and clear the Include This Account When Receiving Mail Or Synchronizing option on the General tab.) To check a particular account only, choose Tools, Send And Receive (or click the down arrow at the right of the Send/Receive button on the toolbar), and then select the account you want to check.

Windows Mail also ordinarily looks for mail at startup (that is, when you launch the program) and plays a sound to announce the arrival of a message (unfortunately, you get the sound even when all the arriving messages are deemed to be junk). You can disable these defaults by clearing check boxes on the General tab of the Options dialog box. If you want sound notification but prefer a different tune, choose Change System Sounds in Control Panel and change the sound associated with the New Mail Notification event.

Chapter 8

Controlling the Format of Outbound Messages

Most e-mail client programs can read HTML. Many newsgroup clients cannot. There-fore, Windows Mail formats outbound mail by default in HTML, leaving news posts in plain text. You can change these defaults on the Send tab of the Options dialog box.

If you keep the HTML default, but some of your regular correspondents prefer that you do not send HTML, you can send plain-text messages to those recipients by choosing Format, Plain Text in the New Message window as your composing each message. Un-fortunately, the option to set a recipient's address-book (aka Contacts folder) entry for plain text has been dropped in Windows Mail.

Setting Security Options

Before you begin using Windows Mail, you should click Tools, Options, and then select the Security tab in the Options dialog box to review your security settings. Make sure that the following options are selected:

- Restricted Sites Zone (More Secure)
- Warn Me When Other Applications Try To Send Mail As Me

Both are selected by default, but it's a good idea to check anyway.

Windows Mail shares the settings for the two most restrictive security zones avail-able in Internet Explorer—the Internet zone and the Restricted Sites zone. By setting Windows Mail to follow the security restrictions observed in the Restricted Sites zone, you get the maximum protection that you have set for this zone in Internet Explorer. This setting goes a long way toward warding off potential viruses and Trojan horses. If something does make it past your defenses, the Warn Me option will provide protection against those viruses that replicate themselves by trying to hijack Windows Mail and its mail-sending capabilities.

It's worth noting that ActiveX controls and scripts are always disabled in Windows Mail, even if you've enabled them in the corresponding security zone for Internet Ex-plorer. Also, the Warn Me capability is useless against modern viruses and worms that incorporate their own SMTP server to send infected messages without getting involved with Windows Mail.

Managing Contacts

The Windows Address Book application familiar to Outlook Express users has been replaced in Windows Vista by a folder called Contacts. This ordinary Windows Explorer folder is part of your user profile, stored (by default) alongside such other profile folders as Documents, Music, Pictures, and Videos. (For more about user profile folders, see "What's What and Where in a User Profile," Chapter 7.) You can get to it in a variety of ways. For example, typing **contacts** in the Start menu's Search box and pressing Enter will take you there. If you're already in Windows Mail, you can open the Contacts folder by pressing Ctrl+Shift+C, by choosing Tools, Contacts, or by clicking the Contacts icon on the Command Bar.

As Figure 8-5 shows, the Contacts folder collects contact information in a simple tabbed dialog box, similar to the one used by the superseded Windows Address Book. To create a new contact, click New Contact on the Contacts folder toolbar, or right-click empty space in the Contacts folder and choose New, Contact.

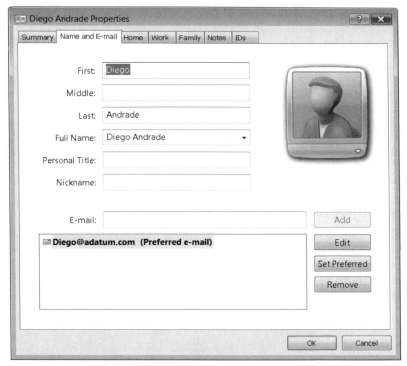

Figure 8-5 The Contacts folder collects data in a simple tabbed dialog box. If you have multiple e-mail addresses for a contact, be sure to select the one you want Windows Mail to use, and then click Set Preferred.

Creating a Distribution List

The Contacts folder lets you create named groups of contacts to simplify mail that you send repeatedly to the same set of recipients. To create such a group entity, click New Contact Group on the Contacts folder Command Bar. Enter a name for the group, then click Select Members to populate the group. The Select Contacts To Add dialog box, which appears when you click Select Members, initially lists all the contacts that already exist in your Contacts folder. By clicking on All Contact Types in the lower right corner of this dialog box, you can change the display to show only previously created contact groups. This allows you to add existing contact groups to the group you're currently creating.

Organizing Your Contacts

Because contact information resides in a standard Windows Explorer folder, you can use standard Windows Explorer methods to organize your folder store and customize its display. For example, you can create subfolders for business, personal, and family contacts, and use them to segregate your contact entries. As long as a contact is stored in a subfolder of Contacts (or in Contacts itself), Windows Mail will find the information it needs when you address an e-mail message to that contact.

All the standard Windows Explorer viewing options are available in your Contacts folder and subfolders, so you can switch easily between iconic and tabular display styles. If you have assigned a picture to a contact (by clicking on the picture frame in the Name And E-Mail tab of the contact's properties dialog box and supplying the name of a picture file), that picture will appear in the various iconic displays. If you've enabled the Preview Pane (choose Organize on the Command Bar, then Layout, Preview Pane), you can read most of the essential details about any contact simply by highlighting the contact's entry; that is, you can save yourself the trouble of opening the contact's properties dialog box.

Dealing with Multiple E-Mail Addresses

You can handle contacts with multiple e-mail addresses in a couple of different ways. You can simply list all the contact's addresses in a single contact entry and let Windows know which address is the default (select that address in the big window at the bottom of the Name And E-Mail tab and click Set Preferred). Or you can create multiple Contacts entries, one for each e-mail address.

The advantage of the first approach is that you can see all of a person's various addresses in one place. The disadvantage is that if you want to address a message to an address other than the one you have marked as preferred, you will have to type the actual e-mail address on the To line of the New Message window. If you type the recipient's name instead of his or her e-mail address, Windows Mail will direct your message to the preferred address without asking for confirmation. (To mitigate the annoyance of making you type an e-mail address instead of a recipient's name, the program uses AutoComplete. As you begin typing an address that you have used before, Windows Mail proposes to complete it for you.)

If you regularly use more than one address for a recipient, you might find it expedient to create separate contact entries. You can create multiple entries for the same person either in the same Contacts folder (Windows will append numbers to names to avoid having duplicate file names) or in separate subfolders. For example, if you use one address to contact a person on business and another for non-business communication, you could segregate the multiple contact entries into personal and business subfolders. Either way—same folder or different folders—if you address a message to a person who has multiple contact entries, Windows Mail will prompt you to choose when you send your message.

Adding Contacts from Windows Mail Messages

By default, when you reply to an e-mail message, Windows Mail adds the name of person you reply to (and of everyone else who received that message, if you click Reply All) to your Contacts folder. In everyday situations, this can be a useful service. Junk senders don't land in your Contacts folder, because you don't reply to their spam, but contacts you find worth responding to are added. If you frequently reply to "one off" messages from strangers, however, this setting can clutter your Contacts folder with irrelevant names. To turn the feature off, in Windows Mail, choose Tools, Options, go to the Send tab, and clear Automatically Put People I Reply To In My Contacts List.

You can also add senders to your Contacts folder without replying to their mail. In the message list, you can right-click a message and choose Add Sender To Contacts. Alternatively, you can open the message in its own window (double-click the message in the message list) and then, in the message window, choose Tools, Add To Contacts. There's an important difference between these two approaches. If you add the sender to your Contacts folder from the message list, the new contact is added forthwith. If you do it from the message window, you get to see and edit the new record before committing it to the Contacts folder. Also, when you choose Add To Contacts in the message window, a submenu gives you the opportunity to add other recipients (people who also received the message) to your Contacts folder selectively.

Exchanging Electronic Business Cards (vCards)

Windows Mail and the Contacts folder support the vCard format, which enables you to exchange electronic business cards with other users via e-mail. To send your business card to another user, first create a contact entry for yourself (if your Contacts folder does not already include that entry). Then right-click your contact record and choose Send Contact (vCard). Windows Mail will open a New Message window with your card as an attached vCard file. Supply the address of the person to whom you're sending your card, add a subject and some message text if you wish, and click Send.

If someone sends a business card to you, it will arrive in your inbox as an attachment to an e-mail message. Open the attachment, click Open in the Mail Attachment dialog box (if that dialog box is displayed), and then click Add To My Contacts in the Contacts folder properties dialog box that appears.

You can have Windows Mail include your business card in all outgoing mail or news messages. To do this, first be sure your Contacts folder includes an entry for yourself. Then, in Windows Mail, choose Tools, Options, and go to the Compose tab. In the Business Cards section of the dialog box, select Mail, News, or both, and then select the contact name from the list.

> **Note**
>
> If opening a vCard attachment does not display the contact in a Contacts folder properties dialog box, then your .vcf files are probably associated with some other application (such as Outlook). You can fix this by going to the Programs section of Control Panel, choosing Make A File Type Always Open In A Specific Program (under the heading Default Programs), selecting .vcf in the list of file types that appears, and clicking Change Program. In the Open With dialog box, then, select Windows Contacts and click OK.

Importing Contacts

If you already have a collection of contacts stored in a Windows Address Book (.wab) file, you don't need to recreate it in Windows Mail. You can import the existing contacts into your Contacts folder. The only challenging part of this process is likely to be locating your .wab file. On a Windows XP system, Outlook Express stores the address book by default in an out-of-the-way place, the folder %AppData%\Microsoft\Address Book. You can get there by using the Start menu's Run command and typing that string. Typically the Address Book file has your user account name and the extension .wab (for example, Craig.wab).

Once you know where your .wab file lives, you can import its contents by clicking Import on the Contacts folder's command bar or choosing File, Import, Contacts in Windows Mail. Either way, you'll see the dialog box shown in Figure 8-6. Choose Windows Address Book File (Outlook Express Contacts), click Import, and tell the ensuing dialog box where to find your file. Note that the import process will disregard the folder structure of your .wab file.

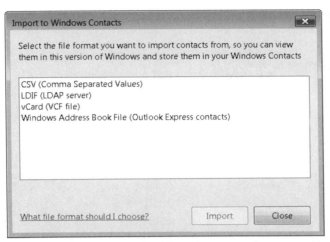

Figure 8-6 Contact data in these four formats can be imported into your Contacts folder.

As Figure 8-6 shows, the Contacts folder can import data in three other formats in addition to .wab. Unfortunately, the VCard (VCF File) option allows you to import only one contact at a time. As we'll see, Windows Mail can export an entire folder of contacts en masse to .vcf files, but it lacks a corresponding bulk-import capability.

One popular contact format not included in the import list is Microsoft Outlook. To use contacts stored in an Outlook .pst file, you must first export them from Outlook. Use Outlook's File, Import And Export command to save your contacts in a Comma Separated Values (Windows) file, then use the CSV (Comma Separated Values) option in Windows Mail to import the data. While you're at it, you can also open the exported contact file in any other application—Microsoft Excel, for example—that accepts comma-separated data.

> **Note**
>
> With the help of a registry edit, it was possible for Windows XP users to share a common set of contacts between Outlook and Outlook Express. That handy, though undocumented, feature has disappeared from Windows Vista.

A comma-separated values file stores tabular data in plain text, with the columns of the table (name, address, and phone fields, for example) demarcated by commas. Because the source of this data (Outlook, for example) may not use the same fields in the same order as your Contacts folder does, you need to do a little interpreting for the import tool. You'll see a dialog box like the one shown in Figure 8-7 on the next page.

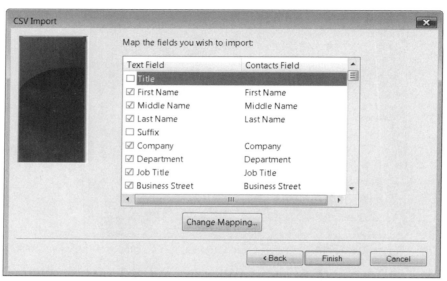

Figure 8-7 Before you can complete the import of comma-separated data, you need to "map" source fields to fields used by your Contacts folder.

Figure 8-7 shows the CSV Import dialog box for Outlook data. Outlook's fields are listed in the column on the left; the fields used by the Contacts folder are listed in the column on the left. In some cases (Company and Department, for example) there is an exact correspondence between Outlook and the Contacts folder—and these are selected and mapped by default. The rest is up to you. To map a field, select it in the column on the left and click Change Mapping. In the Change Mapping dialog box that appears, select a Contacts folder field from the drop-down list, select Import This Field, and click OK. When your map is fully drawn, click Finish in the CSV Import dialog box to complete the job.

Exporting Contacts

The Contacts folder can export data in two formats—vCard and Comma-Separated Values. The former is useful for creating business card files that can be attached to e-mail messages. The latter is handy for such things as copying contact data to a spreadsheet table or database program, or for migrating your information to another contact-management program, such as Outlook.

To carry out an export, click Export on the Contacts folder's command bar, or choose File, Export, Contacts in Windows Mail. Then choose your format and specify a target folder (for vCard files) or filename (for .csv). If you choose the vCard format, each contact in the current folder will be exported to a separate .vcf file. If you choose the comma-separated format, you will see an additional dialog box asking you which of the source fields you want to export. You don't need to export them all. If you're creating a simple telephone list in Excel, for example, you don't need to include address fields.

Using Windows Calendar

Windows Calendar is a straightforward, easy-to-use scheduling application in which you can record appointments and tasks. The program's principal virtue is its support for iCalendar, a standard protocol for sharing calendar information. The iCalendar functionality lets you share your own schedule with others. You can e-mail specific appointment information or an entire calendar to a colleague, for example, or publish your calendar to a website. You can also use Windows Calendar to subscribe to public schedules (arts calendars, calendars of athletic events, notices of public meetings, and so on); subscribed calendar information can be updated automatically at specified time intervals.

Creating an Appointment or Task

The simplest way to create a new appointment is to navigate to the appropriate day (use commands on the View menu to switch as needed between month, week, and day views), then begin typing in a time slot on the calendar page. Windows Calendar responds by displaying your appointment data in the Details pane, at the right side of the program window:

If the appointment is a recurring event, you can use the Recurrence button to specify a time interval. To request a reminder (at a interval that can range from 0 minutes to two weeks), click the Reminder button. If others are involved in the event and their names are included in your Contacts folder, click Attendees. You'll see a form similar to the following:

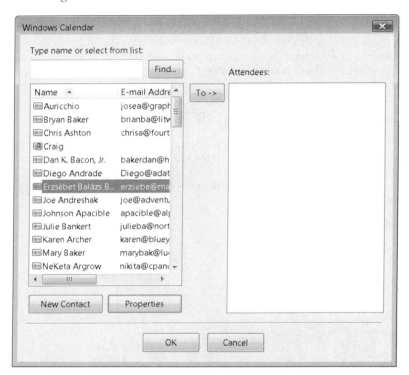

Once you have added some attendees to your event, the Invite button becomes available; clicking here opens a message window in Windows Mail (or your default e-mail client, if that's not Windows Mail), addressed to everyone on your attendees list. An .ics file is attached to the message, suitable for important into your recipients' calendars.

To create a task, click New Task on the command bar, then fill out the form that appears in the Details pane:

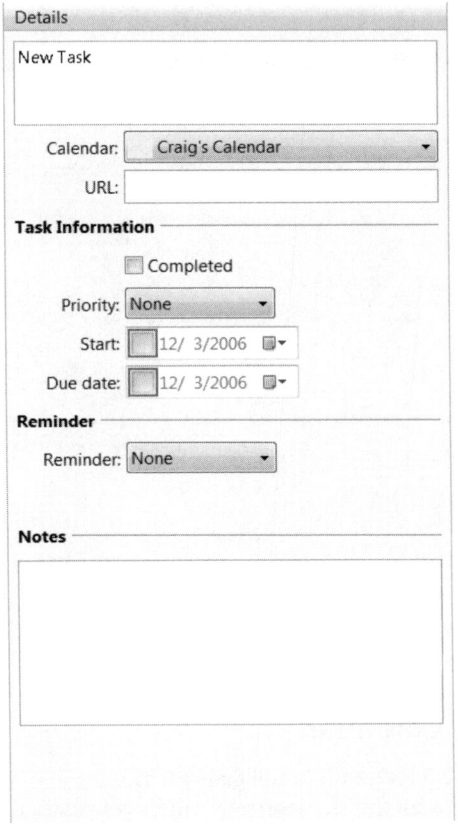

Chapter 8

Details

New Task

Calendar: Craig's Calendar   ▼
URL:

Task Information

☐ Completed
Priority: None   ▼
Start: ☐ 12/ 3/2006 ▦▼
Due date: ☐ 12/ 3/2006 ▦▼

Reminder

Reminder: None   ▼

Notes

Your tasks will appear in the Tasks box of the Navigation pane, to in the lower left corner of the window (see Figure 8-8 on the next page). When you've completed the task, you can select the check box beside the task name in the Navigation pane or the Completed check box in the Details pane; the two are linked. Although the program does not have a specific mechanism for assigning tasks to others, you can select a task in the Navigation pane and then choose Share, Send Via E-Mail to provide a colleague with an importable .ics attachment.

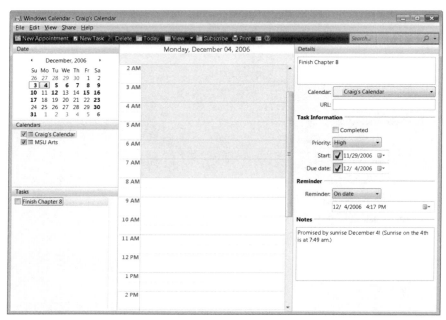

Figure 8-8 Windows Calendar lets you accumulate unfinished tasks in the Tasks section of the Navigation pane, at the left side of the window.

Sharing or Publishing a Calendar

To share your entire calendar, select its name in the Calendars section of the Navigation pane. Then choose Share, Send Via E-Mail. A message form in your default e-mail program will appear, with an .ics file attached. Address the form and send. Your recipients will be able to import the attachment into their calendar programs (Windows Calendar or Outlook 2007, for example) by double-clicking and responding to a confirmation prompt.

To publish a calendar to a web host, select the calendar name in the Calendars section of the Details pane, and then choose Share, Publish. A dialog box similar to the following will appear:

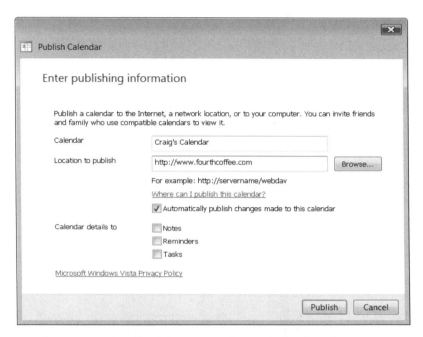

Supply a URL, select check boxes to indicate the level of detail you want to include, and then click Publish.

Subscribing to a Calendar

A growing number of websites make calendars available in the iCalendar format. You can use Windows Calendar to subscribe to schedules published in this manner, and you can control the frequency at which those schedules are updated. If you know the URL of a publicly available calendar, you can subscribe to it by clicking the Subscribe button on the Command bar and filling out a form like the following:

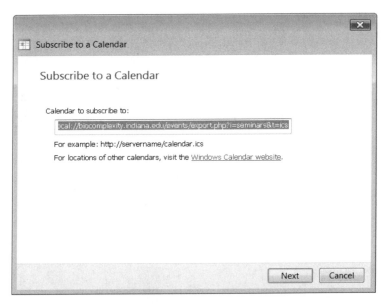

A subsequent form will give you the opportunity to name the incoming calendar and specify an update interval:

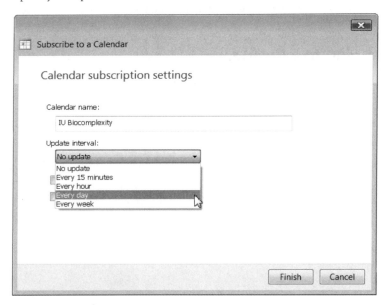

You can also subscribe to many published calendars by visiting their sites, clicking a Download button, and answering a confirmation prompt from Windows Calendar.

Managing Multiple Calendars

Windows Calendar can handle as many imported or subscribed calendars as you care to give it, along with your own schedule. All of your calendars are listed in the Calendars section of the navigation pane, with a check box beside each one. If you want to focus on a particular calendar and hide the others, clear the check boxes for the ones you don't want to see. As Figure 8-9 shows, you can also assign distinctive colors to each calendar to help you tell what's what.

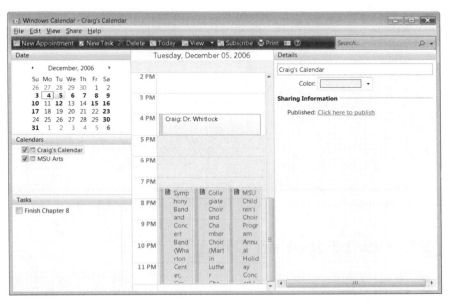

Figure 8-9 If you work with multiple calendars, you can use colors to set them apart.

If you work with more than a few calendars, you might want to use groups to organize them. To create a group, right-click in the Calendars section of the navigation pane, and then choose New Group. After you have created one or more groups, you can use your mouse to move existing calendars into groups.

You can also use multiple calendars to deal with the complexity of your own schedule. To create a new calendar, right-click in the Calendars section of the navigation pane and choose New Calendar. You can name the calendars, organize them into groups, and use colors to distinguish them. Then, when you want to focus on a particular aspect of your schedule, you can do so by means of the check boxes in the Calendars section. Figure 8-10 on the next page shows an example of this strategy, applied to the busy life of a high school student.

Figure 8-10 You can use multiple calendars to organize the complexity of your own schedule.

Using Windows Meeting Space

Home Basic
Home Premium
Business
Enterprise
Ultimate

Windows Meeting Space is a program that facilitates the sharing of documents, images, and desktops between as many as ten users in a peer-to-peer setting. Each of the meeting participants must be running Windows Vista. As Figure 8-11 shows, the first time each user runs Windows Meeting Space, he or she will be prompted to enable file replication and sign into People Near Me. These steps require administrative credentials.

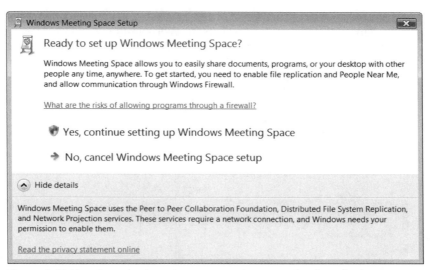

Figure 8-11 Your first use of Windows Meeting Space entails a firewall adjustment.

In the program's opening screen, shown in Figure 8-12, you can either start a new meeting or join one in progress. If you choose to start a new meeting, you'll be asked to name it (the default is your own name plus the current time) and declare a password that your attendees will have to supply.

Figure 8-12 In the opening screen of Windows Meeting Space, you can start your own meeting or join a meeting in progress.

By default, a meeting you create will be "visible" to others on your network who have signed in to People Near Me and happen to be running Windows Meeting Space. This visibility saves you the trouble of issuing formal invitations (but your attendees will still need the password). If you prefer that your meeting not be visible to those you have not explicitly invited, click Options on the screen where you establish your meeting. Then select Do Not Allow People Near Me To See This Meeting:

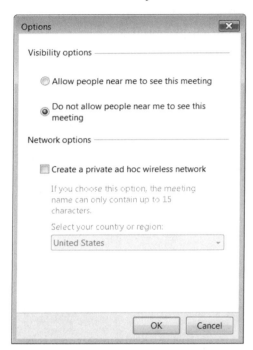

After you have named the meeting and specified the password, clicking the green arrow to the right of the Password box takes you to the meeting screen. Here you can use the Invite button on the command bar (or an Invite People link at the right side of the window) to let people know about the meeting. The Invite People dialog box lists everyone on your local network who has signed in to People Near Me:

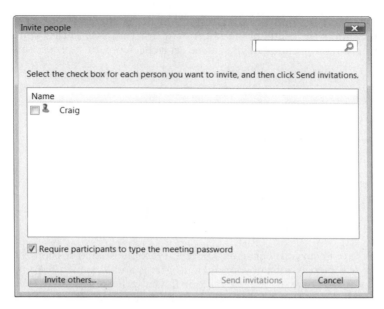

To invite someone who is not on this list, click Invite Others. The ensuing screen will let you send invitations by e-mail or instant messaging.

As people join your meeting, their names appear in the upper right corner of the meeting screen:

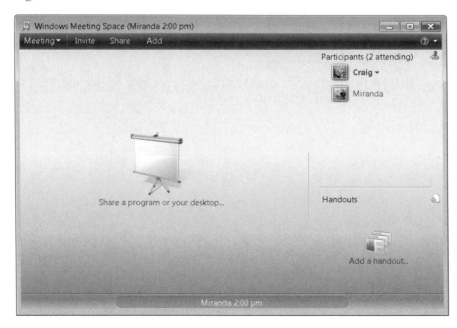

To begin sharing programs or your desktop, click the Share button on the command bar or the link in the center of the screen. The first time you do this, you'll see an elaborate confirmation prompt, but you can select a check box to suppress this on future occasions:

After you have given your consent (if necessary) to the shared session, Windows Meeting Space will display a list of your open programs and documents. You can select the item you want to share (or select Desktop). If what you want to share isn't on the list, you can click Browse For A File To Open And Share.

If you initiate the sharing, you control the action. If you're sharing a document, for example, the others in your meeting are passive observers of whatever you care to show. A banner across the top of your screen indicates that you are sharing, and a Give Control button in the upper right corner allows you to pass the baton to another participant:

To leave the meeting, choose Meeting, Leave Meeting or Meeting, Exit. The conference continues until all participants have left.

CHAPTER 9

Obtaining Help and Support

Home Basic ●
Home Premium ●
Business ●
Enterprise ●
Ultimate ●

As the Windows operating system becomes more complex—even while it's supposedly more intuitive with each successive version—inevitably some parts will be unclear to some users, creating a need for help and support systems.

Creating a help system that meets the needs of all users has been the subject of much research, and the help system in Windows has evolved as dramatically as has Windows itself. Most experienced Windows users quickly learned to skip right past the help files in Windows 95 and 98, which were aimed at novices and were hampered by a help engine that's extremely awkward to navigate. The reservoir of help content in Windows Me and Microsoft Windows 2000 was much deeper, and the HTML-based interfaces were slicker and easier to use than their predecessors. However, in both of those Windows versions, the online help file was still essentially a user manual that had been carved into small pieces and grew increasingly outdated with each Windows update. Windows XP added a Help And Support Center, which serves as an entry point to a tremendous collection of resources for Windows users at every level of experience.

Help And Support in Windows Vista uses a greatly simplified interface to provide paths to more information that is more current than ever before. Improvements in this version include:

- Guided Help topics, which show you how to complete perform a particular task by leading you through it, step by step—or performing the task for you

- Narrated video demonstrations (along with text transcripts) that explain key concepts for new users

- Updated help topics, which are available whenever your computer is connected to the internet

What's in Your Edition?

The help system works identically in all editions of Windows Vista. Topics that relate only to a particular edition are omitted from the help system of other editions, naturally. Windows Remote Assistance also works identically in all editions.

- More extensive help available online at the new Windows Online Help And Support website (*http://windowshelp.microsoft.com*), as well as other online resources

- Handy links to online help resources

The other help component that we discuss in this chapter, Windows Remote Assistance, is also greatly improved in Windows Vista. It's no longer integrated into Help And Support Center, and the new stand-alone program offers substantially better performance and security enhancements. But the biggest change is its far superior network connectivity, which makes it easier to connect to another person's computer to offer or request assistance—even when both computers are behind routers that use network address translation (NAT).

Using Windows Help And Support

To open Windows Help And Support, open the Start menu and click Help And Support. Your initial view of Help And Support is its home page, which is shown in Figure 9-1. (The first time you seek help, Windows Help And Support asks whether you want to obtain online content. For more information, see "Online Help vs. Offline Help," later in this chapter.)

Figure 9-1 The Help And Support home page has austere navigation and search tools, along with links to a variety of resources. Many computer manufacturers add their own links and content to this page.

The toolbar at the top of each help window includes only a few buttons:

- The browser-style Forward and Back buttons enable retracing your steps through the help system.

- The Help And Support Home button returns you to the home page.

- The Print button prints the currently displayed topic.

- The Browse button displays your current location within the table of contents, from which you can navigate up or down the hierarchy to a topic of interest.

- The Ask button leads to a page with links to other help resources, including places where you can ask for help (such as Windows communities, or newsgroups) and places where you can look for more help on your own (such as the Microsoft Knowledge Base). The Ask Someone Or Expand Your Search button that appears at the bottom of each help window leads to this same topic.

- The Options button opens a short menu of commands, two of which duplicate the function of toolbar buttons. Other commands let you adjust the size of text displayed in the help window and find a word or phrase within the currently displayed page.

INSIDE OUT   Start Windows Help And Support without the Start menu

If your Start menu doesn't include a Help And Support command, you can restore it by customizing the Start menu. (Right-click the Start menu, choose Properties, and, on the Start Menu tab, click Customize. In the Customize Start Menu dialog box, select Help.)

If you use Windows Help And Support rarely and you prefer to keep your Start menu lean and clean, you can avoid that rigmarole by simply typing **help** in the Start menu Search box.

Online Help vs. Offline Help

In previous versions of Windows, help was essentially static. The help files that were produced when a particular Windows version was released continued to be installed on new computers years after that original release. Windows XP was the first version to address the problem of outdated help files; it included some dynamically updated text on the Help And Support Center home page and updates to help content were included in some service packs and Windows updates.

The periodic updates via Windows Update continue, but Windows Vista goes a step further. Help content on Microsoft web servers is continually updated; at your option, whenever your computer is connected to the internet, you'll see the latest version of each help topic. The first time you open Windows Help And Support, it asks whether you want to get the latest online content, as shown in Figure 9-2. Unless you have a dial-up internet connection, there's seldom a reason to click No.

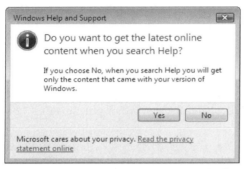

Figure 9-2 This dialog box appears only the first time you open Windows Help And Support. Regardless of how you answer, you can switch at any time.

To change between online content (that is, the content from Microsoft web servers) and offline content (the content stored on your computer's hard drive), click the button in the lower right corner of the Help window, which is labeled with your current status—either Offline Help or Online Help.

Note
Updated online help content is not stored on your computer; it's available only while you're connected to the server. When you disconnect from the server, the updated content is gone.

You should also be aware of another important online resource that is also updated frequently: the Windows Online Help And Support web site (*http://windowshelp.microsoft.com*). This web site covers many topics that aren't included in Windows Help And Support and offers greater depth as well.

TROUBLESHOOTING

You can't display help from older programs

The original format for help files is the .hlp file format. This long-lived and widely used format has been used in help files for all versions of Windows from Windows 3.1 (in 1992) through Windows XP (still available in 2007), along with all types of applications for Windows. There's a good chance that you'll find some .hlp files on your computer's hard drive. Alas, the program needed to display those files, Winhlp32.exe, is not included in Windows Vista. The Winhlp32.exe program has not been updated for many years and has officially been put out to pasture. Newer programs, as well as Windows itself, now use one of the newer help engines to display help files saved in one of the newer formats.

If you have some ancient .hlp files that you must use, you can download Winhlp32.exe from the Microsoft Download Center. For details, see Microsoft Knowledge Base (MSKB) article 917607 *(http://www.vista-io.com/0903)*.

Browsing Through Windows Help And Support

If you're reading this book from front to back, you might be the type who'd like to read through Windows Help And Support as well. Or you might find it easier to find a subject by drilling down through a table of contents–like hierarchy. Either way, the Browse button (or the Table Of Contents link on the home page) is the ticket to the help topics that interest you.

To explore the available help, click a subject heading. You'll be rewarded with links to more narrowly focused subject headings as well as links to detailed help topics, as shown in Figure 9-3. Links near the top of the page trace your path to a topic; you can use these "bread crumbs" to quickly find your way back to an intermediate subject page.

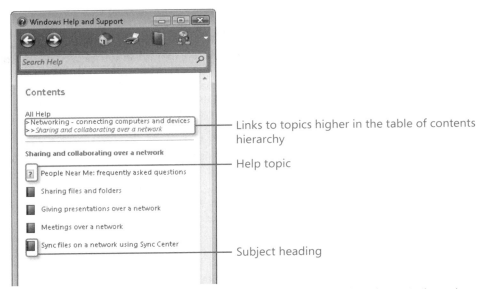

Figure 9-3 The Browse button lets you explore help topics organized by subject, similar to the table of contents in a printed book.

Searching for Help Topics

Finding a particular help topic in Windows Vista is a straightforward task. This is in sharp contrast to Windows XP, which offered a confusing process of selecting a topic, entering a search term, and specifying search options, with the search results then displayed in three categories. In Windows Vista you simply type your search word or phrase in the Search box (in the toolbar at the top of the Help window) and press Enter. No advanced options to set, no special operators to remember; just clean, simple search.

Windows then displays links to up to 30 of the best results, with the ones most likely to be useful to you at the top of the list. If you're using online help, it searches the online topics; otherwise, it looks only at your local (offline) content.

> **Note**
>
> At the bottom of the search results window, you'll see an Ask Someone Or Expand Your Search button. If you're expecting this to let you refine your search, you're in for a letdown. In fact, this button (which is a standard component of every Windows Help And Support window) merely takes you to the "ask someone" topic. Some of those online resources, fortunately, do offer ways to narrow your search as well as broaden it.

INSIDE OUT   Find articles in the Microsoft Knowledge Base

Unlike Help And Support Center in Windows XP, when you search help in Windows Vista, it does not search for articles in the Microsoft Knowledge Base, even when you're using online help. That's a shame, because the MSKB is a repository of thousands of articles with detailed troubleshooting solutions and other useful information. Nonetheless, you can use Help And Support as a launchpad for MSKB searches. Instead of using the Search box, click the Ask button, and then click the Knowledge Base link under "Other resources." To go directly to the advanced search page for MSKB, use this link: *http://www.vista-io.com/0902*

Using Guided Help and Demos

Help And Support in Windows Vista includes two new features that are useful primarily to users who are inexperienced with computers or with Windows: Guided Help and Demos. You'll find Guided Help, indicated by a compass icon, included in a number of help topics. To view a list of all Demos, type **demos** in the Search box; in the results list, click "Windows Vista demos."

Guided Help

Guided Help can be handy even for computer gurus, particularly ones who are not yet familiar with tasks in Windows Vista that are performed differently than in previous Windows versions. Guided Help provides automated assistance in one of two fashions: It can show you, step by step, how to perform a task; or it can just complete the task for you.

You find Guided Help links embedded into certain topics, as shown in Figure 9-4 on the next page. When you see the Guided Help icon, click one of its links to begin the tour. Figure 9-5 on the next page shows an example of how Guided Help shows you the way.

Chapter 9

Figure 9-4 The compass icon in a help topic is your indication that Guided Help is available.

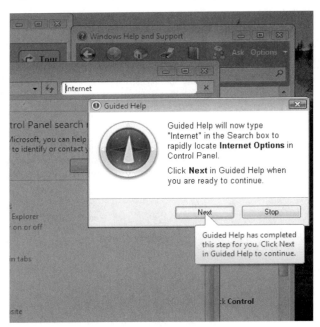

Figure 9-5 Guided Help tells you exactly what to click, and even does the typing for you.

> **Note**
> Guided Help is available only when you're using online help.

INSIDE OUT   Create a shortcut to a Guided Help procedure

You might come across a Guided Help procedure that you find particularly useful and worthy of sharing with others. You can do that by creating a shortcut. The trickiest part is finding the command to enter as the shortcut location. Here's how:

1. In Help And Support, display the topic that links to the Guided Help procedure.

2. Right-click anywhere in the topic and click View Source. The HTML source code for the topic opens in Notepad.

3. In Notepad, search for the text of the link you want to encapsulate as a shortcut— "Do it automatically" or "Show me step-by-step."

4. Select the command, which is normally between quotation marks immediately to the left of the link text you found. The command begins with "shortcut:" and ends with "DoIt" or "ShowMe."

5. Copy the command text to the Clipboard.

6. Right-click the desktop (or a folder where you want to save the shortcut) and click New, Shortcut.

7. In the Create Shortcut dialog box, paste the command text. Do not click Next.

8. Edit the command text to the proper form for command-line entry: Delete "shortcut:" and change each occurrence of "%25" to a single percent sign. The complete command should look something like this:

   ```
   %SystemRoot%\system32\acw.exe -Extensions GuidedHelp.dll -taskID mshelp://
   windows/?id=d031e17d-59aa-4862-9280-74a17bbb5d9c -ExecutionMode DoIt
   ```

9. Click Next, type a name for your shortcut, and then click Finish.

Before you distribute your new shortcut, double-click it to be sure that it runs properly.

Demos

Demos are narrated video presentations that explain various topics—mostly basic ones. When you jump to a demo page, you can click "Watch the demo" to run the video in Windows Media Player. If you're not ready for a multimedia experience, click "Read the transcript" to display the demo's narrative text.

Finding Help Outside Help And Support Center

Help And Support Center isn't the only path to local help resources. In windows and dialog boxes throughout Windows, you'll encounter other links to help. A colored text link (which might or might not be underlined) or a question mark in a circle or square indicates a link to help.

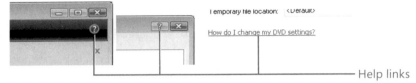

Temporary file location: <Default>

How do I change my DVD settings?

——————————— Help links

Control Panel has its own path to help: type text in the Search box in Control Panel, and the search results include not only links to relevant Control Panel pages, but also a link to relevant topics in Help And Support.

Most programs—those that come with Windows as well as those you obtain separately—have their own help system that's separate from Help And Support Center. To access these help resources, look for links like those shown above and look on the program's Help menu, if it has one. Also, in most programs pressing the F1 key summons help.

Yes, help is available in lots of places, many of them unexpected. Keep your eyes peeled for various signposts.

Connecting to Another PC with Windows Remote Assistance

If you've ever tried to help a novice user troubleshoot a Windows problem over the phone, you know how frustrating the entire process can be. It's usually difficult for an inexperienced user to accurately communicate detailed configuration information, especially if the problem involves technically challenging areas, such as hardware drivers or network protocols. Because you're not looking over the user's shoulder, you can't see error messages or informational dialog boxes, so you have to rely on the user to read this crucial information back to you. Even when you successfully pin down the problem and find a solution, you have to walk the user through a potentially daunting repair process. And if the registry needs editing—well, good luck.

With Windows Vista, on the other hand, you can eliminate most of those headaches using a cool support tool called Remote Assistance. This feature, available in all versions of Windows Vista (as well as Windows XP and Windows Server 2003), lets you open a direct connection between two machines over the internet or over a local area network. Even if you're hundreds or thousands of miles away, you can watch as the user demonstrates the problem and take control of the screen to make repairs quickly and accurately. You can investigate Control Panel settings, run diagnostic tools, install updates, and even edit the registry of the problem-plagued PC. Repairs that might have taken hours the old-fashioned way can be accomplished in a few minutes using this tool.

Remote Assistance in Windows Vista is substantially different from, yet interoperable with, Remote Assistance in earlier Windows versions. To begin with, it's no longer embedded in the Help And Support Center; instead, it's a stand-alone executable (Msra.exe) that is smaller and faster than its predecessor. It supports several command-line arguments, which makes it practical to use in scripts, batch programs, and shortcuts. (At a command prompt, type **msra /?** for details.)

Remote Assistance is designed for informal, peer-to-peer use by Windows users without an extensive technical background. Although the user interface hides most of its complexities, a basic understanding of how Remote Assistance connections work can help you make reliable connections without compromising the security of either computer.

Remote Assistance vs. Remote Desktop Connection

Remote Assistance in Windows Vista uses some of the same underlying technology as Remote Desktop Connection, a program that allows you to connect to your computer from a remote location and use it as if you were sitting right it front of it. Some of the key differences that set apart these programs:

- In a Remote Assistance session, both users must be present at their respective computers and must agree to establish the connection. Remote Desktop Connection can be initiated from one computer without the assent of someone at the remote target computer.

- With Remote Assistance, you can connect to a computer running any edition of Windows Vista. The target computer for a Remote Desktop Connection session must be running the Business, Enterprise, or Ultimate edition. (You can initiate the connection from any Windows Vista edition. You can even initiate the connection from a web browser, which is not possible with Remote Assistance.)

- Remote Assistance provides a shared view into an existing session (that is, the users at each end see the same screen and can share control), whereas Remote Desktop Connection starts a new session on the remote computer. The remote session takes over completely, and the local user loses interactive access, seeing instead a logon screen with a label indicating the user account that is logged on from a remote location.

- In a Remote Assistance session, the remote user has the same rights and privileges as the local user. With Remote Desktop Connection, remote users can do whatever their account credentials allow them to do.

- Remote Assistance connections can be established over the internet, even when each computer is behind a different router that uses NAT. With Remote Desktop Connection, the target computer must be on the same network (including a virtual private network, or VPN) and it cannot be behind a NAT router.

These two programs, of course, are intended to serve very different needs. But their similarities sometimes make it possible to use one in place of the other.

How Remote Assistance Works

The two parties in a Remote Assistance session are called the *novice* and the *expert*. (On some screens and in some documentation, the expert is referred to as the *helper.*) To use Remote Assistance, both parties must be using a Windows version that includes Remote Assistance (Windows Vista, Windows XP, or Windows Server 2003) and both must have an active internet connection or be on the same local area network, and neither can be blocked by a firewall.

To create a Remote Assistance session, the novice sends a Remote Assistance invitation, typically using an instant messenger program or e-mail. The expert then accepts the invitation and enters an agreed-upon password. Finally, the novice approves the expert's acceptance. A terminal window on the expert's computer that displays the desktop of the novice's machine then opens. The expert views the desktop in a read-only window and exchanges messages with the novice using text chat. In order to work with objects on the novice's computer, the expert must request control, and the novice must approve the request.

In a slight variation of this process, the expert can initiate the Remote Assistance session, perhaps in response to a telephone plea for help from the novice. We describe both connection processes in detail in the sections that follow.

At the heart of each Remote Assistance connection is a small text file called an *RA ticket*. (More formally, its type is Windows Remote Assistance Invitation and its extension is .msrcincident.) This file uses encrypted data in XML fields to define the parameters of a Remote Assistance connection. When you use Windows Live Messenger to manage the connection, the RA ticket is never visible. (In fact, Messenger uses a connection string that includes only part of the of the RA ticket information—just enough to establish connection.) When a novice sends a Remote Assistance request via e-mail, however, the RA ticket rides along as an attachment to the message. The expert has to double-click this file to launch the Remote Assistance session.

What happens next behind the scenes is the biggest improvement in the Windows Vista version of Remote Assistance: Without the use of a relay server, Remote Assistance is able to reach computers behind nearly any NAT router. It simultaneously attempts several types of connections until it finds one that works:

- **IPv4 address** is used when both computers can be directly addressed using IPv4, such as on a local area network or when both computers have public IP addresses.

- **IPv6 address** is used when both computers are on an IPv6 network; most routers and switches currently in use do not support IPv6 addressing.

- **UPnP NAT address** is used to connect through a UPnP router, which provides NAT traversal.

- **NAT traversal via Teredo** is used when all the other methods fail. After using a public Teredo server to determine NAT port mapping and to initiate communication, this connection then encapsulates IPv6 data in IPv4 packets, enabling it to tunnel through an IPv4 network.

For more information about NAT, IPv4, IPv6, and Teredo, see Chapter 12, "Setting Up a Small Network."

TROUBLESHOOTING

Teredo can't make a connection

If you can't make a connection and you're certain that a firewall isn't blocking the connection, be sure that UPnP is enabled on your router. (See the instructions for your router for details. If you no longer have the manual, check the manufacturer's website.) Teredo doesn't work with routers that use symmetric NAT. To find out if you have an incompatible router, at a command prompt type **netsh interface teredo show state** (this can be abbreviated as **netsh int ter sho st**). If the Type line shows Symmetric or Port Restricted, your best bet is UPnP.

With previous versions of Remote Assistance, connecting two systems behind NAT routers was difficult at best. Trying to explain to an inexperienced user who's already flustered because of computer problems all the complex configuration steps needed to bypass NAT made Remote Assistance impractical for most such setups. NAT is a great system for extending the limited number of available IP addresses and for securing computers on a small network. But it is the bane of users trying to make peer-to-peer connections, whether for voice, video, gaming—or Remote Assistance. Now, the only obstacle to end-to-end connections for Remote Assistance on computers running Windows Vista is a firewall.

Windows Firewall has an exception defined for Remote Assistance. (An exception is a group of rules that enable an application to communicate through the firewall.) By default, the exception is enabled only for private networks, such as a workgroup in a home or small office. The exception is disabled for public networks (such as an internet cafe or public Wi-Fi hotspot) and for domain networks. If you try to make a Remote Assistance connection when the exception is disabled, you'll see a message like the one shown in Figure 9-6.

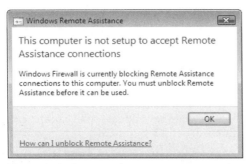

Figure 9-6 If you see this message, you need to enable the Remote Assistance exception in Windows Firewall.

To enable the exception in Windows Firewall, open Windows Firewall. In the left pane, click Allow A Program Through Windows Firewall (requires administrator privileges). On the Exceptions tab, select Remote Assistance and then click OK.

INSIDE OUT Know the rules

The specific rules that make up the Remote Assistance exception vary depending upon the profile type. For example, UPnP connections are enabled only in the private and domain profiles—not in the profile for public networks. Teredo connections are enabled only in the private and public profiles to prevent its use on corporate domains. The domain profile contains additional rules that enable help-desk personnel to offer assistance using DCOM. You might want to examine the rules that define the Remote Assistance exception, whether it's to satisfy your innate curiosity or to configure comparable rules for a third-party firewall. To do so:

1. Open Windows Firewall With Advanced Security (requires administrator privileges).
2. In the console tree, select Inbound Rules or Outbound Rules.
3. In the Actions pane, click Filter By Group, Filter By Remote Assistance.
4. In the details pane, double-click a rule to review its specifics.

Asking for Remote Assistance

To begin a Remote Assistance session, the novice must ask for help. That's done through either an instant messaging program or by opening the Remote Assistance program and sending an invitation file.

Using Instant Messaging

The simplest way to use Remote Assistance is through an instant messenger connection. The novice initiates the session by following these steps:

1. Sign in to Windows Live Messenger and open a chat window with your prospective helper, if one is not already open.
2. In the chat window, click the Activities button and then click Request Remote Assistance. Alternatively, click the Show Menu button and then click Actions, Request Remote Assistance. Your request appears as part of the conversation.
3. Specify a password for the session; the expert will be asked to enter the same password. If you have any doubt at all that the person at the other end of the instant messaging connection is who they appear to be, call the expert and provide the password by phone or send it by e-mail.
4. If the expert accepts the request (by clicking the Accept link in the chat window and correctly entering the agreed-upon password), Remote Assistance then

attempts to make a connection and, if successful, displays a prompt on the novice's computer.

5. Check the e-mail address in the prompt to be certain that you're chatting with who you think you are—after all, this person will be able to see and (with your additional consent) operate your computer—and then click Yes.

Once the Remote Assistance connection has been established, you no longer need the instant messenger session; you can close that window if you wish. You can resume your online discussion in the Remote Assistance chat pane.

> **Note**
>
> At the time of this book's publication, full support for Remote Assistance connections in Windows Vista is available only in Windows Live Messenger version 8. (Windows Live Messenger is available as a free download; use the link in the Windows Vista Welcome Center or visit *http://www.vista-io.com/0904*.) By the time you read this, however, other instant messaging applications might include this capability. The Rendezvous API allows any instant messaging application to be written in a way that integrates with Remote Assistance.

Sending an Invitation

If the expert and novice don't use the same instant messaging system, the novice can create an invitation file. The invitation file can be transferred to the expert via e-mail, a shared folder on the network or internet, or even on physical media, such as a USB flash drive. The novice follows these steps:

1. Open Remote Assistance, which can be done in any of the following ways:

   ○ On the Start menu, click All Programs, Maintenance, Windows Remote Assistance. (More simply, type **remote** in the Start menu Search box and click Windows Remote Assistance).

   ○ At a command prompt, type **msra**.

○ In Windows Help And Support, click the Ask button and then click the Windows Remote Assistance link.

2. In the Windows Remote Assistance window, click Invite Someone You Trust To Help You.

3. If you have an e-mail program set up on your computer, click Use E-mail To Send An Invitation. If you use a web-based e-mail program, or if you want to transfer the invitation file to a shared location on your network, click Save This Invitation As A File.

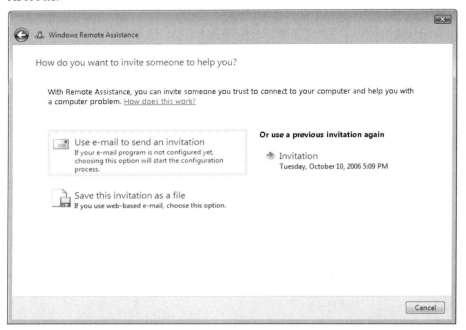

4. Provide the remaining information that Remote Assistance requests, such as a password that you create for the invitation, the location and name of the file to create, and the recipient's e-mail address.

5. If you chose the file option, get the file to the expert; send it as an e-mail attachment or store it in a location where the expert can open it. With the e-mail option, Remote Assistance takes care of this detail in its last step.

6. Give the password to the expert, preferably in person or by phone. (If you include the password along with the invitation file, anyone who intercepts the message can pose as the expert and connect to your computer.)

After you click Finish, Remote Assistance displays the window shown in Figure 9-7 and awaits a response from your invited expert. By default, the window (and the invitation) remains open for six hours. When the expert opens the invitation file, the expert's computer attempts to connect to the novice's computer, and displays on the novice's computer a message like the one shown in Figure 9-8.

Figure 9-7 If this window gets in your way while you wait for the expert to respond, minimize it. If you close it, the Remote Assistance session closes and the expert won't be able to connect.

Figure 9-8 After the expert opens the invitation file and enters the correct password, Remote Assistance negotiates a connection between the computers and then notifies the novice with this prompt.

INSIDE OUT   Change the invitation duration

By default, a Remote Assistance invitation expires six hours after it's created. For the best security, reduce the expiration time if the expert can respond quickly to your request. Conversely, you might need to create a longer lasting invitation if you don't expect your chosen expert to be available during that time. To modify the duration of invitation files you create:

1. Open System in Control Panel. (In the Start menu Search box, type **system**.)

2. In the Tasks list, click Remote Settings (requires administrator privileges).

3. On the Remote tab, click Advanced to display the dialog box shown in Figure 9-9 on the next page. Specify the amount of time that you want invitation files to remain valid.

Chapter 9

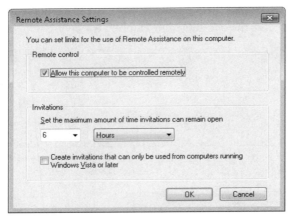

Figure 9-9 You can specify the time in minutes, hours, or days, up to a maximum of 99.

CAUTION

Don't make your invitation lifespan longer than necessary. Although there are several protections in place to prevent its misuse, a Remote Assistance file is an invitation to connect to your computer. It's best to keep the window of opportunity as small as possible. Note that when you close the Remote Assistance window on the novice's computer, you effectively cancel the invitation, regardless of the time.

Offering Remote Assistance to Someone Else

A weakness of Remote Assistance is that it ordinarily depends on the novice—someone who is having trouble using his or her computer—to initiate a Remote Assistance session by sending an invitation. Depending on how the novice and expert computers are connected and the novice's general computer aptitude, this hurdle might prevent the novice from ever getting the needed help.

With Windows Vista and Windows Live Messenger, the process can be driven entirely from the expert's end of the connection, making it much easier to assist inexperienced users. The process is nearly identical to the one initiated by the novice.

In a chat window with the person you want to help, click the Activities button and then click Offer Remote Assistance. The novice must accept the request and then, after a bit of handshaking, you're off to the races.

If you start Remote Assistance (type **msra** at a command prompt), you'll see the option to offer assistance; if you click that option, a screen appears that asks for the computer name or IP address of the user you want to assist. The ability to offer assistance in this way is intended primarily for corporate help desks and technical support centers within large organizations. It uses DCOM connectivity and requires prior configuration of the novice's computer, including configuration of that computer's firewall and user accounts; this is most easily done through group policy on a domain-based network. If you're trying to assist someone on a small network in a home or business, this option isn't for you; your best bet is to establish the Remote Assistance connection through Windows Live Messenger or other compatible instant messaging software. (The reason DCOM connectivity is not readily available in workgroups is primarily security. Allowing anyone to offer assistance to someone else is rife with danger.)

INSIDE OUT **Make it easier for the novice to request assistance**

The offer assistance feature is impractical except for experts in a domain environment or those with Windows Live Messenger connections to their friends in need of help. If you must rely on your novice friends to initiate a request by sending you an invitation, help them out by creating a shortcut on their desktop that creates an invitation and attaches it to an e-mail message; all they need to do is click Send. To do that, use the /Email option with Msra.exe. For details, at a command prompt type **msra /?**

Working in a Remote Assistance Session

After a Remote Assistance connection has been established as described in the previous sections, a Remote Assistance window opens on the expert's machine, as shown in Figure 9-10.

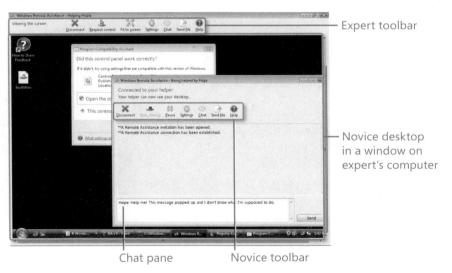

Figure 9-10 The novice's desktop appears on the expert's computer in a window topped with a toolbar containing Remote Assistance controls.

As the expert, you'll use the toolbar at the top of the Remote Assistance window to take control of the remote desktop, open a chat window, send a file, or disconnect when the session is complete. The novice has similar options available.

● Either party can terminate the session by clicking Disconnect.

● Request Control allows (with the novice's consent) the expert to take control of the novice's computer. For details, see the following section, "Taking Control of the Novice's Computer." While the expert has control, each party's toolbar has a Stop Sharing button, with which either user can return exclusive control to the novice.

● Clicking Fit To Screen toggles the expert's view of the novice's screen between actual-size and a scaled view that fits in the Remote Assistance window without the use of scroll bars.

● The Settings button appears on the Remote Assistance toolbar for both users, but it summons a different set of options, as shown in Figure 9-11. For details about these settings, see the following sections, "Taking Control of the Novice's Computer" and "Improving Remote Assistance Performance."

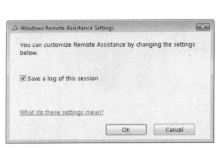

Figure 9-11 The expert (left) can make only one setting, whereas the novice (right) can also control performance and security options.

● Clicking Chat opens a chat pane that works much like an instant messaging program.

● Either party can send a file from their own computer to the other. The recipient must approve the transfer before it begins.

● Clicking Help displays a list of Remote Assistance topics in Help And Support.

- When the novice clicks Pause, the expert's view of the novice's screen is blacked out until the novice clicks Continue.

Taking Control of the Novice's Computer

For obvious security reasons, clicking Request Control sends a request to the novice, who must grant permission before the expert can actually begin working with the remote desktop. (See Figure 9-12.) While the expert has control, the novice's computer responds to input from the keyboard and mouse of *both* the expert and the novice. At any time, the novice can cut off the expert's ability to control the session by tapping the Esc key; alternatively, either party can return exclusive control to the novice by clicking Stop Sharing.

Figure 9-12 The novice must decide whether to allow the expert to take control, and whether the expert should be able to perform administrative tasks.

Regardless of his or her expert credentials, the expert's actions in a Remote Assistance session are governed by the privileges assigned to the novice user's account. When connecting to a machine belonging to a user with a standard user account, for instance, you might be unable to edit the registry or make necessary configuration changes unless you can supply the password for an administrator account on the novice's computer.

The setting of the check box shown in Figure 9-12 determines what happens whenever a User Account Control (UAC) prompt (that is, the secure desktop) appears on the novice's computer:

- If the novice selects the check box, the expert sees any UAC prompt that appears once control is granted, and can respond to it just as the local user (that is, the novice) can.

- If the check box is clear (the default), whenever a UAC prompt appears on the novice's screen, the expert's screen is blacked out, exactly the same as if the session was paused. The expert's screen remains blacked out until the novice closes the UAC prompt.

The novice can change the setting after control has been granted by visiting the Settings dialog box. (See Figure 9-11.)

For more details about UAC, see "Preventing Unsafe Actions with User Account Control" in Chapter 10.

Using Remote Assistance with Earlier Windows Versions

Windows Vista is not the first version of Windows to include Remote Assistance; it's also available in Windows XP and Windows Server 2003. For the most part, experts and novices on any of these three platforms can use Remote Assistance to help each other. There are some limitations:

- If either computer is running an earlier version of Windows, Remote Assistance in Windows Vista reverts to the capabilities of the earlier version. New connectivity features such as NAT traversal using Teredo are unavailable, as are the performance enhancements introduced with Windows Vista.

- Remote Assistance in Windows Vista does not support voice chat, which was supported in earlier versions.

- Pausing a session (the expert can't see what occurs while a session is paused) is a feature that's new to Windows Vista. If a novice running Windows Vista pauses a session, an expert running an earlier version receives no indication that the session has been paused.

- You cannot offer assistance from a computer running an earlier version, nor can you use instant messenger to offer assistance from a computer running Windows Vista to a computer running an earlier version.

- Invitation files created on a computer with the "Windows Vista–only" option enabled (see Figure 9-11) are completely encrypted and cannot be used on computers running earlier versions.

Maintaining Security

Remote Assistance is a powerful tool. In the wrong hands, it's also potentially dangerous, because it allows a remote user to install software and tamper with a system configuration. In a worst-case scenario, someone could trick an unsuspecting novice into allowing access to his or her machine, and then plant a Trojan application or gain access to sensitive files.

Remote Assistance was designed and built with security in mind, and several enhancements have been made in the Windows Vista version. For example:

- A password is required for all connections, whether by invitation file or instant messenger.

- The novice must agree to accept each incoming connection, and must approve each request to share control.

- Invitation files expire six hours after they're created or when the Remote Assistance session is closed.

- Remote Assistance uses a dynamic port assignment.

- By default, the Windows Firewall exception for Remote Assistance is enabled only on private networks.

For these reasons and more, Remote Assistance is sufficiently secure out of the box. You can take some additional precautions to completely slam the door on Remote Assistance–related security breaches.

- Set a short expiration time on Remote Assistance invitations sent via e-mail. An expiration time of one hour should be sufficient for most requests. (Note that the invitation must be accepted within the specified time; you don't need to specify the length of the Remote Assistance session.) An expired RA ticket file is worthless to a potential hacker.

- Assign a strong password to Remote Assistance invitations. Because e-mail is fundamentally insecure, do not send the password with the invitation. Instead, communicate the password by telephone or in a separate e-mail message.

- Manually expire an invitation when it's no longer needed. To do so, simply close the Remote Assistance window.

- If both the expert and novice use Windows Vista, use encrypted invitation files. Open System in Control Panel. In the Tasks list, click Remote Settings. On the Remote tab, click Advanced. Then select Create Invitations That Can Only Be Used From Computers Running Windows Vista Or Later.

- Disable Remote Assistance on any machine where the possible benefits of a Remote Assistance session are outweighed by potential security risks. To completely disable Remote Assistance on a given machine, open System, click Remote Settings, click the Remote tab, and then clear Allow Remote Assistance Connections To This Computer. If that step seems too drastic, you can limit Remote Assistance capabilities so that an expert cannot take control of the remote machine. On the Remote tab, click Advanced and then clear Allow This Computer To Be Controlled Remotely.

Improving Remote Assistance Performance

You might shudder at the thought of accessing another desktop over a dial-up connection. Surprisingly, the performance can be quite usable. You wouldn't want to use this sort of connection for everyday work, but for troubleshooting, it's good enough.

You can maximize Remote Assistance performance over a slow link by observing these guidelines:

- If possible, use Windows Vista for both novice and expert. Its version of Remote Assistance incorporates a number of performance enhancements compared to the version included in Windows XP, but most of these improvements are effective only when both computers are running Windows Vista.

- Close any unnecessary applications on the novice machine.

- Don't let the novice move the mouse on the novice machine, if possible, when the expert is in control of the screen.

- Reduce the visual complexity of the novice machine as much as possible. Reduce the display resolution to 800 × 600 and use only as many colors as is absolutely necessary.

- Turn off desktop animations and other sophisticated visual effects, and avoid opening windows that contain complex graphics unless absolutely necessary.

The last two suggestions can be implemented by using the Settings button on the novice machine (see Figure 9-11). The Bandwith Usage slider has four settings; for details about each setting, move the slider. The slower your connection, the lower you should set this slider.

PART II

Security and Networking

Security Essentials

Home Basic ●
Home Premium ●
Business ○
Enterprise ○
Ultimate ●

In the early days of personal computing, security—if it was considered at all—was a mere afterthought. But as personal computers have become more powerful, more complex, and more connected, they've also become more vulnerable. Because Microsoft Windows is so widely used, computers running any version of Windows make an especially juicy target for those who would like to steal your valuable personal data, appropriate your computing resources and bandwidth, or simply create havoc. Security can no longer be an afterthought, but it needn't be an all-consuming passion for you either.

In part, that's because security is an all-consuming passion for the developers of Windows Vista. Countless new features (some are visible, such as User Account Control and Windows Defender; but there are also many under-the-hood improvements) have significantly raised the bar for those malcontents who try to attack your computer. The bad guys don't give up easily, however.

In this chapter, we examine in detail each of four essential security steps—using a firewall, getting updates, blocking viruses, and blocking spyware—for ensuring that your computer is protected from those who would do it harm. We also explain how to use new tools in Windows Vista that can help to keep your kids out of trouble.

What's in Your Edition?

Parental Controls is included only in the Home Basic, Home Premium, and Ultimate editions. All other security components of Windows Vista described in this chapter work identically in all editions.

Chapter 10

Understanding Security Threats

With advances in security technology and increased user awareness of security threats and how to mitigate them, the good guys seem to be getting the upper hand. Nonetheless, 52 percent of the companies participating in the 2006 Computer Crime and Security Survey, conducted by the Computer Security Institute and the Federal Bureau of Investigation, reported one or more incidents of "unauthorized computer use" during the prior year. (To be clear, many of the respondents represent large corporations with thousands of computers. The results don't suggest that 52 percent of *all computers* were attacked—not even close. But they do suggest that security is a widespread problem that, to some degree, affects many, many people who administer computers.)

When people talk about security threats these days, they're generally referring to viruses, worms, and spyware. Understanding how these programs work is essential to keeping them out of your computer and network. Let's start with some definitions:

- A *virus* is a piece of code that replicates by attaching itself to another object. A virus doesn't have to be a self-contained program; in fact, many outbreaks of seemingly new viruses actually involve rewritten and repackaged versions of older virus code. When a virus infects a computer running Windows, it can attack the registry, replace system files, and take over e-mail programs in its attempt to replicate itself. The virus payload is the destructive portion of the code. Historically, viruses have been written to destroy or corrupt data files, wipe out installed programs, or damage the operating system itself.

- A *worm* is an independent program that replicates by copying itself from one computer to another, usually over a network or through e-mail attachments. Many modern worms also contain virus code that can damage data or consume so many system resources that they render the operating system unusable.

- *Spyware* is a term that originally referred to software that uses an internet connection without the user's knowledge or consent. It soon came to encompass *adware*, which is advertiser-sponsored software that typically tracks a user's web surfing habits, which it then reports to the advertiser. Today, the term is used in a much broader sense, as a catch-all for many types of potentially unwanted software. Some such programs display pop-up ads; others redirect Internet Explorer to a search engine or home page that's different from the one you specify; still others replace the advertisements in webpages you visit with ads of their own. For the purposes of this chapter, our definition of spyware is "any program that is installed without the user's full and informed consent, often through deceptive means, and that displays advertising, records personal information, or changes a computer's configuration without the user's explicit permission."

The most pernicious form of spyware is the *Trojan horse program*, which acts as a stealth server that allows intruders to take control of a remote computer without the owner's knowledge. (For example, a Trojan horse program making the rounds in late 2006 caught the attention of Securities and Exchange Commission investigators because it was being used to monitor users' activities and to capture account numbers and passwords for brokerage accounts, which were subsequently cleaned out.) Like the Greek myth after which they're named, Trojan horse programs typically masquerade as benign programs and rely on gullible users to install them. Computers that have been taken over by a Trojan horse program are sometimes referred to as zombies. Armies of these zombies can be used to launch crippling attacks against websites.

Computer viruses date back to the 1980s, when they were most commonly transmitted through infected floppy disks. In recent years, though, virus outbreaks have become faster and more destructive, thanks to the ubiquitous nature of the Windows platform and popular e-mail programs such as Microsoft Outlook and Outlook Express (the predecessor to Windows Mail), coupled with the soaring popularity of the internet. Virus writers have become more sophisticated, too, adding smart setup routines, sophisticated encryption, downloadable plug-ins, and automatic web-based updates to their dangerous wares. Polymorphic viruses can mutate as they infect new host files, making discovery and disinfection difficult because no two instances of the virus "look" the same to virus scanners. A new class of so-called stealth viruses can disguise themselves so that installed antivirus software can't detect them. If you know where to look in the virus underground, you can find point-and-click virus-authoring software, which lets even a nonprogrammer build a fully functional, destructive virus.

Many viruses and worms spread by attaching themselves to e-mail messages and then transmitting themselves to every address they can find on the victim's computer. Some bury the virus code in an executable file that masquerades as something innocuous, such as an animated greeting card. When the victim opens the attachment, the animated file plays in its own window, disguising the virus activity.

Other viruses hidden in e-mail attachments try to cloak their true identity by appending an additional file name extension to the infected attachment. This strategy relies on the intended victim using the default settings of Windows Explorer, which hides extensions for known file types. With file name extensions turned off, the attachment might appear to be an innocuous Microsoft Word document, for example, and an unwary recipient would be more likely to open it.

Chapter 10

Securing Your Computer: Four Essential Steps

1. **Keep your firewall turned on.** You can use Windows Firewall, which is included with Windows Vista, or a firewall that you obtain elsewhere. For details, see "Blocking Intruders with Windows Firewall," later in this chapter.

2. **Keep Windows Vista up to date.** Windows Update can do this for you automatically. For details, see "Keeping Your System Secure with Windows Update."

3. **Use an antivirus program.** You'll need to obtain one, as none is included with Windows Vista. For more information, see "Blocking Viruses and Worms with an Antivirus Program."

4. **Use an antispyware program.** Windows Defender, which is included with Windows Vista, serves this function well. For details, see "Stopping Spyware with Windows Defender."

Windows Security Center monitors each of these four areas to be sure you're protected, and displays an alert if something needs attention. For details, see "Monitoring Security in Windows Vista," later in this chapter.

Beyond those essential steps, it's important that you learn to avoid installing potentially risky software. User Account Control (UAC) helps in this regard by limiting the administrative tasks (installing any type of program is an administrative task—even though it is not always performed by an "administrator") that less knowledgeable users can perform. (For details, see "Preventing Unsafe Actions with User Account Control.") In addition, Internet Explorer makes getting into trouble more difficult than in previous versions. (For more information, see "Internet Security and Privacy Options," in Chapter 6.) Windows Security Center also monitors your UAC and internet security settings.

Finally, if you have children who use your computer, you'll want to help them to stay safe while on the computer, and you might want to restrict their computer activities in other ways. Parental Controls in Windows Vista can help with those tasks; for details, see "Controlling Your Children's Computer Access."

What's New in Windows Vista

In a word: plenty.

Several security features, such as User Access Control and Parental Controls, are completely new to Windows Vista; they're unavailable in any earlier version of Microsoft Windows. Even some of the features with familiar names, such as Windows Firewall and Windows Update, have been completely overhauled in Windows Vista. Among the key improvements:

- **User Account Control (UAC)** UAC reduces the inherent danger of using an administrator account for everyday tasks by requesting your consent when an application needs to do something with system-wide effect—which includes virtually all administrative tasks. Furthermore, architectural changes wrought by UAC make it practical for most people to use a standard account for daily computing.

- **Windows Firewall** Windows Firewall is substantially changed from the version in Windows XP. Significantly, it is now a "two-way" firewall, monitoring outbound traffic as well as inbound. With its advanced configuration console, administrators have much greater control over firewall rules and other settings.

- **Windows Defender** Windows Defender, an antispyware program, continuously monitors to prevent the installation of known spyware and to alert you to the presence of spyware-like activity.

- **Internet Explorer** Internet Explorer runs in Protected Mode, which lessens the likelihood of installing malicious code. Effectively, it runs isolated in a "sandbox" with reduced privileges, able to write data only in a temporary files folder unless you grant permission to act outside the protected area. Other security improvements to Internet Explorer include a phishing filter and restrictions on ActiveX controls. (For more information, see "Internet Explorer Security and Privacy Options," in Chapter 6.)

- **Parental Controls** Parental Controls provide tools to help parents guide their kids' use of the internet, games, and other programs.

- **Data redirection** While running under a standard user's account, an application that attempts to write to a protected system folder (such as %ProgramFiles% or %SystemRoot%) gets transparently redirected to a virtual file store within the user's profile. Similarly, if an application attempts to write to system-wide areas of the registry (such as the HKEY_LOCAL_MACHINE hive), it gets redirected to virtual keys within the user's section of the registry. Applications that attempt to read from these protected file and registry locations look first to the virtual stores. File and registry virtualization allows standard users to run older applications—including many of those that required administrator access under Windows XP—while at the same time preventing malicious applications from writing to areas that could bring down the entire system.

- **Buffer overrun protection** Address Space Layout Randomization (ASLR) is one of several underlying technologies, new to Windows Vista, that defend against buffer overrun exploits. With ASLR, each time you boot Windows Vista, system code is loaded into different locations in memory. This seemingly simple change stymies a class of well-known attacks in which exploit code attempts to call a system function from a known location. ASLR and numerous other esoteric programming changes are one result of Microsoft's adoption of the Security Development Lifecycle (*http://www.vista-io.com/1002*), a process that minimizes security bugs in program code.

- **Additional security on 64-bit computers** With the 64-bit versions of Windows Vista, only digitally signed device drivers can be installed. This feature, called PatchGuard, ensures that kernel-level code is from a known source and has not been altered, as a means to prevent the installation of rootkits.

Chapter 10

- **Data encryption** BitLocker Drive Encryption (available only in Enterprise and Ultimate editions) encrypts entire hard drives—making the data they contain completely inaccessible to a thief who makes off with a computer. The Encrypting File System (EFS) has been improved in Windows Vista with smart card support, page file encryption, and additional group policy options.

- **Restrictions on removable drives** Through the use of group policy, administrators can control the use of removable storage devices, such as USB flash drives and external hard drives. These restrictions can help prevent the theft of sensitive or proprietary data. In addition, they can be used to seal an entry point for viruses and other malware brought in from home.

> **Note**
>
> For more details about the underlying architecture and new security features in Windows Vista, see the "Windows Vista Security Enhancements" white paper at *http://www.vista-io.com/1001*.

Preventing Unsafe Actions with User Account Control

One of the most visible security changes, at least while you're setting up and configuring a new computer, is User Account Control (UAC). It's also one of the most controversial—and potentially most effective. In short, UAC intercedes whenever a user or program attempts to perform a system administrative task and asks for the consent of a computer administrator before commencing what could be risky business. A typical request looks like the one shown in Figure 10-1.

Figure 10-1 The UAC prompt appears on the darkened secure desktop, centered on the location where you clicked the shortcut, button, or link that triggered the prompt.

To understand why UAC is effective you need to look at security before Windows Vista. Computer security experts have long espoused *least privilege*, a rule that states that you give only enough access for a person to perform his or her job. (This basic security tenet is sometimes referred to as LUA, an acronym that, depending upon whom you ask, stands for "limited user account," "least user access," "least-privileged user account," or something similar.) In earlier versions of Windows, by default all accounts are set up as administrator accounts, with full privileges to do anything on the computer—including the ability to easily and inadvertently install viruses and perform other harmful tasks. This is a clear violation of LUA, and security experts recommended setting up users with limited accounts (comparable to standard accounts in Windows Vista); because these accounts have fewer rights and more restrictive permissions, users and programs running with limited accounts can do less damage. As it turns out, however, using a limited account in Windows XP is practically impossible, primarily because most applications of the day were written with the assumption that users would have full administrative privileges and don't run properly (or at all) with a limited account.

By contrast, in Windows Vista, accounts after the first one are nonadministrator standard accounts by default; while they can carry out all the usual daily computing tasks, they're prevented from performing potentially harmful operations. These restrictions apply not just to the user; more important, they also apply to any programs launched by the user. Even administrator accounts run as so-called "protected administrator" accounts, in which they run with standard-user privileges except when they need to perform administrative tasks. (This is sometimes called Admin Approval Mode.)

For information about user accounts, see Chapter 11, "Managing User Accounts, Passwords, and Logons."

Newer, security-aware programs are written so they don't require administrator privileges for performing everyday tasks. Programs that truly need administrative access (such as utility programs that change computer settings) request elevation. And what about those older programs—many still in use—that require administrator privileges? Windows Vista has several ways of making most of them work properly. In one way or another, the program is made to act as if it's being run by an administrator. One method, for example, is file and registry virtualization (also known as data redirection); when a program attempts to write to (and subsequently read from) a file or registry key on which only administrators have write access, Windows Vista instead uses a file or key within the current user's profile. In some cases, a program must be marked as requiring elevation, in which case it triggers a UAC prompt each time it runs—and then actually runs as an administrator.

For more information about program compatibility, see "Dealing with Compatibility Issues," in Chapter 4.

IT professionals, network administrators, and the extremely curious can find detailed information about UAC in two white papers available on the Microsoft TechNet website: "User Account Control Overview" (*http://www.vista-io.com/1003*) and "Understanding and Configuring User Account Control in Windows Vista" (*http://www.vista-io.com/1004*).

Chapter 10

What Triggers UAC Prompts

The types of actions that require elevation to administrator status (and therefore display a UAC elevation prompt) include those that make changes to system-wide settings or to files in %SystemRoot% or %ProgramFiles%. Among the actions that require elevation:

- Installing and uninstalling applications
- Installing device drivers
- Installing ActiveX controls
- Installing Windows Updates
- Changing settings for Windows Firewall
- Changing UAC settings
- Configuring Windows Update
- Adding or removing user accounts
- Changing a user's account type
- Configuring Parental Controls
- Running Task Scheduler
- Restoring backed-up system files
- Viewing or changing another user's folders and files

Within Windows Vista, you can identify in advance many actions that require elevation. A shield icon next to a button or link indicates that a UAC prompt will appear.

Dealing with UAC Prompts

At logon, Windows creates a token that is used to identify the privilege levels of your account. Standard users get a standard token, but administrators actually get two: a standard token and an administrator token. The standard token is used to open Explorer.exe (the Windows shell), from which all subsequent programs are launched. Child processes inherit the token of the process that launches them so, by default, all applications run as a standard user—even when you're logged on with an administrator account. Certain programs request elevation to administrator privileges; that's when the UAC prompt is displayed. If you provide administrator credentials, Windows then opens the program using the administrator token. Note that any processes that the successfully elevated program opens also run as administrator.

As an elevation-requesting application attempts to open, UAC evaluates the application and the request and then displays an appropriate prompt. As an administrator, the most common prompt you're likely to see is the *consent prompt*, which is shown in Figure 10-1. Read it, check the name of the program, click Continue, and carry on.

If you use a standard account, when a program requires elevation, you'll see the *credentials prompt*, which is shown in Figure 10-2. If the user is able to provide the credentials (that is, user name and password, smart card, or fingerprint, depending on how logon authentication is configured on the computer) of an administrator, the application opens using the administrator's access token.

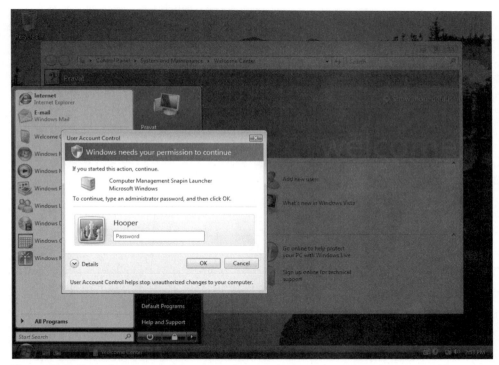

Figure 10-2 To perform an administrative task, a standard user must enter the password for an administrator account.

You'll encounter other UAC prompts as well. A colored background near the top of the prompt dialog box provides a quick visual clue to the type of program that's requesting elevation.

- **Red background and red shield icon** Identifies an application from a blocked publisher or one that is blocked by Group Policy; be extremely wary if you see one of these

- **Yellow-orange background and red shield icon** Identifies an application (signed or unsigned) that is not yet trusted by the local computer (see Figure 10-3)

- **Blue-green background** Identifies an administrative application that is part of Windows Vista (see Figures 10-1 and 10-2, earlier in this chapter)

- **Gray background** Identifies an application that is Authenticode signed and trusted by the local computer

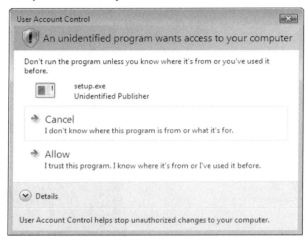

Figure 10-3. When you install a new program, you'll see a UAC prompt.

In all cases, the UAC dialog box sits atop the *secure desktop*, a separate process that no other application can interfere with. (If the secure desktop wasn't secure, a malicious program could put another dialog box in front of the UAC dialog box, perhaps with a message encouraging you to let the program proceed. Or a malicious program could grab your keystrokes, thereby learning your administrator logon password.) When the secure desktop is displayed, you can't switch tasks or click the windows on the desktop. (In fact, they're not really windows. When UAC invokes the secure desktop, it snaps a picture of the desktop, darkens it, and then displays that image behind the dialog box.)

> **Note**
>
> If an application other than the foreground application requests elevation, instead of interrupting your work (the foreground task) with a prompt, UAC signals its request with a flashing taskbar button. Click the taskbar button to see the prompt.

It becomes natural to click though dialog boxes without reading them or giving them a second thought. But it's important to recognize that security risks to your computer are real, and that actions that trigger a UAC prompt are *potentially* dangerous. Clearly, if you know what you're doing and you click a button to, say, set the Windows Update settings, you can blow past that security dialog box with no more than a quick glance to be sure it was raised by the expected application. But if a UAC prompt appears when you're not expecting it—stop, read it carefully, and think before you click.

Disabling UAC—and Why You Shouldn't

You don't like it when UAC asks for your approval to do something you just told it to do? No problem; you can turn it off—but you'll have to respond to one last UAC prompt in order to do so! Here's how:

1. In Control Panel, open User Accounts.

2. Click Turn User Account Control On Or Off.

3. Respond in the affirmative to that pesky UAC prompt.

4. Clear the check box and click OK.

5. Restart your computer.

With UAC disabled, the shield icons still appear throughout Control Panel, but you won't see any UAC prompts. Clicking a button or link identified with a shield immediately proceeds with the desired action. Administrators run with full administrator privileges; standard users, of course, still have only standard privileges.

> **Note**
>
> It's important to recognize that UAC is more than annoying prompts. Only when UAC is enabled does an administrator run with a standard token. Only when UAC is enabled does Internet Explorer run in a low-privilege Protected Mode. And, of course, only when UAC is enabled does it warn you when a rogue application attempts to perform a task with systemwide impact.

Are you beginning to miss UAC yet? To turn it back on, follow the same procedure as above (except you select the check box, of course). But note: This is one of those settings that a standard user can't make. You must log on as an administrator to restore UAC.

Although the UAC prompts are sometimes intrusive, that's the point. First, they provide a not-so-subtle reminder that what you're about to do has systemwide effect. But most important, it prevents a malicious application from silently installing without your knowledge. Most spyware, viruses, and other malware get installed as a direct, albeit unintended, result of a user action, such as clicking a link. When you click a link that you think is going to display some pretty pictures, wouldn't you be pleased to have UAC tell you that it's attempting to install a program?

One misperception about UAC is that it doesn't let you do certain things, or that it "locks you out" of your own computer. In fact, UAC doesn't prevent anything—all it does is inform you when an application requires administrator access. Remember that, even though you're logged in with an administrator account, you ordinarily run as a standard user. Need to run something that requires full administrator privileges? Simply respond to the prompt. (If you find that you can't access certain folders and files, it's likely that the restriction is imposed by NTFS permissions—which are unrelated to UAC. For information about NTFS, see Chapter 29, "Controlling Access to Files and Folders.")

Working Around UAC Without Disabling It

Most people encounter lots of UAC prompts while setting up a new computer, configuring it, and installing programs. After that, they seldom see a prompt from UAC and forget that it's even there. But if you frequently tweak your computer's settings or install new programs, consider these tricks for running into fewer prompts:

- **Use an administrator Command Prompt window** Because child processes inherit the access token of the process that opens them, programs that you run from an administrator command prompt run as an administrator without further prompting. You'll need to respond to just a single prompt when you open the Command Prompt window. Then you can enter commands, open MMC consoles, start programs, and edit the registry without further prompting.

  To open an administrator Command Prompt window, use one of these methods:

  - In the Start menu Search box, type **cmd**. Then press Ctrl+Shift+Enter. (This little-known shortcut is equivalent to right-clicking a shortcut and clicking Run As Administrator.)

  - Create a shortcut to Cmd.exe. Open the shortcut's properties dialog box and, on the Shortcut tab, click Advanced. Select Run As Administrator.

Naturally, you can only run programs for which you know the name and location of the executable file, as well as any required command-line parameters. (You can often glean this information by examining an application's shortcut.) Also note that Windows Explorer, Internet Explorer, and Control Panel do not run as administrator, even when started from an administrator command prompt. (You can run Control Panel applications if you know the command line; it's just the main Control Panel window that does not run with elevated privileges.)

- **Run as a standard user** As a standard user, you'll actually encounter *fewer* elevation prompts than you do as an administrator. In this situation, many applications refuse to run or run with limitations (for example, they might not display all settings or they might not save settings you make). On those occasions when you do need to use such an application with full capabilities, right-click and choose Run As Administrator. Or, in the Start menu Search box, type the program name and press Ctrl+Shift+Enter.

- **Use a fingerprint reader** If you ordinarily use a standard user account—always a good practice—and you're required to type the password for your administrator password when UAC presents a credential prompt, you'll find it easier to use biometric authentication, such as a fingerprint reader. With this inexpensive peripheral, you can simply swipe your finger instead of typing a lengthy password.

- **Use the Administrator account and fast user switching** Longtime Windows veterans know that each computer has a special administrator account named Administrator. In Windows Vista, the Administrator account is disabled by default. You can enable the account (for details, see "Working with User Accounts," Chapter 11) and then, whenever you need to perform an administrative task, switch users to the Administrator account. By default, the Administrator account is not affected by UAC.

INSIDE OUT   Business users can customize UAC behavior

Users of the Business, Enterprise, and Ultimate editions of Windows Vista can use the Local Security Policy console to modify the behavior of UAC. Start Local Security Policy (Secpol.msc) and open Security Settings\Local Policies\Security Options. In the details pane, scroll down to the policies whose names begin with "User Account Control." For each policy, double-click it and click the Explain tab for information before you decide upon a setting.

Chapter 10

Monitoring Security in Windows Vista

In Windows Vista, security-related options have been gathered in an application called Windows Security Center. Ordinarily, the only indication of this program's presence is its shield icon in the notification area, which serves as a reminder that Security Center is on the job, monitoring your computer's essential security settings. You can open Security Center by double-clicking its notification area icon (or clicking one of the messages that emanate from that icon when your computer's security settings need attention). You can also open Security Center via its icon in Control Panel or by typing **wscui.cpl** at a command prompt. Figure 10-4 shows the various elements in Security Center.

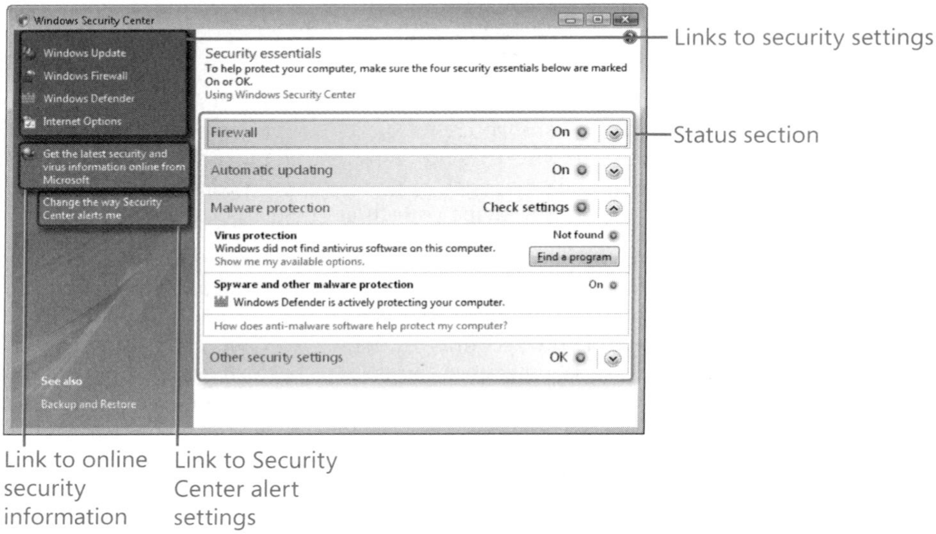
Windows Security Center
Windows Update
Windows Firewall
Windows Defender
Internet Options
Get the latest security and virus information online from Microsoft
Change the way Security Center alerts me
See also
Backup and Restore
Security essentials
To help protect your computer, make sure the four security essentials below are marked On or OK.
Using Windows Security Center
Firewall On
Automatic updating On
Malware protection Check settings
Virus protection Not found
Windows did not find antivirus software on this computer.
Show me my available options.
Find a program
Spyware and other malware protection On
Windows Defender is actively protecting your computer.
How does anti-malware software help protect my computer?
Other security settings OK
Links to security settings
Status section
Link to online security information
Link to Security Center alert settings

Figure 10-4 Security Center collects security related information and settings in a single window.

The status section provides at-a-glance information about your security settings. For each item, if everything is okay, you'll see a green bar with the word *On*. Clicking the green bar expands it to display descriptive information. Items that need your attention have a yellow or red bar, and status is indicated by phrases such as *Off*, *Check settings*, *Out of date*, *Not found*, *Not automatic*, or *Not monitored*. Below the bar appear explanatory text and buttons that let you correct the problem (or configure Security Center so that it won't bother you).

INSIDE OUT   **Use Security Center on a domain member computer**

If your computer is joined to a domain, Security Center is turned off by default. Although you can still summon it from Control Panel in this situation, the status section is absent. No icon appears in the notification area, and Security Center does not monitor your computer's security status. The only function of Security Center while it's turned off is to provide an attractive container for links to security-related Control Panel applications and online security information. Security Center is neutered by default in a domain-based computer because the domain administrator typically has more powerful security tools available and will want to centrally administer security settings. However, by making a group policy change, you can enable Security Center for a domain-based computer and use it just as if you're working on a computer that is not joined to a domain. Here's how:

1. At a command prompt, type **gpedit.msc** to open Group Policy Object Editor; you'll need administrative privileges.

2. In Group Policy Object Editor, open Computer Configuration\Administrative Templates\Windows Components\Security Center.

3. Double-click the Turn On Security Center (Domain PCs Only) policy.

4. Select Enabled and click OK.

This procedure uses the local Group Policy object to enable Security Center for all users on a computer. Note that this policy can be overridden by policies set on the domain controller.

Security Center is designed to work with third-party firewall, antivirus, and antispyware programs as well as with the programs built in to Windows Vista (Windows Firewall and Windows Defender) and those available separately from Microsoft, such as Windows Live OneCare. (Even programs that include their own control panel are monitored by Security Center and can be controlled—at least for basic functionality—from Security Center if you prefer.) Systems with more than one program installed in any of these categories include a link to show a list of such programs, as shown in Figure 10-5 on the next page. The dialog box that appears allows you to turn on any installed program that is currently not enabled.

Chapter 10

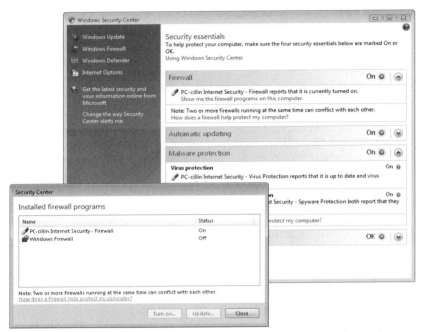

Figure 10-5 Security Center is designed to manage security settings from other vendors in addition to those included with Windows.

> **Note**
>
> Running more than one firewall or more than one antivirus program can cause problems as the programs compete with each other to process each bit of information that passes through the computer. (In fact, many firewall and antivirus programs refuse to install until other protective software is removed.) For this reason, Security Center doesn't allow you to turn on a firewall or antivirus program until all others in that category have been turned off. Antispyware programs, on the other hand, generally don't have such conflicts, so you can safely run multiple programs if you really feel the need to do so.

Although Security Center is designed to work with other security programs, some such programs are not properly recognized by Security Center. Using Windows Management Instrumentation (WMI) queries, it checks for the presence of other software, and also checks to see if the software (including its virus and spyware definitions) is up to date and whether real-time scanning is enabled. Some third-party security programs don't respond in an expected way, so Security Center doesn't recognize their existence.

If you've turned off Windows Firewall in favor of an unrecognized third-party firewall, Security Center indicates with a red bar that your computer has no firewall protection.

Click Show Me My Available Options to display the dialog box shown in Figure 10-6. If you don't want to use Windows Firewall and you don't want to be bothered with alerts from Security Center, click I Have A Firewall Program That I'll Monitor Myself. You won't receive any further alerts, and thereafter Security Center passively indicates the status as Not Monitored. If you decide you'd rather use Windows Firewall, instead of clicking Show Me My Available Options, simply click Turn On Now to enable Windows Firewall for each of your network connections, without so much as a visit to Windows Firewall or Network And Sharing Center.

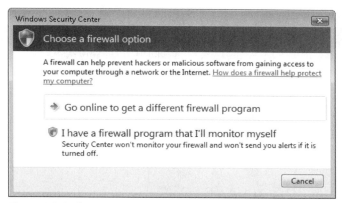

Figure 10-6 If you use a third-party firewall that Security Center doesn't recognize (or you'd like to find a firewall program), choose one of these options.

> **Note**
>
> Security Center does not detect any type of hardware firewall device. If your network has one, you can stop monitoring to avoid the warnings—or, better yet, you can enable Windows Firewall. Although it's not a good idea to run more than one software firewall on a computer, you should run a software firewall as an extra layer of protection behind your hardware firewall. This helps to protect your computer in case other computers on your network contract a virus or spyware infection.

Likewise, if you use an antivirus program that Security Center doesn't recognize, you can avoid incessant warnings from Security Center with a workaround similar to the one for unrecognized firewalls: Under Virus Protection, click Show Me My Available Options and then click I Have An Antivirus Program That I'll Monitor Myself. A second option, Don't Monitor My Antivirus Software State, does exactly the same thing (but isn't it nice to have a choice?!). The options for antispyware are similar to those for firewalls: go online to find a program, or simply stop monitoring.

Chapter 10

INSIDE OUT Disable Security Center alerts

Selecting the I Have... option in any of the "available options" dialog boxes, as described in the preceding paragraphs, causes Security Center to stop monitoring a particular security component and, therefore, to stop displaying security alert messages that sprout from the notification area. However, you might want to disable the alerts but not disable Security Center monitoring. This ensures that alerts don't pop up at inopportune times, such as during a presentation. To disable alerts, in Security Center click Change The Way Security Center Alerts Me, the last link on the left side. In the dialog box that appears, shown below, you can disable Security Center alerts and, if you like, repress the notification area icon. (The shield icon provides a quick status check; a red shield with an X or a yellow shield with an exclamation point indicates that Security Center isn't satisfied with your current settings.)

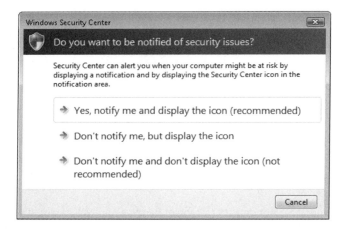

Naturally, you can use the links in the upper left corner of the Security Center window to open Control Panel applications in which you can refine your security settings. As shown in Figure 10-4, by default Security Center includes icons for Windows Update, Windows Firewall, Windows Defender, and Internet Options. At the time of this book's publication, we're not aware of any third-party firewall, antivirus, or antispyware programs that add their own icons to the mix. But Security Center is designed to easily accommodate them, so that with a complement of properly designed programs, it serves as the heart of your basic security operations.

Keeping Up with Security News

It's an unfortunate fact of life: Security has become an unwanted but essential part of the computing experience. Therefore, you might want to schedule periodic visits to security-related websites and subscribe to security-related newsletters or RSS feeds. Some resources you might want to check out include:

- Microsoft's security home page at *http://www.vista-io.com/1009* offers links to information about the latest security updates (which you already have installed if you use Windows Update), current security threats, security training sessions, guidance centers, and other information. The link to online information in Security Center leads to this page.

- Microsoft TechNet Security (*http://www.vista-io.com/1010*) provides more technical details, aimed primarily at information technology (IT) professionals. You can view the latest issue of the Microsoft Security Newsletter at *http://www.vista-io.com/1011*; to subscribe, visit *http://www.vista-io.com/1012*.

- You can sign up for alerts (sent via e-mail, RSS, or instant messenger) of security information from Microsoft at *http://www.vista-io.com/1013* and *http://www.vista-io.com/1014*.

- You can also find valuable technical information on current security threats at *http://www.cert.org*, a site maintained by the CERT Coordination Center, a research institute operated by Carnegie Mellon University.

Blocking Intruders with Windows Firewall

Your first line of defense in securing your computer is to protect it from attacks by outsiders. Once your computer is connected to the internet, it becomes just another node on a huge global network. A *firewall* provides a barrier between your computer and the network to which it's connected by preventing the entry of unwanted traffic while allowing transparent passage to authorized connections.

Using a firewall is simple, essential, and often overlooked. You'll want to be sure that all network connections are protected by a firewall. You might be comforted by the knowledge that your portable computer is protected by a corporate firewall when you're at work and that you use a firewalled broadband connection at home. But what about the dial-up connection you use when you travel? Viruses like Sasser and its ilk find unprotected dial-up connections to be an easy mark. In fact, although dial-up users are less vulnerable to certain types of attacks just because of their relatively short connection time, they are particularly vulnerable to internet worms like Sasser because many internet service providers (ISPs) don't offer effective firewall protection for this type of connection.

And it makes sense to run a firewall on your computer (sometimes called a *personal firewall*) even when you're behind a residential router or corporate firewall. Other people on your network might not be as vigilant as you are about defending against viruses, so if someone brings in a Sasser-infected portable computer and connects it to the network, you're toast—unless your network connection has its own firewall protection.

Chapter 10

CAUTION

This bears repeating. In today's environment, you should run firewall software on each networked computer; don't rely on corporate gateway firewalls and gateway antivirus solutions to protect your computer from another infected computer inside the perimeter. It was this kind of vulnerability that led to the Blaster worm's quick and wide proliferation throughout supposedly protected networks in 2003. Administrators who fret about installing, maintaining, and restricting usage of yet another application on every desktop throughout an enterprise can take solace in the fact that Windows Firewall can be centrally managed through Group Policy.

Windows Vista includes a two-way stateful-inspection packet filtering firewall called, cleverly enough, Windows Firewall. Windows Firewall is enabled by default for all connections, and it begins protecting your computer as it boots. By default:

- The firewall drops all inbound traffic except traffic sent in response to a request sent by your computer, and unsolicited traffic that has been explicitly allowed by creating an exception.

- All outgoing traffic is allowed unless it matches a configured exception.

You notice nothing if a packet is dropped, but you can (at your option) create a log of all such events.

Stateful-Inspection Packet Filtering Explained

Most firewalls work, at least in part, by *packet filtering*—that is, they block or allow transmissions depending on the content of each packet that reaches the firewall. A packet filter examines several attributes of each packet and can either route it (that is, forward it to the intended destination computer) or block it, based on any of these attributes:

- **Source address** The IP address of the computer that generated the packet
- **Destination address** The IP address of the packet's intended target computer
- **Network protocol** The type of traffic, such as Internet Protocol (IP)
- **Transport protocol** The higher level protocol, such as Transmission Control Protocol (TCP) or User Datagram Protocol (UDP)
- **Source and destination ports** The number that communicating computers use to identify a communications channel

Packet filtering alone is an inadequate solution; incoming traffic that meets all the packet filter criteria could still be something you didn't ask for or want. *Stateful-inspection packet filtering* goes a step further by restricting incoming traffic to responses to requests from your computer. Here's a simplified example of how stateful-inspection filtering works to allow "good" incoming traffic:

1. You enter a URL in your browser's Address Bar.

2. The browser sends one or more packets of data, addressed to the web server. The destination port is 80, the standard port for HTTP web servers; the source port is an arbitrary number between 1024 and 65535.

3. The firewall saves information about the connection in its state table, which it will use to validate returning inbound traffic.

4. After the web server and your computer complete the handshaking needed to open a TCP connection, the web server sends a reply (the contents of the webpage you requested) addressed to your computer's IP address and source port.

5. The firewall receives the incoming traffic and compares its source and destination addresses and ports with the information in its state table. If the information matches, the firewall permits the reply to pass through to the browser. If the data doesn't match in all respects, the firewall silently discards the packet.

6. Your browser displays the received information.

Compared with the firewall included in Windows XP, Windows Firewall has been enhanced in several ways:

- Windows Firewall supports both incoming and outgoing network traffic.

- Through its Windows Firewall With Advanced Security console, Windows Firewall provides far more configuration options, and it can be configured remotely. A new wizard makes it easier to create and configure rules. Configuration of Internet Protocol Security (IPsec), a mechanism that provides for authentication, encryption, and filtering of network traffic, is also done in the Windows Firewall With Advanced Security console.

- In addition to the usual criteria (addresses, protocols, and ports), firewall exceptions can be configured for services, Active Directory accounts and groups, source and destination IP addresses for incoming and outgoing traffic, transport protocols other than TCP and UDP, network connection types, and more.

- Windows Firewall maintains three separate profiles, with the appropriate one selected depending on whether the computer is connected to a domain, to a private non-domain network, or to a public network.

Tools for Managing Windows Firewall

Windows Vista includes no fewer than four different tools for configuring and controlling Windows Firewall:

- Windows Firewall, a Control Panel application, is the simplest—and the least capable. Nonetheless, with it you can complete routine tasks, such as allowing a program through the firewall or blocking all incoming connections.

- Windows Firewall With Advanced Security is a snap-in and predefined console for Microsoft Management Console (MMC). It offers much more granular control over rules, exceptions, and profiles.

Chapter 10

- Group Policy Object Editor (available only in Business, Enterprise, and Ultimate editions) incorporates the Windows Firewall With Advanced Security snap-in (under Computer Configuration\Windows Settings\Security Settings\Windows Firewall With Advanced Security). In addition, Windows Firewall can be managed with a number of policies, which can be found in Computer Configuration\Administrative Templates\Network\Network Connections\Windows Firewall.

- The Netsh utility (in particular, its Firewall and Advfirewall contexts) lets you make firewall settings from a Command Prompt window or a batch program.

This chapter, remember, is about security *essentials*. Therefore, we discuss only the Control Panel application, which is shown in Figure 10-7.

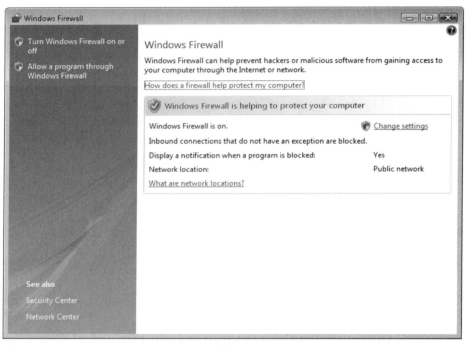

Figure 10-7 You can open Windows Firewall from Control Panel or Security Center, as well as the Start menu.

> **Note**
>
> Veteran users of Windows Firewall in Windows XP with Service Pack 2 might notice the omission of a few features and settings in the Windows Firewall Settings dialog box in Windows Vista. Specifically, the settings for firewall logs and for configuring services and Internet Control Message Protocol (ICMP) traffic (such as Ping and other diagnostic tools) are not to be found. Instead, to view and modify those settings, use Windows Firewall With Advanced Security.
>
> **For information about the advanced tools for managing Windows Firewall, see Chapter 31, "Advanced Security Management."**

Using Windows Firewall in Different Network Locations

Windows Firewall maintains a separate profile (that is, a complete collection of settings, including rules and exceptions for various programs, services, and ports) for each of three network location types:

- **Domain** Used when your computer is joined to an Active Directory domain; in this environment, firewall settings are typically (but not necessarily) controlled by a network administrator

- **Private** Used when your computer is connected to a Home or Work network in a workgroup configuration

- **Public** Used when your computer is connected to a network in a public location, such as an airport or library; it's common—indeed, recommended—to have fewer exceptions and more restrictions when you use a public network

Settings you make in the Windows Firewall Settings dialog box affect only the firewall profile for the network location you're currently using. The settings in a profile apply to all networks of the particular location type to which you connect. (For example, if you allow a program through the firewall while connected to a public network, that program exception is then enabled whenever you connect to any other public network. It is not enabled when you're connected to a domain or private network, unless you enable the exception in those profiles.) To make settings for a different network location, either connect to that network or use Windows Firewall With Advanced Security.

For more information about network locations, see "Understanding Location Types," Chapter 12.

Chapter 10

Enabling or Disabling Windows Firewall

The main Windows Firewall application, shown in Figure 10-7, is little more than a status window and launchpad for the Windows Firewall Settings dialog box, which is shown in Figure 10-8. To enable Windows Firewall for all network connections, select On. To disable Windows Firewall, of course, select Off. In general, the only reason to turn off Windows Firewall is if you have installed a third-party firewall that you plan to use instead of Windows Firewall.

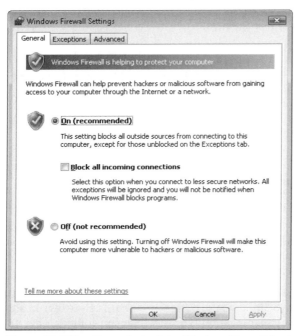

Figure 10-8 The General tab of the Windows Firewall Settings dialog box houses the main on/off switch for Windows Firewall.

Preventing All Incoming Traffic

The Block All Incoming Connections check box on the General tab provides additional safety. When it's selected, Windows Firewall rejects *all* unsolicited incoming traffic—even traffic that would ordinarily be permitted by an exception. (For information about exceptions, see "Allowing Connections Through the Firewall," on the next page.) Invoke this mode when extra security against outside attack is needed. For example, you might disable exceptions when you're using a public wireless hotspot or when you know that your computer is actively under attack by others.

> **Note**
>
> Selecting Block All Incoming Connections does not disconnect your computer from the internet. Even in "no exceptions" mode, you can still use your browser to connect to the internet. Similarly, other outbound connections—whether they're legitimate services or some sort of spyware—continue unabated. If you really want to sever your ties to the outside world, open Network And Sharing Center and disable each network connection. (Alternatively, use brute force: physically disconnect wired network connections and turn off wireless adapters.)

Disabling Windows Firewall for Individual Connections

Windows Firewall ordinarily monitors all network connections for unwanted traffic. In some situations, you might want to disable its protection for one or more connections while leaving it on for others. (For example, you might have a print server on your internal LAN connection that refuses to work with Windows Firewall—but you still want to protect your external dial-up connection.) That's easily done, as follows:

1. In Windows Firewall, click the Advanced tab.

2. Clear the check box of each connection for which you want to disable Windows Firewall.

Allowing Connections Through the Firewall

In some situations, you want to allow other computers to initiate a connection to your computer. For example, you might use Windows Meeting Space, play multiplayer games, or chat via an instant messaging program; these types of programs typically require inbound connections so others can contact you. In each of these cases, you set up an *exception* in Windows Firewall. An exception pokes a small hole in the firewall and allows a certain type of traffic to pass through the firewall.

Working with Exceptions

You manage exceptions that apply to all connections on the Exceptions tab, shown in Figure 10-9 on the next page. The list of programs and services that initially appears on the Exceptions tab depends on which services and programs are installed on your computer; you can add others, as described in the following sections. In addition, exceptions are created (but not enabled) when a program tries to set up an incoming connection. To enable an exception for a program or service that's already been defined, simply select its check box.

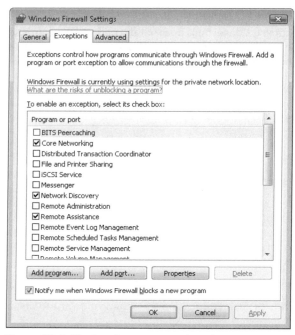

Figure 10-9 The list of programs and services on your computer might not include all those shown here, and it might include others.

Each exception increases your security risk to some degree, so you should clear the check box for all exceptions you don't need. If you're confident you won't ever need a particular exception, you can select it and then click Delete. (A handful of predefined exceptions don't allow deletion, but as long as their check boxes are not selected, there's no danger.)

Creating an Exception for a Program

When you run a program that needs to allow an inbound connection, you can create an exception in any of three ways:

- You can click Unblock when Windows Firewall blocks a program and asks if you want to keep blocking.

- You can set up a program exception on the Exceptions tab in Windows Firewall.

- You can open a port on the Exceptions tab in Windows Firewall. (For details, see "Opening a Port," later in this chapter.)

> **Note**
>
> A *port* is a somewhat arbitrary number that two computers use to identify a particular communications channel. In order for two computers to connect to each other using TCP/IP, both have to agree on which port number (from 1 to 65535) each computer will use.

Creating an exception for a program using either of the first two methods is usually the easier and more secure approach. You don't need to know which port (or ports) the program uses. And Windows Firewall allows the exception only while the program is running, whereas an exception created for a port you open is allowed whenever Windows itself is running, regardless of whether the affected program is actually running.

The first time you run a program that tries to set up an incoming connection, Windows Firewall asks for your permission by displaying a dialog box like the one shown in Figure 10-10.

Figure 10-10 When this dialog box appears, Windows Firewall creates an exception. But it enables the exception only if you click Unblock.

When such a dialog box appears, read it carefully:

- Is the program one that you knowingly installed and ran?

- Is it reasonable for the program to require acceptance of incoming connections?

- Are you currently using a network location where it's okay for this program to accept incoming connections?

If the answer to any of these questions is no—or if you're unsure—click Keep Blocking. If you later find that a needed program isn't working properly, you can open Windows Firewall Settings and enable the exception.

From the Exceptions tab, you can set up a program exception without waiting for the Windows Security Alert dialog box to appear. Follow these steps:

1. Click Add Program. The Add A Program dialog box appears.

2. In the Add A Program dialog box, select the program for which you want to allow incoming connections. Or click Browse and navigate to the program's executable file if it isn't shown in the Programs list.

3. Click Change Scope to display the dialog box shown in Figure 10-11.

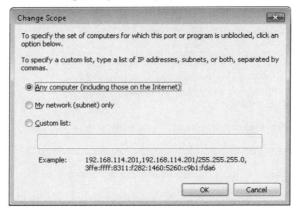

Figure 10-11 The scope options are the same for creating a program exception or opening a port.

4. Select the range of computers from which you want to allow incoming connections.

○ Any Computer means just that—any computer on your network or on the internet. (Other defenses, such as NTFS permissions or some form of password authentication, might keep out unwanted users, but Windows Firewall will not.)

○ My Network (Subnet) Allows inbound connections inbound connections only from computers in the same subnet as yours. (For information about subnets, see "Troubleshooting TCP/IP Problems," Chapter 14.)

○ Custom List lets you specify one or more computers by their IP address (IPv4 or IPv6). These can be computers on your local area network or computers with public IP addresses on the internet.

Opening a Port

Another way to create an exception for an incoming connection is to open a port. If the instructions for a program or service you want to use indicate that it needs to use a particular port, use the following procedure to open the specified port.

1. In Windows Firewall, click the Exceptions tab.

2. Click Add Port. The Add A Port dialog box appears.

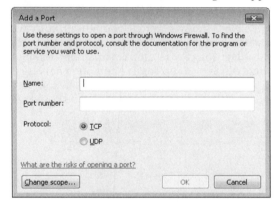

3. In the Add A Port dialog box, make the following entries:

○ In the Name box, type a descriptive name for the program or service.

○ In the Port Number box, type the port number needed by the program or service.

○ Select either TCP or UDP to match the protocol needed by the program or service.

4. Click Change Scope.

5. In the Change Scope dialog box (see Figure 10-11 and step 4 in the previous section), select the range of computers from which you want to allow incoming connections.

Chapter 10

Keeping Your System Secure with Windows Update

Windows Update is a service that provides online updates for Windows Vista. With it, you can obtain updates to Windows that include security updates, performance improvements, and support for new devices. Completely overhauled in Windows Vista, Windows Update is now a Control Panel application instead of using a web-based interface. (Of course, it still requires an active internet connection.) As before, it can be opened from the All Programs menu or the Tools menu in Internet Explorer as well as from Control Panel.

> **Note**
>
> Keeping Windows up-to-date is an absolutely essential step in maintaining a secure computer and avoiding malware. In recent years, the most widely exploited vulnerabilities in Windows have been patched quickly—usually *before* the issue became a widespread problem. Windows users who installed the updates promptly were able to avoid infection, whereas legions of others (who failed to keep their systems updated) fell victim.

Depending on how you have Windows Update configured, you might not need to visit the Windows Update window at all, as it does its work quietly in the background, keeping your computer up-to-date with the latest fixes and improvements. You can view its current settings, see what it has been up to, and find out what else it has in store for you by starting at its main window, shown in Figure 10-12. The top part of the window displays the current status and alerts you to any actions you should take.

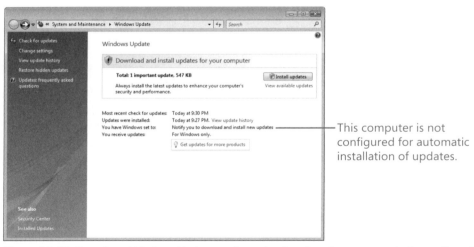

Figure 10-12 If you have Windows Update configured to install updates automatically, you'll rarely need to visit its Control Panel application.

INSIDE OUT   **Get updates for other Microsoft products**

In this chapter, we talk about the ability of Windows Update to download and install updates for Windows Vista. You can also merge the functionality of Microsoft Update, a service for managing updates to Microsoft Office and several other Microsoft products, into Windows Update so you no longer need to visit Office Online to get updates. To enable checking of other products, on the Windows Update home page, click Get Updates For More Products, which takes you to the Microsoft Update website for some quick installation steps. (You only need to do this once. Thereafter, the "more products" link doesn't appear, and the Windows Update home page indicates that you receive updates "for Windows and other products from Microsoft Update.")

Although security updates are routinely released on the second Tuesday of each month (informally known as "patch Tuesday"), other updates are not distributed on a regular basis. Instead, they're published when the need arises, such as when a fix is developed for a newly discovered problem. You can make a habit of regularly visiting Windows Update to see what's new, but there's an easier way: install updates automatically. To review in greater detail (and modify, if you wish) your current Windows Update settings, click Change Settings. The page that appears (shown in Figure 10-13), lets you specify the degree of automation.

Figure 10-13 For set-it-and-forget-it convenience, select the first option.

With one of the first three options selected, you don't need to remember to visit Windows Update periodically. Instead, Windows Update checks for you and (depending on your settings) downloads updates in a way that throttles its use of your internet connection bandwidth to avoid interfering with your normal use of the connection. If you use the automatic installation option, Windows Update installs any updates it has downloaded at the time you specify (3:00 AM by default). If your computer is in a low-power "sleep" state at that time *and* if your computer is connected to AC power, Windows Update wakes the computer to perform the installation. (If your sleeping computer is not plugged in, Windows Update waits until the next scheduled installation time.)

If you have either the "download, but don't install" or "check, but don't download or install" options selected, Windows Update notifies you with a pop-up message when new updates are available for your review.

Click the message to open Windows Update. If you miss the pop-up message, the information awaits you the next time you open Windows Update. When you arrive there, click Install Updates to finish installing all updates or, if you want to review them first, click View Available Updates. See Figure 10-14.

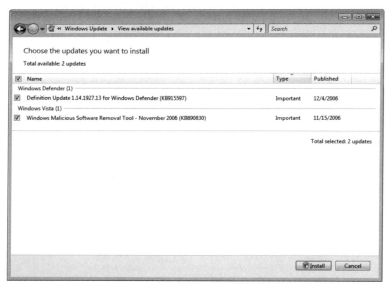

Figure 10-14 Clear the check box for any updates you do not want before you click Install.

INSIDE OUT   Hide updates that you don't ever want to install

If you choose not to download and install an update, it's available for you the next time you visit Windows Update...and the next time, and the next time after that, too. You might have a good reason for not accepting a particular update—perhaps it makes improvements to a Windows component you never use—and there's no reason it should clutter your list of available updates. To remove an item from the list without installing it, you hide it. But the trick for hiding updates in the list is itself somewhat hidden.

In the list of updates (see Figure 10-14), right-click any update that you don't want to see again, and choose Hide Update. If you later change your mind—or if you just want to see a list of the updates you've chosen to hide—on the main Windows Update page, click Restore Hidden Updates.

Windows Update classifies updates into three categories: important (which includes security and critical performance updates), recommended (typically, updates to signed drivers that affect performance or reliability, as well as fixes to noncritical bugs), and optional (updated drivers for nonessential components, interesting but unnecessary enhancements, and so on). Important updates are always included in automatic updates. The setting near the bottom of the Change Settings page determines whether recommended updates are included. Optional updates are never included in automatic updates. To review, download, and install optional updates, you must open Windows Update.

TROUBLESHOOTING

Windows Update fails to download and install updates

When Windows Update fails, it displays an error code on its home page, along with a link to get help about the problem. The first place to start solving the problem, of course, is with the Get Help link. Sometimes that doesn't work either.

In that case, check your internet connection. If it's not working, that would not only account for the failure of Windows Update, but also for the failure of the link to additional help.

Using Windows Update Manually

Whether you choose one of the automatic update options or choose the "never check" option, you can always manually check for updates to Microsoft products. To check for updates to Windows Vista, open Windows Update and click Check For Updates (in the left pane).

Chapter 10

Removing an Update

If you find that a particular update creates a problem, you can try removing it. Not all updates can be removed, however. (In particular, security-related updates usually cannot be removed. In addition, updates upon which other updates or other components are dependent cannot be removed.) To find out if an update can be removed—and to go ahead and do the deed, if you choose—in Windows Update, click Installed Updates (in the left pane). Doing so takes you to a page within the Programs section of Control Panel that lists all uninstallable updates.

> **Note**
>
> The installed updates page might lead you to believe that no updates have been installed. (For some reason, the "No updates are installed on this computer" message gives people that impression.) In fact, this page lists only the updates that can be uninstalled. To see a list of all updates that have been installed, return to Windows Update and click View Update History.

Updating More Than One Computer

The simplest way to keep all the computers on your network up to date is to enable automatic updating on each computer. If you have a small network in a home environment, go to each computer, open Windows Update, click Change Settings, and be sure it's set to download and install automatically.

But that's not always practical or efficient. If you have a dial-up connection to the internet, for example, you'll spend a lot of time connected as each computer independently downloads large updates. And in larger networks, even those with lightning-fast internet connections, administrators might want to control which updates get installed (and when) rather than leaving it up to individual users.

Microsoft provides the following ways to manage updates in situations where setting Windows Update to automatic on all computers is impractical:

- Microsoft Update Catalog (*http://www.vista-io.com/1018*) is a website that offers stand-alone installable versions of each update for Windows. Microsoft Update Catalog offers updates for all currently supported versions of Windows, which means you can also use this service to find updates for computers on your network that are not running Windows Vista. You can search for updates based on operating system, language, date posted, content, and type of update. After you find the updates of interest, download them once and store them in a shared network folder, where they can be installed from any computer.

- Administrators of large networks can use Windows Server Update Services (WSUS) to manage and deploy updates throughout an organization. The WSUS server, which runs on a computer running Windows Server 2003 or Windows Server "Longhorn," manages downloading updates from Microsoft; computers on the network then obtain updates from the WSUS server instead directly from Microsoft's update servers. For details about WSUS, visit *http://www.vista-io.com/1017.*

Blocking Viruses and Worms with an Antivirus Program

A *virus* is a computer program that replicates by attaching itself to another object. Viruses can infect program files, documents (in the form of macro viruses), or low-level disk and file-system structures such as the boot sector and partition table. Viruses can run when an infected program file runs; they can also reside in memory and infect files as the user opens, saves, or creates the files. A *worm* is a stand-alone program that replicates by copying itself from one computer to another, usually over a network or through e-mail attachments. The distinction between viruses and worms can be blurry, and for practical purposes, is unimportant.

Historically, the most common source of widespread computer virus outbreaks is the class of hostile software that replicates by sending itself to other potential victims as an attachment to an e-mail message. The accompanying message often uses "social engineering" techniques designed to lure inattentive or gullible users into opening the infected attachment. Several variants of the Mydoom virus, which spread like wildfire throughout 2004, arrived as attachments that mimicked delivery failure reports from an e-mail server administrator. The attachment, in .zip format, ostensibly included details of the failed message but actually contained the virus payload.

INSIDE OUT   Beware of .zip files attached to e-mail messages

These days, most mail servers reject all incoming messages with executable files attached; even if the server doesn't stop such messages, modern e-mail clients make it difficult or impossible to run executable attachments. That simple measure completely stops most viruses written before 2003. To work around the blockade, attachment-based viruses now typically send their payloads using the standard .zip format for compressed files. If the user opens the attachment, the contents of the compressed file appear—in Windows Explorer or in the third-party utility assigned to handle .zip files. Double-clicking the executable file within the compressed archive sets the virus in motion. Virus writers use a variety of tricks with .zip files. In some cases, they include a bogus extension in the file name and then append a large number of spaces before the real file name extension, so that the actual file type doesn't appear in the window that displays archived files. Some viruses even encrypt the .zip attachment and include the password as part of the message. That allows the infected attachment to slip past some virus scanners. Most real-time scanners will detect a virus in a .zip file, either when it arrives or when the user tries to extract the file. The moral? Be wary of all attachments, even when they appear to be innocent.

Although viruses that spread through e-mail attachments have been to blame for the majority of attacks in recent years, some security experts believe that other modes of transmission represent a far greater threat and will become more prevalent in the future. By their nature, attachments (as well as files transferred with an instant messenger program, a more recent attack vector) require some cooperation from an unwitting or distracted user; that requirement dramatically limits their potential to spread unchecked. As a result, authors of hostile software are always on the lookout for techniques they can use to spread infections automatically.

One popular mechanism is the use of scripts, written in languages such as JavaScript, JScript, or Microsoft Visual Basic Scripting Edition (often abbreviated as VBScript or VBS), that automatically take actions on the intended victim's computer when he or she visits a webpage or views an HTML-formatted e-mail message. Protected Mode in Internet Explorer is one defense against this type of intrusion.

For details about Protected Mode and other defensive measures in Internet Explorer, see Chapter 27, "Advanced Internet Explorer Security and Administration."

Viruses and worms are not necessarily, by their very nature, dangerous. Most are, however—why else would a programmer need to resort to such sneaky techniques?—and you don't want them on your computer. Besides replicating itself, a virus can be programmed to do just about anything that the current user account is allowed to do, such as erase files, make registry changes, and send information over the internet. An important layer in a basic PC protection strategy, therefore, is to use up-to-date antivirus software. Windows Vista does not include any antivirus software, but it's readily available from Microsoft and many other vendors.

Finding an Antivirus Program

Plenty of good antivirus programs are available. You can start your search at the Windows Vista Antivirus Providers page, *http://www.vista-io.com/1025*, which provides brief summaries and links to publishers of Windows Vista–compatible antivirus software. (If you haven't yet installed antivirus software, you'll find a link to this site in Windows Security Center. Under Malware Protection, click Find A Program.) CERT Coordination Center also maintains a list of antivirus vendors on its Computer Virus Resources page at *http://www.vista-io.com/1022*.

Both of these resources provide lists of products but little or no independent evaluation. Besides the usual review sites managed by computer magazines, you should look to ICSA Labs, which tests antivirus programs and certifies those that meet its criteria for effectiveness. You can find lists of certified programs at *http://www.vista-io.com/1020*.

> **Note**
>
> Microsoft's entry in the antivirus arena is Windows Live OneCare *(http://www.windowsonecare.com)*. In addition to antivirus protection, Windows Live OneCare provides other tools for keeping your computer secure and healthy, including a replacement for Windows Firewall, backup capabilities, and automated "tune-ups" that perform maintenance tasks such as defragmenting your hard disks.

Using an Antivirus Program

Installing an antivirus program is a good first step. But you're not done yet! The initial setup enables the antivirus scanning engine—the code that checks files for possible viruses. The most important part of the package is the database of virus definitions (sometimes called the signature file). After installing an antivirus package on a new computer, update it to the latest definitions immediately. Then configure the program to enable these features:

- Install updates to program files and virus definitions at least weekly.

- Scan each file that you access in any way. This feature is typically called real-time scanning, virus monitoring, or something similar. Don't confuse this type of scanning with scheduled scans, which periodically scan the files stored on your computer to find infected files.

- Scan e-mail attachments and block access to infected files.

Learning More About Viruses and Virus Protection

The internet is a rich source of complete and accurate information about viruses, worms, and other hostile software. Unfortunately, a random search of the internet for information about "computer viruses" also turns up a long list of links to sites that are incomplete, out-of-date, or run by scam artists. We recommend that you start your search for definitive information with the vendor that supplies your antivirus software, because that company is most likely to have information and step-by-step instructions that are directly applicable to your system configuration. Virtually every major company that produces antivirus software offers a searchable web-based list of viruses. In addition, we suggest bookmarking the CERT Coordination Center site, which offers up-to-date, unbiased information about currently active viruses *(http://www.vista-io.com/1021)*.

The CERT Coordination Center Computer Virus Resources page at *http://www.vista-io.com/1022* provides lots of general information about viruses—how they've evolved, how they work, how you can protect against them, and how you can recover from an infection. Another good resource is "The Antivirus Defense-in-Depth Guide" *(http://www.vista-io.com/1019)*, which was produced by the Microsoft Solutions for Security group. Although this white paper is targeted primarily at IT professionals working on a

Chapter 10

corporate network, its information is useful (and understandable) for people without a computer science degree too.

Scanning for Viruses—Without an Antivirus Program

On the second Tuesday of each month, as part of its normal security releases, Microsoft releases an updated version of a utility called the Malicious Software Removal Tool (MSRT). This utility is not designed to block new viruses from entering a computer; rather, its function is to clean up systems that have been infected with well-known and widespread viruses and other forms of malware. The MSRT is delivered by Windows Update, and on most computers, this tool runs silently and then deletes itself; it keeps a record of its actions, including details of any viruses it detected and removed, in a file called Mrt.log in your %SystemRoot%\Debug folder.

If you prefer to scan one or more systems manually, you can download the current executable version of the MSRT from *http://www.vista-io.com/1026*. Because this utility is updated at least monthly, we do not recommend that you save this file. For details about this tool, read Microsoft Knowledge Base article 890830 *(http://www.vista-io.com/1028)*.

As an alternative to the MSRT, free web-based virus scanning services are available from several antivirus vendors. The Windows Live OneCare safety scanner can be run from *http://www.vista-io.com/1027*. Because this tool uses an ActiveX control, you must run the web-based scan using Internet Explorer and not an alternative browser.

CAUTION
Periodic scanning by the MSRT or an online tool does not provide continuous protection against virus infections. For that, you need to install and run an antivirus program.

Do You Need an Antivirus Program?

Some computer experts—computer *security* experts, even—proudly point out that they don't use antivirus software. Why not? Some question its efficacy, particularly at blocking zero-day exploits for which virus definitions have not been created. (A *zero-day exploit* is one that exploits a security vulnerability on the same day that the vulnerability becomes widely known among security researchers.) Others point to the fact that, like every additional running program, an antivirus program adds another level of complexity and another potential attack surface for malicious software. Indeed, at one time or another, virtually every major antivirus program has been found to have some vulnerability to remote exploits. Finally, what puts some folks over the edge is the performance hit imposed by antivirus programs that constantly work in the background to examine each file as it's read from disk; the slowdown is small, but measurable.

How is it possible to maintain a virus-free computer without the assistance of an antivirus program? Remember that antivirus protection is just one of many security layers in a well-protected computer network. To have any hope of surviving unscathed without that layer, several other forms of protection must be in place. The network's internet gateway should provide filtering that prevents viruses from entering through a web browser or instant messenger connection; this capability is typically available only in commercial-grade firewall appliances or in a separate gateway computer that's configured for this purpose.

The e-mail server should also have virus blocking capability. (Many ISPs and web-based mail services block all mail that contains a virus.) In theory, those network-level layers should prevent any malware from reaching your computer, but the computer itself must be properly secured in other ways: all patches up to date, firewall enabled, User Account Control enabled, and a standard account set up for each user. The most important protective layer—and the one that is most easily overlooked—is user education and self control. *Everyone* who uses the computer must have the discipline to read and evaluate security warnings when they're presented and to allow the installation only of software that is known to be safe. (Although a user with a standard account is incapable of installing or running a program that wipes out the entire computer, they can still inflict enough damage on their own corner of the computer to cause considerable inconvenience.) Countless successful virus attacks worldwide have proven that most users do not have adequate awareness of safe computing methods. Indeed, our standard advice for most users is *don't even think of connecting to the internet without antivirus software!* Only people who really know what they're doing, and who remain vigilant, should consider joining those anti-antivirus experts.

Stopping Spyware with Windows Defender

Spyware is a term that has come to describe a variety of undesirable software, ranging from annoying pop-up ads to programs that surreptitiously send your private information to other people. Indications of common spyware infections include:

- Unexpected new toolbars, favorites, and links in your web browser
- Changes to your browser's home page and default search provider
- Numerous pop-up ads
- Sudden occurrence of computer crashes or slow performance

Note that spyware doesn't necessarily "spy" on you. A common characteristic of anything dubbed spyware is that it does its deeds—malicious or otherwise—without your informed consent. (Spyware typically gets installed by deceitfully asking permission to do something other than what it actually does or, in some cases, by exploiting browser vulnerabilities. In this regard, most spyware is fundamentally different from earlier types of malware; it typically relies on social engineering to install instead of exploiting vulnerabilities.)

That's where Windows Defender comes in. For known malicious programs that have no redeeming value to you, it intercedes without disturbing you and then quarantines or removes the offending program. Other "spyware" programs, along with programs that perform activities that are suspiciously similar to known spyware tactics, fall into a gray area; when Windows Defender encounters one of these programs knocking at your door, it offers some advice and asks what you want to do. By participating in Microsoft SpyNet, you can also learn from the experience of other users.

> **Note**
> For detailed information about the criteria that Windows Defender uses to identify spyware, visit *http://www.vista-io.com/1030*.

In addition to its real-time protection for spyware-like behavior, Windows Defender (shown in Figure 10-15) also scans your computer's files periodically, looking for known spyware. Once installed, most spyware programs are configured to run automatically each time you start your computer. Windows Defender includes a Software Explorer component that provides comprehensive information about all startup programs and other risk-prone program types, along with tools for disabling any of these programs.

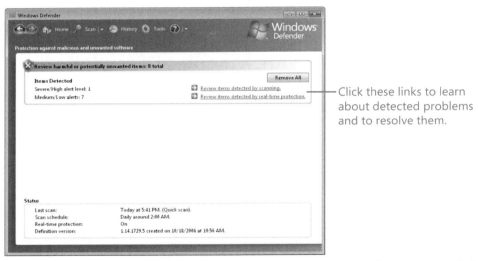

Click these links to learn about detected problems and to resolve them.

Figure 10-15 The Windows Defender home page shows the current status of your system, including links to information about detected problems, the scan schedule, and the date of the spyware definition file.

For information about managing programs with Software Explorer in Windows Defender, see "Managing Startup Programs," Chapter 4.

Windows Defender runs as a service, which allows it to provide protection for all users on your computer. The Windows Defender user interface runs in the context of the current user (therefore, UAC elevation is required for some actions), but the scanning and spyware removal is done by the service—and without the need for administrative privileges.

> **Note**
>
> Windows Defender is a good antispyware solution for computers in homes and in small business networks. If you use a domain-based networks, you might want to look into Microsoft Forefront Client Security *(http://www.vista-io.com/1032)*, which provides spyware protection with centralized control, management, and reporting.

Scanning Your Computer for Spyware

Scanning is one of the two primary detection mechanisms in Windows Defender. (The other is real-time protection.) When Windows Defender scans your computer, it checks applications it finds against a database of spyware definitions. The database, which is frequently updated via Windows Update, contains detailed information about known spyware, including file names and version numbers, a description of the threat presented by each program, and a recommended action to take if the program is found on your computer.

TROUBLESHOOTING

Spyware definitions don't update properly

Microsoft Knowledge Base article 918355 *(http://www.vista-io.com/1031)* explains how to troubleshoot and resolve definition update problems.

Chapter 10

Scanning Automatically

By default, Windows Defender scans your computer automatically once a day; your current scan schedule appears near the bottom of the home page in Windows Defender, shown in Figure 10-15. You can modify the schedule and set other scanning options by clicking Tools and then clicking Options. The Options page is shown in Figure 10-16.

Figure 10-16 Scheduling options are near the top of the page; you must scroll down to set other scanning options.

The Automatic Scanning section of the Options page is where you specify a schedule and specify the type of scan: quick or full. A *quick scan* checks only the places on your computer that spyware is most likely to infect, and is the recommended setting for frequent regular scans. A *full scan* checks all files on your local hard disk drives and all running programs, and is likely to slow down your computer during its sometimes lengthy run. Before you leave the Options page, scroll down to the Advanced Options section, where you'll find some additional, less intuitive options, two of which affect scanning:

- **Scan the contents of archived files and folders for potential threats** When selected, Windows Defender scans the compressed contents of .zip archives—the storage mechanism for compressed folders.

- **Do not scan these files or locations** In this box, you can specify files or folders that you know to be safe. Generally, the only reason to consider excluding files in this way is if you have a program that you knowingly run regularly—typically at startup—and that is detected by Windows Defender every time it runs, despite your telling it to allow the program. If this happens, you should exclude the detected file (or files) rather than their containing folder; if you do that, and later some real spyware ends up in the folder, Windows Defender won't detect it.

Scanning Manually

Regular automatic scanning is normally sufficient for identifying and resolving spyware problems. However, if you suspect that you've been infected—or if you've disabled automatic scanning—you can scan on demand. To immediately run a quick scan, simply click the Scan button in the toolbar. If you want to run a full scan, which is a better option if you suspect infection, click the arrow next to the Scan button and click Full Scan. The Custom Scan option lets you narrow your scan to the drives and folders you specify.

INSIDE OUT   **Run Windows Defender from a batch program**

Windows Defender also includes a command-line utility, %ProgramFiles%\Windows Defender\Mpcmdrun.exe, that you can use to automate the use of Windows Defender. For details about using the utility, open a Command Prompt window and run the program with no parameters.

Chapter 10

Using Real-Time Protection

Real-time protection runs in the background, always on the lookout for spyware that attempts to install itself or to run. If it encounters spyware (or suspected spyware), it displays an alert, similar to the one shown here:

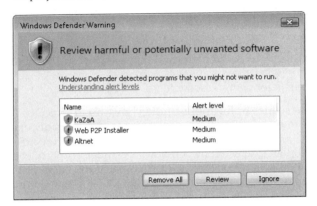

When you see an alert like this, you generally have three options:

- **Remove All** Windows Defender permanently removes the detected spyware from your computer.

- **Review** Windows Defender opens to a page that has detailed information about the detected spyware program. On that page, you decide what to do with the program; your options include Remove and Ignore—just like the warning dialog box—plus Quarantine and Remove All.

- **Ignore** Windows Defender allows the program to be installed or to run—for now. You'll see the same warning the next time the program attempts to run or to change security-related settings.

INSIDE OUT   Choose Review

If you need more information to make your decision, you can click Understanding Alert Levels to open Windows Help And Support, which offers a detailed description of each alert level. Unfortunately, the warning dialog box remains on top, making it difficult to read the help text. Although you can try rearranging the windows, your best bet is to click Review, which closes the warning dialog box and opens Windows Defender. The review page offers more details about the detected software and includes a link to more information online. (Meanwhile, you can bring the Help And Support window to the fore.)

Although there's seldom reason to modify the default options for real-time protection, it's worth reviewing them just to gain a better understanding of exactly what real-time protection does. Click Tools, click Options, and then scroll down to the Real-Time Protection Options section, shown in Figure 10-17.

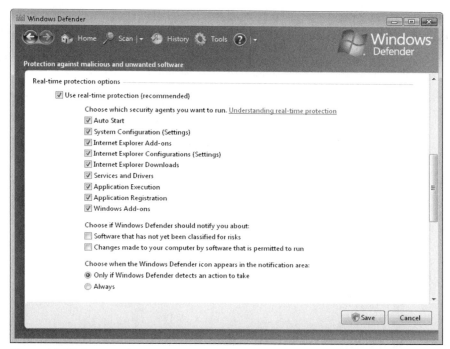

Figure 10-17 To see a description of each real-time protection agent, click Understanding Real-Time Protection.

Responding to Windows Defender Alerts

When Windows Defender informs you that your computer has a problem, if you're un-sure what to do, choose the "review" option. In addition to the button in the warning dialog box, this option appears on the Windows Defender home page after Windows Defender detects spyware, whether during a scan or as a result of real-time protection. (See Figure 10-15, earlier in this chapter.) The review page, shown in Figure 10-18, of-fers detailed information about each detected program. At the bottom of the description area (not shown in the figure) is a link to a website with still more details about this particular spyware program.

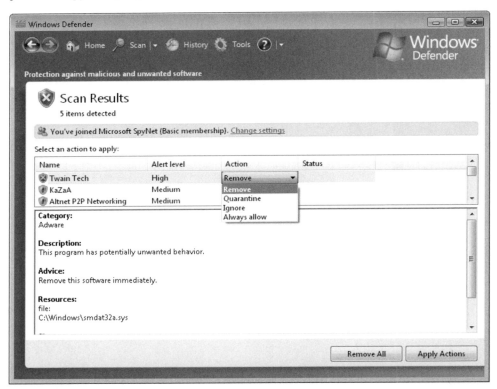

Figure 10-18 You can specify an action for each detected program (click Apply Actions when you're done), or vanquish them all at once by clicking Remove All.

INSIDE OUT   Take action—but which action?

How do you decide what to do based on the rather cryptic information that's presented? Begin with the SpyNet Community Rating for the selected item, if one is shown; that gives you an indication of how others have handled the same program. (You get more information from SpyNet if you change your membership to advanced. Click Tools and then click Microsoft SpyNet for more information and to make the change. There's no charge for membership at either level.) Then look to the Windows Defender advice, if shown. Consider the publisher of the program: Is it a company that you've heard of and trust? Examine each of the details and, for the ones you can understand, consider if that's a reasonable action for the type of program you *think* you're installing. If you're still unsure, search the web for the names of any programs or files shown; you're likely to find many sites that better describe the source and potential risks with a particular file or program. (You're also likely to find a number of sites packed with misinformation, and it's sometimes hard to tell the difference. Until you find a site that gives you confidence, check several sites to find a consensus. And when you do find one of those good sites, bookmark it for the next time you have to deal with an uncategorized risk.) Dealing with potentially risky software is not clear-cut. First, not everyone agrees on what constitutes a risky program. Some are willing to accept the risk in return for benefits derived from the program. Finally, some perfectly safe, perfectly legitimate programs work in ways similar to some spyware, and they could be flagged as spyware. Ultimately, you have to decide.

The review page offers two actions in addition to Remove and Ignore, described earlier.

- **Quarantine** Windows Defender moves the program to a different folder and prevents the program from running. If you later decide what you want to do with the quarantined program, click Tools and then click Quarantined Items. When you visit the quarantine, you can choose to restore an item (that is, return it to its prequarantine condition) or remove it from your computer.

- **Always allow** Windows Defender adds the program to the allowed list, and no longer alerts you to its presence and its risks. You should allow only software that you know to be safe. If you later change your mind, click Tools and then click Allowed Items. When you remove an item from the allowed list, Windows Defender does not remove the program from your computer—but it does resume monitoring it and warning you when the program does something provocative.

Note

By default, Windows Defender alerts you only when known spyware or potentially unwanted software is detected. You can broaden its reach by joining SpyNet with an advanced membership or by selecting the option (under Real-Time Protection Options) to receive notification about software that has not yet been classified by Microsoft analysts.

Stopping Offending Programs

Throughout Windows Defender, the emphasis is on removing spyware. You'll often see prominent Remove and Remove All buttons, and Remove is the first choice on the list of available actions. If removal is the action you want to take, Windows Defender makes it easy to do.

In Software Explorer, Windows Defender offers another effective tool for reviewing and, optionally, removing programs. Click Tools and then click Software Explorer. The initial view is of programs that run automatically at startup, because spyware programs are often configured thusly. After reviewing the details of a program here, you can (of course) remove it. Alternatively, you can disable a program from launching at startup without removing it from your computer. Unlike the quarantine option, the program can still be run.

The other views—Currently Running Programs, Network Connected Programs, and Winsock Service Providers—provide similar options for arresting wayward programs, if not removing them altogether. For example, Figure 10-19 shows network connected programs. On that page, you can block a program's incoming connection or stop it from running. (Surprisingly, there's no option to remove here. Potentially risky programs that are running will be listed on the review page or allowed list, either of which can be used to remove the program.)

Figure 10-19 Software Explorer shows all active programs—not just spyware—and includes options for dismissing them.

For more information about using Software Explorer to manage programs that run at startup, see "Managing Startup Programs," Chapter 4.

TROUBLESHOOTING

You can't get rid of a spyware program

Some spyware is pernicious and uses every trick in the book to avoid being removed and to reinstall itself—much like a monster in a horror movie. After you take action to disable spyware (either remove or quarantine), be even more vigilant in case it rears its ugly self again. After you restart your computer (usually required by Windows Defender after cleanup), run a full scan. Be sure that all real-time protection agents are enabled. And watch out for the sequel.

If spyware does return, you're dealing with a tough one, and you're going to need some up-to-date expert advice to help you through the process of manually removing it. Because the advice depends on the particular spyware as well as other factors, we can't provide it here—but we can point you to an excellent resource: the Spyware Warrior website *(http://www.spywarewarrior.com)*, operated by Suzi Turner and Eric Howes. It offers a wealth of resources, including links to tools, forums for discussing specific problems, and links to other sites with additional spyware information.

Disabling Windows Defender

As you can see in Figures 10-16 and 10-17, choices on the Options page let you turn off automatic scanning and real-time protection. Even if you turn off both options, however, the Windows Defender service continues to run and the program remains available for manual scans. If you want to disable Windows Defender altogether, go to the Options page, scroll all the way to the bottom, and clear Use Windows Defender.

Chapter 10

Controlling Your Children's Computer Access

Home Basic ●
Home Premium ●
Business ○
Enterprise ○
Ultimate ●

Parental Controls is a feature, new to Windows Vista, that enables parents to help manage how their children use the computer. As a parent, you can set restrictions (different for each child, if you like) on which websites your children can visit, which games they can play, and which programs they can run. You can set hours of use for the computer. Perhaps most importantly, you can view activity logs that detail each child's computer activity, including when they logged on and off, which programs they ran, which websites they visited, whom they've corresponded with via e-mail and instant messaging, and so on.

> **Note**
>
> In addition to technological measures in Windows Vista and other products, Microsoft also offers plenty of educational information for parents and kids to assist them in staying safe online. Visit the "Protect your family" page at *http://www.vista-io.com/1029* to view parent's guides, safety tips, and more.

The requirements for using Parental Controls are simple:

- You must be using the Home Basic, Home Premium, or Ultimate edition of Windows Vista.

- You must have at least two user accounts set up on your computer—an administrator account for the parent and a standard account for the child. (More adults? More kids? Create a separate account for each person. Be sure that each child to whom you want to apply Parental Controls has a standard account, as parental controls can't be applied to administrator accounts.)

- All administrator accounts on the computer should be protected by a password. (This isn't an absolute requirement, but without password protection, anyone can bypass or turn off Parental Controls. Note also that you need only one password-protected administrator account to manage Parental Controls. Other parents with standard accounts can use the administrator parent's credentials to run Parental Controls.)

For information about creating and managing user accounts, see "Working with User Accounts," Chapter 11. For information about password protection for user accounts, see "Setting a Logon Password," Chapter 11.

Configuring Parental Controls

To begin using Parental Controls, open it in Control Panel. (It's in the User Accounts And Family Safety category.) After consenting to the User Account Control prompt (or entering an administrator password if you're logged on as a standard user), you'll see a window like the one shown in Figure 10-20.

Figure 10-20 If any of your administrator accounts is not password-protected, Windows displays a prominent warning—and a link to correct the problem—in this window.

To set restrictions for a child, click the child's account name and then click On, Enforce Current Settings, as shown in Figure 10-21.

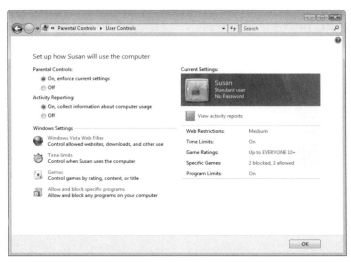

Figure 10-21 Using a window like this one, you can set different restrictions for each child.

Chapter 10

INSIDE OUT Use Parental Controls on an Ultimate system joined to a domain

Parental Controls, naturally, is designed to be used in a home environment, and is not really an appropriate way to restrict users on a corporate network. (Administrators of corporate networks can use group policy and other tools to place restrictions on employees of all ages and maturity levels.) For that reason, the Parental Controls feature is not included in the Business and Enterprise editions of Windows Vista. Similarly, when you join a computer running Windows Vista Ultimate to a domain—a capability that is unavailable in the Home Basic and Home Premium editions—Parental Controls disappears from Control Panel and the feature is no longer accessible.

It's not uncommon, however, for a "corporate" network, such as one based on Windows Small Business Server, to be set up in a home. Small Business Server comes with many components and management tools (and an attractive price) that provide additional capabilities, greater security, and easier control of a larger home network. (If you have more than about five computers, it's worth investigating.) If you're a leading-edge user with a domain network, does that mean you can't use Parental Controls? Fortunately, if you use Windows Vista Ultimate edition, you can.

To enable Parental Controls on a domain-joined Ultimate computer:

1. At a command prompt, type **gpedit.msc** to open Group Policy Object Editor.

2. In the console tree, open Local Computer Policy\Computer Configuration\ Administrative Templates\Windows Components\Parental Controls.

3. In the Details pane, double-click Make Parental Controls Control Panel Visible On A Domain, the only policy in this folder.

4. Select Enabled and click OK.

5. Restart your computer.

Restricting Access to Websites

To control your child's internet browsing, in the User Controls window (shown in Figure 10-21), click Windows Vista Web Filter. The web restrictions, which you configure in the window shown in Figure 10-22, can be imposed in either or both of two ways:

- You can specify a list of sites to allow and sites to block. By clicking Edit The Allow And Block List, you can manually enter URLs for sites you want to explicitly allow or prohibit, and you can also export and import the list for easy replication to other computers. For the most restrictive browsing, enter a list of allowable sites, and then select Only Allow Websites Which Are On The Allow List.

- You can use automatic blocking, which relies on site lists maintained by Microsoft. Automatic blocking provides three levels of blocking:

  o **High** Allows only sites that are specifically intended for children. These sites use language and content that is understandable by and appropriate for preteens.

  o **Medium** Filters websites based on various types of content. The intent of this setting is to allow free exploration of the web, without the risk of encountering inappropriate content.

  o **Custom** Filters websites based on various types of content, which you specify. As shown in Figure 10-22, you decide which types of content you want to ban.

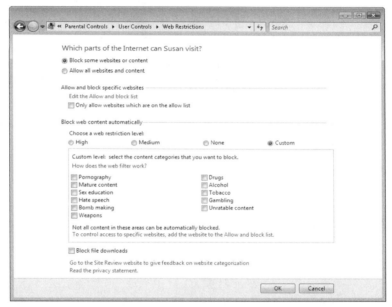

Figure 10-22 To enable website filtering, select Block Some Websites Or Content, and then specify the types of sites you want to block.

If, after reviewing your child's activity logs, you find a site that you feel was inappropriately allowed (or blocked), visit the Family Safety site review website (*http://www.vista-io.com/1023*), where you can suggest a change to the classification. Instead of waiting for the automatic filters to be updated appropriately, add the site in question to the allow list or block list; settings in the allow and block lists supercede automatic blocking controls.

Chapter 10

> **Note**
>
> Website restrictions set up in Parental Controls work independently of Content Advisor in Internet Explorer, and there are some important differences in the approach taken by these two tools. Because it's part of Internet Explorer, Content Advisor has no effect when another web browser is being used, whereas Parental Controls monitors the use of any browser. Content Advisor uses ratings systems created by independent ratings boards; for the most part these systems rely on site owners to rate their own site and embed the ratings information in each page. Unfortunately, many sites—including some of the raunchiest—don't bother to take this step. Content Advisor has one other drawback: its settings apply to all users on a computer, whereas Parental Controls lets an administrator apply separate settings to each standard user. For more information about Content Advisor, see "Blocking Objectionable Content," Chapter 27.

Once web restrictions are in place, if your child strays to a site that is blocked, the web browser displays a page similar to the one shown in Figure 10-23. Your child can gain access to the site by clicking the Ask An Administrator For Permission link and persuading you (or anyone with an administrator account) to enter your password.

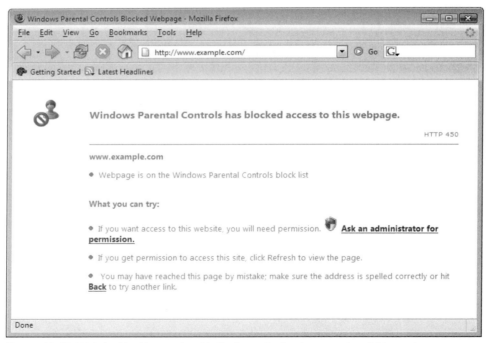

Figure 10-23 Website blocking works with Firefox and other browsers in addition to Internet Explorer.

Restricting Logon Hours

To control the times at which your child can use the computer, in the User Controls window (shown in Figure 10-21), click Time Limits. You can then specify, for each day of the week, which hours are allowed, and which are blocked.

Thereafter, if your child tries to log on outside of the allowable times, a simple message appears: "Your account has time restrictions that prevent you from logging on at this time. Please try again later."

While a child with a restricted account is logged on, as the end of the allowable time approaches, a message pops up from the taskbar.

If your child is still logged when the blocked time arrives, he or she is unceremoniously logged off. Note, however, that this logoff is akin to switching users; open windows and running applications remain open, and no work is lost. When your child logs on again during an allowable time, everything is just as it was before being logged off.

INSIDE OUT   Find out how much time is left

When Parental Controls is in effect, it displays an icon in the notification area. Hovering the mouse pointer over the icon displays the current status of Parental Controls, including how much time remains until the user will be logged off.

Parental Controls are turned on. Time left: 1hrs, 7mins

By double-clicking the icon, your child can view (but not modify) all of the Parental Controls settings imposed on his or her account.

Controlling Access to Games

To control which computer games your child is allowed to play, in the User Controls window (shown in Figure 10-21), click Games. From the window shown in Figure 10-24, click Set Game Ratings to specify the ratings codes for allowable games. You can also block games that contain specific types of objectionable content, even if the game's rating falls into the acceptable range. (Scroll down on the game ratings page to see these types of content, many of which you probably never imagined could appear in something called a "game.") In addition, you can review a list of installed games and explicitly block or allow certain titles.

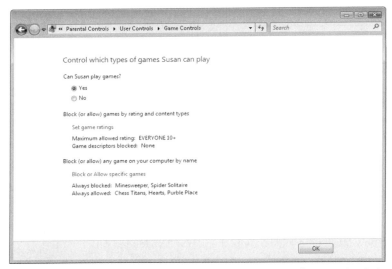

Figure 10-24 Time for a timeout? You can block access to all games simply by selecting No near the top of this window.

By default, Parental Controls uses the game rating system established by the Entertainment Software Rating Board (ESRB), which has been widely adopted by publishers of games sold in the United States. To use a different rating system, return to the main

Parental Controls page (see Figure 10-20 earlier in this chapter). In the Tasks list, click Select A Games Ratings System.

> ### Protecting Your Family Against Other Threats in the Digital Home
>
> Parental Controls in Windows Vista is part of a broader Microsoft effort to protect children from inappropriate content in the digital world. The effort includes providing technology such as the Family Settings feature in the Microsoft Xbox 360, which enables parents and caregivers to set access restrictions to content on Xbox 360, the Xbox Live service, and Xbox Live Vision camera. For example, you can use Family Settings to block unwanted contacts and specify which video games can be played. In addition, there's an educational component for parents and caregivers, so that they can learn how to understand ESRB ratings, how to use Family Settings, and how to take other steps to protect their family. You can learn more about the "Safety is no game. Is your family set?" campaign at *http://www.vista-io.com/1024*.

Blocking Programs

To control which programs your child is allowed to run, in the User Controls window (shown in Figure 10-21), click Allow And Block Specific Programs. The Application Restrictions window, shown in Figure 10-25, lists the executable files for programs installed on your computer, grouped by storage location (folder).

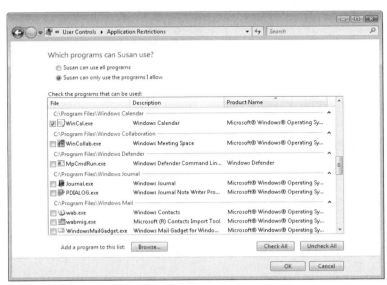

Figure 10-25 Blocking programs through Parental Controls does not remove them from the child's Start menu; it just prevents their use.

If you want to restrict your child's use to just a handful of programs, you can easily do so here. Conversely, if you want to give free rein *except* for a handful of programs (for example, you might want to prevent the use of Microsoft Money so your financial records aren't inadvertently compromised), click Check All—and then clear the check box by the programs you want to block.

> **Note**
>
> Most of the basic accessory programs included with Windows—such as Notepad, Calculator, and Help And Support—are not included in the list of blockable programs, nor can you add them to the list. These programs are always allowed.

When your child attempts to run a blocked program, a dialog box appears.

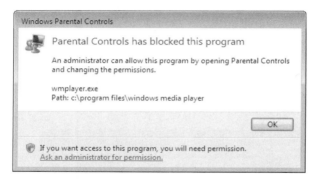

Clicking OK dismisses the dialog box, whereas clicking the Ask An Administrator For Permission link requests the password of an administrator, and then gives you a chance to change your mind by clicking Keep Blocking. If you click Always Allow, the program is added to the list of allowed programs, and your child won't be prompted again.

Checking Up on Your Children's Computer Activities

Besides imposing restrictions on computer usage, another important step in making your computer safe for children is monitoring their activities. Of course, it's important to let them know that you're doing so—which in itself can be a deterrent to misuse. Parental Controls provides detailed reports on your children's computer activities.

To enable this feature, be sure that, in the User Controls window (Figure 10-21 earlier in this chapter), Activity Reporting is turned on. To view a log of your children's computer usage, click View Activity Reports. Your initial view is a summary of your child's activities, as shown in Figure 10-26.

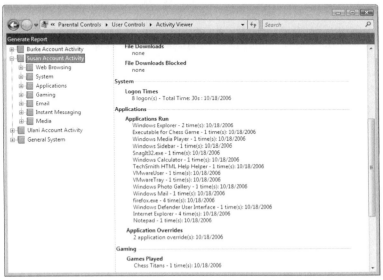

Figure 10-26 For details on each item, click a plus sign and select a subreport.

By delving into report details, you can see precisely which websites have been visited (and which files each site has displayed), which programs have been run (and for how long), a list of e-mail messages received and sent, instant messaging activities, and much more. Activity reports also detail attempts to visit blocked sites or run blocked programs or games. You—and your child—are likely to be shocked by the amount of detail that's recorded.

> **Note**
>
> The Activity Viewer displays all standard accounts, including those for whom you haven't enabled Parental Controls (such as parents with a standard account). However, if activity reporting is turned off for an account, no data is collected.

The activity viewer shows activity only for the past seven days. If you want to save the information in the activity viewer for later viewing, in the left pane select the view you want to save, and then click Generate Report. The report includes everything in the selected view, including all subordinate views. Windows saves the report as an HTML page, which you can view in any web browser or send to someone else via e-mail.

INSIDE OUT   Open the Parental Controls activity viewer the easy way

Unfortunately, Windows doesn't make it easy to go directly to the activity viewer in Parental Controls. However, you can get there without traipsing through the lengthy path from Control Panel to the Parental Controls page for a particular user before you find a link to activity reports. Here's how: Open activity viewer. In the Address bar, right-click the text and choose Copy Address. On the desktop (or another folder where you want to create a shortcut), right-click and choose Paste Shortcut. Thereafter, to view activity reports, simply double-click this shortcut.

CHAPTER 11

Managing User Accounts, Passwords, and Logons

Home Basic ○
Home Premium ○
Business ○
Enterprise ○
Ultimate ●

The *user account*, which is used to uniquely identify each person who uses the computer, is an essential component in security and in providing a personalized user experience in Windows Vista. In the tradition of Microsoft Windows NT, Windows 2000, and Windows XP, Windows Vista allows you to restrict access to your computer so that only people you authorize can use the computer or view its files. (This is a sharp departure from Windows 95/98/Me, in which bypassing security was as simple as pressing Esc when Windows asked you for a password.) With Windows Vista, user accounts provide the means by which you can:

- Require each user to identify himself or herself when logging on

- Control access to files and other resources that you own

- Audit system events, such as logons and the use of files and other resources

What's in Your Edition?

For the most part, the tools for managing user accounts work the same in all Windows Vista editions. The core Control Panel application for managing user accounts works slightly differently in the business editions compared with the home editions; Ultimate works like the business editions when joined to a domain, like the home editions otherwise. We point out the differences, which are relatively unimportant. Some account-management tasks are most easily performed with a console called Local Users and Groups; it's not available in the Home Basic and Home Premium editions. All these tasks can be performed with one or more other tools, however, and we describe each one in this chapter. We also mention a handful of policies you can use to lock down accounts using Local Security Policy; again, it's not available in the Home Basic and Home Premium editions. None of these policies is critical, especially in a home environment.

Of course, if your computer is in a secure location where only people you trust have physical access to it, you might not have such concerns. Because the designers of Windows Vista were able to provide for the needs of those who want convenience as well as those who need security, Windows Vista works for you, too. You'll still probably want to create a user account for each person who uses the computer, because associated with each account is a user profile that stores all manner of information unique to that user: favorite websites, desktop background, document folders, and so on. With features such as the Welcome screen and Fast User Switching, described in this chapter, you can log on or switch between user accounts with only a few clicks.

Introducing Windows Security

The Windows Vista approach to security is discretionary: Each securable system resource—each file or printer, for example—has an owner, who has discretion over who can and cannot access the resource. Usually, a resource is owned by the user who created it. If you create a file, for example, you are the file's owner under ordinary circumstances. (Computer administrators, however, can take ownership of resources they didn't create.)

> **Note**
>
> To exercise full discretionary control over individual files, you must store those files on an NTFS volume. For the sake of compatibility, Windows Vista supports the FAT and FAT32 file systems used by MS-DOS, Windows 95, Windows 98, and Windows Me, as well as by most USB flash drives. However, the FAT and FAT32 systems were not designed with security in mind. To enjoy the full benefits of Windows Vista security, you must use NTFS. For more information, see "Choosing a File System" in Chapter 28.

To determine which users have access to a resource, Windows assigns a *security ID* (SID) to each user account. Your SID (a gigantic number guaranteed to be unique) follows you around wherever you go in Windows. When you log on, the operating system first validates your user name and password. Then it creates a *security access token*. You can think of this as the electronic equivalent of an ID badge. It includes your user name and SID, plus information about any security groups to which your account belongs. (Security groups are described later in this chapter.) Any program you start gets a copy of your security access token.

In Depth: Security Identifiers

Windows security relies on the use of a security identifier (SID) to identify a user. When you create a user account, Windows assigns a unique SID to that account. The SID remains uniquely associated with that user account until the account is deleted, whereupon the SID is never used again—for that user or any other user. Even if you re-create an account with identical information, a new SID is created.

A SID is a variable-length value that contains a revision level, a 48-bit Identifier Authority value, and a number of 32-bit subauthority values. The SID takes the form S-1-*x*-*y1*-*y2*-.... S-1 identifies it as a revision 1 SID; *x* is the value for the IdentifierAuthority; and *y1*, *y2*, and so on are values for subauthorities.

You'll sometimes see a SID in a security dialog box (for example, on the Security tab of a file's properties dialog box) before Windows has had time to look up the user account name. If a SID on a Security tab doesn't change to a name, it's because it's a SID for an account that has been deleted; you can safely delete it from the permissions list because it'll never be used again. You'll also spot SIDs in the hidden protected operating system folder \Recycler (each SID you see in this folder represents the Recycle Bin for a particular user) and in the registry (the HKEY_USERS hive contains a key, identified by *SID*, for each user account on the computer), among other places. The easiest way to determine your own SID is with the Whoami command-line utility. For details, see "Learning About Your Own Account with Whoami" in this chapter.

Not all SIDs are unique (although the SID assigned to your user account is always unique). A number of commonly used SIDs are constant among all Windows installations. For example, S-1-5-18 is the SID for the built-in Local System account, a hidden member of the Administrators group that is used by the operating system and by services that log on using the Local System account. You can find a complete list of such SIDs, called *well-known SIDs*, in Microsoft Knowledge Base article 243330 (*http://www.vista-io.com/1101*.)

With User Access Control (UAC) turned on, administrators who log on get two security access tokens—one that has the privileges of a standard user, and one that has the full privileges of an administrator.

Whenever you attempt to walk through a controlled "door" in Windows (for example, when you connect to a shared printer) or any time a program attempts to do so on your behalf, the operating system examines your security access token and decides whether to let you pass. If access is permitted, you notice nothing. If access is denied, you get to hear a beep and read a refusal message.

In determining whom to let pass and whom to block, Windows consults the resource's *access control list* (ACL). This is simply a list of SIDs and the access privileges associated with each one. Every resource subject to access control has an ACL.

This manner of allowing and blocking access to resources such as files and printers is essentially unchanged since Windows NT. With UAC, Windows Vista introduces another layer of restrictions based on user accounts. Although UAC is sometimes confused with (blamed for?) the restrictions imposed by discretionary access control lists (described in the preceding paragraphs), it's actually unrelated. UAC is a method of implementing the rule of least-privilege user access—a fancy way of saying that a user account should have the minimum privileges required to perform a task; this practice is intended to prevent malicious programs from using the power of an account to do bad things.

With UAC turned on, applications are normally launched using an administrator's standard user token. (Standard users, of course, have only a standard user token.) If an application requires administrator privileges, UAC asks for your consent (if you're logged on as an administrator) or the credentials of an administrator (if you're logged on as a standard user) before letting the application run. With UAC turned off, Windows Vista works in the same (somewhat dangerous) manner as previous versions: administrator accounts can do just about anything (sometimes getting them in trouble), and standard accounts don't have the privileges needed to run many older programs.

For more information about UAC, see "Preventing Unsafe Actions with User Account Control," Chapter 10.

A new feature in Windows Vista places one more doorway on the way to object access. Somewhat like the discretionary ACLs used to secure file objects, registry keys, and the like, in Windows Vista each securable object has an Integrity Level (IL) access control entry, which can be low, medium, or high. (Objects that don't have an IL specified have an implicit value of medium.) Each process (program) is also marked with an IL: protected mode ("low rights") Internet Explorer is low, standard processes are medium, and processes that require elevation to administrator are high. A process can open an object for write access only if its IL is equal to or higher than that of the object.

Permissions and Rights

Windows distinguishes two types of access privileges: permissions and rights. A *permission* is the ability to access a particular object in some defined manner—for example, to write to an NTFS file or to modify a printer queue. A *right* is the ability to perform a particular systemwide action, such as logging on or resetting the clock.

The owner of a resource (or an administrator) assigns permissions to the resource via its properties dialog box. For example, if you are the printer owner or have administrative privileges, you can restrict someone from using a particular printer by visiting the properties dialog box for that printer. Administrators set rights via the Local Security Policy console. (This console is available only in the Business, Enterprise, and Ultimate editions of Windows Vista. In the home editions, rights for various security groups are predefined and unchangeable.) For example, an administrator could grant someone the right to install a device driver.

> **Note**
>
> In this book, as in many of the Windows messages and dialog boxes, *privileges* serves as an informal term encompassing both permissions and rights.

User Accounts and Security Groups

The backbone of Windows Vista security is the ability to uniquely identify each user. While setting up a computer—or at any later time—an administrator creates a user account for each user. The *user account* is identified by a user name and is (optionally) secured by a password, which the user provides when logging on to the system. Windows then controls, monitors, and restricts access to system resources based on the permissions and rights associated with each user account by the resource owners and the system administrator.

Account type is a simplified way of describing membership in a security group, a collection of user accounts. Windows Vista classifies each user account as one of three account types:

- **Administrator** Members of the Administrators group are classified as administrator accounts. By default, the Administrators group includes the first account you create when you set up the computer and an account named Administrator that is disabled and hidden by default. Unlike other account types, administrators have full control over the system. Among the tasks that only administrators can perform:

    - Create, change, and delete user accounts and groups
    - Install and uninstall programs
    - Configure automatic updating or install Windows updates manually
    - Install an ActiveX control
    - Install or remove hardware device drivers
    - Share folders
    - Set permissions
    - Access all files, including those in another user's folder
    - Take ownership of files
    - Copy or move files into the %ProgramFiles% or %SystemRoot% folders
    - Restore backed-up system files
    - Grant rights to other user accounts and to themselves
    - Configure Parental Controls
    - Configure Windows Firewall

- **Standard user** Members of the Users group are classified as standard user accounts. (In Windows XP, Users group members are called limited accounts.) Many tasks that were available only to administrators in previous Windows versions can be performed in Windows Vista by standard users. These additional tasks do not affect overall system security, and their prohibition in earlier versions made it impractical for most people to run without full administrative privileges; in Windows Vista—finally—it makes sense to use a standard account. A partial list of tasks available to standard user accounts includes:

- Change the password and picture for their own user account
- Use programs that have been installed on the computer
- Install approved ActiveX controls
- Configure a secure Wi-Fi connection
- View permissions
- Create, change, and delete files in their document folders and in shared document folders
- Restore their own backed-up files
- View the system clock and calendar, and change the time zone
- Configure power options
- Log on in Safe Mode

- **Guest**   Members of the Guests group are shown as guest accounts. Guest accounts have privileges similar to standard accounts, with some limitations. A user logged on with the Guest account (but not any other account that is a member of the Guests group) cannot create a password for the account.

> **Note**
>
> User accounts that are not a member of the Administrators, Users, or Guests group do not appear in User Accounts in Control Panel. There's seldom reason to set up an account that doesn't belong to one of these groups, but if you do need to work with such accounts, you must use one of the other user account management tools. For details, see "Advanced Account Setup Options" in this chapter.

Assigning an appropriate account type to the people who use your computer is straightforward. At least one user must be an administrator; naturally, that should be the person who administers the computer. All other regular users should each have a standard user account. Use a guest account if you have guests or occasional users; that way, they can use your computer without gaining access to your files.

Groups allow a system administrator to create classes of users who share common privileges. For example, if everyone in the accounting department needs access to the Payables folder, the administrator can create a group called Accounting and grant the entire group access to that folder. If the administrator then adds all user accounts belonging to employees in the accounting department to the Accounting group, these users will automatically have access to the Payables folder. A user account can belong to one group, more than one group, or no group at all.

On a computer that is shared by many users, groups can be a valuable administrative tool. They simplify the job of ensuring that all members with common access needs have an identical set of privileges. Although you can grant privileges to each user account individually, doing so is tedious and prone to errors—and usually considered poor practice. You're better off assigning permissions and rights to groups and then adding user accounts to the group with the appropriate privileges.

Permissions and rights for group members are cumulative. That means that if a user account belongs to more than one group, the user enjoys all of the privileges accorded to all groups of which the user account is a member.

Local Accounts and Groups vs. Domain Accounts and Groups

Windows stores information about user accounts and security groups in a security database. Where the security database resides depends on whether your computer is part of a workgroup or a domain.

A *workgroup* setup (or a standalone computer) uses only local user accounts and local groups—the type described in this chapter. The security database on each computer stores the local user accounts and local groups that are specific to that computer. Local user accounts allow users to log on only to the computer where you create the local account. Likewise, a local account allows users to access resources only on that same computer. (This doesn't mean that you can't share your resources with other network users, even if you're not part of a domain. For details, see Chapter 14, "Managing Shared Folders and Printers.") With such a setup, you avoid the initial expense of purchasing and configuring Microsoft Windows Server 2003—but because you must manage user accounts on each individual computer, this process becomes unwieldy with more than five or ten computers.

The alternative is to set up the network as a domain. A Windows *domain* is a network that has at least one machine running Windows Server 2003, Windows 2000 Server, or Windows NT Server as a domain controller. A *domain controller* is a computer that maintains the security database, including user accounts and groups, for the domain. With a *domain user account*, you can log on to any computer in the domain (subject to your privileges set at the domain level and on individual computers), and you can gain access to permitted resources anywhere on the network.

In general, if your computer is part of a Windows domain, you shouldn't need to concern yourself with local user accounts. Instead, all user accounts should be managed at the domain controller. But you might want to add certain domain user accounts or groups to your local groups. By default, the Domain Admins group is a member of the local Administrators group, and Domain Users is a member of the local Users group; members of those domain groups thereby assume the rights and permissions afforded to the local groups to which they belong.

Domain-based accounts and groups are also known as *global accounts* and *global groups*.

Working with User Accounts

When you install Windows Vista on a new computer, you create one user account, which is an administrator account. If you upgrade to Windows Vista from Windows XP and you had local accounts set up in your previous operating system, Windows migrates those accounts to your Windows Vista installation. Accounts that you migrate from Windows XP maintain their group memberships and passwords.

Through User Accounts in Control Panel, Windows Vista provides a simple post-setup method for creating new accounts, making routine changes to existing accounts, and deleting accounts. If your computer is not a member of a domain, when you launch User Accounts in Control Panel you'll see a window similar to the one shown in Figure 11-1.

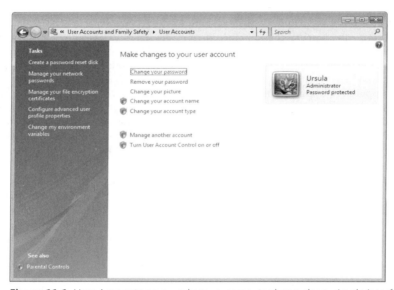

Figure 11-1 User Accounts on a workgroup computer has a clean, simple interface.

INSIDE OUT Access User Accounts quickly

You can jump straight into User Accounts without going through Control Panel. Simply open the Start menu and click the account picture in the upper right corner of the Start menu.

If your computer is a member of a domain, User Accounts is even more pristine, offering less information about your account and fewer options, as shown in Figure 11-2. In a domain environment all management of user accounts beyond the basic tasks shown in User Accounts is normally handled at the domain level. You can manage local accounts using the Advanced User Accounts Control Panel. For more information, see "Advanced Account Setup Options" in this chapter.

Figure 11-2 On a computer joined to a domain, click Manage User Accounts to get to meatier options.

Creating a New User Account

To create a new user account, in the User Accounts window shown in Figure 11-1, click Manage Another Account. The Manage Accounts window appears, as shown in Figure 11-3. (To get there directly, in the main Control Panel window click Add Or Remove User Accounts, under User Accounts And Family Safety.)

Figure 11-3 The Manage Accounts page shows all local user accounts that are a member of the Administrators, Users, or Guests groups.

Click Create A New Account, which takes you to the window shown in Figure 11-4, where you can create a new account with a minimum of fuss. You need to supply only a name for the account and decide whether you want to set up the account type as standard user or administrator.

Figure 11-4 Creating an account couldn't be much easier; just specify a name and account type.

> **Note**
> The name you provide when you create a new account with Windows is used for both the user name and the full name. The *user name* is the primary name used internally by Windows. You use it when you log on without the benefit of the Welcome screen (such as in certain networking situations) and when you specify the account name in various commands and dialog boxes for setting permissions. The *full name* is the name that appears on the Welcome screen, at the top of the Start menu, and in User Accounts. You can change either name at any time after the account is created.

If you want to specify any other information about the account—including setting a password—you must make changes after you create the account, as described in the following section. Alternatively, you can use the Local Users And Groups snap-in or the Net User /Add command, both of which allow you to create an account and make several other settings simultaneously. For more information, see "Advanced Account Setup Options" in this chapter.

INSIDE OUT   **Don't use spaces in the user name**

User Accounts allows you to include spaces in the user name when you create an ac-count. Don't do it. Spaces in user names cause complications with some applications and when you use command-line tools for managing user accounts. If you want a space to appear on the Welcome screen and on the Start menu (for example, if you want to display your full name, including first and last name), create your account name without a space. (For example, use just your first name or, if that's the same as another account name, use your first name and last initial without a space.) After you create the account, you can change the full name without changing the user name, as described in the fol-lowing section.

Changing Account Settings

Making routine changes to an account is easy with User Accounts. To change your own account, start at the main User Accounts page, shown in Figure 11-1. To change another user's account (you must have administrative privileges to do so), click Manage Another Account to display the page shown in Figure 11-3, and then click the name of the ac-count you want to change. You'll see links to options similar to those you can make to your own account.

In this window, you can make the following account changes to your own account or (if you're an administrator) other accounts on your computer:

- **Account name** Although User Accounts doesn't explain the distinction, when you change the name here you're changing the full name (the one that appears on the Welcome screen, on the Start menu, and in User Accounts), not the user name. Changing the name here—after creating a short user name without spac-es—allows you to create a friendly name that appears on-screen. (You must have administrator privileges to change the account name.)

- **Password** You can create a password and store a hint that will provide a remind-er for a forgotten password. If the account is already password protected, User Accounts allows you to change the password or remove the password. For more information about passwords, see "Setting Logon Passwords" in this chapter.

- **Picture** If you don't want a user to be identified as a kitten (or whatever icon Windows selects for the account), you can change the picture associated with the account name on the Welcome screen, at the top of the Start menu, and in User Accounts. Clicking the change-picture link shows all the pictures stored in %AllUsersProfile%\Microsoft\User Account Pictures\Default Pictures, but you're not limited to those choices (most of which are no more or less appropriate than the kitten icon). Click Browse For More Pictures, and you can select any picture in bitmap format (.bmp extension), Graphics Interchange Format (GIF), Joint Photo-graphic Experts Group (JPEG) format, or Portable Network Graphics (PNG) format, such as a picture of yourself or a favorite scene. Windows reduces and crops the picture to fit the picture box.

- **Parental Controls** Clicking this link takes you to Parental Controls, where you can place restrictions on the user by limiting the hours of use, filtering web content, and specifying which games and other programs can be run. You must have administrator privileges to view or change Parental Controls settings, and you can't configure Parental Controls settings for administrator accounts. For details about Parental Controls, see "Controlling Your Children's Computer Access," Chapter 10.

- **Account type** With User Accounts, you can change the account type to Administrator (which adds the account to the Administrators group) or Standard User (which adds the account to the Users group). If you want to add the account to other groups, you must use Advanced User Accounts, Local Users And Groups, or the Net Localgroup command. For more information about those alternatives, see "Advanced Account Setup Options," In this chapter. (You must have administrator privileges to change the account type.)

For your own account (that is, the one with which you're currently logged on), you can make the following additional changes by clicking links in the Tasks pane:

- **Password reset disk** This link launches the Forgotten Password wizard, from which you can create a password reset disk. For more information, see "Recovering from a Lost Password" in this chapter.

- **Network passwords** This link opens Stored User Names And Passwords, which lets you manage stored credentials that you use to access network resources and websites.

- **File encryption certificates** This link opens a wizard that you can use to create and manage certificates that enable the use of Encrypting File System (EFS). EFS is a method of encrypting folders and files so that they can be used only by someone who has the appropriate credentials.

- **Advanced user profile properties** This link is used to switch your profile between a local profile (one that is stored on the local computer) or a roaming profile (one that is stored on a network server in a domain environment). With a local profile, you end up with a different profile on each computer you use, whereas a roaming profile is the same regardless of which computer you use to log on to the network. Roaming profiles require a domain network based on Microsoft Windows Server. To work with user profiles other than your own, in Control Panel open System, click Advanced System Settings; on the Advanced tab, click Settings under User Profiles.

- **Environment variables** Of interest primarily to programmers, this link opens a dialog box in which you can create and edit environment variables that are available only to your user account; in addition, you can view system environment variables, which are available to all accounts. For more information, see "Using Environment Variables," Appendix B.

Using the Guest Account for Visitors

The Guest account is designed to allow an infrequent or temporary user such as a visitor to log on to the system without providing a password and use the system in a restricted manner. By default, the Guest account is disabled; no one can use an account that's disabled.

To enable the Guest account, open User Accounts, click Manage Another Account, and click the Guest account icon. In the window that appears, click Turn On. The Guest account thereafter shows up on the Welcome screen, and anyone can use it. Users of the Guest account have access to items in the Public folder as well as those in the Guest profile.

Deleting an Account

You can delete any account except one that is currently logged on. To delete an account, open User Accounts, click Manage Another Account, and click the name of the account you want to delete. Then click Delete The Account. User Accounts gives you a choice, shown in Figure 11-5 on the next page, about what to do with the account's files:

- **Delete Files** After you select Delete Files and confirm your intention in the next window, Windows deletes the account, its user profile, and all files associated with the account, including those in its Contacts, Desktop, Documents, Downloads, Favorites, Links, Music, Pictures, Saved Games, Searches, and Videos folders.

- **Keep Files** Windows copies certain parts of the user's profile—specifically, files and folders stored on the desktop and in the Documents, Favorites, Music, Pictures, and Videos folders—to a folder on your desktop, where they become part of your profile and remain under your control. The rest of the user profile, such as e-mail messages and other data stored in the AppData folder; files stored in the Contacts, Downloads, Saved Games, and Searches folders; and settings stored in the registry, will be deleted after you confirm your intention in the next window that appears.

> **Note**
> User Accounts won't let you delete the last local account on the computer, even if you're logged on using the account named Administrator. This limitation helps to enforce the sound security practice of using an account other than Administrator for your everyday computing.

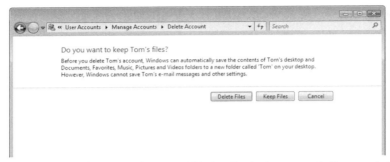

Figure 11-5 Select Keep Files to avoid losing files in the account's Documents folder.

After you delete an account, of course, that user can no longer log on. Deleting an account also has other effects you should be aware of. You cannot restore access to resources that currently list the user in their access control lists simply by re-creating the account. This includes files to which the user has permission and the user's encrypted files, personal certificates, and stored passwords for websites and network resources. That's because those permissions are linked to the user's original SID—not the user name. Even if you create a new account with the same name, password, and so on, it will have a new SID, which will not gain access to anything that was restricted to the original user account.

You might encounter another predicament if you delete an account. If you use a tool other than User Accounts to delete the account, the user's original profile remains in the Users folder. If you later create a new account with the same name, Windows creates a new profile folder, but because a folder already exists with that user's name (for example, C:\Users\Tom), it appends the computer name to the user name to create a convoluted folder name (for example, C:\Users\Tom.Sequoia). The extra folder not only consumes disk space, but leads to confusion about which is the correct profile folder. (In general, the one with the longest name is the most recent. But you can be certain only by examining files in the profile folder.) To avoid this problem, use User Accounts to delete accounts because it properly deletes the old profile along with the account.

INSIDE OUT Delete an unused profile when you delete an account

If you delete an account with a tool other than User Accounts, the account's profile continues to occupy space in the Users folder and in the registry. You don't want to delete the files or registry entries directly because a simple mistake could affect other accounts. Instead, in Control Panel open System and click Advanced System Settings. Click the Advanced tab and then click Settings under User Profiles. Select the account named Account Unknown (the deleted account), and click Delete.

Effectively Implementing User Accounts on a Shared Computer

Whether you're setting up a computer for your family to use at home or to be used in a business, it's prudent to set it up securely. Doing so helps to protect each user's data from inadvertent deletions and changes as well as malicious damage and theft. When you set up your computer, consider these suggestions:

- **Control who can log on.** Create accounts only for users who need to use your computer's resources, either by logging on locally or over a network. Delete or disable other accounts (except the built-in accounts created by Windows).

- **Change all user accounts except one to standard accounts.** You'll need one administrative account for installing programs, creating and managing accounts, and so on. All other accounts—including your own everyday account—can run with standard privileges.

- **Be sure that all accounts are password protected.**   This is especially important for administrator accounts and for other accounts whose profiles contain important or sensitive documents. You might not want to set a password on your toddler's account, but all other accounts should be protected from the possibility that the tyke (or your cat) will accidentally click the wrong name on the Welcome screen.

- **Restrict logon times.** You might want to limit the computing hours for some users. The easiest way for home users to do this is with Parental Controls; for details, see "Restricting Logon Hours," Chapter 10. You can also limit logon times with the Net User *username* /Times command; for details, see "Using the Net User and Net Localgroup Commands," later in this chapter. (Users of the Business and Enterprise editions must use this method—or domain-based policies—because those editions do not include Parental Controls.) Administrators of Business, Enterprise, and Ultimate edition computers can forcibly log off users if they are still logged on at the end of their allowable logon time by using Local Security Policy (Secpol.msc). Open Local Policies\Security Options and enable the policy named Network Security: Force Logoff When Logon Hours Expire.

- **Restrict access to certain files.** You'll want to be sure that some files are available to all users, whereas other files are available only to the person who created them. The Public folder and a user's personal folders provide a general framework for this protection. You can further refine your file protection scheme by selectively applying permissions to varying combinations of files, folders, and users. For details, see Chapter 29, "Controlling Access to Files and Folders."

- **Restrict the amount of disk space available to each user.** You can set disk quotas for each user, thereby preventing your teenager from filling the whole hard drive with downloaded music files or a coworker from gobbling up disk space with scanned photographs, for example. To implement a quota system, in Windows Explorer right-click the drive icon, click Properties, and click the Quotas tab.

- **Turn on the Guest account only when necessary.** You might occasionally have a visitor who needs to use your computer. Rather than logging on with your own account and exposing all your own files and settings to the visitor, turn on the Guest account in such situations.

Setting a Logon Password

Associating a password with your user account is your first line of defense against those who would like to snoop around in your files. Because the Welcome screen shows every user account, if you don't set passwords, anyone who has physical access to your computer can log on by simply clicking a name on the Welcome screen. If the chosen name belongs to an administrator account, the person who clicks it has full, unfettered access to every file and setting on the computer. Requiring a password for each account (particularly administrator accounts) goes a long way toward securing your computer.

> **Note**
>
> You needn't worry about someone logging on to your computer remotely (over the network, the internet, or with Remote Desktop Connection, for example) if your account doesn't have a password. Security features in Windows Vista prevent remote logon by any account with a blank password. When you don't have a password in Windows, the risk comes only from people who have physical access to your computer.
>
> This feature is enforced by a policy, which is enabled by default. If you have the Business, Enterprise, or Ultimate edition, you can confirm that the policy is enabled, as follows. At a command prompt, type **secpol.msc** to open Local Security Settings. Open Local Policies\Security Options and be sure that the Accounts: Limit Local Account Use Of Blank Passwords To Console Logon Only policy is enabled. (If you use the Home Basic or Home Premium edition, you needn't worry; the policy can't be disabled.)

Creating a Secure Password

A password is of little value if it's easily guessed by an intruder. Obviously, you shouldn't use your name or something equally transparent. However, even a random word provides little security against a determined intruder—some hackers use tools that try every word in the dictionary. By observing the following guidelines, you can create a password that's difficult to crack in a reasonable amount of time:

- Use at least eight characters. Longer is better, which is why some security experts suggest using a *pass phrase*. A password or phrase can include spaces and punctuation; the maximum length is 127 characters.

- Use a mixture of uppercase letters, lowercase letters, numbers, and punctuation.

- Avoid including your name or user name in the password.

- Use random sequences instead of words, or intersperse numbers and punctuation within words (for example, v!stA 1ns!dE ()uT).

With a little thought, it's pretty easy to come up with a password that is memorable and secure. For example, start with a phrase about yourself or your hobbies—one that you can easily remember, such as *I'm addicted to Solitaire.* Make a few letter substitutions, misspell a word or two, and you come up with *I'm + Icted 2 $ol!ta!re.* It's long, uses all four types of characters, contains no dictionary words, and is easy to remember—so you won't be tempted to write it on a sticky note attached to your monitor.

Setting a Password

The simplest way to set a password for yourself or for another user (if you have administrator privileges) is with User Accounts in Control Panel. Click the name of the user for which you want to set a password and then click Create A Password. A window like the one shown in Figure 11-6 appears.

Figure 11-6 User Accounts allows you to provide a password reminder hint that becomes available on the Welcome screen.

To change your password, you must provide your old password as well as a new one.

INSIDE OUT
Use Ctrl+Alt+Delete to access password options

The fastest path to a password-setting screen is to press Ctrl+Alt+Delete and then click Change Password. There you can set a password along with an updated hint.

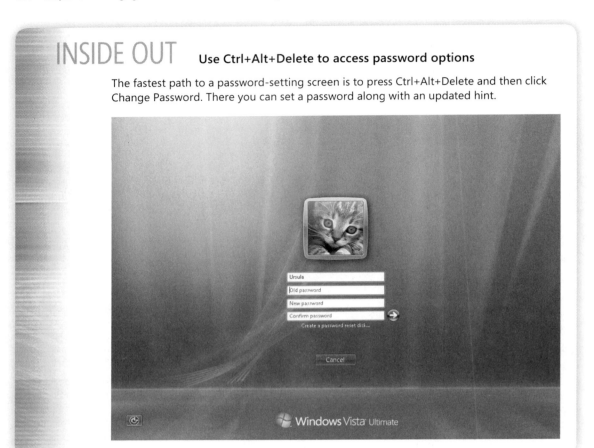

You can set a password with the other account management tools, but User Accounts is the only tool (along with Ctrl+Alt+Delete, described above) that lets you specify a password hint. The password hint appears after you click your name on the Welcome screen and type your password incorrectly. Be sure your hint is only a subtle reminder—not the password itself—because any user can click your name and then view the hint.

CAUTION

If another user has files encrypted with EFS, do not create a password for that user; instead, show the user how to create a password for their own account. Similarly, do not remove or change another user's password unless the user has forgotten the password and has absolutely no other way to access the account. (For more information, see the following section, "Recovering from a Lost Password".) If you create, change, or remove another user's password, that user loses all personal certificates and stored passwords for websites and network resources. Without the personal certificates, the user loses access to all of his or her encrypted files and all e-mail messages encrypted with the user's private key. Windows deletes the certificates and passwords to prevent the administrator who makes a password change from gaining access to them—but this security comes at a cost!

TROUBLESHOOTING

You can't access encrypted files because an administrator changed your password

When an administrator removes or changes the password for your local account, you no longer have access to your encrypted files and e-mail messages. That's because your master key, which is needed to unlock your personal encryption certificate (which, in turn, is needed to unlock your encrypted files), is encrypted with a hash that includes your password. When the password changes, the master key is no longer accessible. To regain access to the master key (and, by extension, your encrypted files and e-mail messages), change your password back to your old password. Alternatively, use your password reset disk to change your password.

When you change your own password (through User Accounts or with your password reset disk), Windows uses your old password to decrypt the master key and then re-encrypts it with the new password, so your encrypted files and e-mail messages remain accessible.

Recovering from a Lost Password

It's bound to happen: Someday when you try to log on to your computer and are faced with the password prompt, you will draw a blank. Windows Vista offers two tools that help you to deal with this dilemma:

- **Password hint** Your hint (if you've created one) appears below the password entry box after you make an incorrect entry and then click OK. You can create a hint when you set a password with User Accounts.

- **Password Reset Disk** A password reset disk allows you (or anyone with your password reset disk) to change your password—without needing to know your old password. As standard practice, each user should create a password reset disk and keep it in a secure location. Then, if a user forgets the password, he or she can reset it using the password reset disk.

> **Note**
>
> You can make a password reset disk only for your local user account. If your computer is joined to a domain, you can't create a password reset disk as a back door to your domain logon password. However, in a domain environment, a domain administrator can safely reset your password and you'll still have access to your encrypted files. Also, on a computer joined to a domain, password hints are never shown, even for local user accounts.

Both solutions require a little forethought on your part. You must create the hint when you set your password, and you must create the password reset disk before you actually need it.

To create a password reset disk, you'll need to know your current password and you'll need to have removable media available. (You can use a floppy disk, USB flash drive, external hard drive, or memory card.) Follow these steps:

1. Log on using the account for which you want to create a password reset disk.

2. In Control Panel, open User Accounts.

3. In the Tasks pane, click Create A Password Reset Disk to launch the Forgotten Password wizard.

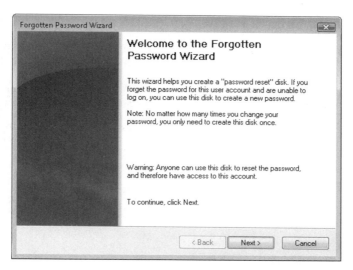

4. Follow the wizard's instructions.

You can have only one password reset disk for each user account. If you make a new one, the old one is no longer usable.

To use the password reset disk when password amnesia sets in:

1. On the logon screen, make an entry in the password box. If you guess right, you're in! If you're wrong, Windows informs you that the password is incorrect.

2. Click OK. The logon screen reappears, but with additional text below the password box.

3. If the first bit of additional text, your password hint, jogs your memory, enter your password. If not, click Reset Password to open the Password Reset wizard.

   The Password Reset wizard asks for the location of the password reset disk, reads the encrypted key, and then asks you to set a new password, which it then uses to log you on. Your password reset disk remains usable for the next attack of forgetfulness; you don't need to make a new one.

If you can't remember the password, the hint doesn't refresh your memory, and you don't have a password reset disk, you're out of luck. An administrator can log on and change or remove your password for you, but you'll lose access to your encrypted files and e-mail messages and your stored credentials.

Chapter 11

Enforcing Secure Password Practices

Even if you convince everyone who uses your computer to use a password, you can be sure that they won't always follow the secure practices of choosing a difficult-to-crack password and changing it periodically. If security is a serious concern in your organization, you might want to set password policies that place restrictions on the types of passwords users can provide and how often users can (or must) change them.

For users of Windows Vista Business, Enterprise, or Ultimate edition, the easiest way to set password policies is with the Local Security Policy console, shown in Figure 11-7. To open Local Security Policy, in Control Panel open Administrative Tools, Local Security Policy. Alternatively, type **secpol.msc** at a command prompt.

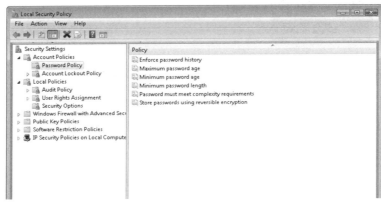

Figure 11-7 With Local Security Policy, you can set password requirements for all local user accounts.

To see the policies that set password behavior for all accounts, open Account Policies\Password Policy. Table 11-1 describes each of these policies.

As an alternative to the Local Security Policy console, you can set most of these policies using the Net Accounts command. (For users of the Home Basic or Home Premium edition, this is the only option.) In Table 11-1, the appropriate switch to set a policy is shown next to the policy name as it appears in Local Security Policy. For example, to set the maximum password age to 21 days, type **net accounts /maxpwage:21** at a command prompt.

Table 11-1. Account Policies

Policy	Net Accounts Switch	Description
Enforce password history	/Uniquepw:*number*	Specifying a number greater than 0 (the maximum is 24) causes Windows to remember that number of previous passwords and forces users to pick a password different from any of the remembered ones.
Maximum password age	/Maxpwage:*days*	Specifying a number greater than 0 (the maximum is 999) dictates how long a password remains valid before it expires. (To override this setting for certain user accounts, open an account's properties dialog box in Local Users And Groups and select the Password Never Expires check box.) Selecting 0 means the password never expires. (With the Net Accounts command, use the /Maxpwage:unlimited switch if you don't want a password to ever expire; 0 is not an acceptable value.)
Minimum password age	/Minpwage:*days*	Specifying a number greater than 0 (the maximum is 999) lets you set the amount of time a password must be used before a user is allowed to change it. Selecting 0 means that a user can change the password as often as he or she likes.
Minimum password length	/Minpwlen:*length*	Specifying a number greater than 0 (the maximum is 14) forces a password to be longer than a certain number of characters. Specifying 0 permits a user to have no password at all. *Note: Changes to the minimum password length setting do not apply to current passwords.*
Password must meet complexity requirements	N/A	Enabling this policy requires that a new password be at least six characters long; that the password contain a mix of uppercase letters, lowercase letters, numbers, symbols, and upper range Unicode characters (at least one character from three of these five classes); and that the password does not contain the user name or any part of the full name. *Note: Enabling password complexity does not affect current passwords.*
Store password using reversible encryption for all users in the domain	N/A	Enabling this policy effectively stores a password as clear text instead of encrypting it, which is much more secure. The only situation in which you should even consider enabling this policy is when you have a particular application that needs access to the user password for authentication.

Chapter 11

Managing the Logon Process

Unlike Windows XP, which provides a radically different logon experience for computers joined to a domain compared with those in a workgroup or not connected to a network, the process is similar for all users of Windows Vista. The key differences:

- By default, on a computer joined to a domain, users must press Ctrl+Alt+Delete before the logon screen appears. This requirement can be removed from domain computers or added to others, as described below.

- The Welcome screen for a workgroup or standalone computer shows an icon for each account on the computer, as shown in Figure 11-8. By contrast, after pressing Ctrl+Alt+Delete, a domain user sees only one user account, along with a Switch User button that enables you to log on using an account other than the one shown. (This is the same screen that a workgroup user with a password-protected account sees after clicking his or her account name.)

Figure 11-8 At startup, a workgroup computer—but not a computer joined to a domain—shows all user accounts on the Welcome screen.

INSIDE OUT   Skip the Ctrl+Alt+Del requirement

On a domain-based computer, if you don't want to be bothered by pressing Ctrl+Alt+Del to reach the logon screen, make the following change:

1. Open User Accounts in Control Panel, and then click Manage User Accounts to open Advanced User Accounts.

2. In the User Accounts dialog box that appears, click the Advanced tab.

3. Under Secure Logon, clear Require Users To Press Ctrl+Alt+Delete.

Be aware that doing so removes a security feature. Because a component of the Windows security system prevents any other application from capturing this particular key combination, pressing Ctrl+Alt+Delete ensures that the next screen that appears, the logon screen, is displayed by the operating system and not by a rogue application that's trying to capture your password, for example.

INSIDE OUT   Hide the name of the last user to log on

On a computer joined to a domain, by default the name and picture of the last user who logged on appears on the logon screen. On a system that's used primarily by a single user, this is a convenient feature that allows the user to log on again without typing his or her name each time. For a computer that's shared by many users, you might prefer not to show the last user. You can prevent the last-used name from appearing by typing **secpol.msc** at a command prompt to open Local Security Policy. In Local Security Policy, open Local Policies\Security Options. Then enable the policy named Interactive Logon: Do Not Display Last User Name.

Bypassing the Logon Screen

If your computer has only one account (aside from built-in accounts, such as Administrator and Guest), and if that account doesn't have a password, Windows Vista automatically logs on as that user during startup. You won't see the Welcome screen or any other logon screens; Windows launches straight to your desktop.

You might want to set up your computer to log on this way even if it has more than one user account. This kind of logon can be convenient in several situations: if you're the primary user of the computer but other people occasionally need to use it; if you occasionally need to log on as a different user to install software or perform other tasks; or if you have set up a password for your account (so that you could use scheduled tasks or connect remotely, operations that are available only to accounts with passwords), but you still want it to log you on automatically at startup.

CAUTION

> *Automatically logging on* means that the system effectively enters your user name and password when you turn on the power. Anyone who has physical access to your computer can then log on as you and have access to all computer resources (including websites for which you've saved passwords) that you normally have.

If your computer is not joined to a domain, you can set it up to log on automatically by following these steps:

1. At a command prompt, type **control userpasswords2** to open Advanced User Accounts.

2. On the Users tab, clear the Users Must Enter A User Name And Password To Use This Computer check box and then click OK. Note that the Users Must Enter A User Name And Password To Use This Computer check box doesn't appear if your computer is a member of a domain. Only computers that aren't part of a network or are part of a workgroup can bypass the logon screen. Domain users must enter a user name and password, even to log on locally.

The Automatically Log On dialog box appears.

3. Type the user name and password for the account that you want to be logged on to each time you start your computer.

After you make this change, you can use other accounts on the computer by logging off and then logging on to another account or by using Fast User Switching.

Users of any computer—those joined to a domain as well as workgroup and standalone computers—can configure automatic logon by downloading and using a free command-line utility. Two good ones are available, and they're both named Autologon. One was created by Mark Russinovich at Sysinternals (now part of Microsoft); it can be downloaded from *http://www.vista-io.com/1103*. The other was created by the Windows Vista shell team; it's available at *http://www.vista-io.com/1104*. Either one must be run from an elevated Command Prompt window.

INSIDE OUT   Bypass automatic logon or prevent others from bypassing

If you've configured your system to log on automatically, you can suppress the automatic logon by holding down the left Shift key as the system boots. If you want to prevent users from bypassing the automatic logon (thereby ensuring that your system always starts with a particular account), you can use a registry setting to make the system ignore the Shift key. Use Registry Editor to navigate to HKLM\Software\Microsoft\ WindowsNT \CurrentVersion\Winlogon. If the string value IgnoreShiftOverride doesn't exist, create it. Set this value to 1 to ensure that your system always starts with its auto-logon account.

Logging Off, Switching Users, or Locking Your Computer

When you're finished using your computer, you want to be sure that you don't leave it in a condition in which others can use your credentials to access your files. To do that, you need to log off, switch users, or lock your computer.

- **Log off** With this option, all your programs close and dial-up connections are ended. To log off, click the arrow in the lower right corner of the Start menu and click Log Off. (See Figure 11-9.)

Figure 11-9 The Lock icon provides a pretty big target, but to log off or switch users, you must click the arrow to the right of the lock.

- **Switch users** With this option (sometimes called Fast User Switching), your programs continue to run. Your account is still logged on, but (if it's protected by a password) only you can return to your session. To switch users, click the arrow in the lower right corner of the Start menu and click Switch User. On a computer that is not joined to a domain, this takes you to the Welcome screen, where you can click the name of the account you want to switch to.

  Fast User Switching, a feature that made its first appearance in Windows XP, allows multiple users to be logged on to a computer at the same time. As the feature name suggests, you can quickly switch among users. This might be convenient, for example, if one user logs on, opens several documents, and begins downloading a huge file from the internet. Meanwhile, another user comes along and wants to quickly check e-mail. No problem: the second user can log on, log off, and return control to the first user. While the second user is logged on, the first user's applications (such as the download process) continue to run.

- **Lock your computer** With this option, your programs continue to run, but the logon screen appears so that no one can see your desktop or use the computer. Only you can unlock the computer to return to your session; however, other users can log on in their own sessions without disturbing yours. To lock a computer, click the lock icon in the lower right corner of the Start menu.

In any case, if you want to prevent others from using your account, you must protect your account with a password. When you choose any of these options, Windows hides whatever you were working on. Your computer continues to run (subject to power management settings), and any resources shared by your computer remain available to other users on the network.

INSIDE OUT   Use keyboard shortcuts

To lock your computer, you can press Windows logo key+L. (You might also find it more convenient to use this shortcut for switching users; the only difference is that it takes you to the logon screen—which has a Switch User button—instead of to the Welcome screen.)

For any of these actions—log off, switch users, or lock—you can start by pressing Ctrl+Alt+Delete, which displays a menu that includes all three options.

What Happened to the Administrator Account?

Every computer running Windows Vista has a special account named Administrator. Traditionally in Windows, Administrator has been the primary account for managing the computer. Like other administrator accounts, the Administrator account has full rights over the entire computer. There's one key difference in Windows Vista: the Administrator account is disabled by default.

> **Note**
>
> Upon installation of Windows Vista, the Administrator account is disabled, with one exception: If you upgrade from Windows XP and Administrator is the only active local administrator account, then Administrator remains enabled. In that situation, it is placed in Admin Approval Mode for purposes of User Access Control (UAC).

Chapter 11

Use of the Administrator account is being phased out in Windows Vista, and there's seldom a need to use it instead of another administrator account. With default settings in Windows Vista, it does have one unique capability: it's not subject to UAC, even when UAC is turned on for all other users. That is, it runs with full administrative privileges at all times and never needs your consent for elevation. (For this reason, of course, it's rather risky. Any application that runs as Administrator has full control of the computer—which means applications written by malicious or incompetent programmers can do significant damage to your system.)

For other ways to live with UAC, see "Working Around UAC Without Disabling It," Chapter 10.

Logging On as Administrator

If you feel compelled to use the Administrator account, it's easy enough to do. Simply open an elevated command prompt window (easiest way: in the Start menu Search box type **cmd**, press Ctrl+Shift+Enter, and respond in the affirmative to the UAC prompt) and enter the following command:

```
net user administrator /active:yes
```

Thereafter, the Administrator account appears on the Welcome screen, and you can use it like any other account. We strongly suggest using it sparingly; use it only when you need to perform several administrative tasks and don't want to be bothered with UAC prompts.

CAUTION

Initially, Administrator account does not have a password—a deadly vulnerability for a full-strength administrator account. Your first action upon logging on, therefore, should be to assign a strong password to the account.

When you decide that enabling the Administrator account wasn't such a good idea after all, use the same Net User command to disable it, except replace *yes* with *no*.

Using the Administrator Account in Safe Mode

With default settings (that is, with the account disabled), the Administrator account cannot log on to the computer in Safe Mode. This is a departure from earlier Windows versions, in which the Administrator account was often the account used for recovery operations in Safe Mode.

On a computer that is not joined to a domain, as long as there is at least one other administrator account, if you need to use Safe Mode you must use one of the other administrator accounts to log on and perform administrative tasks. (Standard users can log on in Safe Mode, but the face the same restrictions as when Windows is running normally.) If you somehow manage to delete, disable, or demote the last administrator account (User Accounts in Control Panel won't let it happen, but it is possible with the other account management tools), then Safe Mode allows the Administrator account to log on, even if it's disabled.

On a computer that's joined to a domain, you can never log on in Safe Mode using a disabled Administrator account. Recovery in a domain environment relies on members of the global Domain Admins group. Any member of that group can log on and create a local administrator account for further repair work if necessary. If the Domain Admins account has logged onto the computer previously, its cached credentials can be used to log on in Safe Mode. If the domain administrator has never logged onto the computer, cached credentials don't exist; in that situation, you must start Safe Mode With Networking.

For more information about Safe Mode, see "Using Advanced Boot Options," Chapter 24.

Learning About Your Own Account with Whoami

Windows Vista includes a new command-line utility, Whoami (Who Am I?). You can use Whoami to find out the name of the account that's currently logged on, its SID, the names of the security groups of which it's a member, and its privileges. To use Whoami, open a Command Prompt window. (You don't need elevated privileges.)

Then, to learn the name of the logged-on user, type **whoami**. (This is particularly useful if you're logged on as a standard user, but running an elevated Command Prompt window.) If you're curious about your SID, type **whoami /user**. To see a list of your account's group memberships, type **whoami /groups /fo list**. To learn which privileges are enabled for the logged-on account, type **whoami /priv /fo list**. For a complete list of Whoami parameters, type **whoami /?**.

Advanced Account Setup Options

Windows Vista includes no fewer than four different interfaces for managing users and groups:

- **User Accounts** Located in Control Panel, User Accounts provides the simplest method to perform common tasks. For more information, see "Working with User Accounts" in this chapter.

- **Advanced User Accounts** If your computer is joined to a domain, clicking Manage User Accounts opens Advanced User Accounts. (The title bar of the dialog box doesn't include the word Advanced, however.) If your computer is not joined to a domain, you can open this version by typing **control userpasswords2** at a command prompt.

The capabilities of Advanced User Accounts are few (you can remove local user accounts, set passwords, and place a user account in a single security group), but it has a handful of unique features that you might find compelling. With Advanced User Accounts, you can:

○ Change an account's user name (for information about the difference between the user name and the full name, see "Creating a New User Account" in this chapter.

○ Configure automatic logon (for more information, see "Bypassing the Logon Screen" in this chapter.

○ Eliminate the Ctrl+Alt+Delete requirement on domain-joined computers (for details, see "Managing the Logon Process" in this chapter.

● **Local Users And Groups** This Microsoft Management Console (MMC) snap-in provides access to more account management features than User Accounts and is friendlier than command-line utilities. For more information, see "Using the Local Users And Groups Snap-In" in this chapter.

● **Command-line utilities** The Net User and Net Localgroup commands, though not particularly intuitive (starting with the name—we're talking about local accounts and groups, not network-based accounts!), provide the most complete and direct access to various account tasks. For more information, see "Using the Net User and Net Localgroup Commands" in this chapter.

With varying degrees of ease, all of these options allow an administrator to create, modify, and delete local user accounts and security groups. The availability and appearance of each of these options depends on which edition of Windows Vista you have (the Local Users And Groups console is not available in Home Basic and Home Premium editions) and whether your computer is a member of a domain. Which interface you choose depends in part on whether you prefer a graphical interface or a command prompt.

But you'll also find that each tool offers capabilities that the others do not. To help you decide which tool to use for a particular task, Table 11-2 shows the common account-management tasks that can be performed with each interface.

Table 11-2. Account-Management Tool Tasks

Task	User Accounts	Advanced User Accounts	Local Users And Groups	Command-Line Utilities
Local User Accounts				
Create user account	✓	✓	✓	✓
Delete user account	✓	✓	✓	✓
Place account in a group	✓ [1]	✓ [1]	✓	✓

Task	User Accounts	Advanced User Accounts	Local Users And Groups	Command-Line Utilities
Change user name		✓	✓	
Change full name	✓	✓	✓	✓
Change description		✓	✓	✓
Change picture	✓			
Set a password	✓	✓[2]	✓	✓
Set a password hint	✓			
Set password restrictions			✓	✓
Set logon hours				✓
Enable or disable account	✓[3]		✓	
Unlock account			✓	✓
Set account expiration date				✓
Specify profile and logon script			✓	✓
Local Security Groups				
Create			✓	✓
Delete			✓	✓
Rename			✓	✓
Set group membership			✓	✓
Add a domain account to a group		✓[1]	✓	✓

[1]With User Accounts or Advanced User Accounts, you can add an account to only one group. With User Accounts, you can add an account only to the Administrators or Users group.

[2]With Advanced User Accounts, you can set the password only for a local account other than the one with which you're currently logged on.

[3]With User Accounts, you can enable or disable the Guest account, but not other user accounts.

Using the Local Users and Groups Snap-In

Local Users And Groups, an MMC snap-in, offers more advanced capabilities than either version of User Accounts. Local Users And Groups is not available in Windows Vista Home Basic and Home Premium editions.

You can start Local Users And Groups, shown in Figure 11-10, in any of the following ways:

- In Computer Management, open System Tools, Local Users And Groups.

- At a command prompt, type **lusrmgr.msc**.

- In Advanced User Accounts, click the Advanced tab, and then click the Advanced button.

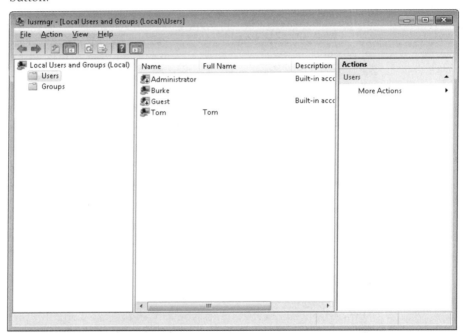

Figure 11-10 Through its austere interface, Local Users And Groups offers more capabilities than User Accounts.

Table 11-3 lists the procedures for performing various tasks with the Local Users And Groups snap-in.

Table 11-3. Local Users And Groups Procedures

Task	Procedure
Local User Accounts	
Create	Right-click Users and choose New User.
Delete	In Users, right-click the account and choose Delete.
Change user name	In Users, right-click the account and choose Rename.
Change full name or description	In Users, double-click the account to display the General tab of the properties dialog box.
Set or change password	In Users, right-click the account and choose Set Password.
Set password restrictions	In Users, double-click the account to display the General tab of the properties dialog box.
Enable or disable	In Users, double-click the account to display the General tab of the properties dialog box, and then clear or select the Account Is Disabled check box. (When an account is disabled, the user can't log on or access resources on the computer.)
Unlock after too many unsuccessful logon attempts	In Users, double-click the account to display the General tab of the properties dialog box, and then clear the Account Is Locked Out check box.
Set group membership	In Users, double-click the account and then click the Member Of tab.
Specify profile and logon script	In Users, double-click the account and then click the Profile tab.
Local Security Groups	
Create	Right-click Groups and choose New Group.
Delete	In Groups, right-click the group and choose Delete.
Rename	In Groups, right-click the group and choose Rename.
Set group membership	In Groups, double-click the group to display the properties dialog box. You can add local user accounts, domain user accounts, and domain groups to a local group. In the Select Users, Computers, Or Groups dialog box that appears when you click Add, use the Locations button to specify the computer name (for local users) or domain name (for domain users and groups).

Using the Net User and Net Localgroup Commands

If you prefer a terse Command Prompt window to a gooey utility, you'll want to use Net.exe for managing local users and groups. To change any local user account or group information, you'll need to use an elevated Command Prompt window. (In the Start menu Search box, type **cmd** and press Ctrl+Shift+Enter. Alternatively, right-click a Command Prompt shortcut and click Run As Administrator.)

In the following sections, we describe only the most common Net commands (and their most common parameters) for managing local users and groups. This isn't an exhaustive reference, however. You can get that information from online help or by typing **net help** *command*, replacing *command* with the word that follows *Net* in the examples below. For instance, to get more information about the Net Localgroup command, type **net help localgroup**. This provides more help than typing **net localgroup** /?, which shows only the command syntax.

Net User

The Net User command lets you view, add, modify, or delete user accounts.

Viewing User Account Information

Typing **net user** with no parameters causes the program to display the name of your computer and a list of local user accounts. If you follow *Net User* with the name of a local user account (for example, **net user jan**), Net User displays all information about the user account, as shown in the sample that follows.

```
C:\>net user

User accounts for \\SEQUOIA

-------------------------------------------------------------------------------
Administrator            Carl                     Guest
Jan
The command completed successfully.


C:\>net user jan
User name                Jan
Full Name                Jan
Comment
User's comment
Country code             000 (System Default)
Account active           Yes
Account expires          Never

Password last set        1/4/2007 12:43:12 PM
Password expires         Never
Password changeable      1/4/2007 12:43:12 PM
Password required        Yes
User may change password Yes
```

```
Workstations allowed        All
Logon script
User profile
Home directory
Last logon                  1/4/2007 11:54:30 AM

Logon hours allowed         All

Local Group Memberships     *Users
Global Group memberships    *None
The command completed successfully.
```

Adding or Modifying a User Account

Following Net User *username*, you can append any or all of the parameters shown in Table 11-4. For example, you can add a new account for a user named Josie, create a complex password, and prevent Josie from changing the password with the following command:

```
C:\>net user Josie /add /random /passwordchg:no
Password for Josie is: nkHRE$oU

The command completed successfully.
```

Table 11-4. Useful Parameters for the Net User Command

Parameter	Description
password or * or /Random	Sets the password. If you type an asterisk (*), Net User prompts for the password you want to assign; it does not display the password as you type it. The /Random switch generates a hard-to-crack, eight-character password.
/Add	Creates a new user account. The user name must be 20 characters or fewer and can't contain any of these characters: " / \ [ ] : ; | = , + * ? < >
/Fullname:"*name*"	Specifies the user's full name.
/Comment:"*text*"	Provides a descriptive comment (maximum length of 48 characters).
/Passwordchg:yes or /Passwordchg:no	Specifies whether the user is allowed to change the password.
/Active:no or /Active:yes	Disables or enables the account. (When an account is disabled, the user can't log on or access resources on the computer.)
/Expires:*date* or /Expires:never	Sets the expiration date for an account. For *date*, use the short date format set in Regional Options. The account expires at the beginning of the day on the specified date; from that time on, the user can't log on or access resources on the computer until an administrator sets a new expiration date.

Parameter	Description
/Passwordreq:yes or /Passwordreq:no	Specifies whether the user account is required to have a nonblank password.
/Times:*times* or /Times:all	Sets the times when an account is allowed to log on. For *times*, enter the days of the week you want to allow logon. Use a hyphen to specify a range of days or use a comma to list separate days. Following each day entry, specify the allowable logon times. For example, type **M-F,8am-6pm; Sa,9am-1pm** to restrict logon times to normal working hours. Use All to allow logon at any time; a blank value prevents the user from ever logging on.

> **Note**
>
> The last three switches in Table 11-4 (/Expires, /Passwordreq, and /Times) allow you to make settings that you can't make (or even view) using Local Users And Groups. These switches provide some powerful options that are otherwise available only with Windows 2000 Server or Windows Server 2003.

Deleting a User Account

To remove a user account from the local security database, simply use the /Delete switch with the Net User command, like this:

```
C:\>net user josie /delete
The command completed successfully.
```

Net Localgroup

The Net Localgroup command lets you view, add, modify, or delete local security groups.

Viewing Group Information

Type **net localgroup** with no parameters to display the name of your computer and a list of local groups. If you follow Net Localgroup with the name of a group (for example, **net localgroup "event log readers"**), Net Localgroup lists the members of the group.

Adding or Deleting a Group

Following Net Localgroup *groupname*, append /Add to create a new group or append /Delete to remove an existing group. When you add a group or view its information, you can optionally add a descriptive comment (maximum length of 48 characters) by appending the /Comment:"*text*" switch.

Adding or Deleting Group Members

You can add local user accounts, domain user accounts, and global groups to a local group (although you can't add other local groups). To do so, enter the names of the users or groups you want to add after the group name (separate multiple names with a space) and include the /Add switch. For example, to add Jan and Josie to the Users group, use this command:

```
C:\>net localgroup users jan josie /add
The command completed successfully.
```

To delete one or more group members, use the same syntax, replacing the /Add switch with /Delete.

Working with Domain Accounts

By appending the /Domain switch to any of the Net User or Net Localgroup commands described in this chapter, you can view, add, modify, or delete domain user accounts and global groups—as long as you log on as a member of the Domain Admins group. You don't need to specify the domain name; the Net User and Net Localgroup commands always work with the primary domain controller of your computer's domain.

CHAPTER 12

Setting Up a Small
Network

Home Basic   ○
Home Premium ○
Business   ○
Enterprise   ○
Ultimate   ○

Setting up a network is no longer the complex and sometimes frustrating process it used to be. With Microsoft Windows XP, a Network Setup wizard performed many of the tasks necessary to configure network computers—tasks that required diving deep into obscure dialog boxes and using arcane commands. Because of advances in hardware technology as well as in Windows itself, the wizard isn't necessary for configuring wired networks in Windows Vista. On a network where every computer is running Windows Vista, in fact, you might find that your wired network requires no configuration at all—after you finish setting up Windows, your network is available for immediate access. A wizard brings similar ease of configuration to wireless networks. Even on networks that include a mix of different Windows versions, getting everything connected is usually a straightforward process. (For advice on what to do when the pieces of your network don't fit together so neatly, see Chapter 14, "Tweaking and Troubleshooting a Small Network.")

You can maximize your chances of a trouble-free network setup by selecting the right hardware and installing it properly. When you start Windows after connecting your network, a quick visit to the Network And Sharing Center is usually all that's necessary to confirm that IP addresses, workgroup names, Windows Firewall settings, registry settings, and system policies are properly configured to facilitate a working network. Although Windows does all this with nary a nudge from you, you can always fine-tune network settings to suit your networking needs.

What's in Your Edition?

This chapter explains how to configure a peer-to-peer network for a small workgroup (typically consisting of 10 computers or fewer)—a network of computers that are not part of a domain running Windows Server "Longhorn," Windows Server 2003, or Windows 2000 Server. In this environment, the steps for setting up and configuring a network are the same in all editions of Windows Vista.

Capabilities of a Small Network

With a minimal investment in hardware, you can connect two or more computers and form a simple peer-to-peer network. Because these networks aren't built around a server, they don't allow you to manage users and shared resources centrally; instead, each computer contains its own database of authorized user accounts and shared folders, drives, and printers. Setting up a workgroup-based network offers the following advantages:

- **Shared storage** By designating certain folders as shared resources, you avoid the need to swap files on removable media or to maintain duplicate copies of files; instead, everyone on the network can open a shared report or access a collection of digital photos or music files from a single location.

- **Shared printers** Sharing a printer allows any authorized network user to print to that device.

- **Shared internet connection** Using Internet Connection Sharing (ICS), you can set up internet access on a single computer and allow every computer on the network to share that connection. This capability is most useful if you have a dial-up connection to the internet; ICS lets you control it from any computer on the network.

As we discuss in this chapter, using a hardware router offers significant security and performance advantages over ICS, and is clearly the way to go if you have high-speed, always-on internet service, such as that provided by cable or DSL.

What's New in Windows Vista

Networking in Windows Vista is based on a protocol stack that has been completely rewritten. Dubbed the Next Generation TCP/IP stack, this redesign of the network underpinnings provides improvements in security, performance, and convenience that are largely invisible to ordinary users.

For example, additional security comes in the new ability of the Windows Filtering Platform to implement packet filtering at all levels of the TCP/IP protocol stack. Performance is enhanced by Receive Window Auto-Tuning, which dynamically determines the optimal receive window size based on changing network conditions; in previous versions, you can tweak the registry to set a fixed-size receive window that is generally appropriate for your type of internet connection. The Next Generation TCP/IP stack implements IPv6 in a dual-stack architecture; instead of having to install a separate protocol (with its own transport and framing layers) as in previous versions, IPv4 and IPv6 are incorporated in a single Windows driver, with a shared transport layer and framing layer. Enabling IPv4 and IPv6 by default is more convenient for the user who needs both—nothing extra to install—but also easier for developers. Native support for wireless devices is now built in to the Next Generation TCP/IP stack, which also reduces demands on developers and users who must deal with add-in support in earlier versions of Windows.

And if all of the preceding jargon means nothing to you—well, that's the point. Improvements like these (and dozens of others) have made networking almost transparent to users, so that you don't need to spend time understanding how the layers in a protocol stack communicate and, worse, how to configure them to do so.

> **Note**
>
> For a detailed look at the Next Generation TCP/IP stack and related networking changes, see "New Networking Features in Windows Server 'Longhorn' and Windows Vista" on the Microsoft TechNet website: *http://www.vista-io.com/1201*.

Concurrent with the changes in the protocol stack, implementation of new features in networking hardware makes configuration easier than ever. Windows Rally technologies are designed to provide secure, reliable networks that are easy to set up and use, and they're now showing up in new network infrastructure devices (such as routers and wireless access points). These technologies include:

- **Windows Connect Now** The Windows Connect Now specifications enable simple and secure configuration of the gamut of wireless network devices, including wireless access points, computers, printers, cameras, game consoles, media extenders, and personal digital assistants (PDAs). With Windows Connect Now, users can create network configuration settings and transfer them to an access point via a wired Ethernet connection, a USB flash drive (UFD), or a USB cable. Windows Connect Now incorporates the Microsoft implementation of the Wi-Fi Simple Configuration Protocol, a standard promulgated by the Wi-Fi Alliance (*http://www.wi-fi.org*).

- **Link Layer Topology Discovery (LLTD) protocol** The LLTD protocol enables applications to find devices at the data-link layer. Windows Vista uses LLTD to create the network map, which shows a graphical view of the network topology, including links to each supported device's web interface. LLTD is also the enabling technology for quality media-streaming, even on relatively slow networks; audio and video playback devices that implement LLTD can use its Quality of Service (QoS) extensions to ensure that those devices use prioritized streams.

- **Plug and Play Extensions (PnP-X)** Just as Plug and Play provides automatic discovery and configuration of devices plugged directly into a computer (for example, by connecting to a USB port), PnP-X enables discovery and configuration of network-connected devices.

Windows Vista, of course, provides full support for these technologies. Windows XP added partial support for Windows Connect Now (UFD transfer only) in Service Pack 2. A more recent update to Windows XP provides LLTD support for computers running that operating system.

Chapter 12

Using Network And Sharing Center

Many of the tasks related to configuring the hardware and software for a network, viewing network resources, setting up shared resources on your own computer, and diagnosing network problems can be managed from the Network And Sharing Center. Figure 12-1 shows Network And Sharing Center.

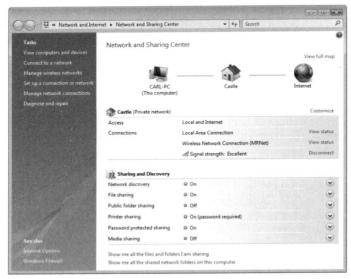

Figure 12-1 Clicking one of the icons at the top of Network And Sharing Center opens your Computer folder, Network folder, or internet home page.

You can open Network And Sharing Center in any of the following ways:

- In the Start menu Search box, begin typing **network** until Network And Sharing Center appears; click it.

- In Control Panel, click Network And Internet, and then click Network And Sharing Center.

- In Windows Explorer, with the Network folder displayed, click the Network And Sharing Center button in the Command bar.

- In the notification area, click the Network icon and then click Network And Sharing Center.

> **Note**
>
> Many of the tasks related to configuring networks require administrator privileges, as indicated by the shield icon next to commands and on command buttons.

Hardware, Cabling, and Connections

Before you can set up the networking software in Windows, you need to assemble and configure the proper hardware. In addition to two or more computers, you'll need the following components to set up a home or small office network:

- **Network adapters** Each computer needs an adapter to communicate with the other computers on the network. (An adapter is sometimes called a *network interface card*, or NIC.) Network adapters can be internal (usually installed in a PCI slot) or external (typically connected to a USB port). Most wired network adapters conform to the Ethernet standard. Wireless adapters conform to one of several 802.11 (Wi-Fi) standards.

- **A central connection point** Use a *hub* or *switch* to connect the computers in an Ethernet network. This function is sometimes integrated in a *router* or *residential gateway*. On a wireless network, a *wireless access point* handles these duties. Networks that use the Home Phoneline Networking Alliance (HomePNA) standard do not require a central connection point.

In this chapter, we sometimes use the term *hub* in its generic sense to refer to a central connection point for networks that use a star-bus topology, such as Ethernet. However, a *hub* (using its more precise definition) is just one of several types of connection points commonly used in home and small office networks:

- **Hub** A hub is the simplest and slowest of these devices, all of which have several jacks (called *ports*) into which you can plug cables attached to computers and other network devices. In a hub (which is sometimes called a *repeater*), data that is received on one port is broadcast to all its ports, which produces a lot of unnecessary network traffic.

- **Switch** By keeping track of the MAC address for each connected device, when a switch receives data, it sends it only to the port to which the destination device is attached. A switch is faster and more secure than a hub.

- **Router** Unlike hubs and switches, which are used to connect computers on a single network, a router is typically used to connect two or more networks. In a small network, a router typically is used to connect the local area network to the network at an internet service provider (which, in turn, uses routers to connect to the internet backbone).

  A *residential gateway* is a router that typically adds network address translation (NAT) and Dynamic Host Configuration Protocol (DHCP) capabilities. (NAT enables multiple computers on a network to share a single public IP address. DHCP is a system for assigning an IP address to each computer on a network.) In addition, many residential gateways include a stateful packet inspection firewall and other security features.

  A *wireless gateway* adds wireless capability to a residential gateway, thereby enabling connections to computers with Wi-Fi adapters as well as computers with wired adapters. To add wireless capability to a network centered around a nonwireless residential gateway, use a *wireless access point*.

Chapter 12

- **Cables** On an Ethernet network, you connect each network adapter to the hub using an eight-wire Category 5, Category 5e, or Category 6 patch cable with RJ-45 connectors on each end. (Cat 5 is designed for Fast Ethernet, with speeds up to 100 Mbps, whereas Cat 5e and Cat 6 cable are designed for Gigabit Ethernet, with speeds up to 1 Gbps.) HomePNA networks connect to an existing telephone jack with a standard telephone connector (RJ-11). By definition, wireless networks require no cables, except between the wireless access point and the internet.

Although it's not required, most networks also include one additional hardware component: a modem or other device to connect your network to the internet.

INSIDE OUT   Connect two computers without a hub

If your home network consists of two computers and you have no plans to expand it, you can save yourself the cost of a hub and use a *crossover cable* instead. A crossover cable is identical to a standard patch cable, except that two wires are reversed, simulating the connection that would take place if the wires were plugged into a hub. Using a crossover cable is an acceptable solution when you want to connect two computers directly to transfer files quickly with a minimum of hassle; using Windows Explorer and a two-computer network is much easier than cumbersome solutions that require null-modem cables and extra software. A crossover cable can also serve as a permanent connection between two computers if one computer has an internet connection and the other doesn't. But as soon as you add a third computer to the network, you'll need additional hardware to serve as a hub.

Windows Vista has another option if your intent is to create a temporary connection between computers with wireless network adapters, say, for exchanging files with another user: an ad hoc network. For details, see "Setting Up an Ad Hoc Network," later in this chapter.

Ethernet, Wireless, or Phone Line?

When setting up a network, you can choose from three popular technologies, all of which are supported by Windows Vista:

- **Ethernet** This popular networking standard, developed in the mid-1970s, has stood the test of time. The original Ethernet standard (also known as 10Base-T) is capable of transferring data at maximum speeds of 10 megabits per second. The Fast Ethernet standard (also known as 100Base-T) can transfer data at 100 megabits per second, and is currently the mainstream system used in most homes and small office networks. A newer standard called Gigabit Ethernet allows data transfers at 1 gigabit (1,000 megabits) per second. In an office or home that is wired for Ethernet, you can plug your network adapter into a wall jack and install a hub at a central location called a *patch panel*. In a home or office without structured wiring, you'll need to plug directly into a hub.

- **Wireless** In recent years, wireless networking technology has enjoyed an explosion in popularity, thanks to its convenience and steadily decreasing prices. Although wireless local area networks (WLANs) were originally developed for use with notebook computers, they are increasingly popular with desktop computer users, especially in homes and offices where it is impractical or physically impossible to run network cables. The most popular wireless networks use one of several variants of the IEEE (Institute of Electrical and Electronics Engineers) 802.11 standard, also known as Wi-Fi. Using base stations and network adapters with small antennas, Wi-Fi networks using the 802.11g standard transfer data at a maximum rate of 54 megabits per second using radio frequencies in the 2.4 GHz range. (Some manufacturers of wireless networking equipment have pushed the standard with proprietary variations that approximately double the speed.) Currently the most popular, 802.11g-based networks have largely supplanted those based on an earlier standard, 802.11b, which offers a maximum speed of 11 megabits per second. Nipping at the heels of 802.11g is 802.11n, which offers approximately a tenfold improvement in speed as well as significantly greater range. At the time of this book's publication, the 802.11n specification has not been adopted, although that hasn't stopped manufacturers from selling equipment based on the draft standard. Nobody is certain whether these devices will be compatible with the final specification. Most 802.11g hardware works with 802.11b networks as well. Likewise, most 802.11n (draft) hardware is backward compatible with 802.11g and 802.11b devices. (Note, however, that all traffic on your network runs at the speed of the slowest wireless standard in use; if you've just bought an 802.11n router, you might want to pony up a few dollars more to replace your old 802.11b network adapter.)

  Another Wi-Fi standard in wide use is 802.11a, which can reach maximum speeds of 54 Gbps. It broadcasts in a different frequency range (5 GHz), and is therefore incompatible with 802.11b, 802.11g, and 802.11n equipment, except for specialized dual-band gear.

  A number of other wireless network standards promulgated by the IEEE's 802.11 Working Group promise benefits such as better security. Be aware that, despite the confusingly similar names, network equipment using one of the wireless standards is generally compatible only with other equipment using the exact same standard. For the latest technical details, you can read the sometimes dense and dry commentary at the official site of the 802.11 Working Group, *http://www.ieee802.org/11*. For a more readable summary, try the website run by the Wi-Fi Alliance at *http://www.wi-fi.org*.

- **Phone Line** Networks that comply with early versions of the Home Phoneline Networking Alliance (HomePNA) standard operate at speeds of roughly 10 megabits per second; the HomePNA 3 standard claims to work at speeds of up to 128 megabits per second. HomePNA networks don't require a central connection point such as a router or hub; instead, they employ a daisy-chain topology in which all network adapters communicate directly by plugging into existing telephone jacks and transmitting data on the same wires that carry telephone and fax signals, without interfering with those communications. The availability of inexpensive wireless network gear has relegated HomePNA technology to a tiny niche;

Chapter 12

it's most attractive in older homes where adding network cable is impossible and wireless signals are impractical because of distance or building materials. For more information, visit the Home Phoneline Networking Alliance at *http://www. homepna.org.*

In many homes and offices, it's impractical to rely exclusively on one type of network. For example, it might not be feasible to run cables to every location where you want a computer. Yet, a wireless network might not be adequate because the signal can't reach all locations due to the number and type of walls and floors that separate computers. In such a case, you can install two or more networks of different types, and use a router or a bridge to connect the disparate networks.

Installing and Configuring a Network Adapter

On most systems, you don't need to take any special configuration steps to set up a network adapter, regardless of whether it's for an Ethernet, wireless, or HomePNA adapter. The Plug and Play code in Windows handles all the work of installing drivers. If you install an internal adapter and Windows includes a signed driver for that adapter, the driver should be installed automatically when Windows detects the adapter (if Windows cannot find a built-in driver, you'll be prompted to supply the location of the driver files). For an external adapter connected to a USB or IEEE 1394 port, the driver installs like one for an internal adapter, and thereafter loads and unloads dynamically when you attach or remove the adapter.

For more details about installing hardware, see "Installing and Configuring a New Device," Chapter 5.

As with all hardware devices, you can inspect the properties of a network adapter from the Device Manager console. (See "Changing Settings for an Installed Device," Chapter 5, for details.) Most network adapters include an Advanced tab in the properties dialog box, from which you can configure specialized hardware settings. These settings are invariably hardware-specific, and they can vary dramatically, as the two examples in Figure 12-2 illustrate. In general, you should accept the default settings on the Advanced tab of the network adapter's properties dialog box except when you're certain a change is required.

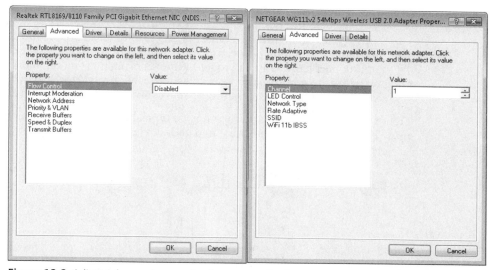

Figure 12-2 Adjust Advanced properties for a network adapter only when required for performance or compatibility reasons.

Making Connections

On a standard Ethernet network, all computers must be connected via one or more routers, switches, or hubs.

If you're going to connect your network to a broadband internet service, you should use a router or residential gateway as the primary hub. Most such products designed for use in homes and small offices combine a router and hub; in this type of device, you connect your external DSL or cable modem to the internet connector (often labeled as wide area network, or WAN) on the router and then connect each computer on the network to a port on the local area network (LAN) side.

If you use a dial-up connection for internet service, you can use any type of hub to connect your computers.

On wireless networks, a wireless access point serves as a hub.

Here are some guidelines to follow when connecting your network to a hub:

- Place the hub in a central location. You must be able to run a cable from the hub to each computer on your network. It's not always feasible to make a direct connection from each computer or other networked device to the central hub. (Furthermore, the central hub might not have enough ports to connect all devices.) To make additional connections in an Ethernet network, use another hub or switch.

- The total length of all cables used on the network should not exceed 100 meters (approximately 328 feet). For most home networks, this is not an issue.

Chapter 12

- It usually doesn't matter which ports you use on the hub, unless one is identified as *uplink*. Uplink ports are used to expand a network's capacity by connecting two hubs or sometimes to connect a hub to a router or broadband modem. On most hubs an uplink port cannot be used to connect to a computer, unless the uplink port has a switch to toggle it into a normal port mode. The uplink port achieves the same purpose as a crossover cable, and a toggle switch simply reverses the crossed-over lines to be able to accept a standard patch cable.

Figure 12-3 shows a schematic diagram of a typical network in a home or small business. This network includes both wired and wireless segments.

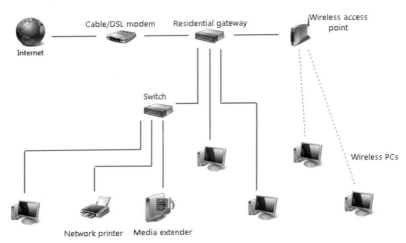

Figure 12-3 The residential gateway device can also provide the functionality of a cable modem, wireless access point, or both, eliminating the need to have separate devices.

Setting Up a Wireless Network

Configuring each device on a wireless network so that they all communicate with each other (and not with nearby networks that share the same airwaves) has traditionally been a tricky task. Understanding the alphabet soup of abbreviations—SSID, WEP, WPA, PSK, and MAC, to name a few—and providing appropriate values for each is a task for a true wizard. Fortunately, Windows Vista includes a wizard for each configuration task in wireless networking. These wizards, along with configuration support such as Windows Connect Now in modern wireless networking equipment, truly make setup simple:

1. Run the wizard to configure the wireless access point.

2. Transfer the configuration settings to the wireless access point, either through a wired connection or by using a USB flash drive.

3. Configure each computer and other wireless network device. This is most easily done by using a USB flash drive to transfer the configuration settings, but can also be done by running a wizard on each computer.

Before we get into the details of setup and configuration, however, we discuss security. Because wireless signals potentially expose your network to anybody who comes near, it's important to understand and consider security implications before you make your first wireless connection.

Understanding Security for Wireless Networks

On a conventional wired network, physical security is a given: If someone plugs a computer into your hub, you'll know about it immediately, and you can trace the physical wire back to the intruder's computer. On wireless networks, however, anyone who comes into range of your wireless access point can tap into your network and intercept signals from it. Finding open access points has become something of a sport; participants call it *war driving*. Although some war drivers seek open access points just for fun, other users who find their way into your network present several risks:

- **Theft of service** An intruder might be able to access the internet using your connection, which could degrade the quality of your internet service.

- **Denial of service** An intruder who is unable to connect to your network can still cause some degree of havoc by flooding the network with connection requests. With enough persistence, an attacker could completely deny legitimate users access to the network.

- **Privacy violations** An intruder with the right tools can monitor all data sent over the network, and can therefore see which websites you visit (along with your passwords for those sites), documents you download from a shared network folder, and so on.

- **Theft or destruction of data** Outsiders who successfully connect to your network can browse shared folders and printers. Depending on the permissions assigned to these resources, they can change, rename, or delete existing files, or add new ones.

- **Network takeover** An intruder who manages to log on to the network and exploit an unpatched vulnerability can install a Trojan horse program or tamper with permissions, potentially exposing computers on the LAN to attacks from over the internet.

To prevent any of these dire possibilities, you can and should configure the best available security for your access point and all wireless devices on your network. Depending on your hardware, you should have a choice of one or more of the following options:

- **Wired Equivalent Privacy (WEP)** WEP is a first-generation scheme for protecting authorized users of a wireless network from eavesdroppers by encrypting the data flow between the networked computer and the access point. To enter a WEP key, you supply a string of ASCII or hex characters (5 ASCII or 10 hex characters for a 64-bit key; 13 ASCII or 26 hex characters for a 128-bit key). The key you provide when setting up your wireless adapter must match the key on your access point, and all devices on the network must use the same encryption strength—either 64 or 128 bits. WEP suffers from some known security flaws that make it relatively easy for an attacker to "crack" the key using off-the-shelf hardware. As a result, WEP is inappropriate for use on any network that contains sensitive data. Most modern Wi-Fi equipment supports WEP for backward compatibility with older hardware, but you should use it only if none of the newer standards is available.

- **Wi-Fi Protected Access (WPA)** WPA is a newer, stronger encryption scheme that was specifically designed to overcome weaknesses of WEP. On a small network that uses WPA, clients and access points use a shared network password (called a *pre-shared key*, or *PSK*) that consists of a 256-bit number or a passphrase that is between 8 and 63 bytes long. (A longer passphrase produces a stronger key.) With a sufficiently strong key based on a truly random sequence, the likelihood of an outside attack is very, very slim. Most network hardware that supports the 802.11g standard also supports WPA. With older hardware, you might be able to add WPA compatibility via a firmware upgrade.

- **Wi-Fi Protected Access 2 (WPA2)** Based on the 802.11i standard, WPA2 provides the strongest protection yet for wireless networks. It uses 802.1x based authentication and Advanced Encryption Standard (AES) encryption; combined, these technologies assure that only authorized users can access the network, and that any intercepted data cannot be deciphered. WPA2 comes in two flavors: WPA2-Personal and WPA2-Enterprise. WPA2-Personal uses a passphrase to create its encryption keys, and is currently the best available security for wireless networks in homes and small offices. WPA2-Enterprise requires a server to verify network users. WPA2 can work with all flavors of Wi-Fi, including 802.11b, 802.11g, and 802.11a. (WPA2 support will undoubtedly be included in 802.11n devices also when the specification is finalized in 2007.) All wireless products sold since early 2006 must support WPA2 in order to bear the Wi-Fi CERTIFIED label.

You must use the same encryption option on all wireless devices on your network—access points, routers, network adapters, print servers, cameras, and so on—so choose the best option that is supported by all your devices. If you have an older device that supports only WEP (and it can't be upgraded with a firmware update) consider retiring or replacing that device.

The alternative to these encryption methods is to use no security at all, an option that produces an "open" network. If you own a coffee shop or bookstore and your goal is to provide free internet access for your customers, this option is acceptable as long as you make sure to protect other computers on your network from unauthorized access. (The primary tools for doing so are a firewall, sharing permissions, and folder permissions.) But for most people, the risks of running an open network are unacceptable.

Configuring a Wireless Access Point or Router

You begin setting up your wireless network by configuring the wireless access point (or a router that includes a wireless access point), which is the hub of your Wi-Fi network. What used to be a complex process is quite simple if you use a device that supports Windows Connect Now. The D-Link DIR-655 router is one of the first to fully implement Windows Connect Now, but we anticipate that most residential gateway devices sold in 2007 and later will include full support.

To configure a wireless access point or router that supports Windows Connect Now, follow these steps:

1. Open Network And Sharing Center; in the Tasks list, click Set Up A Connection Or Network.

2. In the Set Up A Connection Or Network wizard, select Set Up A Wireless Router Or Access Point and click Next. On the next page, click Next.

3. Click Create Wireless Network Settings And Save To USB Flash Drive.

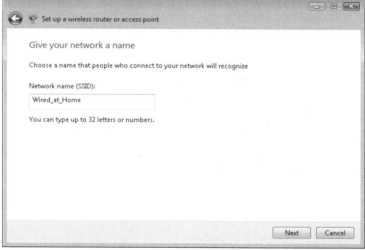

4. Enter a name for your wireless network. This name, also known as the SSID (for service set identifier), may contain only letters, numbers, and underscores. Windows suggests using the name of your computer with "_Network" appended; because it's the name by which all devices on a WLAN identify the network, you might want to come up with something more meaningful.

5. Click Show Advanced Network Security Options. Then select the best security method supported by all your wireless devices—WPA2-Personal (best), WPA-Personal, WEP, or No Security. (If you don't display the advanced options, Windows defaults to WPA-Personal.)

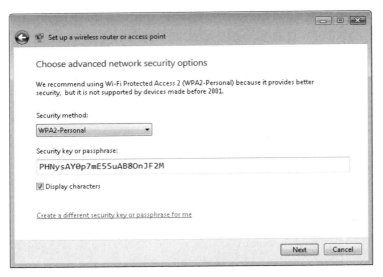

6. Enter a passphrase, which Windows uses to generate a security key. Windows suggests a gobbledygook "phrase," but you can replace it with one of your own choosing. (You might prefer to use a memorable phrase instead of random characters. If you do, choose a phrase that's not easily guessed, make it long, and consider incorporating letter substitution or misspellings to thwart attackers. Because you seldom have to type the passphrase—it's ordinarily needed only during setup, and even then it's usually transferred automatically from a UFD or, at worst, by cut and paste—using a memorable phrase for WPA is less appealing than it is for, say, a login password.) A passphrase for WPA or WPA2 can be up to 63 characters long and may contain letters (case-sensitive), numbers, and spaces (no spaces at the beginning or end, however). A WEP security key must be 26 hexadecimal characters (numbers 0–9 and letters A–F) or 10 letters (case-sensitive), numbers, and symbols. Click Next.

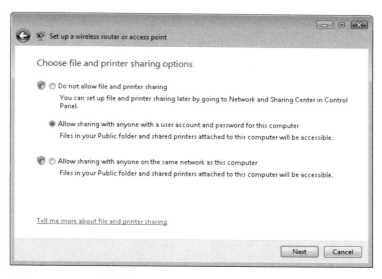

7. Select an option for file and printer sharing over the network. (You can change this setting at any time later. For more information, see Chapter 13, "Managing Shared Folders and Printers.")

8. Plug a USB flash drive into your computer, select it from the list, and click Next. You don't need to use a UFD dedicated to the purpose; all the files (Autorun.inf and Setupsnk.exe in the root folder, plus a handful of files in the \Smrtntky folder) take only a few kilobytes of space, and don't interfere with other files on the UFD.

9. Remove the UFD from your computer and plug it into the router. Most routers give some indication when they have accepted the information from the UFD, such as a pattern of blinking lights or a message in an LCD panel. Check your router's documentation for details.

INSIDE OUT   Print configuration details

Before you close the Set Up A Wireless Router Or Access Point wizard, click the "For more detailed instructions" link. Doing so opens a document in WordPad that includes the network name (SSID) for your wireless network and the passphrase or security key that you created. In addition, the document includes instructions for adding a computer or other device—wireless or wired—to your network. You might want to save or print this document for future reference.

If you click Close before you open the document, you have another option: Open the \Smrtntky\Wsetting.txt file on the UFD. Although this plain-text document doesn't include the instructions, it does include all the details of your WLAN configuration.

INSIDE OUT
Save the configuration files

After you use the configuration files you saved on a USB flash drive to configure your router and then set up each of the wireless computers on the network, you might be tempted to delete the files from the UFD. For security purposes, you should; if you leave the files in place, an attacker who ends up with the UFD has instant and unfettered access to your wireless network.

However, we recommend that you first copy the \Smrtntky folder to one of your profile folders on your computer's hard disk drive. (There's no security risk in doing so; if the attacker has your hard disk, he already has access to your network.) You might need these files again for any of several reasons, including:

- You add a new computer or device to your network
- A visiting friend wants access to your wireless network to use its internet connection
- You upgrade the firmware in your router or other wireless device, and it loses all its settings
- You reinstall Windows Vista on one of your networked computers

Many routers that don't support Windows Connect Now have comparable, proprietary systems for configuring the router's SSID, encryption, and other settings. Check the instructions that came with your router.

With others, configuring an access point to support encryption requires that you use a web-based configuration utility. Figure 12-4, for instance, shows configuration settings for a Linksys WRT54G, which combines a wired router and a wireless access point.

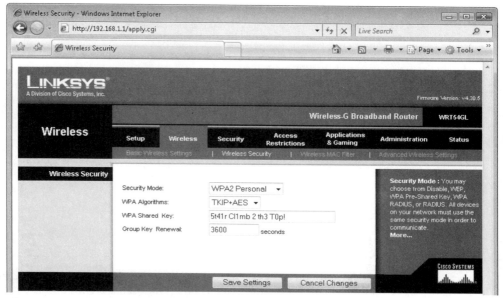

Figure 12-4 Security settings and keys for a wireless access point must match those for your wireless network adapter. The WPA Shared Key setting here works with the Security Key Or Passphrase setting in the Connect To A Network wizard that you use to configure an adapter.

To get to the configuration webpage for your router, start from the Network And Sharing Center, as you would for a Windows Connect Now–enabled router.

1. In the Tasks list, click Set Up A Connection Or Network.

2. In the Set Up A Connection Or Network wizard, select Set Up A Wireless Router Or Access Point and click Next. On the next page, click Next.

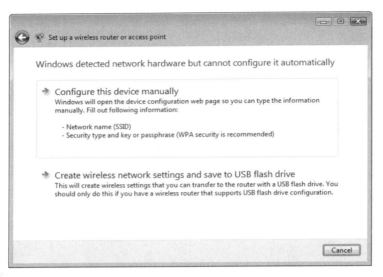

3. Click Configure This Device Manually. You'll then have to provide the user name and password for your router's configuration page; check its documentation for details.

INSIDE OUT **Create a configuration UFD even if your router requires manual configuration**

Even if your router doesn't support the use of a USB flash drive for configuration, you can use one to configure your wireless computers and other wireless devices that allow configuration by UFD. That way, you won't need to type the network name and security passphrase on each computer.

After you complete the manual configuration of your router, run the Set Up A Wireless Router Or Access Point wizard again. This time, click Create Wireless Network Settings And Save To USB Flash Drive and complete the wizard, as described earlier in this section.

INSIDE OUT **Beef up security at the access point**

If your data is sensitive and your network is in an apartment building or an office complex where you can reasonably expect other people to wander into range with wireless adapters, you should take extra security precautions in addition to enabling WPA. Consider any or all of the following measures to protect your wireless access point from intruders.

- Change the network name (SSID) of your access point to one that doesn't match the hardware defaults and doesn't give away any information about you or your business.

- Consider disabling remote administration of the access point; if you need to change settings, you can do so directly, using a wired connection.

- If you allow remote administration of the access point, set a strong password.

- Upgrade the firmware of your wireless hardware (access point and adapter) to the most recent versions, which may incorporate security fixes.

- If your pool of PCs is small and fixed, use your access point's configuration tools to restrict access to computers using the unique MAC address of each computer's wireless adapter.

- Consider using virtual private networks for wireless connections.

On larger networks with one or more domain servers available, you can set up a Remote Authentication Dial-In User Service (RADIUS) server to allow the most secure option of all, 802.1x authentication. In addition, consider enabling Internet Protocol Security (IPsec).

Connecting to a Wireless Network

In this section, we assume that you have already connected a wireless access point to your network and set it up using the instructions in the previous section or the instructions provided by the manufacturer. Here we explain how to connect a computer that has a wireless network adapter to your wireless network.

Note

These instructions describe the process in Windows Vista specifically, although the process is nearly identical on computers running Windows XP. For computers running other operating systems, the process of configuring a wireless network connection varies; see the operating system documentation or the documentation for the wireless network adapter for more information.

If you created a USB flash drive with configuration settings for your wireless network, plug it into the computer that you want to add to the wireless network. When the AutoPlay dialog box appears, click Wireless Network Setup Wizard. Click OK a couple of times, and you're done! To confirm that your computer is part of the network, open the Network folder (click Start, Network), and you should be able to see other computers and devices on your network.

Chapter 12

TROUBLESHOOTING

No other computers appear

If you're connecting to a network in your home or office (as opposed to a public hotspot, such as an internet café), be sure that the network is defined as a private network. If you don't specify a network location the first time Windows detects a network, by default it sets the location type as public, which is safer. However, on a public network, network discovery is turned off—which means you won't be able to see other computers on the network. To see if this is the problem (and to resolve it), open Network And Sharing Center. If "(Public network)" appears next to the name of your network, click Customize. In the Set Network Location dialog box, select Private, and click Next.

Connecting to a Network Without Using a USB Flash Drive

Having configuration settings on a UFD makes it dead simple to add a computer to a wireless network. However, this option isn't always available. This might be the case if you're visiting someone else's WLAN, if you didn't create a UFD when you configured your wireless network, or if the UFD is simply not available. Whenever your computer's wireless network adapter is installed and turned on, Windows scans for available wireless access points. If it finds at least one, it displays a status message in the notification area as the network icon alternately displays a signal-strength indicator.

Click the notification area's Network icon and then click Connect To A Network to display a dialog box similar to the one shown in Figure 12-5. (If you're already connected to one wireless network and you want to switch to another, click Connect Or Disconnect.) Select the network to which you want to connect, and then click the Connect button to join the network.

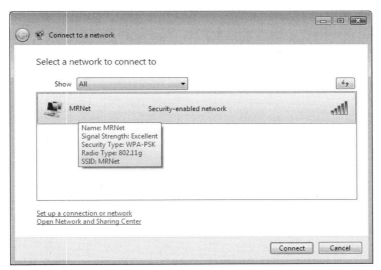

Figure 12-5 Any nearby networks that are broadcasting their network names (SSIDs) are visible here, with secure networks clearly noted.

If the network you select is secure and you haven't already entered its security key or passphrase, you'll be prompted to enter that information at this point, as shown in Figure 12-6 on the next page. (Note that Windows offers another opportunity to use a USB flash drive that has WLAN configuration settings.) After you successfully enter the key, you can begin using the shared internet connection and any available shared resources on the network.

Figure 12-6 When you attempt to connect to a secure wireless network, Windows prompts you to enter the appropriate WPA passphrase or WEP security key.

INSIDE OUT Don't type, paste!

Although you can carefully enter a 64-character WPA passphrase by typing each character, that method is a recipe for frustration, especially if you have more than one or two computers to set up. The wireless network setup wizard uses a USB flash drive to enter this information automatically on computers running Windows Vista or Windows XP Service Pack 2. If you allow the wizard to generate the encryption key automatically, it saves the key in a text file on the flash drive. To set up a router that doesn't use the flash drive, and for computers running other operating systems, open that text file, copy the key to the Clipboard, and then paste it into the dialog box. This method saves typing and avoids frustrating typos that can cause connections to fail.

Connecting to a Hidden Network

Some wireless networks are set up so that they don't broadcast their SSID. (Configuring a router to not advertise its name has been incorrectly promoted by some as a security measure. Although it does make the network invisible to casual snoops, lack of a broadcast SSID is no deterrent to a knowledgeable attacker. Furthermore, attackers can learn the SSID even when they're not near your wireless access point because it's periodically broadcast from your computer, wherever it happens to be.) Connecting to such hidden networks is a bit more challenging because its name doesn't appear in the list of preferred networks (see Figure 12-8 later in this chapter). Instead, it shows as "Unnamed

Network." To connect to the network, select it and click Connect. You'll then be asked to provide the network's SSID; if you answer correctly, the connection proceeds.

You can also set up your computer so that it connects to a particular nonbroadcasting wireless network whenever you're in range, as follows:

1. Open Network And Sharing Center and in the Tasks list, click Set Up A Connection Or Network.

2. In the Set Up A Connection Or Network wizard, select Manually Connect To A Wireless Network and click Next.

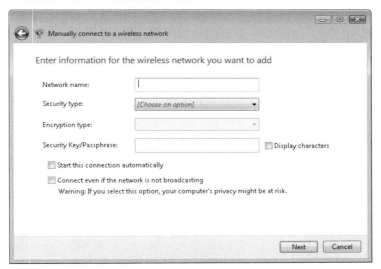

3. Specify the network name (SSID), the type of security used by the network, the encryption type if the network uses WPA or WPA2 security, and the security key or passphrase. Select Connect Even If The Network Is Not Broadcasting. (What is the privacy risk mentioned in the dialog box? When this option is turned on, your computer sends out probe requests to locate the wireless network; an attacker can detect these probe requests and use them to determine the network's SSID. Your computer continues to send these requests even when you're away from your network's access point.) Click Next.

4. If you want to connect to the network right away, click Connect To; otherwise, click Close.

For more information about hidden networks, see "Non-broadcast Wireless Networks with Microsoft Windows" on the Microsoft TechNet website (*http://www.vista-io.com/1202*).

Chapter 12

Setting Up Per-User Wireless Network Connections

By default, when you set up a wireless connection on your computer, it's available to all users of your computer. You can optionally make a connection available only to the user who's currently logged on. To make that option available, you must make a setting before you set up the wireless network connection, as follows:

1. In Network And Sharing Center, click Manage Wireless Networks.

2. In the Command bar of the Manage Wireless Networks window, click Profile Types.

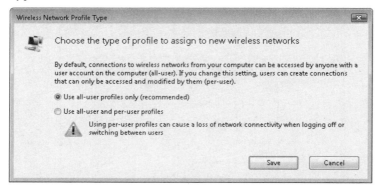

3. In the Wireless Network Profile Type dialog box, select Use All-User And Per-User Profiles.

Thereafter, when you set up a new wireless network, Windows asks whether you want the network to be available to all users or only to yourself. You can't apply this setting to an existing network; to do that, you must delete the network (in Manage Wireless Networks, select the network and click Remove) and then re-create it (in Manage Wireless Networks, click Add).

INSIDE OUT Copy connection information to another computer

Using a USB flash drive as described in the preceding sections is usually the easiest way to set up all the configuration information needed to connect to a wireless network. In some cases, however, you might find it more convenient to use the Netsh Wlan command line tool. Use Netsh Wlan Export to save a profile to a file, and Netsh Wlan Add to install a profile. For details, in a Command Prompt window, type **netsh wlan ?**.

Setting Up an Ad Hoc Network

An *ad hoc network* is a temporary network that connects two or more wireless computers and devices without requiring a hub or wireless access point. The computers' network adapters communicate directly with each other. An ad hoc network is handy when you need to exchange files or share an internet connection with someone who isn't normally part of your network—for example, in a meeting. Another common use: multiplayer games.

Windows Meeting Space provides another way to share files and other information wirelessly. For more information about this alternative, see "Windows Meeting Space," Chapter 8.

To set up an ad hoc network, follow these steps:

1. Open Network And Sharing Center and in the Tasks list, click Set Up A Connection Or Network.

2. In the Set Up A Connection Or Network wizard, select Set Up A Wireless Ad Hoc (Computer-to-Computer) Network and click Next. On the next page, click Next.

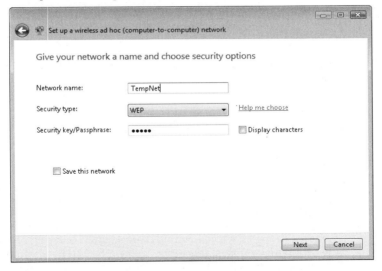

3. Specify a network name. The name can be up to 32 characters long, may contain letters, numbers, and underscores, and is case-sensitive.

4. Specify a security type. Ad hoc networks support only WEP encryption; the only other option is an open, unsecured network. An open network is the easiest for others to join—whether that's an advantage or disadvantage depends on whether potential interlopers might be nearby and whether you expect to transmit sensitive information.

5. If you selected WEP as the security type, enter a security key, which you can enter in any of these forms:

    ○ 5 or 10 case-sensitive characters (letters, numbers, and punctuation)

    ○ A 13-digit or 26-digit hexadecimal number (numbers and letters A–F)

6. If you plan to use the ad hoc network again in the future, select Save This Network. If you do not, Windows automatically deletes the network after the user who set up the network or all other users on the network disconnect.

7. Click Next. If your computer is connected directly to the internet (through a network adapter other than the wireless adapter you're using for the ad hoc network) and you want to share the internet connection, click Turn On Internet Connection Sharing.

8. Click Close.

The network is now set up and ready to use. Others can join the network just as they join any other wireless network: Click the network icon in the taskbar's notification area, click Connect To A Network (or Connect Or Disconnect if already connected to a wireless network). Select the ad hoc network and click Connect. If the ad hoc network is secured with WEP encryption, another dialog box asks for the security key; enter it and click Connect.

To share files, file sharing must be enabled. For more information, see Chapter 13, "Managing Shared Folders and Printers."

Setting Up a Shared Internet Connection

To share an internet connection safely on a small network, you have two options:

- **Install a router or residential gateway** This piece of hardware sits between your network and your internet connection (usually an external DSL or cable modem, although you can also use a conventional modem in this configuration). To the outside world, the residential gateway appears to be a computer with its own IP address, although it's considerably more secure because it does not have any running programs or disk storage that can be attacked by a would-be intruder. This class of hardware typically uses network address translation (NAT) to assign private IP addresses to computers on your network. Because it's always on, any computer can access the internet at any time through the gateway device.

- **Use Internet Connection Sharing (ICS)** In this configuration, the computer with the active internet connection acts as the ICS host computer and shares its internet connection. All computers on your network route their internet traffic through the ICS host computer. ICS is most effective with high-speed (cable or DSL) connections, although it works acceptably with dial-up internet connections. The ICS host computer must have a second network adapter to share a broadband connection. (If your broadband modem is an internal device or if you use a dial-up modem, you don't need a second network adapter.) The shared connection is available only while the ICS host computer is turned on.

For security and convenience, the first option is far superior, and we strongly recommend it. In a time when routers were expensive and difficult to configure, ICS made a lot of sense. For the most part, those days are gone.

> **Note**
>
> Before you can share an internet connection, you must create one. (With some broadband services and some network configurations, that happens automatically when you connect your router or computer to the internet.) To do that, in Network And Sharing Center click Set Up A Connection Or Network. Select Connect To The Internet and click Next to launch the Internet Connection wizard, which leads you the rest of the way.

If you decide to use ICS, here's how:

1. In Control Panel, open Network Connections. (Alternatively, in Network And Sharing Center, click Manage Network Connections.)

2. Right-click your internet connection and click Properties.

3. On the Sharing tab, select Allow Other Network Users To Connect Through This Computer's Internet Connection.

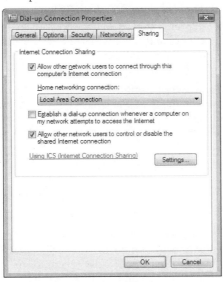

Enabling ICS makes the following changes to your system:

- The shared connection on the ICS host acquires an IP address from the internet service provider.

- An exception for Internet Connection Sharing is created and enabled in Windows Firewall.

- The connection to the local network from the ICS host uses the static IP address 192.168.0.1, configured with a subnet mask of 255.255.255.0.

- The Internet Connection Sharing service runs automatically on the ICS host.

- A DHCP allocator on the ICS host automatically assigns IP addresses to other computers on the network. The default range is 192.168.0.2 to 192.168.0.254, with a subnet mask of 255.255.255.0. A DNS proxy on the ICS host eliminates the need to specify DNS servers on other computers on the network. Network connections on the other computers should be configured to obtain an IP address and DNS server address automatically.

TROUBLESHOOTING

Your shared internet connection isn't working

Any of the following circumstances can prevent ICS from working properly:

- **The Internet Connection Sharing service is not running** Open the Services console, and then check to see that the Status column alongside the Internet Connection Sharing (ICS) service reads Started. If necessary, right-click the Service entry and choose Start or Restart from the shortcut menu.

- **The wrong network adapter is shared** In Network And Sharing Center, click Manage Network Connections and confirm that you've selected the correct adapter. You want to share the adapter that is connected to the internet; the adapter that connects to the rest of your network should not be shared.

- **The settings on other network computers are incorrect** Computers running any version of Windows should be able to connect to the internet through an ICS host when configured to obtain an IP address automatically and obtain DNS server addresses automatically. Leave the default gateway field blank when configuring network settings.

Exploring the Network

With your network hardware installed and the network configured, as described in the preceding sections, you're ready to begin exploring the other computers and devices on your network—without leaving your chair. Start your explorations in the Network folder (see Figure 12-7), which is most easily reached in either of the following ways:

- On the Start menu, click Network.

- In Network And Sharing Center, click View Computers And Devices.

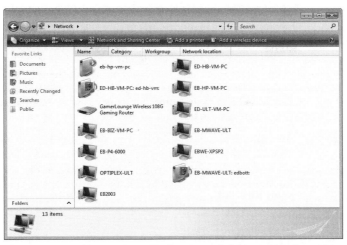

Figure 12-7 Unlike Windows XP, the Network folder in Windows Vista shows all computers on your network, not just those in your workgroup.

Your first foray onto the network might be somewhat less than fully satisfying, as you'll encounter some obstacles:

- When you first connect to a network, you must choose a network location. If you don't make a choice when the opportunity first presents itself, Windows sets the location to Public by default. You can change this setting from Network And Sharing Center. For more information about network locations, see "Understanding Location Types," on the next page.

- Network discovery might be turned off. Network discovery allows you to see other computers and shared devices in the Network folder. It's a two-way street; with network discovery turned off on your computer, it (and any shared devices attached to your computer) can't be seen in others' Network folder. Turning on network discovery enables an exception in Windows Firewall.

  Network discovery is turned on by default when you set up a private network (that is, a network location of Home or Work), and off by default when you set up a public network.

  When network discovery is turned off, an Information bar at the top of the Network folder window lets you know. To turn on network discovery, click the Information bar and then click Turn On Network Discovery And File Sharing. Alternatively, open Network And Sharing Center, where you'll find the Network Discovery setting under Sharing And Discovery.

  Remember, too, that network discovery must be turned on at each computer you want to be visible in your Network folder.

Chapter 12

INSIDE OUT Access network resources without network discovery

Even with network discovery turned off (on your computer or the target computer), you can access "undiscovered" network resources. Although they're not visible in the Network folder, if you type the name of computer preceded by two backslashes in the Windows Explorer Address bar and press Enter, you'll see that computer's shared resources. (For example, to view the resources on a computer named Sequoia, type **\\sequoia**.) If you type another backslash at the end of the computer name, a list of shared resources appears in the Address bar; you can use this trick to "drill down" through a folder hierarchy.

- Sharing settings on the other computers on your network might prevent you from finding anything of interest on those computers. For information about sharing settings, see Chapter 13, "Managing Shared Folders and Printers."

Understanding Location Types

With computers that connect to different types of networks—such as a corporate domain, an internet café, and a private home network, often within the same day—using the same network security settings for all networks would lead to security breaches, severe inconvenience, or both. Windows Vista uses network locations to identify a type of network, and then applies appropriate security settings. When you initially connect to a network, Windows asks you to select a network location.

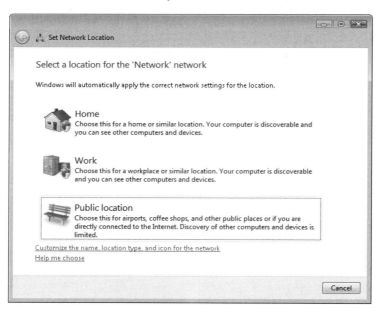

- **Home or Work** The only functional difference between the first two location options is the default icon that Windows uses to represent your network. Select one of these options when you're connecting to a trusted network, such as your own network at home or your company network at work. You should select Home or Work only for a network that is protected by a residential gateway or comparable internet defense, and one where you're confident that malicious users aren't connected. With this choice, Windows turns on network discovery, which lets you see other computers on the network and lets other users see your computer.

- **Public Location** Use this option for networks in public places, such as wireless hotspots in coffee shops, hotels, airports, and libraries. This type of network typically has a direct connection to the internet. Network discovery is turned off for public locations.

If you have a mobile computer that connects to multiple networks, keep in mind that Windows keeps three groups of network security settings: one for private (home or work) networks, one for public-location networks, and one for use when your computer is joined to a domain-based network. As you can see by visiting Windows Firewall With Advanced Security, Windows Firewall maintains three profiles: Public Profile, Private Profile, and Domain Profile; each is associated with a network location type.

For more information about Windows Firewall, see "Blocking Intruders with Windows Firewall," in Chapter 10, and Chapter 31, "Advanced Security Management."

This is important because, for example, when you are connected to a public network and Windows Firewall is turned on, some programs and services ask you to let them communicate through the firewall. Consider carefully whether you want to unblock such programs; if you do, that program is unblocked for all networks identified as "public location" networks. Rather than creating a firewall exception that remains enabled at all public hotspots you visit, you might consider instead changing the location type of the current network to a home or work network. (Alternatively, you can open Windows Firewall and disable the exceptions when you're through using the program or service.)

Table 12-1 shows the default settings for each location. Any changes you make to the current network apply to all networks of the same location type.

Table 12-1. Default Settings for Network Locations

	Private	Public	Domain
Windows Firewall	On	On	On, with settings configured by Group Policy downloaded from the Active Directory domain
Network Discovery	On	Off	Configured by Group Policy downloaded from the Active Directory domain
File, Public Folder, Printer, and Media Sharing	Off	Off	Configured by Group Policy downloaded from the Active Directory domain

Chapter 12

The location of the current network is shown in Network And Sharing Center, next to the name of the network.

To change the network location, in Network And Sharing Center, to the right of the network name, click Customize. Select either Public or Private, click Next, and then click Close.

Workgroups vs. Domains

Computers on a network can be part of a workgroup or a domain.

In a *workgroup*, the security database (including, most significantly, the list of user accounts and the privileges granted to each one) for each computer resides on that computer. When you log on to a computer in a workgroup, Windows checks its local security database to see if you've provided a user name and password that matches one in the database. Similarly, when network users attempt to connect to your computer, Windows again consults the local security database. All computers in a workgroup must be on the same subnet. A workgroup is sometimes called a *peer-to-peer network*.

By contrast, a *domain* consists of computers that share a security database stored on one or more domain controllers running a member of the Windows Server family (Windows NT Server, Windows 2000 Server, Windows Server 2003, and soon, Windows Server "Longhorn"). When you log on using a domain account, Windows authenticates your credentials against the security database on a domain controller.

When you have more than a handful of computers in a network, they become much easier to manage when configured as a domain. For example, instead of re-creating a database of user accounts on each computer, you create each account only once. A domain environment also offers much greater power and flexibility. For example, you can easily set up roaming user profiles, which allow users to log on at any network computer and see the same personalized desktop, menus, applications, and documents. A domain using Active Directory, a feature of all server versions except Windows NT Server, also offers a fully searchable directory service that allows network users to easily find shared resources, contacts, users, and other directory objects. In addition, these server families offer IntelliMirror, a collection of technologies that offer centralized

- User data management
- Software installation and maintenance
- User settings management

In this chapter (and throughout this book) we focus primarily on workgroup networks.

Changing Network Settings

The default network settings in most cases produce a working network environment with minimal fuss and bother. However, you might want to modify some of the settings for your network.

Setting the Workgroup Name

A workgroup is identified by a name; all computers in a workgroup must be in the same local area network and subnet, and all must share the same workgroup name. The workgroup name is strictly an organizational tool, which Windows uses to group computers and shared resources on the same network. As the administrator of a workgroup, you might want to change the workgroup name to something that describes your organization or family; if your network is relatively large but does not include a domain server, you may choose to define more than one workgroup.

In Windows Vista, the workgroup name is largely invisible and irrelevant; when you open the Network folder or look at a network map, Windows Vista displays all computers in the network, regardless of which workgroup they're in. (However, network discovery is faster when all computers are in the same workgroup.)

That was not the case in earlier versions of Windows, which display in their network folders only computers in the same workgroup as your computer. Therefore, if your network includes computers running earlier versions of Windows, you should use the same workgroup name for all computers so they can see each other. The default name for a new workgroup in Windows Vista is WORKGROUP; in Windows XP it is MSHOME.

Joining a workgroup doesn't require a secret handshake or special security settings; you merely need to set the workgroup name on each computer. To set the workgroup name in Windows Vista:

1. In Network And Sharing Center, click the arrow to the right of Network Discovery to expand that section.

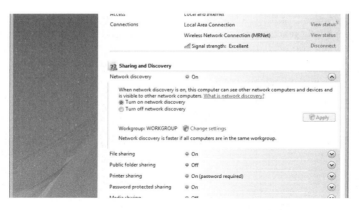

2. Next to the workgroup name, click Change Settings.

3. On the Computer Name tab of the System Properties dialog box, click Change.

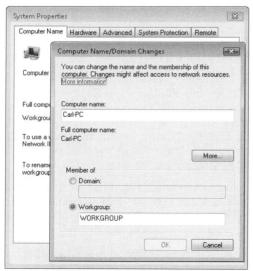

4. In the Computer Name/Domain Changes dialog box, select Workgroup, type the name of the workgroup (15 character maximum; the name can't include any of these characters: ; : < > * + = \ | / ? ,). Then click OK in each dialog box.

5. Restart your computer.

Except for the first step, the process for changing the workgroup name in Windows XP is nearly identical: Right-click My Computer and choose Properties. Then follow steps 3 through 5 above.

Specifying the Order and Connection Properties of Preferred Wi-Fi Networks

The first time you connect to a wireless network, Windows adds that network to the top of the list of preferred networks. (A *preferred network* is simply one to which you have connected before.) If you take your computer to a different location and connect to a new network, that location is added to the list of preferred networks.

Each time you turn on your computer or enable your wireless adapter, Windows attempts to make a connection. The WLAN AutoConfig service tries to connect to each of the preferred networks in the list of available networks, in the order that those networks appear. Unlike Windows XP, which included in its preferred networks list only those networks that broadcast their SSID, Windows Vista includes nonbroadcast networks also. This makes it possible to set a nonbroadcast network to a higher priority than an available broadcast network; Windows XP exhausts the list of broadcast networks before attempting to connect to an available nonbroadcast network.

You can alter the order of networks in the preferred list and configure any entry for manual rather than automatic connection. To manage the settings of entries on the list of preferred networks, in Network And Sharing Center, click Manage Wireless Networks to open the window shown in Figure 12-8.

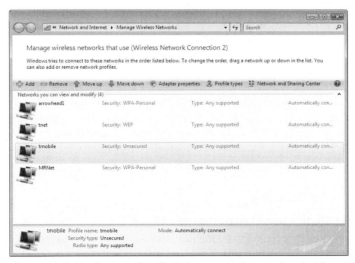

Figure 12-8 The list includes all wireless networks associated with a particular network adapter. If you have more than one wireless adapter installed, the Command bar includes a Change Adapter button.

To change the order of entries in the list, select the entry you want to move and then click Move Up or Move Down. Alternatively, you can drag a network to the desired position.

Manage Wireless Networks is also the place to review and, optionally, change connection settings for a network. To do that, double-click a network, which opens the network's properties dialog box, shown in Figure 12-9.

Figure 12-9 Settings on the Connection tab determine whether Windows should attempt to connect automatically.

To change an entry in the preferred networks list from automatic to manual, or vice-versa, select or clear Connect Automatically When This Network Is In Range. Settings on the Security tab let you specify the type of security and encryption and enter the security key or passphrase; if that information has changed since you set up the connection initially, you can change it here instead of creating a new network.

TROUBLESHOOTING

Windows switches between preferred networks

If you're within range of more than one preferred network, Windows might switch repeatedly between the networks as signal strengths vary. This causes delays as your computer negotiates each new connection, and sometimes drops the connection altogether. To prevent this from happening, in Manage Wireless Networks, double-click one of the interfering networks. On the Connection tab, clear Connect To A More Preferred Network If Available, and then click OK.

Renaming Your Network

You can change the name and the icon for your network. This information appears in Network And Sharing Center and in the information that pops up when you point to the Network icon in the taskbar notification area. The network initially takes on the name of the wireless SSID or, if you join a domain, the domain name. (The default name of a wired network is Network.)

To make the change, in Network And Sharing Center, to the right of the network name, click Customize. Type the name you want in the Network Name box. If you want to select a different icon, click Change Icon, where you'll find icons suggestive of a library, office building, park bench, airport, coffee shop, and more.

> **Note**
> Changing the network name does not affect the workgroup name, wireless SSID, or domain name.

INSIDE OUT   **Rename from Manage Wireless Networks**

The Manage Wireless Networks window (Figure 12-9), can be a more convenient place to change the network name, as it lets you rename networks to which you're not currently connected. Simply right-click a network and choose Rename.

Removing a Network

A computer that travels often is likely to accumulate settings for a large number of networks. Although these collected settings don't have any significant impact on performance or disk space, you might find it helpful to remove from the list entries that you don't plan to use again, such as one for a network at a hotel you don't expect to revisit.

To remove a wireless network, in Network And Sharing Center, click Manage Wireless Networks. Select a network to delete and click Remove.

Windows Vista includes another tool that lets you delete wired networks as well as wireless networks. To use it, in Network And Sharing Center, click Customize. In the Set Network Location dialog box, click Merge Or Delete Network Locations. In the Merge Or Delete Network Locations dialog box (Figure 12-10 on the next page), select the networks to remove and click Delete.

Figure 12-10 Connections to a domain are identified as Managed network locations.

Managing Network Connections

After you've installed your networking hardware (wired or wireless) and configured drivers and other supporting software, Windows creates a local connection that includes the following networking components:

- **Client For Microsoft Networks** A network client provides access to computers and resources on a network; this client allows you to connect to computers running any 32-bit or 64-bit Windows version.

- **QoS Packet Scheduler** This component enables Quality Of Service features provided on corporate networks and by internet service providers. For the most part, these advanced features will not be widely used until Internet Protocol version 6 (IPv6) is also widely used.

- **File And Printer Sharing For Microsoft Networks** This service allows other computers on your Windows-based network to access shared resources on your computer.

- **Internet Protocol Version 6 (TCP/IPv6)** TCP/IP is the default network protocol in Windows Vista, and IPv6 is the latest incarnation. For more information about IPv6, see "Understanding IPv6," later in this chapter.

- **Internet Protocol Version 4 (TCP/IPv4)** The ubiquitous TCP/IPv4 provides easy connectivity across a wide variety of networks, including the internet. Although TCP/IP has plenty of options you can configure, most users can safely accept the default settings without having to make any configuration changes.

- **Link-Layer Topology Discovery Mapper I/O Driver** The Link-Layer Topology Discovery (LLTD) protocol is used to create the network map, which provides a graphical view of the devices on your network and shows how they are connected. The LLTD mapper is one of two components required for creating a network map.

- **Link-Layer Topology Discovery Responder** Besides the mapper, LLTD also relies on a responder, which answers requests from the mapper component.

> **Note**
>
> For more details about TCP/IP configuration, see "Setting IP Addresses," in this chapter, and "Troubleshooting TCP/IP Problems," in Chapter 14. For information about network mapping, see "Diagnosing Problems Using Network Map," Chapter 14.

This default collection of clients, services, and protocols is generally all you need to work with a Microsoft network (that is, one where all computers are running 32-bit or 64-bit versions of Windows).

To see information about currently defined network connections, in Network And Sharing Center, click Manage Network Connections. Figure 12-11 shows the information and configuration options available from this window.

Figure 12-11 Try using Details view to see more information about each connection.

To see more detailed information about a network connection, double-click its icon in the Network Connections window. Figure 12-12 on the next page, for instance, shows the status dialog box for a default Local Area Connection.

Figure 12-12 Click Properties to view or modify the installed clients, services, and protocols.

INSIDE OUT Rename your connections

Windows tags your main network connection with the Local Area Connection or Wireless Network Connection label. When you add connections, they get equally generic titles, like Local Area Connection 2. You can easily replace these labels with text that's more meaningful to you. For instance, on a computer that's serving as an ICS host, you might give your two network adapters distinctive names like "Comcast Cable Modem" and "Home Network Connection." To edit a connection label, right-click the connection icon and choose Rename from the shortcut menu; then type the descriptive name.

Setting IP Addresses

Networks that use the TCP/IP protocol rely on *IP addresses* to route packets of data from point to point. On a TCP/IP network, every computer has a unique IP address for each protocol (that is, TCP/IPv4 and TCP/IPv6) and each network adapter. An IPv4 address—the type used on most networks for many years to come—consists of four 8-bit numbers (each one represented in decimal format by a number between 0 and 255) separated by periods. An IPv6 address consists of eight 16-bit numbers (each one represented in hexadecimal format) separated by colons. In addition to the IP address, each computer's TCP/IP configuration has the following additional settings:

- A *subnet mask*, which tells the network how to distinguish between IP addresses that are part of the same network and those that belong to other networks.

- A *default gateway*, which is a computer that routes packets intended for addresses outside the local network.

- One or more *Domain Name System (DNS) servers*, which are computers that translate domain names (such as *www.microsoft.com*) into IP addresses.

To determine your computer's IP address and other IP settings, in the dialog box shown in Figure 12-12, click Details.

Windows Vista provides several methods for assigning IP addresses to networked computers:

- **Dynamic Host Configuration Protocol (DHCP)** This is the default configuration for Windows Vista. Most internet service providers (ISPs) start with a pool of IP addresses that are available for use by their customers. ISPs use DHCP servers to assign IP addresses from this pool and to set subnet masks and other configuration details as each customer makes a new connection. When the customer disconnects, the address is held for a period of time and eventually released back to the pool so that it can be reused. Many corporate networks use DHCP as well to avoid the hassle of managing fixed addresses for constantly changing resources; all versions of Windows Server include this capability. The Internet Connection Sharing feature in Windows Vista includes a full-fledged DHCP server that automatically configures all TCP/IP settings for other computers on the network. Most routers and residential gateways also incorporate DHCP servers that automatically configure computers connected to those devices.

- **Automatic Private IP Addressing (APIPA)** When no DHCP server is available, Windows automatically assigns an IP address in a specific private IP range. (For an explanation of how private IP addresses work, see the sidebar "Public and Private IP Addresses.") If all computers on a subnet are using APIPA addresses, they can communicate with one another without requiring any additional configuration. APIPA was first introduced with Windows 98 and works the same in all versions of Windows released since that time.

For detailed technical information about APIPA, including instructions on how to disable it, read Knowledge Base article 220874, "How to Use Automatic TCP/IP Addressing Without a DHCP Server" (*http://www.vista-io.com/1203*).

- **Static IP Addressing** By entering an IP address, subnet mask, and other TCP/IP details in a dialog box, you can manually configure a Windows workstation so that its address is always the same. This method takes more time and can cause some configuration headaches, but it allows a high degree of control over network addresses.

  Static IP addresses are useful if you plan to set up a web server, a mail server, a virtual private network (VPN) gateway, or any other computer that needs to be accessible from across the internet. (New features in Windows Vista such as Teredo and Windows Internet Computer Name make it possible to access a computer over the internet even without a static IP address, however.) Even inside a local network, behind a router or firewall, static IP addresses can be useful. For

Chapter 12

instance, you might want to configure the router so that packets entering your network on a specific port get forwarded to a specific computer. If you use DHCP to assign addresses within the local network, you can't predict what the address of that computer will be on any given day. But by assigning that computer a static IP address that is within the range of addresses assigned by the DHCP server, you can ensure that the computer always has the same address and is thus always reachable.

- **Alternate IP Configuration** This feature allows you to specify multiple IPv4 addresses for a single network connection (although only one address can be used at a time). This feature is most useful with portable computers that regularly connect to different networks. You can configure the connection to automatically acquire an IP address from an available DHCP server, and then assign a static backup address for use if the first configuration isn't successful.

To set a static IP address, follow these steps:

1. In the Network Connections folder, select the connection whose settings you want to change.

2. Use any of the following techniques to open the properties dialog box for the selected connection:

   ○ Select the connection and click Change Settings Of This Connection.

   ○ Right-click the connection icon and choose Properties from the shortcut menu.

   ○ Double-click the connection icon to open the Status dialog box and then click the Properties button on the General tab.

3. In the list of installed network components, select Internet Protocol Version 4 (TCP/IPv4) or Internet Protocol Version 6 (TCP/IPv6) and then click the Properties button.

4. In the Internet Protocol (TCP/IP) Properties dialog box, select Use The Following IP Address and fill in the blanks. You must supply an IP address, a subnet mask (for IPv6, the length of the subnet prefix, which is usually 64 bits), and a default gateway.

5. Select Use The Following DNS Server Addresses and fill in the numeric IP addresses for one or more DNS servers as well. Figure 12-13 shows the dialog box with all fields filled in.

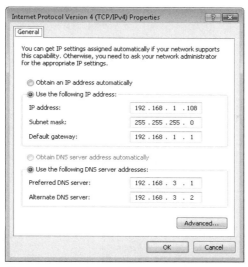

Figure 12-13 When assigning static IP addresses, you must fill in all fields correctly. Make a mistake and you'll lose your internet connectivity.

6. Click OK to save your changes. You do not need to reboot after changing your IP configuration.

To set up an alternate IP configuration, follow these steps:

1. From the Network Connections folder, open the properties dialog box for the connection you want to configure.

2. In the list of installed network components, select Internet Protocol Version 4 (TCP/IPv4) and then click the Properties button.

3. On the General tab of the Internet Protocol (TCP/IP) Properties dialog box, select Obtain An IP Address Automatically.

4. Click the Alternate Configuration tab and then select User Configured.

5. Enter the IP address, subnet mask, default gateway, and DNS servers for the alternate connection, as shown below. (You can safely ignore the fields that ask you to enter a preferred and alternate WINS server. WINS stands for Windows Internet Name Service, a name resolution system that maps a computer's NetBIOS name to an IP address. WINS servers are used on large corporate networks to allow domain servers to communicate with computers running older Microsoft operating systems, including Windows NT, Windows 95, Windows 98, and Windows Me. For virtually all home and small business networks, the WINS server details are unnecessary and irrelevant.)

Chapter 12

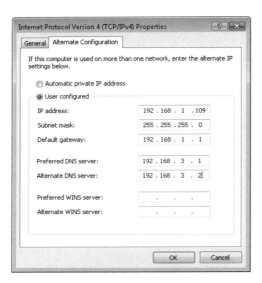

6. Click OK to save your changes. You do not need to restart after setting up an alternate configuration.

When you've configured an alternate IP configuration for a network connection, Windows looks first for a DHCP server to assign an IP address automatically. If no DHCP server is available, the system falls back to the static IP address defined on the Alternate IP Configuration tab.

Public and Private IP Addresses

Any computer that is directly connected to the internet needs a public IP address—one that can be reached by other computers on the internet, so that information you request (webpages and e-mail, for instance) can be routed back to your computer properly. When you connect to an internet service provider, you're assigned a public IP address from a block of addresses registered to that ISP. If you use a dial-up connection, your ISP probably assigns a different IP address to your computer (drawn from its pool of available addresses) each time you connect. If you have a persistent connection to your ISP via a DSL or cable modem, your IP address may be permanent—or semi-permanent, if you turn off your computer when you leave your home or office to travel and your assigned IP address is changed when you reconnect on your return.

On a home or small office network, it's not necessary to have a public IP address for each computer on the network. In fact, configuring a network with all public addresses can increase security risks and often requires an extra fee from your ISP. A safer, less costly solution is to assign a single public IP address to a single computer (or a router or residential gateway). All other computers on the network connect to the internet through that single address. Each of the computers on the local network has a private IP address that is not directly reachable from the outside world. To communicate with the internet, the computer or router on the edge of the network uses a technology called network address translation (NAT) to pass packets back and forth between the single public IP address and the multiple private IP addresses on the network.

The Internet Assigned Numbers Authority (IANA) has reserved the following three blocks of the IP address space for use on private networks that are not directly connected to the internet:

- 10.0.0.0 – 10.255.255.255
- 172.16.0.0 – 172.31.255.255
- 192.168.0.0 – 192.168.255.255

In addition, the Automatic Private IP Addressing feature in all post-1998 Windows versions uses private IP addresses in the range of 169.254.0.0 to 169.254.255.255.

Routers and residential gateways that use NAT almost always assign addresses from these private ranges. Linksys routers, for instance, typically assign addresses starting with 192.168.1.*x*. The Internet Connection Sharing feature in Windows Vista (as in previous versions of Windows) assigns private IP addresses in the 192.168.0.*x* range. If you're setting up a small business or a home network that will not be connected to the internet, or that will be connected through a single proxy server, you can freely use these addresses without concern for conflicts. Just make sure that all the addresses on the network are in the same subnet.

Understanding IPv6

Internet Protocol version 6 (IPv6) is a network layer that is designed to overcome shortcomings of the original Internet Protocol, IPv4. (That's right; the first version was dubbed IPv4, and the second version is IPv6.) The most significant difference is the much larger address space. The 32-bit IPv4 addressing scheme provides for a theoretical maximum of approximately 4 billion unique addresses, which seemed like a lot when the internet and Internet Protocol were conceived over three decades ago. (Because of the way IP addresses are allocated, the actual number in use is far less.) As a stopgap measure to overcome the limited number of IP addresses, private IP addresses and network address translation were implemented, as this system allows a large number of computers to share a single public IP address.

There will be no shortage of addresses with IPv6, which uses 128-bit addresses—providing a pool of 3.4×10^{38} addresses. (That's over 50 octillion addresses for every person on earth. Not many people have that many computers and other electronic devices, each of which will ultimately be addressed by its IPv6 address.)

Although NAT has been promoted as a security measure that shields networked computers behind a NAT firewall from external attack—which it does reasonably well—the security benefit was largely an afterthought; its real *raison d'être* is to ease the address shortage. IPv6 brings true security improvements, achieving the long-sought goal of security implemented at the network layer level; standards-based IPsec support is part of every IPv6 protocol suite.

Chapter 12

Other improvements in IPv6 include easier configuration and more efficient routing.

Unfortunately, although IPv6 is being rapidly rolled out in many Asian countries, its adoption in the West is likely to take many years. Full implementation requires not only support at the host operating system—which we now have in Windows Vista and other recent versions of Windows—but application and hardware support as well, including the routers that tie together the various nodes of the internet and the firewalls that keep them apart. Replacing the existing hardware (not just routers, but also printers and other network-connected devices) and other infrastructure will require huge investment and much time.

Until the transition to IPv6 is complete many years hence, you can gain several of its benefits with Windows Vista. Today, computers running Windows Vista can communicate over IPv4 and IPv6 networks at the same time. This means that, if your local area network (or your ISP) supports IPv6, Windows will use it, as IPv6 is the primary protocol in Windows Vista. You can also access IPv6 websites and other resources even if the intervening network infrastructure doesn't support IPv6, as Windows will automatically fall back to a tunneling system such as Teredo. (Teredo is an IPv6 transition technology that allows end-to-end communication using IPv6 addresses; NAT translation tables on Teredo client computers allow it to communicate through routers that use NAT. Other tunneling systems effectively embed IPv6 data in IPv4 packets.)

While you wait for the transition to IPv6 to be complete, you can find plenty of detailed information about IPv6 at the Microsoft IPv6 website, *http://www.microsoft.com/ipv6*.

CHAPTER 13

Managing Shared Folders and Printers

Home Basic ◐
Home Premium ◐
Business ●
Enterprise ●
Ultimate ●

By sharing your computer's resources, such as its folders, printers, and media library, you let other people who use your computer and other people on your network use these resources. With Windows Vista, using shared resources and sharing your own resources with other users—either locally or across the network—is simple and straightforward. Browsing a network folder is just like browsing a folder on your own hard disk. Sending a document to a network printer is just like printing at your own computer. Playing music and viewing photos from a shared media library lets you benefit from the hours *somebody else* spent ripping CDs and tagging photos!

Windows Vista puts a new face on the sophisticated security settings for resource sharing that have been an integral—and often confusing—part of earlier versions of Windows. This face, in the form of the Sharing wizard, makes it easy to implement security appropriate for computers shared by multiple users and for many small network workgroups. And for the first time, settings for local sharing (via NTFS permissions) and network sharing can be set in one place—and with greater flexibility and improved security compared with the Microsoft Windows XP solution, Simple File Sharing.

This chapter covers the full gamut of sharing options: from the simplicity of Public folder sharing (select one option and immediately other network users can view and use files on your computer), to the nitty-gritty details of setting access permissions on a printer, to the arcane command-line tools that let you control shares from a batch program. It's all here.

What's in Your Edition?

Sharing with other users of your computer and other users on your network works identically in all editions of Windows Vista. One feature mentioned in this chapter, the Print Management console, is not available in Home Basic and Home Premium, but all its functionality is available in other tools.

> **Note**
>
> In this chapter, we describe resource sharing as it applies in a workgroup environment. We do not cover sharing in a domain-based environment.

Understanding Sharing and Security Models in Windows Vista

Windows Vista offers two ways to share file resources, whether locally or over the network:

- **Public folder sharing** When you place files and folders in your Public folder or its subfolders, those files are available to anyone who has a user account on your computer. (The Public folder in Windows Vista replaces the functionality of the Shared Documents folder in Windows XP.) Each person who logs on has access to their own profile folders (Documents, Music, and so on), and *everyone* who logs on has access to the Public folder.

  By making a single setting in Network And Sharing Center, the contents of your Public folder become available on your network. If you turn on password-protected sharing, only people who have a user account on your computer (or know the user name and password for an account on your computer) can access files in the Public folder. Without password-protected sharing, everyone on your network has access to your Public folder files if you enable network sharing of the Public folder.

- **"Any folder" sharing** By choosing to share folders or files outside of the Public folder, you can specify precisely which user accounts will be able to access your shared data, and you can specify the types of privileges those accounts enjoy. You can grant different access privileges to different users. For example, you might enable some users to modify shared files and create new ones, enable other users to read files without changing them, and lock out other users altogether.

You don't need to decide between Public folder sharing and any folder sharing, as you can use them both simultaneously. You might find that a mix of sharing styles works best for you; each has its benefits:

- Any folder sharing is best for files that you want to share with some users, but not others—or if you want to grant different levels of access to different users.

- Public folder sharing provides a convenient, logical way to segregate your personal documents, pictures, music, and so on, from those that you want to share with everyone who uses your computer or your network.

- Public folder sharing is the easiest to set up, although with the benefit of the Sharing wizard, any folder sharing certainly isn't complex.

INSIDE OUT   Use any folder sharing to access your own files over the network

Naturally, because you have a user account on your computer, if you choose to share files over the network, you'll have access to your own shared files from other computers on the network. If you use Public folder sharing, other people also have access to those files, but if you use any folder sharing, you can configure sharing so that only you can remotely access your files.

What Happened to the Windows XP Sharing Models?

Windows veterans know that, in a workgroup environment, Windows XP has two sharing models, dubbed *Simple File Sharing* and *classic sharing*.

Simple File Sharing is the preferred (by Microsoft) method, as it is the default sharing model on all versions of Windows XP, except on computers that are joined to a domain. In fact, with Windows XP Home Edition, Simple File Sharing is the *only* way to share files over a network. As it turns out, Simple File Sharing is a little too simple, as it is notoriously inflexible. With Simple File Sharing, you can share only folders, not files. When you do, they're available to all network users; you can't specify different access permissions for different users. And your choice of permissions for a shared folder is limited: full control or read only.

On the other hand, classic sharing (which is largely unchanged from the sharing model used in Microsoft Windows NT and Microsoft Windows 2000) can be quite complex. Although it has tremendous flexibility, it also causes lots of confusion. This confusion often leads to configuration errors that end up with files being inaccessible to legitimate users, or wide open to anybody who stumbles onto your computer. Further complicating matters is the poorly understood relationship between share permissions (which control network access to shared objects) and discretionary access control lists (DACLs) or NTFS permissions (which control all access to a secured object, from network and local users alike).

The same technologies that underlie Simple File Sharing and classic file sharing in Windows XP—namely, DACLs, share permissions, and user rights—power sharing in Windows Vista. Yet the implementation, primarily through the Sharing wizard and Network And Sharing Center, is radically different. We think that in Windows Vista, you'll find the right balance of simplicity and flexibility.

> ### Another Model: Share-Level Access in Windows 95/98/Me
>
> If you shared folders or printers in Windows 95/98/Me, you might be familiar with a completely different sharing model. When not joined to a domain, those operating systems use *share-level access control*. With this type of access control, passwords (one for read-only access and one for full access) are assigned to each shared resource. When a network user tries to use a shared resource, Windows requests a password. Which password the user enters—the full control password, the read-only password, or an incorrect password—determines the user's level of access to the share. Windows makes no attempt to determine who the user is; therefore, anyone on the network who obtains (or guesses) the password has access to the share.
>
> Windows Vista, by contrast, always uses *user-level access control*, which means each shared resource allows access only by specified user accounts. To gain access to a shared resource over the network, a user must log on using an account that has access to the share.
>
> You cannot set a password for a particular folder or printer in Windows Vista; all access is controlled by permissions granted to specified users.

Configuring Your Network for Sharing

If you plan to share folders and files with other users on your network, you need to take a few preparatory steps—steps you might've already taken when you set up your network. (If you plan to share only with others who use your computer by logging on locally, you can skip these steps.) Each of the following steps can be performed from Network And Sharing Center. (For a list of ways to open Network And Sharing Center, see "Using Network And Sharing Center," Chapter 12.)

1. **Be sure that all computers use the same workgroup name.** If all computers on your network use Windows Vista, this step isn't absolutely necessary, although it does improve network discovery performance. However, if you have a mixed network that includes some computers running Windows XP or other earlier versions of Windows, it's essential for enabling computers on the network to see each other. For details, see "Setting the Workgroup Name," Chapter 12.

2. **Be sure that your network's location type is set to Private.** This setting provides appropriate security for a network in a home or office. For details, see "Understanding Location Types," Chapter 12.

3. **Be sure that Network Discovery is turned on.** This should happen automatically when you set the location type to Private, but you can confirm the setting—and change it if necessary—in Network And Sharing Center.

4. **Select your sharing options, as described below.** You set network sharing options in the Sharing And Discovery section of Network And Sharing Center, which is shown in Figure 13-1.

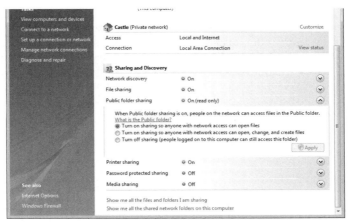

Figure 13-1 To view or modify any settings under Sharing And Discovery, click the arrow to the right of the setting name.

○ **File Sharing** Turn on file sharing (the only options for this setting are On and Off) if you want to use any folder sharing, Public folder sharing, or printer sharing. In other words, file sharing must be turned on if you plan to share any files (other than media sharing) over your network. If you subsequently turn off file sharing, Public folder sharing and printer sharing turn off automatically.

The mere act of turning on file sharing does not expose any of your computer's files or printers to other network users; that occurs only after you make additional sharing settings.

○ **Public Folder Sharing** If you want to share items in your Public folder with all network users (or, if you enable password protected sharing, all users who have a user account and password on your computer), select one of the options under Public Folder Sharing. The first option, Turn On Sharing So Anyone With Network Access Can Open Files, provides read and execute access to network users, meaning they can view any files, play media, and run programs—but they can't create, change, or delete files in the Public folders. The second option grants these additional capabilities to network users.

The contents of Public folders become available to network users immediately after you select one of the "on" options.

○ **Printer Sharing** If you have one or more printers attached to your computer, you can share them with other network users by turning on printer sharing. (You don't need to select this option to share printers that connect to a network hub.)

○ **Password Protected Sharing** When Password Protected Sharing is turned on, network users cannot access your shared folders (including Public folders, if shared) or printers unless they can provide the user name and password of a user account on your computer. With this setting enabled, when another user attempts to access a shared resource, Windows sends the user name and password that the person used to log on to his or her own computer. If that matches the credentials for an account on your computer, the user gets immediate access to the shared resource (assuming permissions to use the particular resource have been granted to that user account). If either the user name or the password does not match, the user will be asked to provide credentials, in a dialog box like the one shown below.

With Password Protected Sharing turned off, Windows does not require a user name and password of network visitors. Instead, network access is provided using the Guest account. This is essentially the same as Simple File Sharing in Windows XP.

○ **Media Sharing** Media sharing uses Windows Media Player to stream music, video, and pictures to other computers on your network. For more information, see "Sharing a Media Library with Other PCs," Chapter 19.

5. **Set up user accounts.** If you use password protected sharing, each person who accesses a shared resource on your computer must have a user account on your computer. They could, of course, use somebody else's existing account as long as they know the user name and password. However, they'll be required to enter that information each time they access the shared resource. Although it requires some extra preparation time up front, in the long run, you'll find it much easier to share resources over the network if, on each computer that will have shared resources, you create a user account for each user who will access those resources. Use the same user name as that person uses on their own computer, and the same password as well. If you do that, network users will be able to access shared resources without having to enter their credentials after they've logged on to their own computer.

Sharing Files with Public Folders

To share items in your Public folder and its subfolders with other users of your computer, you don't need to do a thing. By default, all users with an account on your computer can log on and create, view, modify, and delete files in the Public folders. The person who creates a file in a Public folder (or copies an item to a Public folder) is the file's owner, and has Full Control access. All others who log on locally have Modify access.

> **For more information about access levels, see "Controlling Access with NTFS Permissions," Chapter 29.**

To share items in your Public folder with network users, in Network And Sharing Center, turn on Public Folder Sharing, as described in the preceding section. You can't select which network users get access, nor can you specify different access levels for different users. Sharing via the Public folder is quick and easy—but it's rigidly inflexible.

Sharing Files and Folders from Any Folder

Whether you plan to share files and folders with other people who share your computer or those who connect to your computer over the network (or both), the process for setting up shared resources is the same, as long as the Sharing wizard is enabled. We recommend that you use the Sharing wizard, even if you normally disdain wizards. It's quick, easy, and is certain to make all the correct settings for network shares and NTFS permissions—a sometimes daunting task if undertaken manually. Once you've configured shares with the wizard, you can always dive in and make changes manually if you desire.

To be sure the Sharing wizard is enabled, open Folder Options. (Type **folder** in the Start menu Search box or, in Windows Explorer, click Organize, Folder And Search Options.) Click the View tab, and near the bottom of the Advanced Settings list, see that Use Sharing Wizard (Recommended) is selected.

With the Sharing wizard at the ready, follow these steps to share a folder or files:

1. In Windows Explorer, select the folders or files you want to share. (You can select multiple objects.)

2. In the command bar, click Share. (Alternatively, right-click and choose Share.)

3. In the File Sharing box, enter the names of the users with whom you want to share. You can type a name in the box or click the arrow to display a list of available names; then click Add. Repeat for each person you want to add.

The list includes all users who have an account on your computer, plus Everyone. If you want to grant access to someone who doesn't appear in the list, click Create A New User, which takes you to User Accounts in Control Panel.

> **Note**
>
> If you select Everyone and you have password protected sharing enabled, the user must still have a valid account on your computer. However, if you have turned off password protected sharing, network users can gain access *only* if you grant permission to Everyone or to Guest.

4. For each user, select a permission level. Your choices are:

- ○ **Reader** Users with this permission level can view shared files and run shared programs, but cannot change or delete files. Selecting Reader in the Sharing wizard is equivalent to setting NTFS permissions to Read & Execute.

○ **Contributor** This option, which is available only for shared folders (not shared files), allows the user to view all files, add files, and change or delete files they add. Selecting Contributor sets NTFS permissions to Modify.

○ **Co-owner** Users assigned the Co-owner permission have the same privileges you do as owner: they can view, change, add, and delete files in a shared folder. Selecting Co-owner sets NTFS permissions to Full Control for this user.

> **Note**
>
> You might see other permission levels if you return to the Sharing wizard after you set up sharing. Custom identifies NTFS permissions other than Read & Execute, Modify, or Full Control. Mixed appears if you select multiple items and they have different sharing settings. Owner, of course, identifies the owner of the item.

5. Click Share. After a few moments, the wizard displays a page like the one shown in Figure 13-2.

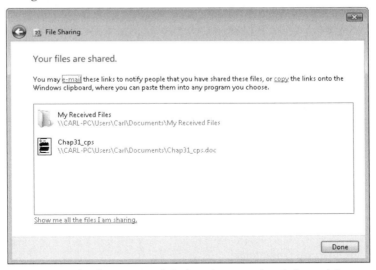

Figure 13-2 The Sharing wizard displays the network path for each item you've shared.

6. In the final step of the wizard, you can do any of the following:

○ Send an e-mail message to the people with whom you're sharing. The message includes a link to the shared folder or file.

- ○ Copy the network path to the Clipboard. This is handy if you want to send a link via instant messenger or other application.
- ○ Double-click a share name to open the shared item.
- ○ Open a search folder that shows all the folders and files you're sharing.

When you're finished with these tasks, click Done.

Creating a share requires privilege elevation, but after a folder has been shared, the share is available to network users no matter who is logged on to your computer—or even when nobody is logged on.

INSIDE OUT Use advanced sharing to create shorter network paths

Confusingly, when you share one of your profile folders (or any other subfolder of %SystemDrive%\Users), Windows Vista creates a network share for the Users folder—not for the folder you shared. This isn't a security problem; NTFS permissions prevent network users from seeing any folders or files except the ones you explicitly share. But it does lead to some long UNC paths to network shares. For example, if you share the My Received Files subfolder of Documents (as shown in Figure 13-2), the network path is \\CARL-PC\Users\Carl\Documents\My Received Files. If this same folder had been anywhere on your computer outside of the Users folder, no matter how deeply nested, the network path would instead be \\CARL-PC\My Received Files. Other people to whom you've granted access wouldn't need to click through a series of folders to find the files in the intended target folder.

Network users, of course, can map a network drive or save a shortcut to your target folder to avoid this problem. But you can work around it from the sharing side too: Use advanced sharing to share the folder directly. (Do this after you've used the Sharing wizard to set up permissions.) For more information, see "Setting Advanced Sharing Properties," later in this chapter. (And while you're doing that, be sure the share name you create doesn't have spaces. Eliminating them makes it easier to type a share path that works as a link.)

Stopping or Changing Sharing of a File or Folder

If you want to stop sharing a particular shared file or folder, select it in Windows Explorer and click Share. The Sharing wizard appears, as shown in the following figure.

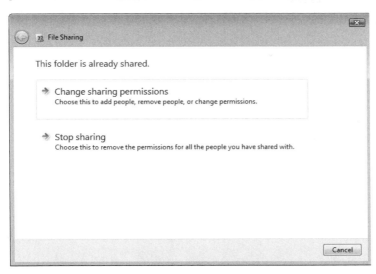

If you click the first option, Change Sharing Permissions, the wizard continues as when you created the share, except that all existing permissions are shown. You can add or remove names, and change permissions.

The second option, Stop Sharing, removes access control entries that are not inherited. In addition, the network share is removed; the folder will no longer be visible in another user's Network folder.

Setting Advanced Sharing Properties

If you disable the Sharing wizard, Windows Vista reverts to a process similar to that employed by earlier versions of Windows (except the aberration in Windows XP called Simple File Sharing—nothing before or since is similar to that!). Without the Sharing wizard, you configure network shares independently of NTFS permissions. (For more information about this distinction, see the sidebar, "How Shared Resource Permissions and NTFS Permissions Work Together.")

With the Sharing wizard disabled, when you select a folder and click Share, rather than the wizard appearing, Windows opens the folder's properties dialog box and displays the Sharing tab, which is shown in Figure 13-3 on the next page. Even with the Sharing wizard enabled, you can get to the same place; right-click the folder and choose Properties.

> **Note**
> The Sharing tab is part of the properties dialog box for a folder, but not for files. Also, when the Sharing wizard is disabled, the Share button appears on the Command bar only when you select a single folder. Only the Sharing wizard is capable of making share settings for files and for multiple objects simultaneously.

Figure 13-3 The Share button under Network And Folder Sharing summons the Sharing wizard, but it's available only when the Sharing wizard is enabled.

To create or modify a network share using advanced settings, follow these steps:

1. On the Sharing tab, click Advanced Sharing to display the Advanced Sharing dialog box.

2. Select Share This Folder.

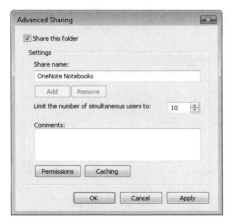

3.   Accept or change the proposed share name.

> **Note**
>
> If the folder is already shared and you want to add another share name (perhaps with different permissions), click Add and then type the name for the new share.

The share name is the name that other users will see in their own Network folders. Windows initially proposes to use the folder's name as its share name. That's usually a good choice, but you're not obligated to accept it. If you already have a shared folder with that name, you'll need to pick a different name.

4.   Type a description of the folder's contents in the Comments box.

Other users will see this description when they inspect the folder's properties dialog box in their Network folder (or use Details view).

5.   To limit the number of users who can connect to the shared folder concurrently, specify a number in the box. Windows Vista permits up to 10 concurrent users. (If you need to share a folder with more than 10 users at once, you must use a server version of Windows.)

6.   Click Permissions.

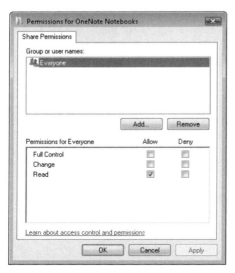

The default shared resource permission associated with a new share is Read access to Everyone.

CAUTION

When you share a folder, you also make that folder's subfolders available on the network. If the access permissions you set for the folder aren't appropriate for any of its subfolders, either reconsider your choice of access permissions or restructure your folders to avoid the problem.

7. In the Group Or User Names list, select the name of the user or group you want to manage.

The shared resource permissions for the selected user or group appear below in the permissions list.

8. Select Allow, Deny, or neither for each access control entry:

- **Full Control** Allows users to create, read, write, rename, and delete files in the folder and its subfolders. In addition, users can change permissions and take ownership of files on NTFS volumes.

- **Change** Allows users to read, write, rename, and delete files in the folder and its subfolders, but not create new files.

- **Read** Allows users to read files but not write to them or delete them.

If you select neither Allow nor Deny, it is still possible that the user or group can inherit the permission through membership in another group that has the permission. If the user or group doesn't belong to another such group, the user or group is implicitly denied permission.

Note

To remove a name from the Group Or User Names list, select it and click Remove. To add a name to the list, click Add to open the Select Users Or Groups dialog box, where you can enter the names of the users and groups you want to add.

9. Click OK in each dialog box.

How Shared Resource Permissions and NTFS Permissions Work Together

The implementation of shared resource permissions and NTFS permissions is confusingly similar, but it's important to recognize that these are two separate levels of access control. Only connections that successfully pass through both gates are granted access.

Shared resource permissions control *network* access to a particular resource. Shared resource permissions do not affect users who log on locally. You set shared resource permissions in the Advanced Sharing dialog box, which you access from the Sharing tab of a folder's properties dialog box.

NTFS permissions apply to folders and files on an NTFS-formatted drive. They provide extremely granular control over an object. For each user to whom you want to grant access, you can specify exactly what they're allowed to do: run programs, view folder contents, create new files, change existing files, and so on. You set NTFS permissions on the Security tab of the properties dialog box for a folder or file. For more information, see "Controlling Access with NTFS Permissions," Chapter 29.

It's important to recognize that the two types of permissions are combined in the most restrictive way. If, for example, a user is granted Read permission on the network share, it doesn't matter whether the account has Full Control NTFS permissions on the same folder; the user gets only read access when connecting over the network. In effect, the two sets of permissions act in tandem as "gatekeepers" that winnow out incoming network connections. An account that attempts to connect over the network is examined first by the shared resource permissions gatekeeper. The account is either bounced out on its caboodle or allowed to enter with certain permissions. It's then confronted by the NTFS permissions gatekeeper, which might strip away (but not add to) some or all of the permissions granted at the first doorway.

In determining the effective permission for a particular account, you must also consider the effect of group membership. Permissions are cumulative; an account that is a member of one or more groups is granted all the permissions granted explicitly to the account as well as all permissions granted to each group of which it's a member. The only exception to this rule is Deny permissions, which take precedence over any conflicting Allow permissions. For more information, see "Testing the Effect of Permissions," Chapter 29.

Managing Shared Folders

Windows Vista includes several tools for managing your shared folders. Naturally, you can use Windows Explorer to find the items you've shared; icons for shared items have a sharing indicator in the lower left corner.

Although you can manage your shared folders from Windows Explorer, Network And Sharing Center provides a more centralized approach; a link near the bottom opens a search window that includes all folders and files you've shared. Figure 13-4 shows an example. Simply select a shared item in this window (or in Windows Explorer) and click Share to modify its settings.

Figure 13-4 This search shows at a glance who has been granted access to each shared folder or file.

If you're concerned only with folders shared over the network, the Shared Folders snap-in for Microsoft Management Console (MMC) provides the best tool. With this snap-in, you can manage all the shared folders on your computer.

Start the Shared Folders snap-in by opening Computer Management (right-click Computer and choose Manage) and then navigating to System Tools\Shared Folders. Figure 13-5 shows the Shared Folders snap-in.

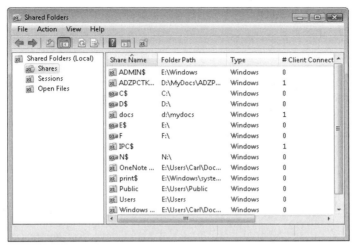

Figure 13-5 You can open the Shared Folders snap-in in its own console window—without all the clutter of Computer Management—by typing **fsmgmt.msc** at a command prompt.

Viewing and Changing Share Properties

When you open the Shared Folders snap-in, all the shared folders on your computer are visible in the Shares folder. You can modify the properties of any folder by right-clicking it and choosing Properties. The associated properties dialog box appears, as shown in Figure 13-6.

Figure 13-6 The properties dialog box is similar to the Advanced Sharing dialog box, except you access share permissions on a separate tab instead of clicking the Permissions button. The Security tab lets you view and set NTFS permissions.

Understanding Administrative Shares

Some of the shares you see in the Shared Folders list are created by the operating system. Most of these share names end with a dollar sign ($), which makes them "invisible"—they do not appear in the browse list when another Windows user looks at the shares on your computer. You can't view or set permissions on most of these shares, as you can for shares you create; the operating system restricts access to them to system accounts.

You can stop sharing these administrative shares only temporarily. The share reappears the next time the Server service starts or you restart your computer. Table 13-1 describes the administrative shares that appear on most systems.

Table 13-1. Administrative Shares

Share Name	Description
C$, D$, E$, and so on	Each of these shares allows certain system accounts to connect to the root folder of a hard drive. You will see one of these (with the appropriate drive letter) for each hard drive on your computer. These shares are often used by backup programs.
ADMIN$	This share is used during remote administration. It maps to the %SystemRoot% folder (C:\Windows on most systems).
IPC$	This share provides the named pipes that programs use to communicate with your computer. It is used during remote administration and when viewing a computer's resources.
PRINT$	This share is used for remote administration of printers.

Creating a New Share Using the Shared Folders Snap-In

To share a folder, right-click Shares in the Shared Folders console tree and choose New Share. The Create A Shared Folder wizard—not to be confused with the Sharing wizard—appears. This wizard helps you find the folder you want to share and assists in setting up basic security options, as shown in Figure 13-7.

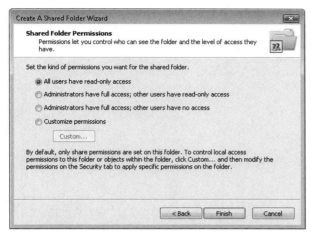

Figure 13-7 The Create A Shared Folder wizard provides an alternative to sharing a folder from Windows Explorer.

Removing a Share

Removing a share is as easy as right-clicking the share and choosing Stop Sharing. This is equivalent to visiting the folder's properties dialog box in Windows Explorer and clearing the Share This Folder check box.

Viewing and Disconnecting Sessions

Each user who connects to your computer creates a session. You can use Shared Folders to see who is currently connected to the computer as well as what files they have open. Click Sessions in the console tree to have the current sessions appear in the details pane, as shown in Figure 13-8 on the next page.

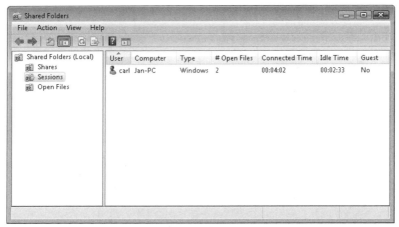

Figure 13-8 The Sessions folder shows all open connections.

INSIDE OUT   See who is authenticated

If you're trying to determine why some users have access to certain folders and others don't, it's helpful to know whether they're being authenticated as themselves or as Guest. That's easy to do with Shared Folders. In the Sessions folder, the rightmost column is titled Guest; its value is either Yes (authenticated as Guest) or No (authenticated as named user).

Besides seeing who is connected, you can also disconnect any or all sessions. Right-click a session and choose Close Session to close a single session. Right-click Sessions in the console tree and choose Disconnect All Sessions to close all the open sessions. Don't do this capriciously; users can lose information if you close a session while they have documents open.

Viewing and Closing Files

Click Open Files in the Shared Folders console tree to see a list of shared files that are currently open for other users, as shown in Figure 13-9.

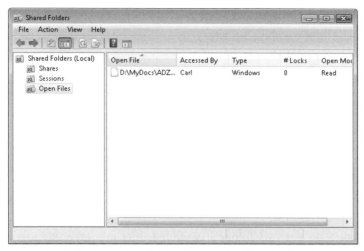

Figure 13-9 The Open Files folder shows all the files that have been opened by current users.

You can close an individual file by right-clicking it and choosing Close Open File. You can close all the open files at once by right-clicking Open Files in the console tree and choosing Disconnect All Open Files. If you close a document file before the user has saved new information, you might cause the information to be lost.

Accessing Shared Folders

The Network folder is your gateway to all available network resources, just as Computer is the gateway to resources stored on your own system. The Network folder contains an icon for each computer on your network; double-click a computer icon to see that computer's shared resources, if any.

Gaining Access to Shared Folders on Another Computer

To open a shared folder on another computer, double-click its icon in the Network folder. If you have the proper permissions, this action displays the folder's contents in Windows Explorer. It's not always that easy, however. If the user account with which you logged on doesn't have permission to view a network computer or resource you select, a dialog box asks you to provide the name of an account (and its password, of course) that has permission.

Perhaps the trickiest part of using shared folders is fully understanding what permissions have been applied to a folder and which credentials are in use by each network user. The first rule to recognize is that *all network access is controlled by the computer with the shared resources*; regardless of what operating system runs on the computer attempting to connect to a network share, it must meet the security requirements of the computer where the resource is shared.

Working with Mapped Network Folders

Mapping a network folder makes it appear to Windows as though the folder is part of your own computer. Windows assigns the mapped folder a drive letter, making the folder appear like an additional hard drive. You can still access a mapped folder in the conventional manner, by navigating to it through the Network folder. But mapping gives the folder an alias—the assigned drive letter—that provides an alternative means of access.

Drive mapping offers benefits in some situations:

- **It makes the network folder available to programs that don't use the Windows common dialog boxes.** With programs that use the common dialog boxes, you can navigate to network folders just as you would with the Network folder. But to read a document from, or save a document to, a network folder using earlier programs, you will probably need to map the folder to a drive letter.

- **It makes the network folder accessible from Computer.** Because a mapped folder becomes a virtual drive on your local computer, an icon for the folder appears in the Computer folder, right alongside your local drives. If you do most of your work with files stored locally but need access to particular network folders, you might find it convenient to map them. That way, you won't have to bother opening Network to find the network folders you need.

Mapping a Network Folder to a Drive Letter

To map a network folder to a drive letter, follow these steps:

1. Open Computer in Windows Explorer, and in the Command bar, click Map Network Drive. (Alternatively, after you open a computer in the Network folder, right-click a network share and choose Map Network Drive.)

2. Select a drive letter in the Drive box. You can choose any letter that's not already in use.

3. In the Folder box, type the path to the folder you want or, more easily, click Browse and navigate to the folder.

4. Select Reconnect At Logon if you want Windows to connect to this shared folder automatically at the start of each session.

5. If your regular logon account doesn't have permission to connect to the resource, click the Different User Name link, enter a user name and password, and click OK. (This capability is useful if you personally have multiple user accounts. For example, you might have an administrator account that has access to some folders that are not available to your regular logon account.)

6. Click Finish.

In the Computer folder, the "drive" appears in the Network Location group. As a top-level item in Computer, it also appears in the breadcrumb bar when you click the arrow to the right of Computer, as shown in the following figure.

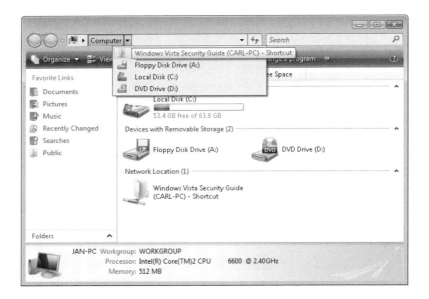

Add network shortcuts to your Computer folder without mapping drives

If you've run out of drive letters or don't want to map network drives for some reason, you can create a shortcut to a network share and place it in the Network Location group in the Computer folder. To do that, in Windows Explorer, open %AppData%\Microsoft\ Windows\Network Shortcuts. Open Network in a separate window, and navigate until you find a network folder you use often. Drag the network folder to the Network Shortcuts folder. The shortcut appears in the Computer folder, next to your mapped drives. Note that, with this method, you can create shortcuts only to the top-level folder of a network share, whereas with drive mapping you can assign a drive letter to a deeply nested subfolder.

As an alternative to this method, right-click an empty space in the Computer folder and choose Add Network Location. A wizard opens to lead you through the process of creating a network shortcut.

Unmapping a Mapped Network Folder

If you change your mind about mapping a network folder, simply right-click the folder's icon in your Computer folder. Choose Disconnect in the resulting shortcut menu, and the connection will be severed.

Sharing a Printer

Although Windows Vista doesn't have a Sharing wizard for sharing a printer over the network, the process is pretty simple. You configure all options for a printer—whether you plan to share it or not—using the printer's properties dialog box, which you access from the Printers folder in Control Panel.

To make a printer available to other network users, right-click a printer and click Run As Administrator, Sharing. (If you right-click and choose Sharing without first clicking Run As Administrator, you're likely to encounter more elevation prompts before you complete your task than if you just bite the bullet and start out running with administrator privileges.) On the Sharing tab, select Share This Printer, and provide a share name, as shown in Figure 13-10. Windows Vista (as well as Windows XP) permits spaces and other characters in printer names.

Figure 13-10 On the Sharing tab, specify a share name.

Setting Permissions on Shared Printers

Unlike shared folders, which maintain separate share permissions and NTFS permissions, a single set of permissions controls access to printers, whether by local users or by network users. (Of course, only printers that have been shared are accessible to network users.)

When you set up a printer, initially all users in the Everyone group have Print permission for documents they create, which provides users access to the printer and the ability to manage their own documents in the print queue. By default, members of the Administrators group also have Manage Printers and Manage Documents permission.

Table 13-2 shows the basic permissions and associated privileges that Windows provides for printers.

Table 13-2. Basic Printer Permissions and Privileges

Permission	Privileges
Print	Print documents Control properties of owned documents Pause, restart, and remove owned documents
Manage Printers	Share printer Change printer properties Remove printer Change printer permissions Pause and restart the printer
Manage Documents	Pause, restart, move, and remove all queued documents

A user account that doesn't have any of these permissions can't connect to the printer, print to it locally, or view its queue.

If you have Manage Printers permission for a printer, you can change other users' permissions for that printer. To do so, click the Security tab of the printer's properties dialog box and change permissions by clicking Allow or Deny (or neither) as necessary. To add another user or group to the list, click Add. After you type the names of users or groups you want in the Select Users Or Groups dialog box, return to the printer's properties dialog box. Then select each new user or group and assign permissions by clicking Allow, Deny, or neither. (If you select neither, permissions are determined by the user's group membership.)

Setting Hours of Availability and Other Options

The Advanced tab of the printer's properties dialog box, shown in Figure 13-11, includes a number of options that are both intriguing and confusing. Making changes to these options requires Manage Printers permission.

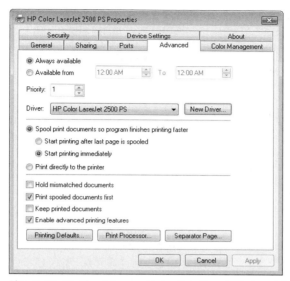

Figure 13-11 The Advanced tab offers the ability to set the hours of operation for a printer, along with a number of unrelated options.

- **Always Available and Available From** To restrict the availability of the printer to certain times of day, choose Available From and specify the range of times. Print jobs that are sent outside of these hours are held in the queue until the appointed time.

- **Priority** If you create multiple printers for a single print device, documents sent to the printer with the higher Priority setting print ahead of those sent to the other printers. You might want to create a high-priority printer that certain users have permission to use when they need to cut in line to get a document printed quickly. Or you might want to assign Print permission to the high-priority printer to one group of users, and permission to the lower-priority printer to another group of users with different (less urgent) needs.

- **Driver** This list includes all the printer drivers currently installed on your system; use it to select the correct driver for the print device. If the correct driver isn't in the list, click New Driver to start the Add Printer Driver wizard.

- **Spool settings** The four option buttons in the center of the dialog box determine whether a document should be spooled to a hard disk before sending it to the printer. (For information about specifying the location of spool files, see "Setting Server Properties," in this chapter.) Spooled documents are then sent to the print device in the background. Ordinarily, you should select the first and third options, which cause fastest return of control to your application and fastest printing completion. But if you have trouble with complex print jobs being interrupted by pages from another document, select Start Printing After Last Page Is Spooled.

- **Hold Mismatched Documents** Selecting this option tells the spooler to check a document's properties against the printer properties and to hold the document in the queue if the properties don't match. For example, a mismatched document can occur when an application specifies a form that's not currently assigned to a printer tray. Correctly matched documents continue to print normally, bypassing any mismatched documents in the queue.

- **Print Spooled Documents First** Selecting this option directs the spooler to print documents that have completed spooling ahead of documents that are still spooling, even if the latter documents have a higher priority. When this option is cleared, the spooler selects the next document to print based only on its priority. Selecting this option maximizes printer efficiency because the print device doesn't have to wait for an incomplete, high-priority document to finish spooling before it can begin printing a complete, lower priority document.

- **Keep Printed Documents** When this option is selected, the spooler doesn't delete documents from the queue after they print. You can then reprint a document from the queue rather than from the program that created it, or you can delete the document manually.

- **Enable Advanced Printing Features** Selecting this option turns on metafile spooling for print jobs from Windows Vista, Windows XP, and Windows 2000 clients using Windows-based applications. Of more interest to most users, selecting this option enables new options in the common Print dialog box for some printers and some applications, such as Booklet Printing and Pages Per Sheet. The only reason to clear this option is if you have problems printing.

- **Printing Defaults** Clicking this button displays the printing defaults dialog box—the same one that appears if you right-click a printer and choose Printing Preferences. In this dialog box, you specify default document settings for options such as orientation, two-sided printing, paper tray selection, and so on. Your settings here become the default settings for all users of the printer. (Another reason to create multiple logical printers for a single device: You might want to create printers with different default settings for different types of documents or for users with different needs.)

- **Print Processor** Clicking this button opens the Print Processor dialog box, a place you'll probably never need to venture. In a nutshell, it displays the available print processors (a *print processor* tells the spooler how to alter a print job depending on the document data type) and the default data type for the selected print processor.

- **Separator Page** Click this button to specify a separator page. A *separator page* prints before each document (much like a fax cover page) and identifies the name of the user who printed the job, the date and time it was sent, and other details. Using separator pages makes finding your document among a stack of others in the printer's output bin easier.

INSIDE OUT   **Use the Print Management console**

Users of Windows Vista Business, Enterprise, or Ultimate edition have a tool that places all print management in one convenient console. Print Management (Printmanagement.msc), shown here, provides a place for managing printers, drivers, queues, and shares. If your edition includes Print Management, you can start it by typing **print** in the Start menu Search box and then clicking Print Management.

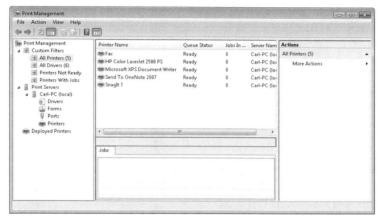

Setting Server Properties

In addition to setting properties for individual printers by using their properties dialog boxes, you can set other properties by visiting the Print Server Properties dialog box. To get there, right-click a blank area of the Printers folder and then choose Run As Administrator, Server Properties.

The first three tabs control the list of items you see in the properties dialog box for a printer:

- The Forms tab controls the list of forms that you can assign to trays using the Device Settings tab in a printer's properties dialog box. You can create new form definitions and delete any that you create, but you can't delete any of the predefined forms.

- The Ports tab offers the same capabilities as the Ports tab in a printer's properties dialog box.

- The Drivers tab offers a list of all the installed printer drivers and provides a centralized location where you can add, remove, or update drivers.

The Advanced tab, shown in Figure 13-12, offers a potpourri of options:

- You can specify the location of spool files. You might want to change to a folder on a different drive if, for example, you frequently run out of space on the current drive when you attempt to print large documents.

- The first three check boxes on the Advanced tab determine which types of events merit entries in the Windows System log, which you can view with the Event Viewer snap-in. For more information, see Chapter 22, "Monitoring System Activities with Event Viewer."

- The Beep On Errors Of Remote Documents check box causes the print server to notify you audibly of problems with a remote printer.

- The two Show Informational Notifications check boxes control pop-up status messages near the notification area.

Figure 13-12 Settings you make here affect options available in all printer properties dialog boxes.

TROUBLESHOOTING

Your document won't print

If a document gets stuck in the print queue and you can't delete it, open the Services snap-in in the Computer Management console, and stop the Print Spooler service. Then restart the service.

INSIDE OUT   **Set spool folders for individual printers**

Your Spool Folder setting on the Advanced tab is stored in the DefaultSpoolDirectory value in the HKLM\Software\Microsoft\Windows NT\CurrentVersion\Print\Printers registry key, and it determines the spool folder for all your local printers. If you want to use a different folder for a particular printer, you must edit the registry directly. Go to the HKLM\Software\Microsoft\Windows NT\CurrentVersion\Print\Printers*printer* key (where *printer* is the name of the printer you want to modify), and set the SpoolDirectory value to the path you want to use.

Command-Line Utilities for Managing Shared Resources

Some users prefer a terse command prompt to a wizard or even an MMC window. If you're in that group, you'll want to use Net.exe for managing resource sharing. With these commands, you can create batch programs to automate some network sharing tasks.

In the following sections, we describe only the most common Net commands (and their most common parameters) for managing network connections. This isn't an exhaustive reference, however. You can get more information from online help or by typing **net help** *command*, replacing *command* with the word that follows *net* in the examples. For instance, to get more information about the Net Use command, type **net help use**. This provides more help than typing **net use /?**, which shows only the command syntax.

Net Share

The Net Share command lets you view, create, modify, or delete shared resources on your computer.

Viewing Share Information

Typing **net share** with no parameters causes the command to display a list of the shared resources on your computer, as shown in the following sample:

```
E:\>net share

Share name   Resource                          Remark
-------------------------------------------------------------------
ADMIN$       E:\Windows                        Remote Admin
print$       E:\Windows\system32\spool\drivers
                                               Printer Drivers
C$           C:\                               Default share
D$           D:\                               Default share
E$           E:\                               Default share
N$           N:\                               Default share
IPC$                                           Remote IPC
```

```
ADZPCTKO 2006
                D:\MyDocs\ADZPCTKO 2006
F               F:\
OneNote Notebooks
                E:\Users\Carl\Documents\OneNote Notebooks

Public          E:\Users\Public
Users           E:\Users
Windows Vista Security Guide
                E:\Users\Carl\Documents\Windows Vista Security Guide

HP Color LaserJet 2500 PS
                192.168.1.101           Spooled  HP Color LaserJet 2500 PS
The command completed successfully.
```

If you follow Net Share with the name of a local shared resource, it displays information about that share. For example, the command **net share "adzpctko 2006"** displays the following:

```
E:\>net share "adzpctko 2006"
Share name      ADZPCTKO 2006
Path            D:\MyDocs\ADZPCTKO 2006
Remark
Maximum users   No limit
Users
Caching         Manual caching of documents
Permission      Everyone, FULL
                Carl-PC\Carl, FULL
                Carl-PC\Jan, READ

The command completed successfully.
```

Adding or Modifying a Share

You can share the folder C:\Spreadsheets, for use by an unlimited number of users, and add the comment "Budgets" with the following command:

```
C:\>net share Spreadsheets=C:\spreadsheets /unlimited /remark:"Budgets"
Spreadsheets was shared successfully.
```

Setting a share name "equal" to a folder creates a share. To modify an existing share, you use only the share name (and no folder), as in the following command, which changes the remark on the Spreadsheets share to "Year 2008 Budgets":

```
C:\>net share Spreadsheets /remark:"Year 2008 Budgets"
The command completed successfully.
```

Several parameters can be used with the Net Share command, as shown in Table 13-3.

Table 13-3. Useful Parameters for the Net Share Command

Parameter	Description
/Grant:*user*,	Sets access permission for the share; after the comma, type Read, Change, or Full
/Users:*number*	Sets the maximum number of concurrent users
/Unlimited	Lets the maximum number of users connect to the share at one time
/Remark:*"text"*	Adds or changes a comment that appears in Details view in Windows Explorer

Deleting a User Share

To remove a share, simply use the /Delete switch with the Net Share *sharename* command:

```
C:\>net share spreadsheets /delete
spreadsheets was deleted successfully.
```

Net Use

The Net Use command connects your computer to shared resources on other computers. It can also disconnect, or display, all the resources to which you are connected.

Viewing Connections

Type **net use** with no parameters to display the resources to which you are currently connected:

```
C:\>net use
New connections will be remembered.

Status       Local  Remote  Network
-------------------------------------------------------------------------
OK G:\\everglades\programs   Microsoft Windows Network
OK K:\\everglades\document   Microsoft Windows Network
OK P:\\everglades\company    Microsoft Windows Network
OK LPT2\\badlands\lj4000      Microsoft Windows Network
   \\www.msnusers.com\xxxxx@msn.com
                    Web Client Network
The command completed successfully.
```

Adding a Mapped Network Drive

You can create drive mappings with a command like this:

```
C:\>net use e: \\badlands\spreadsheets
The command completed successfully.
```

This maps the network share Spreadsheets on the computer named Badlands to the local drive letter E. If you want to use the next available drive letter, use an asterisk (*) instead of the drive letter and colon. You can add any of the parameters shown in Table 13-4.

Table 13-4. Useful Parameters for the Net Use Command

Parameter	Description
password	Enter your password following the share name if a password is required.
/User:*domain\username*	To connect with a user name that is different from the one you are currently logged on with, you can use the /User parameter. The domain name is necessary only if you are not in the same domain as the resource you're connecting to. You can also enter the domain and user name in the format of an e-mail address (for example, *user@domain*).
/Delete	Disconnects the connection. You need only specify the drive letter and /Delete to disconnect.
/Persistent:yes or /Persistent:no	The yes option causes connections to persist so that they are reconnected the next time you log on.

Disconnecting a Mapped Drive

To disconnect a mapped drive, simply use the /Delete switch with the Net Use command:

```
C:\>net use e: /delete
e: was deleted successfully.
```

Net Session

The Net Session command lets you view or disconnect connections between your computer and clients that are accessing it.

Viewing Session Information

Type **net session** with no parameters to display the current connections to your computer:

```
E:\>net session

Computer          User name        Client Type       Opens Idle time
-------------------------------------------------------------------
\\EATONCANYON      Carl                                3 00:00:03

The command completed successfully.
```

Disconnecting a Session

Following Net Session *computername*, append /Delete to disconnect a session. If you don't include *computername*, all active sessions are disconnected.

Net File

The Net File command lets you view or close the open shared files on your computer. Typing **net file** with nothing following it causes Net File to list all the open files, including a file ID, the user name of the person who has the file open, and the number of locks each has:

```
E:\>net file
```

ID	Path	User name	# Locks
1275068754	D:\MyDocs\...	Carl	0
1275068766	d:\mydocs\	Carl	0
1275069404	d:\mydocs\...	Carl	0

```
The command completed successfully.
```

Net Statistics

The Net Statistics command displays the statistics log for the local Workstation or Server service. Type **net statistics workstation** to view the Workstation statistics. Type **net statistics server** to view the Server statistics.

The Workstation statistics log looks like this:

```
E:\>net statistics workstation
Workstation Statistics for \\CARL-PC

Statistics since 11/29/2006 7:13:42 PM

    Bytes received                              11925791
    Server Message Blocks (SMBs) received       1002
    Bytes transmitted                           110878
    Server Message Blocks (SMBs) transmitted    1001
    Read operations                             600
    Write operations                            0
    Raw reads denied                            0
    Raw writes denied                           0

    Network errors                              0
    Connections made                            130
    Reconnections made                          8
    Server disconnects                          12
```

```
Sessions started              0
Hung sessions                 0
Failed sessions               0
Failed operations             0
Use count                     348
Failed use count              43
```

The command completed successfully.

CHAPTER 14

Tweaking and
Troubleshooting a Small
Network

Home Basic ○
Home Premium ○
Business ○
Enterprise ○
Ultimate ○

With Windows Vista, most simple networks of 10 computers or fewer work just fine. When you encounter network problems, however, the troubleshooting process can be tricky, because it's difficult to determine where the fault lies. In some cases, network problems are directly related to hardware, either on the local computer, elsewhere on your network, or at another stop on the connection between your computer and an internet destination. But the problem is just as likely to be caused by a faulty configuration on your computer.

In this chapter, we explain how to identify and repair common network configuration problems, including TCP/IP address errors, improper subnet settings, and domain name server (DNS) problems. We also explain how to identify situations where a network is performing at less than its optimum speed, and we show you how to quickly and easily bridge two networks.

What's in Your Edition?

The networking features described in this chapter work identically in all Windows Vista editions.

Viewing Status in Network And Sharing Center

Windows Vista has built-in network diagnostic capabilities unlike those in previous versions of Windows. In many cases, if there is a problem with your network connection, Windows Vista knows it before you do and displays a message, perhaps like the one shown in Figure 14-1 on the next page. Most such message boxes include a Diagnose button or a similar path to resolving the problem. Sometimes, however, that path leads to a dead end, often to a message asking you to check with your system administrator. That's of little help when you *are* the system administrator.

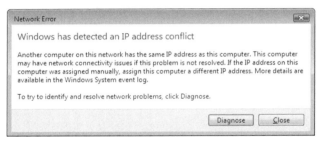

Figure 14-1 When Windows Vista detects network problems, it displays a message box that explains the problem and offers hope for a solution.

To discover and resolve problems, Windows Vista uses the new Network Diagnostics Framework (NDF). When a network-dependent activity (for example, browsing to a website) fails, NDF automatically springs into action. NDF is designed to address the most common network-related issues, such as problems with file-sharing, website access, newly installed network hardware, connecting to a wireless network, and using a third-party firewall.

For more information about NDF, see "Network Diagnostics Framework in Windows Vista," an article by The Cable Guy at TechNet (*http://www.vista-io.com/1401*).

You might find more information about a networking problem with a visit to Network And Sharing Center. And, at the very least, it serves as a launchpad to various diagnostic tools.

For details about opening Network And Sharing Center, see "Using Network And Sharing Center," Chapter 12.

When connectivity is broken between your computer and the rest of your network, or if your internet connection is broken, Network And Sharing Center displays a red X or a yellow caution sign in the line that symbolized the connection, as shown in Figure 14-2. (The same symbol appears in the network icon in the taskbar notification area.)

Figure 14-2 An X indicates trouble.

Click the X or caution sign to launch network diagnostics, which tries to determine the cause and fix the problem or suggest a solution. Alternatively, in the tasks list click Diagnose And Repair. Sometimes, the problem is as simple as a loose connection.

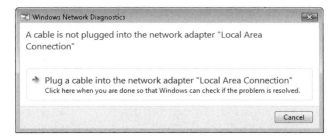

Other problems produce lengthier descriptions and more repair options.

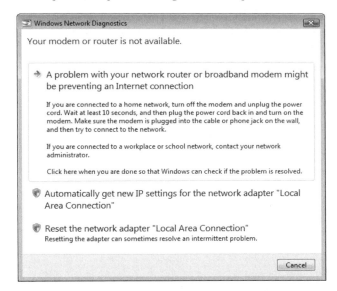

This feature of Network And Sharing Center—the X that indicates a broken connection—is suggestive of the basic troubleshooting process for many connectivity problems: namely, isolate the problem. If the NDF diagnostics leave you at a dead end, you'll find that restarting the affected network hardware often resolves the problem, as the hardware is forced to rediscover the network. Here is a good general procedure:

1. Isolate the problem: Does it affect all computers on your network, a subset of your network, or only one computer?

2. If it affects all computers, try restarting the internet device (that is, the cable or DSL modem). If it doesn't have a power switch, unplug it for a few moments and plug it back in.

3. If it affects a group of computers, try restarting the router to which those computers are connected.

4. If it affects only a single computer, try repairing the network connection for that computer. In Network Connections, select the connection and click Diagnose This Connection. For more details, see "Repairing Your TCP/IP Configuration," in this chapter.

Diagnosing Problems Using Network Map

Another feature new to Windows Vista is network mapping. Network mapping uses the Link Layer Topology Discovery (LLTD) protocol to find the other computers and devices on your network, and then displays them in a schematic representation. To display the map, in Network And Sharing Center click View Full Map. Figure 14-3 shows an example.

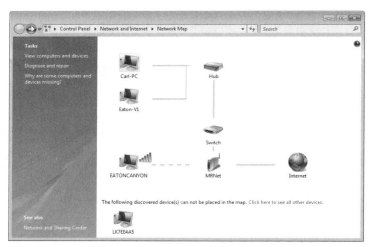

Figure 14-3 The computer you're using is always shown in the upper left corner of Network Map.

Network mapping works with wired and wireless networks, but only on private and domain network locations; you can't view a map of a public network. LLTD maps only the computers in a single subnet—the typical setup in a home or small office.

You might notice that some computers and devices are shown separately at the bottom of the window, or they might be missing altogether. (For example, the device at the bottom of the display shown in Figure 14-3 is a wireless network print server that supports UPnP, but not LLTD.) This occurs because not all operating systems and devices include LLTD support, or because the devices might not be configured properly.

Devices shown at the bottom generally fall into one of the following categories:

- **Computers running Windows XP** LLTD is installed by default in Windows Vista, but is not included in earlier Windows versions. An LLTD client is available for Windows XP, and it should be available through Windows Update. (To find out if it's installed, look at the properties for the network connection and see if LLTD appears in the list of installed protocols.) You can download and install the protocol without Windows Update; for details, see Knowledge Base article 922120 (*http://www.vista-io.com/1402*). LLTD components are not currently available for other versions of Windows.

- **Other network devices** LLTD (along with another network discovery–related technology, Plug and Play Extensions, or PnP-X) is part of the Windows Rally technologies, an initiative for network hardware devices that gained steam in 2006. Devices that include LLTD support are expected to be widely available in 2007 and later, but earlier devices are not fully recognized by Network Map. Most devices sold in recent years support UPnP, which should get the device somewhere in the map window; however, Network Map displays only limited information about the device and offers only limited control of the device.

- **Configuration problems** In Network And Sharing Center, be sure that your network is not identified as a public network, and be sure that network discovery is turned on. In Network Connections, view the properties of your network connection and be sure that two LLTD-related protocols, Link-Layer Topology Discovery Mapper I/O Driver and Link-Layer Topology Discovery Responder, are installed and enabled. (That is, their check boxes are selected.) Whether you use Windows Firewall or another firewall, be sure it has an exception enabled for file and printer sharing.

Network Map is more than a pretty picture. If you hover the mouse pointer over a computer or other device, you get more information about the device, including information such as its IPv4 and IPv6 addresses and its MAC address. Network infrastructure devices (such as routers) that include Windows Rally support offer a menu of choices when you click them, usually including one that leads to the device's configuration page. For computers with shared resources, you can double-click them in Network Map to open them, just as you can in the Network folder.

Network Map, like the "mini-map" in Network And Sharing Center, indicates broken network connections with an X. Click Diagnose And Repair to attempt a solution.

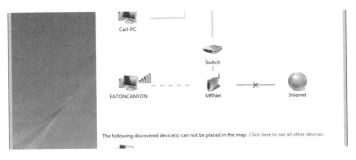

Troubleshooting TCP/IP Problems

TCP/IP is the default communications protocol of the internet; in Windows Vista it's installed and configured automatically and cannot be removed. Most of the time, your TCP/IP connection should just work, without requiring any manual configuration. When you encounter problems with TCP/IP-based networks, such as an inability to connect with other computers on the same network or difficulty connecting to external websites, the problems may be TCP/IP-related. You'll need at least a basic understanding of how this protocol works before you can figure out which tool to use to uncover the root of the problem.

Checking for Connection Problems

Anytime your network refuses to send and receive data properly, your first troubleshooting step should be to check for problems with the physical connection between the local computer and the rest of the network. Assuming your network connection uses the TCP/IP protocol, your most potent weapon is the Ping utility. When you use the Ping command with no parameters, Windows sends four echo datagrams, small Internet Control Message Protocol (ICMP) packets, to the address you specify. If the machine at the other end of the connection replies, you know that the network connection between the two points is alive.

> **Note**
>
> Where does the name *Ping* come from? Some claim that it's short for Packet INternet Groper. However, the author of this utility, which was written for BSD UNIX in 1983, says it was originally named after the sound a submarine's sonar system makes when it sends out pulses looking for objects in the sea.

To use the Ping command, open a Command Prompt window (Cmd.exe) and type the command **ping *target_name*** (where *target_name* is an IP address or the name of another host machine). The return output looks something like this:

```
C:\>ping www.example.com

Pinging www.example.com [192.0.34.166] with 32 bytes of data:

Reply from 192.0.34.166: bytes=32 time=31ms TTL=48
Reply from 192.0.34.166: bytes=32 time=30ms TTL=48
Reply from 192.0.34.166: bytes=32 time=30ms TTL=48
Reply from 192.0.34.166: bytes=32 time=33ms TTL=48
```

```
Ping statistics for 192.0.34.166:

    Packets: Sent = 4, Received = 4, Lost = 0 (0% loss),
Approximate round trip times in milli-seconds:
    Minimum = 30ms, Maximum = 33ms, Average = 31ms
```

If all the packets you send come back properly in roughly the same time, your TCP/IP connection is fine and you can focus your troubleshooting efforts elsewhere. If some packets time out, a "Request timed out" message appears, indicating that your network connection is working, but that one or more hops between your computer and the target machine are experiencing problems. In that case, repeat the Ping test using the –n switch to send a larger number of packets; **ping –n 30 192.168.1.1**, for example, sends 30 packets to the computer or router at 192.168.1.1.

> **Note**
>
> The –n switch is case-sensitive; don't capitalize it.

A high rate of timeouts, also known as *packet loss*, usually means problems elsewhere on the network and not on the local machine. (To see the full assortment of switches available for the Ping command, type **ping** with no target specified.)

If every one of your packets returns with the message "Request timed out," the problem may be the TCP/IP connection on your computer or a glitch with another computer on that network. To narrow down the problem, follow these steps, in order, stopping at any point where you encounter an error:

1. Ping your own machine using any of the following commands:

    ```
    ping ::1
    ping 127.0.0.1
    ping localhost
    ```

    This standard IP address corresponds to your computer. (The first is the IPv6 address for your own computer; the second is the IPv4 address.) If you receive an error, then TCP/IP is not configured properly on your system. For fix-it details, see "Repairing Your TCP/IP Configuration," in this chapter.

2. Ping your computer's IP address.

3. Ping the IP address of another computer on your network.

4. Ping the IP address of your router or the default gateway on your network.

5. Ping the address of each DNS server on your network. (If you don't know these addresses, see the next section for details on how to discover them.)

6. Ping a known host outside your network. Well-known, high-traffic websites are ideal for this step.

7. Use the Pathping command to contact the same host you specified in step 6. This command combines the functionality of the Ping command with the Traceroute utility to identify intermediate destinations on the internet between your computer and the specified host or server.

INSIDE OUT   Choose your test site carefully

In some cases, pinging an external website results in a string of "Request timed out" messages, even when you have no trouble reaching those sites. Don't be misled. Some popular sites, including Microsoft's home page, *http://www.microsoft.com*, block all ICMP traffic, including Ping packets, as a routine security measure. Try pinging several sites before concluding that your internet connection is broken.

If either of the two final steps in this process fails, your problem may be caused by DNS problems, as described later in this chapter. (For details, see "Resolving DNS Issues," in this chapter.) To eliminate this possibility, ping the numeric IP address of a computer outside your network instead. (Of course, if you're having DNS problems, you may have a hard time finding an IP address to ping!) If you can ping a website using its IP address but not by using its name, DNS problems are indicated.

If you suspect that there's a problem on the internet between your computer and a distant host or server, use the Traceroute utility (Tracert.exe) to pinpoint the problem. Like the Ping command, this utility works from a command line. You specify the target (a host name or IP address) using the syntax **tracert *target_name*** and the utility sends a series of packets out, measuring the time it takes to reach each "hop" along the route. Timeouts or unusually slow performance indicate a connectivity problem. If the response time from your network to the first hop is much higher than the other hops, you might have a problem with the connection to your ISP; in that case, a call to your ISP's support line is in order. Problems farther along in the traceroute might indicate congestion or hardware problems in distant parts of the internet that are out of your ISP's hands and that might disappear when you check another URL that follows a different path through the internet.

If your testing produces inconsistent results, rule out the possibility that a firewall program or network address translation (NAT) device (such as a router or residential gateway) is to blame. If you're using a third-party firewall program, disable it temporarily. Try bypassing your router and connecting directly to a broadband connection such as a DSL or cable modem.

If the Ping test works with the firewall or NAT device out of the picture, you can rule out network problems and conclude that the firewall software or router is misconfigured. After you complete your testing, be sure to enable the firewall and router again!

Diagnosing IP Address Problems

On most networks, IP addresses are assigned automatically by Dynamic Host Configuration Protocol (DHCP) servers; in some cases, you need to use static IP addresses, which are fixed numeric addresses. Problems with DHCP servers or clients can cause network connections to stop working, as can incorrectly assigned static IP addresses.

To see details of your current IP configuration, follow these steps:

1. In Network And Sharing Center, click Manage Network Connections.

2. Double-click the icon for the connection about which you want more information. (Alternatively, you can select the icon and click View Status Of This Connection in the command bar.)

3. Click Details to see the currently assigned IP address, subnet mask, and default gateway for that connection. (If you have IPv4 and IPv6 connectivity, the Network Connection Details dialog box shows information for both.) In the following example, you can tell that the IP address was automatically assigned by the DHCP server in a router; details indicate that DHCP is enabled, and DHCP server address matches that of the router.

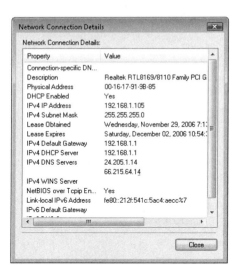

You can also get details of your IP configuration by using the IP Configuration utility, Ipconfig.exe, in a Command Prompt window. Used without any parameters, typing **ipconfig** at a command prompt displays the DNS suffix, IPv6 and/or IPv4 address, subnet mask, and default gateway for each network connection. To see exhaustive details about every available network connection, enter **ipconfig /all**.

> **Note**
>
> To see a full list of options for the Ipconfig command, use the /? switch.

The actual IP address you see may help you solve connection problems:

- If the address is in the format 169.254.x.y, your computer is using Automatic Private IP Addressing (APIPA). This means your computer's DHCP client was unable to reach a DHCP server to be assigned an IP address. Check the connection to your network.

- If the address is in one of the blocks of IP addresses reserved for use on private networks (for details, see "Setting IP Addresses," Chapter 12), make sure that another computer (an Internet Connection Sharing host) or a router or residential gateway is routing your internet requests to a properly configured public IP address.

- If the address of your computer appears as 0.0.0.0, the network is either disconnected or the static IP address for the connection duplicates an address that already exists on the network.

- Make sure you're using the correct subnet mask for computers on your local network. Compare IP settings on the machine that's having problems with those on other computers on the network. The default gateway and subnet mask should be identical for all network computers. The first one, two, or three sets of numbers in the IP address for each machine should also be identical, depending on the subnet mask. A subnet mask of 255.255.255.0 means the first three IP address numbers of computers on your network must be identical—192.168.0.83 and 192.168.0.223, for instance, can communicate on a network using this subnet mask, but 192.168.1.101 will not be recognized as belonging to the network. Likewise, with a subnet mask of 255.255.0.0, the first two numbers in each address must match—172.16.2.34, 172.16.4.56, and 172.16.83.201 are all valid addresses on a subnet with this mask. In every case, the gateway machine must also be a member of the same subnet. (If you use a router, switch, or residential gateway for internet access, the local address on that device must be part of the same subnet as the machines on your network.)

> **Note**
>
> Are you baffled by subnets and other related technical terms? For an excellent overview of these sometimes confusing topics, read Knowledge Base article 164015, "Understanding TCP/IP Addressing and Subnetting Basics" *(http://www.vista-io.com/1403)*, which offers information about IPv4. For comparable details about IPv6, see the "Introduction to IPv6" white paper at TechNet *(http://www.vista-io.com/1404)*.

Repairing Your TCP/IP Configuration

If you suspect a problem with your TCP/IP configuration, try either of the following repair options:

- **Use the automated repair option.** Right-click the connection icon in Network Connections and click Diagnose.

- **Renew your IP address.** Use the **ipconfig /renew** command to renew your IPv4 address from the DHCP server; use **ipconfig /renew6** to renew the IPv6 address.

Resolving DNS Issues

The Domain Name System (DNS) is a crucial part of the internet. DNS servers translate host names (*http://www.microsoft.com*, for instance) into numeric IP addresses, so that packets can be routed properly over the internet. If you can use the Ping command to reach a numeric address outside your network but are unable to browse websites by name, the problem is almost certainly related to your DNS configuration.

Here are some questions to ask when you suspect DNS problems:

- **Do your TCP/IP settings point to the right DNS servers?** Inspect the details of your IP configuration and compare the DNS servers listed there with those recommended by your internet service provider. (You may need to call your ISP to get these details.)

INSIDE OUT Translate names to IP addresses and vice versa

The Nslookup command is a buried treasure in Windows. Use this command-line utility to quickly convert a fully qualified domain name to its IP address. You can tack on a host name to the end of the command line to identify a single address; type **nslookup ftp.microsoft.com**, for instance, to look up the IP address of Microsoft's FTP server. Or type **nslookup** to switch into interactive mode. From this prompt, you can enter any domain name to find its IP address. If you need more sophisticated lookup tools, you can find them with the help of any search engine. A good starting point is *http://www.dnsstuff.com*, which offers an impressive collection of online tools for looking up domains, IP addresses, and host names. The site also offers form-based utilities that can translate obfuscated URLs and dotted IP addresses, both of which are widely used by spammers to cover their online tracks.

- **Is your ISP experiencing DNS problems?** A misconfigured DNS server (or one that's offline) can wreak havoc with your attempts to use the internet. Try pinging each DNS server to see whether it's available. If your ISP has multiple DNS servers and you encounter problems accessing one server, remove that server from your TCP/IP configuration temporarily and use another one instead.

- **Have you installed any "internet accelerator" utilities?** Many such programs work by editing the Hosts file on your computer to match IP addresses and host (server) names. When Windows finds a host name in the Hosts file, it uses the IP address listed there and doesn't send the request to a DNS server. If the owner of the server changes its DNS records to point to a new IP address, your Hosts file will lead you to the wrong location.

INSIDE OUT Match machines and IP addresses quickly

A Hosts file can be useful on a mid-size network where all computers have static IP addresses. By entering computer names and IP addresses in a Hosts file, you eliminate the need to broadcast messages around the network looking for each machine. Instead, Windows finds the machine name and matching IP address in the Hosts file and goes straight to the correct address. To edit the Hosts file, use Notepad or another text editor. Open the Hosts file (it has no extension) in %SystemRoot%\System32\Drivers\Etc. The comments in this file explain its syntax and are very easy to follow.

Temporary DNS problems can also be caused by the DNS cache, which Windows maintains for performance reasons. If you suddenly have trouble reaching a specific site on the internet and you're convinced there's nothing wrong with the site, type this command to clear the DNS cache: **ipconfig /flushdns**.

Network Troubleshooting Tools

Windows Vista contains a huge assortment of utilities you can use to diagnose, monitor, and repair network connections. Table 14-1 lists the available utilities and summarizes how you can use them.

Table 14-1. Windows Network Utilities

Utility Name	What It's Used For
Get MAC Address (Getmac.exe)	Discovers the Media Access Control (MAC) address and lists associated network protocols for all network cards in a computer, either locally or across a network
Hostname (Hostname.exe)	Displays the host name of the current computer
IP Configuration Utility (Ipconfig.exe)	Displays all current TCP/IP network configuration values and refreshes DHCP and DNS settings
Name Server Lookup (Nslookup.exe)	Displays information about Domain Name System records for specific IP addresses and/or host names, so that you can troubleshoot DNS problems
Net services commands (Net.exe)	Performs a broad range of network tasks; type **net** with no parameters to see a full list of available command-line options
Netstat (Netstat.exe)	Displays active TCP connections, ports on which the computer is listening, Ethernet statistics, IP routing table, and IPv4/IPv6 statistics
Network Command Shell (Netsh.exe)	Displays or modifies the network configuration of a local or remote computer that is currently running; this command-line scripting utility has a huge number of options, which are fully detailed in Help
PathPing (Pathping.exe)	Combines functions of Traceroute and Ping to identify problems at a router or network link
TCP/IP NetBIOS Information (Nbtstat.exe)	Displays statistics for NetBIOS over TCP/IP (NetBT) protocol, NetBIOS name tables for both the local computer and remote computers, and the NetBIOS name cache
TCP/IP Ping (Ping.exe)	Verifies IP-level connectivity to another internet address by sending ICMP packets and measuring response time in milliseconds
TCP/IP Route (Route.exe)	Displays and modifies entries in the local IP routing table
TCP/IP Traceroute (Tracert.exe)	Determines the path to an internet address and lists the time required to reach each hop; useful for troubleshooting connectivity problems on specific network segments

Chapter 14

Fine-Tuning Network Performance

Is your network running more slowly than it should? A fast, easy way to measure the performance of all active network connections is to use Windows Task Manager. To view current networking statistics, open Windows Task Manager by pressing Ctrl+Shift+Esc, and then click the Networking tab.

For more information about how to use Windows Task Manager, see "Using Windows Task Manager," Chapter 21.

In the example shown here, two network connections are active, so two graphs appear, one for each connection. Note that neither connection is close to saturating available network bandwidth.

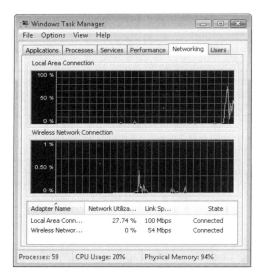

INSIDE OUT   Rename network connections for clarity

In the Network Connections folder, Windows automatically creates generic names for every connection—Local Area Connection, for instance. Get in the habit of renaming all connections in this folder with descriptive names. The names you assign will appear in Windows Task Manager graphs, notification area icons, status dialog boxes, and any other place where you can expect to see information about connections. Descriptive names make it much easier to troubleshoot, especially when you have multiple connections active.

On most networks, the speed of the connection to the internet is the limiting factor for network performance. Fast Ethernet connections, with a theoretical maximum transfer speed of 100 megabits per second, run 10 to 30 times faster than even the fastest cable or DSL connections. You might see excessive network utilization on the local network connection for an Internet Connection Sharing host machine when several other computers on the network are transferring large files such as video clips directly from that machine and not from the network. Wireless connections that are having difficulty reaching a base station may also display performance problems as they automatically throttle down to lower connection speeds. Again, this slowdown will be most obvious when trying to transfer large files between two computers on the network.

CAUTION

In theory, at least, you may be able to improve the performance of a TCP/IP-based network by tweaking specific settings in the registry. The TCP Receive Window (RWIN) and Maximum Transmission Unit (MTU) settings control technical details of how your TCP/IP connection transfers and receives packets. The internet is awash with sites that claim to offer helpful advice and utilities that you can use to reset these values. Beware! Most of these articles are based on TCP/IP settings from previous Windows versions and do not apply to Windows Vista, which generally does a good job of configuring connections properly. In fact, tweaking settings without understanding their consequences is a near-certain route to slower performance, and it may result in connection problems when your tweaked packets hit routers and other connection points on the internet that can't handle them. If you feel compelled to experiment, set a System Restore checkpoint first, and read the definitive and exhaustive Tweaking FAQ at the Broadband Reports site, *http://www.vista-io.com/1405*, before you fire up Registry Editor.

Bridging Two Networks

As we noted in Chapter 12, "Setting Up a Small Network," Windows Vista supports a variety of network media types, including Ethernet, Home Phoneline Networking, and wireless connections. In some cases, your home or small business network may consist of two or more different types of physical networks. For instance, you might have two desktop computers (we'll call them A and B) in your upstairs den connected to an Ethernet hub, with Computer A also serving as your Internet Connection Sharing host. In the basement, you have another computer (call it C) that you want to add to the network. Running network cable to that distant location is impractical, and it's too far away for a reliable wireless connection. You do have a phone jack in that location, however, so you've installed a phone-line network adapter and plugged in to that jack. Upstairs, you've installed a phone-line adapter in Computer B.

You now have two networks. Computer A and Computer B can communicate easily, and Computer B and Computer C can do so as well. But Computer A and Computer C have no way to reach each other, which means Computer C is cut off from the internet as well. How do you bring all three computers into the same network? You create a network bridge, which brings the two networks together seamlessly and creates a virtual connection between the separate network segments. In this example, you would bridge the two network connections on Computer B. In this configuration, Computer C could communicate directly with Computer A, even sharing its internet connection.

> **CAUTION**
>
> In most home and small business setups, a network bridge is unnecessary and you should use Internet Connection Sharing or a router or residential gateway instead. If you plug a wireless access point into a router, for example, instead of hooking it directly to a broadband connection, it will join the other machines on your Ethernet network. Turn off network address translation on the wireless access point, and allow each networked computer equipped with a wireless adapter to receive its IP address directly from the router's DHCP server. This configuration requires that you dive into the access point's setup software and set some advanced options, but the results are worth it from a security and ease-of-administration point of view.

Although the steps to create a bridge are simple, the concepts behind it are potentially confusing. Here's what you need to know:

- You can create a bridge using any two (or more) Ethernet, IEEE-1394, or Ethernet-compatible wireless adapters. You cannot add a VPN connection, a dial-up internet connection, or a direct cable connection to a network bridge.

- Although it's technically possible, you should never bridge a connection that has a public internet address with one that connects to a private network. In that configuration, you should use Internet Connection Sharing instead.

- When you use a network bridge, the machine that has the bridge enabled must be turned on to allow other computers to communicate across the virtual network. If you shut down that computer, you also shut down the bridge.

To create a bridge, in Network Connections select the first connection, hold down Ctrl, and then select each additional connection. Right-click and choose Bridge Connections from the shortcut menu.

After you create the bridge, a new device, Network Bridge, appears in the Network Connections folder, as shown here.

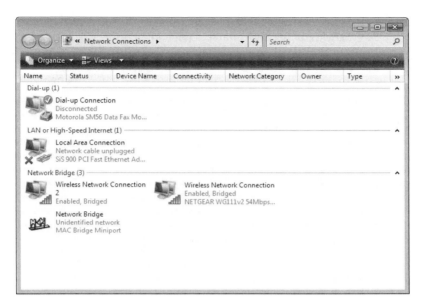

After you create the bridge, the settings for individual connections are no longer available. To view details of your network configuration, double-click the Network Bridge icon. To change details of the bridged connection, right-click the Network Bridge icon and click Properties. The resulting dialog box, shown in Figure 14-4, lets you adjust configuration details for individual adapters or configure IP settings for the bridged connection.

Figure 14-4 To remove adapters from the network bridge, clear the appropriate check boxes in the Adapters section of this dialog box.

You can have only one network bridge on a single computer, although you can, in theory, have as many as 68 network adapters joined in a bridge. To add or remove network adapters from the bridge, right-click the connection icon in the Network Connections window and choose Add To Bridge or Remove From Bridge. If you decide you no longer want to use the network bridge, you can remove it by right-clicking the Network Bridge icon and clicking Delete.

PART III
Digital Media

CHAPTER 15

Digital Media Essentials

Home Basic ○
Home Premium ◉
Business ○
Enterprise ○
Ultimate ◉

I f you can see it, hear it, and convert it into a stream of digital bits, Windows Vista can probably handle it. With a modest amount of practice and education, you can use the assortment of tools and features in Windows Vista to create, download, rip, edit, copy, tag, find, organize, synchronize, burn, play, and share digital media files, including music, video clips, and digital photos. The ability to play back recorded TV and music with full fidelity helps explain why the latest generation of computers running Windows Vista are just as much at home in the living room as in the office.

In the five chapters that make up this section, we show you how to use and customize the individual programs and features that make up the Windows Vista digital media toolkit:

- **Windows Media Player 11** is the playback engine for music and video files and includes the CD-ripping engine for saving music in digital formats. It's where you connect with Windows-compatible download services and where you manage your library of digital music (songs, albums, and playlists) and movie files.

- **Windows Photo Gallery** provides the tools for importing images from digital cameras, performing minor touchup and cropping, and tagging the image files with keywords that make it easier to find them later. From the Photo Gallery, you can burn photos to a data CD or DVD or (in Home Premium and Ultimate editions only) a Video DVD. You can also share photos via e-mail and create a Windows Movie Maker project starting with a selection of image files from the Windows Photo Gallery.

What's in Your Edition?

The most versatile digital media tool of them all, Windows Media Player, is available in every edition of Windows Vista, including Home Basic. Like Windows Photo Gallery, Windows Media Player is absolutely identical in appearance, feature set, and operation for all editions. Windows Movie Maker is also available in all versions, but you can save a project in high-definition formats or burn it to a DVD using Windows DVD Maker only in the consumer-oriented Home Premium and Ultimate editions.

- **Windows Movie Maker** allows you to import, edit, and mix digital photos and video clips into slick movies that can be played back on a computer screen or on a TV display. You can make a DVD-quality movie from any Windows Vista version. To create and save high-definition movie projects you must be running Windows Vista Home Premium or Ultimate.

- **Windows Media Center** adds a so-called 10-foot interface to Windows Vista. Using a remote control, you can record and play back TV, listen to songs, albums, and playlists from your music library, and view slide shows, videos, and downloaded movies, all from across the room. With a direct connection to a widescreen TV—or an indirect connection through a Microsoft Xbox 360 or other media extender device—you can turn a computer running Windows Vista Home Premium or Ultimate into a high-definition, audiophile-friendly digital media hub.

- **Windows DVD Maker** allows you to assemble audio files, video clips, and digital photos and burn them onto recordable DVD disks that can be played back in most consumer DVD players. It is available only in Windows Vista Home Premium and Ultimate editions.

In addition to the applications in the above list, Windows Vista also includes a Media Sharing feature, which allows you to designate some or all of the media files stored in your library for sharing with other computers and devices on your network.

Throughout this chapter, we assume you've correctly installed and configured all the hardware necessary to use the features under discussion, including sound cards, speakers, DVD burners, and TV tuners.

For details on how to configure hardware and install drivers to unlock the functionality of those devices, see Chapter 5, "Setting Up and Troubleshooting Hardware."

Using Windows Media Player

Windows Media Player has been a part of Microsoft Windows for more than a decade. In its earliest incarnation, the Media Player program was a bare-bones 16-bit utility that performed only one trick: playing uncompressed Windows Audio (WAV) files. Through the years, Microsoft has steadily improved the capabilities of Windows Media Player, enhanced its design, and tightened its links to Windows. All versions of Windows Vista include Windows Media Player 11.

> **Note**
>
> Windows Media Player 11 is also available in a version for Windows XP. The two programs are functionally identical.

You can use Windows Media Player to play sound and video files stored on a local disk or streamed from Internet sites. You can *rip* tracks from audio CDs (that is, copy them to your hard disk) in a broad range of quality levels, create custom CDs using a CD or DVD drive that has recording capabilities, and download songs to a portable audio player. You can use the Player as a jukebox to listen to all of your favorite songs, in custom sequences that you devise (called playlists) or in random order. If you have a properly configured DVD drive, you can use the Player to screen your favorite movies and concert videos on a desktop or portable PC.

Windows Media Player is also designed to serve as a gateway to web-based media—especially online stores that sell music and movies. If you click the Media Guide option from the menu at the far right of the Player taskbar (the horizontal panel of options at the top of the Player window), the Player becomes a special-purpose web browser that loads *http://www.windowsmedia.com*, an internet "magazine" that provides access to all manner of news and entertainment content. You can use links on this site to watch news clips, listen to music, check out previews of current movies, and find internet-based radio stations. In Windows Media Player 11, the Online Stores button allows you to connect to sites that will be happy to sell you various kinds of media items.

INSIDE OUT   How to locate, save, and tune in to internet radio stations

Previous versions of Windows Media Player included internet radio as a top-level option. In Windows Vista, this option is much harder to find, but it's still possible to add internet radio stations to the Player, if you know where to look. Although you can navigate to online radio stations from the Windows Media guide within a Player window, it's easier to do so from Internet Explorer. Start at *http://www.vista-io.com/1501*, which takes you to the WindowsMedia.com Radio Tuner page. Use the Featured Stations list or the categorized listings to find a station you're interested in. When you find an interesting station, click Play to open the audio stream in Windows Media Player. To add the station to your media library, save the stream's URL as a playlist. With the radio station playing, tap the Alt key or press Ctrl+M to make the Player's menus visible, and then click File, Save Now Playing List As. Give the new playlist a descriptive name and click Save. You can return to that station anytime by opening the saved playlist.

The basic layout of the Windows Media Player interface hasn't changed much in the past five years, although its visual design is greatly streamlined compared to its predecessors. As Figure 15-1 shows, the Player window consists of six main elements (some of which may be hidden) when content is playing and Now Playing is selected:

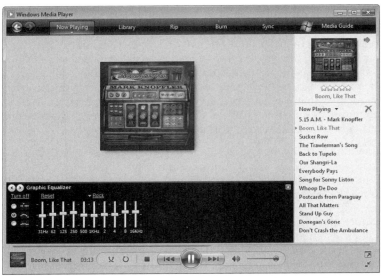

Figure 15-1 Six basic elements of the Windows Media Player interface.

- **Player taskbar**   Contains tabs that activate key features and customization options. Beneath each tab's indicator is a small arrow, visible only when the mouse pointer aims directly at it, that reveals a menu of options for that feature. The Back and Forward buttons at the left of the Player taskbar work just as they do in Internet Explorer.

- **Menu bar**   Offers access to Windows Media Player features and options. In Windows Media Player 11, the menu bar is normally hidden. To make these menu choices visible temporarily in the form of a cascading menu, tap the Alt key. To show or hide the menu bar with its traditional pull-down menus, press Ctrl+M or tap Alt and click Show Classic Menus.

- **Main Player window**   The contents of this area change depending on which tab is selected. When the Library tab is active, this area displays the Navigation and Details panes, where you can organize, edit, and play files. When Now Playing is selected, the Player window may include the Visualizations pane (showing album art in this example) and the Enhancements pane (with the graphic equalizer visible here).

- **List pane**   This pane, which appears to the right of the Player window, displays the contents of the Now Playing list (if Now Playing or Library is selected), the Burn list (if the Burn tab is selected), or the Sync list (if Sync is selected). Use this list to add or remove items from the Now Playing list, change the order of items on the list, sort or shuffle the entire list, or save the current list as a playlist. An info box above the list shows album art for the current track. Click the arrow at the right of this box to hide the List pane. To make the List pane visible again, click the arrow beneath the Now Playing tab and click Show List Pane.

- **Playback controls**   Manage playback of audio and video files, using VCR-style controls to play, pause, fast-forward, and rewind files; this area also includes a variety of special-purpose buttons that control volume and the appearance of the Player. If a file is playing, details appear to the left of the controls.

- **Full/Compact mode button**   Displays a customizable drop-down list from which you can choose an item to play back; available options include CDs, audio and video clips, playlists, and Media Library categories.

When you click an option other than Now Playing, the Player window allows you to work with your library of digital media and create playlists for playing back music and video, ripping CD tracks to the library, burning custom CDs, and synchronizing with portable devices. We cover these options in more detail later in this chapter.

Windows Media Player 11 offers an extensive array of customization and configuration options. Some of these options simply change the Player's look and feel, but others have a major impact on the quality of your experience. For instance, the file format you choose to use when recording CD audio tracks affects both the quality of the recorded files and the amount of space they take up. In this section, we look at how Windows Media Player works and how you can fine-tune it for your own preferences. In Chapter 16, we examine the program's most popular use: creating and managing a digital music collection.

Customizing the Player's Look and Feel

Windows Media Player offers fewer customization options than its predecessors, and most of those options are well hidden. The most radical customization option allows you to completely change the Player's appearance by using an assortment of custom visual designs, known as *skins*.

Even without using a skin, you can do a few things to modify the Player's appearance. In Now Playing, you can display or hide the List pane. You can change the color that appears behind the Player taskbar and in the Now Playing pane from its default blue to any shade. You can collapse the full Player to compact mode, leaving only the playback controls visible, or enable a Mini Player toolbar that embeds playback controls in the Windows taskbar. You can show or hide advanced controls (also known as Enhancements). And you can display one or more of the Player's many visualizations while your music plays. (*Visualizations* are animated designs that Windows Media Player displays while playing music.)

For more information about visualizations, see "Using Visualizations," later in this chapter.

Chapter 15

Switching Display Modes

Windows Media Player has five display modes: full (the default view, described in the previous section), compact, skin, mini Player, and full screen.

Compact mode shrinks the Player window to its absolute smallest size, as shown in Figure 15-2, with only the title bar and playback controls visible. The button in the lower right corner toggles between Full and Compact modes. When playing music in Compact mode, the title bar changes every few seconds to show the artist name, album, and track title in rotation.

Figure 15-2 Compact mode displays only those controls that are essential for playback.

To switch from Full or Compact mode to skin mode, press Ctrl+2 or click Skin Mode from the View menu. To return to the previous mode, press Ctrl+1. When you switch to skin mode, the Player applies the current skin. To choose a different skin, start from full mode and click Skin Chooser on the View menu. Select the skin you want, and then choose Apply Skin. Unlike its predecessors, Windows Media Player 11 includes only two skins, both of which are designed to pare the Player down to a more conservative look. Figure 15-3 shows the Corporate skin.

Figure 15-3 The no-frills corporate skin is one of two included by default with Windows Media Player 11.

To select a different skin, click Skin Chooser on the View menu. To add skins to the list shown in the Skin Chooser, click More Skins. This link takes you to a web page where you can find a long alphabetical list of downloadable skins approved by Microsoft.

Downloading is straightforward, and the skins are automatically added to the Player's Skin Chooser list as soon as they're downloaded. Choose a new skin from the list and click Apply Skin to begin using it.

All skins include the most essential controls—for playing, pausing, stopping, skipping to the next track or previous track, adjusting volume, and so on. Beyond these, skin features vary considerably. Some can show the current playlist or the graphic equalizer. Some show the current visualization and let you move to a different one. Some show the name of the current track. You'll need to experiment to see what the different skins can do and where each control is located.

Most of the Player's menu commands are available in the skin-mode shortcut menu. Right-click anywhere on a skin to display this menu.

INSIDE OUT

To make the Player window stay on top of all other windows, whether it's in full, compact, or skin mode, click Options from the Tools menu. On the Player tab, select Keep the Player On Top of Other Windows.

What do you do if the phone rings while you're playing one of your favorite tunes? If the Player is open in any mode (full, compact, or skinned), you have to bring it to the foreground to reach the Pause or Mute button. For easier access, you have the option to minimize the player to a tiny toolbar that docks on the Windows taskbar. With the Mini Player toolbar enabled, you can control playback and volume without restoring the full Player window. Figure 15-4 identifies each of the toolbar's controls.

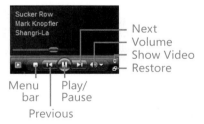

Figure 15-4 The Mini Player toolbar offers access to basic playback and volume controls.

To enable the Mini Player toolbar, right-click any empty space on the Windows taskbar, click Toolbars, and then click Windows Media Player. With this toolbar selected, the Mini Player toolbar will tuck into the right side of the taskbar any time you minimize the Player. Point to the Mini Player to see a pop-up window that provides details about the currently playing content; click the Show Video And Visualization Window button to display a slightly larger window that shows a miniature version of the contents of the Now Playing pane.

INSIDE OUT

The officially documented method to restore the player window is to click the tiny Restore button in the lower right corner of the toolbar. We think it's much easier to click the large Windows Media Player icon at the left side of the toolbar, which is approximately four times the size of the official button.

The final mode, Full Screen, is available only when the Now Playing tab is selected and a music track or video clip is playing. When you play a DVD movie, the Player automatically enters full screen mode after a few seconds. To switch into Full Screen mode manually, press Alt+Enter or click the View Full Screen button, just above the Full/Compact mode button in the lower right corner of the Player window. In Full Screen mode, the Playback controls automatically hide but reappear in a bar at the bottom of the window when you move the mouse. To exit Full Screen mode, click the button at the right side of the Playback controls, or right-click the Player window and choose Exit Full Screen, or just press Escape.

Working With the Enhancements Pane

When you click Now Playing on the Player taskbar, the contents of the main Player window change to show information about the current album, track, or video clip. Just below this display, you can show or hide the Enhancements pane, which hosts a variety of advanced controls. To make it visible, choose View, Enhancements and select the Show Enhancements option. You can choose one of eight available options by selecting it from the Enhancements menu, or use the Previous Controls and Next Controls arrows in the pane's top left corner to cycle through all eight options in order.

The Quiet Mode option, shown below, allows you to reduce the dynamic range of sounds during playback. This option is especially useful when listening to music at low volumes or when using headphones to listen to an album with a wide dynamic range. This feature works only with media that was originally encoded with Windows Media Audio Lossless or Windows Media Audio Professional, however. For MPEG-2 movies and compressed audio files in MP3 or WMA format, it has no effect.

We describe the effect of other Enhancements pane options later in this chapter.

Changing the Player's Color

In a default installation, the background of the full Player window is blue—a dark blue for the background of the currently selected tab and the Back and Forward buttons on the Player taskbar, and a pale blue for the window frame, the playback controls, and the background of the Now Playing area when album art is visible or a video clip is playing. To change the background color, click the arrow beneath the Now Playing tab and choose Color Chooser from the Enhancements menu. In the Color Chooser pane, click Next Preset to cycle through more than 20 color combinations, or choose a color manually by using the Hue slider control to select a color and the Saturation slider to adjust the intensity of the selected color. Click Reset to restore the default blue.

INSIDE OUT   **Go gray**

> To make the Player background a neutral gray, slide the Saturation control to the far left. In this setting, Windows Media Player completely ignores the Hue setting and uses a light gray background. The border around video clips is always black.

Using Visualizations

Visualizations are designs of light and color that change with the frequency and volume of your music, in a style reminiscent of Sixties-era psychedelic light shows. The Player displays visualizations in Now Playing and in many skins. (Not all skins support visualizations, but most do.) Visualizations are grouped into collections which in turn contain individual settings that control colors, shapes, movement, and other attributes of the display. To change the active visualization, click the arrow beneath Now Playing, click the Visualizations menu, and choose any entry from the list. Some visualization collections contain a randomization option that rotates among all the collection's visualizations in random order and timing patterns. Previous versions of Windows Media Player allowed you to cycle through variations in the current collection without returning to the menu; that option is not in Windows Media Player 11.

Many, but not all, visualizations can be displayed in Full Screen mode and are much more effective that way. The built-in Battery collection, for instance, allows you to specify the display size when used in full-screen mode. To access these settings, click the arrow beneath Now Playing and click Options on the Visualizations menu. Select Battery and click Properties to display the dialog box shown in Figure 15-5. The resolution settings allow you to specify how many pixels to use in the Player window and in Full Screen mode.

Figure 15-5 For better performance and display characteristics, adjust the settings for a Full Screen visualization.

To turn off visualizations, select No Visualization or Album Art from the Visualizations menu.

INSIDE OUT

The simplest way to find more visualizations is to click Download on the Tools menu and then choose Visualizations. This takes you to Microsoft's official list of supported downloadable visualizations.

For even more skins and visualizations, visit Microsoft's Windows Media Plug-ins site, *http://www.wmplugins.com*. For a lengthy list of links to non-Microsoft sites that offer Windows Media Player add-ins, see Microsoft Windows Media developer Zach Robinson's excellent Windows Media Player Mini FAQ at *http://www.vista-io.com/1502*.

TROUBLESHOOTING

Visualizations do not appear in Now Playing

If you don't see visualizations in Now Playing, choose View, Visualizations. If No Visualization is selected, choose a different menu option. Also, note that the Player cannot display visualizations during playback of MIDI files, and visualizations might not work for CD tracks when the CD drive is set for analog playback.

Tweaking Performance and Playback Options

In general, Windows Media Player produces output that is commensurate with your hardware. The better the sound card, speakers, display adapter, and monitor, the better the performance you can expect. However, you can tweak a variety of settings to improve performance and to change the type of sound and video that Windows Media Player delivers.

Varying Playback Speed

Buried several layers beneath the Player's basic interface is an advanced playback control, first introduced in Windows Media Player 9 Series, that allows you to vary the speed of playback. This feature does much more than simply rewind or fast-forward a media clip; it performs time compression and expansion, slicing out short pauses, speeding up or slowing down the pace of playback but maintaining audio and video fidelity—keeping a narrator's voice from sounding like a cartoon character when a video clip is played at faster than normal speed, for instance. This feature is especially useful in "speed listening" to podcasts, allowing you to blast through a downloaded program in a fraction of its normal running time while still being able to understand what the host and guests are saying.

To adjust playback speed, click the arrow beneath the Now Playing tab and then choose Play Speed Settings from the Enhancements menu. The main Play Speed Settings control, as shown in Figure 15-6, is a slider that you can drag along a wide range. Drag to the right to speed up playback, to the left to slow things down. (Choosing a negative number causes a video clip to play backwards.) The Slow and Fast presets above the slider work at half-speed and 1.4X normal speed, respectively. Clicking the Previous Frame and Next Frame buttons, just below the slider in the Enhancements pane, pauses playback and steps through a video clip one frame at a time.

Figure 15-6 Click the slider (or use the preset Slow/Normal/Fast options) to change playback speed without distorted audio.

Variable-speed playback doesn't work for all types of content; it's unavailable with streaming audio and video clips that are progressively downloaded, for instance. It's effective with Windows Media Video clips and audio files in WMA and MP3 formats. In addition, audio and video fidelity is only maintained at playback rates between 0.5 and 2.0.

Adding Surround Sound Support

With the right hardware, you can adjust your PC's sound from a simple two-speaker stereo setup to full 5.1, 6.1, or 7.1 surround sound. The difference is most noticeable when watching DVDs in a home theater setup or playing games that take advantage of surround sound. Previous versions of Windows Media Player supported analog surround sound, which artificially creates surround effects from conventional stereo tracks. In Windows Media Player 9 Series and later, you can take advantage of digital surround sound, in which each channel contains discrete audio information specifically recorded for that channel. To play back digital surround sound, you need a compatible sound card, proper drivers for that card, and the proper number of speakers, connected appropriately.

When the hardware and drivers are correctly configured, Windows Media Player automatically recognizes and plays back sounds that are encoded for surround sound. Typically, software utilities included with high-end sound cards allow you to tweak audio performance settings, including adjustments to compensate for less-than-optimum speaker placement. You'll also need to enable advanced speaker configurations in Windows: Open Control Panel and click Sound. On the Playback tab, click Configure and follow the instructions to set your speakers up correctly.

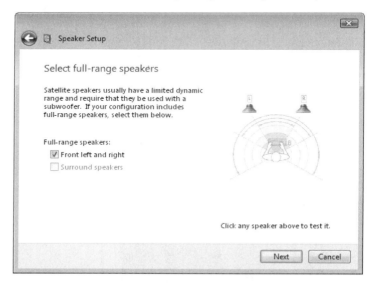

Using the Graphic Equalizer and SRS WOW Effects

Windows Media Player includes a 10-band graphic equalizer with numerous preset equalizer settings, shown in Figure 15-7. To adjust the balance of the various frequency bands in your playback, click Graphic Equalizer from the Enhancements menu. If the frequency sliders appear dark, click Turn On to enable the equalizer (click Turn Off to disable the equalizer).

Figure 15-7 Windows Media Player's graphic equalizer includes presets for many kinds of music.

To choose one of the preset equalizer configurations, click the Select Preset list, located just above the equalizer controls (in Figure 15-7, Blues is selected), and make a selection. If none of the preset options quite matches your aural preferences, drag one or more frequency-band sliders upward or downward. When you drag a slider, other sliders might move with it, depending on which of the three options stacked to the left of the sliders is selected. For example, to move one slider without affecting any others, click the top slider option. The Player can "remember" one (and only one) custom equalizer preset. To save your settings, choose Custom from the bottom of the Preset list and then adjust the frequency-band sliders.

If your sound equipment can take advantage of SRS WOW settings, you can control them in Windows Media Player. To learn more about SRS WOW Effects, which can provide a 3-D sound experience from only two speakers, click the SRS button to open the SRS Labs Web site. To access the effects, choose View, Enhancements, SRS WOW Effects. The Turn On/Turn Off control allows you to toggle the effects. With SRS WOW Effects on, you can select the kind of speakers you're using (normal, large, or headphones), adjust TruBass, and adjust WOW Effect.

Tweaking Video Performance

By default, video clips play back at their original size, and the Player window resizes itself to fit the video clip. You can adjust the default size of the video playback window, change the way the Player window responds to resizing, and adjust the color (hue and saturation), brightness, and contrast of the video image. To access these controls, choose Video Settings in the Enhancement pane.

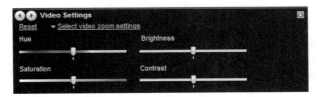

Optimizing Streaming Media Playback

Streaming media servers allow you to enjoy lengthy web-based audio or video clips without having to first download a large file. After establishing a connection to the server, Windows Media Player downloads the beginning of the clip and stores it in a *buffer*, which is then used for playback while the Player continues downloading the remainder of the media file. If all goes well, this buffer supplies a steady stream to the Player, masking any momentary glitches in the connection. If the connection should falter long enough that the buffer runs out of content, however, playback stalls as the Player tries to re-establish the connection and fill up the buffer once again.

In general, Windows Media Player does a fine job of automatically sensing the speed of the connection and setting playback parameters for optimal performance. In some cases, you may need to tweak these settings. This is especially true if your connection speed is erratic. If you find that streaming media playback is frequently interrupted, you may want to increase the size of the buffer slightly. To do so, choose Tools, Options. On the Performance tab, click Buffer *nn* Seconds of Content. Try increasing the buffer size in 5-second increments until streaming clips play back reliably.

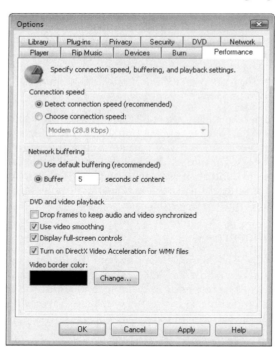

Updating the Player

As with most Windows components, Microsoft periodically issues updates that fix bugs or address security issues identified in Windows Media Player. You can check for the availability of an update at any time by choosing Help, Check For Updates. If updates or new components are available, a list will be displayed, and you can choose to install or not install any item on the list.

Windows Media Player checks for updates automatically at regular intervals. To customize the interval at which it performs these checks, choose Tools, Options. On the Player tab, select Once A Day, Once A Week, or Once A Month. The default is Once A Week.

Using Plug-Ins and Extensions

Windows Media Player supports *plug-ins*—software add-ins that enhance existing features or add new ones. With relative ease, you can find a wide selection of supported plug-ins for Windows Media Player from Microsoft and from third parties. Microsoft's Windows Live Messenger Plug-in, for example, allows you to display the name of the currently playing track along with your name and online status in a Windows Live Messenger window. You can find this and many other plug-ins at Microsoft's Windows Media Plug-ins site at *http://www.wmplugins.com*.

To work with installed plug-ins, choose Tools, Plug-ins, and select from the menu. To adjust the configuration of a plug-in, choose Tools, Plug-ins, Options. Select a category from the list on the left and then select the plug-in whose settings you want to adjust from the list on the right. Select or clear the check box to enable or open the plug-in; click Properties to change its settings.

TROUBLESHOOTING

Plug-ins stop working

If the Player is closed without being shut down properly, the program assumes that the crash may have been the result of a damaged or faulty plug-in and disables all third-party plug-ins. To re-enable a plug-in, choose Tools, Plug-ins, Options, select the plug-in from the list, and click the check box to its left.

Adding and Updating Codecs

A *codec* is a software component used to compress and decompress digital media. Before a sound or video clip can be streamed to your computer from an Internet site or played back from a saved file, your computer must be equipped with a suitable codec. For the most part, you don't have to be concerned about finding and installing codecs for widely supported media types. By default, Windows Media Player is configured to handle this chore automatically. To verify that this option is set, and to change it if necessary, click More Options on the Now Playing menu (or click Options from the Tools menu). On the Player tab, select the check box labeled Download Codecs Automatically. With this option enabled, providers of some types of streamed media will download needed codecs to you without any necessary action on your part. If the check box is clear, you will be prompted for permission before the Player attempts to download and install a new codec.

You can also download and install third-party codecs that are designed to work with Windows Media Player but not endorsed or supported by Microsoft. You do so at your own risk—a buggy codec can cause the Player to crash, freeze, or suffer reduced performance, even when working with clips in a completely different format than the one supported by the rogue codec. In some cases, especially when playing content that was encoded using an older media-authoring program, you may decide to take the risk and install an untested codec. If you do, be sure to set a restore point using System Restore first. (For more details on how to use System Restore, see "Configuring System Recovery Options," Chapter 2, and "Making Repairs with the Windows Recovery Environment," Chapter 24)

TROUBLESHOOTING

A video file does not play back properly

If the Player is unable to play back a particular video clip because a codec is missing, you should see an error message in the following format:

Video not available, cannot find 'vids:XXXX' decompressor.

where *XXXX* is the official Four-Character Code (FOURCC) that uniquely identifies video stream formats. You can use that code to search for an appropriate codec at Dave Wilson's well-organized FourCC.org Web site, *http://www.vista-io.com/1503*. If your hunt is successful, follow the developer's instructions to install the codec.

The two most commonly used and officially unsupported video codecs, both of which are frequently used in AVI files, are DivX and XviD. For more information about these codecs along with download and installation instructions, visit the DivX Movies website at *http://www.divx.com* and the XviD home at *http://www.xvid.org*.

Which File Formats Are Supported?

Windows Media Player 11 plays back a wide variety of media file formats, but its coverage is not exhaustive, and a handful of very popular formats (mostly from companies that compete with Microsoft) are not supported in the Player. When you first run Windows Media Player, one of the setup options allows you to pick and choose which file formats will be associated with it; you can review and change these options any time by opening the Default Programs option from Control Panel or the Start menu, clicking Set

Your Default Programs, choosing Windows Media Player from the list of programs, and finally clicking Choose Defaults For This Program.

The list includes the following supported formats:

- **Advanced Systems Format (ASF)** files can contain audio, video, or both. Files in this format that are encoded with the Windows Media Audio codec typically use the .wma file name extension; those encoded with the Windows Media Video code typically use either the .wmv or .wm file name extension. The generic .asf file name extension indicates that the file was compressed with a different codec.

- **Windows Media Audio (WMA)** and **Windows Media Video (WMV)** are ASF files that have been compressed using Windows Media Audio and Windows Media Video codecs, respectively. WMA files typically use the .wma file name extension, and WMV files can use either .wmv or .wm as the extension. Files in either format can be packaged using digital rights management and can be encoded at various levels of quality (which in turn affects disk space used per file).

- **Windows Media metafiles** are XML files that can be created and viewed in a plain text editor. They're typically designed to be redirectors, which allow Windows Media Player to open and play streaming media sources on Web servers. The file name extensions typically end in x: .asx, .wax, .wvx, .wmx.

- **Windows Media Player playlists** are client-side XML metafiles that define static or dynamic lists of files to be played back. They typically use the .wpl file name extension.

- **Microsoft Digital Video Recording** is the file format used by the TV recording engine in Windows Media Center. Files stored in this format use the file name extension .dvr-ms and can be recorded at any of several quality levels. Converting these files to the more highly compressed WMV format typically results in significant savings in disk space.

- The **Windows Media Download Package** format combines Windows Media Player skin borders, playlist information, and multimedia content in a single downloadable file that uses a .wmd extension.

- **Audio Video Interleave (AVI)** is the most common format for playback of video clips on Windows-based computers. Developed by Microsoft, this format can accommodate content encoded using a number of popular codecs from Microsoft and from third parties. Windows Media Player can play back an AVI file only if the codec it uses is installed.

- A group of widely used formats from the Moving Pictures Experts Group are supported in Windows Media Player. **MPEG-1** is a relatively low-quality video format that uses the .mpeg, .mpg, and .m1v file name extensions. **MPEG-2** encoded video files are DVD quality; Windows Vista is the first Windows version to include a built-in MPEG-2 decoder (in Home Premium and Ultimate editions only; other editions must purchase and install a third-party decoder). **MPEG Audio Layer II (MP2)** is an audio encoding format that is rarely used today. **MPEG Audio Layer III**, more popularly known as **MP3**, is the most popular audio encoding format in use today. Digital media files that use this format typically have the.mp3 file name extension and can be played back in nearly any audio player or portable music jukebox. **M3U** files use a text-based metafile format to define playlists, typically made up of MP3 files.

- **Musical Instrument Digital Interface (MIDI)** files use a standard protocol to create and play back synthesized music files that mimic common instruments. MIDI files typically use the .mid and .midi file name extensions.

- The **Audio for Windows (WAV)** format can use a number of codecs but in everyday use typically stores uncompressed audio files encoded using Pulse Code Modulation.

Popular media file formats that are not supported in Windows Media Player include the following:

- **Real Networks** distributes music and movies in a variety of formats, typically compressed with RealAudio and RealVideo codecs and using the .ra, .rm, and .ram file name extensions. You are most likely to encounter the RealMedia format, which can be used with audio, video, or both, when playing streaming media from a website. Most sites that support this format also offer a Windows Media stream as an option. For sites that offer only RealMedia streams, you need to visit the Real.com website and download a compatible player from Real Software.

- The **QuickTime** file format, developed by Apple Computer, can contain video, audio, graphics, and animation and use the file name extensions .mov and .qt. Windows Media Player can play back ancient files created using QuickTime version 2.0 or earlier. For virtually all QuickTime files you're likely to encounter on the web, you must use Apple's QuickTime Player (*http://apple.com/quicktime*).

- **MPEG-4** is a wide-ranging International Standards Organization (ISO) standard for media files. Windows Media Player offers limited support for some forms of MPEG-4 video compression, but in its default configuration does not play back the more popular video file format, which uses the .mp4 file name extension.

- **Advanced Audio Coding (AAC)** evolved from the popular MP3 standard and boasts higher quality with significantly smaller file sizes. It is the default format used with Apple Computer's iPod portable music players and the iTunes online store. Windows Media Player does not play any AAC-formatted files.

- **Free Lossless Audio Codec (FLAC)** and **Shorten (SHN)** provide lossless compression of audio files. Some portable music players and consumer audio devices support the FLAC format, and the WinAmp music player supports both formats for playback.

- **Ogg Vorbis (OGG)** is an all-purpose compressed media format suitable for audio, video, and games. It is most widely used for audio tracks and is functionally similar to AAC and WMA in this application. (For more information about this format, visit the Vorbis site at vorbis.com.) Some websites offer unsupported releases of the Ogg Vorbis code that reportedly allow clips in this format to play in Windows Media Player 9 Series or later.

And finally: When is a media file format not a file format at all? When it's a CD Audio track. If you open an audio CD using Windows Explorer, you'll see each track listed as a CD Audio file, with the file name extension .cda. These files are representations of audio tracks, and cannot be copied to the Windows file system in their native format or played back except from an audio CD.

Managing Your Media Library

The Library tab in Windows Media Player displays your collection of media files in a single window where you can find, organize, and play media files in any combination that strikes your fancy.

As Figure 15-8 shows, the Library tab displays media items in a window that works much like Windows Explorer. An Address bar just below the Player taskbar allows you to narrow your selection. The Navigation pane on the left shows a hierarchical view of the selected media category, and the Details pane to its right shows what's included in the current selection. (If the List pane is visible, it appears to the right of the Details pane.)

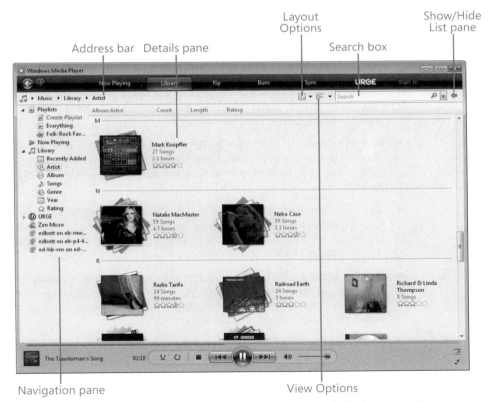

Figure 15-8 Windows Media Player uses a Windows Explorer-style display to organize your media library.

Chapter 15

The drop-down arrow at the far left of the Address bar allows you to choose one of five categories to display: Music, Pictures, Video, Recorded TV, and Other Media. (The latter category includes, among other things, digital images that are stored in your Music folder and are not included in the Windows Photo Gallery index.)

Items in the Navigation pane are organized into a consistent hierarchy:

- The **Playlists** heading allows you to create, organize, edit, and select Auto Playlists and custom lists of music tracks and video clips for later playback. This heading is always at the top of the list and its contents are the same no matter which category is selected.

- Click **Now Playing** to display the contents of the current Now Playing list in the Details pane.

- Items under the **Library** heading offer alternate views of the current category. When viewing the Music category, for example, you can view your collection by Artist, Album, Genre, Year, or Rating.

- If you've signed in to an online service that is integrated with Windows Media Player, such as the MTV URGE service, it appears as a heading in the Navigation pane. Not all online services are capable of hooking into the interface in this fashion.

- Any currently connected portable devices that have been set up for synchronization appear below portable devices in the Navigation pane. If the device is currently connected and not synchronizing, you can browse its contents using the list of views in the Navigation pane.

- Finally, any shared libraries that you can access from other computers on your network appear at the bottom of the Navigation pane. You can display the contents of a shared library and play items from it only if you have been given permission by the user who owns that library.

INSIDE OUT

The lists of options shown in the Navigation pane under the Playlists and Library headings are not complete. The Playlists heading includes only Recent Playlists and the Library shows only so-called Primary Views in the Navigation pane. To see the expanded list of options available for each of these categories, click the name of the heading in the Navigation pane. In the Music category, this option allows you to view your music collection by folder, or you can choose the Online Stores view to see all protected music that you've downloaded from a particular store.

The Layout Options and View Options menus above the Details pane allow you to customize the display of information in the library, in much the same way that Windows Explorer works with files. From the Layout Options menu, you can show or hide the Navigation and List panes and the Classic Menus. You can also customize the list of columns visible in the Details pane. From the View Options menu, you can switch between Icon, Tile, and Details view, the latter providing a plain list with no album art or thumbnails.

The Search box allows you to search the library for any item in the currently selected category. If you begin your search with a particular view already selected, the text you enter in the Search box filters that view only. If you start from the main library heading, however, the search results appear as a list showing how many matches appear in each view.

Where is all this information stored? Most of the information associated with an individual music track or video clip is stored as metadata in the file itself. The library database gathers this metadata when you add the tracks to your library and also collects some additional information, including details about DVDs you've watched, TV shows you've recorded, CDs you've played, and tracks you've purchased from an online service. It stores this information in a single database file, which is organized in a proprietary format and cannot be edited using any tools except Media Player itself.

INSIDE OUT   Manage the media library database

Although the items in your media library consist of individual files, the display of infor-mation in the Player window is drawn from a single indexed database file. In Windows Vista, each local user account has a separate media library database named CurrentDa-tabase_360.wmdb. This file is stored in the folder %LocalAppData%\Microsoft\Media Player. The inner details of this format are not publicly available, and we know of no way to view or edit its data using anything other than Windows Media Player. (When you upgrade to Windows Vista on a computer running a previous version of Windows Media Player, the old database file remains; you can delete it if you're fussy about small amounts of wasted file space, but it isn't necessary to do so.)

Most information in the library is initially drawn from the WindowsMedia.com database or from metadata (tags) stored in the media files themselves. If you change any of the details displayed in the media library window for a given track, that information is saved in your database and is also written as metadata within the underlying files. If the file is in a shared location (on your computer or on a network server), your changes will be re-flected in any other user's media library the next time they play that track.

Details about when and how often you've played each track are stored only in the media library database file and not as metadata. If you erase the library database, this informa-tion is irretrievably lost.

Although you can't edit the media library database, you can clean it up easily if it be-comes corrupted (or if you simply want to get a fresh start). After closing Windows Media Player, open Windows Explorer and browse to the hidden folder %LocalAppData% \Microsoft\Media Player. Rename or delete the database file, CurrentDatabase_360. wmdb. Then reopen Windows Media Player and use the Search facility to import music and other media files stored on your computer (see the following section, "Adding Items to Your media library," for more details). This step erases the stored details (including cus-tomizations) of any CDs and DVDs you've played but have not added to the library; you'll need to download these details again for each CD in your collection. It also wipes out the play counts for any tracks in your library and erases any ratings except those stored as metadata within the file itself.

Adding Items to Your Media Library

When you rip a CD to your hard disk, purchase an album from an online store, or re-cord a TV program using Windows Media Center, those files are automatically added to the library. Those aren't the only ways to expand the library, however.

Adding Items Automatically

By default, Windows Media Player monitors media-related folders (Music, Pictures, and Videos) in your user profile and in the Public folders on your computer. (If your com-puter includes a TV tuner and you've set up Media Center, the Recorded TV folder is monitored as well.) When you add any files in supported formats to these locations, the files are automatically added to the library without any intervention on your part. To adjust these options, click the arrow beneath the library tab on the Player taskbar and click Add To Library (you can also open this dialog box by opening the Options dialog box and then clicking Monitor Folders).

To have media files from other users on your computer appear in your library, select My Folders And Those Of Others That I Can Access. This option adds the Users folder and all its subfolders to the library and is thus an all-or-nothing option; you can't add one user's files and reject those from another using this method.

You can have Media Player check other folders, too—for instance, if you create your own music files or download tracks from the internet and store them in a separate subfolder, consider adding that location to the list of monitored folders. Click Add to browse for folders to make the list longer. Click Remove to clear entries from the list. You cannot remove the media folders for your user profile or the Public profile from this list.

By default, Windows Media Player ignores audio files smaller than 100 KB and video files smaller than 500 KB. These defaults filter out very short clips. To adjust these options, click the Advanced Options button to expand the Add To Library dialog box and make these options visible.

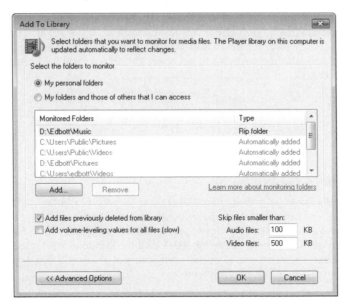

After you close the Add To Library dialog box, even if you made no changes, Windows Media Player searches through all folders listed in the Add To Library dialog box. You can close this dialog box and the search will continue in the background.

INSIDE OUT **Decide where to store your media files**

Are your media files scattered all over your hard disk, in a mishmash of folders? Before adding them to your library, why not reorganize them into a more manageable collection of folders? The best place to store your own collection of music files, of course, is in the Music folder, which is a part of your personal profile. However, if you have a large collection of specialized media files, such as live music recordings, you might want to keep them in their own folder, separate from the tracks you rip from CDs. For extra-large music collections, consider dedicating a separate volume or even a separate physical drive to music only.

If several users share your computer and you also want to share all or part of a music collection, try saving your files in the Public Music folder.

Adding Items When They Are Played

If you download media from the internet, you have a choice as to whether to add such items to your media library automatically. If you want every item you play to take up residence in the library, open the Options dialog and click the Player tab. Then select Add Media Files To Library When Played. Note that this setting does not affect files played from shared network folders or from removable media such as CDs, DVDs, and flash memory cards, which are never added to the library. Clear this check box to specify that you want to add files only when you copy them to a local folder that is in your Monitored Folders list.

If you don't add media items automatically the first time you play them, you can drag a media file from Windows Explorer (or your desktop) and drop it onto Media Player's Details pane to bring the item into your library.

Using Windows Explorer with Media Files

Windows Media Player, Windows Photo Gallery, and Windows Explorer are tightly integrated, so that you can easily manipulate your library in either context. If you rename, move, or delete a media file in Windows Explorer, Windows Media Player dutifully records the change in the media library database (and the Windows Photo Gallery, if necessary); you shouldn't have to rebuild or edit your library in any way. If you delete an item using Windows Explorer, the item will remain in your library.

In addition, the Details tab of the Properties dialog box for any media file contains metadata stored within that file. With rare exceptions, you can edit the information stored here by clicking in the field on the Details tab and adding, deleting, or changing the value stored there. Any changes you make here are reflected immediately in the library database and in Windows Photo Gallery.

The fact that you *can* edit metadata in Windows Explorer doesn't mean you should. In general, we recommend that you use Windows Media Player or Windows Photo Gallery as the primary tool for editing metadata for music, video, and photo files. Use Windows Explorer for small-scale tasks, like cleaning up a misspelled tag or title that you notice in the Details pane in Windows Explorer, or for editing tags that are not readily accessible from Windows Photo Gallery or Windows Media Player, such as the Comments tag associated with a digital photo file.

You'll find other links between Windows Explorer and media-related utilities as well. Right-click any item in Windows Media Player or Windows Photo Gallery and click Open File Location to open the underlying file for that item in Windows Explorer. When you select a media file (or view the contents of a folder containing multiple media files) in Windows Explorer, options on the folder toolbar allow you to play the selected files, burn them to a CD, or perform other tasks appropriate for that file type.

Deleting Items from Your Media Library

When you delete a file or playlist from your media library by right-clicking its entry in the Details pane and choosing Delete, Windows Media Player displays a dialog box asking you to specify whether you want to remove the item from the library or whether you also want to delete the underlying file or files.

If you delete a track from the library but leave its underlying file present in a monitored folder, the Player will add it again if you open the list of monitored folders and click OK, even if you make no changes. You can override this decision by opening the Add To Library dialog box and clearing the Add Files Previously Deleted From Library box.

Using Media Center

Windows Media Center uses many of the same underlying technologies that we discuss in this chapter, but overlays an interface that is intended for use with a remote control. It's worth noting that Media Center uses the same library database as Windows Media Player. Thus, any changes you make in Windows Media Player are available immediately in Media Center, and vice-versa.

For a more detailed discussion of how to set up and use Media Center, see Chapter 19, "Using Windows Media Center."

Synchronizing and Sharing Media with Portable Devices

Do you own a portable music player? If so, you may be able to synchronize the contents of that device with the digital music collection on your PC. Windows Media Player 11 allows you to establish a working relationship between your device and your music collection. After you complete the initial configuration, you can connect the device to your PC (typically via USB cable) and synchronize the contents of the device automatically or manually.

> **Note**
> Don't let the term "synchronization" fool you. In this case, synchronization is not a two-way street. If you add songs to your portable device from another source, they will not be automatically copied to your computer the next time you synchronize. You'll have to perform that operation yourself.

When you perform a synchronization, Windows Media Player uses the settings on the Sync tab, most notably the Sync list, which appears in the List pane. During initial setup, Windows Media Player makes some choices automatically, based on your device configuration. If the storage capacity on the device is more than 4GB and your entire media library occupies less space than the total capacity of the device, the Player sets up a sync relationship in which your entire library is automatically synchronized to the device each time you connect. If the device has a capacity of less than 4GB, or if your library is larger than the total capacity of the device, the Player sets up a manual sync.

The Player can automatically generate a Sync list, or if you prefer you can create a custom Sync list manually. Based on settings you define, the Player may first convert files stored in your library into a format that is more appropriate for the limited space on a portable device. It then copies the tracks from the PC to the device, erasing any files on the device that are no longer part of the Sync list.

In general, supported devices are those that use the Media Transfer Protocol (MTP). Storage may be on flash memory (Compact Flash or Secure Digital cards, for instance) or on a hard disk. For compatible devices, Windows Vista supplies drivers automatically—just connect the device to your computer. After driver installation is complete, Windows Media Player displays a dialog box similar to the one shown in Figure 15-9.

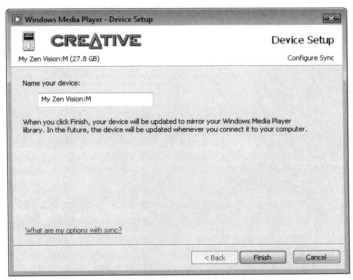

Figure 15-9 When setting up a new portable media device, give it a descriptive name so you can distinguish it from other devices you might add later.

You can set up synchronization partnerships with up to 16 devices on a single computer, each with its own unique settings. To adjust device-specific settings after the initial setup, the device must be connected. Click the arrow beneath the Sync button on the Player taskbar and choose More Options, select the correct device from the list, and then click Properties. In the resulting dialog box, shown in Figure 15-10, you can change the device's name without having to go through initial setup again.

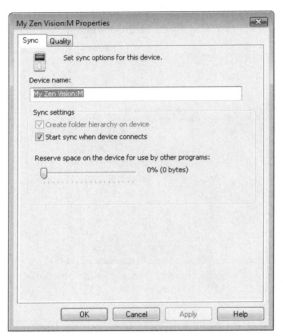

Figure 15-10 Some synchronization options are unavailable when the hardware doesn't support changes to those features.

In Figure 15-10, note that not all of the synchronization options are available. This situation occurs because Windows Media Player correctly detected that this device requires the use of folders to store media files properly. After you sync the device for the first time, the option to reserve storage space on the device becomes available; use this option to restrict the amount of space used for storing music or video files, if you use a portion of a hard-disk-based device to to store backup copies of data files that you carry on the road.

Depending on the capabilities of your device, you may be able to sync only music files, or you may be able to include photos, video clips, and recorded TV shows.

If your portable device has limited storage space, you can make the best use of it by adjusting options on the Quality tab of its properties dialog box, shown in Figure 15-11. Under Music Quality Level, choose Select Quality Level and then use the slider to choose the bit rate you want to use for all tracks copied to the device (all in WMA format). If you set this option to its lowest level, 64 Kbps, you can significantly increase the number of tracks that fit on your portable music player, albeit at a cost in audio quality.

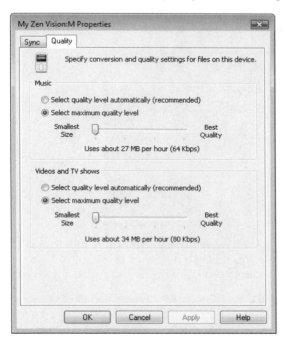

Figure 15-11 To squeeze more media onto a portable player (at a cost in audio or video quality), move either of these two sliders to the left.

INSIDE OUT   Speed up file syncs

Each time you sync with a portable player whose quality settings are lower than those of your music library, Windows Media Player transcodes those tracks—converting them to the lower bit rate in a temporary folder before copying them to the device itself. If you have ample space on your primary hard disk, you can speed up this process by allowing more room for the Transcoded Files Cache and configuring Windows Media Player to perform this operation in the background. To find these options, open the Options dialog box and click Advanced on the Devices tab. Transcoded files are stored in the default location (in your profile). Buttons in this dialog box let you move the cache to another folder or even another drive, and to delete the files for space-saving purposes.

When you connect a device that has a defined relationship with one PC to a different computer, you see a dialog box that allows you to transfer the partnership to the new computer or just synchronize the device one time using the current Library. All other actions are the same after you make this choice.

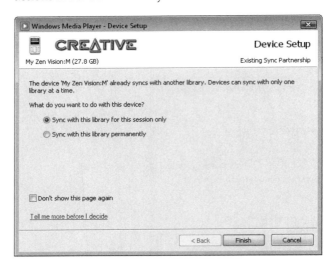

To change sync options after initial setup, right-click the device icon in the Navigation pane and click Set Up Sync. This dialog box, shown in Figure 15-12, allows you to control how automatic synchronization takes place or disable it completely.

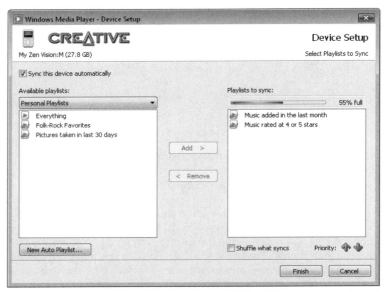

Figure 15-12 Clear the check box at the top of this dialog box to specify that you always want to sync your portable device manually.

After a device is set up, you have three options for synchronizing it with your library:

- **Automatic sync** When the Sync This Device Automatically box is selected, you can select one or more playlists in Windows Media Player to use when synchronizing, as in Figure 15-12. The Player adds media files in the order in which they appear in the Playlists To Sync list and continues until it runs out of tracks in the selected playlists or storage space on the device.

- **Manual sync** When you clear the Sync This Device Automatically box, the Player awaits your instructions each time you connect the device. Select the Sync tab, build a Sync list manually or by selecting an existing playlist, and then click Start Sync.

- **Shuffle music** This option is available in the Sync list pane or from the shortcut menu that appears when you right-click the portable device in the Navigation pane. It completely replaces the contents of the device with a random selection of music files from your existing library.

If your device supports pictures, recorded TV, and video files, you can add playlists for those items to the Sync list.

Chapter 15

INSIDE OUT   What if you don't own a compatible device?

If your portable player isn't on the list of supported devices, you'll need to find an alternate strategy for filling it with music. Most devices include some sort of software designed to help with this task. If you're not happy with that software, visit Red Chair Software (*http://www.redchairsoftware.com*) and see if this innovative company has released a custom package for the device in question. If you choose to use Windows Explorer, use the Desktop Search tools to create a saved search and copy those files to your device. You can specify settings by file or folder and filter out certain types of files (so that album art doesn't waste disk space on your device, for instance).

TROUBLESHOOTING

Your portable device isn't working properly

If your compatible device loses its ability to sync with Windows Media Player, you may be able to restore its function by removing and reinstalling the device. Turn the device on and connect it to your computer. Click Start, right-click Computer, and choose Manage; in the Computer Management console, select Device Manager. Find your device under the Portable Devices category, right-click its entry in the list, and click Uninstall. Now disconnect the device, wait a minute or two, and (with the device still on) reconnect it to your computer.

Understanding and Protecting Your Digital Rights

In Windows Vista, you're likely to encounter media files that use Microsoft's Windows Media Digital Rights Management (DRM) technology—that is, digital content that has been encrypted using digital signatures and whose use is governed by a licensing agreement with the content provider—whenever you acquire music or movies from an online store or when you record TV shows from premium cable or satellite channels using Windows Media Center. The media usage rights (previously called a license) that are associated with DRM-protected files specify how you can use the file and for what period of time; these rights are designed to prevent unauthorized copying or distribution of the media item. The media usage rights are determined by the content vendor and should be disclosed when you agree to purchase or download the item; Windows Media Player enforces the terms of that agreement.

Living Without DRM

We recognize that copy protection and digital rights management schemes that restrict your right to use media files are controversial. If you're philosophically opposed to the idea of restricted usage rights, you have the option to purchase music on unprotected physical media such as CDs and rip it in unprotected digital form to your computer. You can also do business with online stores that sell unrestricted content—the most notable example is eMusic (*http://www.emusic.com*), which has a rich but offbeat collection of music from independent artists and labels.

If you do look for music from sources that don't use Windows Media DRM, be aware that those other sources may use alternative DRM technology that is incompatible with Windows Media Player. Apple's iTunes Store, for example, sells tunes protected with its proprietary FairPlay technology, which are designed to be played in Apple's iTunes player or on an iPod. Check with the supplier of the protected content to see which media player software and devices support the DRM scheme used in that content.

We don't recommend the extreme option of downloading bootleg tools and utilities to decrypt digitally protected files. Under the Digital Millennium Copyright Act of 1998, distributing and using those tools to circumvent access protection on copyrighted material is a criminal offense. As a result, most such tools are hard to find, and finding them requires that you search in some very dark corners of the internet, where you may download more than you bargained for.

When you download a song, movie clip, or other protected media file from an online store, the content provider might encrypt the file with a wrapper that defines your media usage rights. Alternatively, if you try play a file that incorporates usage restrictions without satisfying the terms of the agreement (by signing in with your user account on an authorized computer, for instance), the Player might attempt to obtain an authorization for that file. You might have to register or pay for the license before being able to play the file.

INSIDE OUT

If you want to avoid acquiring licensed media, choose Tools, Options. On the Privacy tab in the Options dialog box, clear Download Usage Rights Automatically When I Play Or Sync A File. In recent years, some unscrupulous Web sites have pushed protected files that spawned pop-up windows and ActiveX installers trying to lure a visitor into accepting a spyware program or worse. The security features in Windows Vista make this tactic much more difficult to pull off, but it's worth closing this potential risk if you never use digitally protected files.

Windows Media DRM agreements can be for an indefinite period of time or can be set to expire after some period of time. In some cases, the media usage rights agreement will allow you to play the media item only on the computer on which the item was originally downloaded. In other cases, the agreement allows you to copy or move the item to other computers and personal music players (but not necessarily to CDs). You can read the terms of an item's license by examining the item's properties dialog box. Find the file in the Player's media library, right-click it, choose Properties, and click the Media Usage Rights tab. Figure 15-13 shows the rights assigned to a downloaded music file.

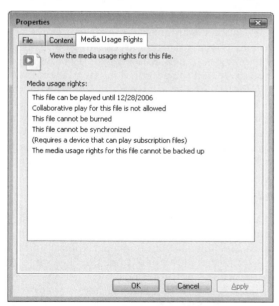

Figure 15-13 You can read the terms of a file's media usage rights agreement by displaying its properties dialog box in the Player's media library.

If you have bought licenses that allow you to play the items for an indefinite period of time on a single computer, how do you move the media item to another computer? Using Windows Media Player 10 and earlier, you could back up licenses on one machine and restore them on another (giving up your privileges on the original computer, of course). In Windows Media Player 11, this feature no longer exists. To move protected files from one computer to another, you must use whatever procedure the original content provider specifies. In extreme cases, you may be unable to play back the original file.

> **Note**
>
> Previously, Microsoft allowed you to restore licenses on a maximum of four unique computers with a counter on the protected file that stripped copying right away after the license had been moved the maximum number of times. This restriction is still in effect for music files that have been ripped to disk using copy protection.

Security and Privacy Issues

Like all internet-enabled applications, Windows Media Player creates a two-way channel between your computer and an ocean of content. Clicking on a link to a media file can take you to a trusted site or a viper's den. Known security holes in previous versions of Windows Media Player created the potential for an attacker to install a virus or Trojan horse program by exploiting the Player's web-browsing capabilities. In addition, because the Player is capable of using the internet to download information about the content you watch or listen to, it raises worrisome privacy issues. Some privacy advocates, for instance, argue that the same connection that downloads information about a music track or DVD is also, at least in theory, capable of sending information about a user's viewing habits to websites that have no legitimate need for that information.

Configuring Security Options

Most security issues associated with Windows Media Player arise because of its role as a host for web-based content. Specifically, a URL on a web page or in an e-mail message, when opened in the Player, can exploit a flaw in Internet Explorer and install hostile code. In addition, malicious scripts can attempt to force the Player into running hostile code, either from a web-based location or from a local file. The most effective way to guard against this sort of exploit is to ensure that all Windows security patches are installed. In addition, default security settings provide extra layers of protection against hostile code. To implement these protections, open the Options dialog box, click the Security tab, and verify that the settings are as shown in Figure 15-14.

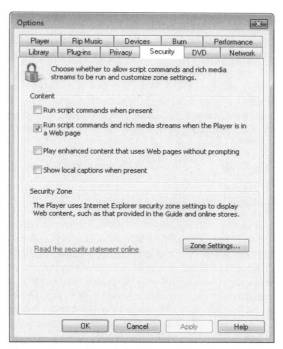

Figure 15-14 These default settings block Windows Media Player from executing scripts, which can contain hostile code.

By default, Windows Media Player 11 blocks the execution of all scripts within the Player window. This feature is designed to prevent a would-be attacker from burrowing into your computer by way of a streaming media file. In one such scenario, an attacker could create a script file using an ASF file, which can contain streaming media (such as an audio or video clip), along with links to URLs and script commands. By enticing you to click one of these links, the attacker might be able to exploit a security hole and load a hostile program. Disabling scripts prevents such an attack from succeeding via Windows Media Player, even if the security hole is unpatched.

This security precaution can, unfortunately, catch innocent web-based content in its dragnet. For instance, some sites offer online audio tutorials that are synchronized with a web-based slide show. As the audio narration plays, the speaker's slides reinforce the underlying messages. If the default security settings are enabled, Windows Media Player 11 cannot control Internet Explorer in this fashion. The solution is to open the Options dialog box, click the Security tab, and select the Run Script Commands When Present check box. (Be sure to restore this setting to its more secure level after playing the web-based presentation.) If an ASF file is embedded in a web page, the capability to process scripts is enabled. To increase security settings in this scenario, clear the second check box, Run Script Commands And Rich Media Streams When The Player Is In A Web Page.

Configuring Privacy Options

As we noted earlier, the connection between Windows Media Player and the Web works both ways. When you connect to a streaming media file or update your digital music collection with information from an online database, you run the risk that someone, somewhere will connect your computer—and by extension, you—with the content you're viewing. Voluntarily surrendering some personally identifiable information is part of the price you pay for certain transactions. In those cases, you have to decide whether you trust the company you're about to do business with to safeguard your personal information.

INSIDE OUT   Pay attention to the privacy statement

Most people click right past web-based privacy statements, which typically are written in legalese and obscure more than they inform. The Windows Media Player privacy statement is a noteworthy exception. It's written in plain, nontechnical terms. It's organized by topic, with hyperlinks that let you jump to a specific part of the document. And it includes step-by-step instructions that explain how to disable features that might affect your privacy, with clear explanations of the consequences of doing so. The information isn't buried, either. When you first run Windows Media Player 11, a wizard steps you through setup options; on the Select Your Privacy Options page of that wizard, you'll find a Privacy Statement tab that contains links to the most up-to-date version of this document. If you've already been through this initial setup process, open the Player's Options dialog box. On the Privacy tab, you'll find a Read The Privacy Statement Online link that leads to the same up-to-date document. (A similar webpage that explains security features is available from a link on the Security tab of the Options dialog box.)

But privacy concerns can also pop up in simple activities that don't involve a commercial transaction. If that's an issue that concerns you, one drastic option is to disable the Player's connection to the Internet. Of course, doing so makes it impossible to update music files or acquire content that has been protected with a media usage rights agreement. For a set of less extreme privacy-protecting options, consider the following three potential privacy risks:

- **Cookies**   Because Windows Media Player uses the same underlying components as Internet Explorer, individual sites (including WindowsMedia.com) can, at least in theory, use cookies to track the content played by a particular computer. By using the cookie-management features in Internet Explorer (described in "Managing Cookies," Chapter 27), you can eliminate this possibility. Note that blocking cookies may break some Windows Media Player features, such as saving your login credentials for an online store.

- **Player ID**   When you connect to a streaming media server, the Player sends a log of the session to the server. This log contains your unique IP address as well as details about your connection. It also includes a unique identifier called a Player ID.

By default, this ID is anonymous in Windows Media Player 11. In some rare cases, a site may require that you use a unique Player ID that is capable of identifying your computer. In that case, choose Tools, Options, and select the Send Unique Player ID To Content Providers check box on the Privacy tab.

- **History Tracking**   For each user account, Windows Media Player maintains a history that identifies media files and URLs you play. In addition, it keeps a list of CDs and DVDs you play. Anyone with physical access to your computer can inspect those lists and possibly draw conclusions based on their contents. To eliminate this possibility, you need to adjust several settings on the Privacy tab of the Options dialog box, as shown in Figure 15-15. Clearing the check box at the top, Display Media Information From The Internet, prevents the Player from compiling a list of discs you play. Clearing the Save File And URL History In The Player check box at the bottom disables the history list. Finally, the Clear History and Clear Caches buttons erase the current contents of those lists for the logged-on user.

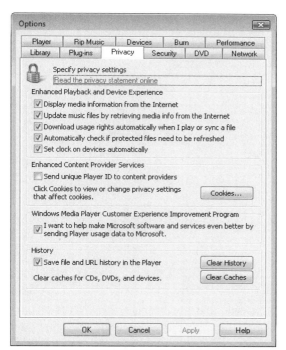

Figure 15-15 Adjust options here if you're concerned about threats to your privacy from Windows Media Player.

CHAPTER 16

Playing and Organizing a Digital Music Collection

Home Basic   ⦿
Home Premium   ⦿
Business   ⦿
Enterprise   ⦿
Ultimate   ⦿

Windows Media Player works with all sorts of media, but it's especially well suited for the task of managing digital music files. Using only Windows Media Player and no other software, you can download songs from the internet, copy tracks from CDs, edit song titles and other information stored within files, rate your favorite tunes, create custom playlists, copy music to portable devices, and burn custom CDs.

In Chapter 15, we explained how to use the core functions of Windows Media Player with media clips in all formats. In this chapter, our emphasis is on the unique tools and techniques that help you acquire, play, and organize digital music files.

> **What's in Your Edition?**
>
> Windows Media Player works identically in all editions of Windows Vista, and all the information in this chapter applies to all versions.

Playing Music in Windows Media Player

When you play back a music file or an audio CD in Windows Media Player, the playback controls, shown in Figure 16-1, look and function like those on common consumer devices, such as CD and DVD players.

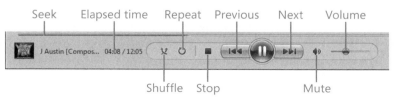

Figure 16-1 The Player uses playback controls like those of other consumer devices.

The Play button becomes a Pause button while the Player is playing. The Mute button is a toggle; click one time for silence, a second time for sound. The Next and Previous buttons move ahead and back one item within the current playlist. Click and hold the Next button to fast-forward through the current track. You can drag the slider in the Seek control to move to a different place within the item that's currently playing. For example, to start the current track over again, you would drag the Seek slider all the way to the left. The time display to the left of the playback controls cycles through three different modes relative to the current track: elapsed time, countdown to the end of the track, and a combination that shows elapsed time and total track time.

TROUBLESHOOTING

Windows Media Player skips when you play a CD

If you get "skippy" performance when playing a CD, the most likely culprit is a damaged or scratched disc. In some cases, you can force the Player to retrieve and play back data (albeit less than perfectly) by using error correction. Open the Options dialog box and then click the Devices tab. Select your CD drive and click Properties. In the Playback section of the Properties dialog box, select Use Error Correction.

The Player plays the current playlist—which might be an album from your library, or a CD, or a selection of tracks you've picked individually—in order, once, unless you turn on Shuffle or Repeat (or both):

- If you turn on Shuffle by pressing Ctrl+H or by choosing Play, Shuffle, the Player moves through the playlist in random order.

- If you turn on Repeat by pressing Ctrl+T or by choosing Play, Repeat, the Player plays the current playlist continuously—that is, it repeats the playlist each time it finishes the final track.

Because the Player generates a different random sequence each time you start the program, the shuffle order will be different each time you play a particular album or playlist or insert a CD. If you repeat the playlist or CD multiple times in a given listening session, you'll shuffle through the tracks in a different sequence each time.

While a CD is playing, use the Now Playing window to enjoy visualizations, album art, or details about the current track as provided by an online music store. You can also see what tracks are coming up in the List pane. If the List pane is not displayed along the Player's right side, click the arrow beneath the Now Playing button and then click Show List pane. When the Now Playing list is visible, you can switch to a different track by double-clicking the track.

TROUBLESHOOTING

Your computer slows down while playing music

Visualizations might have a noticeable impact on system performance on computers with limited resources, especially those with slow CPUs or inadequate video memory. If your other programs slow down while you play a CD or playlist, turn off visualizations: Click the arrow beneath the Now Playing button, click Visualizations, and then click No Visualization from the top of the list.

Playing Audio CDs

Playing an audio CD in Windows Media Player is almost as easy as playing it on any conventional CD player: Insert disc, close drive, enjoy music. The *almost* has to do with your CD (or DVD) drive's AutoPlay settings. As we explained in "Setting Default Programs, File Type Associations, and AutoPlay Options," Chapter 3, you can configure the way Windows responds to the insertion of removable media (including CDs or DVDs). If you have set up your system so that the default AutoPlay action for audio CDs is Windows Media Player, your disc starts playing more or less the moment you insert it (provided it's not busy doing something else).

If you haven't chosen a default AutoPlay action for audio CDs, Windows displays the AutoPlay dialog box shown in Figure 16-2. To set the AutoPlay default and begin playing the CD in one action, leave the Always Do This For Audio CDs box selected and click Play Audio CD Using Windows Media Player.

Figure 16-2 Click the first option to change the default action so that Windows Media Player always begins playing a newly inserted audio CD.

For more details on how to change default AutoPlay settings for specific media types, see "Setting Default Programs, File Type Associations, and AutoPlay Options," Chapter 3.

Chapter 16

What happens when you insert an audio CD and the AutoPlay default is set to Take No Action? That depends:

- If Media Player is open and is not currently playing any content, it will detect the audio CD you just inserted and begin playing it automatically.

- If Media Player is open and is playing a music track or video clip from your library, it will continue playing. Click Stop, switch to the Library tab, and double-click the CD/DVD icon (at or near the bottom of the Navigation Pane) to begin playing your CD.

- If Media Player is not currently running, you'll need to start the Player manually, switch to the Library tab, and double-click the CD/DVD icon.

What happens if you just click Play? In that case, the Player begins playing the first item in the current playlist—which might or might not be your CD. (For more information about playlists, see "Working with Playlists," later in this chapter.) If something other than your CD starts playing, click Stop and double-click the CD/DVD icon in the Navigation Pane.

Viewing Media Information and Album Art

If you're connected to the internet and you've accepted the default settings for Windows Media Player, the Player automatically downloads information about the CD you're currently playing, including the album cover, track names, and information about the artists and composers on the CD. For more information, right-click the album cover and click Find Album Info; this displays the dialog box shown in Figure 16-3. To read a bio of the artist or group and a review of the album, click the Buy CDs link, which opens your default web browser and takes you to a Microsoft-operated shopping site.

Figure 16-3 The Buy CDs link opens a webpage containing detailed information and a review of the CD you're playing.

Details about artists and albums are provided by All Media Guide (AMG) (*http://www.allmediaguide.com*). Windows Media Player uses this information to automatically tag and name tracks you rip to your collection from CD, a topic we discuss in more detail later in this chapter; see "Organizing a Music Collection.")

The algorithm that identifies tracks is truly sophisticated. It actually plays back the track, creates a "fingerprint" for it, and then searches the online database based on that identifier. The result is that the Player is uncannily accurate at finding the correct track. In fact, the fewer details that are available in metadata, the more accurate it's likely to be.

Album art, once retrieved from the internet, is cached on your computer. Thereafter, even if you're no longer online, you can display the album art in the visualization area of Now Playing. To do this, right-click the Now Playing window and click Album Art; or click the arrow beneath Now Playing and then click Album Art on the Visualizations menu. Figure 16-4 shows Now Playing with album art in the visualization area.

Chapter 16

Figure 16-4 The Player's visualization area shows album art that it previously retrieved from the internet, even if you're not currently online.

INSIDE OUT   Add your own album art

What do you do if the Windows Media database doesn't have an album cover for your album? If you can find the correct album art anywhere online, you can add it to the library with just a couple of clicks. Start by locating the album art (ideally at a size that is at least 200 pixels square) at your favorite online music store or fan site. In the browser window, right-click the cover image and copy it to the Clipboard. Now return to the Player, right-click the generic album cover image in the Library tab, and click Paste Album Art. This saves the copied image as a JPEG file in the folder for that album and also caches copies of the JPEG file for individual tracks in an Art Cache subfolder in the %LocalAppData%\Microsoft\Media Player folder.

Building a Digital Music Library

Windows Media Player 11 can handle truly large music collections, consisting of tens of thousands of tracks, thanks to its efficient indexing and search routines. How do you build a library that large? If you already have a CD collection, that's the most logical starting point. You can also download tracks from the internet and share files with friends. In any case, you'll need to pay attention to the details to ensure that your music sounds its best and is stored correctly.

Ripping CDs

Windows Media Player can copy, or *rip*, tracks from audio CDs and store them as files on your hard disk. The copies you make are completely unrestricted: You can listen to the saved tracks on your PC, burn a collection of tracks to a custom CD, or download tracks to a portable player. Before you rip your first CD, however, it's smart to answer the following questions:

- What format do you want to use?
- At what bit rate should you copy?
- Where should your files be stored?
- What naming convention do you want to use?

For a list of music formats supported by Windows Media Player, see "Which File Formats Are Supported?," Chapter 15.

Your answers to the questions in the list above dictate specific settings in Windows Media Player. We discuss each of these settings in more detail in this section. You can adjust settings any time—changing to a different, higher-quality format before ripping a CD you're especially fond of, for instance.

To copy an audio CD to your hard disk using the currently selected file format, naming scheme, and location, click Rip on Windows Media Player's taskbar and then insert the disc. (If the disc is already in the CD drive, just click Rip.) Windows Media Player might begin playing your CD. That's not a problem; the Player can play and copy at the same time.

When you're connected to the internet, Windows Media Player consults its online data sources to determine the name of your disc, as well as the names of the artist(s) and tracks and the genre of music the disc contains. Figure 16-5 shows the Rip tab after Windows Media Player has successfully found all of this information for a newly inserted CD.

Figure 16-5 If your CD is among the nearly 1 million or so in the Windows Media database, album details appear at the left side of the Rip tab, with tracks on the right.

INSIDE OUT   Find a classical music database

The Windows Media online database uses information from a variety of suppliers, including AMG (originally called All Music Guide) and Muze (for UK titles). As of November 2006, AMG's database includes more than 1 million albums and nearly 8 million tracks and is constantly growing. The service is heavily skewed in favor of pop and rock titles and has much less information about classical music CDs. If you want to copy a classical collection to your hard disk, your best bet is to find a third-party CD player that uses an alternative internet service called the Gracenote Media Recognition Service (formerly CDDB). The Gracenote Media Database of classical discs is extensive, and after you have ripped your discs using the other product, you can save the resulting files in a folder monitored by the Player to add them to your library. For more information, visit *http://www.gracenote.com* and search in the Powered By Gracenote section.

By default, Windows Media Player selects the check boxes to the left of all track names when you choose to copy a CD to disk. To copy particular tracks only, clear the check boxes beside tracks that you don't want to copy. To clear or select all the check boxes at once, click the check box in the column heading.

To begin ripping, click Start Rip. Copying begins immediately. Entries in the Rip Status column tell you which tracks are pending, which are being copied, and which have already been ripped to the library. You can do other things in Windows Media Player while this is going on, including listening to an album or playlist from your library.

Windows Media Player copies each CD track to a separate file and stores it, by default, in the Music folder of the currently logged-on user (%UserProfile%\Music). The Player uses the information about each track—the name of the artist, album, and song, for instance—as downloaded from the WindowsMedia.com database and inserts that information into the saved file as metadata. It then uses these details to organize your collection of saved files into a hierarchy, with a folder for each artist and a subfolder for each album by that artist.

In fact, your digital media collection can be drawn from multiple folders. You might keep your favorite tunes—the ones your spouse and kids don't enjoy all that much—in the Music folder in your personal profile and store ripped tunes from CDs you all enjoy in the Public Music folder. Windows Media Player automatically keeps track of where your media files are physically stored and updates your library if you use Windows Explorer to move files after adding them to the library. As a result, you can change your mind about file locations at any time, and you won't have to rebuild your library if you eventually decide to move it to another drive. You should give some consideration in advance to the naming convention that Windows Media Player will use when you rip files (we cover your options in "Deciding How to Name Your Files and Where to Store Them," later in this chapter); however, it's relatively easy to update the names and locations of existing files if you decide that a new naming scheme is more appropriate.

Avoiding copy protection hassles

Copy-protected CDs are still, thankfully, rare. Music publishers have been trying for years to figure out how to keep their customers from making copies of music tracks and giving them to friends or posting them in file-sharing sites for anyone to snag. Unfortunately, most copy protection schemes interfere with your legitimate rights (under the "fair use" doctrine) to make copies for your personal enjoyment or for backup. Today, few commercial CDs are sold with digital rights management of any kind. You can probably thank Sony BMG Music Entertainment, a leading music label and an early pioneer in producing copy-protected CDs, for that state of affairs. In late 2005 and early 2006, Windows expert Mark Russinovich, now a Microsoft employee, discovered that some Sony-produced CDs included software that stealthily installed itself on computers where the CD was played; the software behaved like a rootkit and represented a serious security threat to consumers, Russinovich argued. The resulting uproar and class-action settlement caused Sony to recall virtually all its copy-protected discs, distribute software to remove the rights-management code, and (at least for now) return to producing standard, unrestricted CDs.

Currently, there is no single standard that applies to copy-protected CDs. If you discover that a CD you've purchased doesn't allow you to rip copies, you'll have to read the instructions to find out how the record label expects you to make digital copies and store them on your computer. Or you can check with independent sources to find more creative workarounds, which invariably exist.

Surprisingly, Windows Media Player includes its own copy protection scheme, which allows you to rip tracks in any variation of the Windows Media format to your hard disk that can't be played by anyone without a license. (The copy protection option is not available with the MP3 or WAV formats.) When you rip a track from a CD with copy protection enabled, Windows Media Player adds media usage rights restrictions for each track. You can play these protected files or burn them to a custom CD, as long as you do so on the current computer; the license prevents you from playing the track on another computer or copying it to an SDMI-compliant portable device (such as an MP3 player).

The Windows Media Player copy protection scheme dates back nearly a decade. In early versions of Windows Media Player (including those first included with Windows XP), copy protection was enabled by default. Beginning with Windows Media Player 10, this setting is disabled and must be explicitly enabled before your ripped tracks will be encrypted with media usage rights. For the average music lover, these restrictions serve absolutely no purpose and are an unnecessary hassle. In fact, with Windows Media Player 11, Microsoft has eliminated the capability to back up and restore license rights from copy-protected music files. If you copy the file to another computer or reformat your hard disk and reinstall Windows, you'll be sent to a Microsoft-operated page when you first try to play the protected file on the new PC. You can download a license for the track and begin playing it, but there's a hard limit of 10 license renewals that can be granted; when you hit that number, the track can no longer be transferred to a new computer. We recommend that you leave Windows Media Player configured to copy CDs without copy protection.

To verify that you aren't inadvertently recording copy-protected files, open the Options dialog box, click the Rip Music tab, and make sure Copy Protect Music is cleared. Click Apply or OK to save the setting.

Choosing an Audio Format and Bit Rate

For practical purposes, files copied from audio CDs to your hard disk must be compressed; if you rip tracks to your hard disk using the uncompressed WAV format, a typical 60-minute CD will consume more than half a gigabyte of disk space. Compressing the files means you can store more music on your hard disk, and it makes the process of backing up music files easier and more efficient.

When it comes to compression, your first choice is simple: lossy or lossless? Most popular algorithms used to compress audio (and video) files are *lossy*, which means that they achieve compression by eliminating data. In the case of audio files, the data that's tossed out during the compression process consists mostly of frequencies that humans don't ordinarily hear. However, the more you compress a file, the more likely you are to degrade its audio quality to the point where you'll notice it. Windows Media Player also includes a lossless compressed format, which stores music files more efficiently than uncompressed WAV files, without sacrificing any information. In theory, at least, a track ripped in lossless format should be indistinguishable from the original.

Deciding on the type and amount of compression involves making a trade-off between disk space and audio quality. The level of compression is determined by the bit rate you select for your copied files. Higher bit rates preserve more of the original sound quality of your audio tracks but result in larger files on your hard disk or portable player. Lower bit rates allow you to pack more music into limited space, especially on portable devices with limited storage, at a cost in fidelity.

To express your preferences, click the arrow beneath the Rip button on the Player task-bar. Click Format and choose one of the six available formats; if you choose a format that allows lossy compression, click the Bit Rate option to select from choices available for that format. The following options are available:

- **Windows Media Audio**, which uses fixed bit rates, is the default choice. You can keep the default bit rate of 128 Kbps or choose one of five other settings ranging from 48 Kbps to 192 Kbps.

> ## INSIDE OUT Increase the maximum bit rate for WMA
>
> The maximum rate of 192 Kbps for the Windows Media Audio format is all you can see in the Player's Options dialog box. But you can go higher if you're willing to make a small edit to the registry. (The usual disclaimers apply here: Editing the registry involves risks. Don't do it unless you know what you're doing.) Open Registry Editor (Regedit.exe) and navigate to HKCU\Software\Microsoft\MediaPlayer\Preferences. In the right pane, find the WMARecordRate key and double-click it. Select the Decimal option and enter the bit rate you want to use. To rip WMA tracks at 320 Kbps, for example, enter 320000. Exit Registry Editor and rip away. The Options dialog box will still read 192 Kbps, but your ripped tracks will be stored at the higher rate you entered.

- **Windows Media Audio Pro** is designed for high fidelity output on a very wide range of devices, especially phones and other devices with limited storage capacity. Its default bit rate is 64 Kbps, although you can choose options ranging from 32 Kbps to 192 Kbps. This relatively new format is not supported by all devices, so check compatibility carefully before choosing it.

- **Windows Media Audio (Variable Bit Rate)** allows the encoder to vary the compression applied to portions of a file, depending on the amount of information in it. Using variable bit rate (VBR) can result in files of much higher quality compared to files of similar size created using fixed bit rates. Options on the Bit Rate menu are expressed in ranges, starting with 40 to 75 Kbps and topping out at 240 to 355 Kbps.

- Choose **Windows Media Audio Lossless** if you plan to use Windows Media Player to burn custom CDs that are essentially equal in quality to the music source. This is also your best choice if you want to play tracks on a high-end audio system (including a home theater system connected to Windows Media Center) without compromising quality. Because this format is lossless, no options are available on the Bit Rate menu.

- **MP3** is the longtime standard for digital music files and has nearly universal support. If you want the widest freedom to share, play, and reuse files this is a safe choice. The MP3 format supports variable bit rate encoding, but Microsoft's MP3 codec allows you to rip tracks at fixed bit rates only, in four steps ranging from the default setting of 128 Kbps up to 320 Kbps.

- **WAV (Lossless)** is the correct choice if you want nearly perfect copies of the tracks on a CD and you want those copies to be usable with any burning program. WAV files use nearly twice the space as Windows Media Audio Lossless files and cannot be streamed as easily as compressed formats, making them unsuitable for for all but temporary storage.

INSIDE OUT   Make a perfect copy of a CD track

If you right-click the icon for an audio CD and choose Explore from the shortcut menu, you'll see that each track is listed as a small file with the file type CD Audio Track, the .cda extension, and a date and time stamp of December 31, 1994, at 5:00 PM. Most of that information is completely wrong and represents a confused attempt by Windows Explorer to make sense of a format it wasn't designed to read.

CD Audio is not a file format; instead, these pointers serve as shortcuts to the actual files, which are stored in a format that is essentially identical to a WAV file. You can't copy a CD track directly to your hard drive from Windows Explorer, and the default Rip options compress the resulting file so that it loses some quality. Using Windows Media Player 11, you can rip a track using the WAV (Lossless) format or specify the Windows Media Audio Lossless format which produces a file that is smaller than a WAV file but still quite large. Either format will work if your goal is to create a nearly identical copy of a CD using burning software. The WAV format is certain to work with all third-party CD-burning programs, unlike Windows Media Audio Lossless.

Notice we said "a *nearly* identical copy." The process of ripping a track from a CD is not perfect, especially if the media is scratched. Tiny errors caused by the mechanical operation of the drive components—a single bit here and a couple of bits there—will inevitably creep in when you rip a file. Similar errors can result when you use the "copy CD" option available in most commercial CD-burning software. These errors are mostly imperceptible to the human ear, but if you repeat the rip/mix/burn cycle several times the errors can add up and create a click, pop, or other noticeable glitch during playback. Perfectionists who want to make a perfect copy of a single music track or an entire CD need to take special precautions to prevent these errors from occurring. For these tasks, we recommend Exact Audio Copy, written by Andre Wiethoff and available for download from *http://www.exactaudiocopy.de*; this highly regarded program can reliably extract every bit of digital information from the disc, without allowing any data to be lost.

Most of the options available on the Rip menu are also available in a slightly different arrangement on the Rip Music tab of the Options dialog box. Instead of choosing the Bit Rate from a menu, you use the Audio Quality slider, shown in Figure 16-6, to select a bit rate. Moving the slider to the left produces smaller files with lower quality; moving it to the right produces larger files with better audio quality.

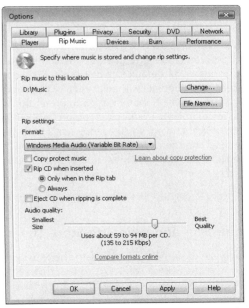

Figure 16-6 The Rip Settings section of this dialog box duplicates choices available from the Rip menu on the Player taskbar.

MP3 or WMA?

The WMA format supported by Windows Media Player achieves audio quality equivalent to that of the original MP3 standard, at higher compression rates. According to Microsoft, a CD track encoded with WMA generally uses no more than half the disk space of an MP3 file of comparable quality. (In some cases, the size of the WMA file is closer to one-third the size of the equivalent MP3.)

The Compare Formats Online link on the Rip Music tab in the Options dialog box, shown previously in Figure 16-5, brings you to a website where you can read Microsoft's official estimation of the relative strengths and weaknesses of MP3 and WMA. (Third-party analyses of the two formats typically find a smaller difference between the two formats.)

Which format is best for you? It depends on how big your disk is (and how many CDs you intend to copy), how much you care about preserving the full spectrum of sound recorded on your CD, the quality and capabilities of your playback equipment, and how you intend to use the ripped tracks. Among Windows Media formats, WMA Lossless offers the best quality, but at a potentially prohibitive cost in disk usage. The WMA VBR format offers higher quality than fixed bit rates, but some portable devices and external media players designed to connect to home audio systems don't support these formats. If you intend to copy the tracks to a portable music device with limited storage, choosing a lower bit rate means you can pack more songs onto the device; however, as we explain in "Synchronizing and Sharing Media with Portable Devices" (Chapter 15), Windows Media

Player can perform this conversion on the fly when synchronizing with a portable device, allowing you to keep higher-quality copies on your computer.

Thankfully, hard disk storage is no longer the limiting factor for digital music collections that it once was, making higher bit rates (and higher file sizes) much more palatable. For most users who care about music, the WMA default rate of 128 Kbps is the minimum acceptable choice. If you're a discerning audiophile with high-quality playback equipment, you will almost certainly want to choose a higher bit rate. If you prefer the MP3 format, we recommend a minimum bit rate of at least 192 Kbps; if you prefer the efficiency and audio quality of variable bit-rate MP3 encoding, you'll need to use a third-party product that supports this encoding method and then add the tracks to the library. To determine your own minimum acceptable audio quality, you'll need to perform comparative tests using your own ears and speakers.

Deciding How to Name Your Files and Where to Store Them

By default, Windows Media Player saves ripped CD tracks in the Music folder within your user profile. If you decide you want ripped tracks to go to a different location, click the arrow beneath the Rip button and choose More Options. On the Rip Music tab of the Options dialog box, click Change. This capability is especially useful if you share a home computer with other family members and want everyone to have access to the same music library. In this case, specify that you want ripped tracks to be stored in the Public Music folder instead.

If you are online when you copy a CD, Windows Media Player connects to the Windows Media online database and gets whatever information is available about that CD. Typically, this information includes the name of the album and the songs it contains, the names of performers and composers, information about musical genres, and album art. Windows Media Player uses some of this information to create file names for your copied CD tracks. (All of the information Media Player gets from this online repository of information can be used in one way or another, even if it doesn't become part of your file names. The album art, for example, appears in the Library tab, in the Now Playing list when you play tunes from that album, and in Windows Explorer when you use Thumbnails view.)

By default, the file names for your tracks are made up of the track number, followed by a space character, followed by the song title (which probably includes spaces). Such a file name might look like this: 09 Tell Me All The Things You Do.wma.

Because the library uses metadata to sort, group, and display items in your collection, it's not vital that you include a lot of detail in the actual file name. Using the track number as the beginning of the file name ensures that the tracks on an album always sort correctly within their folder, even when you copy that folder to another drive, device, or media-playing program. However, if you copy a group of songs to a portable player that doesn't use subfolders, that device may display and sort by only the file name. Therefore, when you choose a file-naming convention in Windows Media Player, give some thought to how your files will work in your portable device. In that context, if you want to keep all songs from a given artist or album together, the most important information is probably the artist or album name, followed by the track number.

INSIDE OUT   **Avoid generic file names**

If Windows Media Player cannot connect to the internet to identify your CD tracks by accessing the Windows Media online database, it uses generic names such as Unknown Album, Unknown Artist, and Track 1. To keep your files recognizable in Windows Explorer and Windows Media Player's Library, do not accept these generic names. Edit the track information *before* Windows Media Player begins copying tracks and creating disk files. If you've already ripped some tracks with these generic names, you can update the album information to add album art, album title, and track details; you can then rename and rearrange the files using the downloaded media information. See "Organizing a Music Collection," later in this chapter, for more details.

In any event, you can tell Media Player how you want your files named as follows:

1. Click the arrow beneath the Rip button on the Player Taskbar to open the Options dialog box with the Rip Music tab selected.

2. Click File Name to open the File Name Options dialog box.

3. Select the check boxes for the information categories that you want to include in your file names, and clear the other check boxes. As you adjust your choices here and in the following two steps, the example in the Preview area of the dialog box shows you the effect on file names..

4. If desired, use the Move Up and Move Down buttons to change the order in which name elements appear.

5. Use the Separator menu to choose the character that appears between elements of a track name, if you don't want to use spaces. You can choose dashes, dots, underlines, or no separator character at all.

6. Click OK.

Downloading Tracks

Tracks you download from the internet can come from a variety of sources:

- Some artists and record labels make unrestricted copies of songs available for download as samples through their own websites or through partners. Typically, these downloads are available in MP3 format with no technical restrictions on their use.

- Some artists expressly permit online distribution of their music, especially live performances. You can find archives of these freely downloadable files, usually in MP3, FLAC, or SHN format, at sites like the Live Music Archive run by Etree.org. (For more details, visit *http://www.vista-io.com/1601*.)

- You can also purchase the rights to download songs from online stores. Although a small number of independent stores sell unrestricted tracks in MP3 format (most notably the excellent Emusic.com), most such stores limit your usage rights with some form of digital rights management. If you download tracks from a source such as the Apple iTunes Store, whose copy-protection scheme is not compatible with Windows Media Player, you'll need to listen to those tracks in a different player or find a way to convert them to a compatible format. The most common workaround is to burn the downloaded tracks to a CD and then rip that CD into unprotected tracks.

Regardless of where you download music files from, you'll need to pay special attention to file names and to metadata saved as part of the track. If you find errors or inconsistencies—or if you just want to make sure the downloaded tracks follow the same standards you've chosen for your library—you might need to manually edit the saved metadata and rename tracks.

Sharing Files

As we noted in Chapter 15, Windows Vista makes it possible for you to share your library with other computers on your network. It does not include any tools for sharing files over the internet. If you decide to install a third-party program to enable so-called peer-to-peer file sharing for your music collection, we recommend that you pay close attention to security and copyright issues.

Peer-to-peer sharing networks are notorious for delivering more than you bargained for, in the form of music and video files that include hostile code—viruses, Trojan horse programs, and spyware. Don't assume that a file is innocent because it appears to be a media file; be alert for unexpected security warnings and keep your antivirus and anti-spyware programs up to date.

Violating copyright restrictions can lead to unpleasant consequences as well. Music industry associations have filed high-profile lawsuits against ordinary consumers who participate in file-sharing networks; even if you win such a lawsuit, the costs of a legal defense can be crushing. On the issue of file sharing, we don't offer any legal or moral guidance, but we do recommend that you understand what the risks are before you decide to make your music collection available to strangers.

Organizing a Music Collection

Regardless of the source of your music files, errors and inconsistencies are bound to creep in to your library. Simple misspellings of track names are probably the most common error, but other problems can occur, too: Variations in the spelling or styling of an artist's name can result in that artist's work being filed in two different places.

The good news with Windows Media Player 11 is that it's relatively simple to fix tagging errors anytime, without having to jump through too many hoops. In this section, we explore how to fix the most common errors. After you whip the metadata into shape, you can turn your attention to more esoteric aspects of your music collection. We cover the full spectrum of organizational tools and techniques in this section.

How and where is metadata stored?

All editable data that appears in your library is stored as metadata within your media files. In addition, some information that is specific to your collection is stored in the library index—details about the play count for a specific track, for instance, or when the track was added to the library. When you edit details about a track in the library, such as the name of a song or an artist, Windows Media Player rewrites the information in the underlying file. (To change file names, you need to work in Windows Explorer.) For music files, Windows Media Player can read and write these details by way of tags stored directly in the file, using one of the following three formats:

- **ID3v1**   This relatively old format is still in wide use for MP3 files. It consists of six fields, each of fixed size, stored in 128 bytes at the end of the file. Windows Media Player can read ID3v1 tags but does not write them.

- **ID3v2**   Modern media players that use the MP3 format typically store metadata using these tags, which can contain dozens of fields, each holding an unlimited

number of characters. Because these tags are often used to help identify streaming media, they are stored at the beginning of the media file. If you edit the details
associated with an MP3 file in Windows Media Player, it writes the data to the file
using this type of tag.

- **WMA** These tags are the native format used for Windows Media Audio files.
  The metadata is stored at the beginning of the file, and the format is functionally
  equivalent to ID3v2 tags.

When you import files into Windows Media Player, the data stored in these tags is used
to populate the fields in the library. When you edit details of a track in your library,
Windows Media Player writes the information back to the file containing that track, using
either an ID3v2 or WMA tag. This change is permanent. The Player continually scans for
changes to metadata within files. If you use an external tag editor or Windows Explorer
to change information stored in a WMA or MP3 file, the changes are reflected in your
Library the next time you open it, usually within a few minutes.

INSIDE OUT   Expand your search for artists

Windows Media Player contains two fields where you can enter information about the
artists on a CD. The Album Artist field is used to group individual tracks for a single album and is the one used for the Artist field in the Navigation Pane. The Contributing Artist field allows you to highlight performers on individual tracks. On a compilation CD, for
instance, enter Various Artists in the Album Artist field, and then enter the names of individual performers in the Artist field for each track, separating multiple artists with semi-
colons. On an album that consists of duets with a star artist and various guests, enter the
star's name in the Album Artist field. In the Navigation Pane, click Contributing Artist (if
this view isn't visible, right-click Library and choose Show More Views) and then use the
Search box to find tracks where a favorite performer is a guest; the search will return results for any track where that artist's name is listed in the Contributing Artist field.

What to Do If Windows Media Doesn't Recognize Your Disc

If the Windows Media online database doesn't recognize your disc or if you don't have
an internet connection to retrieve the information, Windows Media Player proposes to
use generic information in the library and in the ripped files. If you agree to this, the
ripped tracks are named by their order on the disc (Track 1, Track 2, and so on), the
Album Artist field is identified as Unknown Artist, and the Album and Genre fields
are left blank. Windows Media Player creates a new folder called Unknown Artist (if it
doesn't already exist), and then creates a subfolder in that location using the current
date and time as part of the folder name—*Unknown Album (11-17-2006 8-26-52 AM)*, for

instance. The ripped files are saved in that new folder. Figure 16-7 shows what the Rip tab looks like while you're copying tracks to CD.

Figure 16-7 If the Windows Media database doesn't contain information for your CD (or if you can't connect to the internet), your ripped tracks end up with generic names.

If you accept the generic names, your music will sound fine, but you'll have a hard time finding your way back to it, either in Windows Media Player or in Windows Explorer. In Windows Explorer, your file and folder names will be a jumble of Unknowns.

If Windows Media Player can't supply the usual information, you can add it manually before you copy, or you can go ahead and worry about track names and metadata later. If you're unable to connect to the internet to download album information but you're reasonably certain that the CD you're about to copy is in the WindowsMedia.com database, rip away. Windows Media Player will replace the generic information automatically the next time you connect to the internet. However, if the CD is a custom mix, or if it was created by an obscure artist or record label and isn't in the online database, consider entering the album and track information now, before you start ripping (see the next section for details). This will save you a step or two later. If you're pressed for time, though, don't worry—you can update the information later without a lot of hassle.

And what about those not-so-helpful generic file and folder names? You can use the techniques we describe later in this chapter to have Windows Media Player rename the ripped files automatically. (See "Renaming Ripped Files," later in this chapter, for details.)

INSIDE OUT **Double-check the database**

If you have access to an internet connection and you suspect that your CD is actually in the database, try searching for it from this screen before you enter information manually. Right-click the generic album cover icon in the Rip tab and click Find Album Info. In the How Do You Want to Search? box, select Artist or Album, enter a portion of the artist or album name in the respective box, and then click Next. Follow the prompts to narrow down the Results list to the correct album. If track information appears, review the track listings to be sure they're correct. If no track information appears or if you notice any errors, click the Edit button, enter the correct track names and other details, and click Finish. If you're unable to find a match, select The Artist (or Album) I'm Looking For Is Not Here, click Next, and continue with the steps we list in the next section.

Fixing Minor Errors in Album and Track Information

If the Windows Media online database recognizes your disc but doesn't have all the track names and album details the way you want to see them in your Library, you can edit any of the incorrect information directly. You can do this in the Rip tab (if you're tackling this task before ripping a CD) or in the Library tab, if you've already added the tracks. Right-click the Album, Album Artist, Genre, or Release Date fields on the left side of the Rip tab and click Edit to change these details for all tracks. Right-click the Title, Contributing Artist, or Composer tracks in the track list and choose Edit (or select the track name and press F2) to edit these details for individual tracks.

While you're editing, you can move from column to column by pressing Tab or Shift+Tab, and move from row to row by pressing Up Arrow or Down Arrow.

If you want to change the Contributing Artist or Composer information for a group of track or an entire album, select all of the rows first (click the first entry and then Shift+click the last entry, or press Ctrl+A to select all items in the currently visible list). Then right-click and choose Edit. Move to the column you want to edit by pressing Tab or Shift+Tab, make the edit in one row, and then press Enter to duplicate the edit to the entire column.

> **Note**
>
> The Rating and Track Number fields cannot be edited until you have actually added the tracks to your Library. The Length field is always determined by the file itself and can never be manually edited.

Manually Adding Details for an Album

If you've already ripped one or more tracks using generic file and folder names, the first thing you should do before editing these details manually is to check the Windows Media database. If the track information hasn't already been updated for you, right-click the album title (Unknown) in the Media Library and choose Update Album Info. If this isn't successful, you'll need to edit the track information manually. Before you begin the following procedure, decide whether you want the associated files to be renamed automatically, based on the information you enter. If the answer is yes, skip ahead to the next section and adjust the options for renaming and organizing files before continuing.

If you're ripping tracks from a custom CD, or if you've determined that the Windows Media database doesn't contain details for the CD you're ripping, you can open a convenient form that allows you to enter album and track information manually. You can do this before or after ripping a CD.

Follow these steps:

1. Right-click the generic album icon in the Rip tab or in the Library tab and click Find Album Info.

2. In the How Do You Want to Search? box, choose Enter Information For a CD That You Burned, and then click Next.

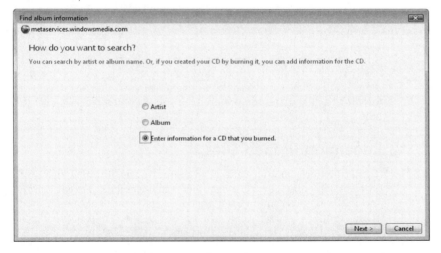

3. Fill in the Edit Album Information form, shown in Figure 16-8 on the next page. At a minimum, you must enter text in the Album and Artist fields and fill in the Title field for each track. The drop-down list to the right of the Album field allows you to choose one of the predefined genres. If you're entering information for a compilation CD with tracks by several artists, choose the Various Artists heading from the drop-down list to the right of the Artist field. Click the Performer and Composer headings to make either column available for editing. Click Next to continue.

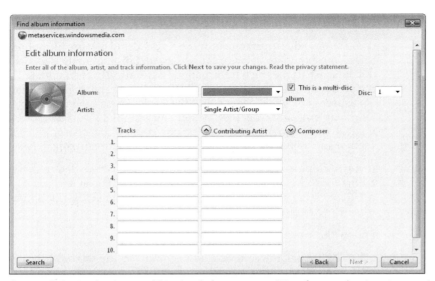

Figure 16-8 Use this form to fill in details for a custom CD or for one that is not recognized in the Windows Media database.

4. Review the information you have entered. If you see any errors or omissions, click Back and repeat Step 3. When you're satisfied with the information entered, click Finish.

If the album was already in your library, you're done. If you've added these details for a newly inserted CD, click Start Rip to begin copying the tracks to your hard disk. Windows Media Player will use the information you entered when it creates the file names for your tracks, using the preferences you set on the Rip Music tab of the Options dialog box.

Renaming Ripped Files

If you diligently clean up and then maintain the album, artist, and track information for tracks in your Library, it becomes a masterpiece of organization—but the original file and folder names remain unchanged. Even if you're not concerned about all filenames being completely consistent, you'll probably want to rename files if you ripped the tunes originally using generic tags (Unknown Artist, Unknown Album), or if you downloaded the track from a source that used cryptic filenames rather than informative ones.

By adjusting two settings, you can tell Windows Media Player to rename ripped files and move them to new folders based on the information in the library. These options are disabled in a default installation. To turn them on, click the arrow beneath the Now Playing button and then click More Options. On the Library tab, select one or both of the following options:

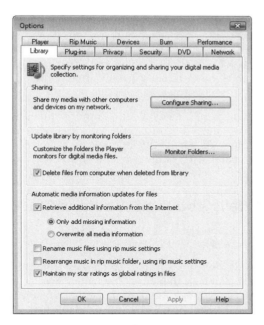

- **Rename Music Files Using Rip Music Settings**   This option renames each individual file, using the current tags and the settings defined in the File Name Options dialog box under Rip Music. It is effective whether you update track information automatically from the WindowsMedia.com database or enter track information manually.

- **Rearrange Music In Rip Music Folder, Using Rip Music Settings**   This option creates new folders and subfolders in the Music folder, using the artist and album information downloaded from the WindowsMedia.com database, and then moves those files as needed. It does not work when you edit track information manually.

When you select these two checkboxes, existing file names remain intact until one of the following events take place:

- Windows Media Player automatically updates information for an existing album or track. If you've ripped a CD using generic file and folder names while disconnected from the internet, each file will be renamed and, if necessary, moved to a new folder as soon as you reconnect and download the correct album details.

- You manually edit information for an album or track. If you change the name of an artist *and* the artist name is part of your file naming settings *and* the Rename Music Files Using Rip Settings option is selected, all tracks associated with that album will be renamed immediately.

How do you force the Player to rename all tracks in your library? After adjusting the settings in the File Name section of the Rip Music tab and enabling either or both of the rename/rearrange options, click the Library tab on the Options dialog box, click Monitor Folders, and immediately click OK without making any changes. This action forces the Player to rescan all folders that contain tracks in your library and will rename and reorganize files to match your current settings.

If you select the Rearrange Music In Rip Music Folder, Using Rip Music Settings option, any change to an artist or album name will result in the tracks associated with that artist or album moving to a new folder. As part of this operation, the Player does not delete the now-empty folder for the original artist or album name. If you're a fanatic about neatness, you'll need to locate and delete these empty folders manually.

Adding Additional Details About an Album or Track

The details visible in the default Library views barely scratch the surface of what types of metadata you can store and access using Windows Media Player.

In any view, you can right-click a column heading, click Choose Columns, and select from a list of columns that are available in that view. For some views, such as Artist and Album views, this list is strictly limited. But in other contexts, such as Songs view or Recently Added, you can choose from the entire list of available tags, as shown in Figure 16-9.

Figure 16-9 In some (but not all) views, you can customize the display to view and edit additional details about the current selection.

Some bits of metadata in these additional columns are editable, others are not. For instance, you can view but not change the values stored in the Protected, Bit Rate, and

Date Added columns. But you can edit values in the Subgenre and Mood fields. You can also fill in a free-form Keywords field or use one or both Custom columns.

What's the best use for these custom fields? Use the data contained there to create Auto Playlists for slicing and dicing your music collection. For example, if you have a basic subscription to a rental service such as MTV URGE that doesn't allow you to copy down-loaded tracks to a portable device, you can create a playlist using the criteria Protection Is Not Present and then use that playlist as the basis for synchronizing your device.

An alternative tool for editing these additional tags is the Advanced Tag Editor, which exposes all the tags in your library for editing. You can edit a single file or a group of files, or work through your entire library to add details missing from your collection. To use this tool, select one or more files from the library (you can use the Search box for this task as well), right-click, and choose Advanced Tag Editor. As Figure 16-10 shows, this utility organizes all available tags into a set of five tabs.

Figure 16-10 Use the Advanced Tag Editor to add and edit details that can't easily be changed in the Library itself, such as Beats Per Minute or Key (both useful for DJs).

For music files, the Track Info and Artist Info tabs contain all standard tags. Select a single track, change the value in a field, and then click Apply (to save the changes and continue editing tags) or OK (to save your changes and close Advanced Tag Editor).

CAUTION

Advanced Tag Editor doesn't include an undo feature. If you make a mistake when editing tag information, those changes become part of the underlying files. Before doing any serious tag editing, we strongly recommend that you back up your music collection.

Chapter 16

If you select multiple tracks, the interface changes slightly. By default, all fields are unavailable for editing. This is a safety precaution, designed to prevent you from inadvertently renaming a group of tracks with a title you intended to apply to just one. To enable editing for fields that typically are identical for an entire group (such as Genre, Album, or Album Artist), select the check box to the left of the field you want to edit. Make your change and click Apply or OK; the new value you entered replaces the existing contents of that field for all selected tracks.

> **Note**
>
> The combination of basic tag editing functions in the Player window and the Advanced Tag Editor is powerful enough for all but the most obsessive music fans. It's far from perfect, however. For instance, you can't use any built-in tools to search and replace values in a library (useful when you've misspelled an artist's name). Although you can edit the Track Number field, you can't automatically renumber tracks based on the order in your playlist. You can't manually rename files based on tag information, nor can you extract tag information from the names of downloaded files. And you'll be unable to edit files in formats other than MP3 and WMA, such as OGG or AAC. If you want those features and many more, we recommend an inexpensive third-party utility called eMusic Tag Editor, available from AbyssAudio at *http://www.abyssaudio.com*. It uses an easy, Explorer-style interface and supports virtually any type of music file. For serious music collectors, it's a must-have, if only for its undo/redo capability!

You can also edit metadata directly in Windows Explorer. For more details, see "Using Windows Explorer with Media Files," Chapter 15.

Using Ratings

Every music track in your library has a star rating, assigned on a scale of 1 star (lowest) to 5 stars (highest). Auto ratings are assigned by default and appear in the Rating column with a soft blue tint over the stars. Ratings you assign explicitly appear in gold. By default, all new tracks are Auto Rated at 3 stars; tracks in WMA format that are listed in the WindowsMedia.com database are auto-rated using values from that source. When you first play a track, its Auto Rating increases to 4 stars. (The rating goes up only if you play all the way through a track; if you click the Next button while a track is playing, Windows Media Player assumes you did so because you didn't like the selection.)

If you choose to do so, you can assign ratings to tracks, one at a time or in groups. To adjust a rating, switch to the Library tab, select one or more tracks, choose Rate, and pick a rating from the list. You can also assign a rating by pointing to the Rating column for a track and choosing the correct number of stars. As soon as you assign a rating, Windows Media Player stops using Auto Rating for that track. (To completely remove a rating you've assigned, choose Unrated. In this case, the track will once again have an Auto Rating of 3 stars.)

The Rated Songs category in the Library's Navigation Pane allows you to sort your Library by user rating (or to see all tracks that you have not yet rated).

Adding Lyrics and Other Details

You can add lyrics to a song's metadata and then display those lyrics in the Now Playing window as you play the song. Start by right-clicking a song's entry in the Library tab or in the List Pane. Choose Advanced Tag Editor from the shortcut menu and then click the Lyrics tab. Enter or paste the lyrics in the text box provided.

If you want the lyrics to appear karaoke-style, synchronized with music tracks, select the group of lyrics and click the Synchronized Lyrics button. Click Play to hear the song; in the window at the bottom of the dialog box, drag the indicators for each line so that they appear at the appropriate time.

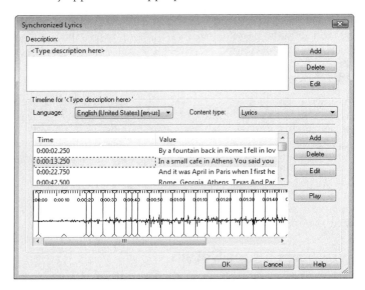

To display the song's lyrics in Now Playing while you play it back, choose View, Now Playing Tools, Lyrics. You can add both static and synchronized lyrics to a file. Static lyrics appear in the Now Playing window in Info Center view when you begin playing the file. Synchronized lyrics take over when you reach the defined markers. (You don't have to enter lyrics in this space. You can synchronize the playback of a song with web-pages, trivia questions, or choreography instructions; just change the Content Type list to reflect your changes.)

Likewise, use the Pictures tab in Advanced Tag Editor to insert your own pictures into a ripped file. You can add an unlimited number of pictures to a WMA or MP3 file. These can also be viewed in the Now Playing window.

Working with Playlists

A *playlist* is a customized list of digital media files that Windows Media Player can play back as a unit, in either linear or random order. If you want to combine tracks from multiple albums or rearrange the order of tracks on a CD, you use a playlist. Windows Media Player 11 supports three distinct uses for playlists: Now Playing lists are for play-back, Burn lists are for creating custom CDs, and Sync lists are for synchronizing files with a portable device.

You can build a playlist on the fly for a specific purpose—to play some files or burn a CD, for example. After the task is done, you can clear the list or save it for reuse. Saved lists are stored by default in the Playlists folder. You can also create and save Auto Playlists, which are essentially saved searches whose results are updated automatically each time you open them..

Creating and Editing Custom Playlists

The current playlist appears in the List pane at the right of the Player window. (If the List pane isn't visible in the Library window, click the arrow beneath Now Playing on the Player Taskbar and then click Show List Pane; this menu choice is a toggle that you can also use to hide the List pane if it's currently showing.) Use the Navigation bar, the Search box, or another Playlist to choose which tracks you want to include, and then use any of the following techniques to create a custom playlist:

- Drag individual songs, albums, or artists from anywhere in the Library tab and drop them in the List pane.

- Select one or more tracks, albums, or artists, right-click, click Add To, and then click Now Playing. If you click Burn or Sync on the Player Taskbar first, the shortcut menu includes Add To Burn List or Add To Sync List options as well.

- Double-click any album or existing playlist. Its contents appear in the Now Playing list in the List pane, where you can add or remove tracks or rearrange the order of tracks on the album.

- Select one or more tracks in Windows Explorer, right-click, and click Add To Windows Media Player List on the shortcut menu. Click the Play or Burn buttons in the Command bar to add the selected tracks to the Now Playing or Burn lists, respectively.

Regardless of which of the above methods you use, your selections appear in the List pane at the right of the Library tab. You can drag items up and down in the list to change their order. Use the drop-down menu above the list contents (see Figure 16-11) to clear the current list, sort items by artist or other criteria, randomly shuffle the list, or save the playlist as a file. The Red X to the right of this menu clears the list contents immediately, with no warning.

Chapter 16

Figure 16-11 Use this drop-down menu to sort, shuffle, or save the current playlist. Clear the list to start over.

Saved playlists appear at the top of the Navigation pane. By default, the Playlists section of the Navigation pane shows only the most recently used playlists. Click the Playlists heading to see all saved playlists in the contents pane, or right-click the Playlists heading and select Show All to see all saved playlists in the Navigation pane. (Click the Show All option again to toggle back to the shorter list.)

When you select a playlist from the Navigation pane, the items that make up the list appear in the contents pane, where you can edit the properties of individual items or assign star ratings. Playlists display in Details view only. In this view, you can right-click and use the Remove From List option on the shortcut menu to winnow the list down, and you can sort by any heading. To manually change the order of items in the playlist or save the playlist under a new name, click the Edit In List Pane button at the bottom of the contents pane. To stop editing in the List pane and return to the full view in the contents pane, click Clear List from the menu at the top of the List pane.

Change the playlist order—permanently

The only way to permanently customize the order of items in a playlist is to save it as a custom playlist, using the same name or a different one. For instance, you might have copied a CD to your disk, in which case the track numbers define the order in which songs on that album are played. Or you might have created an Auto Playlist that finds tracks from your three favorite female vocalists that you've rated with 4 or 5 stars. If you want to play the tracks in a sequence that can't be set by sorting a column in Details view, define your preferred custom order by following these steps:

1. Make sure the Now Playing list is empty. If it's not, click Clear List on the menu above the List pane.

2. Right-click the album, playlist, or artist in the contents pane and choose Add To Now Playing Playlist.

3. In the List pane, drag individual tracks up or down in the list. To remove items from the playlist, right-click the item in the List pane and click Remove From List.

4. Click Save List As from the menu above the List pane and give the new playlist a name.

Your custom list will contain the same tracks as the original, but you can now always play back your list in your custom order, and you can rearrange the order whenever you like.

Using Auto Playlists

Playlists you create using Windows Media Player 10 or 11 can retrieve results dynamically, based on criteria you define. Unlike static playlists, which capture a list of specific tracks in the exact order you specify, Auto Playlists are saved searches that return different results depending on the current contents of your library. These saved searches let you zero in on tracks that you've added recently but not yet rated, for instance, or on tracks from a specific genre that you've rated highly. Details of each Auto Playlist you create are stored in an XML file stored in the Playlists subfolder in your Music folder. Copy that file to another computer and the Auto Playlist will be available on that computer as well.

Note

If you upgraded from Windows XP, your collection includes a group of preset Auto Playlists, all of which are stored in the My Playlists folder. Windows Media Player seamlessly combines the contents of these two lists in the library. In fact, selecting Playlists from the Navigation pane shows all saved playlists from any folder in any monitored location.

Chapter 16

To get started, right-click the Playlists heading and click Create Auto Playlist. Enter a name in the box at the top of the New Auto Playlist dialog box and then begin clicking to add criteria to your Search. Start with the first green plus sign and use drop-down lists to define criteria. In the example shown in Figure 16-12, we've created an Auto Playlist that includes songs that are performed by a trio of talented folk-rock artists and are all rated 4 stars or better.

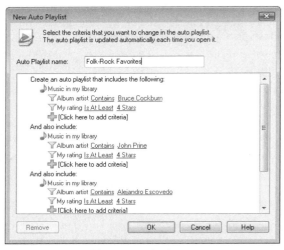

Figure 16-12 Build an Auto Playlist one criterion at a time. Enter each criterion in its own branch and click OK to save.

Note when creating an Auto Playlist that all criteria within a single group must be satisfied for the Player to add matching items to the playlist results. When you create different groups of criteria, the Player combines them with a logical OR. Thus, any track that matches all the criteria within any one group gets added to the list. The group of criteria at the bottom of the Auto Playlist window allows you to restrict the playlist itself to a maximum size, number of items, or playing time.

TROUBLESHOOTING

The filename for an Auto Playlist doesn't match its display name

When you create an Auto Playlist, the text you enter in the Auto Playlist Name box is used in two places. The playlist title appears between the <title> and </title> tags in the XML file that contains the Auto Playlist definition. The Player also uses that text as the filename that gets saved into the Playlists folder. When you right-click the saved Auto Playlist and click Edit, you can change the name in the Edit Auto Playlist dialog box, but that change is only written to the XML file; the filename remains the same. To rename the file itself, right-click the Auto Playlist name and click Open File Location; then rename the file in Windows Explorer.

Importing and Exporting Playlists

As noted in the previous section, playlists are saved by default in files within the Playlists subfolder of the Music folder in your profile. When saving a custom list, you have your choice of several file formats. The default is a file in Windows Media Playlist format, with a .wpl extension. If you suspect you'll play your playlists on a different device or in a program that doesn't support this format, you may need to choose an alternate format, such as an M3U playlist (.m3u). Check the documentation for the other program or device to see what playlist formats it supports.

Windows Media Playlist files use XML tags to specify the file name of each track in the list. Additional information (genre, artist, and so on) are drawn from the Library database using the Globally Unique IDs—the two long alphanumeric strings—that define each track's entry in the WindowsMedia.com database. Note that this playlist format uses relative path references for each track. If you copy the playlist and the files to a CD and play it back on another computer, it should work just fine, even when the current CD drive has been assigned a different letter than on the computer where the playlist was created.

By contrast, older playlist formats such as M3U Playlist (.m3u) use fixed file paths. When you move an M3U playlist to a new computer, Windows Media Player may have trouble locating the files you're trying to play if they're in a different location than they were on the other machine.

Windows Media Player can also import playlists in a wide variety of formats, including formats created by other media programs. Click Open on the File menu and, in the Open dialog box, use the Files Of Type list to specify Media Playlist and then choose the playlist file you want to import. Note that you can choose searches you created and saved from Windows Explorer as well as more conventional playlist formats.

> **Note**
>
> All playlist formats are text files. The Windows Media Playlist format uses XML tags to save your selections. You can open any saved playlist (including Auto Playlists) in a text editor to verify its contents, as shown on the next page.

Chapter 16

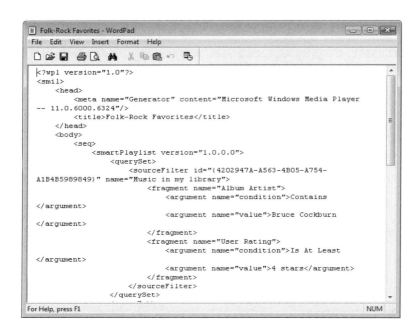

Burning Custom CDs or DVDs

If you have a CD or DVD burner, Windows Media Player can use it to burn a custom selection of songs. You don't need to use Windows Explorer or a third-party CD- or DVD-burning program to do this (although you may choose to use a more powerful program for a variety of reasons, as we explain later in this section).

To start, insert a blank CD or DVD in the drive and click Burn in the Player taskbar. Use the Navigation pane or the Search box to filter the display in the contents pane. Then drag songs, albums, playlists, or artists to the List pane. You'll see a display comparable to the one shown in Figure 16-13.

Figure 16-13 The box above the Burn List keeps a running total of tracks in your list and marks where one disk ends and the next begins.

The Player notes the space available on the blank disc and tallies up the elapsed time of all the tracks you've added to the Burn List. If the total is greater than the capacity of the blank disc, it adds Next Disc markers at the break points. Note the total time figure at the top of the List pane and the remaining time for the last disc at the bottom of the same box. You can accept the disc breaks as defined or edit the playlist. A blue icon to the left of any track indicates that the track contains restricted media usage rights that don't allow burning.

By default, Windows Media Players assumes you want to burn an audio CD that can be played back in most home or car CD players. If you would rather burn a data disk consisting of compressed files, click the arrow beneath the Burn button on the Player taskbar and choose Data CD or DVD from the drop-down list.

Finally, decide whether you want the Player to automatically adjust audio levels for tracks on your custom CD. This option is useful for mix CDs, where the content is drawn from a variety of sources and volume levels may vary widely. Disable this option if you're burning tracks from a single source and you want to maintain their fidelity. To check and change this setting, click the arrow beneath the Burn button and select or clear the Apply Volume Leveling Across Tracks On Audio CDs option.

When you're ready to copy, click the Start Burn button at the bottom of the Burn List. The burning process takes a little while. Windows Media Player first checks each track to make sure that its media usage rights (if any) permit copying. Then it converts each file in turn to a temporary WAV audio file. Because WAV files are uncompressed, you might need as much as 1 GB of temporary storage to accommodate this process. By default, Windows Media Player uses the drive on which Windows is installed. If you don't have enough room there, open the Options dialog box and then click the Advanced button. In the File Conversion Options dialog box, shown in Figure 16-14, select a different location and, if necessary, adjust the space set aside for the Transcoded Files Cache.

Figure 16-14 The File Conversion Options dialog box lets you specify the disk used for temporary storage while Windows Media Player burns CDs and video files.

INSIDE OUT   Don't make the cache too small

You might be tempted to dial the Transcoded Files Cache back to about 1GB or so. That strategy is probably safe if all you ever plan to do is burn music CDs. But this same location is used when you transfer movie clips or recorded TV shows to a portable device or burn them to a DVD, and if you change this setting now you could run into problems later. Our advice? Don't change this value unless you're desperately short of disk space and an upgraded hard disk is not an option.

Finally, after each track is checked and converted, Windows Media Player begins copying files to the CD. You can follow the progress of all of these operations by watching the Status column in the Burn tab, or you can return to another part of Windows Media Player and perform other tasks.

By default, Windows Media Player ejects your disc when the copy is complete. If you've prepared a multi-disc burn list, this option makes it easy to insert a new disc and click Start Burn to continue. The Eject operation can be dangerous, however, if your computer is a tower model stored on the floor next to your knee. If you're unaware that a disc has popped out, you could inadvertently bump the drive and injure your knee, snap the drive tray, or both. If you don't want burned discs to eject automatically, click the arrow beneath the Burn button and clear the Eject Disc After Burning option.

INSIDE OUT Tracks that play continuously in Windows Media Player don't do so on custom CDs

Windows Media Player puts two-second "spacers" between tracks on CDs that it burns, and you don't have the option of eliminating these spacers. Tracks that are intended to be played continuously (such as live music performances or movements in a symphony) will thus be discontinuous when copied to a CD. To eliminate the gaps, use a third-party CD-burning program. (The Nero Fast CD-Burning Plug-in, made for earlier versions of Windows Media Player, is incompatible with Windows Media Player 11.) If you burn CDs with spaces and play them back in Windows Media Player, you can configure the player to use crossfading, which gradually overlaps the end of one track with the beginning of the next on playback. We suggest that you experiment to see if this option is acceptable. Choose Enhancements from the View menu and then click Crossfading And Auto Volume Leveling. In the Enhancements pane, click Turn On Crossfading and specify how much of an overlap you want.

Chapter 16

CHAPTER 17

Viewing, Organizing, and Sharing Digital Photos

Home Basic ◐
Home Premium ◕
Business ◐
Enterprise ◐
Ultimate ●

Windows Vista includes an impressive assortment of new tools for managing digital image files. When you plug in a digital camera, Windows automatically imports any pictures and videos it finds on the devices, moving them to your default Pictures folder, optionally adjusting the orientation and naming the files to suit your preferences. Although you can choose to use third-party image editing tools, we recommend that you seriously consider the new tools in Windows Vista, which are more powerful and flexible than a quick glance might suggest.

If you're familiar with the tools and techniques available to work with digital images in Windows XP, you'll need to know about the following significant changes in Windows Vista, which we cover in detail in this chapter:

- **Windows Explorer enhancements** Many common tasks can be accomplished directly from Windows Explorer. The default Pictures folder appears on the Start menu. Within any folder that contains pictures, you can view images as thumbnails or in the Preview pane (or both), accomplish common tasks by clicking buttons on the Command bar, edit file properties in the Details pane, and use the full assortment of desktop search tools available in Windows Vista. Figure 17-1 shows these enhancements in action.

What's in Your Edition?

The basic tools and techniques for enjoying digital photos are available in all editions of Windows Vista. The premium home-oriented editions—Home Premium and Ultimate—offer themed slide shows and the capability to burn a video DVD from a selection of pictures; in Home Basic, Business, and Enterprise editions, you can adjust the pace of a photo slide show, but you can't add fancy borders and transitions, nor can you burn a video DVD from your photo collection.

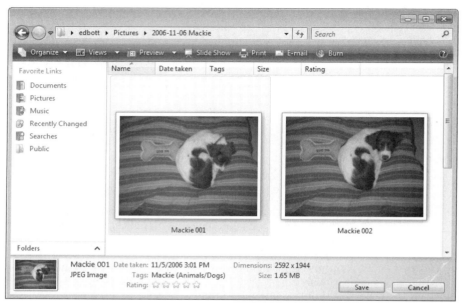

Figure 17-1 In a folder filled with pictures, you can access common tasks from the Command bar and edit properties—including keyword tags—in the Details pane at the bottom of the window.

For more details about using Windows Explorer and its integrated search tools, see "Navigating Your System with Windows Explorer," Chapter 7.

- **Windows Photo Gallery** This application (a replacement for the Windows Picture and Fax Viewer in Windows XP) allows you to import and organize a collection of images and view them individually, as a collection, or as a slide show. It includes basic editing tools and can help you share images via e-mail or as video files.

- **Tags** The single most significant improvement in Windows Vista for digital photo buffs is the capability to tag photos with keywords, which you can then use to organize, filter, and search even an enormous library. For supported file types, including the widely used JPEG format, these tags are stored along with captions, ratings, and details about the image itself as metadata within the file.

- **Printing** Digital images don't have to remain trapped on a disk. Using the layout tools in Windows Photo Gallery, you can print to a local printer—in color or black and white, on plain paper or glossy photo stock. Or use the built-in tools to order prints from online suppliers.

No one will mistake Windows Photo Gallery for a professional image editing program, but its simple, easy-to-use tools are more than sufficient for casual shutterbugs and enthusiasts who want to get images out of a camera and onto the screen with a minimum of hassle. As we explain in the following section, photo fanatics can customize the program to include links to more powerful image editing programs and use them to complement one another.

INSIDE OUT   Give photos some extra room

Want to clear the title bar and Address bar when working with a folder full of images in Windows Explorer? Press F11, the Full Screen shortcut key, to banish these elements. The Command bar remains at the top of the screen; you can show or hide the Navigation, Preview, and Details panes using the Layout option on the Organize menu. To restore the normal interface elements, press F11 again.

Using Windows Photo Gallery

When you click the Windows Photo Gallery shortcut on the Start menu, the program opens in Gallery mode, displaying a thumbnail view of all photos in your collection. By default, this includes the contents of the Pictures and Videos folders in your profile as well as the Public Pictures and Public Videos folder.

As we explain later in this chapter, you can import pictures directly from a digital camera. But you can also build a collection of digital photos by copying files to folders that are part of the gallery, by importing images saved on a CD or DVD, or by transferring files between devices with a memory card, a USB flash drive, or other removable device. As part of the import, you specify how the resulting files are named, instruct Photo Gallery to automatically rotate images to their correct orientation, and delete the pictures from the camera when the import is complete.

Figure 17-2 shows the options available in a gallery containing a large collection of photos.

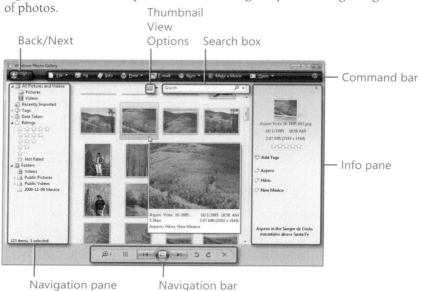

Figure 17-2 Gallery view displays all or part of a photo collection as thumbnails. Allowing the mouse pointer to hover over an item displays this pop-up preview.

Allowing the mouse pointer to hover over any photo or video displays a larger preview window like the one shown here, with details about the item. Normally, the Info pane is hidden; click the Info button on the Command bar to make it visible. Double-clicking any picture or video displays that item full size in the main window, hiding the Navigation pane and the Search box.

Whether you're viewing thumbnails or a single item, the Navigation bar at the bottom of the Photo Gallery window allows you to work with the entire gallery. The controls change slightly, depending on which view is active.

Click the Change Display Size button at the far left of the Navigation Bar to display a slider that you can use to zoom in or out. The smallest thumbnail view (shown at left) allows you to focus on tags, dates, or ratings. In single-image view, the smallest setting on this slider fits the image to the viewer window. The button to the right of the slider changes depending on the current view and the slider's position. In thumbnail view, click it to reset thumbnails to their default size; when viewing individual items, the button toggles between Fit To Window and Actual Size. Regardless of the current view, pressing the keyboard shortcut Ctrl+0 has the same effect as clicking this button.

The group of controls in the center of the Navigation Bar allow you to move through a collection. In either view, click the Previous and Next buttons (or use the left and right arrow keys) to move through the current selection. The large Play Slide Show button in the center displays the current contents of the gallery window in a continuous slide show (its keyboard shortcut is F11).

The group of controls at the right side of the Navigation bar allow you to change the current selection. The Rotate Clockwise and Rotate Counterclockwise buttons shift the image by 90 degrees. (We predict that almost no one will remember the keyboard shortcuts for these two buttons: Ctrl+comma and Ctrl+period, respectively.) Clicking the Delete button send the current selection to the Recycle Bin.

> **CAUTION**
>
> As we note in this section, the popular JPEG format uses "lossy" compression, and each time you make a change and save a file some image data is irretrievably lost. You need to rotate images to view them correctly on the screen, of course, and the impact on image quality is relatively low if you only do it once. Avoid rotating an image repeatedly, which can lead to a noticeable degradation in image quality.

The pane on the right side of the Photo Gallery window allows you to work with image files. Clicking the Fix button switches to Preview mode, showing the most recently selected image, and makes the Edit pane available. Click the Info button to open a pane where you can tag images and edit file properties for one or more items; you can use it whether you're viewing a single image or thumbnails.

You can preview any single picture in Photo Gallery by double-clicking it in Windows Explorer or in the gallery. If you open a picture from Windows Explorer and click the Fix button, you see a display like the one in Figure 17-3.

Figure 17-3 The image editing tools in the Edit pane are useful for basic tasks like cropping an image.

The button at the left of the Command bar takes you to the Gallery view, but its text and associated Action change slightly, depending on how you opened the photo currently on display. It reads Back To Gallery if you started by double-clicking a thumbnail in Gallery view. It reads Go To Gallery if you double-clicked a picture in Windows Explorer that is already in the gallery. If you open a photo from a folder that is not in the gallery, this button reads Add Folder To Gallery; clicking it adds the current image and all others in the same folder to the gallery.

Windows Photo Gallery works well with other image-editing programs, and it's relatively easy to customize these connections. After doing some basic cropping, for instance, you might want to open a picture in a more robust image editing program to do some touchup work. After selecting any item in the gallery, click the Open button on the Command bar or the Open With option on the right-click shortcut menu. If Windows recognizes that the program is associated with the selected file type, you can choose the program from the menu. From Windows Explorer, click the drop-down arrow to the right of the Preview button on the Command bar to choose from a similar list that includes Windows Photo Gallery.

Supported File Formats

You can use Photo Gallery to view pictures saved in any of the formats listed in Table 17-1.

Table 17-1. Image Formats Supported in Windows Photo Gallery

File type	Extension	Comments
Windows Bitmap	.bmp, .dib	Because this format does not support compression, images tend to be very large. Tags created in Photo Gallery cannot be stored within files saved in this format.
Joint Photographic Experts Group (JPEG) File Interchange Format	.jpeg, .jpg, .jpe, .jfif	Because it is highly compressible, this is the most popular format used for web graphics and in digital cameras, and it fully supports tags and other metadata as used in Photo Gallery. The compression normally used in JPEG files results in a permanent loss of detail each time the file is edited and saved.
Tag (or Tagged) Image File Format (TIFF)	.tif, .tiff	TIFF files can be compressed without a great loss of detail; as a result, these files are generally larger than comparable JPEG files and are limited to 4 GB in size. The format is widely used in desktop publishing programs and is frequently used for faxes. Multipage TIFF format merges two or more pages into a single file. TIFF files fully support tags.
Portable Network Graphics Image	.png	This platform-independent, highly compressible format is increasingly popular on webpages because it's supported by virtually all modern browsers. Because it is a bitmap format that uses lossless compression, it tends to produce relatively large images. Tags added to a PNG file are stored in the Photo Gallery index and not in the file itself.
HD Photo (previously known as Windows Media Photo)	.wdp	This format, based on the TIFF standard and devised by Microsoft as a high-performance alternative to JPEG files, is the preferred image format for documents created using the XML Paper Specification (XPS). Files in this format can be viewed in Photo Gallery and can stored tags as metadata within the file. As of this writing, the format is in experimental use only. More details are available at *http://www.vista-io.com/1701*.

For a list of file formats you can play back in Windows Media Player, see "Which File Formats Are Supported?" Chapter 15.

> **Note**
>
> Photo Gallery, using code shared with Windows Movie Maker, can also display videos in the popular ASF, AVI, MPEG, and WMV formats and can save tags as metadata within Windows Media Video files. Don't expect to use Photo Gallery as an all-purpose video playback console; this feature's main purpose is to help download movie files from digital cameras that happen to have basic movie capture built in as well. For any video file more demanding than an occasional short video clip, you'll do better with Windows Media Player for playback and Windows Movie Maker for editing.

Two file formats are notably absent from this table. The GIF format, once a graphic superstar, is now a has-been. Files saved in the venerable GIF format will not open in Photo Gallery at all. At the other end of the quality scale are the uncompressed, super-high-quality RAW formats used in today's professional-grade cameras. Although Windows Vista includes the capability to add support for RAW images, that support isn't in the initial release and will no doubt arrive as a series of driver updates from camera makers, perhaps via Windows Update.

Importing Pictures into the Gallery

The simplest way to add images to the gallery is to copy them to the Pictures folder in your profile or to the Public Pictures folder. Photo Gallery constantly monitors these locations and automatically adds any new image files you copy there to the gallery. You can also add any folder to the list of monitored folders by clicking the File button on the Photo Gallery Command bar and then choosing Add Folder To Gallery.

If the image files are freshly captured in a digital camera or saved on a portable storage device, you have other options.

Connecting a Digital Camera

Any digital camera that was made after 2001 is almost certain to work with Windows Vista. Virtually all recent-vintage cameras support the Windows Image Acquisition (WIA) driver standard introduced in Windows XP or the newer Windows Portable Devices (WPD) standard introduced in Windows Vista. Plug in the camera, connect it to a USB port, and Windows kicks off the Import Pictures wizard.

INSIDE OUT   **Make an indirect connection**

Do you have an older digital camera that won't communicate with Windows Vista? If it still takes perfectly good pictures, don't toss it out. As long as it uses industry-standard memory cards (Compact Flash or Secure Digital, for example), you can plug its cards into a memory reader. External devices connect via the USB port on your computer, and it's not unusual to find multi-format memory card readers installed as internal devices in new computers. Instead of connecting the camera directly to the computer, you transfer the memory card to the reader. Windows recognizes digital memory cards as generic storage devices (look for an icon in the Computer window) and provides the exact same image-handling features you would get with a compatible camera. Card readers also help you conserve your camera's battery power, because you don't have to leave the camera turned on while you transfer pictures.

When you first connect a camera to your computer, you see the AutoPlay dialog box shown here. Click Import Pictures to begin the import process described in this section. If you'd prefer to open the camera's storage folders and copy files to the Pictures folder or another location using Windows Explorer, choose the Open Device To View Files option instead.

For details on how to change actions that take place when you connect a camera or removable storage device, see "Setting Default Programs, File Type Associations, and AutoPlay Options," Chapter 3.

Chapter 17

The Importing Pictures and Videos window is about as lean as a wizard gets. In fact, you can complete the import with a single click if you're in a hurry. Figure 17-4 shows the initial window, which appears in the lower right corner of the primary display.

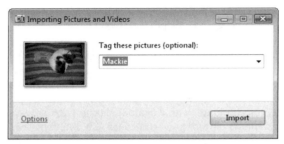

Figure 17-4 The Import Pictures wizard is designed to get pictures into the gallery as quickly as possible, with a minimum of options.

If you click Import without entering any text in the Tag These Pictures box, all the pictures on the connected device are imported into the gallery using the default settings. You can adjust any or all of these settings by clicking the Options link, which leads to the dialog box shown in Figure 17-5. (If you'd prefer to set these options before connecting a camera, click the File button on the Command bar, click Options, and then click the Import tab.)

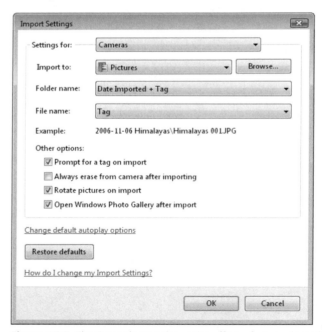

Figure 17-5 The Example text shows the effect of your selected settings on file and folder names.

In the Import Settings dialog box, you can adjust any or all of the following settings:

- **Import To** Designate which folder your imported pictures should be stored in. The default is the Pictures folder in your user profile.

- **Folder Name** The drop-down list lets you choose a variety of combinations of the date imported, the date or date range when the pictures were taken, and the text you enter in the Tag These Pictures dialog box.

- **File Name** The default setting here uses the text you enter in the Tag These Pictures dialog box, plus a sequence number. If you prefer to use the names assigned by your camera, choose either of the Original File Name options.

- **Other Options** The check boxes in this section allow you to specify whether to prompt for a tag on import, whether to rotate pictures automatically when importing, whether to erase pictures from the camera after the import is successful, and whether to immediately open the imported pictures in Windows Photo Gallery.

CAUTION

The option to erase pictures on import is potentially dangerous, especially for irreplaceable photos of once-in-a-lifetime events. If you leave this check box unselected, you can decide on a case-by-case basis whether to erase pictures on the fly. Just select the Erase After Importing option in the status dialog box that appears after you click Import.

If you're a digital camera fanatic, you can skip the wizard altogether and automatically copy all images to your hard drive every time you connect your camera. To set up this option, clear the Prompt For A Tag On Import box in the Options dialog box and configure AutoPlay so that the Import Pictures option runs automatically when the camera is connected. With these two options chosen, Windows Photo Gallery will automatically begin importing pictures as soon as you connect your camera, creating a subfolder in the Pictures folder (using the current date as the folder name), copying all pictures from the camera to that folder using the original filenames, and opening Windows Photo Gallery after the import is complete.

Chapter 17

INSIDE OUT Skip the wizard for faster results

If you don't like the wizard's approach, you can cut straight to the chase and work directly with images stored on a digital camera. After connecting the device, choose Open Folder To View Files from the AutoPlay dialog box, or open the Computer window and double-click the camera icon. In Windows Explorer, select one or more images and then copy the selected items to a folder of your choice. When you use this technique, the image files use the default names supplied by your camera—typically a combination of a prefix and automatic numbering. If necessary, you can change these names afterwards in Windows Explorer or in Photo Gallery.

Importing Images From a Storage Device

When you copy image files to a USB flash drive or similar removable storage device and attach the device to a computer running Windows Vista, the effect is the same as if you have connected a camera. The Import Pictures wizard appears, giving you the option to add a tag, import the files, and erase them from the storage device.

When you insert a CD or DVD containing files in a supported image format, AutoPlay offers the same choices and fires up the same wizard. The default settings are slightly different, however. For one, the option to delete pictures from the source disk is cleared—a logical choice, given that CDs and DVDs are generally read-only media. And instead of creating filenames using the tag you enter, image files copied from a CD or DVD use the original filenames, preserving any subfolders. That's a logical assumption, reflecting the likelihood that a CD/DVD contains files copied from a disk after you've made file-naming decisions.

INSIDE OUT Start over

Is your gallery hopelessly messed up? Need to get a fresh start? That's easy, as long as you don't mind deleting the index and rebuilding it from existing files (and, in the process, wiping out all metadata associated with nonsupported file types like Bitmap and PNG files). First, shut down Windows Photo Gallery. Then open Windows Explorer and navigate to %LocalAppData%\Microsoft\Windows Photo Gallery. Select the index file, Pictures.pd4, and delete it. Now reopen Windows Photo Gallery and wait for the index to rebuild itself.

Organizing and Categorizing Your Digital Pictures

The traditional way to organize photos, just like any file in digital format, is by creating a hierarchy of nested folders and subfolders to hold them all. But that system falls apart rapidly when you try to create a subset of pictures that don't fall into the prearranged hierarchy. If all the pictures from your Hawaiian vacation are in the Hawaii folder and those from your week in Mexico are in the Mexico folder, how do you quickly gather photos of stunning sunsets from both locations?

One useful solution is to tag photos with keywords. Photo viewing programs have been offering the capability to tag or label photos for years, but most suffer from an inherent weakness: the tags are stored in a separate database. If you copy or move the photos to a new computer or send them to a friend as an e-mail attachment, the tags are lost.

Windows Photo Gallery takes a giant step toward solving these problems by embedding user-defined metadata directly in the file itself (depending, of course, on whether the file format supports embedded metadata, as we discussed earlier in this chapter). Windows Vista uses the Extensible Metadata Platform (XMP), developed by Adobe and used in a variety of professional-strength photo-editing applications. Specifically, you can add ratings (on a scale of one to five stars), captions, and an unlimited number of keyword tags to an image file.

When working with individual file or a selection of multiple files in Photo Gallery, you can use the Info pane to add or edit tags and change file details, including the file name and the date and time the picture was taken.

Editing File Properties and Other Metadata

To edit the name of an image or video file in Windows Photo Gallery, use any of the following techniques:

- Click its name at the top of the Info pane

- Choose Rename from the File menu on the Command bar

- Choose Rename from the right-click shortcut menu

- Use the keyboard shortcut Ctrl+M

The name displayed at the top of the Info pane includes a file name extension that identifies the file type. When you click this name to begin editing, the extension goes away and only the name remains. If you select multiple items in the gallery, the number of selected items appears at the top of the Info pane. When you enter a new name, the text you enter is applied to the first selected item; the names of remaining selections are replaced using the same text, with a number in parentheses [(1), (2), (3)] appended to the end of the file name before the file name extension.

As Figure 17-6 shows, the stacked thumbnails at the top of the Info pane show how many items are selected, and you can edit a surprising amount of metadata here.

Figure 17-6 In the Info pane, you can change the file name, adjust the date and time the picture were taken, add a rating and caption, and add an unlimited number of keyword tags.

The date and time the photo was taken appear just below the filename at the top of the Info pane. Both settings are fully editable; click the date and then click the arrow to display the calendar shown here, or click the time to adjust using spinner controls. This capability works with multiple images selected, a capability that can come in handy if you discover that the date and time were set incorrectly on a camera that took a series of images in your collection.

If you discover that the date and time stamps are incorrect for a group of photos because you traveled to a different time zone without adjusting the camera's clock, here's an easy solution. Select the images in Photo Gallery, right-click, and then click Change

Time Taken on the shortcut menu. The resulting dialog box (see Figure 17-7) allows you to add or subtract up to 24 hours from the time saved with each photo.

Figure 17-7 Use the Change Time Taken dialog box to compensate for time-stamp errors that are caused when you travel to a new time zone and don't change the camera's clock.

To add a rating for one or more selected files, click the stars in the Info pane. To add a caption, click the link at the bottom of the Info pane and begin typing. Captions can be up to 255 characters in length.

You can also view and edit file properties using the Details tab of the Properties dialog box. In Windows Explorer or in Windows Photo Gallery, right-click any file icon and click Properties. Figure 17-8 shows the properties saved for a JPEG file.

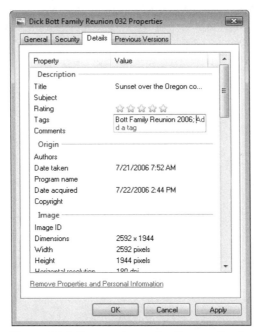

Figure 17-8 You can view and edit properties for a supported image file using the Properties dialog box. The Title field here is the same as the Caption in Photo Gallery.

INSIDE OUT **Convert to a different file format**

Need to convert a graphics file after saving it to your hard disk? Open Paint (click the Start button, choose All Programs, Accessories, and click Paint). The Windows Vista version of Paint works with all file formats that open in Photo Gallery, plus GIF and a few less common Bitmap formats. If you want to choose custom options such as compression levels for any of these formats, you'll need a third-party image-editing tool.)

Adding Keyword Tags to Image Files

Tags are an extraordinarily flexible way to organize files, especially digital photos. A tag can consist of a single word (*Hawaii, sunset, Judy*) or a phrase of up to 255 characters, and if there's a theoretical limit to the number of tags you can add to an image file, we haven't found it. (In practice, of course, you'll rarely want to use more than a handful of tags for any given picture.)

To add a tag to an image, use any of the following techniques:

- In Photo Gallery, select one or more photos and click Add Tags in the Info pane (or use the keyboard shortcut Ctrl+T). The drop-down list shows up to ten tags you've used most recently. As you type, Photo Gallery's AutoComplete feature displays a list of existing tags that match your input; press the down arrow to move to one of these tags and then press Enter. If you enter a keyword or phrase that isn't already defined as a tag and press Enter, Photo Gallery adds it to the list of available tags.

- In Photo Gallery or in Windows Explorer, select one or more images, right-click, and choose Properties. On the Details tab, click in the Tags field and enter as many tags as you want, using semi-colons to separate tags.

- In Windows Explorer, with the Details pane visible, click in the Tags field and enter as many tags as you want, using semi-colons to separate them.

- In Photo Gallery, select one or more photos, drag them into the Navigation pane, and drop them on the tag you want to assign to the selected images. If you need confirmation that you've selected the correct tag, wait a few seconds before releasing the mouse button and a Property tag will appear.

When you select multiple files that are tagged differently, Photo Gallery breaks down the display of tags to show which are assigned to all selected photos and which are assigned to only some. If you add a tag using the Add Tags box, it is assigned to all items in the current selection. To tag all the selected photos with a tag from the Assigned To Some group, right-click the tag and click Assign To All. To remove tags from one or more photos, make a selection, right-click the tag name in the Info pane, and click Remove Tag.

Use the Tags list in the Navigation Pane to manage existing tags. Right-click a tag name to choose from a shortcut menu that lets you create a new tag, rename an existing tag, or delete a tag. If you delete a tag from this list, it also deletes that tag from all files to which the tag is currently applied.

Tags can be organized into hierarchies. Figure 17-9 shows a top-level Animals tag, with subtags for Cats, Dogs, Dolphins, Meerkats, and other types of animals, and subtags for the names of individual pets under the Cats tag. You can drag an existing tag and drop it onto another to create a hierarchical relationship, or create a new hierarchy on the fly by using forward slashes: Animals/Cats/Bianca.

Figure 17-9 Tags can be arranged into hierarchies. When you select a top-level tag (Animals, in this case) all of the tags beneath it are selected as well.

CAUTION

Photo Gallery allows you to create multiple tags with identical names, as long as they're in different hierarchies. Be especially vigilant when entering a new tag; it's all too easy to accidentally create a new top-level tag when you mean to apply an existing tag from another hierarchy.

Filtering and Searching Image Files

Photo Gallery's contents pane can show every picture and video in your collection (click All Pictures And Videos at the top of the Navigation Pane). To display a subset of your collection, use any combination of selections from the Navigation pane, or filter the results using the Search box.

You can click any single item in the Navigation pane to see all items in the gallery that match that item. Use Ctrl+click to select multiple discontiguous objects in this pane. The results can be powerful, allowing you to slice and dice your collection using any combination of tags, dates, ratings, and folders. Figure 17-10, for example, shows all photos taken on June 17, 2004 and rated five stars. To choose a top-level tag without selecting all the tags beneath it, right-click the tag and choose Select Top-Level Tag, or use Ctrl+click to clear individual tags you don't want in your selection.

Figure 17-10 Ctrl+click to select multiple items from the Navigation pane and narrow your selection of photos.

INSIDE OUT **Use the Not Tagged tag**

The Not Tagged item at the top of the Tags section in the Navigation Pane can help you keep new photos organized. If you choose not to add a default tag when importing a group of new photos, all your new items show up in this list. Take a quick review of the section, apply tags as needed, and you'll be ready for the next batch.

Use the Search box to narrow down the selection even further. Although the Search interface in Photo Gallery doesn't offer the same range of options as the Advanced Search tools in Windows Explorer, it's fast and ridiculously easy to use. Here are some things you should know about Photo Gallery's Search capability:

- Searches are performed using all available metadata, including tags, captions, file name, file path, and camera name.

- All searches work as logical AND operations. If you enter two terms separated by any delimiter (spaces, commas, periods, and semi-colons all work), both terms must appear in the search index for any item to appear in the results set.

- Photo Gallery search looks for strings, not keywords, so *sun* returns any item with *sunset* or *sunrise* or *sunday* in its file name, path, or metadata.

- Search works on the current set as defined in the Navigation Pane. To expand the result set to for the current search terms to include your full collection, click the arrow to the right of the Search box and click Search All Items in Photo Gallery.

Sorting and Grouping Items in the Gallery

The contents of the gallery, with any filters and searches applied, can be sorted and arranged in a variety of ways. By default, Photo Gallery takes its best guess at sorting and grouping based on the current filters. You can apply manual choices by right-clicking any empty space in the contents pane and choosing from the Group By and Sort By menus.

INSIDE OUT   **Get to hidden metadata with the Group By menu**

The Group By menu includes an assortment of properties that aren't available in the navigation pane, including file size, file type, and camera name. Grouping by camera name is useful if you've combined pictures from several family members in a single folder and you want to sort them out temporarily. As long as each person used a different make and model of camera, you'll be able to see at a glance who shot what.

One well-hidden interface element that comes in handy when viewing a selection of photos is the Table of Contents, which adds a column to the right of the Navigation pane showing all items in the current grouping, with a bar indicating the relative number of item in each category. Figure 17-11 shows the Table of Contents after selecting a year's worth of photos and using the default Group By Month Taken selection.

Figure 17-11 The Table of Contents is live. Click any item to scroll up or down to that grouping. Use the arrows above and below the Table of Contents to scroll through long lists.

A Closer Look at Metadata

Image metadata is nonpicture information that's captured and stored within a picture file. Most digital cameras use the Exchangeable Image File (EXIF) format when saving pictures; images may also include metadata that conforms to the International Press Telecommunications Council (IPTC) standard. Windows Photo Gallery saves additional metadata using Adobe's Extensible Metadata Platform (XMP) standards. (To learn more about the EXIF standard, visit *http://www.exif.org*; for more details about XMP, see *http://www.vista-io.com/1702*.)

EXIF metadata typically includes the date and time the picture was taken, the width and height of the image (in pixels), the resolution (in dpi), and the color depth. Depending on the camera you use, metadata can also include technical information such as the camera model, flash mode, aperture, and exposure time. Some high-end devices even allow you to add audio annotations to images and store them in the same file.

Windows Photo Gallery provides easy-to-access tools for viewing and editing some metadata, but to see all available metadata you need to create a custom view in Windows Explorer. To do so, switch to Details view, right-click any column heading, and then select the names of available fields to make those columns visible. Click More at the bottom of the list to see all possible fields. After selecting all the fields you want to work with, you can group, stack, and search image files just as you would any other file type.

For supported file types (see the full list earlier in this chapter) Windows Photo Gallery saves all metadata in the file itself. During the import process, Exif data is transferred to the XMP metadata store within the file, and any changes you make are written back to the Exif data store to help maintain compatibility.

For file types that don't support saving metadata in the file, Windows Photo Gallery saves tags, captions, and ratings in the Photo Gallery index. If you move image files to a new computer, the accompanying metadata is, unfortunately, left behind.

CAUTION

When you rotate images in Windows Photo Gallery, your metadata is preserved. However, some image-editing programs wipe out metadata when you make changes to the image, such as cropping or resizing. Before using any image-editing software, make a backup copy of some test images first and experiment to see what effect different forms of editing have on tags you've applied.

Editing Image Files

The image-editing tools in Windows Photo Gallery were designed to be as simple as possible, doing enough to make slightly flawed images fit more neatly in your collection. You can't straighten a crooked image, and you can't touch up flaws or add special effects. But you can crop out extraneous details, fix color and exposure problems, and get the red out of the eyes of human and animal subjects.

To begin working with the Edit Pane, select an image and click Fix. Figure 17-12 shows the options available in the Edit Pane.

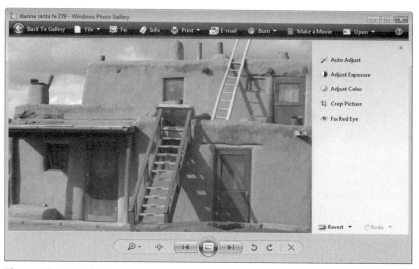

Figure 17-12 Click the Revert button at the bottom of this screen to throw away all changes you've made and restore the original image.

As you make changes using the controls in the Edit Pane, you can use the Undo and Redo buttons at the bottom of the pane to do quick comparisons. You don't need to explicitly save your changes; Windows Photo Gallery saves changes automatically when you close the program or return to Gallery view.

When you first save a change to a picture, Photo Gallery makes a copy of the original image file and saves it in %LocalAppData%\Microsoft\Windows Photo Gallery\Original Images. This cached copy remains available until you explicitly remove it or restore it. It's important to note that each time you make changes to a photo and save those changes, the new copy replaces the previous saved copy; the copy in the Original Omages folder remains unchanges. If you click the Revert button (or press its keyboard shortcut, Ctrl+R), Photo Gallery undoes all changes made in all editing sessions and restores the original image.

Chapter 17

If you're worried about permanently altering an important picture, you can explicitly make a copy before or after doing any editing. Choose Make A Copy from the File menu and give the new copy a name; any changes you make from that point on will affect only the new copy.

As you make changes in each area, Photo Gallery adds a green check mark to the right of the box in the Edit Pane. You can undo any change at any time until you exit the current editing session.

- **Auto Adjust** This one-click fix-it option analyzes the image and makes its best guess about how to adjust brightness, contrast, and color values. It's most useful as a starting point when you're trying to salvage an image with noticeable problems. (Look for the green checkmarks next to the sections where it made changes and adjust its settings if necessary.)

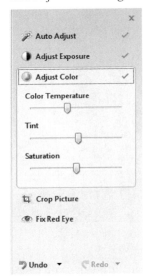

- **Adjust Exposure** The two sliders here adjust brightness (making all pixels brighter or darker) and contrast (changing pixels relative to one another). Generally, you should make only small adjustments in either setting.

- **Adjust Color** These three sliders work in combination to fix color-related problems. Use the Color Temperature slider to make an image appear cooler or warmer and move the Tint slider to change the level of green or red. The Saturation slider adjusts the intensity of an image; move it all the way to the left to simulate a black-and-white photo.

- **Crop** By default, every image appears in the proportions that your camera saved it in. Smart cropping can make an image pop by removing extraneous elements and zeroing in on the details that matter. To begin, click Crop and choose one of the preset cropping frames from the Proportion list, or choose Custom if you don't need the dimensions to match a standard shape. Figure 17-13 shows the cropping frame in place for a 4x6 image.

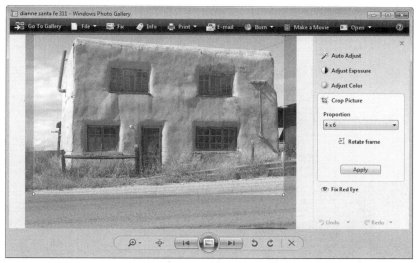

Figure 17-13 Drag the cropping frame so that its upper left corner is in the correct position, then drag the lower right corner to its proper spot.

If you're planning to print your pictures, cropping to the correct dimensions before you print assures the best results. If the image needs to be rotated 90 degrees for printing, click Rotate Frame.

- **Red Eye** Indoor flash photos have a way of making people look downright demonic. Zoom and pan the image to make the eyes more visible, click this option in the Edit Pane, and use the mouse pointer to select the area around the red eyes.

Sharing Digital Images

A collection of digital pictures deserves sharing. You can gather everyone around your PC screen (or connect the computer to a TV), select a group of pictures, and turn it into an instant slide show. Or you can take those pictures and burn them to a CD or DVD, turn the pictures into a movie file that plays on a computer or on a DVD player, print the images on your own printer, send them to a professional service for custom printing, or attach them to an e-mail message.

Chapter 17

Viewing a Slide Show

Basic slide show capabilities are built into every edition of Windows Vista. If you're using Home Basic, Business, or Enterprise edition, clicking the Play Slide Show button in the Navigation Bar (or pressing F11) immediately starts a slide show using the current gallery, with any filters or search results applied. You get no fancy transitions, and every image scales up to fill as much of the screen as possible, with black borders for images that don't fill the screen completely. A handful of options are available when you right-click any portion of the screen while the slide show is running: you can shuffle the slides, change the speed, or pause to admire a particularly nice slide.

With Home Premium and Ultimate editions and the Aero user interface enabled, clicking the Play Slide Show button starts the slide show with a difference. Instead of a simple, no-frills show, you see the Slide Show toolbar, which contains a variety of fancy and useful options. Figure 17-14 shows this toolbar in action.

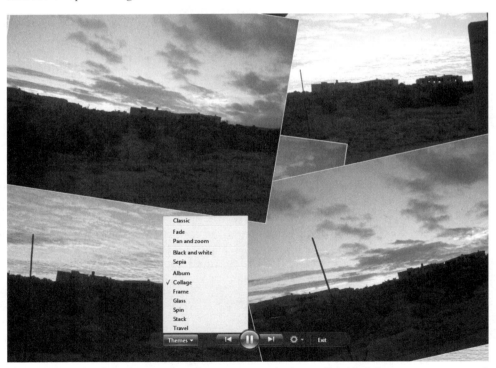

Figure 17-14 The Slide Show toolbar allows you to apply themes like this Collage arrangement and use special effects.

From the Themes list, you can choose one of seven ready-made themes, change the standard transition effects (the subtle Fade or the more dramatic Pan and Zoom), and apply black-and-white or sepia tones to the images in the show. The settings menu to the left of the Exit button offers the same choices as a basic slide show, plus the option to mute any background music that might be playing.

Printing

Digital images are ideal for on-screen viewing, but they're hardly suitable for framing. Sometimes a printed copy is more useful and practical than a digital one. The Print Pictures dialog box in Windows Photo Gallery allows you to arrange images on the printed page and make the most efficient use of expensive photo-quality paper.

After using the Navigation Pane and the Search box to filter the display of images, click Print on the Print menu (or press Ctrl+P). This opens the Print Pictures dialog box, which offers every photo-printing option in a compact dialog box. Figure 17-15 shows this dialog box with all its options already selected.

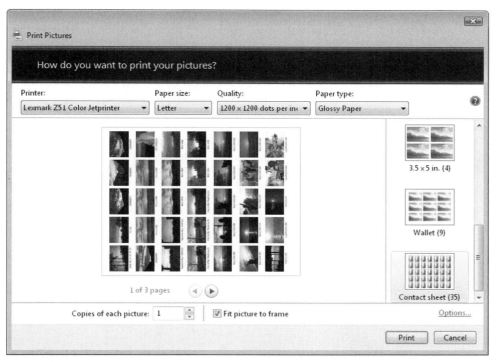

Figure 17-15 Use the Contact Sheet layout to print out thumbnails of selected photos—up to 35 per page.

The options on the Print Pictures dialog box are self-explanatory. Choose a printer, paper size, quality, and paper type. Then scroll through the list of layouts on the right side of the preview window and select the most appropriate one. In Figure 17-15, we've chosen the Contact Sheet layout, which prints 35 thumbnail images per page. Be sure to choose a layout that matches the proportions of the pictures you've chosen. If the layout isn't a near-perfect match, you might wind up with unexpected cropping on the printed photos.

Pay close attention when using the Photo Printing Wizard with images saved using the 4:3 ratio that's standard on most digital cameras. All but one of the nine available layouts crop images during the printing process if the Fit Picture to Frame check box is selected. Depending on the proportions of the selected images, you could be unpleasantly surprised by the final results. For more accurate image printing, clear the Fit Picture to Frame check box.

When using the Print Pictures dialog box, choose layouts carefully and pay close attention to cropping. For casual snapshots, the default cropping might not be noticeable. But for images that are carefully composed, you'll get best results by cropping the image manually in an image-editing program so its proportions match those of the print layout you plan to use.

INSIDE OUT   Avoid wasting paper

Make your choices carefully when choosing a print layout, or you might end up wasting paper accidentally. Pay special attention to the number of photos in your selection and on the layout; if you select three images and then choose the 5 × 7 inch prints layout, which contains slots for two prints, the wizard will put the final image on a page by itself. Rather than waste half a sheet of photo paper, you might want to select a fourth image to fill the remaining space. Or, as an alternative, you could split the job in two. Select two images and print them on a single page; then run the wizard again and print the third image using the same layout, increasing the Number Of Times To Use Each Picture setting to 2.

Exporting to CD, DVD, or Movie File

How do you share a large stack of pictures with someone who has a computer? Slide a blank CD or DVD into a drive that can handle recordable media and then choose Data Disc from the Burn menu. The step-by-step procedure is straightforward and should result in a disc that can be read on any computer.

What if the would-be recipient doesn't have a computer or isn't comfortable with photo-viewing software? What if you want to show the pictures off on your big-screen TV, which isn't connected to a computer? With Home Premium or Ultimate edition, you have an additional option. After filtering your selection of photos, choose Video DVD from the Burn menu to make a Video DVD that will play back on just about any DVD player. Or click the Make A Movie button, which transfers the lot to Windows Movie Maker. From there, you can create a file that can be burned to a video CD or DVD or posted to a network or internet site for playback.

For more details on using Movie Maker and DVD Maker, see Chapter 18, "Creating and Watching Movies and DVDs."

E-Mail

When you initially import a digital image, the size of the file can be enormous, especially on a high-resolution camera. That's all well and good if you want to keep every detail of the original photo intact, but large file size is a serious hindrance if you plan to send an image as an e-mail attachment. In that case, your most important consideration is reducing the image to a size that can be conveniently attached to an e-mail message without sacrificing too much quality.

If you manually attach an image file to a message using some e-mail client programs, including Windows Mail, you'll send the original, uncompressed image. (Outlook 2003 and Outlook 2007 include tools for automatically compressing digital images attached to outgoing messages; if you use either of these programs as your default e-mail program, you can start with Photo Gallery or a new Outlook message and be assured you'll get the correct result.) From Photo Gallery, click the E-mail button to display the dialog box shown here.

You can choose from four predefined settings, or choose Original if you really do want to send the original uncompressed image. By default, this option converts Bitmap, TIFF, and PNG images to JPEG format. (Because JPEG images are already compressible, using this option leaves those file formats alone.) It then compresses the file substantially and resizes the image so that it fits within a space no larger than the size you specified. (The smallest option is 640 × 480 pixels, although the exact dimensions of the resized image depend on the proportions of the original picture.) If you're willing to accept a larger file size in exchange for more detail, you can select a larger image size instead.

> **Note**
>
> In our tests, we found that the compression estimates in this dialog box were incorrect, sometimes wildly so. Use them as a guideline, but be sure to check the size of the file attachment in your e-mail message window before clicking the Send button.

Chapter 17

CHAPTER 18

Home Basic   ◐
Home Premium   ●
Business   ◐
Enterprise   ◐
Ultimate   ●

Creating and Watching Movies and DVDs

O ver the past few years, the computer has moved into the living room—territory once firmly controlled by consumer electronics gear. In Windows Vista, this trend continues and even accelerates. In this chapter, we look at the three main ways you can turn your PC into the centerpiece of a movie-watching experience.

We start with the essentials of watching standard DVDs in Windows Media Player. Some editions of Windows Vista contain everything you need to watch DVDs; for others, you need to add a small but crucial software component before DVDs will play back properly. (In this chapter we *don't* discuss the two nascent high-definition DVD formats, HD-DVD and Blu-Ray. As we write this book, neither technology is ready for prime time, at least not on a computer screen.)

Windows Vista also includes the latest update to Windows Movie Maker, which allows you to create and edit your own movies. You can import footage you shoot yourself, using a digital video camera, and add clips you import or download from other sources. (For that matter, if you use the TV-recording features in Windows Media Center, you

What's in Your Edition?

Most of the activities we touch on in this chapter can be characterized as entertainment, so it's not surprising that several features are available only in Home Premium and Ultimate editions. Although you can watch DVDs using any edition, the required DVD decoder is not included with Home Basic, Business, and Enterprise editions; you'll need to install a third-party decoder or upgrade to a DVD-ready Windows Vista edition before you can watch a DVD. Windows Movie Maker is available with all editions, but support for high-definition formats is included only in Home Premium and Ultimate editions. And finally, if you want to use the Windows DVD Maker program to burn DVDs that will play back in the standalone DVD player in your living room, you'll need Home Premium or Ultimate edition; other editions lack this capability and are only able to burn data DVDs using Windows Explorer.

can edit any recorded TV show, as long as it's not copy-protected.) We provide detailed instructions on how to save movies in a wide variety of formats, from small files suitable for sharing via e-mail or posting on websites to high-quality productions that look great on a big screen.

And to bring the process full circle, we show you how to use the new Windows DVD Maker to turn the movies you create into DVDs that will play back on any consumer DVD player.

Watching DVDs in Windows Media Player

DVD playback in Windows Media Player requires a supported DVD drive and a software decoder. Virtually all new PCs sold today include a DVD drive, so we'll assume that your system includes the correct hardware. How do you know if you have a compatible software decoder installed?

Windows Vista Home Premium and Ultimate editions include a DVD decoder as part of the standard installation. If you're running either of these editions, you're all set.

- If you performed a clean install of Windows Vista Home Basic or Business, a DVD decoder is not included. The first time you insert a DVD disc in your drive, the Player will display the error message shown here. If you have purchased a third-party DVD playback program that includes a DVD decoder, close this dialog box and install the player software; then try again. If you need to purchase a DVD decoder, click Web Help, which leads to a list of Microsoft-approved decoders.

> **Note**
>
> Most DVD drives sold as retail upgrades come with basic DVD playback software that includes a software decoder. If you install a third-party player that includes a DVD decoder, you automatically enable DVD playback in Windows Media Player as well.

- If you upgraded to Windows Vista Home Basic or Business on a Windows XP system that already included a DVD decoder, your previously installed decoder should be available for your use. To check, open a Command Prompt window (type **cmd** in the Search box and press Enter) and then enter the command **dvdupgrd /detect**. This command displays the dialog box shown here. If the message reads "No decoders found," you'll need to install a decoder to continue.

- If you purchased a new computer with Windows Vista Home Basic or Business edition preinstalled, the computer manufacturer might have included a DVD decoder as part of the software bundled with your new PC. Try playing a DVD in Windows Media Player or use the command-line Dvdupgrd tool to check.

After all the requisite hardware and software is in place, playing a DVD movie in Windows Media Player is as transparently simple as playing an audio CD. If Windows Media Player is the AutoPlay application for DVD movies, it will start automatically and begin playing your movie. If it isn't, start Windows Media Player yourself. Then click Library, click the icon for the DVD in the Navigation Pane, and click Play.

For information on using Windows Media Center to play DVDs, see "Using Media Center's 10-Foot Interface," Chapter 19.

While your movie is playing in Windows Media Player, playback controls appear at the bottom of the Player and the DVD chapter list appears in the Now Playing list (see Figure 18-1 on the next page for an example). This list provides one means of navigation within the movie—you can jump to a particular chapter by double-clicking it in Now Playing. You can also get to the movie's own menu screen by clicking the DVD button (to the left of the playback controls in the Navigation bar) and choosing Root Menu from the menu.

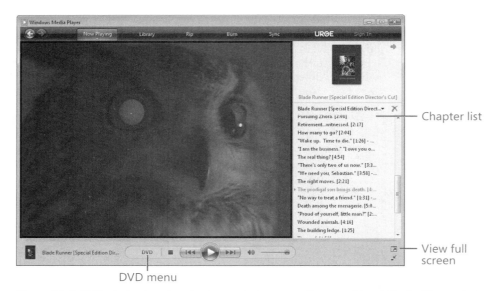

Chapter list

DVD menu

View full screen

Figure 18-1 DVD playback and navigation controls are readily accessible within the Player window, but they distract from the playback experience.

Use the playback controls to play or pause your movie, to fast-forward or rewind, or to adjust the volume. To jump to the DVD menu (which typically includes options for choosing the language of the soundtrack, adjusting audio settings, and showing sub-titles), click the DVD icon at the bottom of the Now Playing screen, to the left of the playback controls, or choose View, DVD Features. You can also adjust the soundtrack and subtitles from the Play menu, by choosing Audio And Language Tracks or Lyrics, Captions, And Subtitles.

To fully appreciate the DVD playback experience, you probably don't want to see any part of the Player except the portion that shows the movie itself. Click the View Full Screen button to switch from the Player window to a full screen display. You can also toggle between these two views by double-clicking the movie or by pressing Alt+Enter.

In full-screen mode, the Player's playback controls appear initially in a transparent bar along the bottom of your screen. The controls normally fade from view after a few seconds and reappear whenever you move the mouse. The controls remain visible when you cause them to reappear while playback is paused. To lock the player into full-screen mode, click the lock button in the lower right corner of the full-screen playback bar. As Figure 18-2 shows, this option requires that you enter a four-digit pin. With the lock in place, you can still use the playback controls, but you can't switch back to the Player window unless you click the Lock icon and re-enter the PIN.

Figure 18-2 Click the lock icon and enter a PIN to prevent accidentally switching back to the Player window during DVD playback.

TROUBLESHOOTING

You forgot your PIN and can't exit full-screen view

Normally, you can return to the Player window from full-screen view by double-clicking the movie itself or by pressing Alt+Enter. Neither of these options work when full-screen view is locked. If you forget your PIN and are unable to return to the Windows desktop, here's the escape sequence: Press Ctrl+Alt+Delete to display the security screen. Click Start Task Manager. This restores the Player window and allows you to access the Windows interface normally. The View Full Screen button on the Navigation bar is unavailable until you restart the Player.

Introducing Windows Movie Maker

If you've owned a video camera for more than a week or two, odds are good that you have a stack of videotapes somewhere in your home or office. Those tapes likely contain nuggets of pure gold—memories of idyllic vacations, perhaps, or recordings of milestone events in your life or the lives of people you love. Unfortunately, those nuggets are probably so deeply embedded in the surrounding gangue that you seldom bother to look for them (let alone look *at* them). It doesn't help that the sequential-access nature of recording tape discourages review, not to mention the fact that much of what most of us put on videotape isn't worth revisiting or inflicting upon others.

But the nuggets are there, so you don't dare discard or reuse those tapes. How to separate the valuable bits from all the rest? Windows Movie Maker can help. This program, originally introduced in Windows XP and extensively updated for Windows Vista, is a highly functional video editing tool. Use it to create polished video presentations, complete with animated titles, credits, narration, background music, professional-looking scene transitions, and special effects. Even if you never use any of those fancy features, you'll find that Windows Movie Maker is a terrific tool for memory-mining. With it, you can import your raw video footage, separate it into scenes, pick out the valuable pieces, and assemble the edited pieces into clips that you'll be at ease delivering to friends and family—and watching again yourself.

Windows Movie Maker is a consumer-oriented program, adequate for most personal purposes. But even though it lacks the exotic features of professional video editing programs (such as Adobe Premiere Pro or Avid Liquid Pro), you can use it to create effective business presentations as well—training videos, short movies to post to your company's website, product demonstrations, and other similar items.

How Much Hardware Does Movie Maker Need?

Creating and editing videos with Windows Movie Maker demands a lot of computing and storage resources. For starters, you need a modern display adapter that supports DirectX 9; if your video card doesn't meet this bar, you'll see an error message when you try to start Movie Maker. After you pass that hurdle, our experience suggests you're more likely to capture video footage from your camcorder successfully, without dropped frames, if you have plenty of usable RAM—at least 1 GB, preferably twice that amount. You'll need a robust CPU as well, ideally a dual-core processor running at 1.6 GHz or better, unless you're willing to allow projects to chug away overnight as they render into usable formats.

What about disk space? Your storage requirements depend on the image quality you want to achieve and the amount of footage you intend to store. Capturing footage from your digital camcorder using the highest quality, least compressed format, called Digital Video Audio-Video Interleaved (DV-AVI), will consume disk space at a rate of 178 MB per minute, or about 13 GB for a one-hour source tape. You'll want to use this format, if possible, if you intend to copy your finished movies back to videotape, to CDs, or to DVDs. If you are planning to prepare videos to watch on a computer, you can choose a more compact format. Capturing digital camcorder footage in the WMV format at the quality level that Windows Movie Maker recommends for computer playback consumes a mere 14 MB per minute—less than a twelfth of the space used by DV-AVI. If you're planning to publish your work on websites, you can choose from a variety of still more compact formats, suitable for downloading at broadband or dial-up speeds. Windows Movie Maker creates large temporary files while it renders projects into movies. As you calculate your disk space needs, it's a good idea to budget 15 GB for this purpose.

Note

Make sure that any partitions on which you plan to capture DV-AVI video are formatted in NTFS. FAT32 partitions have a file-size limit of 4 GB.

However you expect to work, assume that you need a large amount of storage. If you're planning to get into movie making as a serious pastime, get the largest disk you can afford (add another disk to your system if that's an option). That will give you the freedom to capture more of your video library and assemble the best parts into satisfactory movies.

To import footage from a digital camcorder, you should have an IEEE 1394 (FireWire or iLink) interface and cable. If your computer is of recent vintage and has a built-in 1394 adapter, you're set. If not, you can buy an IEEE 1394 card and plug it into a PCI slot. To import video from an analog camera or from VHS tape, you'll need an analog capture device.

You'll find a shortcut for Windows Movie Maker (Moviemk.exe) near the top of the All Programs menu. Figure 18-3 shows the basic layout of Movie Maker in operation.

Figure 18-3 Movie Maker's clean layout allows you to follow a smooth workflow—preview items first, then drag them from the Contents pane onto the Storyboard.

The Tasks pane on the left walks you through the three basic steps in creating a movie. The Contents pane contains thumbnails of images, video clips, and audio files you've imported into the current collection. The Preview monitor allows you to play a video clip, pausing and moving frame by frame through it so you can split it at exactly the right point for your project.

To work most effectively with Movie Maker, it helps to understand its terminology:

- The media elements you import are called *clips*.

- You can organize clips in folders and subfolders called *collections* in the Imported Media folder.

- To create a movie, you drag clips (or collections) onto the *storyboard*, where you can rearrange them as needed.

- To add or edit the audio track, trim video clips, and adjust the timing of each item on the storyboard, switch to the *timeline*, which is shown in Figure 18-4 on the next page. To switch between storyboard and timeline, use the drop-down menu at the top left, or use the Ctrl+T shortcut.

Chapter 18

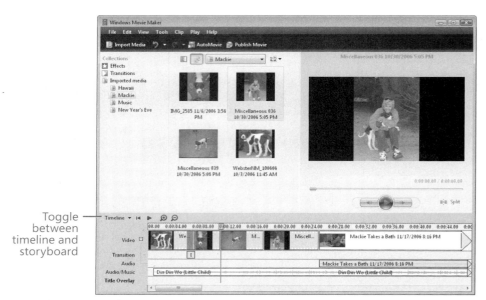

Toggle between timeline and storyboard

Figure 18-4 After getting clips in the correct order on the storyboard, use the timeline to add an audio track and adjust the timing of each clip in your project.

- *Effects* allow you to change the look and feel of a clip—by speeding up or blurring a video clip, for example. *Transitions* control what happens when you move from one clip to the next—wipes, fades, and dissolves are among the many options available here.

At any time, you can replace the Tasks pane with the Collections pane, which displays effects and transitions in addition to a tree view of the Imported Media folder. The two left-most buttons just above the Contents pane allow you to show the Tasks pane or the Contents pane. Click the button for the pane that's currently visible to hide it and allow the Contents pane to occupy the entire space. (The contents of the Collections pane are always available from the drop-down Location menu, just above the Contents pane.)

With the Collections pane open, you can create, copy, nest, and delete folders to suit your own organizational purposes. The mechanics are simple: To create a new top-level folder, right-click the Imported Media entry in the Collections pane, click New Collection Folder, and type a name to replace the default New Folder moniker. To create a new subfolder, right-click an existing folder and then follow the same steps. Drag and drop folders and subfolders (or right-click and use the Cut, Copy, and Paste menus) to move and copy them. If you make a copy of a folder in the same location as the original, Movie Maker gives it a new name consisting of the original name plus a sequential number.

Remember that the clip objects you work with in Windows Movie Maker are merely pointers to file data, so you can copy them freely without incurring meaningful storage expense. To move a clip from one folder to another, drag it from the Collections pane and drop it onto the appropriate entry in the Collections tree. To copy instead of move, hold down Ctrl as you drag.

The large dark area to the right of the Contents pane is the preview monitor. Use this miniature media player to play the selected clip (whether that clip is video or sound) or to preview your work as you put together a movie.

As you assemble materials on the storyboard and timeline, you create a *project*, which Windows Movie Maker will use to render your finished movie. Windows Movie Maker Project files are saved with the extension .mswmm. Unlike your source video files, project files are small and consist mostly of pointers to the original imported files and instructions on how to trim and arrange the pieces of your project. Provided the data objects they reference remain at hand, you can edit and reuse project files indefinitely to make different kinds of movies for different purposes.

INSIDE OUT   Back up the Collections database

Windows Movie Maker records the state of your collections—the names of your folders and clips, and the links between clips and source files—in a single file with the .dat file name extension. Each user account gets its own Movie Maker database, which you'll find in %LocalAppData%\Microsoft\Movie Maker. If you've invested more than a few minutes' work in Movie Maker, be sure this file is included in your regular backup routine. If the file is erased or damaged, you won't lose your captured video (all of which will still be safely stored in WMV or AVI files elsewhere on your hard disk), but you will have to reimport that footage and rebuild your collections structure.

INSIDE OUT   Use AutoRecover

By default, Windows Movie Maker saves your collections database and current project information (if any) every ten minutes in an AutoRecover file. If the programs stops abnormally, the next time you start you'll have the opportunity to return to the state recorded by the last AutoRecover save. You can change the AutoRecover time interval by choosing Tools, Options, clicking the General tab, and entering a new value in the Save AutoRecover Info Every *nn* Minutes check box. You can also turn the feature off, although we can't think of any good reason to do that.

Planning a Movie Maker Project

Creating a digital movie with Windows Movie Maker isn't quite as easy as 1-2-3, but that's how many steps are involved:

1. Gather and organize source materials, including video clips, digital photos, and music clips.

2. Edit the project by trimming video clips, arranging the source material in the correct order on the storyboard and timeline, and adding transitions, visual effects, sound, and titles.

3. Publish the finished movie as a digital video file or burn it to a DVD or CD.

Devoting some thought and energy to the first part of this process—particularly the organization of your raw material—will save you a great deal of time and hassle when you are immersed in the more interesting, creative work. As you work with imported items in the Contents pane (in thumbnail view or as a list, if you click the icon above the pane to switch to Details view), remember that you are manipulating pointers to data, not the data itself. Similarly, when you create collections folders in which to classify your clips, you are dealing with virtual folders, not the folders on your hard disk. Thus, once you have captured or imported an accumulation of video footage, you can copy your clips (and folders) at will, give each copy a meaningful name, and build a conveniently redundant structure that reflects the multiple contexts in which your clips can be used—all without touching your original, efficiently stored and organized data files.

When it comes to converting a finished project into a format that you can view or share with others, you have four or five choices, depending on which edition of Windows Vista is installed on your computer. You can save the movie to a disk file for viewing in Windows Media Player (or a comparable program), burn it onto a recordable CD, save it as an e-mail attachment, or (if you have a digital video camera and an IEEE 1394 connection) send it back to videotape. If you have Home Premium or Ultimate edition installed, a fifth option opens Windows DVD Maker so you can burn the project to a recordable DVD in a format that can be played back on a consumer DVD player. Some of these basic choices have options of their own; for details, see "Saving and Sharing Movies," later in this chapter.

Gathering and Managing Source Materials

Before you can make a movie, you have to import the raw materials you plan to use—pictures, video clips, and audio. If you've previously imported items and saved them in collections under the Imported Media folder, you can reuse them here. When you start a new project, every item in your collection is available. If an item you want to use in the current project isn't in the collection, you need to import it. After a video clip is available in the Imported Media folder or a collection, you can preview it, split it, trim away unwanted material at the beginning or end (or both), and create new clips from existing ones.

You can import media from any of the following sources:

- If the media files you want to import are available on a local or network drive, click the Import Media button. Select items in any compatible format from the Import Media Items dialog box (Ctrl+click to select multiple items) and then click Import. (You can also drag and drop any supported media file into the Collections pane or the Contents pane.) All items you add using the Import Media dialog box are dumped into the Imported Items folder; you can reorganize the imported items in existing folders or create new folders at any time.

- If you've already organized and tagged your photos and video clips, start in Windows Photo Gallery, make your selection, and click the Make Movie button. This action opens Movie Maker (or switches to it, if the program is already open), imports all selected images, and stores them in a new collection folder within the Imported Media folder. Rename the newly created folder and you're done.

INSIDE OUT   Use Photo Gallery to filter imported media

Using Windows Photo Gallery offers a significant advantage over the Import Media option in Movie Maker. In Photo Gallery, you can use the built-in search tools, tags, ratings, and date stamps to gather a selection of photos and video clips from multiple folders. In Movie Maker, you have to repeat the Import Media option for each folder that contains media files. This solution is ideal for throwing together a quick and easy slide show in a shareable format. For more details on how to use Photo Gallery, see Chapter 17, "Viewing, Organizing, and Sharing Digital Photos."

- To import recorded video from a digital camera, switch the camera to Play mode, connect it to your PC, and click the From Digital Video Camera link under the Import heading in Movie Maker's Tasks pane. (If Movie Maker isn't running, you can use the Windows Video Import tool, which uses the same wizard, to import the video.) We discuss this process in more detail in the next section.

- To import live video from a webcam or digital video camera, connect the camera to your computer and turn it on in camera mode. Then use the same Windows Video Import tool to start and stop the camera and capture a file in a supported format.

Note

Earlier versions of Windows Movie Maker included the option to import video content from videocassette recorders and other sources using analog capture devices. This capability is not available in Windows Vista. If you have video clips trapped in an analog format, you'll need to use third-party software to create a digital video file in a supported format and then import that file into Movie Maker. Most analog capture devices include software specifically designed to perform this task.

Table 18-1 lists the media formats that Windows Movie Maker can import.

Table 18-1. File Formats Supported by Windows Movie Maker

Media Type	Supported Extensions
Audio	.aif, .aifc, .aiff, .asf, .au, .mp2, .mp3, .mpa, .snd, .wav, .wma
Still image	.bmp, .dib, .emf, .gif, .jfif, .jpe, .jpeg, .jpg, .png, .tif, .tiff, .wmf
Video	.asf, .avi, .dvr-ms, m1v, .mp2, .mp2v, .mpe, .mpeg, .mpg, .mpv2, .wm, .wmv

You'll notice in Table 18-1 a noteworthy addition and an omission. The good news is that in Windows Vista, for the first time, Movie Maker allows you to use recorded TV (in the .dvr-ms format created by Windows Media Center) as a video format. So, if you're patient and you're not working with a recorded program that has been copy-protected, you can trim commercials and pledge breaks from a documentary on public television or cull a snippet of video from a much longer show. The bad news is that Windows Movie Maker still does not support QuickTime video (files with the extension .mov). If you have QuickTime files that you want to use in your Windows Movie Maker productions, you'll need to convert them to a supported format first. The RAD Video Tools, which you can download from the RAD Game Tools site at *http://www.vista-io.com/1801*, can do this job for you.

INSIDE OUT　Prepare for codecs

If you try to import a video or audio file that uses a codec (a compression/decompression algorithm) that isn't already installed on your system, Windows Movie Maker will not be able to complete the import. To avoid this problem, you can have Windows Movie Maker download any codec it needs without intervention from you. To make use of this service, choose Tools, Options, and click the General tab. Then select Download Codecs Automatically. For some formats, you might have to install a codec manually, and with third-party codecs in particular, you're likely to encounter difficulties that won't occur using the standard codecs and formats included with Windows Vista. For more details on codecs, see "Adding and Updating Codecs," Chapter 15.

Importing Recorded Video

Most digital video cameras record on tape. Movie Maker includes the Windows Video Import utility (Capturewizard.exe), which can transfer all or part of a tape to a digital file on your computer. Before you can successfully import recorded video, you need to first connect the camera to your PC and switch it to Play mode. If Movie Maker is running when you connect the camera, the Import Video wizard starts automatically. If it doesn't start, click the From Digital Video Camera link under the Import heading in Movie Maker's Tasks pane. If Movie Maker is not running, an AutoPlay dialog box offers to import the video using the Windows Video Import utility. The resulting procedure is identical.

> **Note**
>
> If you connect the camera and switch it to camera mode, the Import Video wizard allows you to capture live video. Click the Start Video and Stop Video buttons to turn recording on and off.

In the wizard's first step, shown in Figure 18-5, you need to enter a name for the file you're going to import, choose a location (the default options are the Videos folder or the Public Videos folder), and choose a format.

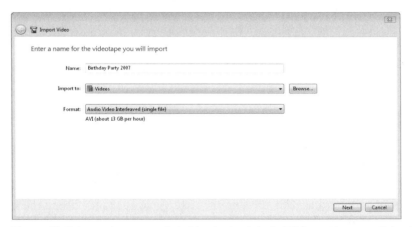

Figure 18-5 Importing a recorded video in the default AVI format is compatible with the widest variety of programs, but it uses a frightful amount of disk space.

Below the selected option in the Format box, Movie Maker displays an estimate of the approximate storage space required. You have three options:

- **Audio Video Interleaved (single file)** imports the recorded video and saves it as a single file in AVI format. Choose this option if you intend to use the digital video file in other video editing programs; the AVI format is universally supported. It consumes 13 GB of disk space per hour of video.

- **Windows Media Video (single file)** imports the recorded video and saves it as a single file in WMV format. If you plan to use the resulting clips only in Movie Maker or other video editing programs that directly support the WMV format, choose this option, which is far more efficient than AVI, at 2 GB of disk space per hour of recorded video.

- **Windows Media Video (one file per scene)** imports the recorded video into multiple WMV files. The Import Video wizard detects each point at which the camera was stopped and started and use those breakpoints to define scenes, which it saves in individual WMV files.

After filling in the blanks, click Next. The wizard's second step, shown in Figure 18-6, allows you to exercise some control over exactly how much of the recorded video ends up stored in files on your hard disk.

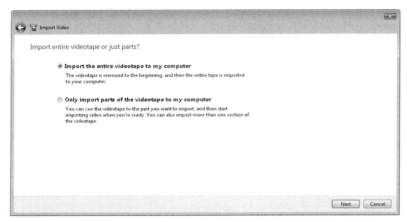

Figure 18-6 Importing the entire tape involves the least hassle; importing parts of a tape takes more work up front but makes for more manageable video collections.

If you choose Import the Entire Videotape To My Computer, the import begins as soon as you click Next. The Import Video wizard rewinds the tape to the beginning and starts transferring the bits and saving them in the format you specified in the previous step. The wizard displays a status dialog box as it works, showing the elapsed time of the video imported so far, the amount of disk space consumed, and the amount of disk space remaining.

INSIDE OUT   You can stop the transfer any time

You don't have to import an entire tape using this option. If you know that the one-hour tape you're using has only 15 minutes of recorded video at the beginning, choose the Import The Entire Videotape To My Computer option and then click Stop after 15 minutes have elapsed. The Import Video wizard warns you that it will only save what's been transferred so far. If you give your approval, the partial tape is saved in the format you chose.

If you choose Only Import Parts of the Videotape To My Computer and click Next, the wizard takes you to a follow-up screen like the one shown in Figure 18-7.

Figure 18-7 The camera controls at the top of this dialog box allow you to cue the tape up to the exact frame where you want the transfer to begin.

Use the camera controls at the top of the dialog box to cue the tape to the precise frame where you want the import to start. While the tape is stopped, click the Rewind and Fast Forward buttons (just to the right of the Stop button) to move quickly through the tape; when the tape is playing, click and hold these buttons to scan through the tape. Use the Previous Frame and Next Frame buttons to advance one frame at a time, stopping when you reach the first frame you want to see in your imported file.

If you know the approximate length of the section you want to import, select Stop Importing After (min) and adjust the number of minutes to a number slightly longer than the clip itself. If you eschew this option, the recording will continue until the end of the tape or until you click Stop Video Import.

When you import video files, Movie Maker saves them in the folder you specified, using the name you entered at the beginning of the wizard and appending the date and time that you imported the recording. It also adds clips for each file imported during the current session to the Imported Media folder. If you're planning to immediately edit the clips into a movie and then discard the original files, you can leave the default names intact. If you want to add one or more clips to a collection that you anticipate reusing, however, we recommend that you rename the clip to something more descriptive; select the item in the Contents pane and press F2, or right-click and choose Rename, or right-click and choose Properties, which displays a box where you can edit the file name and a read-only list of technical details like those shown in Figure 18-8.

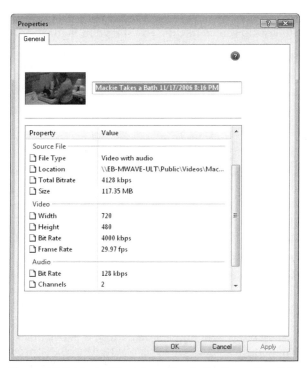

Figure 18-8 Most of the information in the Properties dialog box for a video clip is read-only; the name is a noteworthy exception.

Renaming clips you plan to keep has an additional benefit as well: Assuming you save the underlying files to one of the default folders (Videos or Public Videos), those names will be picked up and indexed in Photo Gallery and in the Windows Search index. Although you can add tags to your WMV files at any time, a good descriptive name requires no additional effort to be searchable.

Now that you have a folder full of imported clips, you can begin tinkering with them:

To preview a clip, select it in the Contents pane and use the controls under the preview monitor to its right, as shown in Figure 18-9. The large Play/Pause button starts and stops playback. Drag the blue indicator on the Seek bar in either direction to move to a particular portion of the clip. Click and hold the Previous Frame and Next Frame buttons to rewind or fast-forward through the clip; click these buttons to move one frame at a time until you reach the right point.

Figure 18-9 Aim the mouse pointer at the Seek bar to see this ScreenTip, which shows the time marker for that point on the bar. Click to jump to that point.

The Split button below the right edge of the Seek bar allows you to create two clips out of the current clip, breaking them at exactly the frame displayed in the preview monitor (the current frame becomes the first in the second clip). When you split a clip, you see two items in the collection, but the single underlying video file is unchanged. If you make a mistake, you can undo the split by clicking the Undo button or pressing Ctrl+Z.

To join two existing clips, click the first clip in the Contents pane and then hold down the Ctrl key and click the second. Choose Clip, Combine (or press N) to combine the two clips into a single file. This option works only if the two clips were originally immediately contiguous; in other words, you can combine two clips that were originally split, but you can't combine two random or disconnected clips.

If you originally imported a recording as a single file and you decide you want to split it into individual clips, select the clip in the Contents pane, right-click, and choose Create Clips. This option works only for WMV and AVI clips and is best suited for tapes that were imported directly from a digital video camera. Movie Maker uses the timestamps inserted by the camera as well as "significant frame changes" in the video to detect where clips should break. If the breaks occur at incorrect locations, use the Combine menu to rejoin the split clips.

Using the Storyboard and Timeline to Assemble a Project

To create a sequence of video clips that Windows Movie Maker can render into a movie, drag those clips from the Collections pane and drop them onto the big rectangles of the storyboard. As Figure 18-10 shows, the storyboard displays a thumbnail of each clip, along with the clip's name. You can add a transition between two clips by dragging it to the small rectangle between those clips, and you can add an effect to a clip by dragging it to the star in the lower left corner of the clip's thumbnail. Windows Movie Maker changes the color of the star from gray to blue when an effect is in use. (For more about video transitions and effects, see "Using Transitions," and "Using Effects," later in this chapter.)

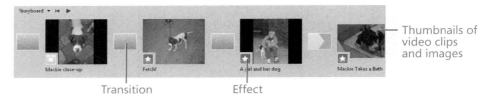

Figure 18-10 The storyboard displays a thumbnail of each video clip in your project. Transitions appear in the small rectangles, and effects are marked by a blue star.

While you're putting the project together, you can use the Preview monitor at any time to see what you have so far. To play the project starting from a particular clip, select that clip before clicking the Play button.

INSIDE OUT Get a fresh start

To clear everything from your project and start fresh, press Ctrl+Delete, or choose Edit, Clear Storyboard (or Edit, Clear Timeline).

The storyboard is always in insert mode. To place a new clip between two clips that are already on the storyboard, simply drop the newcomer in the space between those clips. Windows Movie Maker inserts your clip and moves everything else to the right. To move a clip, drag it to its new location. Windows Movie Maker inserts at the new location, closing the gap at the old location.

INSIDE OUT The secret of renaming clips on the fly

If you don't like the way a clip on the storyboard is named, delete it (select it and press Delete). Rename it in the Collections pane, then drag it back onto the storyboard. You can't rename objects while they're on the storyboard or timeline. And if you rename an object in the Contents pane, your changes are not reflected in any matching item that's already on the storyboard.

The storyboard makes it easy to see the beginning content of each clip in your project, but it doesn't, at a glance, show you the relative durations of your clips. If you hover the mouse over a clip, however, Windows Movie Maker reports the clip's duration in a ScreenTip.

Transitions and effects have names, just as clips do. You can also hover the mouse over a transition rectangle to see the name of that transition or over a blue star to see what effect you've applied.

To get precise information about when events occur in your movie-in-progress, switch to the timeline. Figure 18-11 shows a timeline view of the project displayed in Figure 18-10.

Zoom timeline in/out

Figure 18-11 The timeline shows when events start and stop. It also displays information about sounds and titles. ScreenTips (like the one over the transition) are also useful sources of information.

Because the space devoted to events on the timeline is proportional to the time they occupy in your movie, some clips appear stretched, while others are scrunched into illegibility. To get a better look at items of short duration, you can expand the scale of the timeline by clicking the Zoom Timeline In button (the plus sign near the upper-left corner of the timeline) or pressing Page Down. Press Page Up or click Zoom Timeline Out to return the timeline to a more compressed scale.

As Figure 18-11 shows, the timeline has five separate tracks and conveys some information not shown on the storyboard. (If you don't see the Transition and Audio tracks, click the plus sign to the right of Video. If you still don't see all five tracks, drag the top border of the Timeline pane upward to expand the pane.) These tracks have the following functions:

- **Video** The Video track displays an initial thumbnail for each clip. If you've added an effect to the clip, a blue star appears.

- **Transition** Transitions appear on the Transition track. Depending on how you've adjusted the time scale, your transitions might show up as narrow vertical bars.

- **Audio** The Audio track represents the audio captured or imported with your video—the sounds recorded by your camcorder's microphone, for example, or by your computer's microphone if you captured video from a webcam with a separate microphone. A blue sound graph runs through the middle of the track; the thickest parts of the graph represent the loudest sounds.

- **Audio/Music** If you add narration or background music to your project, those items appear on the Audio/Music track. (For information about managing the sound balance between Audio/Music and Audio, see "Changing the Balance of Sound Between the Audio and Audio/Music Tracks," later in this chapter.)

Chapter 18

- **Title Overlay**   Windows Movie Maker includes a titles/credits editor. If you use it to create titles that appear superimposed on the video of your movie, these titles are represented on the Title Overlay track of the timeline. You can also use the editor to generate a title that appears at the beginning of your movie or credits that appear at the end, those items are represented on the Video track of the timeline. (For more about titles, see "Creating Titles and Credits," later in this chapter.)

The first three of these tracks—Video, Transition, and Audio—are bracketed on the timeline, because you can't adjust the positions of items on these tracks independently. If you move two clips joined by a transition, for example, the transition moves along with the video and audio.

Trimming Clips

One of the handy things you can do on the timeline that you can't do on the storyboard is trim a clip. To lop off the beginning or ending of any clip, audio or video, start by clicking somewhere within the clip to select it. Then move the mouse pointer to the right or left edge of the clip (depending on whether you want to trim the beginning or the end). When you see the trim clip (a double-headed red arrow) drag it to the point where you want to trim.

For a quicker, more precise trim, select the clip in the timeline and click Play. Watch the playback in the Preview pane. When you get to the place where you want to make the cut, pause the player. Use the Previous Frame and Next Frame controls on the Preview pane if necessary to get to the exact frame. Click Clip, then click Trim Beginning or Trim End to remove that portion of the clip.

Using Still Images

Movies don't always need to move. Sometimes a moment of frozen action is just what's needed.

Still images enable you to create interesting narrated slide shows. They can be handy as stationary backgrounds for overlaid titles. (For more about laying titles over clips, see "Creating Titles and Credits," later in this chapter.) Still image clips have a default duration of five seconds. You can increase or decrease this duration for a particular clip by dragging its trim handle on the timeline. To change the default duration, choose Tools, Options, click the Advanced tab, and enter a new value in the Picture Duration box. Note that changing the default does not affect pictures you've already added to your project.

Using Transitions

By default, Movie Maker adds a simple cut between the clips of your movies. To avoid these abrupt changes from one scene to the next, you can choose from 63 stylish transitions in Windows Movie Maker's built-in Transitions collection. For a sampling of what a transition will look like in your movie, open the Transitions collection, select any item in the list, and click the Play button in the preview monitor.

INSIDE OUT   **Set your own default images**

Any JPEG images can serve as the pictures that Windows Movie Maker uses to preview transitions. The default images are stored in %ProgramFiles%\Movie Maker\Shared, as Sample1.jpg and Sample2.jpg (both in 640 x 480 format) and Sample3.jpg and Sample4. jpg (in widescreen format, 640 x 360). To use your own pictures as preview fodder, re-name the respective images in this folder. Then copy the new images into this folder us-ing the names of the images you're replacing. Because this is a system folder, you'll need to approve UAC dialog boxes to rename the existing images and to copy new ones to this location.

The easiest way to add a transition to your project is to drag it to the storyboard. Drop the transition in the small rectangle before the clip that you want to transition to. Al-ternatively, select that clip, select the transition in the Collections pane, and then press Ctrl+D.

Transitions have a default duration of 1.25 seconds. To increase or decrease the time devoted to a particular transition, display the timeline and adjust the time scale (using Page Down and Page Up, or the Zoom Timeline In and Zoom Timeline Out buttons) so that the transition becomes visible as a rectangle on the Transition track. Then click the transition and drag the trim handle to the left or right. To change the default transition time, choose Tools, Options, click the Advanced tab, then adjust the value in the Transi-tion Duration box. Note that changing the default does not affect transitions that you have already added to your project.

To add a Fade transition—in which one video clip simply overlaps another so that the first footage gradually disappears from view while the second emerges—you can work in the manner just described (that is, drag the Fade object from the Transitions collection to the storyboard). But as an alternative, click the second clip on the timeline and then drag that clip to the left so that it partially overlaps the preceding clip. As you do this, a bright blue bar tapers to a point at the timeline position where the fade will begin:

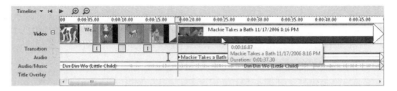

You can see the exact starting time of the fade by reading the ScreenTip. Note that the duration time reported in the ScreenTip is that of the second clip, however, not that of the fade. You can calculate the duration of the fade by noting the timeline position of the playback bar, which marks the start of the second clip. In the example just shown, the playback bar is at 0:00:18.17 and the starting time of the fade is 0:00:16.87, hence the fade will last 1.4 seconds.

Chapter 18

If you right-click a clip on the timeline or storyboard, you'll see the shortcut-menu commands Fade In and Fade Out. You can also use these to achieve fade transitions. But these fade options are different in two ways from the fade transition just described. First, they fade in from or out to black, not in from or out to the adjacent clip. Second, they are of shorter duration and their duration can't be changed. Because of these differences, Windows Movie Maker treats them as *effects*, not *transitions*. (The Effects collection also includes fades into and out of white.) We'll take up the topic of effects next.

Using Effects

With the exception of the four fade effects just mentioned, the effects available in Windows Movie Maker change the entire appearance of video clips, not just their beginnings or endings. You can use effects to do such things as brighten or darken a clip, speed playback up or slow it down, invert or flip the action, achieve a grainy or old-movie appearance—and so on. To see what effects are available, select Effects from the top of the Collections tree. To see what an effect does, select it in the Collections pane and click the Play button in the Preview pane.

Effects, unlike transitions, can be combined. Thus, for example, you can make your clip both dark *and* grainy by adding both the Brightness, Decrease and Film Grain effects. You can use as many as six effects on the same clip. Using the same effect more than once on the same clip intensifies the effect. For example, using Speed Up, Double twice multiplies the playback speed by four.

Note that some effects don't work together at all. The Ease In effect, for example, zooms in on the selected clip (in other words, it crops the clip slowly from the outside toward the center). The speed at which the effect carries out this zoom is timed so that it continues through the duration of the clip. Ease Out does exactly the opposite. With Ease Out, playback of your clip starts zoomed in toward the center, and more and more of the clip is revealed throughout the duration of its playback. If you try to use both these effects together, Movie Maker uses whichever effect is higher in the list and simply ignores the other.

To add an effect to a clip, select the effect you want and drag it to the clip. You can do this with equal facility in both the timeline and the storyboard. Windows Movie Maker darkens the star on the storyboard (in the bottom left-hand corner of the clip) to show that an effect is in place; on the timeline it displays a star that would otherwise not be there. If you apply multiple effects to a clip, the display shows multiple stars, stacked atop one another.

As an alternative method of adding effects, right-click the clip and choose Effects from the shortcut menu. As Figure 18-12 shows, the Add Or Remove Effects dialog box allows you to add multiple effects at once. It's also a handy way to see what effects are already in place. (Another way to do that is to hover the mouse over the blue square in a clip's storyboard frame.)

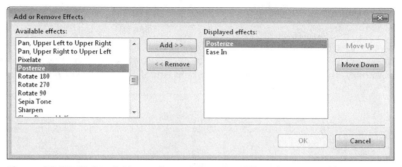

Figure 18-12 Right-clicking a clip and choosing Effects lets you add or remove effects—or just see what effects are already in place.

Working with Sound

As we noted earlier, the timeline in Windows Movie Maker reveals two audio tracks. One of these, the Audio track, represents the sound captured on your video source (your camera's microphone, typically, or the microphone at your computer if you captured video from a webcam). The other, called Audio/Music, lets you add a separate layer of sound—such as background music from a WMA or MP3 file, sound effects recorded in a WAV file, or a narration that you record to accompany your movie. The Audio track is a component of the Video track, in the sense that its objects cannot be moved or trimmed independently of the video they belong to. Objects on the Audio/Music track, in contrast, are freely movable and may be trimmed at either end.

Adding Background Music or Audio

To add music to your project, first be sure that you have that music in the form of a Windows Movie Maker clip. If what you want is a CD track, use Windows Media Player to rip the track, then import the resulting WMA file into Windows Movie Maker. (For information about converting CD audio tracks to digital files, see "Ripping CDs," Chapter 16.)

Display the timeline and, if necessary, expand the timeline upward (drag the blue bar at the top of the pane), so that you have a good view of the Audio/Music track. Then drag the clip onto that track. To position an audio/music object *precisely* within a video track, play the video track from the timeline. When you get to the point where you want the sound to be aligned, click the Pause button in the Preview pane. The playback pointer in the timeline now provides you with an easy-to-hit target for your sound clip. (Adjust the position of this pointer with the Previous Frame and Next Frame buttons if necessary to get it exactly where you want it.)

Note that unlike video, which can only be appended to the last clip on the Video track or inserted between existing clips, sound clips can be positioned anywhere on the Audio/Music track. Before you drop the clip on the track, as you move the mouse left and right, a bright blue insertion pointer shows where the sound will land if you release the mouse button.

> **Note**
>
> If you move the mouse pointer smoothly beneath a set of clips stationed on the Video track, you'll notice that the insertion pointer pauses briefly each time you come to a clip boundary. This behavior is designed to help you align sound clips with video clips.

INSIDE OUT   Clips first, then sound

Clips on the Audio/Music track are not anchored to the video clips with which they're aligned. If the video clips moves (for example, because you insert another video clip or trim a clip), you'll have to realign your sound and video. To avoid frustration, get all your visual blocks in place, and then add sound.

Adding Narration

If you have a microphone connected to your computer, you can play back all or portions of a project and record a narration to accompany what you see. Follow these steps:

1. Display the timeline and make sure that the Audio/Music track is visible.

2. Position the playback pointer (the blue bar that runs through all five tracks) where you want to begin your narration. (The Audio/Music track must be vacant at this place; you cannot record a narration over an existing audio/music clip.)

3. Choose Tools, Narrate Timeline (or click the Narrate Timeline tool on the Timeline toolbar).

4. In the Narrate Timeline window that appears, make sure that the Audio Device option is set correctly.

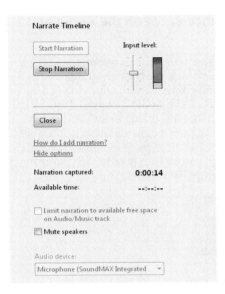

5. Speak into your microphone at the volume level and distance you're comfortable with; adjust either the Input Level setting, your volume level, or your position relative to the microphone if the meter is going into the red zone or not getting off the floor.

   ○ If you have other sound clips on the Audio/Music track to the right of your current position, select Limit Narration To Available Free Space on Audio/Music Track. (Otherwise, if your narration goes on too long, subsequent objects will be moved to the right while you speak.)

   ○ If the video that you're about to narrate has much sound of its own, select Mute Speakers (or turn your speakers off). Otherwise, your microphone will pick up some of that sound along with your voice as you narrate.

6. Click Start Narration. Windows Movie Maker will begin playback of your project at the current playback position, and you can match your words to what you see in the Preview pane. When you've said all you want to say, click Stop Narration.

Windows Movie Maker will prompt you for a file name and location for your newly recorded sound. Then it will import that sound file and create an audio clip for you, deposit that clip in the same folder where the video clip you're narrating resides, and finally place that clip in the desired position on the Audio/Music track. Return the playback pointer to that place and play your project again to make sure everything is the way you want it. Then save your work (or delete the clip from the timeline and try again).

Changing the Sound Balance Between the Audio and Audio/Music Tracks

By default, Windows Movie Maker treats the two sound tracks even-handedly. You can adjust the balance, though, so that the background music or narration gets less or more importance than the sound component of your video clips. To alter the balance, choose Tools, Audio Levels or click the Audio Levels tool, at the left edge of the timeline or storyboard toolbar. The Audio Levels dialog box that appears is modeless, which means you can leave it open on screen, begin a playback, and then move the slider to the left or right until you get the balance you're looking for. Note that the Audio Levels setting is global per project. You can't adjust it separately for different parts of a project, but projects can maintain different balance settings.

Creating Titles and Credits

No movie is complete without titles and credits. Windows Movie Maker includes a rudimentary editor for creating such necessities, complete with a selection of text layout and animation styles. You can use it to create opening titles, closing credits, titles that appear between scenes of your movie, or titles superimposed on still images or video within the movie. In all but the last case, titles join your project on the timeline's Video track, where you can modify their duration by dragging the trim handles. Superimposed titles appear on the Title Overlay track; you can move them to achieve the desired alignment with your video.

To open the title editor, choose Tools, Titles And Credits. The title editor will then ask you to specify where you want your title to appear. After clicking one of the placement options, you'll see the two-box edit screen shown on the next page.

(If you've chosen to place your title at the end of the current project, the editor assumes you want to list credits and gives you spaces to enter names and parts.) After you've written your title text, you can click the other two links on this page to customize the font and color, and to choose one of the available animation styles. Watch the Preview monitor to see your choices in action.

Using AutoMovie to Generate Movies Automatically

The AutoMovie button (also available as the top choice on the Tools menu) concocts a project automatically from the contents of the current Collections folder. AutoMovie might seem more like a gimmick than a useful feature. But if you have a set of clips that tell a coherent story, it's worth letting AutoMovie have a run at your stuff, just to see what it will come up with. Granted, you're not likely to publish the result without modification. But perhaps you'll find it a useful starting point that you can edit into something satisfactory. At the very least it will give you ideas.

To use AutoMovie, start by creating a Collections folder with all the video clips that you want your movie to include. (Don't worry about sound at this point.) Then click the AutoMovie button (or choose Tools, AutoMovie). The following screen appears:

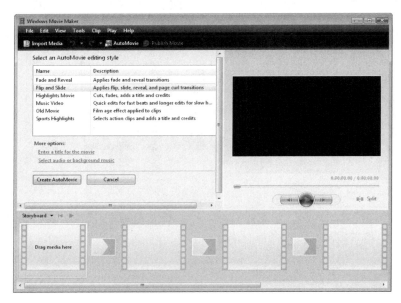

Choose one of the six available movie styles. Click the links at the bottom of the window to specify title text and an audio file for background music (AutoMovie will incorporate the music into your Audio/Music track *without* creating a clip from it—something you can't do on your own!), and then click Create AutoMovie. Windows Movie Maker will take a few minutes to analyze your audio and video, and then present its work on the timeline and storyboard.

Saving and Sharing Movies

With your project fully assembled on the timeline and storyboard, it's time to let Windows Movie Maker make a movie. If the Tasks pane is visible, click one of the links beneath the Publish To heading. Or click the Publish Movie button to open the Publish Movie wizard, shown in Figure 18-13. The wizard's first screen offers the same options available in the Tasks pane.

Figure 18-13 The DVD option shown here is only available with Windows Vista Home Premium and Ultimate editions.

Publish in the Correct Format and Aspect Ratio

Before you begin the sometimes long and tedious task of turning your project into a movie, you might want to confirm that your aspect ratio and video format settings are appropriate. (Choose Tools, Options and click the Advanced tab to see or change your settings.) Windows Movie Maker normally detects the format and aspect ratio of your video footage and sets these parameters accordingly. For the majority of users in the United States, the settings are 4:3 (aspect ratio) and NTSC (video format).

NTSC, which stands for National Television System Committee, is the standard required for broadcast in the United States and hence the standard supported by video devices configured for use in this country. Windows Movie Maker also supports the PAL, or Phase Alternating Line, standard used in some other parts of the world. If you're planning to render your movie back to a digital-video device configured for PAL, you should make sure the video format is set to PAL.

Many recent-vintage camcorders can record in 16:9 widescreen mode as well as the more common 4:3 mode. If your footage was captured at 16:9 and you intend to watch it at that ratio, be sure the aspect ratio setting is 16:9 before you render. You can render 4:3 footage at 16:9 as well, but if you're considering this, be sure to run it through the Preview pane before you render it. Typically, you'll get distortions that you won't be happy with.

Publishing to a File on Your Computer

Your first option is to save the movie as a file on your computer (or on a shared network drive). After you specify a file name and location and click Next, you'll be prompted to make a quality decision. If you don't go with the default choice, Best Quality For Playback On My Computer (Recommended), you can click More Settings and open the drop-down list to see the range of options shown in Figure 18-14.

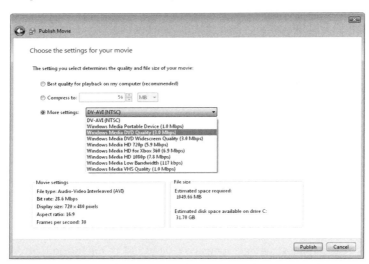

Figure 18-14 Most of the time, the first option is the best. But if you want more control over the size and quality of playback, scroll through these options and watch the bottom of the screen.

If you're having trouble evaluating the size/quality tradeoff, scroll through the list and take a look at the information in the Movie Settings and File Size boxes below. The Compress To option is useful if you want to limit your file size and none of the ready-made approaches will work.

Publishing to a Recordable CD

Previous editions of Windows Movie Maker supported a video CD format called High-MAT. In Windows Vista, this technology is no longer supported. If you choose the option to publish a movie to recordable CD, your file is saved as a Windows Media Video file at a bit rate that will allow the file to fit on a single CD.

You must insert a recordable CD in your CD or DVD drive to proceed with this option. When the wizard finishes publishing the movie, it ejects your disc (in case you want to make another CD copy). To publish another movie to the same disc, close the drive, tee up the next project, and return to the wizard. In the lower right corner of the dialog box, under the File Size heading, you'll find an estimate of the file size you're about to create and a report of the available space on your CD.

Publishing a Movie as an E-mail Attachment

You can save any Movie Maker project as a movie and share it with friends and family as an e-mail attachment. Because many mail systems impose size limits on message attachments, Windows Movie Maker, by default, will not let you create a movie larger than 10 MB. You can increase that threshold in 1 MB increments to as much as 25 MB; to do this, choose Tools, Options, click the Advanced tab, and adjust the Maximum File Size For Sending A Movie As An Attachment In An E-Mail Message option.

When you choose this option and click Next, Windows Movie Maker immediately begins publishing your project—without asking for any quality decisions on your part. When it finishes, it opens your default e-mail program, creates a new message, and attaches the newly created movie file. Add an address and a short message, click Send, and you're done.

Publishing to a Digital Video Camera

The last Publish option returns your movie to digital tape (or other media) in a digital video camera. Your camera must be turned on, set to its playback mode, and connected to an IEEE 1394 port. Put a fresh tape in the camera, click Next, and Windows Movie Maker does the rest.

This option preserves your movie at the maximum possible quality. (Ideally, you want to use this with footage that you've captured at maximum quality, of course.) After you've copied the movie back to DV tape, you can preserve it, transfer it to another medium, export it to another computer, or even re-import it in Windows Movie Maker for further editing as you think of ways to improve it.

Turning Movies and Pictures into Custom DVDs

Home Basic	○
Home Premium	●
Business	○
Enterprise	○
Ultimate	●

In the previous section, we didn't mention the Publish To DVD option. That's because it really isn't a function of Windows Movie Maker. Instead, when you click this option, Movie Maker saves your project, closes it, and sends it to a completely different application: Windows DVD Maker.

As we noted at the beginning of this chapter, DVD Maker is available only with Windows Vista Home Premium and Ultimate editions. Every other edition of Windows Vista can burn data DVDs for backup and for playback on other computers. But you'll need DVD Maker or a third-party equivalent if you want to create DVD disks that can be played back in the living room on a consumer DVD player connected to your TV.

DVD Maker includes no pull-down menus. Instead, you use a two-step wizard: First, you put together the elements that will go into your DVD (digital video files in WMV or AVI format, and photos in any format that Windows Vista recognizes). Next, you add a title and create a DVD menu that can be navigated with a remote control. When both those steps are complete, you burn the project.

If you start by clicking the Publish To DVD option in Movie Maker, DVD Maker opens automatically, with your just-saved project in the list of items that will go into your new DVD. Figure 18-15 shows the available options.

Figure 18-15 Be sure to enter a disc title in the box at the bottom of this dialog box before going on to the next step.

If you start DVD Maker from scratch, or if you want to supplement your DVD with additional content, click the Add Items link above the Contents pane. Use the Remove Items link to delete the current selection from the list of items that will go on your DVD. Enter a disc title in the box at the bottom of the dialog box and click Next to continue.

The Ready To Burn Disc step, shown in Figure 18-16, allows you to choose from a variety of menu styles and then customize the menu to suit your preferences.

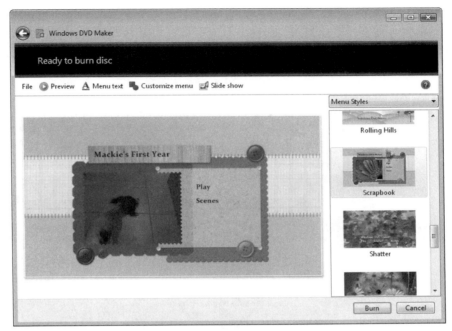

Figure 18-16 You can accept one of the canned menu styles, such as the Scrapbook option shown here, or use the row of buttons along the top to customize the menu.

The four buttons along the top of this dialog box allow you to preview the DVD menu based on its current settings and customize individual elements of the DVD. The following choices are available:

- **Preview** takes you to a page that allows you to test-drive the DVD using on-screen controls that mimic those on a DVD player's remote control. You can see not only what menus look like but how they work. Preview buttons are available from other customization screens as well.

- **Menu Text** includes edit controls where you can change the DVD title, customize the text that identifies the Play and Scenes buttons, choose fonts, font colors, and font styles, and add notes.

- **Customize Menu** includes the same font choices as in the Menu Text option, as well as options to customize the video clips and sounds that play while the menu is visible. By default, DVD Maker picks snippets from the items in your project and uses them to add zing to the menu. If the snippets it chooses are inappropriate, you can create your own short custom video files, save them in WMV format, and use them here. You can also choose an alternate background audio track to play along with the menu. Click Change Style to accept the changes you just made. Note the Save As New Style button, which allows you to add your custom options to the menu list so you can reuse the changes you make here.

- **Slide Show** includes options suitable for creating a DVD from scratch using only photos. You can include audio files as the sound track, change the length of time each picture is visible on the screen, and select transition effects. The most interesting option is the Change Slide Show Length To Match Music Length box, which automatically adjusts the intervals between photos so that the show begins and ends with the music.

When you've finished customizing the menus, insert a blank DVD disc in the drive, click the Burn button, and be prepared to wait.

CHAPTER 19

Using Windows Media Center

Home Basic ○
Home Premium ◉
Business ○
Enterprise ○
Ultimate ◉

Windows Media Center is one of the smoothest, most polished pieces of Windows Vista. But that's not surprising—after all, this is the fourth major release of a product that has been around since 2002, and its immediate predecessor, Windows XP Media Center Edition 2005, earned raves for its user experience and general reliability.

When you picture a Media Center, you probably imagine it in the living room, hooked up to a widescreen high-definition TV and a surround sound system. But a Media Center PC is also right at home in dorm rooms, hotel rooms, offices, bedrooms, and other relatively small places where a computer display is big enough to double as a TV and where you can use a remote control to operate a jukebox filled with music, slide shows, and videos. With the addition of hardware extenders, a single Media Center PC is also capable of feeding live or recorded TV to multiple rooms over a wired or wireless network.

Windows Media Center is included with the two upscale home editions of Windows Vista: Home Premium and Ultimate. By adding the right hardware and an antenna or a satellite connection, you can configure Media Center to act as a digital video recorder whose capacity is limited only by the amount of disk space you give it. Media Center uses the same hardware and media "plumbing" as Windows—the Music Library, for instance, is shared with Windows Media Player, so a CD you rip in Media Player appears in Media Center as well.

Windows Media Center is a large, feature-rich program, so our attempt to cover it in a single chapter is, by definition, going to zoom quickly past some important topics. We apologize in advance to our readers outside the United States as well. Television technology is different overseas, and this chapter covers only the standards commonly used in the United States. Our immediate goal is to help you get Media Center up and running, regardless of what room it's in.

What's in Your Edition?

Windows Media Center is included only in Home Premium and Ultimate editions. All computers can use the shared library feature of Windows Media Player, which allow computers and media players to access all or part of the media library on a Windows Vista computer over a network.

Getting Started with Windows Media Center

If your system configuration is simple—especially if it doesn't include a TV tuner or connect to a fancy surround-sound system—setting up Media Center can take literally two clicks (or two taps on a remote control). The first time you run Media Center, you see the Welcome screen shown here. If you choose Express Setup and click OK, you launch immediately into the Windows Media Center interface, ready to begin playing music, movies, or videos or browsing through your library of digital photos.

If you choose the Custom option, you run through a required setup section that checks your network and internet connection and offers you several opportunities to read the Media Center privacy statement. Assuming your network is set up already, the only substantive option is on the Enhanced Playback page, shown in Figure 19-1, where you get to decide whether to download information from the internet, including cover art for albums and DVDs, information about movies, and TV guide listings. Most people will click Yes here.

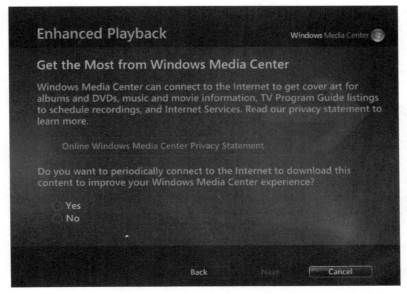

Figure 19-1 If you plan to click Yes here and don't need to customize display or audio options, choose Express Setup instead, which spares you from having to click past a half-dozen intervening screens.

After you finish the Required Setup, you can go through any of the four Optional Setup choices shown on the next page. We cover the process of configuring one or more TV tuners in "Recording and Watching TV," later in this chapter. The second and third options here are straightforward wizards that help you adjust your display settings and speakers to best advantage.

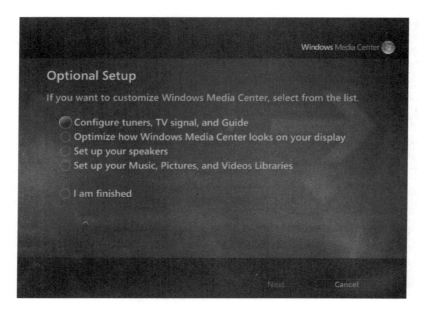

The final option on the menu allows you to specify which folders Media Center should use to build its library. By default, your library contains all folders that are currently being monitored by Windows Media Player in the account with which you're logged on. You can add or remove folders from the list here or in Windows Media Player; the results are reflected in both places.

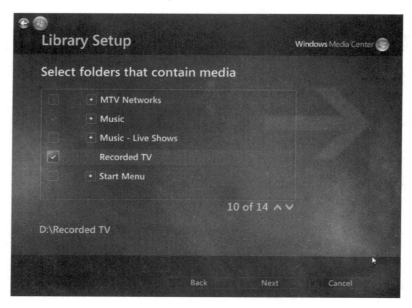

For details on how to change the list of folders monitored in Windows Media Player and Media Center, see "Managing Your Media Library," Chapter 15.

Finally, after you complete both stages of the guided setup, you can choose from a list of additional configuration options on the Settings menu. To display this menu, use any of the following techniques:

- Using the Media Center remote control, press the green button to go to the Start page, and then select Settings from the Tasks menu, or from any music, pictures, or TV page press More Info on the remote control and choose Settings from the shortcut menu.

- Using the mouse and keyboard, click the green button in the upper left corner of the Media Center window to go to the Start page. (If the green button isn't visible, click anywhere within the Media Center window and move the mouse to make it appear.) Then use the Up and Down arrows to move through the main menu options; press the left arrow when you reach Tasks to select Settings, and then press the spacebar or press Enter.

You'll find an assortment of useful options on the General menu, where you can adjust the Media Center settings shown in Table 19-1:

Table 19-1. Media Center General Options

Menu choice	Available options
Startup and Windows Behavior	Tweak the behavior of the Media Center window, including whether it starts automatically with Windows.
Visual and Sound Effects	Choose a color scheme, set a background color to fill the screen when the video signal doesn't fit the display (black or a customizable shade of gray), and turn transition effects and sounds for menu actions on or off.
Program Library Options	Edit the library of Media Center games and add-ins and control how they interact with the Media Center interface.
Windows Media Center Setup	Configure your internet connection, speakers, TV signal, and TV or monitor. The Run Setup Again choice resets all Media Center options and restarts the guided setup you ran through initially.
Parental Controls	Lock out access to programs based on TV or movie ratings; access is controlled by a 4-digit PIN you select.
Automatic Download Options	Control whether and when Media Center retrieves album art and other information from the internet. The Download Now option forces the program guide to refresh immediately.
Optimization	Select the single checkbox here to specify a time, once per day, when Windows will restart the Ehshell.exe process (the Media Center shell). This restart doesn't happen if you're watching or listening to content or if the recorder is busy.
About Windows Media Center	Display the Media Center version number and the terms of service for the online program guide.
Privacy	Read the privacy statement and adjust some privacy settings that affect internet connections and the TV program guide.

INSIDE OUT · Let Media Center start itself

If you have set up a system whose primary function is to run Media Center, why stop at the Windows desktop every time you start? From the Settings menu, choose Startup And Window Behavior and select the Start Windows Media Center when Windows Starts option, which is not selected in the default settings shown here.

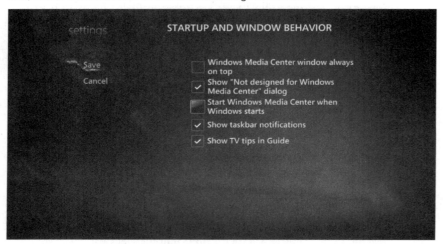

If your user account is the only one on the system and has no password, you'll go straight to the Media Center Start page each time you power up. If you want to start automatically with a password-protected account, open the Run dialog box (press Windows logo key+R) and enter **control userpasswords2**. On the Users tab of the Advanced User Accounts dialog box, clear the Users Must Enter a User Name And Password To Use This Computer dialog box, and enter the user name and password when prompted. This option automatically logs on using the selected account each time you start the computer.

Using Media Center's 10-Foot Interface

Some brilliant observer of technology once made the observation that we work with computers from 2 feet away and from consumer electronics components from 10 feet away. And thus was born the concept of the 10-foot interface, which dictates the design of Windows Media Center. Every menu and option in Media Center was created so that you could see it from across the room and navigate through menus with a remote control using four arrows and a big OK button.

When you first start Windows Media Center, you're taken to the Start page, which contains scrolling menus intended for use with a remote control. The centerpiece of the Media Center remote control is a big green button that returns to this Start page when pressed. Strictly speaking, though, you don't need a remote control to use Media Center functions. You can simulate the experience on a PC keyboard by using the arrow keys to go up, down, right, and left, and by pressing the spacebar or clicking the left mouse button to simulate a press of the OK button on the remote control. Figure 19-2 shows the Media Center Start page.

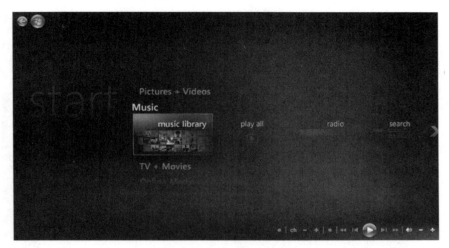

Figure 19-2 Use the up and down buttons on the remote control to change main menu options on the Media Center Start page. Use the right and left buttons to choose other options on each menu.

Did you notice the change of orientation in this figure? The Media Center interface in Windows Vista is optimized for a display that uses a 16:9 ratio rather than the standard 4:3 ration of computer monitors. You can find such a display on an HDTV monitor or a widescreen LCD.

The design of Media Center is also optimized for navigation using the basic menus and the standard arrow keys. In addition to the green button, which opens the Media Center Start page, these special navigation keys are available on the remote control:

- **Back** This button functions just like the Back button in a web browser, taking you to the previous page or menu.

- **Page Up/Page Down** These keys move one screen at a time through the Music Library and the TV program guide.

- **Replay/Skip** While playing back a TV show, these buttons jump 7 seconds back or 30 seconds forward, respectively. Within the TV program guide, they move 12 hours forward and backward.

- **Guide** Press this button to open the TV program guide. If a program is already playing, it continues to play in the background with the guide in the foreground.

- **More Info** If a program or movie is selected, pressing this button brings up more details about the current selection. In library windows, it brings up a shortcut menu instead.

In some cases, the remote control doesn't have all the keys you need to enter the information required for the task at hand. If you select Search from a library window, for example, you need to enter an alphabetical search term. The keyboard works just fine for this task, but using the numeric keypad at the bottom of the remote control is slightly more problematical. The solution is the virtual keyboard included on the remote keypad. When you choose Search in the Music Library, for instance, you see the screen shown here.

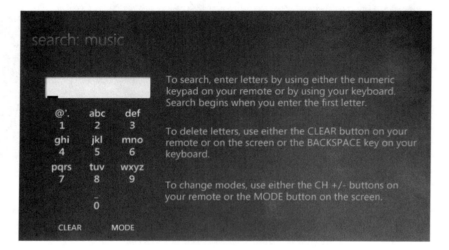

Pressing each key cycles through the options available for that key. Continue pressing the key until you reach the character you want. If the next character you want to enter is assigned to a different key, you can press that key immediately. Otherwise, wait a few seconds until the cursor moves one space to the right. You can switch between three different alphanumeric keypad mappings by pressing the Channel Up and Channel Down keys on the remote control.

You probably noticed two other elements in the screen on the previous page. The back arrow and green button in the top left corner and the playback controls in the lower right corner both appear only when you move the mouse in a Media Center window. When you do this, the program assumes that you don't have access to a remote control and offers these options, which would otherwise be unavailable.

Playing Music

Clicking the Music Library option on the Media Center Start page takes you to the page shown in Figure 19-3. Using the row of options along the top of the contents pane, you can change the view from album art (shown here) to artists, genres, playlists, or years, among other choices.

Figure 19-3 As you use the remote control to move through albums in the Music Library, the highlighted album appears larger than its neighbors; regardless of the view, details about the current selection appear below.

In any view in the Music Library, you can use the keypad to jump directly to the first entry in that list. In Artists view, for example, if you press the 7 key three times in succession, you get the letter R. Press the 6 key three times to show the letter O, and then press 5 three times quickly to get the letter L. As you can see here, that jumps straight to the listing for The Rolling Stones.

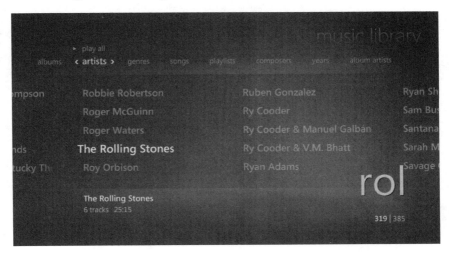

You can add search results, individual songs, or entire albums to the current queue. If you choose Play Album, the current album replaces the contents of the current Now Playing list. Choose Add To Queue if you want the current album to be added to the end of the Now Playing list. Both options are also available from shortcut menus by right-clicking or pressing the More Info button on the remote control.

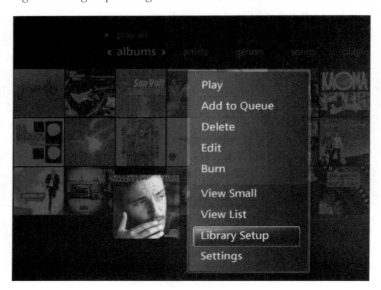

INSIDE OUT   Save and edit playlists in Media Center

Although it's not as easy or convenient as it is within Windows Media Player, you can create, edit, and save playlists from the Media Center interface. Start by adding songs or albums to the Now Playing list. Press the green button to return to the Start page and choose Now Playing + Queue. In the Now Playing window, choose View Queue, and then choose Edit Queue. The editing screen allows you to move individual tracks up or down in the list or delete them completely.

Trouble With My Lover	3:28	∧	∨	✕
Meet Me at Midnight	4:02	∧	∨	✕
Send the Man Back Ho	5:09	∧	∨	✕
Sweet Simple Love	3:29	∧	∨	✕
Power in Music	4:24	∧	∨	✕
Ease the Pain	4:46	∧	∨	✕
Trouble With Love	4:37	∧	∨	✕
Recovered Soul	4:05	∧	∨	✕

1 of 12 ∧ ∨

When you're satisfied with the playlist, choose Done and then choose Save As Playlist. Use the alphanumeric keypad to save the playlist under a name of your choosing.

Watching Pictures and Videos

In the Pictures + Videos category on the Start page, you can select a listing of all pictures or all videos in your library, sorted by folder, by date taken, or by tag. When you open any of these views, you see thumbnails for each picture or video in that category, as in Figure 19-4. Note that the name of the current view—in this case a folder name—appears in the top right corner of the screen, with details about the currently selected picture below.

Figure 19-4 Choose Play Slide Show to display all the photos in the current view in a slide show. Playing a slide show does not interrupt the playback of music.

When you choose an individual picture from the Picture Library, Media Center gives you access to a small set of image editing tools. To access these tools, press More Info and choose Picture Details from the shortcut menu. You can rotate a picture or use the Touch Up menu to crop, change contrast, or remove red eye.

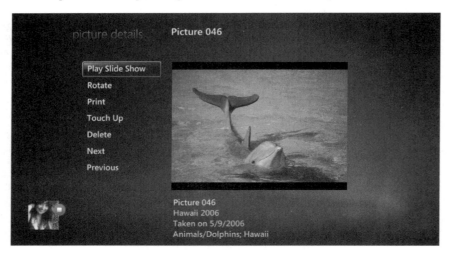

CDs, DVDs, and Devices

If you want music CDs and DVDs to begin playing in Media Center as soon as you insert them into a drive, you need to adjust AutoPlay settings. In the absence of custom settings, Media Center expects you to manually cue up and play these forms of media.

When you insert a music CD into the drive of a PC running Windows Media Center, the new CD appears in the top left slot in the Music Library. When you select the CD, you see information about the CD and a menu gives you the option to play the CD or copy its tracks using the format and bit rate currently set on the Rip Music tab in the Windows Media Player Options dialog box.

> For more details on how to adjust settings for ripped CDs, see "Building a Digital Music Library," Chapter 16.

To play a DVD in Media Center, choose TV + Movies from the Start page and then choose Play DVD. Use the More Info button to display a shortcut menu with additional options, including a Zoom menu that adjusts the image to your screen dimensions and a Title Menu option that jumps to the DVD's menu.

If you've already set up a portable music player for synchronization with Windows Media Player, you can perform the same tasks from the Media Center interface. You'll find the Sync option on the Start page, in the Tasks menu. Prepare to be a little disappointed by the options available here, however. Unlike the rich interface in Windows Media Player, your only option in Media Center is to sync with one or more playlists.

Recording and Watching TV

For music, videos, photos, and DVD playback, Media Center provides a different interface than Windows Media Player, but its feature set is essentially the same. What makes a Media Center really shine is its unique ability to play back live TV, record individual TV shows or series, and allow you to manage a collection of recorded programs from a comfy chair with nothing more than a remote control.

Before you can begin recording TV, you need to have the right hardware. The most important ingredient, of course, is a TV tuner. Tuners can be internal cards (PCI or PCI Express) or external devices that connect through a USB port. After installing a tuner, you next have to provide a television signal (from an over-the-air antenna, a cable TV connection, or a satellite converter box). You'll need a Media Center remote control and its infrared receiver (which plugs into a USB port on the PC and acts as a remote sensor for the signals sent by the remote control)—unless you plan to control everything using your keyboard and mouse. And you'll need disk space, lots of it.

About the DVR-MS Format and Copy Protection

Media Center files are recorded and saved in the Microsoft Recorded TV Show format, more commonly known as DVR-MS, from the file name extension it uses. DVR-MS is a variant of the MPEG-2 format that supports metadata written directly to the files.

This format has the advantage of being reliable and of very high quality. Its singular disadvantage is size. An hour-long TV program can consume well over 3 GB of disk space at the highest quality supported by Media Center. It's not surprising to find movies that consume as much as 9 GB of disk space. That makes it difficult to record a favorite flick and then burn it to a standard DVD, which has a maximum capacity of roughly 4.5 GB. (If you select the Burn DVD option for one of these large files, Media Center offers to burn it at a "lower quality" but gives you no way to know just how much lower the quality will be, nor can you adjust the quality level manually, as you can with Movie Maker.)

Media Center doesn't offer any alternatives for transcoding DVR-MS files to less demanding formats. Your only option using tools included with Windows Vista is to open the recorded TV program in Windows Movie Maker, transcode the file to WMV format, and then burn it to DVD using Windows DVD Maker. Several third party developers offer utilities that promise to convert DVR-MS files to MPEG or WMV formats on the fly, although most require a fairly steep level of technical proficiency and patience to configure. (For a listing of programs in this category, visit the downloads page at The Green Button, *http://www.vista-io.com/1901*.)

The DVR-MS format also supports protected recordings using the Copy Generation Management System Analog (CGMS-A) system. If you connect a cable or satellite converter box to a Media Center TV tuner, you'll quickly discover that some programs—such as those from premium channels like Home Box Office—are protected with CGMS-A. That shouldn't affect your ability to watch the program on the PC on which you recorded it or on a Media Center Extender connected to that PC. But CGMS-A protection definitely affects other things you try to do with that program:

- If you copy the file to another computer and try to play it in Windows Media Player or Media Center, you'll see only an error message. Unprotected files can be freely moved from one PC to another.

- If you install a new, larger hard disk and move recorded programs to the new disk, you'll find that protected files will no longer play.

- You'll be unable to load a protected DVR-MS file into Windows Movie Maker for editing.

- You can't burn a DVD from a protected file.

With a little searching, it's easy to find underground utilities that purport to work around CGMS-A protection. We haven't tried any, and we don't recommend them. But knowing the nature of the problem can help you decide how best to deal with it.

Setting Up a TV Tuner (or Tuners)

Windows Media Center can recognize and use up to four TV tuners—two analog and two digital. The most common configuration is a pair of analog tuners with the possible addition of one or two digital tuners to receive over-the-air (OTA) high-definition TV (HDTV) signals.

> **Note**
>
> Microsoft has announced support for digital cable tuners that can be integrated into computers sold with Windows Vista Home Premium or Ultimate edition. These tuners will use CableCARD technology to allow reception of encrypted content from cable TV companies without using a separate converter box. At the time we wrote this chapter, no such devices were available for us to purchase or test.

If you have two analog tuners installed, both must be connected to the same type of video source: you can't connect one tuner to an analog cable connection and connect the other to the output of a cable converter box. Digital tuners used for OTA HDTV can coexist with one or two analog tuners.

Setting up a TV tuner or two requires the following steps:

- **Install drivers for the tuner hardware.** If you've selected a popular, well-supported card, the drivers should be installed automatically and updated by Windows Update. If no Windows Vista drivers are available, you should be able to use Windows XP drivers on a 32-bit Windows Vista installation.

- **Connect a video source to the tuner.** You can make this connection using RCA cables, coaxial cable, or S-Video connecters.

- **Configure your TV signal.** If you haven't yet set up your hardware, you can do so by choosing Set Up TV from the TV + Movies menu on the Start page. Or choose TV from the Settings menu and then choose Set Up Your TV Signal. In this procedure, you need to identify your signal provider, enter a ZIP code so that you can receive the correct program guide listings, and specify which physical connections your tuner is using. As Figure 19-5 on the next page shows, Media Center can perform some or all of these tasks automatically.

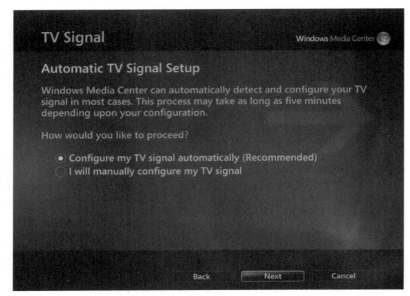

Figure 19-5 Always try to use the automatic setup first. If setup is unsuccessful, you'll be offered the option to start over and choose manual settings.

- **Configure your remote control to work with your hardware.** For an external cable or satellite converter, you will probably need to attach a USB emitter from the infrared sensor used by your remote to the infrared receiver on the converter box. This allows your Media Center remote control to change channels on the external box.

- **Configure the program guide.** For large digital cable and satellite networks, the most important step in this process is removing access to channels you never watch. The options shown at the top of the next page are available by opening the Settings menu, choosing TV, and then choosing Guide.

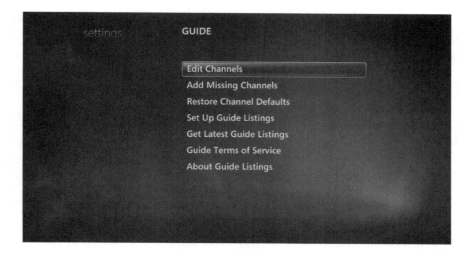

Using the Program Guide

To see what's on TV right now or at any time until approximately two weeks into the future, choose Guide from the Start page or press the Guide button on the remote control. Figure 19-6 shows a typical guide listing.

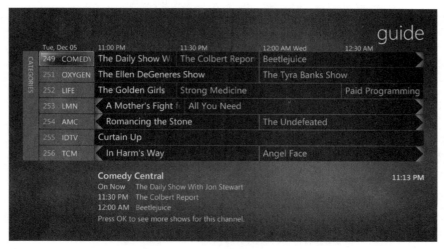

Figure 19-6 Choose the Categories bar on the left to filter guide listings by category. Select a channel name to see what's coming up on that channel. Or select an individual program to see details about that show.

Use the Page Up and Page Down buttons (also called Channel Up and Channel Down) to move up or down a screen at a time. To jump to a particular channel, enter its number on the numeric keypad. Virtually everything on the Guide is "live." If you press OK after selecting the thin Categories bar on the left side, for instance, it expands to show a list of available categories, which you can use to filter the guide's contents.

INSIDE OUT   Use the Search box

Search capabilities aren't available directly from the TV program guide, but you can search current listings by going to the Start page, choosing TV + Movies, and choosing Search. You can search by title, category, keyword, movie actor, or movie director. The same Search box is available from the Add Recording menu.

Recording a Program or Series

The advantage of a digital video recorder over an old-school video tape recorder is twofold: First, you don't need to hassle with finding a tape, rewinding it to the correct position, and switching tapes when you run out of room. More importantly, digital video recorders can interact directly with program listings to record every episode in your favorite series, and the recorder is smart enough to know that this week's episode is on at a different time than usual.

To record an individual upcoming program, highlight its entry in the program guide and press the Record button on the remote control, or press OK to display more details and then choose Record from the menu on the left, as shown in Figure 19-7.

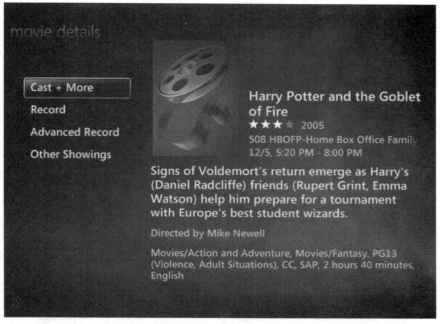

Figure 19-7 To adjust recording options for an upcoming program, select Advanced Record.

> **Note**
>
> The Other Showings option is useful when you want to record an upcoming program that's on at the same time as one you've already chosen to record. Rather than cancel the original recording, choose Other Showings to see a list of alternate times and dates. If you're lucky enough to find an additional showing at a more convenient time, you can choose one of those dates and avoid the conflict.

To record a series, start with any listing in that series. Press OK to see the details for that show and then choose one of the following options:

- **Record Series** Use this option if you want to add the recording to your series list using all the current default settings. (To view and adjust these settings, choose TV, then choose Recorder, and finally select Recording Defaults.)

- **Advanced Record** Select this option if you want the series recordings to always start a minute (or two or three) early or end a little later. You can also choose how many copies of the series to keep on hand at any given time. For a series recording of a nightly news show, for example, you might want to keep only one show, discarding yesterday's news as soon as today's news begins recording.

To see all upcoming recordings, go the Start page, select Recorded TV, and choose View Scheduled. On this list, you can choose Series to see all series recordings you've set up. This list allows you to rank series to determine which one should be recorded in the event that two programs from different series are on at the same time. (If you have two tuners, this sort of conflict is less likely to be a problem, but the rules still come into play if you have *three* shows on at the same time.)

Watching and Managing Recorded TV

To watch programs you've previously recorded, go to the Start page and choose Recorded TV from the TV + Movies category. Figure 19-8 shows all current recordings in List format. Click More Info and choose View Large from the shortcut menu to see much larger thumbnails for each program in a list that scrolls horizontally.

Figure 19-8 This list view of all recorded programs is more efficient than the default Large view—but it's somewhat harder to read.

Select any program from the list and press OK to see details and settings for that program. Options on this menu allow you to change when the program is automatically deleted or burn it to a CD or DVD for archival purposes (if the program isn't copy protected, of course).

Sooner or later—usually sooner—you'll run out of disk space, at which point Media Center begins throwing out old programs to make way for new ones. You can check on available disk space at any time by opening the Settings menu, choosing TV, then Recorder, and finally Recorder Storage. If you want to make sure that you reserve some space on your primary disk for documents and other data files, adjust the Maximum TV Limit.

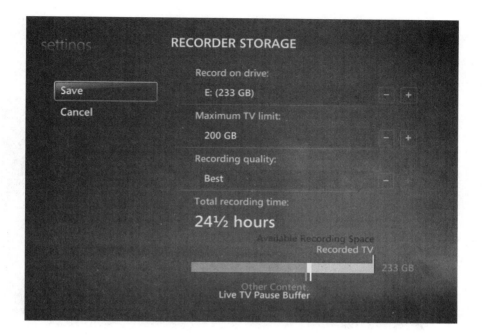

Connecting and Using a Media Center Extender

Your PC is in the den, hooked up to a cable connection and dutifully recording your favorite programs to a large hard disk. Your most comfortable chair is in the living room, opposite a large-screen TV. How do you get the content off the PC and onto the big screen? One excellent option is a Media Center Extender.

A Media Center Extender is a self-contained hardware device that connects directly to your home entertainment system and communicates over a network with a Media Center PC. The first generation of Media Center Extenders arrived in 2004 and are compatible only with Windows XP Media Center Edition. As we write this, the only extender device compatible with Windows Vista Media Center is Microsoft's Xbox 360. However, a new generation of extenders is due to hit the streets in 2007.

The beauty of a Media Center Extender is that it uses an interface that is almost exactly identical to the one on the PC itself. The simple box doesn't need a keyboard; its primary role is to send the input from your remote control in the living room to the PC in the den, office, or basement, which in turn delivers TV or music or digital pictures to your big-screen TV.

When you connect a Media Center Extender to the network and turn it on, your Media Center PC should detect its presence and display a message offering to set up a connection between the PC and the Extender. You can also kick off this process manually, by selecting Add Extender from the Tasks menu.

The setup process is relatively simple: You need to write down an eight-digit code displayed on the Extender screen and enter it in a box on the Media Center setup screen. After Setup is complete, you can verify that everything is working by selecting Extender from the Settings menu. Figure 19-9 shows an Xbox 360 that has been successfully configured as a Media Center Extender.

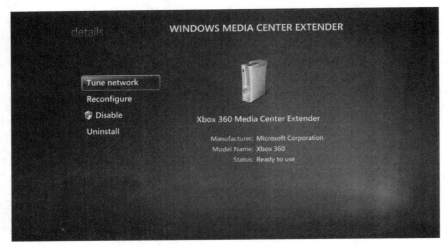

Figure 19-9 Use the Tune Network option to maximize performance of a Media Center Extender, especially if you're using a wireless network connection.

Media Center Extenders operate by setting up Remote Desktop sessions with the Media Center PC. You can connect up to three extenders to a PC running Windows Vista Home Premium; you're allowed to connect as many as five extenders with a PC running Windows Vista Ultimate. Each extender uses resources on the host PC. If you intend to use multiple extenders, you'll want a muscular hardware platform with a fast CPU and plenty of memory.

One option that confuses Extender owners, at least initially, is how the Media Library is built. When you watch content on a Media Center PC, the library is identical to the one for the logged-on user account. But extenders use a different account to log on: MCX1 for the first extender, MCX2 for the next, and so on. These accounts are restricted for use only by the extender. The first time you use the extender, you'll be prompted to set up a library. If you've customized the folders where you store data, you'll need to repeat those customizations on the extender.

Sharing a Media Library with Other PCs

Media Center Extenders aren't the only way to share content over a network. If you have two or more Windows Vista computers, you can keep a library of media on one computer and access it from the other using Windows Media Player.

To enable this option, open Windows Media Player and click Library, Media Sharing. By default, Windows Media Player detects libraries that others on your network are sharing; your libraries remain private unless you specifically choose to make them available to others. To share your library, select the Share My Media To check box in the Media Sharing dialog box, select a computer or device by name, and click Allow. A green check mark indicates that the device now has access to your library.

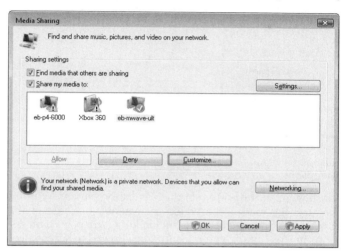

For Media Sharing to succeed, your network must be configured as Private (not Public) so that sharing and discovery can take place. When you're actively sharing a library (as opposed to just making it available for sharing), the Windows Media Player Network Sharing Service (Wmpnetwk.exe) runs, along with the Media Foundation Protected Pipeline (Mfpmp.exe).

Sharing a very large library can drag down performance on both ends of the connection. To limit the amount of traffic, the default settings for Media Sharing filter the list of media files in the library. From the Media Sharing dialog box, click Settings to open the dialog box where you set options for all devices, as shown in Figure 19-10. If you want to restrict access to some types of media, clear the check boxes for Music, Pictures, or Video, or turn on the Parental Ratings restrictions.

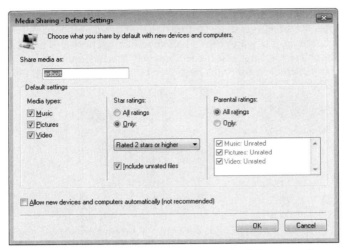

Figure 19-10 The options shown here apply to all devices and computers sharing a media library. You can set similar options for an individual device.

Shared libraries show up at the bottom of the Navigation pane in Windows Media Player. If another user has made a shared library available but has not explicitly enabled access for your machine, you see the icon, but clicking it displays a message: "Before you can play items in this library, you must first be allowed to access the library."

When access is enabled, you see a hierarchy of views that are similar to those in your Library. Access is tied to a user account *and* a machine (you don't need credentials to access the shared library). So, in theory, at least, you could see two or more shared libraries from a single machine, each from a different user account.

It takes a while for the index from a shared library to build and become visible. If you've connected to a new shared library, be prepared to wait for a few hours as Windows Media Player downloads information from the shared library and builds a local index.

PART IV

System Maintenance and Management

CHAPTER 20

Home Basic   ○
Home Premium   ○
Business   ◉
Enterprise   ◉
Ultimate   ◉

Performing Routine Maintenance

Your personal computer is a curious combination of digital data and temperamental machinery. To keep your system running smoothly, it pays to perform some regular maintenance tasks. In particular, it's wise to do the following on a regular basis:

- Check your disks for file system and media errors.

- Defragment your hard disks to optimize file access.

- Make sure that you always have sufficient free hard disk space by deleting or archiving files you no longer need and compressing files where appropriate.

- Perform regular backups of data and system files.

Longtime Windows users will recognize most of the tools and techniques we describe in this chapter. What's different in Windows Vista is that many of them run automatically—or will, after you perform some essential setup steps.

What's in Your Edition?

With one glaring exception, the tools and techniques described in this chapter work identically in all editions of Windows Vista. That exception is the new Windows Backup utility. In Windows Vista Business, Ultimate, and Enterprise editions, you can choose to create a Complete PC Backup, which creates a restorable image of one or more volumes, or you can perform more conventional file-based backups, either on demand or automatically, on a schedule you set. In Home Basic and Home Premium editions, the Backup utility lacks the capability to create image-based backups and instead allows you to perform only file-based backups. In addition, the Backup utility in Home Basic edition blocks creating backups on network drives and allows you to perform interactive file-based backups only; automatic scheduling is not supported.

Checking Disks for Errors

Errors in disk media and in the file system can cause a wide range of Windows problems, ranging from an inability to open or save files to blue-screen errors and widespread data corruption. Windows is capable of recovering automatically from many disk errors, especially on drives formatted with NTFS.

To perform a thorough inspection for errors, you can manually run the Windows Check Disk utility, Chkdsk.exe. Two versions of this utility are available—a graphical version that performs basic disk-checking functions, and a command-line version that provides a much more extensive set of customization options.

To check for errors on a local disk, follow these steps:

1. Open Computer, right-click the icon belonging to the drive you want to check, and then choose Properties from the shortcut menu.

2. On the Tools tab, click the Check Now button. (You must supply credentials for an account in the Administrators group to execute this utility.)

3. In the Check Disk dialog box, shown here, select from the following options.

   ○ **Automatically Fix File System Errors** This option, which is enabled by default, configures Windows to automatically repair any errors it detects in the file system. If this option is not selected, Check Disk reports any errors it finds but does not change them. This option is the equivalent of running the Chkdsk command with the /F switch, as described later in this section.

○ **Scan For And Attempt Recovery Of Bad Sectors**   Select this option to perform an exhaustive check of the entire disk, locate bad sectors, and recover readable information stored in defective locations. Note that selecting this option automatically repairs file system errors as well, even if the previous option is cleared. This option is the equivalent of running the Chkdsk command with the /R switch.

If you simply want to see a report of file system errors without making any changes to disk structures, leave both boxes unselected.

4. Click Start to begin the disk-checking process. The green progress bar provides feedback as the error-checking tool goes through several phases.

If you select the Automatically Fix File System Errors option on a drive that currently has open files, Windows is unable to run the utility immediately. In that case, you see the message shown here.

Click Schedule Disk Check to configure Windows startup so that the disk check utility runs the next time the computer is started. The disk check occurs early in the startup sequence, before Windows shifts into graphical mode; during this period your computer is not available for you to perform any other tasks. When your computer starts, Windows notifies you that it's about to perform a scheduled disk check; by default, you have 10 seconds to cancel the operation and boot normally instead.

After Check Disk completes its operation, it reports its results. If the disk check turns up no errors, you see a Disk Check Complete dialog box. If Check Disk uncovers any errors, it writes a message to the Event log and displays a dialog box listing the errors it found and the repairs it made.

CAUTION

Although Check Disk is a useful tool and sometimes a lifesaver, it can cause you headaches if used without some planning. Once started, the Check Disk operation cannot be stopped except by pressing your computer's power switch. On very large drives (60 GB and larger), the full disk check can take hours or even days to complete.

Check Disk runs automatically after an abnormal shutdown only if a specific bit in the registry is set, indicating that the file system is "dirty"—that is, that some pieces of data were not properly written to the disk when the system was shut down. If the file system wasn't doing anything when the system shut down, the dirty bit will not be set. Because NTFS volumes keep a journal of all disk activities, they are able to recover and remain clean even if you shut down in the middle of a disk write. Check Disk is most likely to run automatically at startup only on FAT32 volumes, after an unexpected shutdown.

INSIDE OUT   Cancel checks with Chkntfs

Two additional and well-hidden Windows commands are crucial to the operation of the Check Disk utility. The first of these, Autochk.exe, runs automatically any time you specify that you want to schedule a disk check to run at startup; it cannot be run interactively. The second, Chkntfs, is especially useful if you change your mind and decide you want to cancel a scheduled check. At a command prompt, type **chkntfs /x *d*:** (where *d* is replaced by a drive letter) to exclude the drive specified. Chkntfs has another nifty trick: It can tell you whether a disk is dirty. At a command prompt, simply type **chkntfs *d*:**. For more details about these commands, see Knowledge Base article 218461, "Description of Enhanced Chkdsk, Autochk, and Chkntfs Tools in Windows 2000" (*http://www.vista-io.com/2001*) and Knowledge Base article 160963, "CHKNTFS.EXE: What You Can Use It For" (*http://www.vista-io.com/2002*).

The command-line version of Check Disk gives you considerably more options. It also allows you to set up regular disk-checking operations using the Task Scheduler (as described in "Using the Windows Vista Task Scheduler," Chapter 30). To run this command in its simplest form, open a Command Prompt window using the Run As Administrator option, and then type **chkdsk** at the prompt. This command runs Chkdsk in read-only mode, displaying the status of the current drive but not making any changes. If you add a drive letter after the command (**chkdsk d:**, for instance), the report applies to that drive.

You can use any combination of the following switches at the end of the command line to modify its operation:

- **/F** Instructs Chkdsk to fix any errors it detects. This is the most commonly used switch. The disk must be locked. If Chkdsk cannot lock the drive, it offers either to check the drive the next time you restart the computer or to dismount the volume you want to check before proceeding. Dismounting is a drastic step; it invalidates all current file handles on the affected volume and can result in loss of data. You should decline the offer. When you do, Chkdsk will make you a second offer—to check the disk the next time you restart your system. You should accept this option. (If you're trying to check the system drive, the only option you're given is to schedule a check at next startup.)

- **/V**   On FAT32 volumes, /V displays verbose output, listing the name of every file in every directory as the disk check proceeds. On NTFS volumes, this switch displays cleanup messages (if any).

- **/R**   Identifies bad sectors and recovers information from those sectors if possible. The disk must be locked. Be aware that this is a time-consuming and uninterruptible process.

The following switches are valid only on NTFS volumes:

- **/I**   Performs a simpler check of index entries (stage 2 in the Chkdsk process), reducing the amount of time required.

- **/C**   Skips the checking of cycles within the folder structure, reducing the amount of time required.

- **/X**   Forces the volume to dismount, if necessary, and invalidates all open file handles. This option is intended for server administrators. Because of the potential for data loss, it should be avoided in normal use with any desktop edition of Windows Vista.

- **/L[:*size*]**   Changes the size of the file that logs NTFS transactions. If you omit the *size* parameter, this switch displays the current size. This option is intended for server administrators. Because of the potential for data loss, it also should be avoided in normal use with any desktop edition of Windows Vista.

TROUBLESHOOTING

When you run Chkdsk in the Windows Recovery Environment, some options are not available

The Chkdsk command used when you boot to the Windows Recovery Environment is not the same as the one used within a full Windows session. Only two switches are available for this version:

- **/P**   Performs an exhaustive check of the current disk

- **/R**   Repairs damage on the current disk

If your system is able to boot to Windows either normally or in Safe Mode and you suspect that you have disk errors, you should use the full Chkdsk command. For more details, see "Making Repairs with the Windows Recovery Environment," Chapter 24.

Defragmenting Disks for Better Performance

On a relatively new system with a speedy processor and plenty of physical memory, hard disk performance is the single biggest bottleneck in everyday operation. Even with a zippy hard disk, it takes time to load large data files into memory so you can work with them. The problem is especially noticeable with movies, video clips, DVD burning projects, databases, ISO image files, and virtual hard disks, which can easily take up multiple gigabytes, sometimes in a single file.

On a freshly formatted disk, files load fairly quickly, but over time, performance can degrade because of disk fragmentation. To understand how fragmentation works, it helps to understand the basic structure of a hard disk. The process of formatting a disk divides it into *sectors*, each of which contains space for 512 bytes of data. The file system combines groups of sectors into *clusters*, which are the smallest units of space available for holding a single file or part of a file.

For more details about how to choose a size and format for disk partitions, see "Formatting Disks," Chapter 28.

On any NTFS volume greater than 2 GB in size, the cluster size is 4 KB. Thus, when you save a 200-MB video clip, Windows divides the file into roughly 50,000 pieces. When you save this file for the first time on a freshly formatted, completely empty hard disk, Windows writes it in contiguous clusters. Because all the clusters that hold individual pieces of the file are physically adjacent to one another, the mechanical components of the hard disk can work very efficiently, scooping up data in one smooth operation. As a bonus, the hard disk's onboard cache and the Windows disk cache are able to anticipate the need for data and fetch nearby clusters that are likely to contain other parts of the file, which can then be retrieved from fast cached memory rather than from the relatively slow disk.

Unfortunately, hard disks don't stay neatly organized for long. When you add data to an existing file, the file system has to allocate more clusters for storage, typically in a different physical location on the disk. As you delete files, you create gaps in the once-tidy arrangement of contiguously stored files. As you save new files, especially large ones, the file system uses all these bits of free space, scattering the new files over the hard disk in many noncontiguous pieces. The resulting inefficiency in storage is called *fragmentation*; each time you open or save a file on a badly fragmented disk, disk performance suffers, sometimes dramatically, because the disk heads have to spend extra time moving from cluster to cluster before they can begin reading or writing data.

The Disk Defragmenter in Windows Vista improves on its predecessor in many ways, not the least of which is you shouldn't need to do anything to benefit from it. Disk Defragmenter runs as a low-priority background task that kicks off once a week, in the middle of the night, without requiring any attention from you. Alas, you'll look in vain for an interactive, color-coded display to show you the progress of the defragmentation operation. That visual gimmick, which has been part of various Windows versions for more than a decade, is now officially retired.

Using Disk Defragmenter

The Disk Defragmenter utility improves performance by physically rearranging files so that they're stored in contiguous clusters. In addition to consolidating files and folders, the utility also consolidates free space, making it less likely that new files will be fragmented when you save them. The Disk Defragmenter process (Dfrgntfs.exe or Dfrgfat.exe, for disks in the NTFS and FAT32 formats, respectively) starts according to a schedule that you can adjust. To view the current settings, click the Disk Defragmenter shortcut (in the System Tools subfolder of the Accessories folder on the All Programs menu), or right-click any drive icon in the Computer window and click Defragment Now on the Tools tab.

Figure 20-1 shows the simple Disk Defragmenter interface. The check box at the top of the dialog box allows you to enable or disable scheduled operation. The button at the bottom of the dialog box starts or stops manual defragmentation operation.

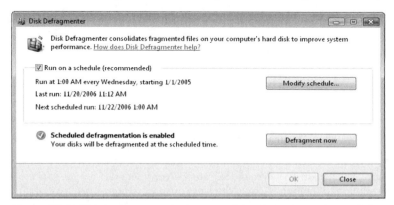

Figure 20-1 Click the button at the bottom of this dialog box to begin defragmenting all local hard disks immediately. If Defragmenter is running, the button text reads Cancel Defragmentation.

Click Modify Schedule to change when Disk Defragmenter runs automatically. By default, this option runs weekly, at 1:00 AM each Wednesday. You can schedule operation to be daily, weekly (you pick the day of the week), or monthly (you pick the date) and choose the time of day (round numbers only), as shown in Figure 20-2.

Figure 20-2 Pick a daily, weekly, or monthly schedule for Disk Defragmenter to begin running as a background task.

For details about managing scheduled tasks, see "Using the Windows Vista Task Scheduler," Chapter 30.

INSIDE OUT Do you need a more powerful defragmenter?

Through every previous Windows version, Disk Defragmenter has been a bare-bones utility, sufficient for average users but frustratingly incomplete for power users. As a result, a thriving if specialized market in third-party disk utilities sprang up, led by Executive Software's Diskeeper utility (*http://www.diskeeper.com*), a full-featured version of the Defragmenter utility bundled with Windows XP. The Norton SystemWorks package (*http://www.vista-io.com/2003*) also includes a capable disk defragmenter, as does Raxco's PerfectDisk (*http://www.raxco.com*). Given the improvements in the Windows Vista Disk Defragmenter, are these third-party tools still necessary? At the time we wrote this, none of the mentioned third-party utilities was available in a Windows Vista-compatible version. If you have an older version written for Windows XP, we recommend you check reviews carefully before getting the upgrade.

INSIDE OUT Dedicate a partition for CD or DVD burning

The best way to avoid disk fragmentation is to start with a completely clean slate. If you routinely work with CD images, for instance, consider creating a separate partition that's big enough to temporarily hold the files you're working with. A 2-GB partition, for instance, is big enough to hold a CD image and all temporary files associated with it. (You'll need roughly 10 GB for a DVD-burning partition.) Keep that drive empty except when you plan to create a CD, at which time you can copy files to it for burning. Using this strategy, you can be certain that fragmentation won't have a deleterious impact on your CD-burning performance.

Running Disk Defragmenter from a Command Line

The command-line version of the Disk Defragmenter allows you to exercise fine-grained control over the defragmentation process and uses the exact same program code as the scheduled version. To use this command for a specific drive, type **defrag d:** at any command prompt, where d is the drive letter or mount point of an existing volume. (For an explanation of mount points, see "Mapping a Volume to an NTFS Folder," Chapter 28.) You can use the following switches with the Defrag command:

- **-c** Defragments all volumes on the computer; use this switch without specifying a specific drive letter or mount point.

- **-a** Analyzes the selected drive or volume and displays a summary of the analysis report.

- **-r** Performs a partial defragmentation by consolidating only file fragments that are below 64 MB in size. This is the default setting.

- **-w** Performs a full defragmentation by consolidating all file fragments, regardless of size.

- **-f** Forces defragmentation of the volume even if the amount of free space is lower than normally required. Use this option with caution, as it can result in slow performance.

- **-v** Displays complete (verbose) reports. When used in combination with -a, this switch displays only the analysis report. When used alone, it displays both the analysis and defragmentation reports.

TROUBLESHOOTING

The Disk Defragmenter utility does not fully defragment the drive

A volume must have at least 15 percent free space before Disk Defragmenter can completely defragment the volume. If you have less free space available, the operation will run, but only partial defragmentation will result. From a Command Prompt window, run Defrag with the –a switch to see statistics (including free space) the specified volume.

You cannot defragment a volume that Windows has marked as possibly containing errors. To troubleshoot this possibility, enter **chkdsk *d:* /f** at any command prompt, substituting the letter of the drive in question. Chkdsk will report and repair any file-system errors it finds (after restarting, in the case of a system or boot volume).

Disk Defragmenter does not defragment files in the Recycle Bin. Empty the Recycle Bin before defragmenting.

Additionally, Disk Defragmenter does not defragment the following files: Bootsect.dos, Safeboot.fs, Safeboot.csv, Safeboot.rsv, Hiberfil.sys, and Memory.dmp. In addition, the Windows page file is never defragmented. (See the text following this sidebar to learn how to work around this issue.)

By default, Disk Defragmenter ignores fragments that are more than 64 MB in size, both in its analytical reports and in operation. According to Microsoft's benchmarks, fragments of this size (which already consist of at least 16000 contiguous clusters) have a negligible impact on performance. Thanks to disk latency, a large file divided into 10 fragments each 64 MB or greater in size will not load measurably slower than the same file in a single unfragmented location; under those circumstances, it's best to leave the fragments alone.

Disk Defragmenter will pass over any files that are currently in use. For best results, shut down all running programs before running the utility. For even better results, log off and log back on (using an account in the Administrators group) before continuing.

In addition to the documented switches listed above, the command-line Defrag utility includes two useful but undocumented switches.

- **-i** The –i switch makes Defrag run in the background and operate only if the system is idle—as it does when run as a scheduled task. If you want to perform the scheduled defrag early, use this switch, but leave it off if you're defragmenting a disk as part of major file operations.

- **-b** The –b switch optimizes boot files and applications while leaving the rest of the drive undisturbed.

The command-line Disk Defragmenter does not provide any progress indicator except for a blinking cursor. To interrupt the defragmentation process, click in the command window and press Ctrl+C.

Getting a Fragmentation Report at the Command Prompt

By opening a Command Prompt session with administrative privileges, you can use the defragmentation program with various command-line options. (For details, type **defrag /?** at the command prompt.) In addition to enabling scripts to incorporate defragmentation tasks, the command-line approach offers an option to analyze and report on the fragmentation status of a disk without actually carrying out the defrag operation. Type **defrag c: –a –v**, for example, to generate a verbose report on the condition of drive C. (You can add **>%temp%\report.txt** to the end of that command string to funnel the report into a text file saved in the Temp folder.) The last line of the report will recommend a defrag run if the system thinks you need it.

Using Disk Defragmenter's Analysis Report, you can determine whether your page file is fragmented. (For an explanation of how the page file works, see "Basic Strategies for Improving Performance," Chapter 21.) Although page file fragmentation is normally not a serious issue, a severely fragmented page file can reduce your system's performance. Disk Defragmenter cannot consolidate your page file, because Windows holds it open while you work. However, if you have more than one volume available (even if the second volume is on the same physical hard disk as your system drive), you can work around the problem as follows:

1. Open Control Panel and double-click the System icon (in the System and Maintenance category).

2. In the task pane on the left side of the window, click Advanced System Settings.

3. On the Advanced tab of the System Properties dialog box, click the Settings button under Performance.

4. On the Advanced tab of the Performance Options dialog box, click Change under Virtual Memory.

5. From the list of available drives, choose a volume other than the one that holds your current page file. This drive will hold your temporary page file.

6. Choose the Custom Size option, choose System Managed Size, and click Set.

7. Select the drive that contains the fragmented page file, choose the Paging File option, and then click Set.

8. Close open dialog boxes to save your settings, and restart the computer to allow it to stop using the old page file and begin using the new one.

9. Defragment the drive that previously held your page file. This consolidates the free space on that volume so that your new page file will be stored in contiguous space.

10. Repeat steps 1 through 8, this time creating a page file on the original disk and eliminating the temporary page file you created. Then reboot to allow the new, defragmented page file to take over.

Managing Disk Space

In the digital era, Parkinson's Law has an inescapable corollary: Data expands to fill the space allotted to it. Gargantuan hard disks encourage consumption, and digital media files (not to mention Windows itself) supply plenty of bits to be consumed. It's surprisingly easy to run low on disk space, and the consequences can be deleterious to your system. If you run low on storage, Windows might not have enough room to expand its page file, or it might be unable to create temporary files. In addition, essential features such as Windows Search and System Restore may stop working properly. At that point, you start seeing ominous error messages and (possibly) degraded performance.

To pare down on disk space consumption, you can do any or all of the following:

- Clear out temporary files that you no longer need.

- Uninstall programs you don't need.

- Uninstall Windows components you don't need.

- Delete documents you don't need.

- On NTFS volumes, use real-time file compression.

Cleaning Up with Disk Cleanup

The simplest way to make room on any drive is with the help of the Disk Cleanup utility, Cleanmgr.exe. If you click a "low disk space" warning, this tool opens automatically. To begin working directly with a single local drive, right-click the drive icon in the Computer window, choose Properties from the shortcut menu, and then click Disk Cleanup on the General tab of the properties dialog box. You'll be given the opportunity to choose between cleaning up your own files only or all files on the disk (including those created by other users). You'll need administrative credentials to go for the latter option.

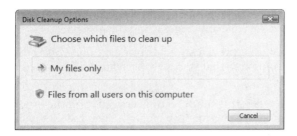

You can also click the Disk Cleanup shortcut (on the All Programs menu, click Accessories and then choose System Tools). When you choose this option, you'll be presented with the same option to choose between your own files and those of all users. After making your decision, you'll then be asked to select a drive to work with.

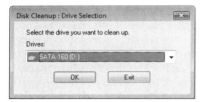

With those preliminaries out of the way, you reach the Disk Cleanup dialog box. Figure 20-3 shows the results after selecting the option to clean files from all users and selecting more than the default settings.

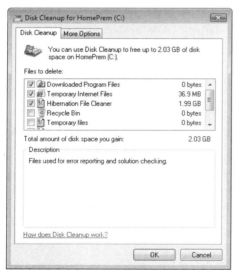

Figure 20-3 Select options from this list to make additional disk space available on the selected drive.

The Disk Cleanup options are fairly self-explanatory and merely consolidate functions already scattered throughout the Windows interface. For instance, you can empty the Recycle Bin, clear out the Temporary Internet Files folder, and purge files from the Temp folder. (Avoid cleaning out the Downloaded Program Files folder, which contains generally useful ActiveX and Java add-ins.) When you simply use these default settings, the Disk Cleanup utility is strictly an interactive tool. Each time you run the utility, you must select options you want to run and then click the OK button to actually perform the cleanup. Removing the Hibernation file can save a large amount of disk space—an amount equal to the amount of RAM installed on your computer; choose this option only if you never hibernate your system.

CAUTION

Disk Cleanup includes one confusing option that can leave an inordinate amount of wasted space on your hard disk if you don't understand how it works. When you run Disk Cleanup, one of the available options offers to delete Temporary Files; the accompanying Help text explains that these are unneeded files in the Temp folder. Unfortunately, this option may display a value of 0, even if your Temp folder contains hundreds of megabytes of useless files. The reason? Although the Help text hints at the answer, it doesn't clearly explain that this value lists only files in your Temp folder that are more than one week old. If you want to completely clean out this folder, you'll need to do so manually. Close all running programs and type **%temp%** in the Run dialog box; from the resulting Windows Explorer window, delete everything you find. You may discover that some files are not available for deletion until you restart your computer.

The options shown in this dialog box reflect a subset of the total options available, based on the actual contents of the drive you're working with. The wizard performs a bit of triage for you, selecting check boxes next to the categories that it thinks you can part with most easily. The program is reasonably cautious about all of this, leaving, for example, categories such as Previous Windows Installation(s) (if you have any such) and Files Discarded By Windows Upgrade unchecked. Look the list over carefully, select any items about which you're curious and read the descriptions at the bottom of the dialog box for each one, click View Files if you want to see the members of a category, and then click OK to carry out the approved deletions.

For information about using restore points, see "Making Repairs with the Windows Recovery Environment," Chapter 24. For an explanation of how to restore previous versions of files and folders, see "Restoring Files and Folders with Previous Versions," Chapter 7.

The overwhelming majority of Windows users never realize that Disk Cleanup offers several cool switches that are documented only here and in a pair of obscure Knowledge Base articles. Through the use of these switches, you can save your preferences and rerun the cleanup process automatically using those settings. To do so, you need to use the following switches with Cleanmgr.exe:

Chapter 20

- **/Sageset:***n*   Opens a dialog box that allows you to select Disk Cleanup options, creates a registry key that corresponds to the number you entered, and then saves your settings in that key. Enter a number from 0 through 65535 in place of *n*.

- **/Sagerun:***n*   Retrieves the saved settings for the number you enter in place of *n* and then runs Disk Cleanup without requiring any interaction on your part.

To use these switches, follow these steps:

1. Open a Command Prompt window and type the command **cleanmgr /sageset:200**. (The number after the colon is completely arbitrary; you can choose any other number from 0 through 65535 if you prefer.) You must supply credentials from a member of the Administrators group to begin this task.

2. In the Disk Cleanup Settings dialog box, shown in Figure 20-4, choose the options you want to apply whenever you use these settings. For this example, the options we've selected include dump files created by Windows Error Reporting, Temporary Files, Temporary Windows Installation Files, and Thumbnails.

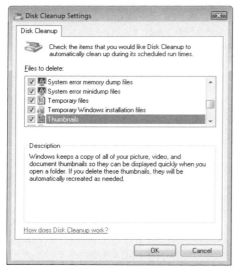

Figure 20-4 When you use the /Sageset switch, you can work with an expanded set of options that are not available interactively.

3. Click OK to save your changes in the registry.

4. Open Task Scheduler from Control Panel and start the Create Basic Task Wizard. Follow the wizard's prompts to name the task and schedule it to run at regular intervals. When prompted to select the program you want Windows to run, enter **cleanmgr.exe** in the Program/Script box and and enter **/sagerun:200** in the Add Arguments box.

5. Repeat steps 1–4 for other Disk Cleanup options you want to automate.

INSIDE OUT   Make the most of Disk Cleanup shortcuts and tasks

Disk Cleanup shortcuts can be tremendously useful for routine maintenance. For instance, you might want to create a shortcut for Cleanmgr.exe with a saved group of settings that automatically empties the Temporary Internet Files folder and Recycle Bin and another that purges installation files and system dump files. If you create a shortcut that empties the Recycle Bin, it's best not to add it to your list of Scheduled Tasks, where it can inadvertently toss files you later discover you wanted to recover; instead, save this shortcut and run it as needed.

Chapter 20

The More Options tab in the Disk Cleanup dialog box provides two additional Clean Up buttons.

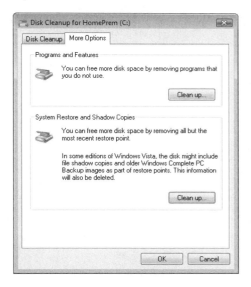

The top button (under Programs And Features) takes you to the Uninstall Or Change a Program dialog box, where you can remove Windows components and programs. (For details, see "Finishing Your Windows Vista Installation," Chapter 2, and "Uninstalling Programs," Chapter 4.) The bottom button, under System Restore and Shadow Copies, lets you remove all but the most recent System Restore checkpoints and Complete PC Backup images. This option can recover a significant amount of space, but you should choose it only if you're certain you won't need to restore a backup or roll back your configuration to one of the saved versions you're about to delete.

While getting rid of programs you no longer use is always a good idea, the option to eliminate all but the most recent restore point should be considered a desperate measure. Restore points can sometimes provide a way to restore stability to a system that has become unruly. In Business, Ultimate, and Enterprise editions, they also provide a way to restore previous versions of documents you have changed. Keep them if you can.

Using NTFS File Compression

One of the many advantages of choosing the NTFS file system over FAT32 is that it offers slick and essentially seamless on-the-fly compression. To compress a file (or an entire folder) stored on an NTFS-formatted volume, all you have to do is set an attribute for that object; Windows decompresses the file or folder automatically when you access it.

To compress a file or folder, right-click its icon in Windows Explorer, choose Properties from the shortcut menu, and click the Advanced button on the General tab. In the Advanced Attributes dialog box, shown in Figure 20-5, select Compress Contents To Save Disk Space.

Figure 20-5 You can compress a single file, a folder full of files, or an entire drive—but only on a drive formatted with NTFS.

INSIDE OUT   Use compression sparingly

A little compression goes a long way. In general, NTFS compression is most effective when used on files that are not already compressed. Bitmap images, Microsoft Word documents, and database files are highly compressible. Because music files (in MP3 and WMA format) and JPEG and GIF images are already compressed, NTFS compression provides little benefit and incurs a noticeable performance hit. By all means, avoid compressing the folders that contain Windows system files and log files that the operating system uses regularly. The negative effect on performance is especially severe here.

To compress an entire volume at once, right-click the drive icon in Windows Explorer and follow the same procedure. You'll be asked to confirm that you really want to do this for every file in the volume. When you say yes, the system begins compressing files, one at a time. The process can take hours to complete; fortunately, it only needs to be done once. You can continue working while Windows is busy compressing files. If the system needs to compress an open file, you'll be notified with a dialog box. At that point, you can close the file in question and click Retry, or click Ignore or Ignore All.

TROUBLESHOOTING

When you select the encryption option, the compression button in the Advanced Attributes dialog box is cleared

For security and performance reasons, encryption and compression are mutually exclusive attributes for files stored on an NTFS volume. If the file is compressed, it can't be encrypted, and vice versa. If you need to combine compression with security, consider using password-protected Zip files, which offer good (but not great) encryption along with efficient compression capabilities. Use the third-party WinZip program (*http://www. winzip.com*) or the Compressed Folders feature in Windows (as described in "Maximizing Storage Space with NTFS Compression and Compressed (Zipped) Folders," Chapter 7).

When you compress a folder, that attribute affects files that you move or copy later, according to the following rules:

- If you create a new file in a compressed folder, the new file is compressed.

- If you copy a file into a compressed folder, the file is compressed.

- If you move a file from a different NTFS volume into a compressed folder, the file is compressed.

- If you move a file into a compressed folder on the same NTFS volume, the file retains whatever compression setting it had originally; in other words, its compression attribute remains unchanged.

- If you move a compressed file into an uncompressed folder on the same NTFS volume, the file retains the compressed attribute. However, if you move a compressed file to an uncompressed folder on a different NTFS partition, the file loses the compression attribute.

Chapter 20

INSIDE OUT **Highlight compressed files**

If you use on-the-fly compression, take advantage of an option in Windows Explorer that displays compressed files and folders in an alternate color. That way, you can see at a glance which files and folders are compressed. To verify that this feature is enabled, open Windows Explorer and choose Organize, Folder and Search Options. On the View tab, make sure that Show Encrypted Or Compressed NTFS Files In Color is selected. By default, the names and other details of compressed files appear in blue within Windows Explorer.

Smart Backup Strategies

Home Basic ◑
Home Premium ◑
Business ◓
Enterprise ◓
Ultimate ◓

Hard disks are amazing yet fragile mechanical devices. Packed with ultra-miniature electronics that zoom along at thousands of revolutions per minute, it's no wonder that they fail more often than any other component in the average computer. When a disk crashes, it's usually impossible to recover your data without spending a small fortune at a data recovery service.

And even if your hardware never lets you down, human error can wreak havoc with data. You can press the wrong key and inadvertently delete a group of files you meant to move. If you're not paying attention, you might absentmindedly click the wrong button in a dialog box, saving a new file using the same name as an old one, wiping out an irreplaceable document in the process.

In any of those circumstances, you're almost certainly going to lose some data. When a hard disk crashes, for instance, all files you've created or saved since your last backup are gone for good. But you can avoid the worst data losses if you get into the habit of backing up regularly. And with the help of new backup tools included with Windows Vista, that's easier than with any previous Windows version.

If you're looking for assistance on how to recover your computer using a Complete PC Backup, see "Making Repairs with the Windows Recovery Environment," Chapter 23.

> **Note**
>
> The Windows Vista Backup Utility, like most backup programs, uses each file's archive attribute to determine whether to include the file in a backup. The *archive attribute* is a single bit in the file's directory entry. When a file is created or modified, its archive attribute is turned on. When a file is backed up using a normal or an incremental backup, the archive attribute is cleared. You can view (and set, if you like) the archive attribute for a file by right-clicking the file in Windows Explorer and choosing Properties. On the General tab, click the Advanced button; the first check box in the Advanced Attributes dialog box represents the archive attribute. (On a FAT-formatted drive, the Archive check box appears on the General tab.)

Using the Windows Backup Program

The Windows Vista Backup utility (Sdclt.exe) is installed by default in all editions. To begin creating a backup, you can start from either of two locations:

- The Backup And Restore Center in Control Panel includes links that allow you to start a backup or restore operation. Figure 20-6 shows the full range of options available in Business, Ultimate, and Enterprise editions.

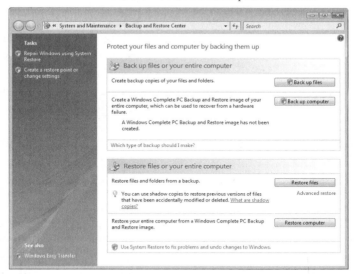

Figure 20-6 The capability to back up an entire drive using Complete PC Backup is unavailable in the two Home editions of Windows Vista.

- Your other option is to start by clicking the Backup Status and Configuration shortcut (on the All Programs menu, click Accessories, then click System Tools). Figure 20-7 shows the options available the first time you run this program on Windows Vista Business, Ultimate, or Enterprise edition.

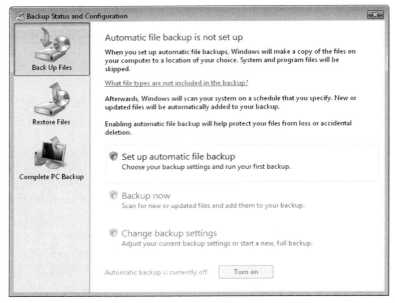

Figure 20-7   The option to schedule file backups to occur automatically is available with all editions of Windows Vista except Home Basic,

The basic steps for performing a backup are simple and straightforward. You have to make some decisions first, which in turn dictate which tools you use and what actions you need to take.

Choose the type of backup. Depending on your Windows Vista edition, you have two options here:

- Complete PC Backup creates an image of your system drive and, optionally, any other drives you specify. The image includes data files, programs, and settings. When you use the Windows Recovery Environment to restore an image, your configuration is identical to the configuration in place when you created the backup. This option is not available in Home Basic or Home Premium editions.

- The Back Up Files Wizard copies data files, but not programs or settings. You can use a backup set created using this wizard to restore individual files or all backed-up data, but in the event of a disk crash you'll need to reinstall Windows and all your programs to get back to work.

INSIDE OUT   Combine the two backup types

The two backup types described above are not mutually exclusive. In fact, one of the smartest strategies uses both backup types. On a PC with a freshly installed copy of Windows Vista Business, Ultimate, or Enterprise, start by creating a Complete PC Backup. Then create an automatic backup program for data files, backing them up daily or weekly to removable media, an external hard drive, or a network location. Every month or two, you can refresh your original Complete PC Backup. In the event of a disk failure, you can replace the disk, boot from the Windows Vista DVD, use Complete PC Restore to copy your backed-up image file with all programs, and finally restore your data files.

Choose what to back up. For a file-based backup, you can specify the types of data files you want to include in your backup. For a Complete PC Backup, you must choose the drive that contains your copy of Windows; optionally you can include one or more drives containing data files as well.

Choose a destination for the backed-up files. The Windows Backup program allows you to save backed-up files to any of the following locations:

- An internal hard drive other than the one that contains your copy of Windows Vista.

- An external hard drive that connects to your system via USB 2.0 or IEEE 1394 connections.

- A shared network location. (This option is not available for Complete PC backups.)

- Removable media, such as writable CDs or DVDs. The Backup program will prompt you to swap media as needed

So, which destination is the right one? There's no correct answer; the choice you make depends on your needs and your hardware configuration. External hard drives are the most convenient, because of their size and portability. Removable media is also portable, but if your backed-up data uses more than 4.5 GB of space (the maximum capacity for a single-layer DVD), you'll have to manually swap media, making it impossible to schedule the backup process for unattended operation. Network locations are unavailable if you're using Windows Vista Home Basic.

CAUTION

We strongly advise against storing backup copies on a disk partition on the same physical disk as the system you're backing up. In the event of a hard disk failure, you lose your files and your backup at the same time.

Chapter 20

Create a backup schedule. For file-based backups using any edition except Home Basic, you can schedule automatic backups to take place daily, weekly, or monthly, on a schedule of your own choosing. After the original full backup, updates to your backup set include only files that have changed since the last backup.

Perform the backup operation. After setting up any form of backup, you should perform a full manual backup immediately.

Backing Up Files and Folders

To get started with a file-based backup, you must supply credentials from an account in the Administrators group. Open Backup and Restore Center and click Back Up Files, or click the Set Up Automatic File Backup link in Backup Status And Configuration. Then follow these step-by-step instructions:

1. Choose the destination where you want to save your backup, as shown in Figure 20-8. The list at the top displays all available internal and external hard drives as well as any writeable CD or DVD drives. Use the box below it to choose a network location. Click Next to continue.

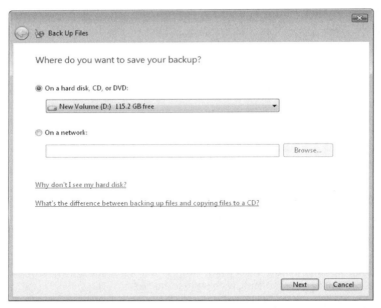

Figure 20-8 The On A Network option is unavailable if you're using Windows Vista Home Basic edition.

2. Choose the file types you want to back up by selecting their check boxes in the list shown in Figure 20-9. As this figure illustrates, moving the mouse pointer over any category displays help text for that category. After making your selections, click Next to continue.

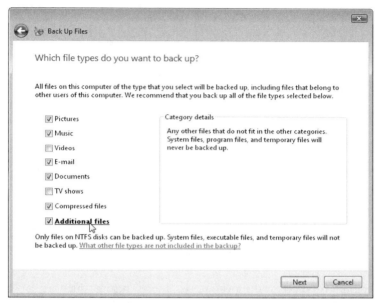

Figure 20-9 Clear the check boxes for types of files that you don't want to back up as part of a scheduled Windows Backup.

INSIDE OUT   What's not backed up?

Every file on your computer that matches the criteria you select is backed up, regardless of which user account it belongs to. But not every file is backed up. Even if you select every box in the list of file types available for backing up, Windows excludes some files. For starters, the disk on which the files are stored must be formatted with NTFS; FAT32 disks don't work with Backup. Files that are encrypted using the Encrypting File System are also excluded, as are system files, program files, and any files in the Recycle Bin or the %Temp% folder.

Create a backup schedule. In the How Often Do You Want to Create a Backup? section, choose Daily, Weekly, or Monthly backups. Change the default day, date, or time if necessary.

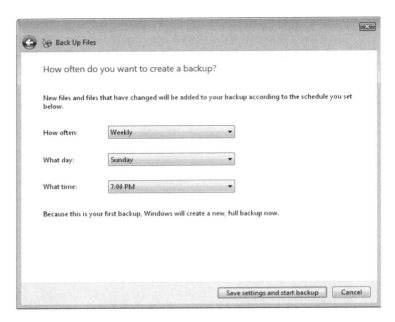

Click Save Settings and Start Backup to continue. The Backup program immediately begins creating your backup file.

Backups are saved to the location you specify, using a naming convention that includes your computer name and the date and time when the backup was saved. The folder for a Complete PC Backup also includes the date when the backup was created. When you update the backup set, the date remains unchanged. To create a new folder and associated files with the current date, create a new backup job.

INSIDE OUT   Make sure you have some free space

At the time it begins saving a backup set, Backup Utility creates a "volume snapshot" using free disk space on any available NTFS drive. If you have sufficient space, you can continue to use the computer while a backup is in progress, and you don't need to close any open files. If your system is short on free space, however, Backup Utility can't create the snapshot, and you may find that open files are not properly backed up.

After the first time you run a backup, the display in the Backup Status and Configuration window changes to indicate when the last backup was performed and where it was stored. If a backup is in progress, you also have the opportunity to stop the current operation.

Creating a Complete PC Backup

To create a Complete PC Backup, open Backup Status And Configuration, click the Complete PC Backup icon in the sidebar on the left, and click Create a Backup Now. Figure 20-10 shows this option, which is available only in Business, Ultimate, and Enterprise editions.

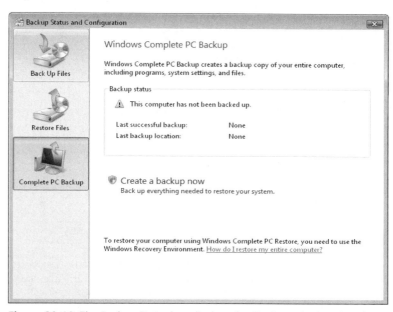

Figure 20-10 The Backup Status box displays details about the last time the computer was backed up. We recommend refreshing the full backup every month or two.

The first step in the wizard asks you to select a destination. Note that the disk space requirements for an image-based backup can be substantial. Windows will warn you if the destination you choose doesn't have sufficient free disk space. (Network drives are, unfortunately, not supported in this release of Windows Vista Backup.)

Choose the disks you want to include in the backup. By default, any system that contains Windows Vista system files is selected. You can optionally choose to include other drives in the backup image as well.

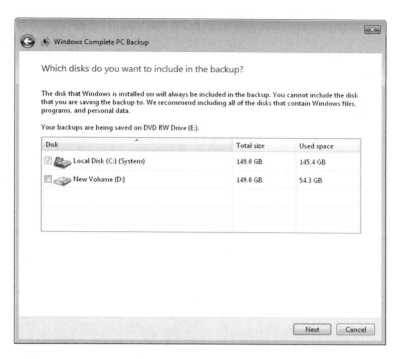

After you confirm your settings, click Start Backup to begin the process of building your image. When the image is complete, save it in a safe location, preferably away from the original system.

CHAPTER 21

**Tuning Up and
Monitoring Performance**

Home Basic ⬤
Home Premium ⬤
Business ⬤
Enterprise ⬤
Ultimate ⬤

> **What's in Your Edition?**
>
> The information in this chapter applies equally to all editions of Windows Vista.

Every Windows user has experienced sudden, mysterious slowdowns in system performance. Routine actions that normally take a few microseconds suddenly cause your computer to stop responding. Your hard disk chatters incessantly. You're forced to wait when switching between programs. Surprisingly, you don't need an engineering degree, an oscilloscope, or expensive third-party software to determine the cause of and solution to problems such as these.

Windows Vista includes a number of tools that you can use to pinpoint performance bottlenecks. Some of these, such as the System Health Report, the Windows Experience Index, and the Reliability Monitor, provide static snapshots showing the resources available to your system and where those resources might not be adequate to your needs. Others, such as the venerable Windows Task Manager, the new Resource Overview, and Performance Monitor (an improved version of the tool known in Windows XP as System Monitor), let you track a variety of performance metrics in real time.

In addition to these snapshot and monitoring utilities, Windows Vista incorporates the following forms of performance-enhancing technology:

- SuperFetch
- ReadyBoost
- ReadyDrive

All three of these are designed to reduce the amount of time your system spends engaged in performance-degrading disk IO. *SuperFetch* is a memory-management technology that observes your computer usage patterns over extended stretches of time (noting the programs you run and the days and times you typically run them) and adjusts caching behavior to accommodate your own particularities. *ReadyBoost* uses external memory devices (such as USB 2.0 flash disks) to cache disk content of all kinds, reducing the need for time-consuming hard disk access. And *ReadyDrive* is technology that supports the use of hybrid hard disk drives—drives that incorporate nonvolatile flash memory (NVRAM) as well as conventional rotating disk media. Hybrid drives are particularly useful for extending battery life on portable computers, because they reduce the need for drive spin.

SuperFetch is useful to anyone running Windows Vista. You don't need to do anything except be glad that it's there. ReadyDrive should be of interest if you're in the market for a new computer and hybrid drives are a purchase option. ReadyBoost, in contrast, is of no value unless you implement it—by attaching a suitable external memory device to your system. For details, see "Using ReadyBoost," later in this chapter.

Basic Strategies for Improving Performance

Before we look at the various diagnostic tools included with Windows, let's cut to the chase and review these basic performance-enhancing strategies:

- Ensuring that you have adequate RAM
- Ensuring that you have an adequate virtual-memory configuration
- Using ReadyBoost
- Managing startup programs
- Keeping your disks defragmented
- Maintaining adequate free space on your disks
- Avoiding tweaks of dubious value

Ensuring That You Have Adequate RAM

Random access memory (RAM) is the vital stuff that keeps Windows running smoothly. Having enough physical (main) memory helps reduce the operating system's dependence on virtual memory, thereby minimizing the number of number of times Windows has to swap information between fast memory chips and your (relatively slow) hard disk. How much memory do you need?

The "Windows Vista Capable" and "Windows Vista Premium Ready" stickers that appear on some new hardware are based on standards expressed at Microsoft's *Microsoft Vista Enterprise Hardware Planning Guidance* site (*http://www.vista-io.com/2101*). According to these standards, a system needs 512 MB to be "Windows Vista Capable" and at least 1 GB to be "Windows Vista Premium Ready." You should consider "Vista Capable" to mean adequate (if barely) for Windows Vista Home Basic. For the more feature-rich editions of Windows Vista—Home Premium, Business, and Ultimate—treat the "Vista Premium Ready" standards as a minimum. In any case, doubling these minimums will provide a better ride for most users.

You can gauge the adequacy of your computer's physical memory by watching the Memory graph in the Resource Overview (see "Using Resource Overview," in the Monitoring Performance in Real Time" section later in this chapter). The blue line on the graph indicates the percentage of your physical memory that's currently in use. If this line hovers in the sub-arctic zone (say, north of 60 percent) most of the time under your typical working conditions, you might want to consider adding memory to your computer, particularly if you are also seeing the green line on the same graph, the line that indicates the number of hard faults per second your system is generating, spike off the top of the graph for extended periods of time. (A *hard fault*, which despite its name is not an error condition, is an instance where a block of memory needed by the operating system has to be fetched from the page file on the hard disk. A high number of hard faults per second indicates a large—perhaps excessive—reliance on virtual memory, with consequent adverse performance effects.)

On the other hand, if the blue line on the Memory graph typically dwells in tropical or temperate regions (say, at 45 percent or less), you're not likely to see sharp performance gains from an increase in physical memory.

Ensuring That You Have an Adequate Virtual-Memory Configuration

Physical memory might be the vital lubricant of a happily humming Windows machine, but Windows is not designed to run on RAM chips alone, no matter how many of them you have. In addition to using physical RAM to store programs and data, Windows creates a hidden file on your primary hard disk and uses that file to swap pages of data out of physical memory when necessary. The "swap file" (these days more commonly called a *page file*) acts as an extension of main memory—or, in other words, as *virtual* memory.

In a default installation, Windows creates the page file in the root folder on the same drive that holds the Windows system files. The size of the page file is determined by the amount of RAM in your system. By default, the minimum size is 1.5 times the amount of physical RAM, and the maximum size is three times the amount of RAM (twice the minimum). You can see the page file in a Windows Explorer window if you configure Windows to show hidden and system files; look for Pagefile.sys in the root of your system drive.

To see the current configuration of your system's virtual memory, open Control Panel, click System And Maintenance, click Performance Information And Tools, click Advanced Tools (in the Tasks pane at the left side of the dialog box), and then click Adjust The Appearance And Performance Of Windows. After answering the UAC prompt, you'll arrive at the Performance Options dialog box. You're nearly there; click the Advanced tab, and then click Change. Figure 21-1 on the next page shows the Virtual Memory dialog box, with default settings for a machine with 2 GB of RAM (default, that is, except that we cleared the Automatically Manage Paging File Size For All Drives check box to make the rest of the dialog box easier to read).

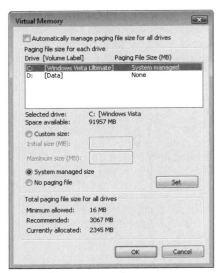

Figure 21-1 By default, Windows manages the page file size for you.

By default, Windows creates a single page file in the root folder on the same volume that holds the Windows system files and manages its size for you. The Currently Allocated number near the bottom of the dialog box shows you how large the file is now. If conditions on your system change (you run an unusually large assortment of memory-intensive applications, for example), Windows might expand the page file. It might then return the file to its original size (or a smaller size) if the demand subsides. All this happens without intervention or notification if you leave the Automatically Manage Paging File Size For All Drives check box selected.

If you don't want Windows to do this for you, you have the following options:

- You can move the page file to a different volume, if you have more than one.

- If you have more than one volume, you can establish more than one page file.

- For any page file, you can choose between System Managed Size and Custom Size.

- If you choose Custom Size, you can specify an initial size and a maximum size.

- You can remove a paging file from a volume by selecting the volume and choosing No Paging File. (You can even get rid of all paging files this way, although doing so is not recommended, even on systems with a lot of RAM.)

Should you get involved in page-file management, and, if so, how?

If you have more than one physical disk, moving the page file to a fast drive that doesn't contain your Windows system files is a good idea. Using multiple page files split over two or more physical disks is an even better idea, because your disk controller can process multiple requests to read or write data concurrently. Don't make the mistake of creating two or more page files using multiple volumes on a single physical disk, however.

If you have a single hard disk that contains C, D, and E volumes, for example, and you split the page file over two or more of these, you might actually make your computer run more slowly than before. In that configuration, the heads on the physical disk have to do more work, loading pages from different portions of the same disk sequentially, rather than loading data from a single contiguous region of the hard disk.

If you are short of hard disk space, you might consider setting a smaller initial page file size. You can use a handy script from Windows MVP Bill James to monitor current page file usage and session peak usage. This tool, a free download at *http://www. vista-io.com/2102*, was written for Windows XP but works fine in Windows Vista. If this script nearly always shows current and peak usage levels well below the current page file size, you might want to consider reducing the initial size to save disk space. On the other hand, if you're not short of disk space, there's nothing to be gained from doing this and you might occasionally overload your custom settings, thereby degrading the performance of your system.

Should you enlarge your page file? Most users won't need to do this. But you might want to keep an eye on the green line in the Memory graph of Resource Overview (see the full discussion under "Monitoring Performance in Real Time" later in this chapter). If that line is spiking off the top of the graph a great deal of the time during your normal work, you might consider increasing the maximum size of your page file. (Disregard page file spikes and disk activity in general that takes place while you're not actually working. This is likely to be the result of search indexing, defragmentation, or other background processes and does not indicate a problem with your actual work performance.)

> **Note**
>
> For more information about page file management in Windows, we recommend the article "Virtual Memory in Windows XP," at *http://vista-io.com/2103* Although the file magnitudes discussed in this article are pertinent to the XP environment rather than to Windows Vista, the basic information about how Windows manages and uses page files is still useful and valid.

Using ReadyBoost

ReadyBoost technology takes advantage of the fact that flash memory offers lower seek times than hard disks. Essentially that means that your system can get to a given location on a flash disk more quickly than it can to a corresponding spot on a hard disk. Hard disks are faster for large sequential reads; flash disks are quicker for small, random reads. When a supported external memory device is available, ReadyBoost caches small chunks in flash memory and is thus able to retrieve those chunks, when needed, more quickly than it could if it relied only on the hard disk.

Because an external memory device can be removed without warning to the system, all data cached via ReadyBoost is encrypted and backed up on the hard disk (as well as being compressed). Encryption ensures that the data can't be read on another system, and backup enables Windows to revert to the hard disk cache in the event that the Ready-Boost drive is removed.

Windows supports the following form factors for ReadyBoost:

- USB 2.0 flash disks
- Secure Digital (SD) cards
- CompactFlash cards

When you connect a device of one of these types to your system, Windows runs a quick performance test to see if the device meets minimum standards required for Ready-Boost. Those standards are:

- 2.5 MB / second throughout for 4 KB random reads
- 1.75 MB / second throughout for 512 KB random writes

In addition, the device must have at least 256 MB available for the ReadyBoost cache.

> **Note**
>
> ReadyBoost does not support external card readers. If Windows Explorer shows a volume letter for a drive without media (as it does, for example, for card-reader drives or floppy drives), inserting flash media for that volume letter will not give you a ReadyBoost drive. In addition, Windows Vista does not support multiple ReadyBoost drives. (Microsoft has indicated that multiple-drive support is under consideration for future versions.)

How much boost will you get from ReadyBoost? As with so many other performance issues, it depends. If your internal memory is well above the amount you actually need, ReadyBoost won't do much for you. If not, you should definitely see some performance improvement. To use ReadyBoost, follow these steps:

1. Plug a suitable external memory device into your computer. An AutoPlay window similar to the following will appear (it won't say READYBOOST, unless you've already assigned that name to the volume, as we have here):

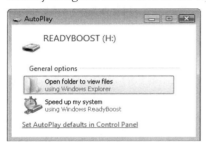

2. Click Speed Up My System. If your system passes an initial ReadyBoost test, the Properties dialog box will appear, with the ReadyBoost tab selected:

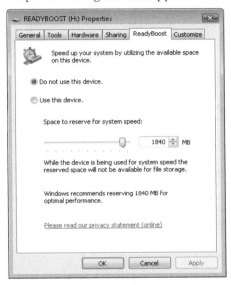

3. Select Use This Device, and then adjust the slider to specify the amount of space you want to use for ReadyBoost. Then click OK.

How much of the external memory device you want to assign to ReadyBoost will depend on whether you also want to use the device for ordinary storage. Microsoft estimates that you can benefit from a ReadyBoost cache equal to approximately 150 percent of your system RAM—for example, a 1.5 GB ReadyBoost cache on a 1 GB system.

INSIDE OUT   Check a flash drive's ReadyBoost performance

When you plug in a USB flash drive or other removable drive and specify you want to use it as a ReadyBoost device, Windows runs a quick performance test to see whether the drive meets the minimum standards. If it fails, you're greeted with a message that says "This device does not have the performance characteristics for use in speeding up your system."

If you think the test is in error, click Test Again to get a second hearing. If the drive fails several tests, look up the performance results for yourself. Open Event Viewer (Eventvwr. msc) and click the Applications And Services Logs category in the console tree on the left. Under this heading, click Microsoft, Windows, and ReadyBoost; under this heading, select Operational. The log entries here include performance test results for both successful and unsuccessful attempts.

To be used as a ReadyBoost device, your flash drive has to pass several tests, including available free space, write performance, and random read performance. If any of these tests fail, the drive is rejected.

Managing Startup Programs

A common performance problem occurs when Windows automatically loads an excessive number of programs at startup. The result, especially on systems with minimal memory, is unpleasant: Startup takes unnecessarily long, applications that you never use steal memory from programs you use frequently, and the page file gets more of a workout than it should. Some programs, such as antivirus utilities, need to start up automatically. But in most cases, you're better served by running programs when you need them and closing them when they're not needed.

Overcrowded startups are most common on computer systems sold in retail outlets, where Windows Vista is preinstalled, along with a heaping helping of applications. In some cases, the bundled programs are welcome, but a free software program is no bargain if it takes up memory and you never use it.

A program can be configured to run at startup in a variety of different ways. For a survey of these many ways—and how to take appropriate defensive action—see "Managing Startup Programs," Chapter 4.

Chapter 21

> ### Save Memory by Switching to Windows Vista Basic
>
> We love the new eye candy that comes courtesy of Windows Aero. But candy is not free, and if memory is tight, consider freeing up some by switching to the Windows Vista Basic color scheme. (Right-click your desktop, choose Personalize, and then click Window Color And Appearance. In the ensuing dialog box, click Open Classic Appearance Properties For More Color Options. Finally, in the Appearance Settings dialog box, select Windows Vista Basic and click OK.)

Keeping Your Disks Defragmented

A "fragmented" hard disk, in which large files are stored in discontiguous sectors, makes read and write heads work overtime and puts a drag on performance. Fortunately, Windows Vista, by default, performs disk defragmentation for you as a weekly scheduled task, so you shouldn't have to worry about fragmentation. The "defrag" utility (defrag.exe) runs as a background task, silently shifting the furniture while your system is idle. (The default schedule has defrag running at 1 am. If your machine is turned off at that hour, the task runs as soon as possible after you come back online. It always runs as a low-priority background task, however, so you shouldn't find it obtrusive.)

For more information about using the defragmentation utility, see "Defragmenting Disks for Better Performance," Chapter 20.

Maintaining Adequate Free Space on Your Disks

A hard disk cluttered with stuff you no longer need may or may not be an impediment to performance (it certainly can be if the disk is home to a page file), but it's a nuisance at best. If a volume is running short of space, you can tidy up a bit with the Disk Cleanup wizard. Open Computer in Windows Explorer, right-click the disk in question, and choose Properties. Then, on the General tab of the properties dialog box, click Disk Cleanup. You'll be given the opportunity to choose between cleaning up your own files only or all files on the disk (including those created by other users). You'll need administrative credentials to go for the latter option. For a more detailed discussion of this utility's features and capabilities, see "Managing Disk Space," Chapter 20.

Avoiding Tweaks of Dubious Value

Among diehard tweakers, the urge to squeeze out every last bit of performance from a computer is irresistible. As a result, even a casual web search turns up dozens of tips intended to help you improve performance in Windows. Many of these tips repeat information that we cover in this chapter, including the truism that the best way to tune up Windows is to throw hardware at it. Nothing speeds up a sluggish system like a healthy dose of extra RAM.

Unfortunately, many of the Windows-tuning tips we've seen are of dubious value, and a few can actually hurt performance when indiscriminately applied. Some of these spurious tips are derived from techniques that worked with older Windows versions but are irrelevant now. Others are based on seemingly logical but erroneous extrapolations of how would-be experts think Windows works.

Page File Confusion

By far the most common instances of performance-related misinformation revolve around the subject of page files, also known as swap files. The following are some widely published myths about the proper configuration of virtual memory in Windows:

- **If your computer has a large amount of memory installed, you should eliminate your page file completely.** This is incorrect. Although you can configure Windows so that it does not set aside any virtual memory, no reputable source has ever published benchmarks establishing any performance gains from doing so, and Windows simply wasn't designed to run without a page file. If the goal is to conserve disk space, a more sensible strategy is to configure Windows to create a page file with a relatively small minimum size and monitor its usage over time to see how much virtual memory the operating system actually uses in daily operation.

- **Creating a page file of a fixed size improves performance.** This is also bad advice. The logic behind this tip dates back to the earliest days of Windows. On 1990s-vintage hardware, dynamically resizing the swap file caused noticeable delays in system response and also resulted in excessive fragmentation. The memory management subsystems in Windows XP and Windows Vista have been tuned to minimize the likelihood of performance problems.

Prefetch Pros and Cons

To improve the speed of starting applications, Windows continually monitors files that are used when the computer starts and when you start applications. It then creates an index (in the %SystemRoot%\Prefetch folder) that lists segments of frequently used programs and the order they're loaded in. This prefetching process improves performance by allowing the operating system to quickly grab program files.

A widely circulated tip of dubious value recommends that Windows users clean out the Prefetch folder and consider disabling the Prefetch function. Some sites even provide links to utilities that automate these functions.

Clearing out the Prefetch folder forces Windows to run programs inefficiently—but only once, since Windows rebuilds the Prefetch layout for a program the next time you run that program. Disabling the Prefetch function eliminates Windows' ability to optimize program loading. In either case, it's hard to find a logical reason why the tweak should result in a performance improvement.

Is it necessary to clear out the Prefetch cache occasionally to eliminate obsolete files and to minimize wasted disk space, as some websites claim? Hardly. A typical Prefetch folder uses 3-6 MB of disk space, and Windows flushes entries that are older than a few weeks. Our take? The developers responsible for the memory management subsystem of Windows did a remarkable job when they devised this feature. Don't turn it off.

Shutting Down Services

We've also seen sites focusing on Windows services. One sensible piece of advice is to minimize the use of unnecessary background applications and system services. A few sites take this advice to an extreme, however, urging Windows users to shut down virtually all system services, including System Restore and Automatic Updates. We don't agree that the average Windows user should perform this sort of radical surgery on Windows. In less-than-expert hands, the Services console is a minefield; some Windows services can be safely disabled, but indiscriminately shutting down services is a prescription for trouble. That advice is doubly true for features designed to protect system reliability and security. In Chapter 25, "Managing Services," we list all standard services and provide our recommended startup settings.

Taking Performance Snapshots

Windows Vista includes several tools that you can use to get a here-and-now picture of your system's health and performance. These tools include the following:

- The Windows Experience Index (and its command-line companion, Winsat.exe)
- The System Diagnostics Report
- The Reliability Monitor

Measuring Satisfaction with the Windows Experience Index

If you installed Windows Vista yourself, you probably noticed that a performance assessment took place near the end of the setup process. You might have seen a report comparable to the one shown in Figure 21-3. If you missed that at setup, you can always display it again by opening System And Maintenance in Control Panel and then clicking Performance Information And Tools.

Figure 21-3 The Windows Experience Index measures five elements of your system's performance and returns a score based on the weakest element.

The Windows Experience Index runs tests of various kinds, returns scores on each performance metric, and then hands you a composite score based on the weakest link in the chain. You can see details about these tests by clicking View And Print Details. Assorted other links provide a modest amount of information about what the scores mean and what you would need to do to boost your score. The most prominent link on the page connects you to Windows Marketplace, where you can exercise your credit card in the service of software acquisition, with software offerings tailored to your system's performance score.

If you upgrade your system in some way and want to tests the effects of your changes on overall system performance, return to the page shown in Figure 21-3 and click Update My Score (you'll need administrative credentials to do this). Alternatively, you can use the command-line utility winsat.exe. Winsat (type **winsat /?**) for syntax details, lets you retest individual components of the Windows Experience Index or rerun the entire suite. You can also save the output as an XML file or redirect the verbal output of the tests to a text file for subsequent review.

Generating a System Diagnostics Report

To obtain a more detailed and more useful report of your system's current state of well-being (albeit one not linked to shopping opportunities), open System And Maintenance in Control Panel, click Performance Information And Tools, and then click Advanced Tools in the Tasks pane at the left side of the dialog box. On the Advanced Tools page, click Generate A System Health Report.

The System Diagnostics utility that appears (after you have presented your credentials to the UAC sentry) runs for about 60 seconds, and then returns a report comparable to the one shown in Figure 21-4 (yours will probably not look as dire as this).

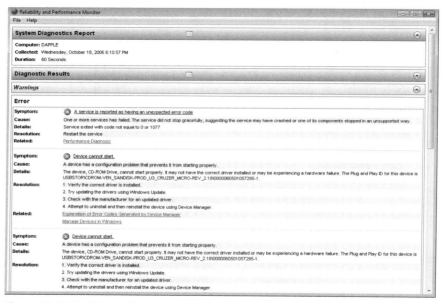

Figure 21-4 The System Diagnostics Report performs a rather detailed physical checkup and puts the bad news (if any) right up front.

Not one to mince words, the System Diagnostics Report starts right out with the worst news it has to deliver. Below this Warnings section, you'll find a section summarizing basic system checks, in which each of five test sets gets a green "Passed" balloon or a red "Failed" balloon:

Basic System Checks		
Tests	**Result**	**Description**
⊞ OS Checks	Passed	Checks for attributes of the operating system
⊞ Disk Checks	Failed	Checks for disk status
⊞ Security Center Tests	Passed	Checks for state of Security Center related information.
⊞ System Service Checks	Failed	Checks for state of system services
⊞ Hardware Device and Driver Checks	Failed	Survey of Windows Management Infrastructure supported devices.

Click the plus-sign outline control next to any item in this list to see a wealth of detail.

Scrolling down further into the report, you'll come to a Resource Overview section, with more green (and possibly red) balloons. If you see a small check box to the right of a Details entry, rest your mouse there to read a "tip" window containing interesting details about the item in question:

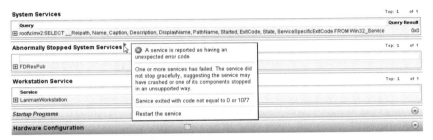

Farther still into the report, you'll see a set of expandable headings: Software Configuration, Hardware Configuration, CPU, Network, Disk, Memory, and Report Statistics. Use the outline controls at the right side of these headings to expand and contract. The headings will open to reveal expandable subheadings, and it's all worth reading, particularly if you run across an item with a red flag next to it. Rally your mouse around the flag for important details and recommendations:

Measuring Stability with the Reliability Monitor

Like the Windows Experience Index, the Reliability Monitor boils its findings down to an index number, but the number might not tell you much you don't already know. (Presumably you don't need a gauge to tell you whether your system is stable or not.) The details can be illuminating, however.

For more about the Reliability Monitor, see "Reviewing the Error History with the Reliability Monitor," Chapter 23.

Monitoring Performance in Real Time

Windows Vista offers three valuable tools for monitoring the performance of your system in real time. The first of these, Windows Task Manager, has been around through many versions of Windows and will therefore probably be familiar to many readers of this book. In addition to showing you what applications, processes, and services are running (and giving you a way to terminate recalcitrant items), it offers performance graphs that show a minute's worth of CPU usage, memory usage, and network capacity usage.

A newcomer in Windows Vista, the Resource Overview component of the Reliability and Performance Monitor shows a similar assortment of performance graphs (along with a graph showing disk activity) but presents the information in a different screen layout. Because the Resource Monitor lets you keep an eye on more different aspects of your system at once, you might find it preferable to Windows Task Manager for all but the most careful scrutiny. By adding nondefault columns to the Processes tab of Windows Task Manager, however, you can examine certain per-process details that are not available in the Resource Monitor.

Finally, the Performance Monitor, also a component of the Reliability and Performance Monitor, is a refurbished, enhanced version of something that was called System Monitor in Windows XP. The Performance Monitor is a heavy-duty tool intended to help IT professionals track and record performance minutiae regarding every aspect of a system.

Using Windows Task Manager

Windows Task Manager pops up in response to the keyboard shortcut Ctrl+Shift+Escape. That alone is one of its more endearing traits, making it almost instantly accessible at times when something appears to have gone awry. If you need to stop an application (or process) that doesn't respond to the usual measures, or if your system suddenly slows down and you want to know who's eating your processor cycles, Windows Task Manager is typically the quickest arrow in your quiver.

The Performance tab of Windows Task Manager, shown in Figure 21-5, gives you a quick overview of CPU and memory usage. The bar graphs at the left report current data—the percentage of your CPU's capacity and the number of megabytes in use—while the line graphs to the right show (by default) one minute's worth of data, with updates at one-second intervals. Numbers below the graphs amplify the graphical presentation. In Figure 21-5, for example, the memory bar graph shows that 717 MB are currently in use, while the Physical Memory item at the bottom of the window reports that those 717 MB represent 35 percent of the system's available RAM. The Physical Memory Usage History line graph, meanwhile, makes it clear that a large chunk of memory has been released within the last several seconds.

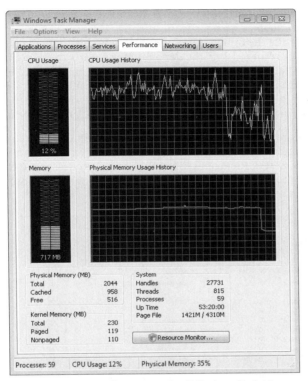

Figure 21-5 The Performance tab of Windows Task Manager gives you a big-picture view of CPU and memory usage.

To change the update speed (and therefore the duration of the line graphs), choose View, Update Speed. You can also use this command's submenu to freeze all the Performance graphs. If you like to work in freeze mode, you can force an update at any time (without resuming continuous updating) by choosing View, Update Now.

If you have a multi-processor system (one using a dual-core CPU, for example), you can choose between seeing a single line graph that represents all processors, or separate graphs for each. Use commands on the View, CPU History submenu to switch between these alternatives.

By default, Windows Task Manager stays on top of other open windows even when another window has the focus. Choose Options, Always On Top to toggle that behavior on or off. Regardless of what settings you choose on the View menu, Windows Task Manager displays, in your notification area, a miniature version of the Memory bar graph. You can minimize Windows Task Manager and still keep an eye on memory usage by glancing over at the notification area as you work. (Be aware, though, that continuous monitoring of your system performance by means of Windows Task Manager—or any other real-time tracking tool—will itself consume some of your processor time.)

The Page File fraction in the lower right corner of Windows Task Manager's Performance tab is useful for helping you gauge the adequacy of your virtual memory setup. Note, however, that while the numerator of the fraction indicates how much page-file space your system is currently using, the denominator reports the sum of physical memory and current page-file size. So, for example, the system depicted in Figure 21-5 is using 1,421 MB of page file at the moment. The total physical RAM is 2,044 MB. The total memory available—physical RAM and allocated page file—is 4,301 MB, which means that the current page file allocation (as distinguished from current page file usage) is 2,257 MB—4,301 minus 2,044.

In its default view, the Processes tab lists programs and services that are directly accessible to the user. Note that in the example shown here 57 processes are currently running (as evidenced by the value in the lower left corner of the dialog box). So why does the list display only 26 entries?

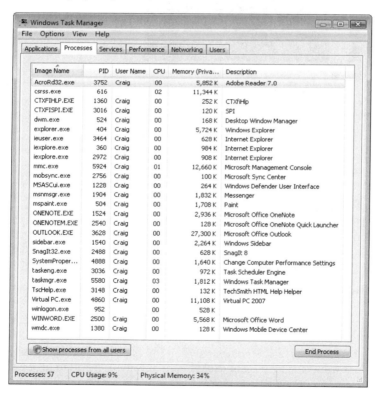

The short list shows only processes that can be directly controlled by the user. If you click Show Processes From All Users, the list expands to include all currently running processes. In this case shown below, the list of all users includes the built-in System, Network Service, and Local Service accounts.

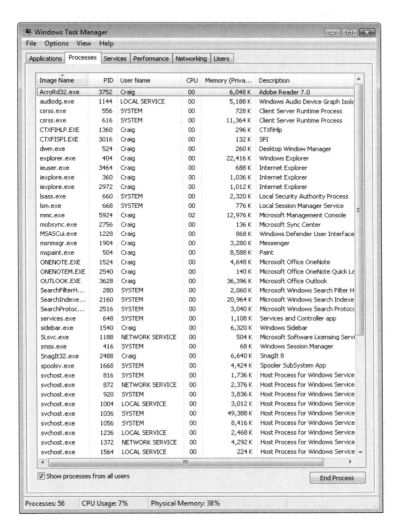

For each process, Windows Task Manager includes the following information by default: Image Name (the name of the process), PID (Process ID), User Name (which user started the process), CPU (the percentage of the CPU's capacity that the process is currently using), and Memory (Private Working Set) (the amount of memory the process requires to perform its regular functions).

Processes are sorted initially by the order in which they were started, with the most recent entries at the top. You can sort by any column by clicking the column heading (click a second time to reverse the sort order). This is a good way to identify processes that using more than their fair share of memory or CPU time.

With a modest amount of work, you can customize the Processes tab so that it shows far more information about each running process than the lean default view. To change the columns displayed on this tab, choose View, Select Columns, and then add or re-move entries from the dialog box shown here:

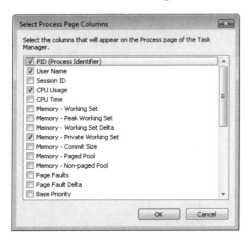

Most of these columns correspond to entries available in the Performance Monitor (described later in this chapter; see "Using the Performance Monitor"). After selecting the columns you want to see, click OK. You can then rearrange the display by dragging column headings to the left or right and dragging the border of any column heading to change its width. If necessary, resize the Task Manager window to see more data. Fig-ure 21-6, for instance, shows the addition of some columns that measure disk reads and writes on a per-process basis. If you hard disk starts thrashing for no apparent reason, switching to a view like this can help you quickly determine which program is respon-sible.

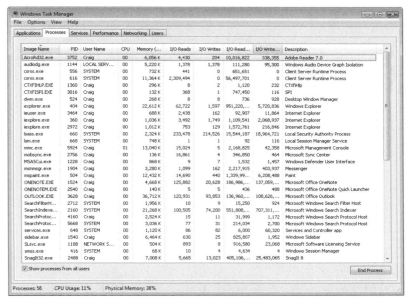

Figure 21-6 Customize the display of data on the Processes tab to identify other performance bottlenecks, such as the disk input/output.

Using Resource Overview

Like the Performance tab in Windows Task Manager, the Resource Overview component of the Reliability and Performance Monitor gives you both instantaneous and recent-history (45 seconds) readouts of key performance metrics. And, like Windows Task Manager, the Resource Overview can show you, per process, who's doing what to whom. The major difference between the two tools is that the Resource Overview shows graphs of more resources, while Windows Task Manager, if you customize the Processes tab, can show you some extra detail not available in the Resource Overview. Unless you need those extra details, you'll probably find the Resource Overview a more informative quick-read.

To get to Resource Overview, open System And Maintenance in Control Panel, click Performance Information And Tools, click Advanced Tools (in the Tasks pane), and then click Open Reliability And Performance Monitor. (You'll need administrative credentials.) Or take the direct route: type **perfmon** at a command prompt. The Reliability and Performance Monitor is a Microsoft Management Console snap-in. To see Resource Overview, click Reliability And Performance in the console pane at the left.

Figure 21-7 shows Resource Overview with the detail about individual processes hidden. At first glance, the tool appears to offer four graphs; closer inspection reveals 16.

Chapter 21

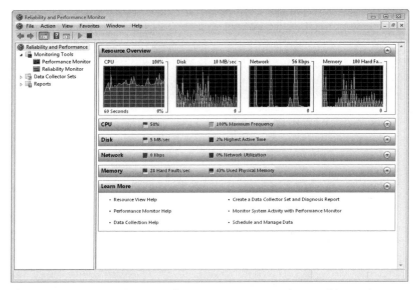

Figure 21-7 Resource Overview shows instantaneous and recent-history data concerning four vital system resources: CPU, disk, network, and memory.

For each of four resources, CPU, disk, network, and memory, the Resource Overview presents instantaneous and recent-history graphs of two metrics. The recent-history data appears in the large rectangles near the top of the window. The instantaneous readouts are in the small squares to the right of the resource headings below the history graphs. Each graph uses colors—green and blue—to distinguish its two data sets. The performance metrics are shown in Table 21-1.

Table 21-1. Resource Overview Performance Metrics

	Green	Blue
CPU	Percent of CPU capacity in use	Percent of full clock speed at which CPU is running
Disk	IO activity for all disks, in MB / sec	Percentage of disks' available throughput in use
Network	Network activity in KB / sec	Percent of network capacity in use
Memory	Hard faults / sec	Percent of physical RAM in use

In Figure 21-7, we see a system whose CPU, running at 100 percent of its clock speed, is currently being used at 58 percent of its capacity, having spent the last 45 seconds at or just below that usage level. The hard disks have seen a flurry of activity in this time slice, ranging from perhaps two megabytes per second up to about eight; the current IO activity stands at five megabytes per second. Disk activity expressed as a percentage of throughout capacity is low, standing currently at 2 percent. Nothing whatsoever is happening on the network at the current moment, although the most recent 45 seconds have seen three spikes of activity above the level of 56 KB per second. At the instant, the system is experiencing hard faults at the rate of 28 per second and using 43 percent of its physical memory. At several points during the last 45 seconds, hard faults have ranged close to 100 per second.

To see per-process details for any of the four resources, click the resource's heading. Figure 21-8 shows the CPU and Disk headings expanded to reveal nine processes each; scroll bars bring the rest into view.

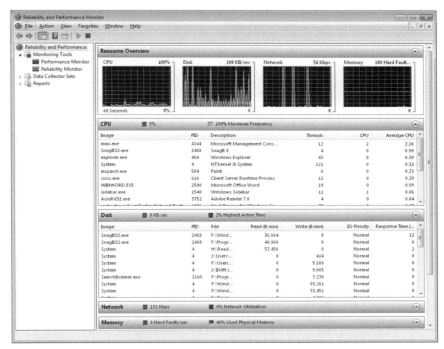

Figure 21-8 Expanding resource headings reveals details about individual processes.

Like the Processes tab in Windows Task Manager, Resource Overview lets you adjust column widths and positions (drag headings left or right to rearrange the column order; drag the dividers between columns to make the columns wider or narrower). You can also change the sorting order by clicking a column heading. You can't add or remove columns, however. If you want to see performance details not included in Resource Overview's display, Windows Task Manager (or the Performance Monitor, discussed next) is what you need.

Using Performance Monitor for Advanced System Analysis

The Windows Task Manager and the Resource Overview provide are great for quick scans of your system performance. A more robust tool, the Performance Monitor, allows you to track a much longer list of performance metrics than is available in either of these simpler tools. You can also use it to log performance data to disk files or export to programs such as Microsoft Excel for detailed analysis.

To get to the Performance Monitor, open System And Maintenance in Control Panel, click Performance Information And Tools, click Advanced Tools (in the Tasks pane), and then click Open Reliability And Performance Monitor. (You'll need administrative credentials.) Or take the direct route: type **perfmon** at a command prompt. When you get to the Reliability and Performance Monitor console, click Performance Monitor in the console pane (the pane at the left).

The Performance Monitor, shown in Figure 21-9, provides graphical displays about your system's current state and recent history. Data Collector Sets, an additional component of the Reliability and Performance Monitor console, allows you to track your system over longer periods of time, recording data in disk files for subsequent analysis. In this chapter, we focus exclusively on using the Performance Monitor. For details about how to use Data Collector Sets, see *Microsoft Windows Vista Resource Kit* (Microsoft Press, 2007).

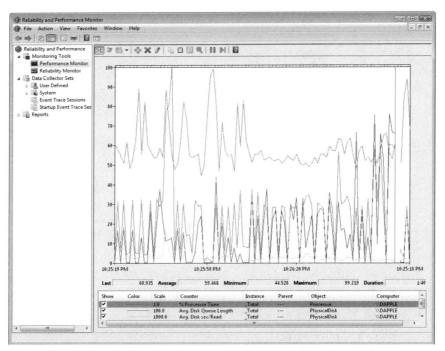

Figure 21-9 The Performance Monitor can provide graphical information about your system's current and recent status.

The Performance Monitor can track everything from relatively mundane but core activities, such as processor time and disk access, to exotic and highly technical measurements, such as the number of nonpaging read bytes per second handled by the network redirector. Whatever you decide to track, you add it to the Performance Monitor in the form of an *object* and a *counter*:

- **Object**   This is any portion of a computer's resources that can be assigned characteristics and manipulated as a single identifiable element. Typical objects on most computers include the processor, memory, page file, and disks. The complete list of objects varies from system to system, depending on what hardware is installed, what network protocols are used, and so on.

- **Counter**   This tracks various types of information about the objects to which they are assigned. The available counters vary from object to object. For the Processor object, for example, the available counters include % C1 Time, % C2 Time, % C3 Time, % DPC Time, % Idle Time, % Interrupt Time, % Privileged Time, % Processor Time, % User Time, C1 Transitions/sec, C2 Transitions/sec, C3 Transitions/sec DPC Rate, DPCs Queued/sec, and Interrupts/sec.

Some counters report instantaneous values. Others report the average of the current value and the value at the previous sampling interval. Still others report the difference between the current value and the previous value. If you're uncertain about what a particular counter represents, select the Show Description check box in the Add Counters dialog box, as explained in "Adding Counters," on the next page.

Some objects can appear more than once in the Performance Monitor; each such counter is considered a separate *instance*, allowing you to measure and compare the same type of performance using different software processes or hardware devices. The Process object has an instance for each process that's running. The PhysicalDisk object has an instance for each physical disk installed in the computer, and so on. Objects that have multiple instances typically include an instance that supplies information about the total of all the individual instances. So, for example, you could create multiple instances of the IO Data Bytes/sec counter, which measures all data that a process reads and writes from all sources (disks, network, and devices). In this example, the counter that tracks total IO Data for all running processes would give you an accurate measurement of overall system performance; by adding counters for each running process, you could see if a particular process is responsible for more than its expected share of this total.

Switching Between Display Types

In its Chart view, the Performance Monitor shows the current state of one or more counters, along with a certain amount of very recent history. (At the default sampling interval of one second, the duration of a Performance Monitor chart is 1 minute and 40 seconds.) Alternative views show the current state of counters as a histogram or a textual report. To switch between Chart, Histogram, and Report views, use the Change Graph Type tool on the toolbar. (More simply, you can press Ctrl+G to cycle through the three display types.)

Adding Counters

To select counters for display in Performance Monitor, right-click the display and choose Add Counters from the shortcut menu. (Or click the green Plus sign in the toolbar.) Figure 21-10 shows the Add Counters dialog box.

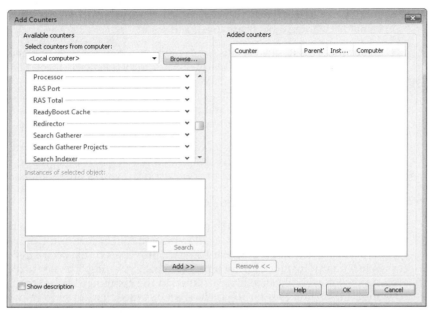

Figure 21-10 To tell Performance Monitor what you want to monitor, select an object. Click one of the available counters that appears, select an Instance, and then click Add.

To monitor your own computer, leave Local Computer selected in the drop-down list in the upper left corner of the dialog box. To monitor a remote computer, select it in this list.

To specify what you want to monitor, begin by clicking the name of an object. The object names function like outline controls; when you click one, its list of available counters appears. At the same time, the list of available instances appears in a separate window below the object list. Select a counter, select an instance, and then click Add. For information about what a counter counts, select the Show Description check box.

Changing the Chart's Display Characteristics

Performance Monitor's Chart and Histogram views plot all counters against a single vertical axis scaled, by default, from 0 to 100. A default scaling factor is applied to each counter so that counters with large values (such as PhysicalDisk(_Total)\Disk Read Bytes/sec, which measures the number of bytes per second read from all physical disks and might reach into the high hundreds of thousands or more) can coexist meaningfully in a chart with low-value counters (such as PhysicalDisk(_Total)\Disk Reads/sec, which measures the number of read operations per second).

It's quite possible that, in order to make a chart intelligible, you will need to adjust its scale or the scaling factor for one or more counters (or both the scale and one or more scaling factors). In particular, you will need to make some kind of adjustment if Performance Monitor represents one or more of your counters as a horizontal line along the top edge of the chart. That's Performance Monitor's way of saying that your data, given its current scaling factor exceeds the highest value of the vertical axis. The following five options represent adjustments that can make the vertical display of performance data more useful.

Changing the Vertical Axis Scale   To change the scale, right-click the chart or histogram and choose Properties from the shortcut menu. On the Graph tab of the Performance Monitor Properties dialog box, type values in the Maximum and Minimum text boxes. Note that because all of Performance Monitor's many counters return positive values exclusively, you cannot set the minimum scale point to less than 0. On this tab, you can also add horizontal or vertical gridlines, supply a descriptive label for the vertical axis, and give the chart a title.

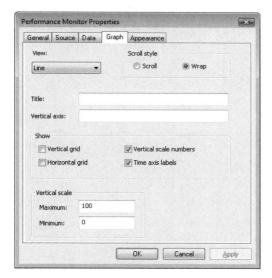

Changing a Counter's Scaling Factor   To change the scaling factor for a counter, go to the Data tab of the Performance Monitor Properties dialog box, select the counter, and then adjust the value of the Scale field. To return to the default scaling factor, choose Default in this field.

Changing Colors, Fonts, and Titles   Other options on the various tabs of the Performance Monitor Properties dialog box let you change colors and fonts for your chart or histogram, as well as for chart elements. You can also use Width, Color, and Style lists on the Data tab to modify the appearance of selected counters.

Emphasizing a Particular Line   With several counters displayed on the same chart, it can sometimes be hard to tell which is which. To make it easier to relate lines to their Counter names in the list below the chart, click the Highlight tool on the toolbar (it's the one directly to the right of the red X). In response, Performance Monitor changes the chart marker (line or histogram bar) that corresponds to the currently item in the Counter list from its current color to black. Now you can use the Up Arrow and Down Arrow keys to move between Counter items, and each one in turn will be drawn in black.

Changing the Sampling Interval   Performance Monitor samples counters at one-second intervals by default and adjusts its display to show 100 sampling intervals. You can alter the sampling interval by going to the General tab of the Performance Monitor Properties dialog box. Integers from 1 to 3888000 (one second to 45 days) are accepted. To set up a console that shows page-file usage over a two-hour period, for instance, you might enter 10 in the Sample Every *nn* Seconds box and 7200 (the number of seconds in two hours) in the Duration box. Note that the duration value must be at least two times and no more than 1,000 times the value in the Sample Every box.

To freeze the current chart (stop sampling), click the Freeze Display tool on the toolbar or press Ctrl+F.

Monitoring System Activities With Event Viewer

Home Basic ●
Home Premium ●
Business ●
Enterprise ●
Ultimate ●

What's in Your Edition?

Event Viewer works exactly the same way in all Windows Vista editions.

In Windows Vista, an *event* is any occurrence that is potentially noteworthy—to you, to other users, to the operating system, or to an application. Events are recorded by the Windows Event Log service, and their history is preserved in one of several log files, including Application, Security, Setup, System, and Forwarded Events. Event Viewer, a Microsoft Management Console (MMC) snap-in supplied with Windows, allows you to review and archive these event logs, as well as other logs created by the installation of certain applications and services.

Why would you want to do this? The most likely reasons are to troubleshoot problems that have occurred, to keep an eye on your system in order to forestall problems, and to watch out for security breaches. If a device has failed, a disk has filled close to capacity, a program has crashed repeatedly, or some other critical difficulty has arisen, the information recorded in the event logs can help you—or a technical support specialist—figure out what's wrong and what corrective steps are required. Watching the event logs can also help you spot serious problems before they occur. If trouble is brewing but hasn't yet erupted, keeping an eye on the event logs may tip you off before it's too late. Finally, you can use one of the event logs (the Security log) to track such things as unsuccessful logon attempts or attempts by users to read files for which they lack access privileges. Such occurrences might alert you to actual or potential security problems in your organization.

Getting Started with Event Viewer

Like Event Viewer in previous versions of Windows, the one in Windows Vista is an MMC snap-in. But the similarity ends there. The interface, shown in Figure 22-1, takes advantage of new features of MMC 3.0, such as the Action pane.

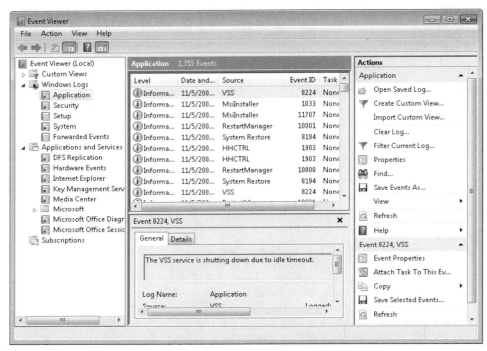

Figure 22-1 In Event Viewer, the Action pane provides a menu of tasks relevant to the items highlighted in the console tree and Details pane.

For more information about MMC, see Appendix C, "Using and Customizing Microsoft Management Console."

In Windows Vista, Event Viewer has several useful new capabilities:

- You can view events from multiple logs simultaneously.

- You can create and save filtered selections as reusable custom views.

- You can create a task to run automatically when a particular event occurs.

- You can create a subscription to specified events on other networked computers.

Running Event Viewer

You'll find a shortcut to Event Viewer in Control Panel's Administrative Tools folder. (Rather than clicking through the Control Panel labyrinth, you can, of course, find Event Viewer via the Search box on the Start menu or in Control Panel.) Event Viewer is also a node of the Computer Management console. To start Event Viewer at a command prompt, type **eventvwr**.

> ### Note
>
> Event Viewer requires administrator privileges for full functionality. If you start Event Viewer while logged on as a standard user, it starts without requesting elevation. However, the Security log is unavailable, along with some other features. To get access to all logs, right-click and choose Run As Administrator if you're logged on with a standard user account. (If you're logged on as an administrator and UAC is turned on, a consent prompt always appears when you start Event Viewer.)

Types of Events

If you've used Event Viewer in previous versions of Windows, you might be overwhelmed initially by the new logs and somewhat cluttered display of the Windows Vista version. As a glance at the console tree confirms, events are now recorded in one of several logs:

- **Application** Application events are generated by applications, including programs you install, programs that come with Windows Vista, and operating system services. Program developers decide which events to record in the Application log, and which to record in a program-specific log under Applications And Services.

- **Security** Security events include logon attempts (successful and failed) and attempts to use secured resources, such as an attempt to create, modify, or delete a file. In Windows Vista Business, Enterprise, and Ultimate editions, an administrator can use the Local Security Policy console (Secpol.msc) to configure audit policies (Local Policies\Audit Policy) to determine which types of events get recorded in the Security log. Then, to specify which objects are monitored for security events, visit the Auditing tab in the Advanced Security Settings dialog box for an object.

- **Setup** Setup events are generated by application installation.

- **System** System events are generated by Windows itself and by installed components, such as device drivers. If a driver fails to load when you start a Windows session, for example, that event is recorded in the System log.

- **Forwarded Events** The Forwarded Events log contains events that have been gathered from other computers. For details about setting up and using the Forwarded Events log, see "Monitoring Events," Chapter 22.

- **Applications And Services** The Applications And Services folder contains logs for individual applications (or application suites, such as Microsoft Office) and services. The other logs generally record events that are systemwide in nature, whereas each log in Applications And Services records the events related only to a particular program or component.

  Within the Applications And Services folder resides a Microsoft\Windows folder, which contains a folder for each of many components that are part of Windows Vista. Each of these folders contains one or more logs.

  Even more logs appear in Applications And Services when you open the View menu and click Show Analytic And Debug Logs. These additional logs are generally needed only for a hard-core troubleshooting session, so they're hidden by default. Also note that these logs do not record events by default. To use either the Analytic or Debug logs, right-click it and choose Enable Logging.

The expansion from three logs (Application, Security, and System) in a base installation of Windows XP or Windows 2000 to the dozens of logs in Windows Vista might seem daunting at first. Fortunately, improvements to the tools for summarizing and filtering events, as well as the ability to view events from multiple log files, make the additional information manageable.

INSIDE OUT   Discover event sources

If you're curious about what elements of your system generate events and where those events are recorded, use Registry Editor to open the following registry key: HKLM\System\CurrentControlSet\Services\Eventlog. Then inspect the subkeys, such as Application, Security, and System. Each entity capable of generating an event has a subkey under one of those keys. (For details about using Registry Editor, see Chapter 26, "Editing the Registry.")

Events in most log files are classified as one of three levels, each identified by a unique icon.

- **Error** These are events that represent possible loss of data or functionality. Examples of errors include events related to a malfunctioning network adapter and loss of functionality caused by a device or service that doesn't load at startup.

- **Warning** These events represent less significant or less immediate problems than error events. Examples of warning events include a nearly full disk, a timeout by the network redirector, and data errors on a backup tape.

- **Information** These are other events that Windows logs. Examples of information events include someone using a printer connected to your computer and a successful dial-up connection to your ISP.

The Security log file uses two different icons to classify events: A key icon identifies Audit Success events, and a lock icon identifies Audit Failure events. Both types of events are classified as Information-level events; "Audit Success" and "Audit Failure" are stored in the Keywords field of the Security log file.

Understanding the Event Logs Summary

When you select the top-level folder in Event Viewer's console tree, the Details pane displays summary information, as shown in Figure 22-2. This view lets you see at a glance if any significant events that might require your attention have occurred in the past hour, day, or week. You can expand each category to see the sources of events of that event type. Seeing a count of events of various types in various time periods is interesting—but not particularly useful in and of itself. However, by selecting an event type or an event source under Summary Of Administrative Events, you can then jump directly to those events, regardless of which logs they're in. In the Action pane, simply click View All Instances Of This Event.

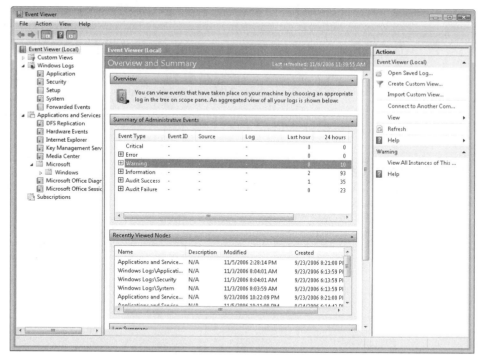

Figure 22-2 Under Summary of Administrative Events, click a plus sign to expand a category of events of a certain type.

Chapter 22

Viewing Individual Logs and Events

When you select in the console tree a log or a custom view, the Details pane shows a single line for each event. By default, five columns of information—each known as an *event property*—are shown:

- **Level** Each event is classified as one of three severity levels: Information, Warning, and Error. (Event Viewer uses the term *level* interchangeably with *event type*.) The icon at the left side of the Level column helps you spot the event types in which you're interested.

- **Date And Time** The Windows Event Log service records the date and time each event occurred in Coordinated Universal Time (UTC), and Event Viewer translates those time values into dates and times appropriate for your own time zone.

- **Source** The Source column reports the application or system component that generated an event.

- **Event ID** Every event is identified by a numerical value. This number is associated with a text description that appears when you view an event's properties. No universal coding system is in use here—each event source's designer simply decides what numbers to use and records those numbers in a file—and there's no requirement that each event source use a unique set of numbers.

- **Task Category** Some event sources use categories to distinguish different types of events they may report. Many sources do not.

Several additional event properties can be displayed. To do so, open the View menu and click Add/Remove Columns.

Viewing Event Details

When viewing events in a selected log or custom view, at the bottom of the Details pane you'll see information about the currently selected event. Except on a monitor with very high resolution, this preview of the full details for a particular event doesn't impart much more information than the columnar display at the top of the Details pane. (If you find the lower part of the Details pane to be useless, you can banish it and use the window's full height for the events list. To do so, open the View menu and click Preview Pane.)

To learn more about an event than Event Viewer's Details pane tells you, you need to display information for the individual event. Select the event you're interested in and double-click it, press Enter, or click Properties in the Action pane. Figure 22-3 shows the Event Properties dialog box for an event in the System log.

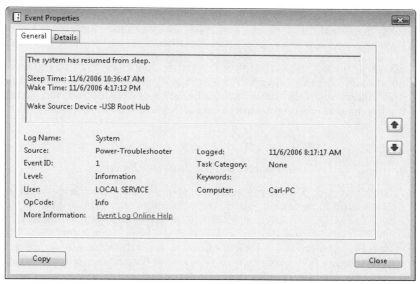

Figure 22-3 The properties dialog box for an event provides a textual description and data that are not shown in the main Event Viewer window.

The summary information in the bottom half of the Event Properties dialog box is identical to the information that appears in Event Viewer's columnar Details pane—except that it includes additional event properties that aren't shown by default in list view. But the most useful features are at the top and bottom of the Event Properties dialog box.

At the top is a plain-language description of what has occurred. For localization purposes, this information is kept separate from the log (.evt) file. Each event type is mapped to descriptive text that lives elsewhere, in whatever file the application's or component's designer chose to use. (The event message file is specified in the EventMessageFile registry value in HKLM\System\CurrentControlSet\Services\Eventlog*logname**eventsource*, where *logname* is the name of the log—System, for example—and *eventsource* is the name of the application or component that generates the event in question.)

Chapter 22

Near the bottom of the Event Properties dialog box is a Copy button. Clicking here sends the entire contents of the Event Properties dialog box to the Clipboard, allowing you, for example, to paste the information into an e-mail message and send it to a support technician. The copied information includes a plain-text rendition similar to the on-screen display as well as the underlying data in XML format. (You can also copy the text in the dialog box by selecting it and pressing Ctrl+C. Use this technique to selectively copy field data from the dialog box as well as information in the Description and Data boxes.)

Also near the bottom of the Event Properties dialog box is a link to more information online. Clicking this link opens a webpage that provides more specific and detailed information about this particular combination of event source and event ID, including further actions you might want to take in response to the event.

INSIDE OUT   Find better descriptions on the web

The description of some events is a model of clarity and completeness. Others, however, leave much to be desired. In addition to the information provided by the More Information link, you can usually find details on the web by searching for "event id" followed by the Event ID number. One particular site deserves mention: EventID.Net *(http://eventid.net)*. Here you can search for information by event ID and source; results typically include a clear description, links to relevant Knowledge Base articles, and comments and suggestions from knowledgeable users.

If you want to view details for other events, you can do so without returning to the Details pane: Click the arrow buttons along the right side of the properties dialog box to move to the previous or next event in the list.

Sorting and Grouping Events

By default, events are sorted chronologically, with the most recent located at the top of the list. You can change the sort order by opening the View menu, clicking Sort By, and then clicking the name of the column you want to sort on. More simply, click a column heading. To revert to the default order, click View, Remove Sorting.

More powerful than sorting is the ability to group events. Grouping not only sorts the event list by the selected column, but it places them under group headings that can be collapsed or expanded, making it easier to find and focus on events of interest. Figure 22-4 shows an example.

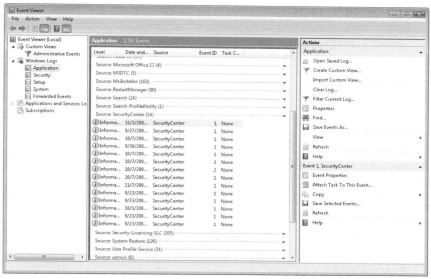

Figure 22-4 The Application log here is grouped by Source. All groups were collapsed, and then a single group was expanded.

To group events in the currently displayed log or custom view, open the View menu, click Group By, and then click the name of the column you want to group by. (Note that Date And Time grouping actually groups by date only.) To find your way more quickly to a group of interest, open the View menu and click Collapse All Groups. To revert to the standard, ungrouped event list, click View, Remove Grouping Of Events.

Filtering the Log Display

As you can see from a cursory look at your System log, events can pile up quickly, obscuring those generated by a particular source or those that occurred at a particular date and time. Sorting and grouping can help you to find that needle in a haystack, but to get the hay out of the way altogether, use filtering. With filtering, you can select based on multiple criteria and, once a view is filtered, nonconforming events are hidden from view, making it much easier to focus on the items you currently care about.

To filter the currently displayed log or custom view, click Action, Filter Current Log. A dialog box like the one shown in Figure 22-5 appears. To fully appreciate the flexibility of filtering, click the arrow by each filter. You can, for example, filter events from the past hour, 12 hours, day, week, month, or any custom time period you specify. In the Event Sources, Task Category, and Keywords boxes, you can type text to filter on (separate multiple items with commas), but you'll probably find it easier to click the arrow and then click each of the items you want to include in your filtered view. In the Event IDs box, you can enter multiple ID numbers and number ranges, separated by commas; to exclude particular event IDs, precede their number with a minus sign.

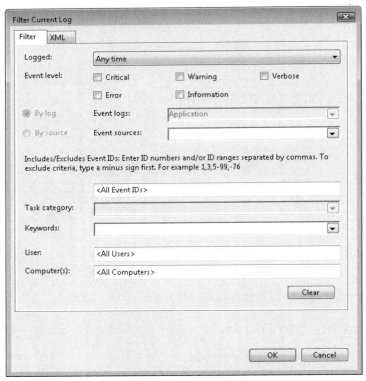

Figure 22-5 If you don't select any Error Level boxes, Event Viewer includes all levels in the filtered results. Similarly, any other field you leave blank includes all events without regard to the value of that property.

When you finish defining the broad strokes of your filter on the Filter tab, you might want to switch to the XML tab, where you can further refine your filter by editing the query.

To restore the unfiltered list, click Action, Clear Filter.

> **Note**
>
> Event Viewer also includes an anemic search capability, which you access by clicking Action, Find. You can perform more precise searches by filtering.

INSIDE OUT   Combine sorting, grouping, and filtering

The sorting, grouping, and filtering actions each work their magic independently. You can apply them in any combination to create exactly the view you want of the events in a log or custom view.

Creating and Saving Custom Views

If you spend much time in Event Viewer or have a particularly troublesome component that sends you back to Event Viewer often, creating ad-hoc filtering, grouping, and sorting criteria becomes tiresome. Custom views to the rescue. To create a custom view, click Action, Create Custom View. You'll see a dialog box nearly identical to the Filter Current Log dialog box shown in Figure 22-5. One key difference: the Event Logs box is available, and you can specify any or all logs to include in your custom view.

After you create filter criteria and click OK, you need to specify a name and location for your custom view. You can store your custom view in the Custom Views folder or any of its subfolders. (To create a subfolder, click New Folder.) Select All Users if you want the view to be available to any user on your computer; clear it if you want it to appear only when you log on.

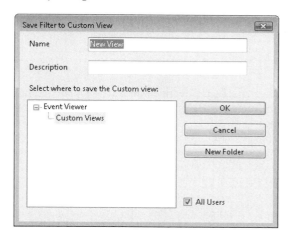

Chapter 22

INSIDE OUT   **Save an existing filtered view as a custom view**

If you've already applied a filter to a log, you can save that filtered view by choosing Action, Save Filter To Custom View.

You can now display your custom view by selecting its name in the console tree. You can apply sorting or grouping, and those changes are stored as part of the custom view. To modify the filter criteria, click Filter Current Log. To change the name or description for your custom view, click Action, Properties.

You can copy the custom view, which is just an XML query, to a file so you can install it on another computer without starting from scratch. Select the custom view in the console tree and then click Action, Export Custom View. To install it, click Action, Import Custom View.

Exporting Event Data

You can save selected events, all events in the current view, or all events in a particular log to a file for archival purposes, for further analysis in a different program, or to share with a technical support specialist. (To select events for exporting, hold down the Ctrl key and click each event you want to include.) The command to do so is on the Action menu, and the command name varies depending on the current view and selection: Save Selected Events, Save Filtered Log File As, Save Events In Custom View As, or Save Events As.

Saving event data in Event Viewer's native (.evtx) format creates a file that you can view only in Event Viewer (or a third-party application capable of reading native event logs). However, Event Viewer can export log data to XML, tab-delimited, or comma-delimited text files, and you can easily import these into database, spreadsheet, or even word processing programs.

Monitoring Events

Traditionally, troubleshooters delve into Event Viewer after a problem has occurred, poring through logs to find clues to the cause of the problem. Event Viewer in Windows Vista includes two new features that take a slightly more proactive approach. First, you can configure a task to be performed automatically when a particular event happens. And if your troubleshooting purview extends beyond your own computer, you can configure Event Viewer so that when certain events occur on other computers on your network, those events show up in Event Viewer on your computer.

Creating a Task to Run When a Specific Event Occurs

You might want to be notified or have a program run if a particular event occurs. Task Scheduler monitors event logs, so that an event can be a trigger to launch a task that runs a program, sends an e-mail message, or displays a message on the screen. To configure such a task from within Event Viewer, find an existing occurrence of the event, select it, and click Action, Attach Task To This Event. Doing so opens the Create Basic Task wizard, with the trigger and event information already completed. If you want to create a task based on an event that isn't currently in your log file, open Task Scheduler and click Action, Create Basic Task.

For more information about creating and configuring scheduled tasks, see "Using the Windows Vista Task Scheduler," Chapter 30.

Monitoring Other Computers' Events with Subscriptions

A subscription lets you collect event records from other computers and store them on your own computer. You can then view them and work with them exactly like events from your computer; you can include them in custom views, filtered views, exported events, and so on.

INSIDE OUT   View all logs on a remote computer

Subscriptions provide a great way to look at specific events from one or more remote computers. As an alternative way to view the complete event logs of a single remote computer, you can open that computer's logs in Event Viewer. To do so, select the top-level entry in Event Viewer's console tree, Event Viewer (Local). Then click Action, Connect To Another Computer. To view all logs, including the Security log, you'll need to use an account that is a member of the Event Log Readers group on the targeted remote computer. In addition, on that computer you must enable the firewall exception for Remote Event Log Management.

To return to viewing your own computer's log files, right-click the top-level entry in the console tree, click Connect To Another Computer, and select Local Computer.

Chapter 22

Configuring Your Systems for Subscriptions

To enable subscriptions, you need to make some changes on the source computers (the remote computers that will send event data to the collector computer) and on the collector computer (the one on which you'll view the source computers' event data). The following instructions explain how to configure computers in a workgroup to use subscriptions. The procedure for configuring computers in a domain is similar, but slightly easier; for details, see Event Viewer help.

On each source computer, follow these steps:

1. Open an elevated Command Prompt window (easiest way: in the Start menu Search box, type **cmd** and press Ctrl+Shift+Enter) and enter this command:

   ```
   winrm quickconfig
   ```

   This command performs the following tasks:

   - Sets the startup type for the Windows Remote Management (WinRM) service to Automatic (Delayed Start)
   - Starts the Windows Remote Management service
   - Creates a WinRM listener to accept incoming requests that use the WS-Management protocol
   - Enables the exception in Windows Firewall for Windows Remote Management

2. Open Windows Firewall and enable the exception for Remote Event Log Management. (For more information, see "Allowing Connections Through the Firewall," Chapter 10.)

3. Create a user account that is a member of the Event Log Readers group. To do this:

   a. At a command prompt, type **control userpasswords2** to open Advanced User Accounts.

   b. On the Users tab, click Add.

   c. In the Add New User wizard, provide a name and password for the new user. Use the same user name and password on each source computer. When you reach the "What level of access" page, select Other and then select Event Log Readers.

To configure the collector computer, open an elevated Command Prompt window and enter these commands:

```
wecutil qc
```

```
winrm set winrm/config/client @{TrustedHosts="computers"}
```

Replace *computers* with the names of the source computers, separated by commas. If you want to be able to subscribe to all computers on your network, replace *computers* with an asterisk (*), which acts as a wildcard.

> **Note**
>
> If you no longer want to view logs on a particular computer, you can close its doors and lock them by doing the following:
>
> 1. At an elevated command prompt, enter the following command to delete the WinRM listener:
>
>    ```
>    winrm delete winrm/config/listener?address=*+transport=http
>    ```
>
> 2. In the Services console, stop the Windows Remote Management service and change its startup type to Manual.
>
> 3. In Windows Firewall, disable the exceptions for Windows Remote Management and Remote Event Log Management.

Creating a Subscription

To create a subscription so that specified events on a source computer are copied to a log file on your computer, follow these steps. (Again, these steps are for a computer in a workgroup; the comparable process on a domain computer is a bit simpler.)

1. In Event Viewer's console tree, select Subscriptions.

2. In the Action pane (or on the Action menu), click Create Subscription.

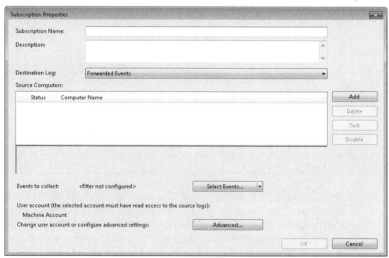

3. Enter a name and, optionally, a description for your new subscription.

4. Select a destination log file. By default, a subscription places events in the Forwarded Events log, but you can select any log. If you select a log other than Forwarded Events, be sure to add the Computer column to the display so that you can differentiate remote events from those generated on your own computer.

5. Click Add and type the name of the source computer. Repeat this step to monitor multiple computers.

6. Click Select Events and specify the types of events you want to monitor.

7. Click Advanced.

8. Select Specific User, click User And Password, and enter the name and password for the user you created on the source computer.

INSIDE OUT   Change the polling interval

By default, event forwarding uses a 15-minute interval, which means that it could be up to 15 minutes between the time an event occurs and the time it shows up on the collector computer. You can adjust the polling interval by setting options in the Advanced Subscription Settings dialog box or by using Wecutil command. (Type **wecutil ss -?** for details.)

Working with Log Files

By default, log files are stored in the %SystemRoot%\System32\Winevt\Logs\ folder. There you'll find the files for the primary Windows logs—Application (Application.evtx), Security (Security.evtx), Setup (Setup.evtx), System (System.evtx), and Forwarded Events (ForwardedEvents.evtx)—as well as the numerous logs in Applications And Services. In general, you don't need to do anything with the log files. But you might want to limit their size, archive their content, or clear them—tasks that are explained in the following sections.

TROUBLESHOOTING

An error message says you don't have enough disk space to record events

If you run out of space on the disk where your log files reside, the Event Log service will be unable to record new events and you will receive an error message to that effect. The best solution, of course, is to create free space on the disk, but if that's not possible you can work around the problem by changing the default location of one or more log files. Doing so requires a modification to your registry, as follows:

1. At a command prompt, type **regedit** to open Registry Editor.

2. Navigate to the subkey within HKLM\System\CurrentControlSet\Services\Eventlog for the log file you want to move.

3. Double-click the File value.

4. Change the File value's data to specify a path to a disk that isn't full. For example, if the current data is located in %SystemRoot%\System32\Winevt\Logs \Application.evtx and you have room to put the Application.evtx file in E:\SomeFolder, change the File value's data to E:\SomeFolder\Application.evtx.

   The folder you specify must exist, or the change won't take effect.

5. Close Registry Editor and restart your computer.

For additional information about modifying the registry, see Chapter 26, "Editing the Registry."

Chapter 22

Setting Log File Size and Longevity

Log files don't continue to pile up new events forever. If they did, they would eventually consume an unmanageable amount of disk space. Each log file has a maximum size setting; the default setting varies by log but some go up to 20 MB—a far cry from the 512 KB in earlier Windows versions. You can adjust the maximum size downward or upward in 64-KB increments.

If a log file reaches its maximum size, by default new events overwrite the oldest ones.

To change either a log file's maximum size or specify the action to take when it reaches capacity, select the log in question in the console tree. Then click Action, Properties. Figure 22-6 shows a log file's properties dialog box. (You must have administrator privileges to use this dialog box; otherwise, all the controls appear dimmed.)

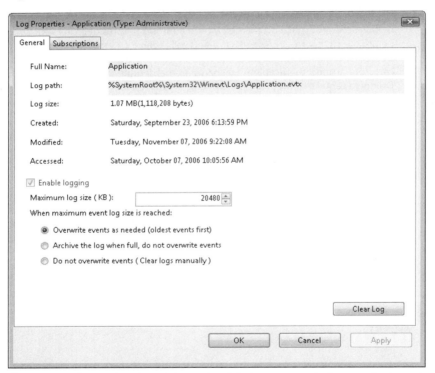

Figure 22-6 If you select the archive option, Windows automatically saves the logged events to a backup file and then clears the log file.

If the Windows Event Log service is unable to add new events to a log because you have told it never to overwrite, you'll receive a warning message. Then you can remedy the situation, either by simply clearing the log or by archiving and then clearing it.

Archiving and Clearing Log Files

To archive a log, select it in the console tree, clear any filters on the log, and click Save Events As on the Action menu. In the dialog box that appears, be sure to select the default file type, Event Files (*.evtx).

To clear a log, either click the Clear Log button in the log's properties dialog box (see Figure 22-6) or select the log in the console tree and click Clear Log on the Action menu. You must have administrative privileges to clear a log.

Displaying an Archived Log File

After you have saved a log file in the .evtx format, it appears under Saved Logs folder in Event Viewer. If for some reason it doesn't appear (for example, if you're trying to view the saved log file on a different computer), in the Action pane click Open Saved Log. You then specify where to put the saved log in the console tree. (It must be in the Saved Logs folder or a subfolder of Saved Logs.)

A reopened archive can be viewed, filtered, grouped, and sorted, just as you can any other log file. You can also delete it—something you can't do to the default logs. When you delete a log from the Saved Logs folder, you're deleting only its entry in the console tree; the file itself remains on disk.

CHAPTER 23

Troubleshooting Windows Errors

Home Basic   ●
Home Premium   ●
Business   ●
Enterprise   ●
Ultimate   ●

> ## What's in Your Edition?
>
> The troubleshooting information in this chapter applies equally to all editions of Windows Vista.

To paraphrase a popular bumper sticker from an earlier era, *stuff happens*. Applications hang (stop responding) or crash (shut down unexpectedly). Once in a while, a component of Windows walks off the job without warning. And on rare occasions, the grim BSOD (the "blue screen of death," more formally known as a Stop error) arrives, bringing your whole system to a halt.

In a fully debugged perfect world, such occurrences would never darken your computer screen. But you don't live there, and neither do we. So the prudent course is to prepare for the unexpected—by making regular backups (including, if possible, a complete image backup of your system drive), letting the Windows Vista System Protection program create daily restore points, keeping Windows Update enabled, and learning to use the other tools that Windows provides for error diagnosis and recovery. Those tools are the subject of this chapter and Chapter 24, "Recovering from a Computer Crash."

For information about creating regular backups and image backups, see "Smart Backup Strategies," in Chapter 20, "Performing Routine Maintenance."

Configuring and Using Windows Error Reporting

Windows Error Reporting has been streamlined and improved in Windows Vista. In Windows XP, the system was essentially manual; when an error occurred, you were invited to send a report to Microsoft. Following up an error report to see if a solution had become available was a cumbersome, discouraging process.

In Windows Vista you can automate this entire reporting and follow-up process. The salient features of Windows Error Reporting in Windows Vista are as follows:

- You now have the option of configuring Windows Error Reporting to transmit basic information to Microsoft automatically when an error occurs.

- You can configure Windows Error Reporting to transmit a more detailed problem report automatically when the system requests it. Or you can provide this additional information on a case-by-case basis.

- You can configure Windows Error Reporting to notify you automatically when an error occurs for which a solution is available.

- Windows Error Reporting maintains a history of errors on your system. You can use this to review dates and events and to see what information has been sent to Microsoft. More important, you can use the history to check periodically for new solutions that might have been developed to problems that have occurred in the past.

In addition to the improvements in Windows Error Reporting, Windows Vista offers application developers a set of application recovery and restart functions that allow them to respond more gracefully to hangs and crashes. An application written with these functions will probably respond to a crash by restarting and reopening the document you were working on. If you use Microsoft Office 2007, you may already have seen these recovery and restart features in action. As time goes by, you can expect to see more and more programs that take advantage of these features.

Understanding Windows Error Reporting and Privacy

The information that Windows Error Reporting transmits to Microsoft is intended primarily to help the company improve its product reliability. Microsoft engineers use this information for solving problems and making improvements, both to Windows and to Microsoft applications, such as Microsoft Office. In the past, a large number of the fixes that arrived in Windows XP Service Pack 1 and Service Pack 2 were the result of submitted error reports. In addition, Windows Error Reporting information involving a third-party application may be made available to that application's publisher.

The basic report that Windows Error Reporting transmits typically include the following information:

- Application name
- Application version
- Module name
- Module version
- Offset
- Exception (error) code

The likelihood that any of these items will convey personally identifiable information is essentially nil. The process does transmit your IP address to a Microsoft server, but Microsoft's Privacy Statement asserts that the IP address is used only to generate aggregate statistics, not to identify you.

If the Windows Error Reporting server requests additional information, that information will consist of one or more files. Typically these are temporary files. If you have configured the system to request your permission to send this additional information, you will see a display similar to the following (You might need to click More Details to see the names of the files):

It is not impossible that one or more of these files might include some data that could be used to identify you. If you are concerned about that possibility, you can use a text editor, such as Notepad, to inspect the files before you make a decision about whether to send them or not. (You can't open the files from within the Windows Error Reporting dialog box, but you can navigate to them via Windows Explorer before responding to the dialog box.)

If privacy is a major concern, you should, of course, read Microsoft's Privacy Statement. You can find a copy of it at *http://www.vista-io.com/2301*.

Understanding the Windows Error Reporting Process

Here is a blow-by-blow description of how Windows Error Reporting responds to a hang, crash, or stop error:

1. Windows Error Reporting gathers the basic information (program name and version, module name and version, and so on) and either transmits this to Microsoft or requests your permission to do so, depending on how you have configured the system.

2. The Microsoft server checks to see if the error has resulted from a known problem. You might see something like this:

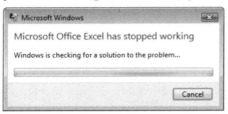

3. If the problem is known and a solution is available, the server sends this information to Windows Error Reporting, which displays it to you. If the problem is known but a solution is still in development, the server reports that. It may also send a request for additional information. In that case, you could see something like the following:

4. If the server has requested more information, Windows Error Reporting gathers the information and either transmits it or requests your permission to do so, depending on how you have configured the system.

5. The application that generated the error restarts if it can.

> **Note**
>
> BadApp.exe, depicted above, is a harmless testing tool that you can download at no charge from *http://www.vista-io.com/2302*.

Setting Windows Error Reporting Options

To configure the behavior of Windows Error Reporting, open Control Panel and click System And Maintenance. Under the heading Problem Reports And Solutions, click Choose How To Check For Solutions. These steps take you to the Problem Reports And Solutions dialog box, shown in Figure 23-1.

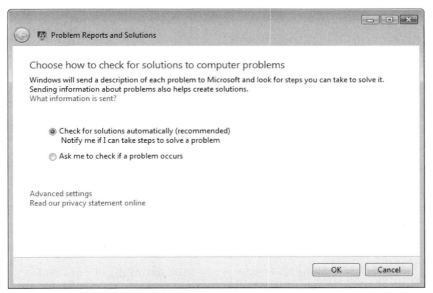

Figure 23-1 By default, Windows Error Reporting transmits basic error reports automatically and prompts for permission if it wants additional information.

The default and recommended option is Check For Solutions Automatically. If you select this option, Windows Error Reporting sends basic information to Microsoft whenever a hang or crash occurs. Note that even with this default in place, the system always prompts for permission if it wants additional details. If you find the default behavior invasive or intrusive, select Ask Me To Check If A Problem Occurs.

If, however, you would rather answer fewer prompts than more, click Advanced Settings in the Problem Reports And Solutions dialog box. In the ensuing dialog box, shown in Figure 23-2, you can select the Automatically Send More Information If It Is Needed To Help Solve Problems check box to reduce the number of permission entreaties that arrive from the Windows Error Reporting server.

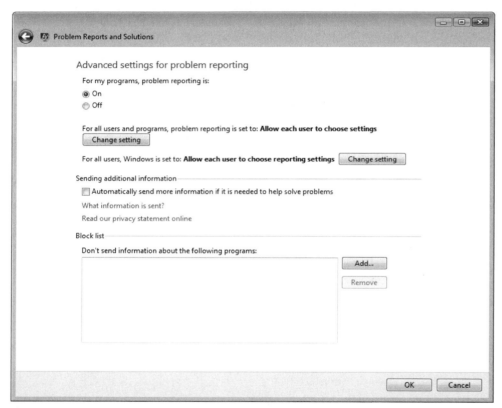

Figure 23-2 Select the check box on this advanced-settings dialog box to reduce the number of prompts you need to reply to.

If you are developing an application yourself (or testing one in development), you probably don't want to be dealing with error-reporting prompts in any way when that application hangs or crashes. You can use the Block list to exclude particular programs from Windows Error Reporting's scrutiny. Click the Add button in the advanced settings portion of the Problem Reports And Solutions dialog box (shown in Figure 23-2) and select the program you want to exclude.

Reviewing the Problem History

Windows Error Reporting maintains a history of the untoward events it has witnessed on your system. To review the log, open Control Panel and click System And Mainte-nance. Then, under the heading Problem Reports And Solutions, click View Problem History. Figure 23-3 shows a portion of the error history for a computer that has been heavily used in a production environment.

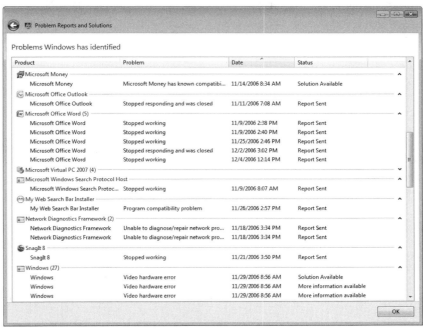

Figure 23-3 Windows Error Reporting maintains a history of errors that occur on your system.

You can see a more detailed report about any event in this log by double-clicking the event. The details might or might not be meaningful to you, but they could be helpful to a support technician. In the following report, for example, the problem description—"Stopped working"—probably tells you nothing that you didn't already know. On the other hand, the version, module name, and other details could be useful.

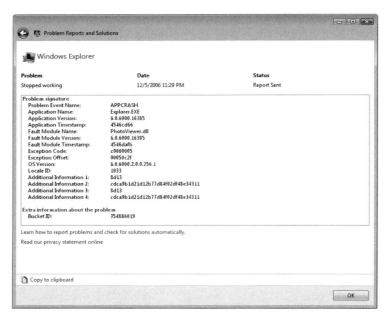

Occasionally you will find an informative nugget in the detailed reports. The second item under Drive Software Installation, in Figure 23-3, for example, reveals the following:

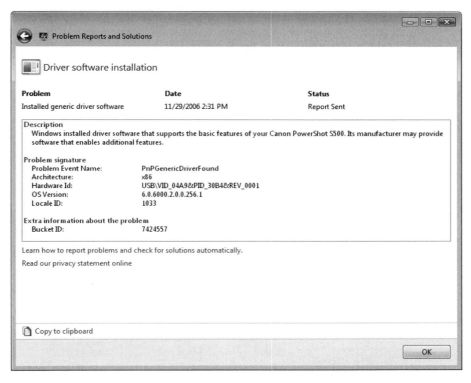

Here, the Description field provides news you can potentially use.

Checking for New Solutions

When you start a session in Windows, you might find a message in your notification area (the clock/calendar display and clump of icons that occupies the rightmost section of your taskbar, assuming the taskbar is arrayed across the bottom of your screen) indicating that Windows has found one or more solutions to problems that you've experienced. If you don't immediately act on this information, you can do so later. Display the history of problems that Windows has identified, as shown in Figure 23-3. If the words *Solution Available* appear in the Status column for an item, right-click that item and choose View Solution from the shortcut menu:

The screen that appears will provide information about how to implement the solution that Windows has found.

Don't assume that an item has no solution unless it is marked *Solution Available*. To check for possible solutions to all the items in your problem history, open Control Panel and click System And Maintenance. Then, under the heading Problem Reports And Solutions, click Check For New Solutions. After a moment or two, you will see a display comparable to the following:

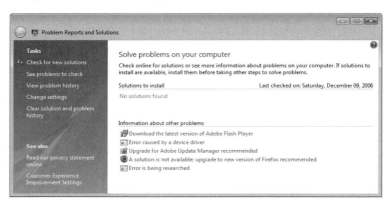

Each item in the sections Solutions To Install and Information About Other Problems is a link to further details. Follow the links to see what information is available.

> **Note**
>
> Don't assume that Windows Update will automatically download solutions to your software problems. If one or more solutions have been incorporated into a Service Pack for Windows Vista and you have enabled Windows Update, then your problems might indeed by solved that way. But solutions developed between Service Packs will not be delivered by Windows Update. Therefore, you should make a practice of revisiting Problem Reports And Solutions from time to time to check for the availability of new solutions.

Reviewing the Error History with the Reliability Monitor

Suppose you suddenly start experiencing errors in a program or Windows component that used to work flawlessly. To troubleshoot a problem like this, you might want to open the Reliability Monitor. Shown in Figure 23-4, the Reliability Monitor is a component of the Reliability And Performance Monitor snap-in, an MMC console. You can get there through Control Panel (Control Panel, System And Maintenance, Performance Information And Tools, Advanced Tools, Open Reliability And Performance Monitor). Or, more simply, you can type **perfmon.msc** at a command prompt. Either way, you'll need elevated privileges.

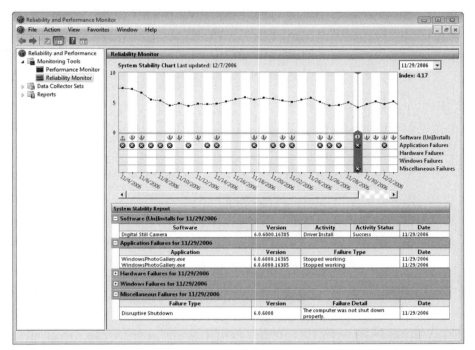

Figure 23-4 The Reliability Monitor can highlight suspicious conjunctions of software installations and application failures.

Chapter 23

Each column in the graphical display at the top of the Reliability Monitor represents events of a particular day. Each red X along the second through fifth line below the graph (the various "Failures" lines) indicates a day on which problems occurred. The first line below the graph, the line marked Software (Un)Installs, identifies days on which an application or other software element (such as an ActiveX control) was installed or removed. You can see the details about the events of any day by clicking on the graph for that day.

In Figure 23-4, we've selected November 29, 2006, a day that witnessed the installation of a new driver for a digital camera, two failures in the Photo Gallery application, and a disruptive shutdown. The alignment of these events could be mere coincidence, but it could also represent the first appearance of a long-term problem. Conjunctions of this sort are worth examining. If you think a new software component has destabilized your system, you can try uninstalling it.

Reviewing the Error History with Event Viewer

You can also examine the history of errors on your system by creating a filtered view of the Application log in Event Viewer. (For details about using Event Viewer, see Chapter 22, "Monitoring System Activities with Event Viewer.") In addition to all the errors reported in Problem Reports and Solutions, Event Viewer can show you errors that are recorded but are not reported (see Figure 23-5).

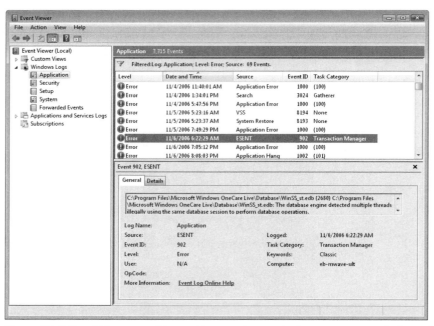

Figure 23-5 Event Viewer provides another way to see what's gone wrong and when—including failures by applications that do not appear in Problem Reports And Solutions.

Rolling Back to a Stable State with System Restore

System Protection is a service that takes periodic snapshots of your system state, including information about user accounts, hardware and software settings, and files required for startup. At regular intervals (once per day, by default), and whenever particular kinds of changes to your system occur (such as the installation or removal of applications or drivers), System Protection creates a *restore point*. If your system becomes unstable, you can sometimes return it to stability by using System Restore to return to one of these restore points.

> **CAUTION**
>
> If you dual-boot Windows Vista with an earlier version of Windows, such as Windows XP, be aware that booting into the alternative operating system *wipes out* all your Windows Vista restore points. New restore points are created at the usual times when you return to Windows Vista, but all previous restore points are erased. If your system has become unstable and you are considering using System Restore, *lay off that other operating system!*

For information about configuring System Protection and creating restore points, see "Configuring System Recovery Options," Chapter 2.

System Restore can't perform miracles, but it can be a lifesaver in the following situations:

- **You install a program that conflicts with other software or drivers on your system.** If uninstalling the program doesn't cure the problem, you can restore your system configuration to a point before you installed the program.

- **You install one or more updated drivers that cause performance or stability problems.** Rather than using the Roll Back Driver command in Device Manager, use System Restore to restore all previously installed drivers.

- **Your system develops performance or stability problems for no apparent reason.** This scenario is especially likely if you share a computer with other family members or coworkers who casually install untested, incompatible software and drivers. If you know the system was working properly on a certain date, you can use a restore point from that date or earlier and be reasonably confident that your system will return to proper operation.

> **CAUTION**
>
> Don't count on System Restore to protect you from viruses, worms, Trojan horses, and other malware. Use a reliable up-to-date antivirus program.

Chapter 23

Using System Restore

The quickest way to get to System Restore is to type **rstrui** at a command prompt. Alternatives:

- Open the Start menu, click All Programs, click Accessories, click System Tools, and click System Restore

- Open Control Panel, type **System Restore** in the Search box, and click Restore System Files And Settings From A Restore Point

A UAC sentry will appear along any of these routes. You need elevated privileges to use System Restore.

When the System Restore wizard appears, it might recommend the most recent restore point. To see a complete list of available restore points, select Choose A Different Restore Point and click Next to get to the dialog box shown in Figure 23-6.

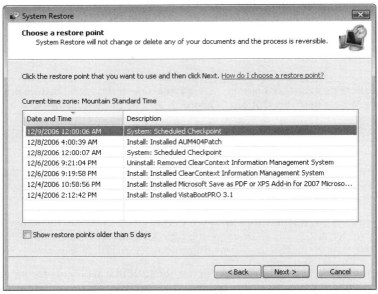

Figure 23-6 System Restore lets you roll your system back to an earlier state.

Note the text near the top of this dialog box. Neither System Protection (the process that creates restore points) nor System Restore (the process that reinstates them) disturbs your documents in any way. And before System Restore returns your system to any restore point, it creates a new restore point—making it easy for you to return to the present if time travel doesn't meet your expectations.

To return to a restore point, select it in the list and click Next. Windows presents the Confirm Disks To Restore dialog box shown in Figure 23-7. Here, if the restore point you want to use encompasses multiple disks, you can select those you want to restore. The only one you must restore is the one where your system files are stored.

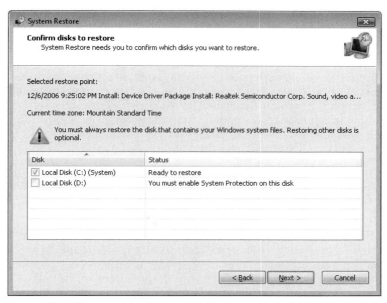

Figure 23-7 If you have enabled System Protection on multiple disks, you can use this screen to select the disks you want to restore.

After you have made your choices on the screen shown in Figure 23-7, click Next again. On the ensuing confirmation screen you'll find a Finish button. Clicking that Finish button takes you to one *more* confirmation prompt, advising you that the restore process must not be interrupted. Answer yes, and the system creates a new restore point, and then restores your system to the restore point you selected. As part of the Restore process, your computer will reboot—and various messages will appear, all counseling you to be patient and not to interfere with the goings on.

When the process is complete and you have logged back on to Windows Vista, check to see if the restoration has improved the stability of your system. If it has not, and you want to return to the state it was in before you restored, retrace your steps to System Restore. At or near the top of the list of available restore points you will find one labeled Undo: Restore Operation. Restore that one and you're back where you started.

Chapter 23

System Restore Do's and Don'ts

You don't have to be a Harry Potter fan to appreciate the hazards of time travel. Here are some to be aware of:

- If you create a new user account and then use System Restore to roll back your system configuration to a point before the new account was created, the new user will no longer be able to log on, and you will receive no warning. (The good news is that the new user's documents will be intact.)

- System Restore does not uninstall programs, although it does remove executable files and DLLs. To avoid having orphaned program shortcuts and files, make a note of any programs that you installed after the date of the restore point you're about to roll back to. If you don't want the program anymore, uninstall it in the normal way before running the restore operation. If you want to continue using the program, reinstall it after the restore is complete.

- Any changes made to your system configuration using the Windows Recovery Environment are not monitored by System Protection. This can produce unintended consequences if you make major changes to system files and then roll back your system configuration with System Restore.

- Although you can restore your system to a previous configuration from Safe Mode, you cannot create a new restore point in Safe Mode. As a result, you cannot undo a restore operation that you perform in Safe Mode. If possible, you should always start Windows normally to perform a restore operation.

For information about the Windows Recovery Environment, see Chapter 24, "Recovering from a Computer Crash."

Dealing with Stop Errors

If Windows has ever suddenly shut down, you've probably experienced that sinking feeling in the pit of your stomach. When Windows Vista encounters a serious problem that makes it impossible for the operating system to continue running, it shuts down immediately and displays an ominous text message whose technical details begin with the word *STOP* in capital letters. Because a Stop error typically appears in white letters on a blue background, this type of message is often referred to as a blue screen error or the Blue Screen of Death (BSOD). When a Stop error appears, it means that there is a serious problem that demands your immediate attention.

Windows Vista includes a variety of information sources and debugging tools that you can use to identify the cause of Stop errors. Many of the tools are intended for use by developers with professional debugging tools. These topics are covered in more detail in *Windows Vista Resource Kit* (Microsoft Press). If you know where to look, however, you can learn a lot from these error messages, and in many cases you can recover completely by using standard troubleshooting techniques.

Customizing How Windows Handles Stop Errors

When Windows encounters a serious error that forces it to stop running, it takes the following actions:

1. The system displays a Stop message.

2. Based on the preferences defined for the current Windows installation, the system writes debugging information to the page file. When the computer restarts, this information is saved as a crash dump file, which can be used to debug the specific cause of the error.

3. Again based on the current preferences, the system either pauses with the Stop message on the screen or restarts when the crash dump information has been saved.

You can customize two crucial aspects of this process by defining the size of the crash dump files and specifying whether you want Windows to restart automatically after a Stop message appears. By default, Windows automatically restarts after a Stop message. That's the preferred strategy in response to a random, isolated Stop error. But if you're experiencing chronic Stop errors, you might have more troubleshooting success by re-configuring Windows to halt at the Stop message and wait for you to manually restart the system. To make this change, follow these steps:

1. Open Control Panel, click System And Maintenance, click System, and then click Advanced System Settings.

2. Respond to the UAC prompt.

3. In the System Properties dialog box, click the Advanced tab.

4. Under Startup And Recovery, click Settings. The following dialog box appears:

5. Clear the Automatically Restart check box and click OK.

From the same dialog box, you can also define the settings for crash dump files. By default, Windows saves a kernel memory dump. This option includes memory allocated to kernel-model drivers and programs, which are most likely to cause Stop errors. Because it does not include unallocated memory or memory allocated to user-mode programs, it will usually be smaller in size than the amount of RAM on your system. The exact size varies, but in general you can expect the file to be approximately one-third the size of installed physical RAM. The crash files are stored in %SystemRoot% using the file name Memory.dmp.

If disk space is plentiful, consider setting the system to store a complete memory dump. This option saves the entire contents of physical memory; as a result, it will be equal in size to your installed RAM.

How to Read a Stop Error

The exact text of a Stop error varies, according to what caused the error. But the format is predictable, as the example in Figure 23-8 shows.

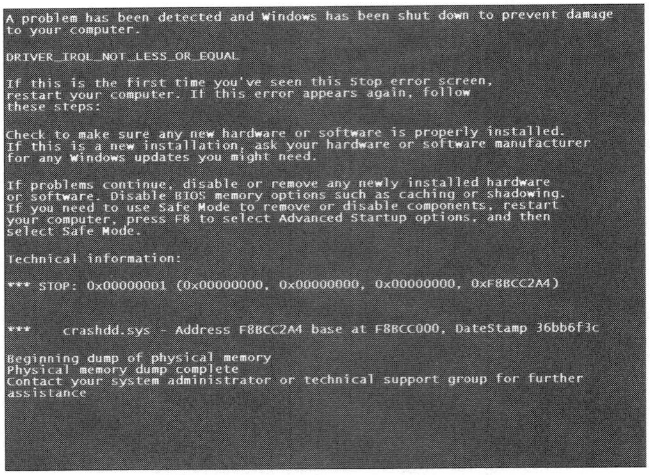

Figure 23-8 Decoding the information in a Stop error can help you find the underlying problem and fix it.

You can gather important information from the following message details.

- **Symbolic error name** This is the message that the error returned to the operating system. It corresponds to the Stop error number that appears at the bottom of the screen. In this example, the symbolic error name is DRIVE_IRQL_NOT_LESS_OR_EQUAL.

- **Troubleshooting recommendations** This generic text applies to all Stop errors of the specified type. Depending on the error number, you may be told to check available disk space, uninstall a piece of hardware, or remove or update recently installed drivers or software.

- **Error number and parameters** Developers call this section *bugcheck information*. The text following the word *STOP* includes the error number (in hexadecimal notation, as indicated by the 0x at the beginning of the code) and up to four parameters that are specific to the error type.

General Advice for Dealing with Stop Errors

If you experience a Stop error, don't panic. Instead, run through the following troubleshooting checklist to isolate the problem and find a solution:

- **Look for a driver name in the error details** If the error message identifies a specific file name and you can trace that file to a driver for a specific hardware device, you may be able to solve the problem by disabling, removing, or rolling back that driver to an earlier version. The most likely offenders are network interface cards, video adapters, and disk controllers. For more details about managing driver files, see "Managing Installed Drivers," Chapter 5.

- **Don't rule out hardware problems** In many cases, software is the victim and not the cause of blue-screen errors. Damaged hard disks, defective physical RAM, and overheated CPU chips are three common hardware failures that can result in Stop errors. If the errors seem to happen at random and the message details vary each time, there is a very good chance that you are experiencing hard problems.

- **Check your memory** Windows Vista includes a memory diagnostic tool that you can use if you suspect a faulty or failing memory chip. To run this diagnostic procedure, open Control Panel and type **memory** in the Search box. Then, under Administrative Tools, click Diagnose Your Computer's Memory Problems. (You will need elevated privileges.) In the Windows Memory Diagnostics Tool, shown here, click Restart Now And Check For Problems (Recommended) or Check For Problems The Next Time I Start My Computer.

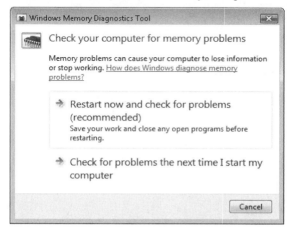

- **Ask yourself, "What's new?"** Be suspicious of newly installed hardware and software. If you added a device recently, remove it temporarily and see whether the problem goes away. Take an especially close look at software in the categories that install services or file-system filter drivers—these hook into the core operating system files that manage the file system to perform tasks such as scanning for viruses. This category includes backup programs, multimedia applications, antivirus software, and CD-burning utilities. You may need to permanently uninstall or update the program to resolve the problem.

- **Search the Knowledge Base** Make a note of the error code and all parameters. Search the Knowledge Base using both the full and short formats. For instance, if you're experiencing a KMODE_EXCEPTION_NOT_HANDLED error, use 0x1E and 0x0000001E as your search keywords.

- **Check your system BIOS carefully** Is an update available from the manufacturer of the system or motherboard? Check the BIOS documentation carefully; resetting all BIOS options to their defaults can sometimes resolve an issue caused by overtweaking.

- **Are you low on system resources?** Stop errors are sometimes the result of a critical shortage of RAM or disk space. If you can start in Safe Mode, check the amount of physical RAM installed and look at the system and boot drives to see how much free disk space is available. You may be able to free space by running the Disk Cleanup utility, as described in "Managing Disk Space," Chapter 20.

- **Is a crucial system file damaged?** To reinstall a driver, restart your computer, press F8, and start Windows in Safe Mode. In Safe Mode, only core drivers and services are activated. If your system starts in Safe Mode but not normally, you very likely have a problem driver. Try running Device Manager in Safe Mode and uninstalling the most likely suspect. Or run System Restore in Safe Mode. If restoring to a particular day cures the problem, use Reliability Monitor (see Figure 23-4) to determine what changes occurred on or after that day.

INSIDE OUT   Try an alternative driver

Experienced support engineers recommend that you use the hardware driver that was made specifically for your device. However, if an unsigned, device-specific driver causes Stop errors, you might have success by using a more recent driver for a product in the same family, even if the model name is not identical. This strategy is most likely to work with printers; it is least likely to be successful with video adapters and network interface cards.

Troubleshooting Specific Stop Errors

The general troubleshooting steps outlined in the previous section apply to all Stop errors. Details provided by specific Stop errors, however, can help you narrow down the cause of the error and get to a solution quickly. This section lists the most common Stop error codes, with suggested troubleshooting actions and external resources for additional information.

> **Note**
> A good online resource for Stop errors can be found at *http://www.vista-io.com/2303*.

STOP 0x0000000A or IRQL_NOT_LESS_OR_EQUAL

A kernel-mode process or driver attempted to access a memory location without authorization. This Stop error is typically caused by faulty or incompatible hardware or software. The name of the offending device driver often appears in the Stop error and can provide an important clue to solving the problem.

If the error message points to a specific device or category of devices, try removing or replacing devices in that category. If this Stop error appears during Setup, suspect an incompatible driver, system service, virus scanner, or backup program.

For more information, see Knowledge Base article 314063, *http://www.vista-io.com/2304*.

STOP 0x0000001E or KMODE_EXCEPTION_NOT_HANDLED

The Windows kernel detected an illegal or unknown processor instruction, often the result of invalid memory and access violations caused by faulty drivers or hardware devices. The error message often identifies the offending driver or device. If the error occurred immediately after installing a driver or service, try disabling or removing the new addition.

STOP 0x00000024 or NTFS_FILE_SYSTEM

A problem occurred within the NTFS file-system driver. A similar Stop error, 0x23, exists for FAT32 drives. The most likely cause is a hardware failure in a disk or disk controller. Check all physical connections to all hard disks in the system and run the Check Disk utility (chkdsk.exe) using the instructions outlined in "Checking Disks for Errors," Chapter 20.

For more information, see Knowledge Base article 228888, *http://www.vista-io.com/2318*.

Chapter 23

STOP 0x0000002E or DATA_BUS_ERROR

Failed or defective physical memory (including memory used in video adapters) is the most common cause of this Stop error. The error may also be the result of a corrupted hard disk or a damaged motherboard.

STOP 0x0000003F or NO_MORE_SYSTEM_PTES

Your system ran out of page table entries (PTEs). The cause of this relatively uncommon error may be an out-of-control backup program or a buggy device driver.

For more information, see Knowledge Base article 256004, *http://www.vista-io.com/2306*.

STOP 0x00000050 or PAGE_FAULT_IN_NONPAGED_AREA

A hardware driver or system service requested data that was not in memory. The cause may be defective physical memory or incompatible software, especially remote control and antivirus programs. If the error occurs immediately after installing a device driver or application, try to use Safe Mode to remove the driver or uninstall the program.

For more information, see Knowledge Base article 894278, *http://www.vista-io.com/2307* or Knowledge Base article 183169, *http://www.vista-io.com/2308*.

STOP 0x00000077 or KERNEL_STACK_INPAGE_ERROR

The system attempted to read kernel data from virtual memory (the page file) and failed to find the data at the specified memory address. This Stop error can be caused by a variety of problems, including defective memory, a malfunctioning hard disk, an improperly configured disk controller or cable, corrupted data, or a virus infection.

For more information, see Knowledge Base article 228753, *http://www.vista-io.com/2309*.

STOP 0x0000007F or UNEXPECTED_KERNEL_MODE_TRAP

Hardware failure is the most common cause of this error. You are most likely to see this Stop error if you have defective memory chips, mismatched memory modules, a malfunctioning CPU, or a failure in your fan or power supply that causes overheating. The error is especially likely to occur on systems where the CPU has been tweaked to run past its rated speed, a process known as "overclocking." The first parameter immediately after this Stop error number identifies the specific cause of the error.

For more information, see Knowledge Base article 137539, *http://www.vista-io.com/2310*.

STOP 0x000000C2 or BAD_POOL_CALLER

A kernel-mode process or driver attempted to perform an illegal memory allocation. The problem can often be traced to a bug in a driver or software. It is also occasionally caused by a failure in a hardware device.

For more information, see Knowledge Base article 265879, *http://www.vista-io.com/2311.*

STOP 0x000000D1 or DRIVER_IRQL_NOT_LESS_OR_EQUAL

This is one of the most common Stop errors. The error typically occurs when a driver tries to access an improper memory address. Check for unsigned drivers, and be especially suspicious of recently installed or updated antivirus programs, disk utilities, and backup programs, which may install a faulty file-system filter driver.

For more information see Knowledge Base articles 810093, 316208, 317216, and 810980, *http://www.vista-io.com/2319, http://www.vista-io.com/2312, http://www.vista-io.com/2313,* and *http://www.vista-io.com/2314.*

STOP 0x000000D8 or DRIVER_USED_EXCESSIVE_PTES

If a poorly written driver causes your computer to request large amounts of kernel memory, you may run out of page table entries (PTEs) and see this error message. The underlying cause of the error and troubleshooting suggestions are identical to those found in the STOP 0x3F message.

STOP 0x000000EA or THREAD_STUCK_IN_DEVICE_DRIVER

You may see this error message after you install a new video adapter or an updated (and poorly written) video driver that causes the system to pause indefinitely while waiting for the video hardware. To resolve the problem, replace the video adapter or use a different video driver.

For more information, see Knowledge Base article 293078, *http://www.vista-io.com/2315.*

STOP 0x000000ED or UNMOUNTABLE_BOOT_VOLUME

Windows was unable to gain access to the volume containing boot files. If you see this Stop message while attempting to upgrade a system to Windows Vista, verify that you have compatible drivers for the disk controller and check the drive cabling to make sure it is configured properly. If you're using ATA-66 or ATA-100 drivers, make sure you have an 80-connector cable, not a standard 40-connector IDE cable. See the troubleshooting suggestions for Stop error 0x7B errors as well. In some cases, this error will spontaneously correct itself after you restart your system.

For more information, see Knowledge Base articles 297185 and 315403, *http://www. vista-io.com/2316* and *http://www.vista-io.com/2317.*

Chapter 23

STOP 0x000000F2 or HARDWARE_INTERRUPT_STORM

This hardware-related Stop error can be extremely frustrating to experience and even more vexing to troubleshoot. The Windows kernel detects an *interrupt storm* when a device fails to release an interrupt request (IRQ). This failure is usually caused by a poorly written device driver or a bug in firmware. To isolate the problem, try to determine which device is associated with the file name listed in the driver information section of the Stop message. Then use Device Manager or the System Information tool to identify other devices using the same IRQ, as described in "Viewing and Changing Resource Assignments," Chapter 5. Remove all the devices identified as using that IRQ and add them back, one at a time, until the problem recurs.

STOP 0xC000021A or STATUS_SYSTEM_PROCESS_TERMINATED

This message indicates a serious security problem with Windows—a user-mode subsystem, such as Winlogon or the Client Server Runtime Subsystem (Csrss.exe), is compromised. The most common cause of this problem is a third-party program, and the solution is usually to remove that program. This error can also occur if a backup set has been partially restored, causing a mismatch in system files, or if system permissions have been incorrectly modified so that the System account no longer has permission to access system files and folders.

STOP 0xC00000221 or STATUS_IMAGE_CHECKSUM_MISMATCH

File or disk corruption problems (including a damaged page file) and faulty hardware are the most common causes of this type of Stop error. The message usually includes the name of the damaged file at the end of the symbolic error name or on a line by itself; you might be able to restore the file from the Windows distribution media, using the Windows Recovery Environment. Restoring the Last Known Good Configuration might also help to resolve this problem.

Home Basic   ◐
Home Premium   ◐
Business   ●
Enterprise   ●
Ultimate   ●

Not every crash is a catastrophe. That might be difficult to remember when you switch on your computer and are confronted by an ominous error message or a black screen instead of the Windows Vista Welcome screen. But if you analyze what caused your system to stop working properly, you have an excellent chance of recovering quickly and completely.

In some cases, the cause is easy to pinpoint. If you install a new scanner or update a video driver and your system hangs at a blank screen when you restart, you can safely bet that the new device or driver is to blame. Error messages sometimes point directly to a file that's causing a problem. Even without a smoking gun, you can use basic troubleshooting techniques to uncover the cause of a crash.

Windows Vista provides a full assortment of troubleshooting and repair options. The circumstances and severity of the problem usually dictate which tool is most appropriate. In this chapter, we cover two broad categories of recovery tools:

- **Advanced Boot Options** If you press F8 while your system is starting up, Windows Vista displays a menu of diagnostic startup options. The first and most important of these is Safe Mode, which lets Windows start with only its most essential drivers and services. After you have started in Safe Mode, you can start and stop services, uninstall programs or drivers that might be causing problems, and run System Restore to return your system to an earlier, more stable, state.

- **The Windows Recovery Environment (WinRE)** New in Windows Vista, the Windows Recovery Environment provides a set of system recovery features in a small-footprint version of Windows. Even if you can't start your system in Safe Mode, you can use the Windows Recovery Environment to repair damaged system files, run System Restore, run memory diagnostics, restore a Complete PC backup, or perform diagnostic and recovery operations at a command prompt. The Windows Recovery Environment is a replacement for the Windows XP Recovery Console.

> **What's in Your Edition?**
>
> The Complete PC Backup and Complete PC Restore programs are not available in Windows Vista Home Basic and Windows Vista Home Premium editions. All other troubleshooting tools described in this chapter are available in all editions.

Using Advanced Boot Options

Pressing F8 during the startup process takes you to the following Advanced Boot Options menu:

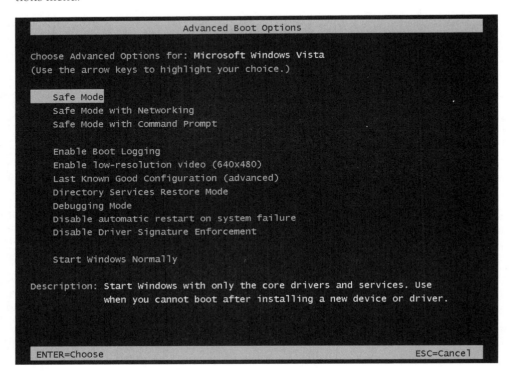

If Windows hangs at startup (that is, if you never get to the desktop or a logon prompt), use the power switch to restart your system. In that case you might see the following Windows Error Recovery menu, which offers some of the same troubleshooting options as the Advanced Boot Options menu:

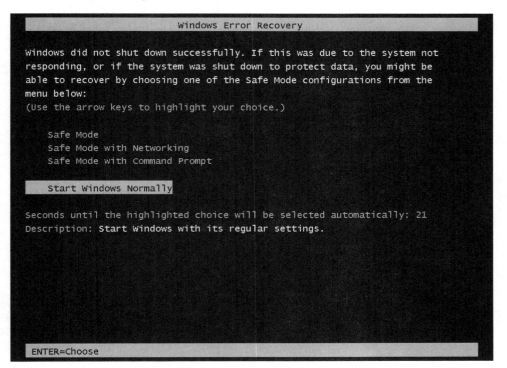

Depending on how your system was set up, it is possible that if Windows can't start you will be taken straight to the Windows Recovery Environment instead of to the Windows Error Recovery menu. We discuss the Windows Recovery Environment later in this chapter.

Using Safe Mode

Like previous versions, Windows Vista gives you the option to start your system in Safe Mode if you're unable to start reliably in the normal manner. In Safe Mode, Windows uses only those services and drivers that are absolutely required to start your system. The operating system runs with a generic video driver at 800 x 600 resolution, with support for keyboard, mouse, monitor, local storage, and default system services. In Safe Mode, Windows does not install support for audio devices and nonessential peripherals. Your USB flash drives, hard disks, keyboard, and mouse will be supported, provided your system BIOS includes the option to recognize and enable these devices. All logon programs (programs in your Startup folder, for example) are bypassed.

Chapter 24

INSIDE OUT   Use an administrative account

To solve problems in Safe Mode, you need administrative credentials. With a Standard account, you'll have read-only access to some diagnostic tools, but you won't be able to take any troubleshooting actions.

In Safe Mode, you can access certain essential configuration tools, including Device Manager, System Restore, and Registry Editor. All local Help And Support features are available; if you choose the Safe Mode With Networking option, you'll have access to online help as well.

One important troubleshooting tool that is not available in Safe Mode is the Backup And Restore Center. To restore a Complete PC Backup, for example, you need to use the Windows Recovery Environment, not Safe Mode.

If Windows appears to work properly in Safe Mode, you can safely assume that there's no problem with the basic services. Use Device Manager, Driver Verifier Manager, and Event Viewer to try to figure out where the trouble lies. If you suspect that a newly installed device or program is the cause of the problem, you can remove the offending software while you're running in Safe Mode. Use Device Manager to uninstall or roll back a hardware driver; use Control Panel to remove a program. Then try restarting the system normally to see whether your changes have resolved the problem.

For information about using Device Manager, see Chapter 5, "Setting Up and Troubleshooting Hardware." For information about using Event Viewer, see Chapter 22, "Monitoring System Activities with Event Viewer." For information about removing programs, see Chapter 4, "Adding, Removing, and Managing Programs."

If you need access to network connections, choose the Safe Mode With Networking option, which loads the base set of Safe Mode files and adds drivers and services required to start Windows networking. Note that this option will do you no good on a portable computer with a PC Card (PCMCIA) network adapter, because PC Card peripherals are disabled in Safe Mode.

The third Safe Mode option, Safe Mode With Command Prompt, loads the same stripped-down set of services as Safe Mode, but uses the Windows Vista command interpreter (Cmd.exe) as a shell instead of the graphical Windows Explorer. This option is unnecessary unless you're having a problem with the Windows graphical interface. The default Safe Mode also provides access to the command line (press Windows logo key+R, then type **cmd.exe** in the Run dialog box).

Restoring the Last Known Good Configuration

Every time you successfully start Windows in normal mode, the operating system makes a record of all currently installed drivers and the contents of the registry key HKLM\SYSTEM\CurrentControlSet. This record comes in handy if you install a driver or make a hardware configuration change that causes your system to hang at startup. When Windows displays the Advanced Boot Options menu, you can choose the Last Known Good Configuration (Advanced) option. This menu choice restores the previous, working registry key, effectively removing the changes that are causing the problem.

In general, System Restore is a more reliable method of restoring a prior, working configuration than the Last Known Good Configuration option. That's because System Restore restores all Windows system files and the entire registry rather than just a single key. (For more information, see "Rolling Back to a Stable State with System Restore," Chapter 23.)

> **CAUTION**
>
> If you suspect that a driver change is causing system problems and you don't have a recent restore point to return to, don't log on in normal mode. As soon as you log on normally, Windows resets the Last Known Good Configuration information, effectively removing your safety net. Be especially careful if you have recently booted this computer into an earlier version of Windows, such as Windows XP. Windows Vista restore points are erased when you boot into an earlier operating system. If you suspect problems, start Windows in Safe Mode and perform basic troubleshooting. Logging on in Safe Mode does not update the Last Known Good Configuration information, so you can safely roll back to the Last Known Good Configuration if Safe Mode troubleshooting is unsuccessful.

Other Startup Options

Six additional choices on the Advanced Boot Options menu are of use in specialized circumstances:

- **Enable Boot Logging** When you select this option, Windows starts up normally and creates a log file that lists the names and status of all drivers loaded into memory. To view the contents of this file, look for Ntbtlog.txt in the %SystemRoot% folder. If your system is hanging because of a faulty driver, the last entry in this log file may identify the culprit.

- **Enable Low-Resolution Video** This option starts the computer in 640 x 480 resolution using the current video driver. Use this option to recover from video problems that are caused not by a faulty driver but by incorrect settings, such as an improper resolution or refresh rate.

- **Directory Services Restore Mode** This option is used only with domain controllers running a server edition of Windows. Ignore it.

- **Debugging Mode** This choice starts Windows Vista in kernel debug mode. To take advantage of this capability, you must connect the system to another computer using a serial connection on COM2. The other computer must run a compatible debugger to perform troubleshooting and system analysis.

- **Disable Automatic Restart On System Failure** Use this option if you're getting a STOP error (a blue-screen crash) every time you start Windows and the operating system is configured to restart automatically after a crash. Under these circumstances your computer will continually reboot, crash, and reboot. To break the cycle, turn the machine off. Then press F8 during startup and choose Disable Automatic Restart On System Failure.

- **Disable Driver Signature Enforcement** Use this option if Windows is refusing to start because of an unsigned driver. Windows will start normally, not in Safe Mode.

If you bought your computer with Windows Vista pre-installed by the computer manufacturer, your Advanced Boot Options might also include a command that starts the Windows Recovery Environment. We discuss the Windows Recovery Environment next.

Making Repairs with the Windows Recovery Environment

If your system won't start even in Safe Mode, all is by no means lost. You can repair many serious problems with the Windows Recovery Environment. If the trouble stems from a corrupted system file, the Windows Recovery Environment might be able to get your system running again with almost no intervention or effort on your part.

Launching the Windows Recovery Environment

If you have a Windows Vista distribution DVD, you can get to the Windows Recovery Environment as follows:

1. Insert the Windows Vista DVD and restart your computer. Let the computer boot from the DVD.

> **Note**
> You might need to change boot settings in your BIOS to enable booting from the DVD drive.

2. When you reach the Install Windows screen, make the appropriate selections for Language to Install, Time And Currency Format, and Keyboard Or Input Method. Then click Next. The following screen appears:

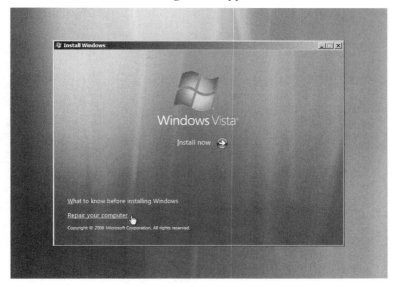

3. Do not click Install Now. Instead, click Repair Your Computer. The System Recovery Options dialog box appears:

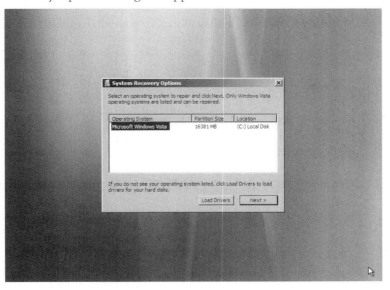

4. Make sure the correct operating system is selected, and then click Next. Note that this dialog box will not list earlier versions of Windows that happen to be installed on the same computer as Windows Vista. After you click Next, the System Recovery Options menu, shown in Figure 24-1, appears.

Figure 24-1 The main menu of the Windows Recovery Environment, titled System Recovery Options, offers a selection of five troubleshooting and repair commands.

If Windows Vista was preinstalled on your computer and you do not have a distribution DVD, your computer's manufacturer has probably set up the Windows Recovery Environment on a hard disk "recovery" volume. In that case, you might find a command called Windows Recovery Environment or System Recovery Options on the Advanced Boot Options menu, the menu that appears when you press F8 during the boot process. It's also possible that your system is set up so that, in the event that Windows can't start, the Windows Recovery Environment loads automatically. In neither of these is the case and you're having trouble finding your way to the Windows Recovery Environment, consult the documentation that came with your computer or call your manufacturer's technical support.

Replacing Corrupted or Missing System Files With Startup Repair

Startup Repair, the first item on the System Recovery Options menu, is designed to get you back up and running when Windows won't start because of damage to (or deletion of) one or more essential system files. Generally speaking, if you're not sure why Windows won't start, you should begin your troubleshooting by running Startup Repair. (Under some circumstances and depending on how your system has been set up, Startup Repair might run automatically when Windows fails to boot.)

Startup Repair will begin by displaying the following:

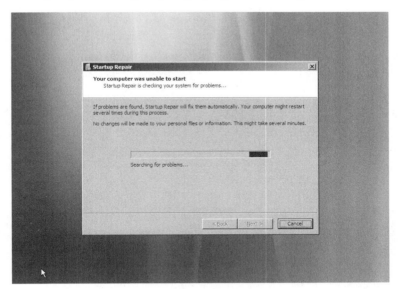

After a few moments, if all has gone well, you might see this message:

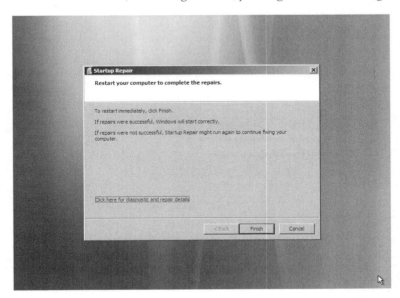

This is not a promise that your system has been fixed—but it is encouraging. If you respond by clicking Finish, the system will reboot. If no problems remain unsolved, you'll be heading straight back into Windows. If more repair is needed, Startup Repair will run again. If you want more information about what Startup Repair has done, click the link at the bottom of the dialog box—Click Here For Diagnostic And Repair Details. Something akin to the following will appear, and you can use the scroll bar to read the full report.

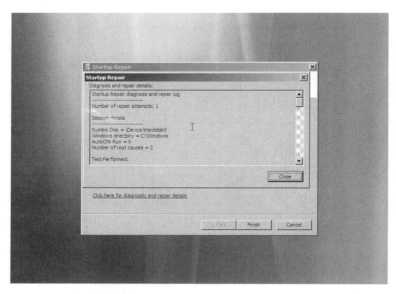

If Startup Repair is unable to solve your problem, you're likely to see the following message, with a request that you consent to informing Microsoft:

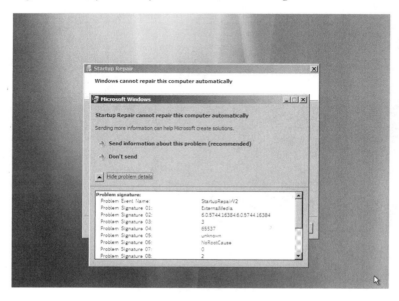

You might also see a message proposing an alternative troubleshooting approach—such as running System Restore.

INSIDE OUT   Check system files while Windows is running

If you receive an error message indicating a damaged system file while you are running Windows and you have an account with administrative privileges (or access to elevated credentials), try running the command-line utility Sfc. Open the Start menu, click All Programs, click Accessories, right-click Command Prompt, and choose Run As Administrator. Respond to the UAC prompt. Then, in the Command Prompt window, type **sfc /scannow**. The utility will scan your system files and attempt to repair any damage that it finds. It might prompt you for Windows Vista distribution media in order to carry out its repairs.

Restoring Stability With System Restore

If Startup Repair doesn't solve your problem, or if you know that your problem is not the result of a damaged system file (for example, if you're reasonably certain that a bad device driver is the culprit), you can try returning your system to a more stable state by means of System Restore. For information about using System Restore, see "Rolling Back to a Stable State with System Restore," in Chapter 23, which describes the use of this tool from within Windows. The one difference between running it in Windows and running it in the Windows Recovery Environment is that in the latter case no new restore point is created at the time you perform the restore. Therefore, if you run System Restore from the Windows Recovery Environment and you're not pleased with the result, you won't have any simple method of undoing the restore. On the other hand, the fact that you're in Windows Recovery Environment to begin with suggests that you have nothing to lose.

Restoring an Image Backup With Complete PC Restore

If, prior to the current emergency, you have used the Complete PC Backup program to create an image backup of your system disk, you can use the Complete PC Restore command in the Windows Recovery Environment to restore that image. Restoring an image backup of a disk completely replaces the current contents of the disk. The restore program, in fact, will format the disk to which it is restoring before it begins the restore process—and it will require your acknowledgement and explicit consent before it begins. This might sound like a drastic step, but it can be a quick and effective way to get Windows running again in circumstances that Startup Repair is unable to address.

For information about the Complete PC Backup program, see "Create a Backup Image," Chapter 2 and "Smart Backup Strategies," Chapter 20.

Chapter 24

The important thing to recognize about using Complete PC Restore is that it will replace the current contents of the disks that it is restoring with the exact contents as they existed at the time of your most recent Complete PC Backup. That means that your Windows system files and registry will be returned to health (provided the system was in good shape when you performed your most recent backup). Whatever programs were installed when you backed up will be restored entirely. All other files on the restored disk, including your documents, will also be returned to their prior states, and any changes made subsequent to your most recent backup will be lost.

CAUTION

> If you keep your documents on the same volume as your system files, performing a Complete PC Restore is likely to entail the loss of recent work—unless, of course, you have an up-to-date file backup or you have the good fortune to have made an image backup almost immediately before your current troubles began. The same is true if you save documents on a volume separate from your system files but you have included that data volume in your Complete PC Backup. If you have documents that have not been backed up, you can avoid losing recent work by copying them to a disk that will not be affected by the restore process—a USB flash drive, for example, or some other form of removable media. You can use the Command Prompt option in the Windows Recovery Environment to copy these documents. (For details about using the Command Prompt option, see "Working at the Command Prompt," later in this chapter.) If you do have a recent file backup, you will be able to restore files after you have used Windows Complete PC Restore to get your system running again.

You can use Windows Complete PC Restore to restore image backups stored on any local hard drive or on a set of CDs or DVDs. If you are planning to restore from optical media, insert the *last* disc in the backup set before you click Windows Complete PC Restore. The program will then find your backup and propose to restore it. If you insert the first (or any other) in a set of CDs or DVDs, the program will not find it.

When you click Windows Complete PC Restore on the System Recovery Options menu (shown in Figure 24-1), the restore program will search for a backup that it can restore. If it finds one, it will identify it by date, time, and location—that is, the drive on which it found the backup. It will then propose to restore that backup. If you have more than one backup available and the program has not proposed the one you want to restore, select the Restore A Different Backup option and click Next. On the ensuing screen, you'll see all available backups and you can choose the one you want to use.

When you have selected the appropriate backup (or confirmed the program's suggested backup), click Next to proceed. On the screen that follows you will find a check box labeled Format And Repartition Disks. If you are restoring to the same hard drive from which you created the image backup, and if you have not changed the partition (volume) structure of that disk since the time you made your most recent backup, you do not need to select this check box. The program will format the drive whether you select the check box or not, but if you leave the check box unselected, the program will not concern itself with the disk's volume structure.

If, on the other hand, you are restoring an image backup to a new hard disk because the original disk crashed, you should select the Format And Repartition Disks check box.

When you are ready to go on, click Next again. This time you will see the Complete PC Restore program's equivalent of an informed consent statement. You don't have to sign anything, but you do have to select the check box labeled I Confirm That I Want To Erase All Existing Data And Restore The Backup. After you've done that, the OK button will become available.

INSIDE OUT   **Using Windows Complete PC Restore with two or more unformatted hard disks**

If you are using Windows Complete PC Restore to restore disk images to two or more "clean" hard disks—that is, disks with no disk signatures and no volumes—the program will fail with a cryptic error message. To work around the problem, go to the Windows Recovery Environment command prompt. Then use the Diskpart command to create and format volumes on the new disks. This workaround is required only when your computer has two or more fixed disks and all of the disks are clean.

Running the Windows Memory Diagnostic Tool

If Startup Repair is unable to get your system running again, and if neither System Restore nor Windows Complete PC Restore has returned your computer to a condition of reliable health, consider the possibility that you have failing memory. To test this hypothesis, click Windows Memory Diagnostic Tool in the Startup Recovery Options menu. The Windows Memory Diagnostic Tool will ask whether you want to restart immediately and check for problems (the recommended option) or check instead on your next startup. Because you're having trouble getting to that next startup, you presumably want the first option.

While the diagnostic program is running, you will see status messages on your screen. These will give you some idea how much longer the tests have to run and whether errors have been found. You can press F1 at any time to get to an options screen. Here you can choose between Basic, Standard, and Extended tests as well as select various other testing parameters. One of these parameters controls the number of test passes the tool will make. If you don't mind letting the tests run a long time—for example, overnight—select a higher number than the default 2. When you have configured the tests to your satisfaction, press F10 to continue.

Your system will restart—if it can—when the testing is complete. The results will be displayed when you log on.

Working at the Command Prompt

To get to the command prompt, click Command Prompt on the System Recovery Options menu. You will land in the Sources subdirectory (folder) of a RAM disk identified by the drive letter X. From here you have access to nearly a hundred command-line tools, including disk-management utilities such as Chkdsk, Format, and Diskpart, as well as file-management items such as Copy, Rename, and Delete.

The Windows Recovery Environment command prompt is a vastly more versatile replacement for the Recovery Console that was introduced in Windows XP. Unlike Recovery Console, which imposed stringent restrictions on your command-line activities, the Windows Recovery Environment command prompt permits you to do just about anything you need to do. Among other things, you can copy, delete, rename, move, and type document files; partition and format hard disks (using Diskpart); run diagnostic utilities; and start and stop services (with Net Start and Net Stop).

INSIDE OUT   Access your network from the Windows Recovery Environment command prompt

Network functionality is not available by default at the Windows Recovery Environment command prompt. To enable it, type **wpeinit**.

Because the command prompt in the Windows Recovery Environment runs in the security context of the SYSTEM account, you have full read-write access there to every file on every accessible disk. This means, among other things, that you can generate backup copies of not only your own documents but those created under other accounts at your computer. It also means that you need to take care of the physical security of your computer, because anyone who knows how to get to the Windows Recovery Environment could wander your system at will, read your documents, take copies away on removable media, and otherwise wreak havoc upon your life.

If you're accustomed to answering UAC prompts for relatively risk-free operations in Windows Vista (such as reading the event logs), or if you've had experience working in the restricted conditions of the Windows XP Recovery Console, the permissive nature of the Windows Recovery Environment command prompt might come as something of a surprise. In reality, though, the Windows Recovery Environment presents no security hazard that wasn't already there. Unless you prevent physical access to your computer by using Windows Bitlocker Drive Encryption (or storing it in a locked closet), anyone with boot media and the appropriate file drivers could enjoy the same access to your resources that the Windows Recovery Environment command prompt affords.

CHAPTER 25

Managing Services

Home Basic   ⦿
Home Premium   ⦿
Business   ⦿
Enterprise   ⦿
Ultimate   ⦿

A service is a specialized program that performs a function to support other programs. Many services operate at a very low level (by interacting directly with hardware, for example) and need to run even when no user is logged on; for this reason, they are often run by the System account (which has elevated privileges) rather than by ordinary user accounts. Windows Vista includes many of the same services as in previous versions of Microsoft Windows but adds several new services as well.

In this chapter, you'll learn how to view the installed services; start, stop, and configure them; and install or remove them. We'll also take a closer look at some of the services used in Windows Vista and show you how to configure them to your advantage. A new (and great, we might add) method for viewing services on your computer is through the Services tab of Task Manager. This chapter also looks at this new feature.

Using the Services Console

You manage services with the Services snap-in for Microsoft Management Console (MMC), shown in Figure 25-1 on the next page. To view this snap-in, type **services.msc** at a command prompt. (You must have administrator privileges to gain full functionality in the Services console. Running as a standard user, you can view service settings, but you can't start or stop most services, change the startup type, or make any other configuration changes.)

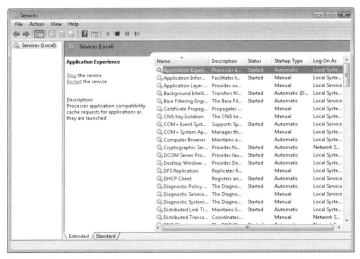

Figure 25-1 Use the Services console to start, stop, and configure services.

The Extended and Standard views in the Services console (selectable by clicking a tab near the bottom of the window) have a single difference: The Extended view provides descriptive information of the selected service in the space at the left edge of the details pane. This space also sometimes includes links for starting, stopping, or pausing the selected service. Unless you need to constrain the console display to a small area of your screen, you'll probably find the Extended view preferable to the Standard view.

The Services console offers plenty of information in its clean display. You can sort the contents of any column by clicking the column title, as you can do with other similar lists. To sort in reverse order, click the column title again. In addition, you can:

- Start, stop, pause, resume, or restart the selected service, as described in the following section

- Display the properties dialog box for the selected service, in which you can configure the service and learn more about it

Most of the essential services are set to start automatically when your computer starts, and the operating system stops them as part of its shutdown process. But sometimes you might need to manually start or stop a service. For example, you might want to start a seldom-used service on the rare occasion when you need it. (Because running services requires system resources such as memory, running them only when necessary can improve performance.) On the other hand, you might want to stop a service because you're no longer using it. A more common reason, however, for stopping a service is because it isn't working properly. For example, if print jobs get stuck in the print queue, sometimes the best remedy is to stop and then restart the Print Spooler service.

INSIDE OUT   **Pause instead of stopping**

If a service allows pausing, try pausing and then continuing the service as your first step instead of stopping the service. Pausing can solve certain problems without canceling jobs in process or resetting connections.

Starting and Stopping Services

Not all services allow you to change their status. Some prevent stopping and starting altogether, whereas others permit stopping and starting but not pausing and resuming. Some services allow these permissions to only certain users or groups. For example, most services allow only members of the Power Users and Administrators groups to start or stop them. Which status changes are allowed and who has permission to make them are controlled by each service's discretionary access control list (DACL), which is established when the service is created on a computer.

To change a service's status, select it in the Services console. Then click the appropriate link in the area to the left of the service list (if you're using the Extended view and the link you need appears there). Alternatively, you can use the VCR-style controls in the toolbar, or right-click and choose the corresponding command.

▷	Start, Resume	Starts a service that isn't running, or resumes a service that has been paused.
■	Stop	Stops a running service.
❙❙	Pause	Pauses a running service. Pausing a service doesn't remove it from memory; it continues to run at a level that varies depending on the service. With some services, pausing allows users to complete jobs or disconnect from resources but does not allow them to create new jobs or connections.
❙▷	Restart	Stops a running service and then restarts it.

You can also change a service's status by opening its properties dialog box and then clicking one of the buttons on the General tab. Taking the extra step of opening the properties dialog box to set the status has only one advantage: You can specify start parameters when you start a service using this method. This is a rare requirement.

Configuring Services

To review or modify the way a service starts up or what happens when it doesn't start properly, view its properties dialog box. To do that, simply double-click the service in the Services console. Figure 25-2 on the next page shows an example.

Figure 25-2 You specify a service's startup type on the General tab, where you can also find the actual name of the service above its display name.

Setting Startup Options

On the General tab of the properties dialog box (see Figure 25-2), you specify the start-up type:

- **Automatic (Delayed Start)** The service starts shortly after the computer starts in order to improve start up performance and user experience.

- **Automatic** The service starts when the computer starts.

- **Manual** The service doesn't start automatically at startup, but it can be started by a user, a program, or a dependent service.

- **Disabled** The service can't be started.

You'll find other startup options on the Log On tab of the properties dialog box, as shown in Figure 25-3.

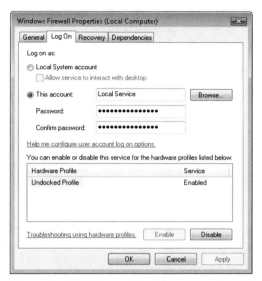

Figure 25-3 On the Log On tab, you specify which user runs the service, and you can also specify which hardware profiles use the service.

> **Note**
>
> If you specify a logon account other than the Local System account, be sure that account has the requisite rights. Go to the Local Security Policy console (at a command prompt, type **secpol.msc**), and then go to Security Settings\Local Policies\User Rights Assignment and assign the Log On As A Service right to the account.

Specifying Recovery Actions

For a variety of reasons—hardware not operating properly or a network connection down, for example—a service that's running smoothly might suddenly stop. Settings on the Recovery tab of the properties dialog box, shown in Figure 25-4 on the next page, allow you to specify what should happen if a service fails.

Chapter 25

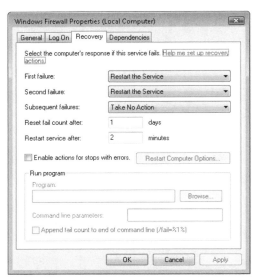

Figure 25-4 Use the Recovery tab to specify what should happen if the service fails.

You might want to perform a different action the first time a service fails than on the second or subsequent failures. The Recovery tab enables you to assign a particular response to the first failure, the second failure, and all subsequent failures, from among these options:

- **Take No Action** The service gives up trying. In most cases, the service places a message in the event log. (Use of the event log depends on how the service was programmed by its developers.)

- **Restart The Service** The computer waits for the time specified in the Restart Service After box to elapse and then tries to start the service.

- **Run A Program** The computer runs the program that you specify in the Run Program box. For example, you could specify a program that attempts to resolve the problem or one that alerts you to the situation.

- **Restart The Computer** Drastic but effective, this option restarts the computer after the time specified in the Restart Computer Options dialog box elapses. In that dialog box, you can also specify a message to be broadcast to other users on your network, warning them of the impending shutdown.

Viewing Dependencies

Many services rely on the functions of another service. If you attempt to start a service that depends on other services, Windows first starts the others. If you stop a service upon which others are dependent, Windows also stops those services. Before you either start or stop a service, therefore, it's helpful to know what other services your action might affect. To obtain that information, go to the Dependencies tab of a service's properties dialog box, shown in Figure 25-5.

Figure 25-5 The Dependencies tab shows which services depend on other services.

Determining the Name of a Service

As you view the properties dialog box for different services, you might notice that the service name (shown at the top of the General tab) is often different from the name that appears in the Services console (the display name) and that neither name matches the name of the service's executable file. (In fact, the executable for many services is either Services.exe or Svchost.exe.) The General tab shows all three names.

> **Note**
>
> A detailed description of Svchost.exe appears in Knowledge Base article 314056, "A description of Svchost.exe in Windows XP Pro" *(http://www.vista-io. com/2501).* The information is applicable to Windows Vista as well.

So how does this affect you? When you work in the Services console, you don't need to know anything other than a service's display name to find it and work with it. But if you use the Net command to start and stop services (as explained in the following section), you might find using the actual service name more convenient; it is often much shorter than the display name. You'll also need the service name if you're ever forced to work with a service's registry entries, which can be found in the HKLM\System \CurrentControlSet\Services*service* subkey (where *service* is the service name).

And what about the executable name? You might need it if certain users have problems running a service; in such a case, you need to find the executable and check its permissions. Knowing the executable name can also be useful, for example, if you're using Windows Task Manager to determine why your computer seems to be running so slowly. Although the Processes tab and the Services tab show the display name (under the Description heading), because of the window size it's sometimes easier to find the more succinct executable name.

As mentioned earlier, you can find the actual name of each service and its executable name by looking at the General tab of the service's properties dialog box. For your reference, Table 25-1 shows the names for all the services that are commonly installed with Windows Vista Ultimate. Note that your system might have other services installed—by Microsoft or by another publisher—or it might not have all of these installed.

Table 25-1. Names of Services in Windows Vista

Display Name	Service Name	Executable Name
Application Experience	AeLookupSvc	Svchost.exe
Application Information	Appinfo	Svchost.exe
Application Layer Gateway Service	ALG	Alg.exe
Application Management	AppMgmt	Svchost.exe
Background Intelligent Transfer Service	BITS	Svchost.exe
Base Filtering Engine	BFE	Svchost.exe
Block Level Backup Engine Service	wbengine	wbengine.exe
Certificate Propagation	CertPropSvc	Svchost.exe
CNG Key Isolation	KeyIso	Lsass.exe
COM+ Event System	EventSystem	Svchost.exe
COM+ System Application	COMSysApp	Dllhost.exe
Computer Browser	Browser	Svchost.exe
Cryptographic Services	CryptSvc	Svchost.exe
DCOM Server Process Launcher	DcomLaunch	Svchost.exe
Desktop Windows Manager Session Manager	UxSms	Svchost.exe
DFS Replication Properties	DFSR	DFSR.exe

Display Name	Service Name	Executable Name
DHCP Client	Dhcp	Svchost.exe
Diagnostic Policy Service	DPS	Svchost.exe
Diagnostic Service Host	WdiServiceHost	Svchost.exe
Diagnostic System Host	WdiSystemHost	Svchost.exe
Distributed Link Tracking Client	TrkWks	Svchost.exe
Distributed Transaction Coordinator	MSDTC	Msdtc.exe
DNS Client	Dnscache	Svchost.exe
Extensible Authentication Protocol	EapHost	Svchost.exe
Fax	Fax	Fxssvc.exe
Function Discovery Provider Host	fdPHost	Svchost.exe
Function Discovery Resource Publication	FDResPub	Svchost.exe
Group Policy Client	Gpsvc	Svchost.exe
Health Key and Certificate Management	Hkmsvc	Svchost.exe
Human Interface Device Access	Hidserv	Svchost.exe
IKE and AuthIP IPsec Keyring Modules	IKEEXT	Svchost.exe
Interactive Services Detection	UI0Detect	UI0Detect.exe
Internet Connection Sharing (ICS)	SharedAccess	Svchost.exe
IP Helper	Iphlpsvc	Svchost.exe
IPsec Policy Agent	PolicyAgent	Svchost.exe
KtmRm for Distributed Transaction Coordinator	KtmRm	Svchost.exe
Link-Layer Topology Discovery Mapper	lltdsvc	Svchost.exe
Microsoft .NET Framework NGEN v2.0.50727_X86	clr_optimization_ v2.0.50727_32	Mscorsvw.exe
Microsoft iSCSI Initiator Service	MSiSCSI	Svchost.exe
Microsoft Software Shadow Copy Provider	swprv	Svchost.exe
Multimedia Class Scheduler	MMCSS	Svchost.exe
Net.Tcp Port Sharing Service	NetTcpPortSharing	SMSvcHost.exe
Netlogon	Netlogon	Lsass.exe
Network Access Protection Agent	napagent	Svchost.exe
Network Connections	Netman	Svchost.exe
Network List Service	netprofm	Svchost.exe

Display Name	Service Name	Executable Name
Network Location Awareness	NlaSvc	Svchost.exe
Network Store Interface Service	nsi	Svchost.exe
Offline Files	CscService	Svchost.exe
Parental Controls	WPCSvc	Svchost.exe
Peer Name Resolution Protocol	PNRPsvc	Svchost.exe
Peer Networking Grouping	p2psvc	Svchost.exe
Peer Networking Identity Manager	p2pimsvc	Svchost.exe
Performance Logs And Alerts	pla	Svchost.exe
Plug And Play	PlugPlay	Services.exe
PnP-X IP Bus Enumerator	IPBusEnum	Svchost.exe
PNRP Machine Name Publication Service	PNRPAutoReg	Svchost.exe
Portable Device Enumerator Service	WPDBusEnum	Svchost.exe
Print Spooler	Spooler	Spoolsv.exe
Problem Reports and Solutions Control Panel	wercplsupport	Svchost.exe
Program Compatibility Assistant Service	PcaSvc	Svchost.exe
Protected Storage	ProtectedStorage	Lsass.exe
Quality Windows Audio Video Experience	QWAVE	Svchost.exe
ReadyBoost	EMDMgmt	Svchost.exe
Remote Access Auto Connection Manager	RasAuto	Svchost.exe
Remote Access Connection Manager	RasMan	Svchost.exe
Remote Procedure Call (RPC)	RpcSs	Svchost.exe
Remote Procedure Call (RPC) Locator	RpcLocator	Locator.exe
Remote Registry	RemoteRegistry	Svchost.exe
Routing And Remote Access	RemoteAccess	Svchost.exe
Secondary Logon	seclogon	Svchost.exe
Security Accounts Manager	SamSs	Lsass.exe
Security Center	wscsvc	Svchost.exe
Server	lanmanserver	Svchost.exe
Shell Hardware Detection	ShellHWDetection	Svchost.exe
SL UI Notification Service	SLUINotify	Svchost.exe
Smart Card	SCardSvr	Svchost.exe

Display Name	Service Name	Executable Name
Smart Card Removal Policy	SCPolicySvc	Svchost.exe
SNMP Trap	SNMPTRAP	snmptrap.exe
Software Licensing	slsvc	SLsvc.exe
SSDP Discovery	SSDPSRV	Svchost.exe
Superfetch	SysMain	Svchost.exe
System Event Notification Service	SENS	Svchost.exe
Tablet PC Input Service	TabletInputService	Svchost.exe
Task Scheduler	Schedule	Svchost.exe
TCP/IP NetBIOS Helper	LmHosts	Svchost.exe
Telephony	TapiSrv	Svchost.exe
Terminal Services	TermService	Svchost.exe
Terminal Services Configuration	SessionEnv	Svchost.exe
Terminal Services UserMode Port Redirector	UmRdpService	Svchost.exe
Themes	Themes	Svchost.exe
Thread Ordering Server	THREADORDER	Svchost.exe
TPM Base Services	TBS	Svchost.exe
UPnP Device Host	upnphost	Svchost.exe
User Profile Service	ProfSvc	Svchost.exe
Virtual Disk	Vds	Vds.exe
Volume Shadow Copy	VSS	Vssvc.exe
WebClient	WebClient	Svchost.exe
Windows Audio	AudioSrv	Svchost.exe
Windows Audio Endpoint Builder	AudioEndpointBuilder	Svchost.exe
Windows Backup	SDRSVC	Svchost.exe
Windows CardSpace	idsvc	infocard.exe
Windows Color System	WcsPlugInService	Svchost.exe
Windows Connect Now - Config Registrar	wcncsvc	Svchost.exe
Windows Defender	WinDefend	Svchost.exe
Windows Driver Foundation User-mode Driver Framework	wudfsvc	Svchost.exe
Windows Error Reporting Service	WerSvc	Svchost.exe
Windows Event Collector	Wecsvc	Svchost.exe

Display Name	Service Name	Executable Name
Windows Event Log	Eventlog	Svchost.exe
Windows Firewall	MpsSvc	Svchost.exe
Windows Image Acquisition (WIA)	Stisvc	Svchost.exe
Windows Installer	MSIServer	Msiexec.exe
Windows Management Instrumentation	Winmgmt	Svchost.exe
Windows Media Center Extender Service	Mcx2Svc	Svchost.exe
Windows Media Center Receiver Service	ehRecvr	EhRecvr.exe
Windows Media Center Scheduler Service	ehSched	Ehsched.exe
Windows Media Center Service Launcher	ehstart	Svchost.exe
Windows Media Player Network Sharing Service	WMPNetworkSvc	wmpnetwk.exe
Windows Modules Installer	TrustedInstaller	TrustedInstaller.exe
Windows Presentation Foundation Font Cache 3.0.0.0	FontCache3.0.0.0	PresentationFont Cache.exe
Windows Remote Management (WS-Management)	WinRM	Svchost.exe
Windows Search	WSearch	SearchIndexer.exe
Windows Time	W32Time	Svchost.exe
Windows Update	wuauserv	Svchost.exe
WinHTTP Web Proxy Auto-Discovery Service	WinHttpAutoProxySvc	Svchost.exe
Wired AutoConfig	dot3svc	Svchost.exe
WLAN AutoConfig	Wlansvc	Svchost.exe
WMI Performance Adapter	WmiApSrv	Wmiapsrv.exe
Workstation	lanmanworkstation	Svchost.exe

Note

Like file names, the names of services are not case sensitive. In Table 25-1, we capitalized the service names exactly as they appear in the registry. Although the capitalization style is sometimes inconsistent, you're likely to see this same capitalization whenever a particular service name is mentioned in documentation.

Recommended Startup Settings for Services

On a typical computer running Windows Vista, literally dozens of services are installed by default. What do all of these services do? Do you really need to have each of these running? Table 25-2 includes a list of services on a typical computer running Windows Vista Ultimate along with a brief description of the service, the account it uses for logon purposes, and our recommendations for setting the startup type (Automatic, Manual, or Disabled).

Note

You may be tempted to try to squeeze extra performance out of your system by disabling many services. However, the amount of performance that can be gained by disabling services is usually quite minimal and can, in some cases, subtly cause performance deterioration. In other cases, disabling a service can make troubleshooting a problem difficult if you forget that the service has been disabled. In general, the default settings proposed by Windows Vista are ideal—and less in need of tweaking than the defaults in earlier Windows versions.

Table 25-2. Service Descriptions and Startup Settings

Service	Log On As	Description	Recommended Startup Type
Application Experience	Local System	Helps to check compatibility of programs run in Windows Vista	Automatic
Application Information	Local System	Part of the User Account Control framework to assist in running applications with Administrator privileges.	Manual. This service will be started as necessary in order to enable Administrator-level access to certain programs.
Application Layer Gateway Service	Local Service	Lets third-party software vendors write plug-ins that enable their protocols to pass through the Windows Firewall and work behind Internet Connection Sharing.	Manual
Application Management	Local System	Provides Assign, Publish, and Remove services for Windows Installer. Also required by the Add New Programs command in the Add Or Remove Programs section of Control Panel.	Manual. The service is stopped until needed by Windows Installer or Add Or Remove Programs, after which it remains running. Do not disable.
Background Intelligent Transfer Service	Local System	Allows queuing and background transfer of files (such as Windows updates) between a local computer and an HTTP server, using otherwise idle network bandwidth.	Manual. The service is started when required, then stopped again when transfer is complete.

Chapter 25

Service	Log On As	Description	Recommended Startup Type
Base Filtering Engine	Local Service	Used by the Windows Firewall as well as IPsec and other security software to implement policies related to the security of the system at the network level.	Automatic
Block Level Backup Engine Service	Local System	Assists in performing backups at a very low level which are sometimes used for Bare Metal Recovery (BMR).	Manual
Certificate Propagation	Local System	In conjunction with a smart card infrastructure, this service assists in distribution of security certificates.	Disabled unless your system uses smart cards.
CNG Key Isolation	Local System	Isolates cryptographic keys in certain highly secure environments using the Common Criteria	Manual
COM+ Event System	Local Service	System services that enable communication between applications using the Component Object Model (COM).	Automatic
COM+ System Application	Local System	Manages COM+ components, including their configuration.	Manual
Computer Browser	Local System	Allows a system to act as a "browse master." In a Windows-based workgroup, one computer is always designated the browse master and keeps a list of which computers are present on the network. If the browse master becomes unavailable, the remaining computers on the network elect a new browse master.	Automatic. (If one computer on your network is always on and is very reliable, you can set the Computer Browser to Automatic on that computer and set it to Disabled on the others.)
Cryptographic Services	Network Service	Provides verification services for digitally signed files (such as device drivers and ActiveX controls), among other system-level cryptographic functions.	Automatic
DCOM Server Process Launcher	Local System	Provides infrastructure for launching of Distributed COM (DCOM) processes.	Automatic
Desktop Window Manager Session Manager	Local System	Provides essential services related to the desktop.	Automatic
DFS Replication Properties	Local System	Keeps files in sync between multiple computers, whether between two client computers or client to server or both.	

Service	Log On As	Description	Recommended Startup Type
DHCP Client	Local Service	Acquires network settings (IP addresses and DNS names) from a Dynamic Host Control Protocol (DHCP) server at startup.	Automatic; may be set to Disabled if network settings are configured manually.
Diagnostic Policy Service	Local Service	An important part of the Diagnostics Framework.	Automatic
Diagnostic Service Host	Local Service	Assists in troubleshooting problems with services and the operating system.	Manual
Diagnostic System Host	Local System	Assists in troubleshooting problems with applications.	Manual
Distributed Link Tracking Client	Local System	Maintains links between shortcuts and target files on NTFS volumes within a computer and on computers within a Windows domain. Ensures that shortcuts and OLE links continue to work if a target file is moved or renamed.	Automatic. (Stopping or disabling this service prevents Windows from repairing shortcut links when target files are renamed or moved.)
Distributed Transaction Coordinator	Network Service	Supports Microsoft Transaction Server (MTS); primarily used in applications based on Microsoft SQL Server.	Manual
DNS Client	Network Service	Caches records of DNS lookups to improve performance. Required if using IPsec.	Automatic; may be set to Manual or Disabled if you prefer not to use DNS caching.
Extensible Authentication Protocol	Local System	EAP is used heavily in wireless network implementations as well as other situations such as Network Access Protection, 802.1x, and with VPNs. This service provides an API into the authentication services.	Manual
Fax	Network Service	Provides fax capabilities; this is an optional service.	Manual; Automatic if you want your computer to receive faxes.
Function Discovery Provider Host	Local Service	Provides a service to discover capabilities of devices regardless of how they're connected to the computer.	Manual
Function Discovery Resource Publication	Local Service	Publishes the resources located on this computer so that they can be discovered by other computers on the network.	Manual
Group Policy Client	Local System	Applies Group Policy-published settings to this computer.	Automatic

Service	Log On As	Description	Recommended Startup Type
Health Key and Certificate Management	Local System	Used in conjunction with Network Access Protection (NAP) to manage security certificates.	Manual
Human Interface Device Access	Local System	Handles the wheels and custom navigation buttons on some mice and keyboards, as well as the volume buttons on USB speakers; a standard 102-key keyboard and PS/2 mouse do not require this service.	Manual
IKE and AuthIP IPsec Keyring Modules	Local System	Runs the modules for Internet Key Exchange (IKE) and Authenticated Internet Protocol (AuthIP) which are related to IPsec.	Disabled if you don't use IPsec.
Interactive Services Detection	Local System	Provides notification framework when user input is required by certain services.	Manual
Internet Connection Sharing (ICS)	Local System	Enables multiple computers to share one internet connection through this computer.	Disabled unless connection sharing is necessary through this computer. Most networks would use a router to provide this functionality.
IP Helper	Local System	Enables Internet Protocol Version 6 (IPv6) connections over the existing Internet Protocol Version 4 (IPv4) network. Not necessary on IPv4 or native IPv6 networks.	Disabled unless IPv6 over IPv4 is in use, which is not common.
IPsec Policy Agent	Network Service	Enforces policies related to IP Security (IPsec) connections.	Disabled unless IPsec is in use.
KtmRm for Distributed Transaction Coordinator	Network Service	Coordinates transactions between the Distributed Transaction Coordinator (DTC) and Kernel Transaction Manager.	Automatic
Link-Layer Topology Discovery Mapper	Local Service	Creates and is responsible for maintaining the Network Map functionality as seen in the Network and Sharing Center	Manual
Microsoft .NET Framework NGEN	Local System	Generates native images of .Net managed applications rather than the Just-In Time (JIT) compiler to improve performance.	Manual
Microsoft iSCSI Initiator Service	Local System	Manages Internet Small Computer Systems Interface (iSCSI) connections between this computer and other iSCSI devices.	Manual

Service	Log On As	Description	Recommended Startup Type
Microsoft Software Shadow Copy Provider	Local System	Helps to prioritize processing tasks in order to help prioritize multimedia applications, which tend to require higher priority.	Manual
Multimedia Class Scheduler	Local System	Helps to prioritize processing tasks in order to help prioritize multimedia applications which tend to require higher priority.	Automatic
Net.Tcp Port Sharing Service	Local Service	Part of the Windows Communication Foundation, this service enables applications written to use the protocol to share the same port.	Disabled
Netlogon	Local System	Used only for authentication of account logon events in Windows domains.	Manual
Network Access Protection Agent	Network Service	Provides Network Access Protection functionality.	Manual
Network Connections	Local System	Manages objects in the Network And Dial-Up Connections folder; unless you disable it, this service starts automatically when it's needed.	Manual
Network List Service	Local Service	Manages properties related to the networks to which this computer is connected in order to inform applications of topology changes affecting the computer.	Automatic
Network Location Awareness	Network Service	Supports the ability to use multiple network configurations; used primarily on notebook computers and when Windows Firewall or ICS is in use.	Manual
Network Store Interface Service	Local Service	Provides vital functionality related to the network connections on this computer.	Automatic
Offline Files	Local System	Enables easier synchronization of files that are normally stored on the network.	Automatic
Parental Controls	Local Service	Helps manage restrictions on what certain accounts can do when using the computer.	Manual
Peer Name Resolution Protocol	Local Service	A component of collaborative network applications such as Windows Meeting Space providing name resolution.	Manual

Chapter 25

Service	Log On As	ion	Recommended Startup Typ
Peer Networking Grouping	Local Service	A component of collaborative network applications such as Windows Meeting Space.	Manual
Peer Networking Identity Manager	Local Service	Provides identity management services to collaborative applications such as Windows Meeting Space.	Manual
Performance Logs And Alerts	Local Service	Collects performance data that you can display and analyze using the Reliability And Performance console. The service also enables you to run a program and send a message when specific performance conditions occur.	Manual
Plug And Play	Local System	Detects and configures Plug and Play hardware devices. This service is an essential part of Windows and should never be disabled.	Automatic
PnP-X IP Bus Enumerator	Local System	Extensions to Plug and Play (PnP) for devices using Windows.	Manual
PNRP Machine Name Publication Service	Local Service	Provides services related to the Peer Name Resoluon Protocol.	Manual
Portable Device Enumerator Service	Local System	Enforces Group Policy settings related to removable storage devices.	Automatic
Print Spooler	Local System	Manages print jobs on local and network printers. If this service is stopped, applications do not see any printers installed.	Automatic
Problem Reports and Solutions Control Panel	Local System	Provides services for the Problem Reports and Solutions applet.	Manual
Program Compatibility Assistant Service	Local System	Assists when running older, legacy applications in this version of Windows and can recommend changes to improve the older application's stability.	Automatic
Protected Storage	Local System	Provides encrypted storage of passwords, private keys, and other sensitive data; Internet Explorer and Windows Mail are two programs that use this service.	Manual
Quality Windows Audio Video Experience	Local Service	Provides enhancements related to streaming media over a local network.	Manual

Service	Log On As	Description	Recommended Startup Type
ReadyBoost	Local System	Works in conjunction with Superfetch to improve performance by using plug-in memory to cache disk contents.	Automatic
Remote Access Auto Connection Manager	Local System	Automatically dials a connection (a connection to a dial-up ISP, for instance, or a VPN connection) when necessary to connect to a remote network.	Manual; may be set to Disabled if you never use dial-up connections of any kind.
Remote Access Connection Manager	Local System	Creates network connections; also required by Windows Firewall and ICS.	Manual
Remote Procedure Call (RPC)	Network Service	Supports RPC functionality that is used throughout Windows. If this service is turned off, Windows will not start.	Automatic
Remote Procedure Call (RPC) Locator	Network Service	Manages the RPC name service database, enabling RPC clients using the RpcNs family of application programming interfaces (APIs) to locate RPC servers. Almost no applications written in the last decade use these APIs.	Disabled unless you have third-party applications that require it.
Remote Registry	Local Service	Lets a user at a remote computer modify the registry on your computer. This feature is typically used only in large organizations and represents a security risk if not carefully configured.	Automatic if your network uses this feature; Disabled on all other computers.
Routing And Remote Access	Local System	Provides support for LAN-based routing, specifically incoming dial-up and VPN connections.	Manual if you use any such connections; Disabled on all other computers.
Secondary Logon	Local System	Allows a user to start a program using an alternative user name and password (using Run As); this service can be effectively used by Scheduled Tasks and by administrators.	Automatic
Security Accounts Manager	Local System	Manages security information for all local accounts. This service is essential to the proper operation of Windows and should never be disabled.	Automatic
Security Center	Local Service	Monitors security settings (such as the status of Windows Firewall).	Automatic
Server	Local System	Supports network file and printer sharing and provides RPC support.	Automatic

Service	Log On As	Description	Recommended Startup Type
Shell Hardware Detection	Local System	Provides AutoPlay support for removable storage media, flash media, PC cards, and external USB and IEEE 1394 fixed drives.	Automatic
SL UI Notification Service	Local Service	Provides the user interface portion of Software Licensing activation.	Manual
Smart Card	**Local Service**	**Supports smart card authentication hardware; typically used in large, security-conscious organizations.**	**Manual**
Smart Card Removal Policy	Local System	Provides framework for a policy related to the removal of smart cards in order to lock the computer.	Manual
SNMP Trap	Local Service	Receives Simple Network Management Protocol (SNMP) traps and forwards them to the SNMP management program.	Manual
Software Licensing	Network Service	Provides tasks related to the licensing of software on this computer.	Automatic
SSDP Discovery	Local Service	The Simple Service Discovery Protocol (SSDP) provides a mechanism for UPnP devices to announce their presence on the network so that other computers can "discover" them. If SSDP is disabled, you can't use Remote Desktop and Remote Assistance to access systems across the internet.	Manual
Superfetch	Local System	Monitors the system to anticipate the data that might be used next in order to precache the data for improved performance.	Automatic
System Event Notification Service	Local System	Tracks system events such as logon, network, screen-saver starts, and power events.	Automatic
Tablet PC Input Service	Local System	Provides pen and ink functionality on Tablet PCs.	Automatic if you have a Tablet PC; Disabled otherwise.
Task Scheduler	Local System	Runs programs in the Scheduled Tasks folder.	Automatic
TCP/IP NetBIOS Helper	Local Service	Provides support for NetBIOS over TCP/IP and NetBIOS name management services; provided for compatibility with Windows 2000.	Automatic

Service	Log On As	Description	Recommended Startup Type
Telephony	Network Service	Supports programs that control telephony devices (typically modems) and IP-based voice connections. ICS and Windows Firewall also start this service.	Manual
Terminal Services	Network Service	Supports a variety of features in Windows Vista that allow multiple users to connect to a computer interactively and to display desktops and applications on remote computers. This service is an essential component in Remote Desktop, Remote Assistance, and Fast User Switching.	Manual
Terminal Services Configuration	Local System	Used when Terminal Services and Remote Desktop settings require a higher level authority under which to run.	Manual
Themes	Local System	Provides support for visual effects associated with the look and feel of Windows Vista.	Automatic; may be set to Disabled if you have chosen the Windows Standard or Windows Classic look (in Personalization, click Appearance Settings) and do not intend to use any of the new interface features.
Thread Ordering Server	Local Service	Enables applications to specify execution of threads in a specific order within a given time frame. Used for high performance applications.	Manual
TPM Base Services	Local Service	Enables access to the Trusted Platform Module (TPM) to provide hardware-based cryptographic services to system components and applications.	Manual
UPnP Device Host	Local Service	Allows the operating system to send UPnP announcements on behalf of non-computer peripherals, such as printers and cameras. The peripheral must provide the drivers and software to support UPnP.	Manual; Automatic if you use any UPnP devices.
User Profile Service	Local System	Loads and unloads User Profiles and is vital to the logon and logoff process.	Automatic

Chapter 25

Service	Log On As	Description	Recommended Startup Type
Virtual Disk	Local System	Enables use of volumes and disk arrays and provides management for such configurations.	Manual
Volume Shadow Copy	Local System	Manages the volume shadow copy, a feature of Windows Vista that backup programs can use to take a "snapshot" of volumes with open files so that they can perform a complete backup without requiring the user to shut down all running programs.	Manual
WebClient	Local Service	Allows Windows programs to create, access, and modify internet files using Web Distributing Authoring and Versioning (WebDAV); uncommon in everyday use.	Manual
Windows Audio	Local Service	Manages audio for programs.	Automatic
Windows Audio Endpoint Builder	Local Service	Manages audio devices that utilize the Windows Audio service.	Automatic
Windows Backup	Local System	Provides services for Windows Backup and Restore.	Manual
Windows CardSpace	Local System	Part of the new digital identity management framework.	Manual
Windows Color System	Local Service	Hosts modules related to the Windows Color System which helps to ensure color consistency across applications.	Manual
Windows Connect Now - Config Registrar	Local Service	Helps to make connection of new devices within a network easier.	Manual
Windows Defender	Local System	Monitors the computer for unwanted software such as spyware and other malware.	Automatic
Windows Driver Foundation User-mode Driver Framework	Local System	Supports management of device drivers at user level, as opposed to kernel level.	Automatic
Windows Error Reporting Service	Local System	Enables logging and other functionality related to errors within the computer. Also works in conjunction with the diagnostic framework.	Automatic

Service	Log On As	Description	Recommended Startup Type
Windows Event Collector	Network Service	Provides functions related to collection and management of events from remote computers or devices.	Manual
Windows Event Log	Local Service	Manages the Event Logs and events going into the Event Logs	Automatic
Windows Firewall	Local Service	Provides Network Address Translation, address translation, and firewall services on networks.	Automatic
Windows Image Acquisition (WIA)	Local Service	Provides image acquisition support for SCSI, IEEE 1394, USB and serial digital still image devices.	Manual
Windows Installer	Local System	Supports installation, repair, and removal of programs that use instructions contained in Windows Installer (.msi) files.	Manual. Applications that need the service will start it.
Windows Management Instrumentation	Local System	Provides information about your system configuration to Windows and to third-party applications; if this service is stopped, most Windows-based software will experience problems.	Manual. Applications that need the service will start it.
Windows Media Center Extender Service	Local Service	Provides functionality related to the Windows Media Center	Disabled.
Windows Media Center Receiver Service	Network Service	Provides services related to reception of television and FM radio signals.	Manual
Windows Media Center Scheduler Service	Network Service	Starts and stops recordings of television programs when used in a Media Center configuration.	Manual
Windows Media Center Service Launcher	Local Service	If the computer is being used in a Media Center configuration, this service manages the startup of other Media Center services.	Automatic (will only start when in a Media Center configuration.)
Windows Media Player Network Sharing Service	Network Service	Enables other devices to use Media Player libraries.	Manual
Windows Modules Installer	Local System	Related to Windows Updates to enable installation-related tasks.	Manual

Chapter 25

Service	Log On As	Description	Recommended Startup Type
Windows Presentation Foundation Font Cache	Local Service	For applications using the Windows Presentation Foundation, this service caches commonly used fonts to improve performance.	Manual
Windows Remote Management (WS-Management)	Network Service	Related to the WS-Management protocol for remote management of this computer.	Manual
Windows Search	Local System	Helps to oprimize computer-wide searching of e-mail and files.	Automatic
Windows Time	Local Service	Allows you to synchronize the date and time on a computer with a remote server using options you set on the Internet Time tab of Control Panel, Date And Time.	Automatic; may be set to Manual or Disabled if you prefer to set the time manually or use alternate synchronization software.
Windows Update	Local System	Provides the core Windows Update functionality in order to receive and install updates to the operating system on this computer.	Automatic
WinHTTP Web Proxy Auto-Discovery Service	Local Service	Provides applications the ability to send HTTP requests and discover a proxy server, when one is used.	Manual
Wired AutoConfig	Local System	Provides 802.1X authentication for wired network connections.	Manual
WLAN AutoConfig	Local System	Provides 802.1X authentication for wireless network connections.	Manual
WMI Performance Adapter	Local System	Implements performance counters as part of Windows Management Instrumentation.	Manual
Workstation	Local Service	Makes network connections with remote computers. Many Windows functions depend on this service being available.	Automatic

Managing Services from a Command Prompt

If you want to control services via a batch program—or if you simply prefer working at a command prompt—you can use variants of the Net command. Don't be dissuaded by the name—the Net command manages all services, not only network services. Table 25-3 shows the Net commands to use for managing services.

Table 25-3. Net Commands for Managing Services

Command	Description
Net Start	Displays a list of running services.
Net Start *service*	Starts the *service* service. For *service*, you can use either the actual service name or its display name. For example, **net start schedule** and **net start "task scheduler"** are equivalent. For a list of services installed by default with Windows Vista, see Table 25-1. Surround multiword service names with quotation marks.
Net Stop *service*	Stops the *service* service. The service must be started before you can stop it.
Net Pause *service*	Pauses the *service* service. The service must be started before you can pause it. Many services don't permit pausing.
Net Continue *service*	Resumes the *service* service. The service must be paused before you can resume it.

Managing Services from Task Manager

The Services tab is a new addition to Task Manager in Windows Vista. Using the Services tab, you can start and stop services and view several important aspects of the services, both running and available, on your computer. You can also use this as a shortcut to the Services console.

Access Task Manager by right-clicking the task bar and clicking Task Manager, by pressing Ctrl+Alt+Delete and clicking Start Task Manager, or by pressing Ctrl+Shift+Esc. The Services tab is shown in Figure 25-6 on the next page.

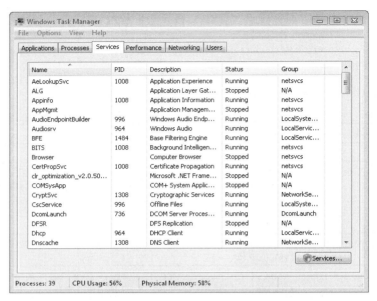

Figure 25-6 To view more of the information displayed on the Services tab, enlarge the Task Manager window and adjust the column widths, as shown here.

To start or stop a service, right-click its name on the Services tab and then click Start Service or Stop Service.

Using the Services tab, you can also associate a running service with its process identifier (PID) and then further associate that PID with other programs and services being run under that PID. For example, Figure 25-6 shows several services running with PID 1008. Right-clicking one of the services with PID 1008 gives two options, one to stop the service and one called Go To Process. By clicking Go To Process, the Processes tab is opened with the particular process highlighted. This solves a problem whereby several processes with the same name might be running (such as Svchost.exe). Where it would've previously been difficult to associate a given service with its PID, the Services tab now makes this rather easy.

> **Note**
>
> Most service-related processes run under an account other than your own and therefore aren't available when you attempt to use the Go To Process option. To view these processes, use the Show Processes From All Users option on the Processes tab in Task Manager before clicking Go To Process.

Editing the Registry

I f you've ever read anything about the registry, you've seen the dire warnings: "Using Registry Editor incorrectly can cause serious problems that may require you to reinstall Windows!" It's true; making changes to the registry directly, as opposed to letting your software do it for you, *can* be hazardous, and an errant edit *can* bring your system down. That's why Windows Vista is set up so that you normally don't have to get involved with the registry. When you change some detail about your system's configuration using Control Panel, Control Panel writes the necessary updates to the registry for you, and you needn't be concerned with how it happens. When you install a new piece of hardware or a new program, a myriad of registry modifications take place; again, you don't need to know the details.

On the other hand, the registry is nothing to fear. With the proper knowledge and a little care, you can work in the registry without worry. Because the designers of Windows couldn't provide a user interface for every conceivable customization you might want to make, sometimes working directly with the registry is the only way to get a job done. And sometimes, even when it's not the only way, it might be the fastest way. Windows includes a registry editor that you should know how to use—safely. This chapter tells you how.

What's in Your Edition?

The basic structure of the registry is identical in all editions of Windows Vista, and Registry Editor, the utility for viewing and editing registry data, works exactly the same way in all editions. The only material in this chapter that does not apply to users of the Windows Vista home editions (Home Basic and Home Premium) is the information about using group policy to prevent unwanted modifications to the registry, because Group Policy Object Editor is not included in those editions.

Understanding the Structure of the Registry

Before you begin browsing or editing the registry, it's good to know a bit about how this database is built. Figure 26-1 shows a portion of a system's registry, as seen through Registry Editor, the registry editor supplied with Windows Vista. As shown in the figure, the registry consists of the following five *root keys*: HKEY_CLASSES_ROOT, HKEY_CURRENT_USER, HKEY_LOCAL_MACHINE, HKEY_USERS, and HKEY_CURRENT_CONFIG. For simplicity's sake and typographical convenience, this book, like many others, abbreviates the root key names as HKCR, HKCU, HKLM, HKU, and HKCC, respectively.

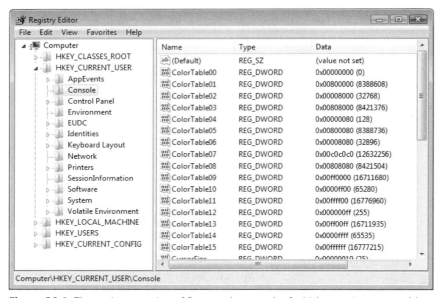

Figure 26-1 The registry consists of five root keys, each of which contains many subkeys.

Root keys, sometimes called *predefined keys*, contain subkeys. Registry Editor displays this structure as an outline. In Figure 26-1, for example, HKCU has been opened to show the top-level subkeys: AppEvents, Console, Control Panel, Environment, EUDC, Identities, Keyboard Layout, Network, Printers, SessionInformation, Software, System, and Volatile Environment. A root key and its subkeys can be described as a path, like this: HKCU\Console. Root keys and their subkeys appear in the left pane in Registry Editor.

> **Note**
>
> The registry is the work of many hands, and capitalization and word spacing are not always consistent. With readability as our goal, we have made our own capitalization decisions for this book, and our treatment of names frequently differs from what you see in Registry Editor. No matter. Capitalization is irrelevant. Spelling and spacing must be correct, however.

Subkeys, which we call *keys* for short, can contain subkeys of their own. Whether they do or not, they always contain at least one *value*. In Registry Editor, that value is known as the *default value*. Many keys have additional values. The names, data types, and data associated with values appear in the right pane. As Figure 26-1 shows, the HKCU\Console key has many values—ColorTable00, ColorTable01, and so on.

The default value for many keys—including HKCU\Console—is not defined. You can therefore think of an empty default value as a placeholder—a slot that could hold data but currently does not.

All values other than the default always include the following three components: name, data type, and data. As Figure 26-1 shows, the ColorTable00 value of HKCU\Console is of data type REG_DWORD. The data associated with this value (on the system used for this figure) is 0x00000000. (The prefix *0x* denotes a hexadecimal value. Registry Editor displays the decimal equivalent of hexadecimal values in parentheses after the value.)

A key with all its subkeys and values is commonly called a *hive*. The registry is stored on disk as several separate hive files. The appropriate hive files are read into memory when the operating system starts (or when a new user logs on) and assembled into the registry. You can see where the hives of your system physically live by examining the values associated with HKLM\System\CurrentControlSet\Control\HiveList. Figure 26-2 shows the HiveList key for one of the systems used for this book.

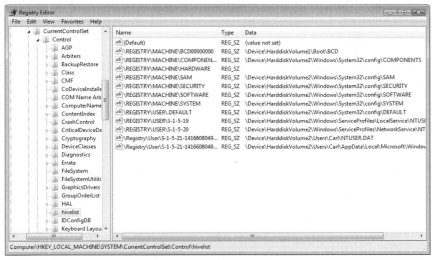

Figure 26-2 You can find the names and locations of the files that make up your registry in HKLM\System\CurrentControlSet\Control\HiveList.

Notice that one hive, \Registry\Machine\Hardware, has no associated disk file. This hive, which records your hardware configuration, is completely volatile; that is, Windows Vista creates it fresh each time you turn your system on. Notice also the path specifications for the remaining hive files. Windows assigns drive letters after assembling the registry, so these paths do not specify drive letters.

Notice also that two predefined keys—HKCR and HKCU—are not shown in the HiveList key at all. Like the file system in Windows, which uses junctions, symlinks, and other trickery to display a virtual namespace, the registry uses a bit of misdirection (implemented with the REG_LINK data type) to create these keys. Both are representations of keys actually stored within HKLM and HKU:

- HKCR is merged from keys within HKLM\Software\Classes and HKU*sid*_Classes (where *sid* is the security identifier of the currently logged on user).

- HKCU is a view into HKU*sid*.

You can view or edit the registry's actual locations or its virtual keys; the results are identical. The HKCR and HKCU keys are generally more convenient to use.

Registry Data Types

The registry uses the following data types:

- **REG_SZ** The SZ indicates zero-terminated string. This is a variable-length string that can contain Unicode as well as ANSI characters. When you enter or edit a REG_SZ value, Registry Editor terminates the value with a 00 byte for you. A quick scan of the registry reveals that REG_SZ is one of the most common data types and that it's often used for numeric as well as textual data. (See, for example, the values of HKCU\Control Panel\Desktop.)

- **REG_BINARY** As its name suggests, the REG_BINARY type contains binary data—0s and 1s.

- **REG_DWORD** This data type is a "double word"—that is, a 32-bit numeric value. Although it can hold any integer from 0 to 2^{32}, the registry often uses it for simple Boolean values (0 or 1) because the registry lacks a Boolean data type.

- **REG_QWORD** This data type is a "quadruple word"—a 64-bit numeric value.

- **REG_MULTI_SZ** This data type contains a group of zero-terminated strings assigned to a single value.

- **REG_EXPAND_SZ** This data type is a zero-terminated string containing an unexpanded reference to an environment variable, such as %SystemRoot%. (For information about environment variables, see "Using Environment Variables," Appendix B.) If you need to create a key containing a variable name, use this data type, not REG_SZ.

Internally, the registry also uses REG_LINK, REG_FULL_RESOURCE_DESCRIPTOR, REG_RESOURCE_LIST, REG_RESOURCE _REQUIREMENTS_LIST, and REG_NONE data types. Although you might occasionally see references in technical documentation to these data types, they're not visible or accessible in Registry Editor.

Registry Virtualization

One of the key elements of security in Windows Vista is that it prevents applications running under a standard user's token from writing to system folders in the file system and to machine-wide keys in the registry, while at the same time enabling users with a standard account to run applications without running into "access denied" roadblocks. Standard advice for security-conscious Windows XP users is to run using a limited account (comparable to a standard account in Windows Vista). In practice, however, most users find this advice inconvenient or impossible to follow because many applications require administrator-level access, even if they don't perform administrative functions. A limited user soon finds that applications don't run as expected (or don't run at all) and switches back to an account with full administrator privileges, putting the computer at greater risk from malicious or poorly written programs.

Many of those applications that require administrator-level access are still in use in Windows Vista, but standard users (and administrators in Admin Approval mode) can run them without hassle. That's because in Windows Vista, User Account Control (UAC) uses *registry virtualization* to redirect attempts to write to subkeys of HKLM\ Software. (Settings in HKLM apply to all users of the computer, and therefore only administrators have write permission.) When an application attempts to write to this hive, Windows writes instead to a per-user location, HKCR\VirtualStore\Machine\Software. Like file virtualization, this is done transparently; the application (and all but the most curious users) never know this is going on behind the scenes.

> **Note**
>
> When an application requests information from HKLM\Software, Windows looks first in the virtualized key, if it exists. Therefore, if a value exists in both the VirtualStore hive and in HKLM, the application sees only the one in VirtualStore.

Note that, because the virtualized data is stored in a per-user section of the registry, settings made by one user do not affect other users. Running the same application in Windows XP, which doesn't use virtualization and therefore looks only at the actual HKLM hive, presents all users with the same settings. This can lead to confusion by users who are accustomed to sharing an application in Windows XP, and find that it works differently in Windows Vista.

INSIDE OUT Copy virtualized registry entries to other user accounts

The hive that stores virtualized registry data, HKCR\VirtualStore\Machine\Software, can also be found in HKU*sid*_Classes\VirtualStore\Machine\Software, where *sid* is the security identifier of the user who is currently logged on. If you want to make sure that a certain application works identically for a different user, you can copy that application's subkey to the corresponding HKU subkey for the other user.

For more information about UAC and virtualization, see "Preventing Unsafe Actions with UAC," Chapter 10.

Avoiding Registry Mishaps

The primary tool in Windows Vista for working directly with the registry is Registry Editor. You won't find it anywhere on the Start Menu, however, and it doesn't show up in the Start Menu Search box when you type its name; you must use the name of its executable file, Regedit.exe. To start Registry Editor, at a command prompt, type **regedit**.

The two most important things to know about Registry Editor are that it copies your changes immediately into the registry and that it has no Undo command. Registry Editor doesn't wait for you to issue a File, Save command (it has no such command) before making changes in the registry files. And after you have altered some bit of registry data, the original data is gone forever—unless you remember it and restore it yourself or unless you have some form of backup that you can restore. Registry Editor is therefore a tool to be used sparingly and soberly; it should not be left open when not in use.

Note

A new technology underlying Windows Vista is Kernel Transaction Manager (KTM), which enables Transactional Registry (TxR). This feature does enable a form of registry rollback, but it's not implemented in Registry Editor. Rather, this feature is designed for use by developers who need to create robust applications using transactional processing. For more information, visit *http://www.vista-io.com/2601*.

So that you can recover from ill-advised edits to the registry, before you make any changes you should back up the registry using one or both of these methods:

- Use the Export command in Registry Editor to back up the branch of the registry where you plan to work.

- Use System Restore to set a restore point.

> **Note**
>
> In Windows XP and Windows 2000, the Backup program has an option to back up (and subsequently restore, if necessary) the "system state," which includes the registry. Backup And Restore Center in Windows Vista has no such option, so it's not a viable method for backing up the registry. Some third-party backup programs do have registry backup capabilities, which provide an alternative to the methods described in the following sections.

Backing Up Before You Edit

One relatively safe way to edit your registry is to back up the section you're interested in before you make any changes to it. If something goes wrong, you can usually use your backup file to restore the registry to the state it was in when you backed up.

Registry Editor can save all or portions of your registry in any of four different formats, described below.

- **Registration Files**   The Registration Files option creates a .reg file, a text file that can be read and edited in Notepad or another similar program. A .reg file can be merged into the registry of a system running Windows Vista, Windows XP, or Windows 2000. When you merge a .reg file, its keys and values replace the corresponding keys and values in the registry. Using .reg files allows you to edit your registry "off line" and add your changes to the registry without even opening Registry Editor. You can also use .reg files as an easy way to share and copy registry settings to other computers. For details, see "Using .Reg Files to Automate Registry Changes," in this chapter.

- **Registry Hive Files**   The registry hive format saves a binary image of a selected portion of the registry. You won't be able to read the resulting file (choose one of the text-file options if that's what you need to do), but if you need to restore the keys you've worked on, you can be confident that this format will do the job correctly.

  Registry hive file is the format of choice if you want to create a backup before working in Registry Editor. That's because when you *import* a registry hive file, it restores the entire hive to exactly the way it was when you saved it. (The .reg file types, when merged, restore all the saved keys and values to their original locations, which repairs all deletions and edits. But the process does not remove any keys or values that you added.) Note, however, that a registry hive file has the potential to do the greatest damage if you import it to the wrong key; see the caution in the following section.

- **Win9x/NT4 Registration Files**   The Win9x/NT4 Registration Files option also generates a .reg file, but one in an older format used by earlier versions of Windows. The principal difference between the two formats is that the current format uses Unicode and the older format does not. Use the Win9x/NT4 Registration

Files option only if you need to replicate a section of your registry in the registry of an older system.

- **Text Files**   The Text Files option, like the Registration Files option, creates a file that can be read in Notepad or another text editor. The principal advantage of this format is that it cannot accidentally (or intentionally) be merged into the registry. Thus it's a good way to create a record of your registry's state at a particular time. Its disadvantage, relative to the .reg file format, is its size. Text files are considerably larger than corresponding .reg files, and they take longer to create.

To export a registry hive, select a key in the left pane, and then on the File menu, click Export. (Easier yet: right-click a key and click Export.) In the Save As Type list in the Export Registry File dialog box, select one of the four file types. Under Export Range, select Selected Branch. The resulting file includes the selected key and all its subkeys and values.

> **Note**
>
> The All option under Export Range in the Export Registry File dialog box sounds useful, but it rarely is. It's an invalid selection for the binary registry hive files type. For any of the three text file types, it generates a gigantic file (often hundreds of megabytes) that is usually not appropriate for registry recovery.

INSIDE OUT   Create hive files using Reg.exe

As an alternative to exporting a hive with the Export command in Registry Editor, you can use the Save operation of Reg.exe, a command-line tool for registry operations. Because Reg.exe is a command-line tool, you can use it in batch programs, which might be useful for backing up a certain hive repeatedly or on a scheduled basis. For more information about Reg.exe, see "Editing the Registry from the Command Line," page 26xx.

Restoring the Registry from an Exported Hive

If you need to restore the exported hive from a registry hive file, select the same key in the left pane of the Registry Editor window, click Import on the File menu, and specify the file. You'll see a confirmation prompt letting you know that your action will overwrite (replace) the current key and all its subkeys. This is your last chance to make sure you're importing the hive into the right location, so take a moment to make sure you've selected the correct key before you click Yes.

> **CAUTION**
>
> Importing a registry hive file replaces the entire content of the selected key with the contents of the file—regardless of its original source. That is, it *wipes out* everything in *the selected key* and then adds the keys and values from the file. When you import, be absolutely certain that you've selected the correct key.

If you saved your backup as a .reg file, you use the same process to import it. (As an alternative, you can double-click the .reg file in Windows Explorer without opening Registry Editor.) Unlike the registry hive file, however, the complete path to each key and value is stored as part of the file and it always restores to the same location. This approach for recovering from registry editing mishaps is fine if you did not add new values or subkeys to the section of the registry you're working with; it returns existing data to its former state but doesn't alter the data you've added.

For more information about using .reg files, see "Using .Reg Files to Automate Registry Changes,"in this chapter.

TROUBLESHOOTING

You mistakenly deleted data from the HKLM\System\CurrentControlSet hive

As those dire warnings pointed out, improper changes to registry can prevent your computer from operating properly or even booting. This is particularly true for changes to the HKLM\System\CurrentControlSet hive. Because keys in that hive are so essential, Windows maintains a backup, which you can restore when necessary. To do that, begin by shutting down your computer. Start your computer and, during the boot process, press F8. Use the arrow keys to select Last Known Good Configuration and then press Enter.

Using System Protection to Save the Registry's State

The System Protection utility takes snapshots of your system's state, at prescribed time intervals or on demand, and allows you to roll your system back to an earlier state (called a *restore point*) if you experience problems. Most of the registry is included in the restore point (the keys that are not included are listed at HKLM\System\ControlSet001\ BackupRestore\KeysNotToRestore). Creating a restore point before you begin working in the registry is an excellent way to protect yourself against mishap.

For information about using System Restore, see "Rolling Back to a Stable State with System Restore," in Chapter 23.

Browsing and Editing with Registry Editor

Because of the registry's size, looking for a particular key, value, or data item can be daunting. In Registry Editor, the Find command (on the Edit menu; also available by pressing Ctrl+F) works in the forward direction only and does not wrap around when it gets to the end of the registry. If you're not sure where the item you need is located, select the highest level in the left pane (Computer, if you're searching your own registry) before issuing the command. If you have an approximate idea where the item you want is located, you can save time by starting at a node closer to (but still above) the target.

INSIDE OUT Search—and replace—faster with third-party tools

To put the matter kindly, the Find command in Registry Editor does not set any speed records (no positive records, at any rate). Nor does it perform the kind of search-and-replace operations that are commonplace in text editors. Given the fact that registry changes take effect immediately, the absence of search-and-replace can be seen as a safety feature. If you don't take the precaution of backing up your registry before editing, you risk the possibility of carelessly replacing all instances of one string with another.

If you take reasonable precautions, however, and if you need to edit your registry more than now and then, you might want to consider using a third-party product to enhance the native capabilities of Registry Editor. "Reasonable precautions" here means backing up and avoiding unprompted search-and-replace. If you're going to replace all instances of one string with another, let the registry tool prompt you before making each replacement.

At the time of this book's writing, third-party registry tools for Windows Vista were still in development, and none that we could recommend were available. By the time you read this, tools that are better and faster than Registry Editor will undoubtedly be available; if you work in the registry often, don't feel locked in to Registry Editor.

After you have located an item of interest, you can put it on the Favorites list to simplify a return visit. Open the Favorites menu, click Add To Favorites, and supply a friendly name (or accept the default). If you're about to close Registry Editor and know you'll be returning to the same key the next time you open the editor, you can skip the Favorites step, because Registry Editor always remembers your last position and returns to that position in the next session.

INSIDE OUT   **Forget the last position!**

Registry Editor remembers your last position by saving it in the LastKey value in the HKCU\Software\Microsoft\Windows\CurrentVersion\Applets\Regedit key when you close the program. For some, the ability of Registry Editor to return to the last-viewed key at startup is a convenient way to pick up where they left off; for others, it's an annoyance. If you're in the latter camp, you can override this behavior by removing Full Control permissions on the HKCU\Software\Microsoft\Windows\CurrentVersion\Applets\Regedit key. Doing so prevents further changes to the LastKey value. (Before you set permissions this way, you should delete the data in LastKey, or else you'll *always* return to that same spot!) This approach is effective, but has some potentially undesirable side effects: Registry Editor no longer saves View or Find settings, nor can you save Favorites in Registry Editor. (You can overcome the last problem by breaking the permissions inheritance chain on the Favorites subkey.)

There's another way to start Registry Editor at the root, without the side effects. Create a simple batch program that clears the LastKey data and then opens Registry Editor, like this:

```
@echo off

setlocal

set key=HKEY_CURRENT_USER\Software
set key=%key%\Microsoft\Windows\CurrentVersion\Applets\Regedit

reg.exe add %key% /v LastKey /d "" /f

start regedit
```

Registry Editor includes a number of time-saving keyboard shortcuts for navigating the registry. To move to the next subkey that starts with a particular letter, simply type that letter when the focus is in the left pane; in the right pane, use the same trick to jump to the next value that begins with that letter. To open a key (revealing its subkeys), press Right Arrow. To move up one level in the subkey hierarchy, press Left Arrow; a second press collapses the subkeys of the current key. To move to the top of the hierarchy (Computer), press Home. To quickly move between the left and right panes, use the Tab key. In the right pane, press F2 to rename a value, and press Enter to open that value and edit its data. Once you get the hang of using these keyboard shortcuts, you'll find it's usually easier to zip through the subkey hierarchy with a combination of arrow keys and letter keys than it is to open outline controls with the mouse.

Changing Data

You can change the data associated with a value by selecting a value in the right pane and pressing Enter or by double-clicking the value. Registry Editor pops up an edit window appropriate for the value's data type.

INSIDE OUT **Use the status bar to figure out where you are**

While you're working in the right pane, Registry Editor doesn't highlight the current sub-key in the left pane. The best way to remind yourself which subkey you're working in is to look at the status bar, which always displays the full path of the current subkey. If you don't see the status bar, open the View menu and click Status Bar.

Adding or Deleting Keys

To add a key, select the new key's parent in the left pane, open the Edit menu, point to New, and click Key. The new key arrives as a generically named outline entry, exactly the way a new folder does in Windows Explorer. Type a new name. To delete a key, select it and then press Delete.

Adding or Deleting Values

To add a value, select the parent key open the Edit menu, and point to New. On the sub-menu that appears, click the type of value you want to add. Table 26-1 shows the value type associated with each command on the submenu. A value of the type you select appears in the right pane with a generic name. Type over the generic name, press Enter twice, enter your data, and press Enter once more. To delete a value, select it and press Delete.

Table 26-1. Menu Names for Registry Data Types

Menu Name	Registry Data Type
String Value	REG_SZ
Binary Value	REG_BINARY
DWORD (32-bit) Value	REG_DWORD
QWORD (64-bit) Value	REG_QWORD
Multi-String Value	REG_MULTI_SZ
Expandable String Value	REG_EXPAND_SZ

Monitoring Registry Changes

Sometimes it can be useful to monitor the changes that take place in your registry—particularly the changes that occur as the result of installing a new program or device. Windows Vista does not provide a registry monitoring tool, unfortunately. Using native Windows tools, the best you can do is employ the venerable command-line program Fc.exe to compare registry export files that you create before and after an important registry change. Export a .txt file or .reg file from the branch of the registry that you expect to change (or the entire registry if you're not sure), install the program or driver (or do whatever it is whose registry effects you want to monitor), repeat the export process (using a different file name), and then, at a command prompt, type

```
fc /u before.reg after.reg > regcomp.txt
```

(Substitute the actual names of your snapshot files for *before.reg* and *after.reg*.)

The /U switch, which tells Fc to use Unicode, is necessary because .reg files use Unicode. The > symbol saves Fc's output to a text file, which you can then inspect in Notepad or another text editor.

If that process seems like too much work (it certainly does to us), take a look at Active Registry Monitor, a product by SmartLine Software that is available at *http://www.vista-io.com/2602*. Active Registry Monitor lets you create any number of before-and-after snapshots of your registry and highlights all differences between any two snapshots.

To track registry changes in real time, we recommend the Sysinternals utility Process Monitor (the successor to the venerable Regmon) (*http://www.vista-io.com/2603*). The Process Monitor can tell you exactly which processes have read or written to your registry and when each such operation has occurred. Filtering commands let you restrict the program's output to particular sections of the registry or to particular kinds of operations. For example, if you expect a program to be making changes to keys within HKCU\Software, you can limit Process Monitor's output to writes within that key.

Using .Reg Files to Automate Registry Changes

The .reg files created by the Export command in Registry Editor are plain text, suitable for reading and editing in Notepad or any similar editor. Therefore, they provide an alternative method for editing your registry. You can export a section of the registry, change it offline, and then merge it back into the registry. Or you can add new keys, values, and data to the registry by creating a .reg file from scratch and merging it. A .reg file is particularly useful if you need to make the same changes to the registry of several different computers. You can make and test your changes on one machine, save the relevant part of the registry as a .reg file, and then transport the file to the other machines that require it.

Figure 26-3 shows a portion of a .reg file. In this case, the file was exported from the HKCU\Software\Microsoft\Windows\CurrentVersion\Explorer\Advanced key, shown in Figure 26-4.

Figure 26-3 A .reg file is a plain-text file suitable for offline editing. This .reg file was exported from the key shown in Figure 26-4.

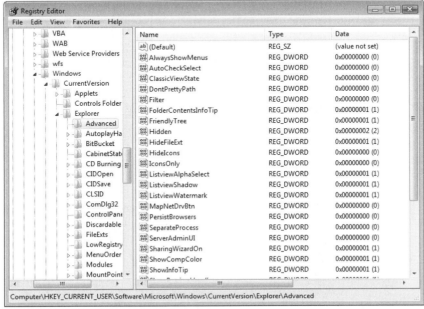

Figure 26-4 This key's name, values, and data are recorded in the .reg file shown in Figure 26-3.

Identifying the Elements of a .Reg File

As you review the examples shown in the two figures, note the following characteristics of .reg files.

- **Header line**   The file begins with the line *Windows Registry Editor Version 5.00*. When you merge a .reg file into the registry, Registry Editor uses this line to verify that the file contains registry data. Version 5 (the version shipped with Windows Vista) generates Unicode text files, which can be used in Windows XP and Windows 2000 as well as Windows Vista. If you want to share registry data with a system running Windows 95/98/Me or Windows NT, select the Win9x/NT4 Registration Files option when you export the file in Registry Editor. To create from scratch a .reg file that's suitable for import into Windows 95/98/Me or Windows NT, use the header *REGEDIT4* instead of *Windows Registry Editor Version 5.00*.

- **Key names**   Key names are delimited by brackets and must include the full path from root key to the current subkey. The root key name must not be abbreviated. (Don't use HKCU, for example.) Figure 26-3 shows only one key name, but you can have as many as you please.

- **The default value**   Undefined default values do not appear in .reg files. Defined default values are identified by the special character @. Thus, a key whose default REG_SZ value was defined as MyApp would appear in a .reg file this way:

    ```
    "@"="MyApp"
    ```

- **Value names**   Value names must be enclosed in quotation marks, whether or not they include space characters. Follow the value name with an equal sign. Notice that the value names shown in Figure 26-3 do not appear in the same order as in Figure 26-4. The .reg file displays values in the order they appear in the registry. Registry Editor, however, sorts them alphabetically for your editing and browsing convenience. If you're creating a .reg file from scratch, the value order is insignificant.

- **Data types**   REG_SZ values don't get a data type identifier or a colon. The data directly follows the equal sign. Other data types are identified as follows:

Data Type	Identifier
REG_BINARY	Hex
REG_DWORD	dword
REG_QWORD	hex(b)
REG_MULTI_SZ	hex(7)
REG_EXPAND_SZ	hex(2)

A colon separates the identifier from the data. Thus, for example, a REG_DWORD value named Keyname with value data of 00000000 looks like this:

```
"Keyname"=dword:00000000
```

- **REG_SZ values** Ordinary string values must be enclosed in quotation marks. A backslash character within a string must be written as two backslashes. Thus, for example, the path C:\Program Files\Microsoft Office\ is written like this:

```
"C:\\Program Files\\Microsoft Office\\"
```

- **REG_DWORD** values DWORD values are written as eight hexadecimal digits, without spaces or commas. Do not use the 0x prefix.

- **All other data types** All other data types, including REG_EXPAND_SZ, REG_MULTI_SZ, and REG_QWORD, appear as comma-delimited lists of hexadecimal bytes (two hex digits, a comma, two more hex digits, and so on). The following is an example of a REG_MULTI_SZ value:

```
"Addins"=hex(7):64,00,3a,00,5c,00,6c,00,6f,00,74,00,00,75,00,73,00,5c,00,
\31,00,32,00,33,00,5c,00,61,00,64,00,64,00,64,00,69,00,6e,00,73,00,5c,00,
\64,00,71,00,61,00,75,00,69,00,2e,00,31,00,32,00,61,00,00,00,00,00,00,00
```

- **Line-continuation characters** You can use the backslash as a line-continuation character. The REG_MULTI_SZ value shown above, for example, is all one stream of bytes. We've added backslashes and broken the lines for readability, and you can do the same in your .reg files.

- **Line spacing** You can add blank lines for readability. Registry Editor ignores them.

- **Comments** To add a comment line to a .reg file, begin the line with a semicolon.

Using a .Reg File to Delete Registry Data

.Reg files are most commonly used to modify existing registry data or add new data. But you can also use them to delete existing values and keys.

To delete an existing value, specify a hyphen character as the value's data. For example, to use a .reg file to remove the value ThumbnailSize from the key HKCU\Software \Microsoft\Windows\CurrentVersion\Explorer, add the following lines to the .reg file:

```
[HKEY_CURRENT_USER\Software\Microsoft\Windows\CurrentVersion\Explorer]
"ThumbnailSize"=-
```

To delete an existing key with all its values and data, insert a hyphen in front of the key name (inside the left bracket). For example, to use a .reg file to remove the key HKCR\.xyz\shell and all its values, add the following to the .reg file:

```
[-HKCR\.xyz\shell]
```

Merging a .Reg File into the Registry

To merge a .reg file into the registry from within Registry Editor, open the File menu and click Import. Registry Editor adds the imported data under the appropriate key names, overwriting existing values where necessary.

The default action for a .reg file is Merge—meaning merge with the registry. Therefore, you can merge a file into the registry by simply double-clicking it in Windows Explorer and answering the confirmation prompt.

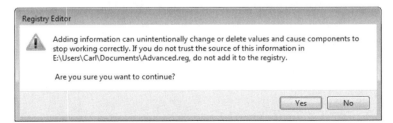

> **CAUTION**
>
> Because the default action for a .reg file is to merge it into the registry, if you want to edit the file, *don't* double-click it. Instead, right-click the file and click Edit on the shortcut menu. (If you accidentally double-click, answer No to the confirmation prompt.)

Chapter 26

Working with a Remote Computer's Registry

You can use Registry Editor to connect to the registry of another computer on your network. Open the File menu, click Connect Network Registry, and then fill out the ensuing dialog box (shown in Figure 26-5) with the name of the computer to which you want to connect. If you don't know the name of the computer, click Advanced and then click Find Now to display a list of computers on your network.

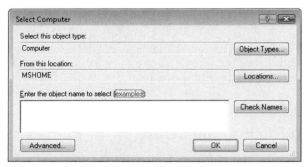

Figure 26-5 Type the name of the target computer in this dialog box.

The remote computer's name appears as a top-level entry in the left pane, with its HKLM and HKU keys listed below, as shown in Figure 26-6.

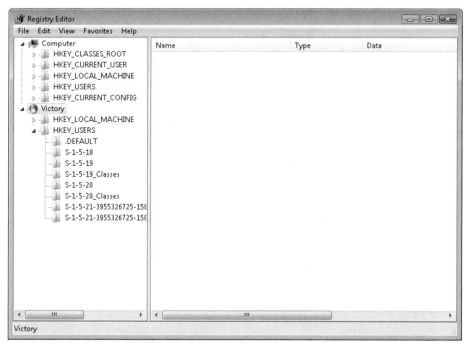

Figure 26-6 With appropriate permissions, you can use Registry Editor to work with a remote computer's registry as well as your own.

> **Note**
>
> To make changes to the remote computer's registry, you must be logged on with an account that is an administrator on both your computer and the remote computer. The Remote Registry service must be started on the remote computer, and its firewall must have an exception enabled for Remote Administration.

Changing Registry Key Permissions

By default, administrators and the System account have full control over all registry keys. The creator/owner of a particular key has full control over that key. (For example, a user typically has full control over all subkeys of HKCU while that user is logged on.) In other registry contexts, a user's default permissions allow read access but nothing more. If you attempt to change a registry key for which you have read access only, Registry Editor presents the appropriate editing dialog box but rejects your edit.

You can prevent changes to an individual registry key and its subkeys (but not to individual values) by editing the permissions for that key. Registry permissions work the same way as permissions assigned to files and folders on an NTFS drive; for each account or group, you can allow full control, allow read access, deny access to the key, or set special permissions. To change permissions for a key, right-click it, and then click Permissions on the shortcut menu. The Permissions dialog box, shown in Figure 26-7, closely resembles the Security tab in dialog boxes in Windows Explorer.

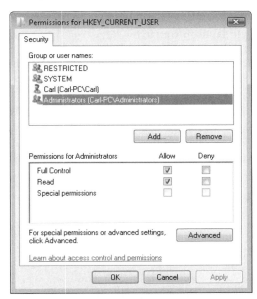

Figure 26-7 In most contexts, administrators have full control over data stored in the registry.

Restricting Access to Registry Editor

Home Basic	◑
Home Premium	◑
Business	●
Enterprise	●
Ultimate	●

On a shared computer running Windows Vista, you might decide that certain users should be denied all access to registry editing tools. To enforce the ban, you can use group policy, which is available only in Business, Enterprise, and Ultimate editions. To set a local group policy, open the Group Policy Object Editor console by typing **gpedit.msc** at a command prompt. In the console tree, open User Configuration \Administrative Templates\System. Double-click the Prevent Access To Registry Editing Tools setting, and change it to Enabled.

> **CAUTION**
>
> These tricks for locking down Registry Editor do only that: prevent the use of Registry Editor (and its command-line sidekick, Reg.exe). Although this practice can be useful for keeping users from poking around where they shouldn't and making inadvertent edits, it does not secure the registry itself. A determined snoop can still work directly in the registry using a third-party registry editor, script, or other tool.

Unfortunately, with local group policy settings, this solution cannot be applied easily to a single user: It locks out all users—you included. To regain access, you must revisit Group Policy Object Editor and change the policy to Disabled or Not Configured. (In a domain environment, you can set group policy at any level to selectively apply restrictions like this.)

It's possible to prevent an individual user from using Registry Editor without using group policy. However, if not done properly, this solution (which works in all Windows Vista editions) can lock out the wrong user—and you'll need another administrator account to undo the damage. To lock out a particular user only, follow these steps (carefully!):

1. If the user whose access you want to disable has a standard account, change it to an administrator account. (You must have administrative rights to perform this change. *Do not use Run As Administrator;* doing so applies the restriction to administrator whose credentials you provide instead of the targeted user.) Then log on using that user's credentials.

2. In Registry Editor, navigate to HKCU\Software\Microsoft\Windows \CurrentVersion\Policies.

3. Select the System subkey. If this key does not exist, create it.

4. Create a new DWORD value named DisableRegistryTools and set it to 1.

5. If you want to change the user to a standard user, log on with your administrator account and demote the user's account.

This user will no longer be able to run Registry Editor or merge a .reg file into the registry. To undo the change and re-enable this user to use Registry Editor, follow these steps:

1. From an administrator account other than the one that is locked out, run Registry Editor. (If you're using a standard account, use Run As Administrator to open Registry Editor.)

2. Browse to HKLM\Software\Microsoft\Windows NT\CurrentVersion\ProfileList.

3. Select each subkey under this key and look at the value ProfileImagePath. At the end of this string is the name of the user. Find the subkey that matches the user whose access you're trying to restore; the name of the subkey is the security identifier (SID) for that user's account.

4. Select the key HKU*sid*\Software\Microsoft\Windows\CurrentVersion\Policies\System, where *sid* is the SID that you identified in the previous step.

5. Change the value for DisableRegistryTools to 0 and close Registry Editor.

Chapter 26

Editing the Registry from the Command Line

All editions of Windows Vista include Reg.exe (sometimes called the Console Registry Tool), a command-line tool that enables you to perform registry operations without using Registry Editor. By incorporating Reg.exe commands in batch programs or scripts, you can automate registry activities, as well as take conditional actions based on the state of a local or remote registry. For example, you can query a registry value and then edit that value (or take another action) if the data meets some criterion. Virtually the entire feature set of Registry Editor is available in Reg.exe (one exception: the Export operation in Reg.exe exports Unicode .reg files only). And you can do at least one thing in Reg.exe that's impossible to do in Registry Editor: Change the data type of a key's default value.

For syntax information about Reg.exe, open a Command Prompt window and type **reg /?**. As you'll see, the tool's basic syntax is

```
reg operation [parameter list]
```

where *operation* is one of the 12 items listed in Table 26-2, and *parameter list* is one or more items (the name of a subkey or value, for example) pertinent to the specified operation. You can get additional syntax details about an operation by typing **reg *operation* /?**. For example, to learn more about how to use the Query operation, type **reg query /?**.

Table 26-2. Reg.exe Operations

Operation	Effect
Add	Adds a key, value, or data item
Compare	Compares one value with another or all values under a particular key with all values under another key
Copy	Copies a value or key from one location in the registry to another
Delete	Deletes a key or value
Export	Exports a key as a Unicode .reg file
Flags	Displays or sets registry virtualization flags for subkeys of HKLM\Software
Import	Imports a .reg file (to the local registry only)
Load	Loads a hive file to a specified new key
Query	Returns the data associated with a specified value or with all values of a specified key
Restore	Loads a hive file into an existing key, overwriting that key
Save	Creates a hive file
Unload	Unloads a hive file

Some guidelines to note about Reg.exe's syntax:

- Reg.exe requires that you abbreviate the names of root keys. Use HKLM, for example, not HKEY_LOCAL_MACHINE.

- If a key or value name includes spaces, enclose the name within quotation marks.

- If you're incorporating a Reg.exe command in a batch program and that command includes an environment variable, enclose the variable name within two pairs of percent signs, not a single pair of percent signs. Otherwise, the command interpreter expands the variable name before passing it to Reg.exe.

All Reg.exe operations issue Errorlevel values that can be tested in batch programs. For all operations except Compare, these values are 0 if the operation is successful and 1 if unsuccessful. Compare returns 0 if the operation is successful and all compared values are identical, 1 if the operation is unsuccessful, or 2 if the operation is successful and there are differences in the compared values. For more information about batch programs, see "Automating Command Sequences with Batch Programs," Chapter 30.

Chapter 26

PART V
Advanced System Maintenance

CHAPTER 27

Advanced Internet Explorer Security and Administration

Home Basic ●
Home Premium ●
Business ●
Enterprise ●
Ultimate ●

E arlier in this book, we discussed the features and capabilities of Internet Explorer 7 and explained how to use and customize those you're likely to work with day in and day out. In this chapter we look in detail at features that improve your security online.

The bedrock of Internet Explorer security in Windows Vista is its consistent use of Windows permissions to limit what webpages and add-ons can do. This security fence around the browser window is called Protected Mode. In this chapter, we explain how Protected Mode defangs potentially dangerous add-ons by restricting their access to system files and redirecting files they save or create to locked-down virtualized locations. We think the minor inconveniences of Protected Mode are far outweighed by its positive effect on your system's security; for that reason, we recommend leaving Protected Mode enabled. A very small minority of Windows Vista users may find that Protected Mode causes a problem that has no easy workaround (such as the inability to run a custom add-on); for that tiny group only, we explain how to disable Protected Mode.

Just as in previous versions, Internet Explorer 7 uses security zones to save and apply groups of settings. Knowing the differences between behaviors that are allowed and prohibited in each security zone is a crucial aspect of protecting yourself and other users of your computer and network. In this chapter, we look in depth at each of the default security zones and explain how to change the permissions to create custom security zones.

What's in Your Edition?

All of the tools and techniques we describe in this chapter are available in all editions of Windows Vista.

Working with (and Around) Protected Mode

Using a web browser exposes you to special security risks; by clicking a link in an e-mail or mistyping a web address, you can find yourself on a site containing hostile script or downloadable code intended to take over your system. To mitigate against these threats, Internet Explorer 7 in Windows Vista runs in Protected Mode; this special mode, which is active in all Internet Explorer security zones except the Trusted Sites zone, takes advantage of a wide range of Windows Vista security enhancements, notably User Account Control. When Protected Mode is enabled (the default setting), Internet Explorer runs with severely limited privileges. The effect of these restrictions is to prevent a website from installing programs without your permission or changing system settings.

In Windows Vista, processes run with integrity levels defined by the Mandatory Integrity Control feature. Protected Mode Internet Explorer runs in the Low privilege process. As a result, Internet Explorer is prevented from writing to areas of the file system or the registry that require a higher privilege. The information sent between processes of different integrity levels is also limited with Protected Mode. Add-ons such as ActiveX controls and toolbars run in the same Low process, preventing them from gaining access to any areas except those specifically created for storing potentially unsafe data and programs.

Behind the scenes, Windows Vista creates a set of folders and files for use with Protected Mode Internet Explorer. These folders and files share the same Low privilege level as Internet Explorer. Four of these Low folders contain files used by the browser in the course of daily operation. They are:

- **Cache** %LocalAppData%\Microsoft\Windows\Temporary Internet Files\Low

- **Temp** %LocalAppData%\Temp\Low

- **Cookies** %AppData%\Microsoft\Windows\Cookies\Low

- **History** %LocalAppData%\Microsoft\Windows\History\Low

Windows Vista also creates virtual folders to store files that Internet Explorer tries to save in protected locations. Instead of causing an add-on to fail when it tries to write a data file to the Program Files or Windows folders, Windows silently redirects the file write operation to a virtual equivalent. The program is able to continue, believing that it wrote the files to a system location and not realizing that the data files actually wound up in a hidden virtualized folder that mirrors the actual path and is stored under the Temporary Internet Files folder. Likewise, any attempt to write to the registry is redirected to a Low-integrity area of the registry.

What happens when Internet Explorer needs to read those virtualized files? A *broker process* intercepts the operation and asks for your consent before continuing. This represents an important concept of Protected Mode: Whenever any action requires a higher privilege level, such as an ActiveX installation or an attempt to save a file, a broker process must be invoked. Typically, this results in Windows displaying a User Account Control dialog box before the process can continue.

Protected Mode fundamentally changes the way that applications intereact with Internet Explorer in Windows Vista. Applications that weren't built for this new environment can perform in unexpected ways. To reduce the likelihood of problems occurring in these situations, Internet Explorer provides a compatibility layer that enables applications built for previous versions of Internet Explorer to work with the new Protected Mode environment.

On rare occasions, Protected Mode may prevent an application or website from working properly. If all attempts to work around the incompatibility fail, you can disable Protected Mode for the current zone. We strongly recommend against taking this measure; if you absolutely must do so, we recommend that you reenable Protected Mode immediately after you finish the activity that conflict with it. Follow these steps to disable Protected Mode for the current zone:

1. From within Internet Explorer, click Tools, and then click Internet Options.

2. Click the Security tab and clear the Enable Protected Mode check box.

3. Click OK to continue and close the Internet Options dialog box. Windows displays a warning that the current security settings will put your computer at risk. Click OK to continue.

When Protected Mode is off, navigating to any webpage displays a warning message in the Information bar, like the one shown in Figure 27-1. To reenable Protected Mode, click on the Information bar and click Open Security Settings. Select the Enable Protected Mode checkbox, click OK and then close and reopen Internet Explorer.

Figure 27-1 The Information bar will alert you if Protected Mode is currently disabled for the current zone.

Another method for working around Protected Mode for a specific website is to add the website to the Trusted Sites zone, where Protected Mode is not in effect. We recommend that you exercise extreme caution before choosing this technique, however; adding a site to the Trusted Sites zone enables a wide range of potentially risky behaviors, and it's all too easy to forget to remove the site from the Trusted Sites zone after you finish working with it. This workaround is most appropriate on enterprise networks, where legacy applications might require older functionality that doesn't work in Protected Mode.

Chapter 27

Using and Customizing Internet Security Zones

Internet Explorer's security zones are key elements to browsing the web and using the internet without fear. By default, all websites you visit are assigned to the Internet zone, and Internet Explorer severely restricts the action of sites in the Internet zone. If you're concerned about security, you can lock down security zones even more tightly if you like.

By default, Internet Explorer allows you to work with four security zones:

- The Internet zone includes all sites that are not included in any other category.

- The Local Intranet zone is for sites on your local network, typically behind a firewall.

> **Note**
>
> Normally, the Local Intranet zone has fewer restrictions than the Internet zone; however, in a default installation of Windows Vista these settings are disabled and the Local Intranet zone has the same settings as the Internet zone. The first time you open a page from an intranet location, you're prompted to relax the intranet settings. In general, you should leave these settings at their default level unless you're running ActiveX controls on an intranet and need the extra functionality that comes with the relaxed settings.

- The Trusted Sites zone (empty on a clean installation of Windows) allows you to specify sites where you allow certain actions—such as running ActiveX controls or scripts—that you might not permit on other sites in which you have a lower degree of trust. The Trusted Sites zone is the only zone where Internet Explorer's Protected Mode security is disabled.

- The Restricted Sites zone (also empty on a clean installation) allows you to specify sites where you want to specifically disallow actions that might otherwise be permitted. This zone is the default for HTML-formatted e-mail you read using Microsoft Outlook or Windows Mail.

How Security Zones Affect the Way You Browse

When you open a webpage using Internet Explorer, Windows checks to see which security zone that page is assigned to and then applies restrictions to that page, based on the settings for that zone. Initially, any sites you connect to internally (that is, your own company's sites, which you access by means of an intranet connection) are automatically assigned to the Local Intranet zone, and if you choose to enable intranet settings the Local Intranet zone is accorded a "medium-low" level of security settings. All other sites on the Internet are lumped into the Internet zone, which is given a "medium-high" level of security settings. As you roam the Internet, if you come upon a site that you trust implicitly, you can move that site into the Trusted Sites zone. Internet Explorer, by default, applies a "medium" level of security settings to the Trusted Sites zone. When you discover a site that warrants a high degree of wariness, you can move that site into the Restricted Sites zone. The security settings that apply there, by default, are described as "high."

Adding Sites to a Zone

To change the zone in which a site resides, or to reconfigure the security settings associated with a zone, you use the Security tab of the Internet Options dialog box (click Tools, Internet Options, and then click the Security tab), which is shown in Figure 27-2. As the figure shows, Internet Explorer uses a different icon to depict each zone.

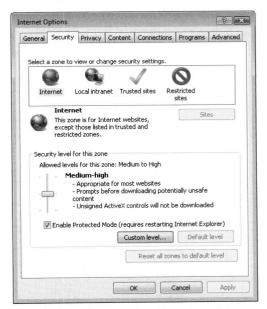

Figure 27-2 Use this dialog box to add sites to particular zones or modify the security settings associated with a zone.

Whenever you visit a site, the icon and name of the site's zone appear at the right side of the status bar, like this:

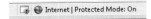

To add a site to your Trusted Sites or Restricted Sites zone, follow these steps:

1. On the Security tab of the Internet Options dialog box (shown in Figure 27-2), select Trusted Sites or Restricted Sites.

2. Click Sites. You'll see the following dialog box (or one similar if you selected Restricted Sites).

3. The URL for the current site appears in the Add This Website To The Zone box. Edit or replace this value if necessary and then click Add.

By design, the Trusted Sites zone is most appropriate for use with secure sites, where you already have a high degree of confidence that the site you're interacting with is legitimate. Thus, the default settings for this zone require that Internet Explorer verify that the site's server is secure (in other words, that it begins with *https:*) before establishing a connection. To add a non-SSL site to the list, clear the check box at the bottom of the Trusted Sites dialog box. (After adding the site, you can select the check box again.) When you add a domain (such as *http://www.microsoft.com*) to either of these zones, all URLs located within that domain are assigned to the zone you selected.

> **Note**
>
> The URLs *http://microsoft.com* and *http://www.microsoft.com* are not considered to be in the same domain; if you want to add all possible pages for a domain to a security zone, you must consider all possibilities. To add all possible pages on a particular domain, enter only the top-level domain name (*microsoft.com*) and leave off the prefix.

By default, Internet Explorer populates the Local Intranet zone with the following:

- All intranet sites that you haven't moved into either the Trusted Sites zone or the Restricted Sites zone

- All sites that bypass your proxy server, if one exists on your network

- All network servers accessed via UNC paths (*server_name*)

To remove one or more of those categories (so that the affected category joins the Internet zone), select Local Intranet in the Internet Options dialog box and then click Sites. You'll see the following dialog box. Clear the appropriate check boxes.

If you want to add a site to the Local Intranet zone, click the Advanced button. Then type the site's URL and click Add.

Changing a Zone's Security Settings

Any site placed in a security zone is subject to the same privileges and restrictions as all other sites in that zone. Thus, if you change the overall security settings associated with the zone, you change the security settings for all of its member sites. You can change the security settings for a zone to one of the predefined groups by following these steps:

1. On the Security tab of the Internet Options dialog box (shown earlier in Figure 27-2), click the icon for the zone you want to adjust.

CAUTION

If you've previously made any customizations to security settings for a particular zone, those settings will be wiped out as soon as you click Default Level. If you've made specific changes to allow a program or site to work correctly, be sure you document those settings so you can reapply them after changing other security settings.

2. In the Security Level For This Zone section of the dialog box, click the Default Level button to reveal a slider control (if the slider isn't already visible).

3. Move the slider up to apply more stringent security measures, or down to be more lenient. As you move the slider from level to level, the description to the right of the slider summarizes the current level's settings.

To fine-tune the settings for a zone, or to read all of the particulars about the current level of settings, click Custom Level. In the Security Settings dialog box that appears, shown in Figure 27-3 on the next page, you can use the option buttons to adjust individual settings.

Figure 27-3 For most security settings, you can choose between Disable, Enable, and Prompt.

If you've customized a security zone's settings and you want to start over from a completely clean slate, open the Security Settings dialog box, choose a predefined level from the Reset To list, and then click Reset.

Protecting Yourself from Unsafe and Unwanted Software

With the addition of Windows Firewall, Internet Explorer's Protected Mode, and Windows Defender, it's become much easier to keep unwanted software off of your computer and to remove it when it does get installed. The use of an antivirus program and sound surfing habits help increase safety and security to a very high level. This section examines some best practices that help to keep your computer free from unwanted software.

To Trust or Not to Trust?

Microsoft offers a digital signing technology, called Authenticode, that can be used to guarantee that an executable item comes from the publisher it says it comes from and that it has not been changed, deliberately or otherwise, since it left the publisher's hands. The digital signature verifies each bit of the signed file by comparing it to a hash value; if even a single bit of the file has changed, the comparison fails and the signature is invalid. Windows Vista blocks installation of any code that has an invalid signature—by definition, this indicates that the program file is corrupt (possibly because it was damaged during downloading) or that it has been tampered with.

A digital signature doesn't promise that the signed item is healthy and benevolent. It confirms only that the bits you're about to download are the authentic work of a particular party and haven't been tampered with on their way to you. However, it is prudent to regard an unsigned item, or an item without a valid signature, as a potential threat.

Assuming the signature is valid, you can use the information contained within that signature to make an additional determination—do you trust the person or organization that attached the signature to the file? If the publisher is reputable and the Security Warning message reports that the item has been digitally signed, you must then decide how much confidence you have in the publisher.

Normally, you make choices about whether or not to install a signed item on an individual basis. But you may choose to trust a particular publisher and allow their software to be installed automatically without any prompting. Or you may decide that the publisher of a particular program is not trustworthy and you do not want any products from that publisher to be installed on your computer, under any circumstances.

To block the installation of add-on programs from a given publisher, you first have to download and run a signed executable file from that publisher or visit a page that attempts to install a signed ActiveX control. To block an ActiveX control, follow these steps:

1. The Information bar should alert you that the website wants to install an ActiveX control. Click the Information bar and then click Install ActiveX Control from the menu. This action calls the Internet Explorer Add-on Installer, which requires an administrator's consent to run:

    ○ If your account is in the Administrators group, click Continue in the User Account Control dialog box.

    ○ If you're running under a Standard account, enter an administrator's user name and password in the User Account Control dialog box.

2. Click More Options to expand the dialog box and display the three options shown here.

3. Choose the Never Install Software from *<publisher>* option and click Don't Install.

After you make this choice, Internet Explorer will notify you any time you visit a site that tries to install or use software from the untrusted publisher. A Manage Add-Ons icon will appear in the status bar, at the right side of the bottom of the browser window. Also, a balloon tip will alert you that an add-on or program has been disabled or blocked.

To remove a publisher from the Untrusted Publishers list, choose Internet Options from the Tools menu in Internet Explorer. On the Content tab, click Publishers. Click the Untrusted Publishers tab, select the publisher name, and click Remove.

CAUTION

> Do not remove the two Microsoft Corporation entries from the Untrusted Publishers list. As the text in the Friendly Name column explains, these two entries represent certificates that were issued several years ago to an untrusted source and were signed with Microsoft's master certificate. The revocation means that a ne'er-do-well can't exploit these phony certificates to install a virus or Trojan horse program that appears to have been published by Microsoft.

Blocking Potentially Unsafe Downloads

Based on a survey of crashes submitted via the Online Crash Analysis tool in Windows XP, Microsoft concluded that roughly half of reported failures in the Windows operating system during the survey period were directly traceable to what it calls "deceptive software." As we explain in this section, spyware, adware, and other similarly unsavory types of software represent a major security risk.

How does deceptive software end up on a computer? The simplest route is the most direct: You click a link on a webpage or in an e-mail message that leads directly to an executable file. For example, an advertisement may make extravagant or alarming claims about a free program, perhaps even embedding the link in a pop-up window that looks like a warning dialog box generated by Windows. When an unsophisticated computer user clicks the ad, the program offers to install as an ActiveX control via an Authenticode dialog box, which can easily be mistaken for an official Windows stamp of approval.

In some cases, the setup routine for one program surreptitiously installs additional programs in the background. When we installed one widely used song-swapping program in a previous version of Windows, for instance, we found that it installed four well-hidden add-ons along with the main application, resulting in an increase in pop-up advertisements and changes to the way the browser handled search requests and mistyped URLs. The most vicious types of deceptive software typically attempt to exploit security holes to install themselves automatically, without your approval or even your knowledge.

It should come as no surprise that the makers of this sort of software employ all sorts of tricks to mislead, deceive, and cajole you into installing their wares, by extolling the program's benefits and glossing over or omitting any mention of its undesirable behavior. For someone with a basic understanding of computer security issues, the principal security concern when browsing is to ensure (insofar as it is possible) that anything you download is safe and that any potentially undesirable behavior is fully disclosed. If you share a computer or network with unsophisticated computer users who cannot reasonably be expected to consistently reject unsafe software, your goal should be to prevent them from having to make potentially confusing choices in the first place.

INSIDE OUT   Spyware? Adware? What's the difference?

Unfortunately, you'll find little consistency in the use of terms and descriptions when you read articles about unsafe or unwanted software. Some sources use the word *spyware* as a broad brush that covers even the most innocuous browser add-ons. In this book, we use the term *deceptive software* to refer to a wide continuum of programs, scripts, and browser add-ons that are typically installed without full disclosure of exactly how they work. Programs in this category interfere with legitimate requests to retrieve information from some websites and, in extreme cases, interfere with the operation of the computer itself. Some developers go out of their way to hide the fact that their program is installed at all and make the process of removing it as difficult as possible.

Depending on how a particular program or add-on works, you may hear it referred to by a number of specialized terms:

- *Spyware* is the term used to describe programs that gather information about you and your browsing activities without your knowledge and informed consent. These programs can store that information and use it to modify your computer's behavior, or they can send the data to the software developer or to a third party.

- *Adware* refers to a class of programs that display advertisements—usually in pop-up windows, on the desktop, or in the browser window. These programs often contain spyware-like features in that they monitor your movements around the web so that they can provide ads that are ostensibly related to your interests.

- *Home-page hijackers* are scripts or programs that modify your browser settings to change your default home page. This type of exploit often affects search settings as well. Some especially egregious offenders modify the registry or place files on the affected computer that block the user's ability to change these settings. The new home page is often disguised to look like a web portal or a legitimate search page, although a minority of programs in this category send the victim to X-rated sites.

In all three categories, the motive for infecting your computer is usually economic, with the owner receiving cash for referrals to webpages that originate from the stealthily installed program. Other examples of deceptive software—less common but more dangerous—include *dialers*, which configure a computer to make unsolicited (and usually expensive) dial-up connections, and *Trojan horses*, which allow an intruder to take over a compromised computer and use it to attack other computers or forward spam.

Chapter 27

For more information on stopping spyware and other such things, see "Stopping Spyware with Windows Defender" and "Blocking Viruses and Worms with an Antivirus Program," both in Chapter 10.

Downloading Executable Files

With each succeeding version of Windows (counting Windows XP Service Pack 2 as a new version), the number of protective layers between your computer and a piece of hostile code grows. In Windows Vista, when you click a link that points directly to an executable program file, Windows displays a Security Warning dialog box like the one shown in Figure 27-4.

Figure 27-4 The first of two separate Security Warnings to download and install a program in Internet Explorer.

If you click Run, Windows downloads the file to a temporary location and, when the download is complete, immediately runs the executable program as if you had double-clicked it yourself. If you click Save, you can download the file to a folder on your hard disk (the default location is the Downloads folder in your user profile). After the file is downloaded, you can click the Run button in the Download Complete dialog box or click Open Folder to open Windows Explorer, display the contents of the folder in which you saved the file, and double-click the file.

What happens next depends on the file type and whether the file is digitally signed.

- If the downloaded file is not executable, you see a warning dialog box asking whether you want to allow the program associated with that file type to open the downloaded file. In the example shown here, Windows is attempting to open a Microsoft Word document using the Microsoft Word Viewer program.

You can allow or refuse the request. If you click Allow and select the Do Not Show Me The Warning For This Program Again option, your choice is saved and applied to all further examples of this type of content. If you click Don't Allow, Windows ignores this option even if you select it.

- If the download is an unsigned executable file, you see a second Security Warning dialog box, shown in Figure 27-5, when you attempt to run it.

Figure 27-5 The second Security Warning dialog asks you to decide whether you want to run a program from an untrusted publisher.

Chapter 27

- If the download is a signed executable file, you see a UAC dialog box (like the one shown here) that requires you to enter an administrator's credentials to continue.

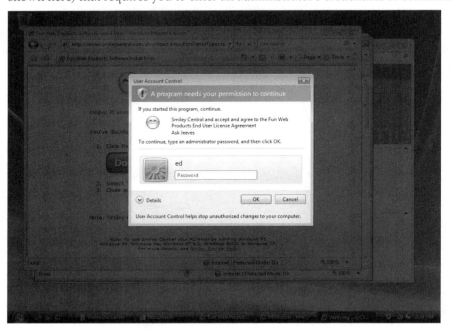

The color of the Windows security icon in each security-related dialog box indicates whether the program is digitally signed: A red icon indicates an unsigned program and a yellow icon identifies a signed program. (Non-executable files are indicated by a blue icon.) If you're certain that the program is safe, you can continue with the installation.

INSIDE OUT   How do you know that a program is safe?

When an executable file isn't digitally signed, it's impossible to make a definitive determination of whether it's safe. In those circumstances, you can't be too cautious. In our experience, you can tip the odds in your favor by using common sense. Make sure the download is from a verifiable source. Use your favorite search engine to look for complaints about the program or its publisher—be sure to search the web and popular newsgroups via MSN Communities (*http://www.vista-io.com/2703*) and Google Groups (*http://groups.google.com*)—and don't install anything until you're comfortable that you can resolve any reported problems if they crop up on your PC. Be sure to scan any downloaded files for viruses and spyware before installing. Finally, set a System Restore point before installing any software, so that you can undo the configuration changes if you're unhappy with the installation.

Keeping ActiveX Under Control

ActiveX controls are small programs that run inside the browser window to enhance the functionality of a website, using a technology developed by Microsoft. They're used for such things as enabling the capability for you to play games with other internet users, displaying stock tickers, and displaying animation. Microsoft's various update sites—Windows Update, Microsoft Update, and Office Update—use ActiveX controls to compare installed patches and updates on your system with those available on Microsoft's servers. ActiveX controls contain binary code and, like executables that you run from the Start menu or a command line, they essentially have full access to your computer's resources, although they are subject to some security restrictions.

> **Note**
>
> You cannot download an ActiveX control, scan it for viruses, and install it separately. ActiveX controls must be installed on the fly. Although the inability to scan for viruses in advance may sound like a security risk, you're protected from known viruses if you've configured your antivirus software to perform real-time scanning for hostile code. If the ActiveX control contains the signature of a known virus or worm or engages in suspicious behavior, the antivirus software will intercept it and refuse to allow the installation to proceed. As with any program you download and install, of course, you need to exercise caution and ensure that the download is safe before allowing it on your computer.

A default installation of Windows Vista contains dozens of ActiveX controls, some of which are highly specialized. In the past, unsavory operators have discovered flaws in these installed controls and devised exploits that take advantage of these flaws on unpatched machines to install unwanted or hostile code. An important security improvement in Internet Explorer 7 requires that you "opt in" with an additional layer of approval for these ActiveX controls. The first time you encounter a webpage that attempts to use a previously installed but never-used ActiveX control, Windows prompts you to give your permission, using a message in the Information bar, as shown in Figure 27-6.

This website wants to run the following add-on: 'Windows Media Player Extension' from 'Microsoft Corporation'. If you trust   ✖
the website and the add-on and want to allow it to run, click here...

Figure 27-6 If an unfamiliar website tries to use an obscure ActiveX control, Internet Explorer blocks the attempt with this display. Approve the action only if you're certain it's safe.

Some businesses refuse to allow the use of any ActiveX control that is not approved by an administrator. Others disallow all ActiveX controls. If you need to tighten the security settings imposed on ActiveX controls in the Internet zone, choose Internet Options from the Tools menu in Internet Explorer. On the Security tab, click Internet, and then click Custom Level. In the ActiveX Controls And Plug-ins section, adjust any of the options shown in Table 27-1 on the next page.

Table 27-1. ActiveX Security Settings

Setting	Description
Allow previously unused ActiveX controls to run without prompt	Disable (default) means that a website can use a previously installed but unused ActiveX control only with your explicit permission (enabling this option turns off the new opt-in ActiveX feature).
Allow Scriptlets	Disable (default) means that potentially dangerous custom objects called DHTML scriptlets won't be allowed to run in webpages.
Automatic prompting for ActiveX controls	Disable (default) displays the Information bar before allowing downloads; choose Enable to skip the Information bar and display a dialog box for all ActiveX controls.
Binary and script behaviors	Enable (default) allows scripts and programs to use an ActiveX control; choose Disable or Administrator Approved to tighten security.
Display video and animation on a webpage that does not use external media player	Disable (default) keeps ActiveX controls from using video and animations without invoking the normal media player context.
Download signed ActiveX controls	Prompt (default) requires that you confirm before installing a signed control; choose Disable to prevent installation. (Note: We strongly caution against choosing Enable, which weakens security to an unacceptable level.)
Download unsigned ActiveX controls	Disable (default) blocks installation of any unsigned control; choose Prompt if you need to install a custom control that is unsigned but trustworthy. (Note: Again, we strongly caution against choosing Enable, which weakens security to an unacceptable level.)
Initialize and script ActiveX controls not marked as safe	Disable (default) blocks any attempt to use an ActiveX control that is not specifically approved for use with scripts; choose Prompt to allow this type of activity on a case-by-case basis. (Note: As noted for the previous two settings, we strongly caution against choosing Enable, which weakens security to an unacceptable level.)
Run ActiveX controls and plug-ins	Enable (default) allows ActiveX controls to function, subject to other security settings; choose Prompt to approve each control as it's used, Disable to block use of all ActiveX controls, or Administrator Approved to allow only those that have been flagged as acceptable by an Administrator Administrator.
Script ActiveX controls marked safe for scripting	Enable (default) allows webpages to use script with certain ActiveX controls; choose Prompt to approve each control as it's used, or Disable to block all scripting of ActiveX controls.

Chapter 27

If you tighten any of these security settings and then visit a page that uses an ActiveX control, you may see one of the following messages in the Information Bar:

- "Your security settings do not allow websites to use ActiveX controls installed on your computer. This page may not display correctly. Click here for options...."

- "Internet Explorer has blocked this site from using an ActiveX control in an unsafe manner. As a result this page may not display correctly."

To work around either of these errors, you need to change the appropriate security setting for the Internet zone or add the site you're visiting to the Trusted Sites zone. For more information, see "Using and Customizing Internet Security Zones," Chapter 6.

Using Scripts Wisely

Scripts are small snippets of code, written in a scripting language such as JavaScript or VBScript, that run on the client computer (that is, *your* computer, not the web provider's) to enhance the functionality of a webpage. (A scripting language is a simple programming language designed to perform limited tasks.) These should be distinguished from Active Server Pages (webpages with the extension .asp or .aspx), which employ a server-side scripting technology and don't, by themselves, represent a security hazard.

Scripts are generally harmless and are widely used in modern web design. However, a would-be attacker can construct a hostile script to take advantage of security holes on a computer running Windows Vista; if the attacker can convince you to click on a link to a webpage that contains the hostile script, it can wreak havoc on an unpatched computer. Security experts sometimes advise users to disable active scripting as a security measure. If you decide to take this extreme step, be prepared for some of your favorite websites to stop working properly. (For instance, you can't search for articles in the Microsoft Knowledge Base when scripting is disabled.) To work around this limitation, you'll have to add sites—manually, one at a time—to the Trusted Sites zone.

With those caveats having been said, if you're still determined to disable scripting, follow these steps:

1. Choose Internet Options from the Tools menu.

2. On the Security tab, click the Internet icon and then click Custom Level.

3. In the Settings list, locate Active Scripting (under the Scripting heading) and click Disable.

4. Click OK to save your settings, and then click OK to close the Internet Options dialog box.

If this option is too extreme but you're still concerned about security risks from scripts, consider choosing Prompt instead of Disable in the Settings list. For sites in the Internet zone that use scripting, you'll be presented with several prompts such as this:

Installing, Removing, and Troubleshooting Add-ons

Internet Explorer is extraordinarily customizable. Developers and their add-ons can extend its capabilities in highly visible ways, by adding new toolbars, Explorer bars, menus, and buttons. A programmer can also hook into the browser's core features to extend its search capabilities, manage the process of filling in forms, and save bookmarks—these are just a few of the tricks that popular add-ons can perform. These add-ons most commonly take the form of browser extensions, browser helper objects (BHOs), toolbars, Java applets, and ActiveX controls.

Unfortunately, add-ons have a dark side as well. A poorly written add-on can interfere with the smooth operation of Internet Explorer, resulting in mysterious crashes and other glitches; a malicious add-on can cause unnecessary pop-up windows, slow system performance, and reveal details about you and your browsing habits to an untrusted third party. Windows Vista offers a Manage Add-Ons dialog box that shows you all currently installed add-ons and allows you to disable those that are suspicious or that you have determined are the cause of problems.

To open this dialog box, choose Manage Add-Ons from the Tools menu and select Enable or Disable Add-ons. Figure 27-7 shows this dialog box on a computer with a relatively small number of installed add-ons.

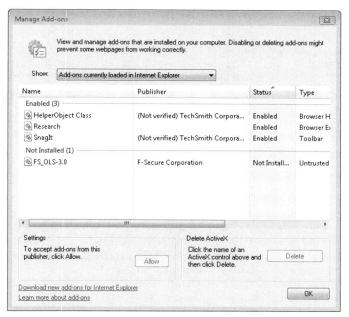

Figure 27-7 This dialog box shows add-ons currently in use by Internet Explorer as well as those you've blocked.

The Manage Add-ons dialog box displays a fair amount of detail about each add-on, including its publisher (if known), type, and the specific file with which it is associated. Use this list to enable or disable add-ons—click an entry in the list and choose Enable or Disable under Settings below. The drop-down Show list at the top of the dialog box allows you to toggle between a full list of all available add-ons and a shorter list of only those that are currently in use. In the case of ActiveX controls installed from websites (choose Downloaded ActiveX Controls from the Show menu to see this list), you can click the Delete button under the Delete ActiveX heading to completely remove the installed code. Note that the Delete option is not available for ActiveX controls that are installed along with Windows or a Windows program such as Microsoft Office or the Windows Live Toolbar; to remove those controls, use the Uninstall Or Change A Program option in Control Panel.

Unfortunately, the Manage Add-ons dialog box does not include a mechanism for removing add-ons. If you want to permanently remove one of the items on this list, you need to find the program that originally installed it and then remove that program. (Windows Defender may also be able to assist in removing known pests.) If you can't identify which program is responsible for a specific add-on, use your favorite search engine to look for clues, using the name of the add-on and the file with which it's associated as search terms. Be aware also that the Manage Add-ons dialog box may not detect all add-ons, especially hostile programs that were deliberately designed to thwart easy removal.

Chapter 27

Managing Cookies

A *cookie* is a small text file that enables a website to personalize its offerings in some way. The website downloads the cookie to your hard disk (Internet Explorer stores it in the folder %UserProfile%\Cookies\Low), and then reads the cookie from your hard disk on your subsequent visits to the site. Cookies can be used for a variety of purposes, such as recording logon information, shopping preferences, pages that you have visited, searches that you have performed, and so on. In general, cookies provide benefits to users as well as to web content providers. They make the websites you visit more responsive to your needs and preferences.

Nevertheless, because cookies can provide websites with personal information about you (an e-mail address or telephone number that you enter in a website when you request information, for example), and because some sites might not use this information in ways that you would regard as beneficial, cookies are a mixed blessing. A cookie can only provide a website with information that you supply while visiting the site (a cookie can't scurry around your hard disk, reading your address book and financial records, for example), and this information can be read only by the site that created the cookie. Nevertheless, because it's not always obvious who's sending you a cookie and what purposes that cookie will serve, many people are understandably wary about allowing cookies on their systems.

In versions earlier than Internet Explorer 6, your cookie management options were limited to allowing all cookies, blocking all cookies, or being prompted every time a site wanted to read or write a cookie. In practice, the second and third of these options created so much inconvenience that most users gave up and accepted all cookies. (Some sites will not even allow you to log on if you block all cookies, and if you request a confirmation prompt for every cookie transaction, you spend most of your web-browsing hours responding to confirmation prompts.)

Like its immediate predecessor, Internet Explorer 7 supports the Platform for Privacy Preferences (P3P) standard. This enables Internet Explorer to filter cookie transactions (that is, block cookies or admit them) on the basis of the cookie's content and purposes, in accordance with your stated privacy preferences. (For information about P3P, visit the World Wide Web Consortium site at *http://www.w3.org/P3P.*)

Sites that support P3P supply information about their use of cookies in the form of a *compact privacy statement*–special HTML tags embedded in the site's HTTP header that indicate what kind of cookies are used and for what purposes. When you access a site, Internet Explorer compares the site's compact privacy statement with your expressed privacy preferences and then accepts, blocks, or *restricts* the cookies. (To restrict a cookie means to allow it for the current session only, deleting it from your hard disk when you leave the website.) Thanks to Internet Explorer's P3P support, you can now choose to block certain kinds of cookies, while allowing the rest. (You can also still choose to be prompted each time a site wants to use a cookie.)

To express your preferences regarding cookies, open the Internet Options dialog box, click the Privacy tab (shown in Figure 27-8), and use the slider to choose one of the following settings:

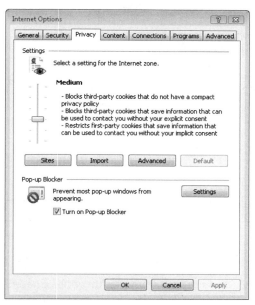

Figure 27-8 Use the slider in this dialog box to select a policy for accepting, rejecting, and restricting cookies based on their source and purpose.

- Block All Cookies
- High
- Medium High
- Medium
- Low
- Accept All Cookies

The default setting is Medium. Table 27-2 on the next page summarizes these options.

> **Note**
>
> If you don't see a slider on your Privacy tab, you are currently using "advanced" or imported privacy settings. You can clear those settings and make the slider appear by clicking Default.

Note

Your privacy setting applies only to sites in the Internet zone. By default, all cookies are accepted in the Trusted Sites and Local Intranet zones. (You can override these defaults by importing custom privacy settings. Doing so requires knowledge of XML programming; for details, see the overview "How to Create a Customized Privacy Import File" at *http://www.vista-io.com/2701*) Cookies from sites in the Restricted Sites zone are always rejected, and you can't override that default. For more information about Internet Explorer's security zones, see "Using and Customizing Internet Security Zones," earlier in this chapter.

Table 27-2. Effects of Privacy Settings on New and Existing Cookies

Privacy Setting	Effects
Block All Cookies	• Blocks all new cookies • Prevents websites from reading existing cookies • Ignores per-site settings
High	• Blocks cookies from sites that do not have a compact privacy statement • Blocks cookies that use personally identifiable information without your explicit consent • Allows websites to read existing cookies • Can be overridden by per-site settings
Medium High	• Blocks cookies from third-party sites that do not have a compact privacy statement • Blocks third-party cookies that use personally identifiable information without your explicit consent • Blocks first-party cookies that use personally identifiable information without your implicit consent • Allows websites to read existing cookies • Can be overridden by per-site settings
Medium (default)	• Blocks third-party cookies that do not have a compact privacy statement • Blocks third-party cookies that use personally identifiable information without your implicit consent • Accepts first-party cookies that use personally identifiable information without your implicit consent, but deletes those cookies when you close Internet Explorer • Allows websites to read existing cookies • Can be overridden by per-site settings

Low	• Blocks third-party cookies from sites that do not have a compact privacy statement
	• Accepts cookies from third-party sites that use personally identifiable information without your explicit consent, but deletes those cookies when you close Internet Explorer
	• Accepts all first-party cookies
	• Allows websites to read existing cookies
	• Can be overridden by per-site settings
Accept All Cookies	• Accepts all new cookies
	• Allows websites to read existing cookies
	• Ignores per-site settings

To make an informed choice, you need to understand the following terms:

- **Compact privacy statement**   Information in a website's HTTP header that indicates the source, purpose, and lifetime of cookies used by that site. (Some cookies, called *session cookies*, are designed to be deleted when you leave a site. Other cookies have a fixed expiration date—usually sometime in the next decade or beyond.)

- **Personally identifiable information**   Information that a site could use to contact you, such as your name, e-mail address, or home or work address; also, the credentials (name and password) you use to log on to a site.

- **Explicit consent**   Giving explicit consent, also known as *opting in*, means that you have taken some kind of affirmative step to allow a site to use personally identifiable information.

- **Implicit consent**   To consent implicitly means not to have *opted out*—that is, not to have taken an affirmative step to deny a website permission to use personally identifiable information.

- **First-party cookie**   A cookie used by the site that you are currently viewing. First-party cookies are generally used to personalize your experience with a website.

- **Third-party cookie**   A cookie used by a site other than the one you're currently viewing—such as an advertiser on the site you're currently viewing.

Chapter 27

Note

Some websites will not function at all if you block their cookies. If you find that a particular site you trust does not let you on with your current privacy setting, you can make an exception for that site, and change your setting in Internet Explorer to accept all of that site's cookies, regardless of your current privacy setting.

Viewing a Site's Privacy Report

When Internet Explorer blocks or restricts a cookie, it displays this icon on your status bar. (Choose View, Status Bar, if your status bar is not visible.)

To find out what cookie was blocked and why, double-click this icon. You will see the site's Privacy Report dialog box, which will indicate which cookies were blocked or restricted. To learn more about why a cookie was blocked or restricted, double-click it in the Privacy Report dialog box.

To read the privacy report for any site, and to find out whether or not Internet Explorer has blocked or restricted cookies from that site, choose Page, Webpage Privacy Policy. Figure 27-9 shows part of the Privacy Report dialog box for the Microsoft Encarta website (*http://encarta.msn.com*). Note that several cookies have been served and that all of them have been accepted—that is, they have met the privacy specifications for this user. If a cookie had been rejected, the word *Blocked* would have appeared in the Cookies column. You can limit the dialog box to show only the names of sites with blocked cookies by selecting Restricted Websites from the Show list.

Figure 27-9 A site's privacy report provides information about all parties contributing content to that site. Double-click a site URL to read its privacy policy (if any).

Double-clicking the entry for the first accepted cookie in this example reveals the privacy statement for Microsoft Corporation, shown in Figure 27-10.

Figure 27-10 This Privacy Policy dialog box shows the privacy policy for an accepted cookie.

Overriding Your Privacy Settings for Particular Websites

If, after reading a site's privacy statement (or discovering that it doesn't have one that conforms to the P3P standard), you decide that you want to block or accept all cookies from that site, regardless of the privacy setting that you have chosen in the Internet Options dialog box, select either Always Allow This Site To Use Cookies or Never Allow This Site To Use Cookies in the site's Privacy Policy dialog box.

You can also specify per-site privacy settings by clicking Sites on the Privacy tab of the Internet Options dialog box. The Per Site Privacy Actions dialog box appears, as shown in Figure 27-11 on the next page. To allow or block all cookies from a site, enter the site's address and then click Allow or Block. As you add settings for individual sites, the sites will be listed in the Managed Websites portion of the dialog box.

Figure 27-11 The Per Site Privacy Actions dialog box lists all sites that you designate to be exceptions to your privacy policy.

Dispensing with Automatic Cookie Handling

If you want, you can tell Internet Explorer to forget about privacy settings assigned on a site-by-site basis and institute uniform policies for all first-party and all third-party cookies regardless of their sites of origin. For example, you can tell Internet Explorer to accept all first-party cookies and to issue a prompt for all third-party cookies (allowing you to block or accept third-party cookies on a case-by-case basis). To override automatic cookie handling, click Advanced on the Privacy tab of the Internet Options dialog box. The Advanced Privacy Settings dialog box appears, as shown in Figure 27-12.

Figure 27-12 Clicking Advanced on the Privacy tab of the Internet Options dialog box lets you institute uniform policies for all first-party and third-party cookies.

This dialog box also includes a check box that tells Internet Explorer to accept all session cookies, which are cookies that a website will delete at the end of your current session. Session cookies are usually benign (they're used for such things as keeping track of what's in your shopping cart), so if you are planning to override automatic cookie handling, this is normally a safe option to select.

Asking Internet Explorer to prompt you for all third-party cookies is an excellent way to learn which of the sites you visit regularly rely on third-party cookies. After a few days' experience with this setting, you can return to automatic cookie handling and tell Internet Explorer to always block cookies from any particularly troublesome third parties that you notice.

> ### Note
>
> Per-site settings trump advanced settings. If you decide to block either first-party or third-party cookies (or both) through the Advanced Privacy Settings dialog box, be sure to remove any per-site settings that allow cookies. Otherwise, the sites to which you gave carte blanche earlier will continue to drop cookies on your plate. To do this, click Edit on the Privacy tab of the Internet Options dialog box. Select specific sites, and click Remove, or simply click Remove All.

Advanced settings don't affect cookies already stored on your computer. Be sure to delete existing cookies for sites that you want to block (or be prompted for). Otherwise, those sites will continue to read your current cookie data. (You might want to back up those cookies before deleting them—just in case you find that a site doesn't work without its cookies.)

Backing Up Cookies

Because cookies—particularly the ones you intentionally allow your system to accept—are more likely to be beneficial than harmful, it's smart to back them up from time to time. Internet Explorer's Import/Export Wizard lets you do just that. Tap the Alt key to make the menu bar visible, and then click Import And Export on the File menu. Follow the wizard's steps to export your cookies. The wizard creates a single text file, stored by default in your Documents folder.

The command to export cookies was included in Internet Explorer to provide users with a way to transfer their cookies to the format used by Netscape browsers. But it works just as well as a backup tool. If you ever need to restore your cookies, run the Import/Export Wizard again, and point the wizard to the file you exported earlier.

Chapter 27

Managing Internet Explorer's Cache and History

Internet Explorer's cache (also known as the Temporary Internet Files folder) and browsing history are items that have changed little since previous versions of Internet Explorer. One notable exception is the location for these items. Since Internet Explorer now uses Protected Mode for most browsing, the cache and history folders are now considered virtual folders with the same low privilege as that of the Internet Explorer process itself. Improvements have also been made to the built-in management of the cache to keep it from growing too large.

Changing the Size of the Cache

Temporary Internet files are stored by default in various subfolders of the hidden system folder %LocalAppData%\Microsoft\Windows\Temporary Internet Files. If you're curious about the contents of the cache, you can take a look at it as follows:

1. Choose Tools, Internet Options, and click the General tab.

2. Within the Browsing History section, click Settings.

3. In the Settings dialog box, shown in Figure 27-13, click View Files.

On some systems you can free up some disk space without suffering any loss of browsing functionality by reducing the cache size. If you have ample free disk space, you can increase the likelihood that a page you visit will be kept in the cache by increasing the cache size. (The minimum allowed size is 8 MB, and the maximum size is 1024 MB. By default, Internet Explorer sets the cache to a reasonable 50 MB.) To adjust the cache size, display the Settings dialog box and use the down arrow to reduce the size of the cache (or enter a smaller number in the edit box).

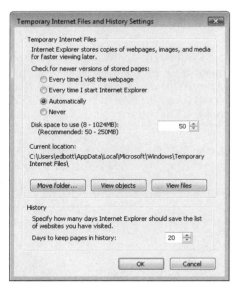

Figure 27-13 The Settings dialog box lets you control how Internet Explorer uses its web cache.

Moving the Cache

If you want to move the cache—to a different disk, for example—you can do that from the Settings dialog box as well. Click Move Folder. In the Browse For Folder dialog box, select the new folder and click OK. Note that you must log off and then log back on again to complete the move.

Controlling How Internet Explorer Uses the Cache

The Settings dialog box gives you four options that control how Internet Explorer exploits its web cache. Each option strikes a different balance between the desire for quick display and the need for current information. As you consider these options, remember that the cache is particularly critical to performance on systems that use a dial-up connection to the internet. If you're working with a broadband connection, the benefit you receive by having Internet Explorer reload pages from the cache is considerably less significant (but still noticeable on some pages, especially those that contain large graphics).

The options are as follows:

- **Every Time I Visit The Webpage**   This option causes Internet Explorer to check the web for newer versions of cached pages every time you visit those pages. If the temporary files are still current, Internet Explorer displays them. Otherwise, it downloads new pages and displays them. This option ensures that the information you see is always current, but it can slow your browsing.

- **Every Time I Start Internet Explorer**   This option causes Internet Explorer to check for newer versions once per Internet Explorer session. A check is made the first time you visit a page after you open Internet Explorer, but not again until you close and reopen the browser. If, however, you have Internet Explorer open over the course of several days and you revisit a page that you visited on a previous day, Internet Explorer does check the files again.

- **Automatically**   This option, the default, is the same as the Every Time You Start Internet Explorer option, except that Internet Explorer tabulates how often pages are actually updated. If a page is not updated frequently, Internet Explorer reduces the frequency with which it checks that page.

- **Never**   With this option, Internet Explorer never checks for newer files and always displays what is in the cache.

Chapter 27

INSIDE OUT   **Ensure that the webpage is up-to-date**

If Internet Explorer appears to be reading from the cache when it should be downloading afresh (for example, if you find yourself looking at yesterday's headlines on a newspaper site), hold down the Shift key while you click Refresh.

Emptying the Cache Automatically

Some users who are particularly concerned with privacy like to cover their tracks by having Internet Explorer purge the web cache whenever they quit the browser. To do this, follow these steps:

1. Choose Tools, Internet Options.

2. Click the Advanced tab.

3. In the Security section of the Settings list, select Empty Temporary Internet Files Folder When Browser Is Closed.

Blocking Objectionable Content

The internet undoubtedly has something to offend every taste and moral standard. Although objectionable content is not a security issue in the sense that it threatens the well-being of your hardware and data, some users might consider it a threat to other aspects of their well-being, so we'll briefly discuss the most important features of Internet Explorer's Content Advisor. When Content Advisor is enabled, if a user tries to go to a webpage that is beyond the limits you set, Internet Explorer won't show the page. Instead it displays a warning message. Users who know the supervisor password (you supply this password when you first enable Content Advisor) can bypass the warning and view the page.

Content Advisor has been a part of Internet Explorer for many years. Windows Vista introduces a separate feature called Parental Controls, which allows you to configure a much more complex set of rules for a child's use of the computer. Using Parental Controls, you can define the hours during which a child can use the internet, which programs can be used, and several other settings related to the safety of the child's computing experience. The use of Content Advisor is more restrictive overall and less flexible than the Parental Controls feature in Windows Vista. You can find more information on Parental Controls in the section "Controlling Your Children's Computer Access," Chapter 10.

Internet Explorer's Content Advisor uses the Internet Content Rating Association (ICRA) system. Content Advisor can be found from within the Content tab of Tools, Internet Options, in Internet Explorer by clicking Enable within the Content Advisor section. The Content Advisor dialog box is shown in Figure 27-14.

Figure 27-14 The Content Advisor is used to set and work with rating systems.

Note

You can also install other rating systems, although ICRA ratings are currently applied to more websites than any other system. To learn about other systems, click the Find Rating Systems button on the General tab.

Blocking Unrated Sites

Not all internet content is rated. By default, Content Advisor blocks pages that don't have a rating, simply because it has no way of knowing what types of content are on such pages. Just as when you attempt to view a site with unacceptable ratings, when you attempt to view an unrated site, you'll see a dialog box similar to the one shown in Figure 27-15 on the next page.

Figure 27-15 Content Advisor blocks pages with ratings beyond the limits you set and pages that aren't rated.

If you don't want this type of protection, you can change the default behavior. Open Internet Options, click the Content tab, and then click Settings within the Content Advisor section. In the Content Advisor dialog box, click the General tab, shown in Figure 27-16, and select Users Can See Websites That Have No Rating.

Figure 27-16 The General tab lets you block unrated sites, bypass blocking, and change the supervisor password.

Because so many sites are unrated—including both "good" sites and "bad" ones—Content Advisor lets you create your own ratings for particular sites. To set up a list of sites that you want to allow or disallow, regardless of their claimed content rating, click the

Approved Sites tab in the Content Advisor dialog box. Type each site's URL and then click Always or Never.

Turning Off Blocking

If you change your mind about blocking offensive material, simply display the Internet Options dialog box, click the Content tab, click the Disable button, and then enter your supervisor password. Blocking will remain turned off until and unless you return and click the Enable button (which alternates with the Disable button).

Saving and Applying Internet Explorer Settings

Businesses have been using the Internet Explorer Administration Kit (IEAK) to customize and control their installations of Internet Explorer for years. Likewise, some internet service providers (ISPs) use this tool to create and distribute custom editions of Internet Explorer that are branded with the name of the ISP and hard-wired with links to the ISP's services. Available in several languages, the IEAK is helpful in situations where you want to customize the Internet Explorer interface and control browser settings, especially those related to security.

IEAK 7 (the version that works with Internet Explorer 7) is a free program that must be installed separately from Windows (details and download links can be found at *http://www.vista-io.com/2702*). The wizard-driven interface, the first stage of which is shown in Figure 27-17, makes the process of creating a custom distribution of Internet Explorer relatively easy.

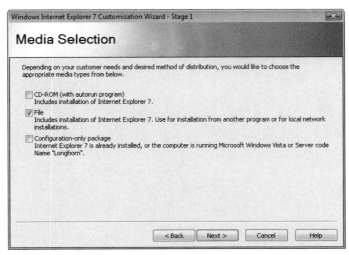

Figure 27-17 IEAK 7 offers a wizard-driven method for customizing an Internet Explorer deployment.

IEAK 7 gives the administrator greater control of the Internet Explorer environment within an organization. For example, a business might use IEAK 7 to create an Internet Explorer installation bundle with custom menu bars. The custom installation packages can be distributed in several different ways, including via CD-ROM, as downloadable files, and in a configuration-only option, where Internet Explorer settings can be applied to a system where Internet Explorer 7 has already been installed.

Some of the customizations available with IEAK 7 enable you to choose which search provider is installed as the default, shown in Figure 27-18. You can also set the default homepage, make IE the default browser, make Security Zone changes, install additional software along with IE, and set Favorites, among many other options. You can even adjust advanced settings, such as defining a custom HTTP User-Agent string which can then be used to help track users who are using the customized browser.

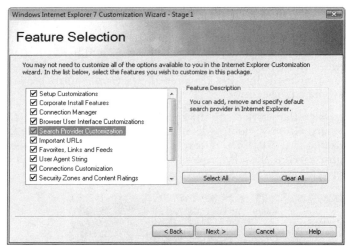

Figure 27-18 Customizing the default search provider is one of many items that can be configured with IEAK 7.

Managing Disks and Drives

Home Basic ●
Home Premium ●
Business ●
Enterprise ●
Ultimate ●

When you get right down to it, storage defines what you can and can't do with Microsoft Windows Vista. A big hard disk (or two or three) makes it possible for you to download and store an enormous amount of digital music, photos, and video; record and preserve television shows; manage large-scale data-intensive projects; and keep your entire collection of digital resources safely backed up.

Using today's gigantic disks effectively, however, often entails partitioning them intelligently, so that separate volumes can be assigned distinct purposes. For a variety of reasons, for example, we recommend that you keep your operating system and personal data on separate volumes, that (if possible) you make a full image backup of the volume on which your Windows system files are stored, and that you make regular and frequent backups of your valuable data. All of this requires some planning and some familiarity with the tools that Windows Vista provides for managing disk resources.

For more information about file management, see Chapter 7, "Managing Files, Folders, and Drives." For more information about backing up, see Chapter 20, "Performing Routine Maintenance."

What's in Your Edition?
Disk management is the same in all editions of Windows Vista.

The principal disk-management tool in Windows Vista and the subject of most of this chapter is the Disk Management console. For those who need to incorporate disk-management tasks in scripts (as well as for those who simply prefer carrying out administrative tasks at the command prompt), Windows also provides a powerful command-prompt program called Diskpart. Everything that you can do with Disk Management you can also do using Diskpart; you just have to work harder (in our opinion) and more carefully.

If you've worked with the disk-management tools in Windows XP or Windows 2000, you'll find significant improvements in Windows Vista. Most notably, you can now shrink partitions as well as expand them from within the console. If you have a writeable CD or DVD drive, you'll also appreciate Windows Vista's support for the Universal Disk Format (UDF). With UDF, you can write folders and files to CDs and DVDs as easily (if not as quickly) as you can write them to a hard disk. And if, like many others, you rely on portable computers or external hard disks (USB or IEEE 1394 drives) you will be pleased to know that Windows now supports dynamic disks as well as basic disks on those devices.

Running Disk Management

To run Disk Management, do any of the following:

- At a command prompt, type **diskmgmt.msc**.

- Right-click Computer and choose Manage. The Computer Management console appears. In the console tree (the left pane), select Disk Management.

- In Control Panel, choose System and Maintenance. Then, under the heading Administrative Tools, choose Create And Format Hard Disk Partitions.

Whatever route you take, you'll pass a UAC prompt along the way. Managing disks requires an administrative token. Figure 28-1 illustrates the Disk Management console.

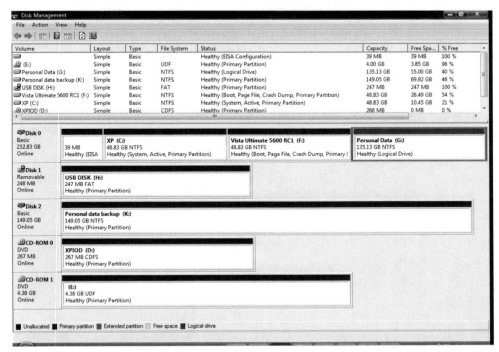

Figure 28-1 Use the Disk Management console to gather information about and manage hard disks and removable disks.

As you can see, Disk Management provides a wealth of information about physical disks and the volumes, partitions, and logical drives in place on those disks. You can use this utility to perform the following disk-related tasks:

- Check the size, file system, status, and other properties of disks and volumes

- Create, format, and delete partitions, logical drives, and dynamic volumes

- Assign drive letters to hard disk volumes, removable disk drives, and optical drives

- Create mounted drives

- Convert basic disks to dynamic disks, and vice versa

- Create spanned and striped volumes

- Extend or shrink partitions

The Disk Management display is in two panes, with a movable horizontal divider between them. In its default arrangement, the upper pane lists each volume on your system and provides information about the volume's type, status, capacity, available free space, and so on. You can carry out commands on a volume by right-clicking in the first column of this pane (the column labeled *Volume*) and choosing from the shortcut menu.

The lower pane provides a graphical display, in which each row is devoted to one physical storage device. In the headings at the left of each row you see the name by which the device is known to the operating system (Disk 0, Disk 1, and so on), along with the device's type, size, and online status. To the right of these headings are rectangles representing the volumes of each device. Note that, although the rectangles are of varying sizes, they are by no means drawn to scale! (In Figure 28-1, for example, the 149 GB drive K appears to be nearly four times as large as the 153 GB drive G.) To assess the size of a volume, read the numbers—and note the units!

Right-clicking a heading at the left in the lower pane provides a menu of commands pertinent to an entire storage device. Right-clicking a volume rectangle provides a menu of actions that can be applied to that volume.

Managing Disks from the Command Prompt

To use the Diskpart command-line tool, start by running Cmd.exe with elevated privileges. You can do that by opening the Start menu and choosing All Programs, Accessories. In the Accessories submenu, right-click Command Prompt, choose Run As Administrator, and then reply to the UAC prompt.

For more about the Command Prompt, see Appendix B, "Working with the Command Prompt."

When you run the Diskpart command, it opens a console window and dumps you at the DISKPART> prompt. If you type **help** and press Enter, you see a screen that lists all available commands, like the one shown here:

Because Diskpart can do everything that the Disk Management console can do, it's invaluable for script writers or anyone who simply prefers working at a command prompt. Even if you fall into neither of those categories, you should know about Diskpart, because if you ever find yourself needing to manage hard disks from the Windows Recovery Environment (WinRE), you will have access to Diskpart but not to the Disk Management console. (WinRE is a special environment that you can use for system-recovery purposes if a major hardware or software problem prevents you from starting Windows.)

> For more about WinRE, see Chapter 24, "Recovering after a Computer Crash."

Windows also includes a second command-line tool for file-system and disk management, called Fsutil. This utility allows you to find files by security identifier (SID), change the short name of a file, and perform other esoteric tasks.

> **CAUTION**
>
> FSUtil and Diskpart are indisputably powerful, but they're not for the faint of heart or for casual experimentation. Both are intended primarily to be incorporated into scripts rather than for interactive use. Diskpart in particular is dense and cryptic, with a complex structure that requires you to list and select objects before you act on them. All but the most experienced Windows users should stick with the graphical tool whenever possible. For more details about Diskpart, see Knowledge Base article 300415, "A Description of the Diskpart Command-Line Utility." Although this article dates from Windows XP days and some of the comparisons it makes between Diskpart and the Disk Management console are out of date, its information about the syntax and usage of Diskpart is still accurate.

Understanding Disk Management Terminology

The Windows Vista version of Disk Management has simplified somewhat the arcane language of disk administration. Nevertheless, it's still important to have a bit of the vocabulary under your belt. The following terms and concepts are the most important.

- **Volume** A *volume* is a disk or subdivision of a disk that is formatted and available for storage. If a volume is assigned a drive letter, as volumes generally are, it appears as a separate entity in Windows Explorer. (See the following paragraph for a type of volume that is *not* assigned a drive letter.) A hard disk may have one, several, or many volumes.

- **Mounted drive** A *mounted drive* is a volume that is mapped to an empty folder on an NTFS-formatted disk. A mounted drive does not get a drive letter and does not appear separately in Windows Explorer. Instead, it behaves as though it were a subfolder on another volume.

- **Format** To *format* a disk is to prepare it for storage using a particular file system (such as NTFS).

- **File System** A *file system* is a method for organizing folders (directories) and files on a storage medium. Windows Vista supports the following file systems: FAT

(File Allocation Table), NTFS (NT File System), CDFS (Compact Disc File System, also sometimes identified as ISO-9660), and UDF (Universal Disk Format).

- **Basic Disk** and **Dynamic Disk** The two principal types of hard-disk organization in Windows are called *basic* and *dynamic*.

  - ○ A basic disk can be subdivided into as many as four partitions. (The four-partition limit applies only to disks that use a Master Boot Record. Disks that use a GUID Partition Table can have more.) What all basic-disk volumes have in common is that their storage space must reside on a single physical disk. That is, their volumes are all *simple* volumes. When you use the Windows Vista Disk Management console to create new simple volumes, the first three partitions it creates are *primary partitions*. The fourth is created as an *extended partition* using all remaining unallocated space on the disk. An extended partition can be organized into as many as 2000 *logical disks*. In use, a logical disk behaves exactly like a primary partition; you format it, assign it a drive letter, and store your stuff on it.

  - ○ A dynamic disk offers organizational options not available on a basic disk. In addition to simple volumes, dynamic disks can contain *spanned* or *striped* volumes. These last two volume types combine space from multiple disks. Dynamic disks cannot be accessed directly from Windows 9x, Windows NT, or Windows XP Home Edition running on the same computer in a dual-boot configuration. (Shared folders on dynamic disks can be accessed across a network from any of these systems, however.)

- **Simple volume** A *simple volume* is a volume contained entirely within a single physical device. On a basic disk, a simple volume is also known as a partition.

- **Spanned volume** A *spanned volume* is a volume that combines space from physically separate disks, making the combination appear and function as though it were a single storage medium. Spanned volumes can be created only on dynamic disks.

- **Striped volume** A *striped volume* is a volume in which data is stored in 64 KB strips across physically separate disks in order to improve performance. Striped volumes can be created only on dynamic disks.

- **Mirrored** and **RAID-5 volumes** Mirrored and RAID-5 volumes are types of dynamic volumes that are *not* available in Windows Vista (they require a server edition of Windows). They use redundant storage methods to provide *fault tolerance*.

- **MBR** and **GPT disks** *MBR (Master Boot Record)* and *GPT (GUID Partition Table)* are terms describing alternative methods for maintaining the information regarding a disk's subdivisions. GPT disks support larger volumes (up to 18 exabytes) and more partitions (as many as 128 on a basic disk). You can convert a disk from MBR to GPT (or vice versa) only before a disk has been partitioned for the first time (or after all partitions have been removed).

- **Active partition, boot partition,** and **system partition** The *active partition* is the one from which an x86-based computer starts after you power it up. It must always

Chapter 28

be on the first physical hard disk attached to the system (Disk 0). The *boot partition* is the partition where the Windows system files are located. The *system partition* is the partition that contains the bootstrap files that Windows uses to start your system and display the boot menu. (That's right; the boot partition contains the system files, and the system partition is the one from which the computer boots.)

Formatting Disks

You have to format a disk before you can put anything on it. The Disk Management wizards that assist you in creating simple, spanned, or striped volumes all include a formatting step (it's assumed that you want to format the new volume so that you can actually do something with it—although the step is optional). You can also format a volume in Disk Management by right-clicking its rectangle in the graphical display (the lower pane) and choosing Format from the shortcut menu. (You cannot format the active, boot, or system partition, however.) Outside of Disk Management, you can format a volume in Windows Explorer (right click, choose Format, and reply to the UAC prompt) or from the command prompt (use the Format command; type **format /?** to see the available options). The formatting dialog box employed by Disk Management looks like this:

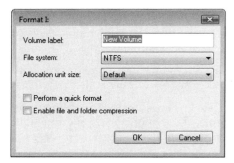

Your choices are as follows:

- **File System** For hard disk volumes larger than 4 GB (4096 MB), your only option is NTFS. For removable media such as USB flash disks, your choices also include FAT and FAT32. For writeable optical media, your choices are limited to UDF in various revisions. All these choices are described in the following section, "Choosing a File System."

- **Allocation Unit Size** The allocation unit size (also known as the cluster size) is the smallest space that can be allocated to a file. The Default option, in which Windows Vista selects the appropriate cluster size based on volume size, is the best choice here.

- **Volume Label** The volume label identifies the drive in Windows Explorer's Computer window. The default label text is New Volume. (You can change this text at any time, as explained in "Assigning or Changing a Volume Label," later in this chapter.

Select Perform A Quick Format if you want Disk Management to skip the sometimes lengthy process of checking the disk media. Select Enable File And Folder Compression if you want all data on the new volume to use NTFS compression. (This option is unavailable if your volume is not to be formatted with NTFS.)

INSIDE OUT   Formatting does *not* remove a volume's data

Whatever formatting options you choose, you will be warned that the action of formatting a volume makes that volume's data inaccessible. That's true. Whatever data is there when you format will no longer be available to you by normal means after you format. Unless you use the /p switch, the data remains in some form, however. If you're really concerned about covering tracks, either use format /p:*x* (where *x* represents the number of passes) or wipe the disk after you format it, by using the command-line program cipher.exe, with the /w switch. (Type **cipher /?** at the command prompt for details.) Curiously enough, the cipher command does not require an administrative token.

Choosing a File System

File system choices available to you depend on the type of media you are formatting. With hard disks, the only option made available by Disk Management is NTFS. If you want to format a hard disk in FAT or FAT32, you need to use the command-prompt Format command, with the /fs switch. (Type **format /?** at the command prompt for details.) The only good reason to do this, however, is for the sake of compatibility with systems running Windows 9x. (See "The Advantages of NTFS," later in this chapter.) If you're dual-booting with Windows 9x and want the data on the volume you're formatting to be accessible to the Windows 9x partition, you should choose FAT32. Note that the 16-bit FAT, while still available, is a relic of much older days when disks were dramatically smaller. It's appropriate for floppy disks and very small hard-disk partitions only.

If you're formatting a USB flash disk, on the other hand, FAT32 is a reasonable choice. In the first place, a flash disk is likely to serve at times as a transfer medium, possibly with systems running earlier versions of Windows. Secondly, because NTFS is a journaling file system, reading and writing files on NTFS disks involves more disk IO than similar operations on FAT32 disks. Flash disks can perform a finite number of reads and writes before they need to be replaced—hence they will likely have a longer life expectancy under FAT32 than under NTFS.

Choosing the Right UDF Version for Optical Media

If you're formatting a writeable CD or DVD disc, your choices are various flavors of the Universal Disk Format (UDF). UDF, a successor to the CD-ROM file system (CDFS), is an evolving specification. The latest version supported by Windows Vista is version 2.50. Other supported versions are 1.50, 2.00, and 2.01. Which to choose? It depends on whether you want the CDs or DVDs that you generate to be readable on systems running earlier versions of Windows or Windows Server 2003. The differences are as follows:

- **Version 1.50** Can be read on systems running Windows 2000, Windows XP, and Windows Server 2003.

- **Version 2.00 or 2.01** Cannot be read on Windows 2000. Can be read on Windows XP and Windows Server 2003. Note that Version 2.01 is a minor revision of version 2.00. There is no reason to prefer version 2.00.

- **Version 2.50** Cannot be read on other versions of Windows.

Note that all of these variants are afforded read-write support by Windows Vista, and that none of them are supported in any form on Windows 9x platforms.

Choosing Between UDF and Mastered Optical Media

You do not have to format a CD or DVD in UDF to store files on it. You can *burn* files to optical media in the manner introduced by Windows XP—by copying files to temporary folder and transferring them *en masse* to the CD or DVD. Using UDF is somewhat more convenient, because it allows you to read and write CD or DVD files as though they were stored on a USB flash disk or floppy disk. But the older method, sometimes called Mastered or ISO, offers greater compatibility with computers running other operating systems, and it's the only method that allows you to burn audio files and play them back on consumer audio devices. For more information, see "Storing Files on CDs and DVDs," Chapter 7.

The Advantages of NTFS

In compensation for its incompatibility with Windows 9x, NTFS offers a number of important advantages over the earlier FAT and FAT32 file systems:

- **Security** On an NTFS volume, you can restrict access to files and folders using permissions, as described in Chapter 29, "Controlling Access to Files and Folders." You can add an extra layer of protection by encrypting files. On a FAT or FAT32 drive, anyone with physical access to your computer can access any files stored on that drive.

- **Reliability** Because NTFS is a journaling file system, an NTFS volume can recover from disk errors more readily than a FAT32 volume. NTFS uses log files to keep track of all disk activity. In the event of a system crash, Windows Vista can use this journal to repair file system errors automatically when the system is restarted. In addition, NTFS can dynamically remap clusters that contain bad sectors and mark those clusters as bad so that the operating system no longer uses them. FAT and FAT32 drives are more vulnerable to disk errors.

- **Expandability** Using NTFS-formatted volumes, you can expand storage on existing volumes without having to back up, repartition, reformat, and restore.

- **Efficiency** On partitions greater than 8 GB, NTFS volumes manage space more efficiently than FAT32. The maximum partition size for a FAT32 drive created by Windows Vista is 32 GB; by contrast, you can create a single NTFS volume of up to 16 terabytes (16,384 GB) using default settings, and by tweaking cluster sizes, you can ratchet the maximum volume size up to 256 terabytes.

- **Optimized Storage of Small Files** Files on the order of a hundred bytes or less can be stored entirely within the Master File Table (MFT) record, rather than requiring a minimum allocation unit outside the MFT. This results in greater storage efficiency for small files.

For more information about the advantages of NTFS and about file-system choices in Windows Vista, see the excellent white paper at *http://www.vista-io.com/2801*.

Converting a FAT32 Disk to NTFS

To convert a FAT or FAT32 disk to NTFS, use the command-line Convert utility. The essential syntax is as follows:

```
convert d: /fs:ntfs
```

where *d* is the drive letter you want to convert. For information about optional parameters, type **convert /?** at the command prompt.

The Convert utility can do its work within Windows if the drive to be converted is not in use. However, if you want to convert the system volume or a volume that holds a page file, you might see an error message when you run Convert. In that case, you must schedule the conversion to occur the next time you start Windows. After you restart the computer, you'll see a prompt that warns you that the conversion is about to begin. You have 10 seconds to cancel the conversion. If you allow it to proceed, Windows will run the Chkdsk utility and perform the conversion automatically. During this process, your computer will restart twice.

CAUTION

Converting your system drive to NTFS makes it impossible to restore your previous operating system, a fact the Convert utility warns you about in no uncertain terms. If you have set up your system using a multiboot configuration so that you can continue to run Windows 9x, do not convert the system drive to NTFS; doing so will make it impossible to start your previous Windows version.

INSIDE OUT **Align clusters before you convert to NTFS**

If you have a drive larger than 512 MB and it was originally formatted as a FAT32 volume using a version of Windows earlier than Windows XP, its 4-KB clusters are probably not aligned on 4-KB boundaries. This situation causes the Convert program to create 512-byte clusters when it converts the drive to NTFS. Because 512-byte clusters generally provide poorer performance than 4-KB clusters, you'll be better off if you realign the partition before you convert, by moving the data area up to a 4-KB boundary. Windows doesn't include a tool for realigning partitions in this manner, but BootIt Next Generation (BootIt NG), a shareware program available at *http://www.vista-io.com/2802*, can perform that task. In BootIt NG, use the Slide button in the Work With Partitions dialog box; be sure to select the Align For NTFS Only check box.

Creating New Volumes

Disk Management allows you to create three kinds of new volumes—simple, spanned, and striped. You'll find the commands for creating these new volumes in the graphical pane of the Disk Management console.

Creating a New Simple Volume

To create a new simple volume on a basic or dynamic disk, you need free space on the disk. In Disk Management, free space is identified by a black bar and the label *Unallocated*. If you add a new hard disk to your system, the entire disk is available for use, and the display in Disk Management's graphical pane will look something like this:

You can choose all or part of the available space for use as the new volume. If no unallocated space is available, you can make room by shrinking or deleting an existing volume. (Be aware that deleting the volume erases the volume's data.)

To create a new simple volume, right-click an unallocated portion of a disk and choose New Simple Volume from the shortcut menu. The New Simple Volume Wizard appears. Click Next to get past the welcome page. On the Specify Volume Size page, you'll be shown the maximum and minimum amounts of space you can devote to the new volume:

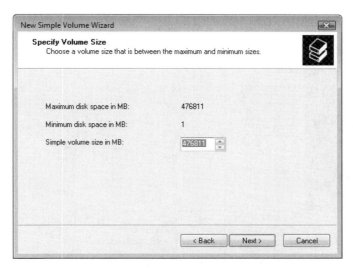

After you have specified the desired size in megabytes and clicked Next, you will be given the opportunity to assign a drive letter to the new volume. Note that the letters *A* and *B*, which used to be reserved for floppy disks, are no longer reserved:

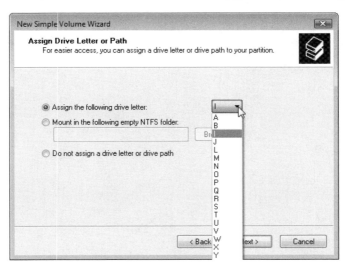

The Format Partition page, which follows the Assign Drive Letter Or Path page, gives you a chance to do just that but does not require that you do so. If you prefer to wait, you can always do the formatting later. The wizard's final page gives you one more chance to review your specifications:

You should actually take a moment to read this display before you click Finish. Make sure you've wheeled the right patient into the operating room before you hand him or her off to the surgeon.

After Disk Management has done its work and the disk formatting is complete, a dark blue bar appears over the new volume in the console's lower pane:

Creating a New Spanned Volume

To create a new spanned volume, right-click an unallocated portion of a disk and choose New Spanned Volume. Spanned volumes can exist only on dynamic disks, but Disk Management will convert a basic disk to a dynamic one for you as part of the spanned-volume creation process, so you can start by right-clicking a basic disk. In the Select Disks page of the New Spanned Volume wizard, shown below, you will be shown the disks available for spanning:

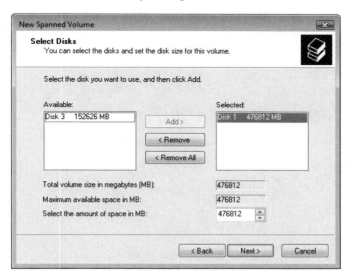

In this example, Disk 1 is the disk we right-clicked to begin the process, and Disk 3 is the only available disk with which we can connect Disk 1. Select the disk or disks that you want to use in the Available list, click Add for each one, and then click Next to continue. If you create a spanned volume involving a single physical disk, Disk Management merely creates a simple volume—but it still converts the disk involved to dynamic if it started out basic. Your completed Select Disks page might look something like this:

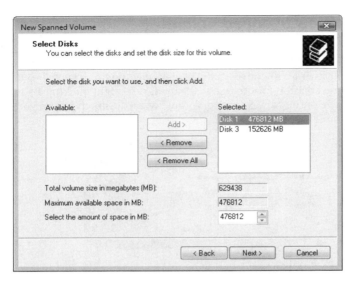

Notice that you can specify the amount of space you want to use on each disk individually, and the Total Volume Size In Megabytes (MB) field shows you how large a combination you are about to create.

The remaining pages of the New Spanned Volume wizard, like the comparable pages in the New Simple Volume wizard, invite you to format the new volume and assign it a drive letter, and give you a final review of your orders. After you click Finish and before the wizard goes to work, however, you will see the following additional warning:

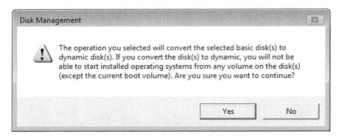

Note the warning. If you are creating a spanned volume involving a disk on which you have an operating system installed (for example, if you dual-boot with Windows XP and Windows XP's boot volume is on the disk you're spanning), you will no longer be able to boot into that operating system. Click Yes if the warning doesn't concern you or No if you need to bail out.

Here's how Disk Management might look after the creation of a new spanned volume (the bar over the new rectangle is magenta). The span uses the maximum possible space on Disk 1 and Disk 3, generating a single volume under the drive letter *I*.

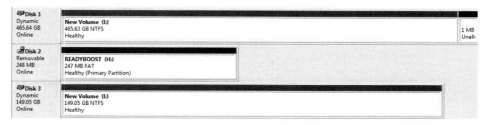

Figure 28-2 shows the General tab of the properties dialog box for this new spanned volume. The Used Space number in this figure, 108 MB, represents overhead associated with the spanning process.

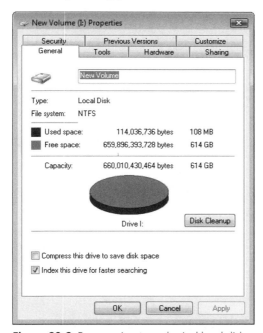

Figure 28-2 By spanning two physical hard disks, you can create a very large volume.

Creating a New Striped Volume

The process for creating a new striped volume is like that for creating a new spanned volume (see the preceding section), except that the total amount of space available is twice the maximum space on the larger of the two disks. Here is how Disk Management would look with the maximum amount of space on Disk 3 (149.05 GB) combined with the same amount of space on Disk 1. The spanned volume is identified by a teal bar over the volume's rectangle.

Disk 1 Dynamic 465.64 GB Online	**New Volume (J:)** 149.05 GB NTFS Healthy	316.59 GB Unallocated
Disk 2 Removable 248 MB Online	**READYBOOST (H:)** 247 MB FAT Healthy (Primary Partition)	
Disk 3 Dynamic 149.05 GB Online	**New Volume (J:)** 149.05 GB NTFS Healthy	

CAUTION

Weigh the risks carefully before creating a volume that combines space from two or more physical disks. If a catastrophic failure occurs on either physical disk, the entire spanned or striped volume and all its data will be lost. Also, you cannot reverse your decision and remove one chunk of space from the spanned or striped volume. Deleting one part of the volume deletes the entire volume.

Assigning or Changing a Volume Label

In Windows Vista, as in previous versions of Windows, you can assign a descriptive text label to any volume. Assigning a label is purely optional, but it's a good practice, especially if you've set up separate volumes to keep your data organized. You can use *Data* as the label for your data drive, *Music* for the drive that holds your collection of digital tunes, and so on. Volume labels appear in the Computer window alongside the drive letter for a volume, as in the in the example shown here:

You can enter a volume label when you format a new volume. Or you can do it at any time afterward, by right-clicking a volume (in Disk Management or in Windows Explorer), choosing Properties, and entering text in the edit field near the top of the General tab.

Assigning and Changing Drive Letters

You can assign one and only one letter to a volume. For all but the following volumes, you can change or remove the drive letter at any time:

- The boot volume

- The system volume

- Any volume on which the page (swap) file is stored

To change a drive-letter assignment, right-click the volume in Disk Management and choose Change Drive Letter And Paths. (You can do this in either the graphical or tabular pane.) To replace an existing drive letter, select it and click Change. To assign a drive letter to a volume that currently has none, click Add. Select an available drive letter from the Assign The Following Drive Letter list, and then click OK twice.

INSIDE OUT   Swapping drive letters between two volumes

The list of available drive letters shows only those that are not currently in use. To swap the drive letters for two volumes, you'll need three steps. For example, to swap the drive letters G and H, first remove the drive letter assigned to drive H. Then change drive G's assignment to H. Finally, add the drive letter G to the currently unnamed former occupant of H.

Mapping a Volume to an NTFS Folder

In addition to (or in place of) a drive letter, you can assign one or more paths to NTFS folders to a volume. Assigning a drive path creates a *mounted volume*. A mounted volume appears as a folder within an NTFS-formatted volume that has a drive letter assigned to it. Besides allowing you to sidestep the limitation of 26 drive letters, mounted volumes offer these advantages:

- You can extend storage space on an existing volume that's running low on free space. For instance, if your digital music collection has outgrown your drive C, you can create a subfolder of your Music folder and call it, say, More Music. Then you can assign a drive path from a new volume to the More Music folder—in effect increasing the size of your original Music folder.

- You can make commonly used files available in multiple locations. Say you have an enormous collection of clip art that you store on drive X, and each user has a folder in his or her Documents folder where they store desktop publishing files. In each of those personal folders, you can create a subfolder called Clipart and assign that folder's path to volume X. That way, the entire clip art collection is always available from any user's desktop publishing folder, and no one has to worry about creating shortcuts to X or changing drive letters while they work.

To create a mounted volume, follow these steps:

1. In Disk Management, right-click the volume you want to change. (You can do this in either the graphical pane or the tabular pane.) Choose Change Drive Letter And Paths from the shortcut menu.

2. Click Add to open the Add Drive Letter Or Path dialog box.

3. Select Mount In The Following Empty NTFS Folder (this is the only option available if the volume already has an assigned drive letter).

4. Click the Browse button. The Browse For Drive Path dialog box that appears shows only NTFS volumes, and the OK button is enabled only if you select an empty folder or click New folder to create one.

5. Click OK to add the selected location in the Add Drive Letter Or Path dialog box and then click OK to create the drive path.

You can manage files and subfolders in a mounted volume just as if it were a regular folder. In Windows Explorer, the folder icon will be marked by a shortcut arrow, like this:

Clip Art

If you right-click the folder icon and choose Properties, the General tab will reveal that the folder is actually a mounted volume. And, as Figure 28-3 shows, if you click the Properties button within that properties dialog box, you'll see the status of the drive to which the folder is mapped.

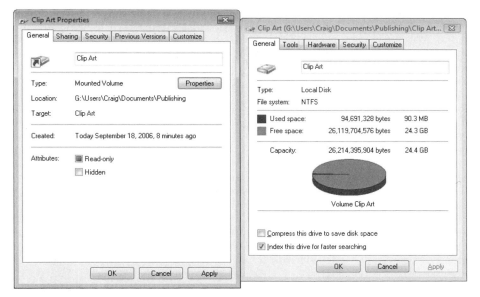

Figure 28-3 The properties dialog box for a mounted drive identifies the volume that actually holds its files. Clicking Properties within that dialog box displays the properties of the volume to which the folder is mapped.

If you use the Dir command in a Command Prompt window to display a folder directory, a mounted volume is identified as <JUNCTION> (for *junction point,* another name for mounted volume), whereas ordinary folders are identified as <DIR> (for *directory,* the MS-DOS term for a folder.)

> **CAUTION**
>
> When creating mounted volumes, avoid establishing loops in the structure of a drive—for example, by creating a drive path from drive X that points to a folder on drive D and then creating a drive path on drive D that points to a folder on drive X. Windows allows you to do this, but it's invariably a bad idea, because an application that opens subfolders (such as a search) can go into an endless loop.

To see a list of all the mounted drives on your system, choose View, Drive Paths in Disk Management. A dialog box like the one shown in Figure 28-4 appears. Note that you can remove a drive path from this dialog box; if you do so, the folder remains in the same spot where it was previously located, but it reverts to being a regular, empty folder.

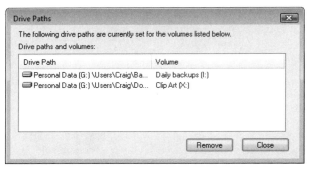

Figure 28-4 This dialog box lists all the mounted drives on a system and shows the volume label, if any, of each mounted drive.

Changing Volume Sizes

Space requirements have a way of changing over time. If you find you need to add space to an existing volume, Disk Management can help—provided space is available, of course. If you need to squeeze an additional volume onto an existing disk, Disk Management can assist with that task as well—again, assuming you have sufficient unused space on existing volumes.

Extending a Volume

Disk Management will be happy to make an NTFS volume larger for you, provided unallocated space is available on the same or another hard disk. To accomplish the expansion, right-click the volume you want to expand, and choose Extend Volume from the shortcut menu. Click Next to move past the Extend Volume Wizard's welcome page. The Select Disks page, shown in Figure 28-5, appears.

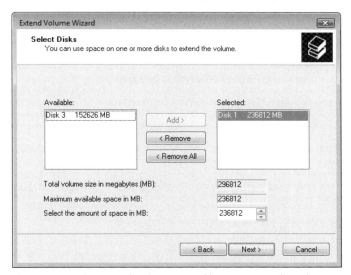

Figure 28-5 The Extend Volume wizard lets you extend a volume into unallocated space on the same or another hard disk.

The Selected list, on the right side of this dialog box, initially shows the disk whose volume you intend to extend. The Maximum Available Space In MB box shows you how much larger you can make the volume, assuming you want to confine your expansion to the current disk. The Select The Amount Of Space In MB box, initially set to equal the maximum available space, is where you declare the number of megabytes you want to add to the volume, and the Total Volume Size In Megabytes (MB) box shows you how big your volume is about to become. When you're ready to continue, click Next, review your orders on the ensuing page, and then click Finish. If your volume resided on a basic disk to begin with, it will remain basic after the expansion—provided the space into which you expanded was contiguous with the original volume. Note that no separate formatting step is required; the new territory acquires the same formatting as the original.

You are not limited to extending a volume in this manner, however. As Figure 28-5 shows, the Select Disks page shows you available unallocated space on other hard disks as well as the one on which the volume you're expanding resides. If you choose to expand into another disk (by selecting it in the Available list and clicking Add), the end result of your expansion will be a spanned volume on a dynamic disk.

What if you want to extend a volume into space on the same disk, but the unallocated space is not contiguous with the volume you want to expand. In that case, Disk Management converts the disk from basic to dynamic (if it was basic to begin with) and displays the extended volume as two non-adjacent rectangles, like this:

Note that the layout of the expanded volume remains *simple*, despite the fact that the volume now spans an intervening volume on the same disk.

Volume extension is subject to the following limitations:

- Only NTFS-formatted volumes can be extended.

- A logical drive can be extended only within the extended partition that contains it.

- The system and boot partitions can be extended only into contiguous unallocated space.

- You cannot extend a striped volume.

Shrinking a Volume

Provided space is available, you can shrink an NTFS-formatted volume to make more space available for other volumes. To do this, right-click the volume in either the tabular or the graphical pane, and choose Shrink Volume from the shortcut menu. Disk Management responds by analyzing the disk, and then reports the amount of shrinkage possible in a dialog box like this:

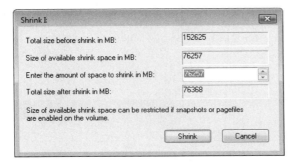

Enter the number of megabytes by which you want to reduce your volume, and then click Shrink. Disk Management defragments the disk, moving all its data to a contiguous block, and then performs the shrink.

Be aware that page files and volume shadow copy files cannot be moved during the defragmentation process. This means that you might not have as much room to shrink as you would like. Microsoft also advises that the amount by which you can shrink a volume is "transient" and depends on what is happening on the volume at the time. In other words, if you are trying to eliminate, say, 10 GB from the volume and Disk Management can manage only 7, take the 7 and then try for more later.

Deleting a Volume

Deleting a volume is easy—and irreversible. All data is lost in the process, so be sure you have backed up or no longer need whatever the volume currently contains. Then right-click the volume and choose Delete Volume. The volume reverts to unallocated space, and if it happens to have been the last volume on a dynamic disk, the disk itself is converted to basic.

Chapter 28

Checking the Properties and Status of Disks and Volumes

As with previous Windows versions, you can check the properties of any drive—including the volume label, file system, and amount of free space available—by right-clicking the drive in Windows Explorer's Computer folder and choosing Properties from the shortcut menu. You can see the same details and more in Disk Management. Most of the crucial information is visible in the volume list, the tabular pane that appears by default at the top of the Disk Management window. Slightly less information is available in the graphical pane at the bottom of the window. Of particular interest is information about the status of a disk or volume. Figure 28-6 shows where to look for this information.

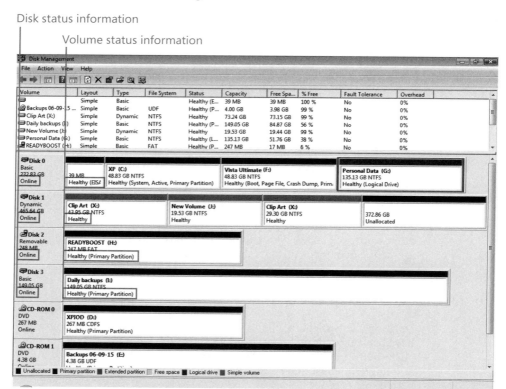

Figure 28-6 Disk Management displays information about the status of each disk and volume.

Under normal circumstances, the status information displayed here should report that each disk is online and each volume is healthy. Table 28-1 lists all possible disk status messages you might see on a system running Windows Vista, along with suggested actions for resolving possible errors.

Table 28-1. Disk Status

Status	Description	Action required
Online	The disk is configured correctly and has no known problems.	None.
Online (Errors)	The operating system encountered errors when reading or writing data from a region of the disk. (This status message appears on dynamic disks only.)	Right-click the disk and choose Reactivate Disk to return its status to Online. If errors continue to occur, check for damage to the disk.
Offline	The disk was once available but is not currently accessible. The disk might be physically damaged or it might be disconnected. (This status message appears on dynamic disks only.)	Check the physical connections between the disk and the power supply or disk controller. After repairing connections, right-click the disk and choose Reactivate Disk to return its status to Online. If the damage cannot be repaired, delete all volumes, right-click the disk, and choose Remove Disk.
Foreign	The disk was originally installed on another computer and has not yet been set up for use on your computer. (This status message appears on dynamic disks only.)	Right-click the disk and choose Import Foreign Disks.
Unreadable	All or part of the disk may be physically damaged, or (in the case of a dynamic disk) the dynamic disk database may be corrupted.	Restart the computer. If the problem persists, right-click the disk and choose Rescan Disks. If the status is still unreadable, some data on the disk may be recoverable with third-party utilities.
Missing	The disk is correupted, disconnected, or not powered on. (This status message appears on dynamic disks only.)	After you reconnect or power on the missing disk, right-click the disk and choose Reactivate Disk to return its status to Online.
Not Initialized	The disk does not contain a valid signature. It may have been prepared on a system running a non-Microsoft operating system, such as UNIX or Linux, or the drive may be brand new.	If the disk is used by another operating system, do nothing. To prepare a new disk for use with Windows Vista, right-click the disk and choose Initialize Disk.
No Media	A disk is not inserted in the drive. (This status message appears only on removable media drives, such as CD and DVD drives.)	Insert a disk in the drive and choose Action, Rescan Disks.

Chapter 28

Table 28-2. describes volume status messages you're likely to see.

INSIDE OUT Tackle disk problems first

Almost without fail, a disk problem will generate a status indicator for both the disk and any volumes on that disk. For instance, if you see a disk with Online (Errors) in the Status column, you're likely to see Healthy (At Risk) as the volume's status. In this case, your best bet is to try to resolve the disk problem first. If you can successfully do so, the problems with the volume will usually clear up as a matter of course.

Table 28-2 Volume Status

Status	Description	Action required
Healthy	The volume is properly formatted and has no known problems.	None.
Healthy (At Risk)	Windows encountered errors when reading from or writing to the underlying disk. Such errors are often caused by bad blocks on the disk. After encountering an error anywhere on the disk, Disk Management marks all volumes on that disk as Healthy (At Risk). (This status message appears on dynamic disks only.)	Right-click the disk and choose Reactivate Disk. Persistent errors often indicate a failing disk. Back up all data and run a thorough diagnostic check using the hardware manufacturer's software; if necessary, replace the disk.
Healthy (Unknown Partition)	Windows does not recognize the partition; this occurs with some partitions created by another operating system or by a computer manufacturer who uses a partition to store system files. You cannot format or access data on an unknown partition.	If you're certain the partition is unnecessary, use Disk Management to delete it and create a new partition in the free space created.
Initializing	Disk Management cannot determine the disk status because the disk is initializing. (This status message appears on dynamic disks only.)	Wait. The drive status should appear in a few seconds.
Failed	The dynamic disk is damaged or the file system is corrupted.	To repair a failed dynamic volume, check to see whether the disk is online. (If not, right-click the disk and choose Reactivate Disk.) Then right-click the volume and choose Reactivate Volume. If the failed volume is on a basic disk, be sure that the disk is properly connected.

Status	Description	Action required
Unknown	The boot sector for the volume is corrupted, and you can no longer access data. This condition may be caused by a virus.	Use an up-to-date virus-scanning program to check for the presence of a boot-sector virus. If no virus is found, boot from the Windows Vista distribution media and use the Windows Recovery Environment's Fixmbr command to fix the Master Boot Record.

CHAPTER 29

Controlling Access to Files and Folders

Home Basic ⚫
Home Premium ⚫
Business ⚫
Enterprise ⚫
Ultimate ⚫

When two or more people use the same computer, how do you keep each user from snooping in files and folders that should be private? How do you allow easy access to files that should be shared? And how do you keep untrained users from accidentally wiping out important files? The Sharing wizard in Windows Vista makes it easy to share files with other users on the same computer, and with users who connect to your computer over the network.

For most people, the Sharing wizard does everything necessary to control access to files and folders.

For information about the Sharing wizard, see Chapter 13, "Managing Shared Folders and Printers."

But there is an alternative: with some advanced access control options, you can exercise precise control over who is able to access any file or folder on any drive. You might find knowledge of NTFS permissions useful, whether it's to limit exactly what a certain user can do with certain files, or if it's to understand how to deal with a message like this:

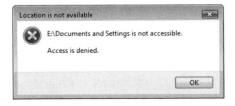

What's in Your Edition?

You can work directly with NTFS permissions in any Windows Vista edition. (This should come as a welcome change to people upgrading from Microsoft Windows XP Home Edition, in which the Security tab is hidden under most circumstances, making it difficult to view or modify NTFS permissions.)

Although the Sharing wizard allows you to control access to files using terms such as Reader, Contributor, and so on, behind the scenes the wizard is applying permissions the old-fashioned way—by creating an access control entry (ACE) for each user to whom you want to grant access and applying the ACE to a folder or file. For each folder or file on an NTFS-formatted volume, Windows Vista uses the same type of discretionary access control list (DACL or, sometimes, just ACL) as Microsoft Windows XP, Windows 2000, and Windows NT. (A DACL comprises the individual ACEs for a secured object.) This system of file security is often called NTFS permissions, and that's the topic of this chapter.

This chapter focuses exclusively on sharing and securing files among users who log on to the same computer. If you're interested in learning how to share files and folders over a network, see Chapter 13, "Managing Shared Folders and Printers."

Changes to NTFS Permissions in Windows Vista

For the most part, the implementation of NTFS permissions in Windows Vista is identical to that of Windows XP (which, in turn, was nearly identical to the Windows 2000 implementation). There are a few important differences:

- The owner of an object no longer implicitly has full control access. If the object includes an ACE that applies to the object owner (for example, an ACE explicitly for the owner's user account or for a group of which the owner is a member), the owner's access is controlled by that ACE. The owner does have two implicit permissions: Read Permissions and Change Permissions.

- Permissions for an object owner can be further modified by the Owner Rights security identifier (SID), which is new in Windows Vista. Permission settings assigned to Owner Rights apply to whatever account currently owns the object. These permissions do not survive a change in ownership, however; when you give or take ownership, the Owner Rights ACE is removed.

- If User Account Control (UAC) is turned on, you might need to respond to a UAC elevation prompt to edit permissions. (You'll know in advance because of the security shield in the Edit button.) That's because ordinarily, you run using the security token of a standard user account, even if you're logged on using an administrator account. If your own account (or a group other than Administrators that includes your account) has full control access (including the ability to change permissions), you won't need to elevate. But if the Administrators group is the only security identifier with Change Permissions permission, you'll need to elevate. For more information about UAC, see "Preventing Unsafe Actions with User Account Control," Chapter 10.

- Operating system files are owned by TrustedInstaller (which is actually a service account, not a user account), and only TrustedInstaller has full control access over these files. In previous versions of Windows, the Administrators group owned these files and had full control access—which put them at risk from a rogue application running in the context of an administrator. Such applications could delete or replace critical operating system files; in Windows Vista, that's possible only if you take ownership of a file and then add an ACE that lets you change or delete it.

- Certain default permissions have changed. Table 29-1 shows the key differences between default permissions in Windows XP and Windows Vista.

Table 29-1. Changes to Default NTFS Permissions

User or Group	Windows XP ACE	Windows Vista ACE
%SystemRoot% Folder		
Administrators	Full Control	Full Control
Users	Read & Execute	Read & Execute
Power Users	Modify	—
System	Full Control	Full Control
Creator Owner	Full Control	Full Control
Newly Formatted Data Drive		
Administrators	Full Control	Full Control

Users	Read
	Special: Create Folders/
	    Append Data
	Special: Create Files/Write
	    Data
		Read & Execute

Everyone	Read	—
Authenticated Users	—	Modify
System	Full Control	Full Control
Creator Owner	Full Control	—

Controlling Access with NTFS Permissions

The full panoply of controls over NTFS permissions that you might have seen in earlier versions of Windows remains available in Windows Vista. And unlike Windows XP, in which you had to disable Simple File Sharing (an act that also made other changes besides exposing the security controls), in Windows Vista, the Security tab is always available—to all users, in all editions, regardless of whether the Sharing wizard is enabled. As an alternative to the Security tab that appears in the properties dialog box for files and folders, you can view and modify NTFS permissions using a command-line utility. (For details, see "Setting Permissions from a Command Prompt," later in this chapter)

With NTFS permission controls, you can:

- Control access to any file or folder on any NTFS-formatted volume

- Allow different types of access for different users or groups of users, include classifications of users not available in the Sharing wizard

- Fine-tune permissions on specific files or folders

CAUTION

Setting NTFS permissions without understanding the full consequences can lead to unexpected and unwelcome results, including a complete loss of access to files and folders. The permission-setting capabilities of the Sharing wizard provide far greater flexibility and power than were possible in the basic Windows XP interface. Before you delve into the inner workings of NTFS permissions on the Security tab, be sure to try the Sharing tab (with the Sharing wizard enabled).

If you do work directly with NTFS permissions without the wizard's assistance, you'll find that working with the built-in permission sets—Full Control, Modify, and so on—is the safest strategy. If you plan to tinker with special permissions, set up a folder and fill it with test files so that you can experiment safely. When you're certain you've worked out the correct mix of permissions, apply them to the folders containing your real working files and delete the test folder.

Applying Advanced Security Settings

To view and edit NTFS permissions for a file or folder, right-click its icon, choose Properties, and then click the Security tab. This dialog box lists all the groups and users with permissions set for the selected object. As the example in Figure 29-1 shows, you can assign different permissions to each user—in this case, Jan can read and play (Execute) files in the Music folder but is forbidden to change existing files (Modify) or create new ones (Write).

Figure 29-1 View permissions for the selected user in the list at the bottom of this dialog box; each user or group can have a different set of permissions.

In Windows Vista, the owner of a file or folder (typically the person who creates the file) has the right to allow or deny access to that resource. In addition, members of the Administrators group and other authorized users can grant or deny permissions. You can add individual users to the list of users and allow or deny specific types of file and folder actions. You can also assign permissions to built-in groups (Administrators, for instance) or create your own groups and assign permissions that way. As we'll explain later in this section, some permissions don't need to be explicitly defined but instead are inherited based on permissions from a parent folder. All permissions are stored in the file system as part of the access control list (ACL).

For more details about creating and managing user accounts and groups, see "Working with User Accounts," Chapter 11.

To make changes to the settings for any user or group in the list, or to add or remove a user or group in the list, click Edit. This extra click, which is new in Windows Vista, reduces the likelihood of inadvertent changes while viewing permissions. The resulting dialog box, shown in Figure 29-2 on the next page, includes Add and Remove buttons, along with check boxes for setting permissions.

Chapter 29

Figure 29-2 Clicking Edit leads to a dialog box that's nearly identical to the Security tab in earlier versions of Windows.

If the user or group whose permissions you want to edit is already listed at the top of the Permissions dialog box, you can select check boxes in the Allow column to add permissions, or clear boxes to remove permissions. Select check boxes in the Deny column only if you want to explicitly forbid certain users from exercising a specific permission. Deny access control entries take precedence over any other permission settings that apply to an account, such as those granted through membership in a group. If you want to completely lock out a specific user or group from access to a selected file or folder, select the Deny check box on the Full Control line.

INSIDE OUT   Be careful with the Deny box

On the average home or small business computer, resist the temptation to select any of the check boxes in the Deny column in the Permissions dialog box. This option is typically used on large, complex networks where many groups of users are defined (individual departments, for example) and administrators want to exercise tight control over sensitive files in specific locations. Unraveling the interactions between Allow and Deny permissions can be a daunting task. On a machine with a handful of users, it's almost always simpler to define permissions by selecting and clearing check boxes in the Allow column.

In most cases, you can safely assign permissions by selecting a user or group name and then selecting one or more of the predefined groups of permissions listed at the bottom of the Permissions dialog box. Table 29-2 describes the function of each of these entries.

Table 29-2. How Permissions Control File and Folder Access

Permission	How It Controls Access to Files and Folders
Full Control	Gives the designated user or group full control over the selected file or folder, as the name implies. Selecting this box selects all check boxes below it as well. Users with Full Control can list contents of a folder, read and open files, create new files, delete files and subfolders, change permissions on files and subfolders, and take ownership of files.
Modify	Allows the user to read, change, create, and delete files, but not to change permissions or take ownership of files. Selecting this check box selects all the options listed below it.
Read & Execute	Allows the user to view files and execute programs. Selecting this check box selects the List Folder Contents and Read boxes as well.
List Folder Contents (folders only)	Provides the same individual permissions as Read & Execute and is available only on the Security tab for a folder. The only difference between the two permissions is in the way they are inherited.
Read	Allows the user to list the contents of a folder, view file attributes, read permissions, and synchronize files. This is the most basic permission of all.
Write	Allows the user to create files, write data, read attributes and permissions, and synchronize files.
Special Permissions	If this permission is selected, the assigned permissions don't match any of the built-in templates shown here. Click the Advanced button on the Security tab to see details.

Note

When the Read & Execute permission is applied to a folder, this permission is inherited by all files and subfolders within the folder. The List Folder Contents permission, on the other hand, though functionally identical, is inherited by subfolders but not by files within the folder or subfolders. For details about inherited permissions, see "Applying Permissions to Subfolders Through Inheritance," later in this chapter.

To set permissions for a group or user who isn't listed in the Group Or User Names box, follow these steps:

1. Open the properties dialog box for the file or folder, and click the Security tab.

2. Click Edit to open the Permissions dialog box.

3. Click Add.

4. Type the name in the Select User Or Group dialog box shown here; when entering multiple names, separate them with semicolons. (Note that you must type the user name, which may be different from the full name that appears on the Welcome screen.)

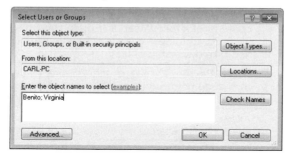

5. Click Check Names to confirm that you entered the names correctly.

6. Click OK to return to the Security tab and set permissions for the newly added user(s).

INSIDE OUT   Entering group and user names

On a standalone computer or on a computer that is part of a workgroup and is not joined to a Windows domain, the list of available group and user names is drawn only from the account database on the local computer—that is, the computer at which you're logged on. If your machine is a domain member, you can click the Locations button and choose whether you want to specify permissions based on users of the local computer or those in the domain's directory. If you're entering names of users on a Windows domain, enter a portion of the name and then click the Check Names button.

Unfortunately, you can't use the same shortcut to select users and groups defined in the local computer's account database; instead, you have to enter the user's name in full, and if you're off by even a single letter you'll get an error message. (Windows will, however, fill in the computer or domain name for you automatically.) To see a list of available local users and groups, click the Advanced button, and then click Find Now. The resulting list includes all user accounts, groups, and special accounts on the local computer.

When adding or removing permissions, follow these basic principles:

- **Start from the top and work down** By default, permissions you set on a folder apply to all files and subfolders within that folder. (For more details, see "Applying Permissions to Subfolders Through Inheritance," later in this chapter.) Managing file access is much easier when you have a consistent set of permissions for all files in a location, with exceptions only where needed.

- **Organize shared data files in common locations** If shared data is scattered over multiple drives and folders, it's too easy to inadvertently let permissions get out of sync. Try to consolidate shared data files into a single group of folders. When data is all in one place, you'll find it easier to manage permissions and make proper backups.

- **Use groups whenever possible** This is especially important in a small business setting. Take advantage of the built-in Administrators and Users groups for basic permissions. If you need to define custom permissions so that several users can access files stored in multiple folders, use group-based permissions to simplify the process. Create a new local group and add the users who need access to the files in question. (For details, see "Using the Local Users and Groups Snap-In," Chapter 11.) Open the properties dialog box for the first folder, click the Security tab, click Edit, add the newly created group, and grant the appropriate permissions to that group. Repeat this process for each additional folder. Later, when one member of the group leaves and another one joins, you can change the group membership and automatically update the permissions for all folders without having to go through each folder's properties dialog box again.

For more information about how to create and manage local groups, see "Working with User Accounts," Chapter 11.

- **Steer clear of special permissions** Unless you're a wizard at understanding the interplay of NTFS permissions, resist the temptation to tweak special permissions for individual files or folders. The built-in security settings (Full Control, Modify, Read & Execute) cover most needs adequately. Note that these settings correlate to those made by the Sharing wizard: Co-Owner, Contributor, and Reader.

- **Grant only the level of access that users require** If a specific user needs to read files stored in a certain location, but does not need to create new files or edit existing ones, grant that user only the Read permission. This precaution is especially important to prevent novices and untrained users from wiping out important data files accidentally.

Chapter 29

TROUBLESHOOTING

You can't change file or folder permissions

If you're unable to set custom permissions, look for the symptom in this list and try the following problem-solving techniques:

- **The Security tab is not visible** Do you see only a Sharing tab? If so, check the properties for the drive; the most likely explanation is that the drive is formatted using the FAT file system. The Security tab is visible only on NTFS drives.

- **Permission settings are unavailable** Check your user account rights. You must be logged on as a member of the Administrators group or be the owner of an object to set its permissions. If you are logged on as a standard user, you can view only your own permission settings; if you select another user and group on the Security tab, the permissions box is empty.

- **The check marks for some users are shaded, and in the Permissions dialog box, the check boxes for those users are unavailable** Those permissions are not set explicitly for the file or folder you're viewing. Rather, they're inherited from the folder in which it's stored. (And that folder might, in turn, inherit its permission settings from its parent folder.) To break the inheritance chain, on the Security tab, click Advanced. In the Advanced Security Settings dialog box, click Edit, and then clear Include Inheritable Permissions From This Object's Parent. For more information, see "Applying Permissions to Subfolders Through Inheritance," later in this chapter

- **You've made changes, but the check marks disappear** This may not be a problem at all. If you set permissions and apply them to anything other than the default location—This Folder, Subfolder, And Files—Windows adds a check mark in the Special Permissions box (when viewing permissions for a folder, you have to scroll to the bottom of the Permissions list to see this box). You can view the applied permissions by clicking Advanced, clicking Edit, selecting the user or group, and clicking Edit.

Working with Built-in Users and Groups

In addition to the standard local groups (Administrators and Users, for instance), Windows Vista includes a number of special identities. These users and groups, which are built into the system and can't be deleted, are used to apply special permissions to system resources (including files and folders); in many cases, these identities are placeholders that apply to user accounts based on the way a given account uses the system.

> **Note**
> Special identities are often referred to as *well-known security identifiers*.

Understanding these built-in accounts and groups is crucial to using advanced NTFS permissions effectively. Table 29-3 lists the most common special identities.

Table 29-3. Special Identities Available in Windows Vista

Special Identity	Description
Everyone	Includes every user who accesses the computer, including Guests. This group does not include Anonymous logons.
Creator Owner Creator Group	Identifies the user or group who created the selected file or folder.
Owner Rights	A special-purpose SID, new in Windows Vista, that is used to specify access rights for whoever currently owns the file or folder. For more information, see "Changes to NTFS Permissions in Windows Vista," in this chapter.
Authenticated Users	Includes any user who logs on with a user name and password. Unlike the Everyone identity, this group does not include users who log on as Guest, even if the Guest account has been assigned a password.
Interactive	Includes any user that logs on locally.
Remote Interactive Logon	Includes any user that logs on through a Remote Desktop connection.
Anonymous Logon	Identifies network logons for which credentials are not provided, such as connections to a web server. Anonymous and Interactive logons are mutually exclusive.
Dialup	Includes any user who accesses the computer over a dial-up connection.
Network	Includes any user that logs on over the network. Does not include interactive logons that use Remote Desktop over a network.

Some of these special identities are esoteric, and the average user will never need to apply them. But others can be extremely powerful additions to your security toolkit. For instance, you can use the following combinations of permissions to tighten security on your computer:

- For shared data folders, assign the Read & Execute permission and the Write permission to the Users group, and the Full Control permission to the Creator Owner special identity. In this configuration, every user who creates a file or folder becomes that object's owner and has the ability to read, modify, and delete it. Other users can read and modify documents created by other users but can't accidentally delete them.

- If you have a second drive in your system that was originally created and formatted with Windows XP and you want to prevent all access to files on that drive by anyone using the Guest account, change the default permissions on the root of the drive. Add the Authenticated Users group and give it Modify permission, and

Chapter 29

then remove the default Everyone group. (On a drive formatted in Windows XP, the Everyone group has Read permission. In Windows Vista, by contrast, Authenticated Users has Modify permission, and the Everyone group has no access by default.)

CAUTION

> One of the most common mistakes made by users who are inexperienced with NTFS permissions is removing the Everyone group from the root of a drive—or worse, selecting the Deny box next to Full Control for this group. Remember, more restrictive permissions always override more lenient permissions. As a rule of thumb, the best strategy for the permissions on the top-level folder for any drive is to make sure that all users who will access files on that drive have the proper level of access. After you've organized data on that drive, tighten up permissions on each subfolder so that it's accessible by the correct users and groups.

Windows Vista includes several special identities that are reserved for software and system processes and are never used by human users. The Batch identity provides permissions for any batch process (such as a job launched via Task Scheduler) that needs to access a resource on the computer. The Service, Local Service, and Network Service identities are used by system services and are controlled by the operating system. (For more information about services, see Chapter 25, "Managing Services.") The System identity allows the operating system itself to access protected resources. Similarly, the TrustedInstaller identity (new in Windows Vista) owns most operating system files. TrustedInstaller (which is a service, not a user; its complete name is "NT SERVICE"\ TrustedInstaller) provides additional protection for those files, because in previous versions of Windows, the Administrators group owned and had full control over them; because most users ran as administrators, a malicious program could run in the context of a user to delete or replace parts of Windows. As a general rule, permissions for these groups are set by the operating system and should never be adjusted by users.

CAUTION

> Tampering with the default permissions on the drive that contains Windows system files is a bad idea. As part of the setup process, Windows Vista applies specific permissions to the root of the system drive; to the Windows, System32, and Users folders; and to specific subfolders within each of these locations. Changing the default permissions will not improve security and will almost certainly cause some users or programs to have problems.

Applying Permissions to Subfolders Through Inheritance

Files and subfolders can inherit permissions from a parent folder. By default, any new permissions you assign to a folder are passed on to subfolders as well. Thus, when you create a new subfolder in your Documents folder, it inherits the permissions you've set for that folder.

You can prevent permissions from being inherited by changing the inheritance options for a folder. You can specify that subfolders or files (or both) no longer inherit permissions that have been assigned to the parent folder containing them. Instead, only permissions you explicitly apply to files and subfolders will apply.

To see the inheritance options for a selected folder, right-click the folder icon, choose Properties, and then click the Security tab. Click Advanced to display the Advanced Security Settings dialog box. The Inherited From column in the Permission Entries list shows the parent folder from which a given set of permissions is inherited. In the example shown in Figure 29-3, the Everyone group inherits Full Control permissions from the ACL on the root folder of drive D, whereas the other permissions, designated as <not inherited>, have been applied directly to this folder.

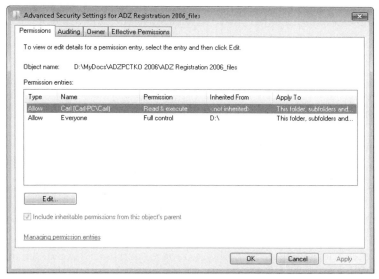

Figure 29-3 The list of permissions shown here helps you identify which permissions are inherited from parent folders.

In this example, the inherited permissions are getting in the way of the tight security we want to apply to this folder. To remove the inherited permissions, click Edit and then clear Include Inheritable Permissions From This Object's Parent. You see the following dialog box, which warns you to specify how you want to reset the permissions on the selected folder.

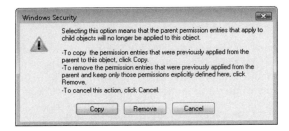

Choose one of the following three options:

- **Copy** This option copies the permissions from the parent folder to the current file or folder and then breaks the inheritance link to the parent folder. After choosing this option, you can adjust the permissions to suit your security needs.

- **Remove** This option removes any permissions that were inherited, keeping only those permissions that you've explicitly assigned to the file or folder.

- **Cancel** This option closes the warning dialog box and leaves the inheritance options intact.

When you remove inherited permissions from a folder, it becomes a new top-level folder in the inheritance chain. By default, any permissions you assign to this folder ripple down the hierarchy of subfolders and to files within those subfolders as well.

In some cases, you may want to apply two or more sets of permissions to the same folder for the same group, with each set of permissions having different inheritance settings. For instance, say that you and several coworkers on a shared computer are working on a top-secret project. You've set up a shared folder called Project X Files for use by everyone who has an account on your computer. In the main folder, you've stored a handful of document templates that you want members of the team to use when creating new documents; you've also set up subfolders to hold files that are currently being worked on.

In this scenario, you might want the Everyone group to have Read & Execute access to files within a top-level folder, and Full Control over subfolders. Using this arrangement of permissions, you can allow users to open templates stored in the top-level folder, while protecting those templates from accidental changes or deletions. By using a different set of permissions on subfolders, you can allow users to create new files and modify previously saved documents. To apply permissions with this level of fine-grain control, follow these steps:

1. Open the properties dialog box for the top-level folder you want to adjust (Project X Files, in this example), and click the Security tab. Click Edit and then Click Add.

2. In the Select Users Or Groups dialog box, enter **Administrators** and click OK.

3. Select Administrators in the Group Or User Names List at the top of the
    Permissions dialog box, and then select the Allow box to the right of the Full
    Control entry in the Permissions list. Click Add again.

4. This time, enter **Everyone** in the Select Users Or Groups dialog box and click OK.

5. Select Everyone in the Group Or User Names List, and then select the Allow box
    to the right of the Read & Execute entry in the Permissions list. Click OK to close
    the Permissions dialog box and return to the Security tab in the properties dialog
    box.

6. Click Advanced to open the Advanced Security Settings dialog box, and then
    click Edit.

7. If necessary, clear Include Inheritable Permissions From This Object's Parent (and
    then select Copy when the security warning appears).

8. Select the entry for Everyone, and click Edit to open the Permission Entry dialog
    box (shown here). Open the Apply To list, select This Folder And Files, and click
    OK.

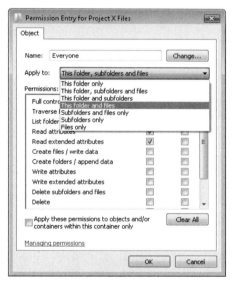

9. From the Advanced Security Settings dialog box, click Add.

10. In the Select User Or Group dialog box, enter **Everyone** and click OK.

11. In the Permission Entry dialog box, select Full Control, select Subfolders Only in
    the Apply To list, and then click OK.

The resulting set of permissions should look like the one shown in Figure 29-4 on the
next page. With these settings, you and other members of the Administrators group can
add and change files in the main folder; you can also add subfolders. All other users can

view and open files in the main folder but can't create new files, change existing files, or delete files or subfolders. They can, however, save files in the subfolders you create.

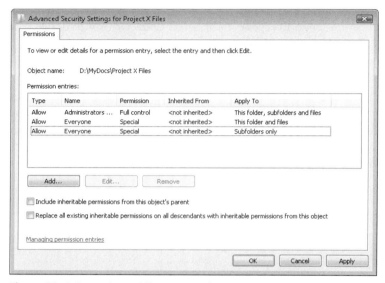

Figure 29-4 By applying different sets of permissions to files and subfolders, you can fine-tune permissions for a group of folders all at once.

What's the advantage of using inherited permissions in this fashion? Each time you create a subfolder, Windows automatically applies the proper permissions to it, using the inheritance settings you defined. Without these settings, you would be forced to define permissions from scratch for each new subfolder. That's a lot of needless work, with the potential for errors and inconsistencies. More important, if you decide to change the permissions later—for instance, changing the Full Control permission for subfolders from the Everyone group to a more limited group of users—you can make a single change and have the changes apply to all the child folders automatically.

Testing the Effect of Permissions

Because file and folder permissions can come from a variety of settings, it's sometimes difficult to figure out exactly what each user can and can't do with a given file or folder. As a general rule, you can figure out *effective permissions* by combining all the NTFS permissions assigned to an individual user account and to all of the groups to which that user belongs. Thus, if a user has Read & Execute permission for a folder set through her user account and is also a member of a group that has been assigned Write permissions for that folder, she has both Read and Write permissions for the folder.

On a scale of complexity, calculating effective permissions is more difficult than programming a VCR and only slightly less taxing than quantum physics. Fortunately, Windows Vista includes a tool that does the calculations for you. To see what the effect of all NTFS permissions will be on a given user or group, follow these steps:

1. Right-click the file or folder in question, and then choose Properties.

2. On the Security tab, click Advanced and then click the Effective Permissions tab.

3. Click Select to open the Select User Or Group dialog box.

4. Enter the name of the user or group for which you want to check effective permissions, and then click OK.

> **Note**
>
> Anyone who's ever struggled to figure out NTFS permissions in Windows 2000 or Windows NT will really appreciate the Effective Permissions dialog box in Windows Vista. It's a wonderful addition, and if you're going to use NTFS permissions you should learn its ins and outs. Unfortunately, it also includes one potentially confusing interface element. The Group Or User Name box looks like a place to enter text directly, but it doesn't work that way in practice. You have to display the Select User Or Group dialog box to enter a name.

The resulting dialog box shows the effective permissions that apply to the user or group you selected. These permissions are presented using the complete list of available permissions from the Advanced Security Settings dialog box, which are far more detailed than those shown on the Security tab. This level of detail can be difficult to decipher, but it's crucial in identifying subtle changes that can compromise security. In the example in Figure 29-5, for instance, the user named Benito has permissions that are equivalent to Read & Execute.

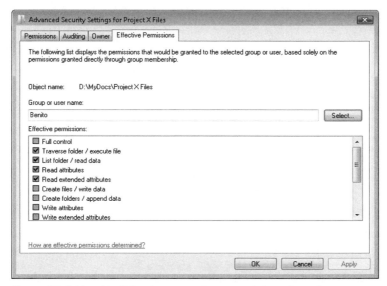

Figure 29-5 Use this dialog box to see how permissions through user accounts and groups combine for a given user. Check marks indicate which permissions are assigned.

The effective permissions calculation looks up all local and domain groups to which a user or group belongs and takes those permissions into account in its summary. A check mark identifies permissions that have been assigned. The resulting display is a snapshot of permissions based on other settings. You can't change any permissions from this dialog box.

> **Note**
>
> The effective permissions calculation does not include the Anonymous Logon or Authenticated Users group, nor does it include settings granted because a user is the Creator Owner of an object. In addition, the calculation does not consider whether you're logging on interactively or over a network. If you've customized any of these permissions, you'll need to account for the differences.

Using Special Permissions

Don't be misled by the long list of so-called special permissions that you see when you click Advanced on the Security tab, click Edit, select a user or group name, and then click Edit. Whenever you use NTFS permissions, whether it's through the Sharing wizard or the more full-featured Permissions dialog box, your actions result in changes to this list. Using the built-in permission options—Full Control, Modify, and so on—actually sets predetermined groups of permissions here. Figure 29-6, for instance, shows the results when you select the Allow box next to the Read & Execute entry—Windows actually sets five individual permissions in response to the single click.

Figure 29-6 In general, you don't need to adjust these so-called special permissions. Using the check boxes in the Permissions dialog box makes the adjustments for you.

When dealing with unusual access control situations, the best solution is usually to start by applying the predefined basic permission that comes closest to the desired result. Then add or remove special permissions as needed. Table 29-4 lists the full set of special permissions that are applied when you set each of the predefined permission options.

Table 29-4. Special Permissions Applied by Basic Permissions

Basic Permission	Special Permissions
Read	List Folder / Read Data Read Attributes Read Extended Attributes Read Permissions
Read & Execute List Folder Contents	All Read special permissions listed above Traverse Folder / Execute File
Write	Create Files / Write Data Create Folders / Append Data Write Attributes Write Extended Attributes
Modify	All Read & Execute permissions listed above All Write special permissions listed above Delete
Full Control	All special permissions listed above Delete Subfolders And Files Change Permissions Take Ownership

Setting Permissions from a Command Prompt

Icacls.exe is a command-line utility that provides another way to view and edit permissions. (Note that the name begins with the letter *i*.) Icacls supplants the original command-line permissions editor, Cacls (short for *Control ACLs*), and the extended version created for Windows XP, Xcacls. With Icacls, you can view existing permissions by typing **icacls** *filename* at a command prompt, replacing *filename* with the name of the file or folder you're interested in (wildcards are acceptable as well). The resulting list of permissions is terse, to say the least. Next to each user account name, Icacls displays codes to identify inherited permissions, if applicable (I for inherited permissions, OI if the inheritance also applies to children objects, or CI if the inheritance applies to children containers/folders), followed by a code to identify basic permission settings (F for Full Control, M for Modify, RX for Read & Execute, R for Read, or W for Write) or a series of comma-separated codes to indicate special permissions. (For a complete list of codes and their meanings, type **icacls** with no parameters in a Command Prompt window.) A simple example might look like this:

```
E:\Users\Carl>icacls documents
documents Carl-PC\Jan:(RX)
          Carl-PC\Carl:(I)(OI)(CI)(F)
          NT AUTHORITY\SYSTEM:(I)(OI)(CI)(F)
          BUILTIN\Administrators:(I)(OI)(CI)(F)
```

In this example, the user Jan has been given Read & Execute permission, which has been applied directly to this folder. The other ACEs are all inherited and all provide Full Control access.

Icacls is useful for quickly finding the permissions for an object—particularly if you're already working in a Command Prompt window. But it does much more:

- You can save existing permission settings to a file, which you can subsequently apply to the same object (a great recovery system for permissions experiments gone awry) or to another object. Use the /Save, /Substitute, and /Restore switches to work with settings files. For example: **icacls music /save musicpermissions** saves the current permission settings for the Music folder to a file named Musicpermissions. Replace /Save with /Restore to reapply the saved settings.

- You can replace explicitly assigned ACLs with default inherited permissions—another good recovery method. Use the /Reset switch. For example, **icacls music /reset** removes existing permissions and restores the Include Inheritable Permissions From This Object's Parent setting.

- You can assign ownership with the /Setowner switch. For example, **icacls bach.docx /setowner jan** grants ownership of the Bach.docx file to the user named Jan.

- You can find all folders and files that have an ACE for a particular user or group. Use the /Findsid switch. For example, **icacls * /findsid benito /t** finds all objects in the current folder and all subfolders (the /T switch adds subfolder processing to any Icacls command) in which there's an entry for the user named Benito.

- You can modify permissions settings using the /Grant, /Deny, /Remove, and /Setintegritylevel switches. Most commonly, you'll use /Grant to add specific permissions (or /Grant:R to replace the existing ACE for a user) or /Remove to remove all permissions for a particular user or group. For example, **icacls music /grant benito:rx /t** grants Read & Execute permission to Benito for the Music folder and its subfolders.

    In conjunction with the /Grant switch, use one of the following codes:

    - F is equivalent to selecting the Allow box next to the Full Control entry in the Permissions dialog box.

    - M is equivalent to selecting the Allow box for the Modify entry.

    - RX is equivalent to selecting the Allow box for the Read & Execute entry.

    - R is equivalent to selecting the Allow box for the Read entry.

    - W is equivalent to selecting the Allow box for the Write entry.

Note that wildcards can be used to specify more than one file in a command and that you can specify more than one user in a command. For instance, if you've created a subfolder called Archives in the Documents folder and you want Carl to have Full Control permissions and Craig to have Read permissions in that folder, open a Command Prompt window, navigate to the Documents folder, and type the following command:

```
icacls archives /grant carl:f craig:r
```

If you then decide that you want to revoke Craig's access rights and give Read permissions to the Administrators group, type this command:

```
icacls archives /remove craig /grant administrators:r
```

For more information about command syntax for Icacls, at a command prompt, type **icacls** with no parameters.

Taking Ownership of Files and Folders

When you create a file or folder on an NTFS drive, Windows designates your user account as the owner of that object. That status gives you the right to allow or deny permission for other users and groups to access the file or folder. As owner, you can lock out every other user, including all members of the Administrators group.

So what happens if you turn over responsibility for a document (or an entire folder full of documents) to another user? As the owner, you can allow the other user to take ownership of the object. In addition, any member of the Administrators group can take ownership of any file or folder.

Turning over the ownership of a file or folder makes sense when you want someone else to be responsible for setting permissions for that object. To ensure a smooth transition of power, use either of the following techniques.

If you're a member of the Administrators group, follow these steps:

1. Right-click the file or folder icon, and choose Properties.

2. On the Security tab, click Advanced to open the Advanced Security Settings dialog box for the file or folder.

3. Click the Owner tab to display a dialog box that identifies the current owner. To change the owner, click Edit. This and allows you to transfer ownership to the Administrators group or to your account.

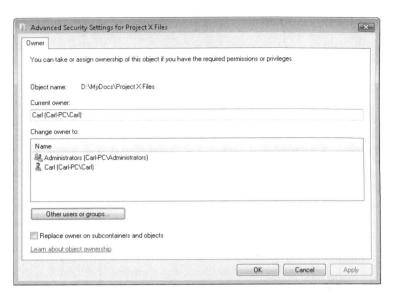

4. Select a name from the Change Owner To list, or click Other Users And Groups to assign ownership to a name not in the list. When you're finished, click OK.

If you're not an administrator, you must first be granted the right to take ownership of a file or folder explicitly. To do this, ask the current owner or any member of the Administrators group to add your account to the ACL for the file or folder and give you the Take Ownership permission. This permission can be found at the bottom of the list of special permissions available by clicking Edit in the Advanced Security Settings dialog box. Ultimately, the ability for an administrator to take ownership of files and folders means that you can't count on absolute privacy for any files stored on an NTFS drive. No matter how securely you lock them up, an administrator can break through the lock by taking ownership of the files. This is a brute force solution, however, and it's not something that can be easily hidden. If you're concerned about security and you want to monitor changes in ownership of file-system objects, configure your system so that Take Ownership events in a particular location are audited. For more information, see "Monitoring Access to Folders and Files," Chapter 31.

Troubleshooting Permissions Problems

If you use only the Sharing wizard to manage permissions, and if you use default settings in Windows Explorer, you're unlikely to run into NTFS permission roadblocks. But if you veer from this path you might sometimes be flummoxed, wondering why you can't access a particular file or folder.

Permissions and File Operations

Sorting out NTFS permissions is complex enough for a static file. But ordinary file management tasks such as moving and copying files can change permissions, which can have unintended and confusing consequences. In fact, even when a user has been granted Full Control permissions for a given folder, he or she may encounter an "access denied" error message when trying to open, rename, delete, or copy a file or folder.

To understand why this problem occurs, you need to understand what happens when you move or copy files or folders from one location to another. During the move, the permissions for the files or folders may change. Note the different results that apply depending on whether you're moving or copying the object and whether the destination is on the same drive or on a different drive:

- **When you copy a file or folder to an NTFS drive...** The newly created folder or file takes on the permissions of the destination folder, and the original object retains its permissions. This is true regardless of whether the destination is on the same NTFS drive as the original file or on a separate NTFS drive. You become the Creator Owner of the new file or folder, which means you can change its permissions.

- **When you move a file or folder to the Public folder or one of its subfolders...** The moved folder or file retains its original permissions *and* takes on the permissions of the destination folder. The owner remains unchanged.

- **When you move a file or folder within a single NTFS drive...** The moved folder or file retains its original permissions and owner.

- **When you move a file or folder from one NTFS drive to another...** The moved folder or file picks up the permissions of the destination folder and you become the Creator Owner.

- **When you copy or move a file or folder from a FAT32 drive to an NTFS drive...** The newly created folder or file picks up the permissions of the destination folder and you become the Creator Owner.

- **When you copy or move a file or folder from an NTFS drive to a FAT32 drive...** The moved or copied folder or file in the new destination loses all permission settings, because the FAT32 file system is incapable of storing these details.

Armed with this understanding, you can change permission settings as needed to regain access. More importantly, you can avoid surprises by anticipating how permissions will be changed, depending on whether you move or copy a file.

Permissions and Windows XP Profile Folders

Windows experts often change display options for Windows Explorer so that it shows "super hidden" files—files with both the system and hidden attributes. (You make this setting in Folder Options. On the View tab, clear Hide Protected Operating System Files [Recommended].) Those who do so invariably discover the profile folders from

Windows XP, including Documents And Settings, My Pictures, Application Data, and so on. But then they're surprised to find that double-clicking one of these folders (or other similar items) results in an "access denied" error message. Similarly, trying to work with any of the files contained within these folders or their subfolders produces the same error. (You can reach those files and subfolders by typing the path name at a command prompt, for example. This is true even if the protected folders are not displayed in Windows Vista.) Using an administrator account makes no difference; all users are blocked from these folders.

In fact, these items are not folders at all; they are junctions or symbolic links that point to their Windows Vista corollary folders. (For example, the Documents And Settings folder is merely a pointer to the Users folder.) These junction points are in place to provide compatibility for older applications for Windows. As part of their implementation, the Everyone group has a Deny ACE for List Folder / Read Data.

> **Note**
>
> Because the access-denied message is reminiscent of the messages displayed by User Account Control (UAC), you might think that UAC is causing the access problem. In fact, this is entirely an NTFS permissions issue, and has nothing to do with UAC. (Don't believe it? You can confirm it by turning off UAC; you still won't have access to these folders.)

The solution is simple: *do not use these folders for navigation!* Aside from application compatibility, they offer nothing that the new folder names do not. Don't delete the folders, and don't remove the Deny permission, as that can have other unintended consequences. To work on the files and folders that appear to be in these folders, instead follow the path of nonhidden folders to find the same files and subfolders. Honestly, the best solution is to hide the protected operating system files, and forget that you ever found these folders.

Other Permissions Problems

You might not be able to access files if you created them in an earlier version of Windows. This is especially likely if you used the Make This Folder Private in Windows XP, or if you've set up a dual-boot system that has a Windows XP partition and a Windows Vista partition. Each Windows installation keeps its own security database, and user accounts created in one Windows installation aren't recognized in the other, even if the user name and password are identical. You can resolve the problem by taking ownership of the file and then adding permission entries for the users who need access. If you plan to continue using the file in the other Windows installation, don't remove the entries that show a security identifier (SID) instead of a user name. Those SIDs represent user accounts in the other Windows installation.

Another common cause of permission problems has a simple solution. After you add a user account to a group that has been assigned permissions for a file or folder, the user must log off and log back on to have access to the files.

INSIDE OUT   Don't overlook inherited permissions

When trying to sort out why a user is having problems accessing a given file or folder, look first in the Advanced Security Settings dialog box. Pay particular attention to the Inherited From column in the Permission Entries list. The data here will often show you the exact source of an unexpected permission problem.

CHAPTER 30

Automating
Windows Vista

Home Basic ⦿
Home Premium ⦿
Business ⦿
Enterprise ⦿
Ultimate ⦿

I f you use your computer very much—and if you're reading this book you probably do—
you likely find yourself certain ordinary tasks repeatedly. Such tasks might include
routine maintenance activities, such as backing up your data or cleaning deadwood
from your hard disk, or they might be jobs that require many steps. Computers excel
at repetitive actions, and Microsoft Windows Vista provides several ways to automate
such tasks:

- **Task Scheduler** Probably the most important automation tool at your disposal
  is Task Scheduler, which is significantly more powerful and easier to use in Windows Vista than it was in Windows XP. Task scheduler lets you set up automated
  routines, to be triggered by events or by a schedule, and requires no programming expertise.

- **Batch Programs** A carryover from the earliest days of MS-DOS, batch programming still offers an easy, reliable way to run sequences of tasks. Most Windows
  programs can be started from a command prompt, which means they can be
  started from a batch program.

- **Windows Script Host** This feature allows you to run scripts written in VBScript,
  JScript, and other languages. Although learning how to use Windows Script Host
  is more difficult than learning to create batch programs, scripts can interact with
  the operating system and with other programs in more powerful ways.

- **Windows PowerShell** Windows PowerShell (known in its pre-release days as
  Monad) isn't actually a component of Windows Vista, but it's available as a free
  download from Microsoft. It's a .NET 2.0-based scripting language tailored to
  work with Windows Vista. If you're serious about scripting Windows Vista, you'll
  want to take a look at Windows PowerShell.

What's in Your Edition?

The options for automating Windows Vista are the same in all editions.

Using the Windows Vista Task Scheduler

If you've used Scheduled Tasks in Windows XP, you'll be pleased by the changes in Windows Vista. To begin with, the user interface to the task scheduler has been implemented as a Microsoft Management Console (MMC) snap-in, giving you access to more information about the properties, status, and run history of your tasks (and those that the operating system and your applications have established for you). Second, the Scheduled Tasks snap-in has been neatly integrated with the Event Viewer snap-in, making it easy for you to use events (an application crash or a disk-full error, for example) as triggers for tasks. Third and most important, the Windows Vista Task Scheduler supports a much more extensive set of triggering and scheduling options. Now, in addition to running programs or scripts at specified times, you can launch actions when the computer has been idle for a specified time period, when particular users log on or off, and so on. You can use these (and other) triggers to send e-mail messages or display message windows, as well as to run programs or scripts.

For information about the Event Viewer snap-in, see Chapter 22, "Monitoring System Activities with Event Viewer." For more general information about using Microsoft Management Console, see Appendix C, "Using and Customizing Microsoft Management Console."

To launch the Task Scheduler snap-in, you can go to Control Panel, click System And Maintenance, and then click Schedule Automated And Periodic Tasks (you'll find that under Administrative Tools). If you have an Administrative Tools folder on your Start menu, you can find the Task Scheduler there. Or, if you're handy at the keyboard, simply press Windows logo key+R and type **taskschd.msc** on the Run line. However you issue the command, you'll need to answer a UAC prompt before the Task Scheduler snap-in appears.

Figure 30-1 shows a sample of Task Scheduler in its default layout. As you can see, the window is divided vertically into three regions—a Console tree on the left, an Action pane on the right, and various informative windows in the center. The Console tree shows you which computer you're working with (the local machine or a network computer to which you have connected) and provides a folder tree of currently defined tasks. You can create your own folders here to organize the tasks that you create yourself, or you can add new tasks to existing folders.

The Action pane provides a menu of things you can do. With rare (and probably unintended) exceptions, items here are also available on the menus at the top of the window, so if you're feeling cramped in the center, you might consider hiding the Action pane. (Choose View, Customize, and then deselect Action Pane.)

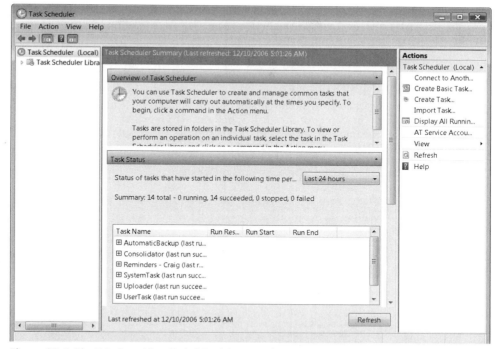

Figure 30-1 The Windows Vista Task Scheduler is implemented via an MMC snap-in.

In the center part of the window, initially, you'll see an overview message (this is a static bit of text; once you've read it, you can hide it by clicking the collapse arrow at the right), a status report of all tasks that have run (or were scheduled to run) during some period of time (by default the most recent 24 hours), and a summary of all the currently enabled tasks. Entries in the Task Status list have outline controls; click an item's plus sign to see more details.

The Task Status and Active Tasks displays are not updated automatically. To get the latest information, click Refresh—at the bottom of the screen, in the Action pane, or on the Action menu.

If this is your first visit to Task Scheduler, you might be surprised by the number of active tasks that Windows and your applications have already established. For example, if you use the Windows Vista Backup program to perform regular full and incremental backups, you'll find some Backup-related items in the list. Unless you or someone else has disabled automatic disk defragmentation, there will be an item in the list. If you rely on Windows Calendar or another program to remind you of appointments or task deadlines, chances are that functionality will be represented in the Active Tasks list.

To see what tasks managed by the Task Scheduler are currently running, click Display All Running Tasks in the Action pane. (If you're looking for that command on the Action menu, be sure that the top node in the Console tree is selected.)

To satisfy your curiosity about what an active task does and how it has been set up, you'll need to locate it in the Console tree. Expand the outline entries as needed and browse to an item of interest. The entries in the Console tree are virtual folders, each of which can contain subfolders or one or more tasks. When you select a folder, the upper pane in the center of the Task Scheduler window lists all tasks stored there. The lower pane, meanwhile, shows a tabbed display of the properties of the current task item. Figure 30-2 shows the WindowsBackup folder selected in the Console tree, the AutomaticBackup task selected in the upper pane, and the General tab of the AutomaticBackup properties display in the lower pane. (The Action pane has been hidden in this figure.)

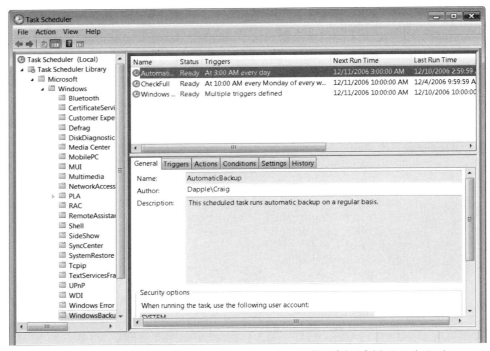

Figure 30-2 Selecting a folder in the Console tree produces a list of that folder's tasks in the upper pane and a properties display in the lower pane.

The properties display that appears in place in the Task Scheduler snap-in (for example, the one shown in Figure 30-2) is read-only. To edit the properties associated with a task, right-click the task name and choose Properties from the shortcut menu. (Or double-click the task's entry.) That will open a read-write dialog box in a separate window.

With the exception of the History tab, the properties dialog box is simply a read-only version of the Create Task dialog box, one of the tools you can use to create a new task; we'll explore that dialog box in some detail, later in this chapter. The History tab allows you to see exactly how, whether, and when a task has run. Figure 30-3 shows the History tab for AutomaticBackup.

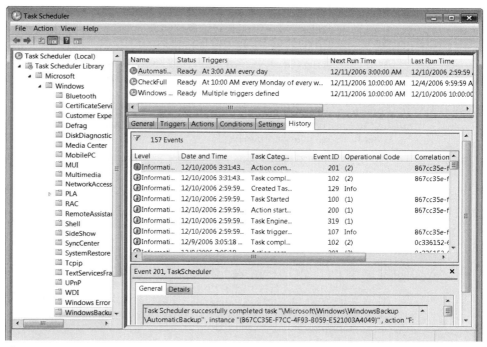

Figure 30-3 The History tab lets you confirm that a scheduled task is running as expected.

When you display the History tab, the relevant portion of the Event Viewer snap-in snaps in, showing you all the recent events relating to the selected task. This is exactly what you would see if you ran Evntvwr.msc, navigated in the Console Tree to Applications And Services Logs\Microsoft\Windows\TaskScheduler\Operational, and filtered the resulting log display to show events relating to the selected task. (Obviously, if you want this information, it's quicker to find it in the Task Scheduler console than in the Event Viewer console.) If a task you've set up is not getting triggered when you expect it to or not running successfully when it should, you can double-click the appropriate event entry and read whatever details the event log has to offer.

Use the History Tab to Troubleshoot Tasks

Unlike the Scheduled Tasks folder in Windows XP (which recorded only the most recent error code generated by a failed task), the Windows Vista Task Scheduler maintains an ample history of the events generated by each task. If a task is failing regularly or intermittently, you can review all the causes by scrolling through the History tab of the task's properties display.

> ### Task Scheduler Terminology
>
> As you go through the steps to create or edit a task, you'll encounter the following terms:
>
> **Trigger** The time at which a task is scheduled to run, or the event in response to which a task is to run. A task can have multiple triggers.
>
> **Action** What the task does. Possible actions include starting a program, sending an e-mail message, and displaying a message on screen. A task can have multiple actions, in which case the actions occur sequentially in the order in which you assign them.
>
> **Condition** An additional requirement that, along with the trigger, must be met for the task to run. For example, a condition might stipulate that the task run only if the computer has been idle for ten minutes.
>
> **Setting** A property that affects the behavior of a task. With settings you can do such things as enable a task to be run on demand or set retry parameters to be followed if a task fails to run when triggered.

Creating a Task

You can set up tasks on your own computer or any other computer to which you have access. If you're administering a remote computer, start by selecting the top item in the Console tree—the one that says Task Scheduler (Local) if you haven't yet connected to a remote computer. Then choose Connect to Another Computer in the Action pane or from the Action menu.

To begin creating a new task, select the folder in the Console tree where you want the task to reside. If you need to create a new folder for this purpose, right-click the folder's parent in the Console tree and choose New Folder from the shortcut menu.

You can create a new task in the Scheduled Tasks snap-in either by using a wizard or by filling out the Create Task dialog box. The wizard, which you launch by choosing Create Basic Task (in the Action pane or from the Action menu), is ideal for time-triggered tasks involving a single action. It's also fine for setting up a task to run when you log on or when Windows starts. For a more complex task definition you'll need to work through the Create Task dialog box. Select the folder where you want the task to appear (in the Console tree), then choose Create Task in the Action pane or from the Action menu. Figure 30-4 shows the General tab of the Create Task dialog box.

The one required entry on the General tab is a name for the task; everything else is optional. The task's author is you (you can't change that), and unless you specify otherwise, the task will run in your own security context. If you want it to run in the security context of a different user or group, click Change User Or Group and fill out the ensuing dialog box.

Figure 30-4 On the General tab, type a name for your new task and indicate whose security context it should run in.

The circumstance under which you're most likely to need to change the security context is if you're setting up tasks to run on another computer. If you intend to run programs with which another user can interact, you should run those in the other user's security context. If you run them in your own, the tasks will run noninteractively (that is, the user will not see them).

Regardless of which user's security context the task is to run in , you have the option of allowing the task to run whether or not that user is logged on. If you select Run Whether User Is Logged On Or Not, you will be prompted for the user's password when you finish creating the task. If you don't happen to have that password, you can select Do Not Store Password. As the text beside this check box indicates, the task will have access to local resources only.

Creating a Task to Run with Elevated Privileges

If the task you're setting up is one that would generate a UAC prompt if run interactively, you'll want to select Run With Highest Privileges. Because you've already dealt with a UAC prompt when you launched Task Scheduler, you won't have to supply any additional credentials or answer any further prompts when you create the task. When your task runs, it will run with administrative privileges.

Creating a Hidden Task

Windows XP Service Pack 2 introduced the ability to create hidden tasks—tasks that did not ordinarily appear in the Windows XP Scheduled Tasks folder. Such tasks could be created only by means of a programming API. In Windows Vista, you can create such tasks without using the API, by selecting the Hidden check box. Presumably the reason to do this would be make tasks that you set up for other users less visible (hence less subject to alteration or deletion) on their target machines.

Note, however, that anyone who has the administrative credentials required to run Task Scheduler can make hidden tasks visible by choosing View, Show Hidden Tasks. And anyone running Task Scheduler can alter or delete tasks at will, regardless of who created them.

Configuring a Task to Run in a Different Operating System

If you're setting up a task on a remote computer that's running an operating system other than Windows Vista, open the Configure For drop-down list and choose appropriately. As of this writing, the Windows Vista Task Scheduler can configure tasks for Windows Server 2003, Windows XP, or Windows 2000, in addition to Windows Vista.

Setting Up a Task's Trigger or Triggers

Tasks can be triggered in the following ways:

- On a schedule
- At logon
- At startup
- On idle
- On an event
- At task creation or modification
- On connection to a user session
- On disconnect from a user session
- On workstation lock
- On workstation unlock

You can establish zero, one, or several triggers for a task. If you don't set any triggers, you can still run the task on demand (unless you clear the Allow Task To Be Run On Demand check box on the Settings tab of the Create Task dialog box). This gives you a way to test a new task before committing it to a schedule, for example. If you set multiple triggers, the task runs when any one of the triggers occurs.

To set up a trigger, click the Trigger tab in the Create Task dialog box, and then click New. On the New Trigger dialog box that appears (shown in Figure 30-5), choose the type of trigger you want from the Begin The Task drop-down list.

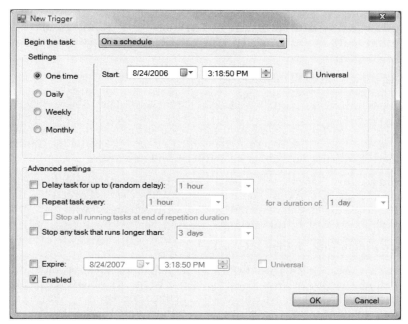

Figure 30-5 A task can have zero, one, or several triggers. Advanced Settings options let you set delay, repeat, and expiration parameters.

Note the Advanced Settings options at the bottom of the dialog box shown in Figure 30-5. These choices, which let you establish delay, repeat, and expiration parameters (among other things), are not so easy to find when you're reviewing a task that you or someone has already created. They don't appear in the read-only version of a task's properties, and if you re-open the read/write version of the properties dialog box, you'll need to select a trigger (on the Trigger tab) and click Edit to see or change the advanced options.

Triggering a Task on Schedule

Time-triggered tasks can be set to run once or to recur at regular intervals. The choices are probably self-explanatory, with the possible exception of the Universal check box. Time triggers are governed by the clock of the machine on which the task is to run, unless you select this check box—in which case they are triggered by coordinated universal time (UTC). You might want to go with UTC if you're trying to coordinate time-triggered tasks on multiple machines in multiple time zones.

Triggering a Task at Logon

Logon tasks can be set for any user or a specific user or user group. If the user whose logon has triggered the task is not the user in whose security context the task is running, the task will be non-interactive—in other words, essentially invisible. (The user can note the presence of the task—and terminate it—by running Windows Task Manager, going to the Processes tab, clicking Show Processes From All Users, and answering the UAC prompt.)

Triggering a Task at Startup

If you set a task to be triggered at startup, the trigger takes effect when you start your own computer (assuming you have Task Scheduler set to configure the local machine), but before you log on. Therefore, if you intend for the task to run on your own system, be sure to choose Run Whether User Is Logged On Or Not, on the General tab of the Create Task dialog box. Otherwise the task will never run.

If you use the Change User Or Group button on the General tab to specify another user on your domain, and you choose Run Only When User Is Logged On, the startup-triggered task will run on the remote system when you restart your own, provided the specified user actually is logged on.

Triggering a Task on Idle

If you set a task to be triggered when your computer is idle, you should also go to the Conditions tab of the Create Task dialog box to specify what you mean by "idle." For information about how Scheduled Tasks defines idleness, see "Starting and Running a Task Only If the Computer Is Idle," later in this chapter.

Note that you only need to set an idle trigger on the Trigger tab if idleness is the only trigger you want to use. If you're setting one or more other triggers but you want to ensure that the task starts only when the computer is idle, select the Start The Task Only If The Computer Is Idle For check box on the Conditions tab.

Using an Event to Trigger a Task

One of the most powerful new features of the Windows Vista Task Scheduler is the ability to have tasks triggered by events. Anything that generates an item in an event log can serve as a task trigger. *(For information about events and event logs, see Chapter 22, "Monitoring System Activities with Event Viewer.")*

The simplest way to use this feature is to launch the Event Viewer snap-in (Eventvwr.msc), find the event that you want to use as a trigger, right-click it in Event Viewer, and choose Attach Task To This Event. This action launches the Create Basic Task Wizard, with the trigger portion of the wizard already filled out. The new task appears in a folder called Event Viewer Tasks (newly created for you if it doesn't already exist), and you can modify it if needed by selecting it there and opening its properties dialog box.

It's possible, of course, to create an event-driven task directly in Task Scheduler—by selecting On An Event in the New Trigger dialog box. If you set up the task in this fashion, however, you'll need to supply the Log, Source, and Event ID information yourself. It's more trouble to do it this way, and there's no need.

Triggering at Task Creation or Modification

The option to trigger a task at task creation or modification gives you an easy way to make a task run the moment you finish setting it up the first time or editing it subsequently. You can use this setting for testing purposes, or by combining it with other triggers, you can use it to make a task run immediately as well as subsequently.

Triggering a Task at User Connection or Disconnection

The options On Connection To A User Session and On Disconnect From A User Session give you some flexible ways to set tasks running in response to user activities. Option buttons associated with these choices let you specify whether the settings apply to any user or to a particular user or group. Additional options make the trigger apply to remote connections and disconnections or to local connections and disconnections. Setting a trigger to a particular user on the local computer, for example, would enable you to run a task in response to that user's connection via Remote Desktop or the Switch User command.

Triggering a Task at Workstation Lock or Unlock

Like several other triggering choices, the On Workstation Lock and On Workstation Unlock options can be configured to apply to a particular user or group or to anyone who locks or unlocks the computer.

Setting Up a Task's Action or Actions

Besides its name (which you supply on the General tab of the Create Task dialog box), the only other task parameter you must provide is the action or actions the task is supposed to perform. This you do by clicking New on the Task tab and filling out the rest of the dialog box. Three types of actions are possible:

- Start a program
- Send an e-mail
- Display a message

You may specify one or several actions. Multiple actions are carried out sequentially, with each new action beginning when the previous one has completed.

The Start A Program option can be applied to anything that Windows can execute—a Windows program, a batch program or script, a document associated with a program, or a shortcut. You can use the Browse button to simplify entry of long path specifications, add arguments for your executable on the Add Arguments line, and specify a start-in folder for the executable. If your program needs elevated privileges to run successfully, be sure that you have selected Run With Highest Privileges, on the General tab of the New Task dialog box.

Chapter 30

If you choose to send an e-mail, Task Scheduler will require the address of your out-bound (SMTP) server. If you opt for a message, the dialog box will provide fields for the window title and message text. The Send An E-Mail and Display A Message options are not available for tasks set to run on Windows XP, Windows 2000, or Windows Server 2003.

Starting and Running a Task Only If the Computer Is Idle

On the Conditions tab of the New Task dialog box, you can require that the computer be idle for a specified period of time before a triggered task can begin. To do this, select the Start The Task Only If The Computer Is Idle For check box, and specify the time pe-riod in the field to the right. Other check boxes in the Idle section of the Conditions tab let you specify what should happen if the task has begun during a required idle period but the computer subsequently becomes active again.

Task Scheduler defines idleness as follows:

- If a screen saver is running, the computer is presumed to be idle.

- If a screen saver is not running, the system checks for idleness every fifteen min-utes, considering the machine to be idle if there has been no keyboard or mouse input during that interval and if the disk IO and CPU usage figures were at 0 per-cent for 90 percent of that time.

In addition to specifying a required period of idleness, you can also tell Windows to wait some period of time after a task has been triggered before beginning to determine whether the computer is idle. Clearly, adjusting the idle parameters is a bit of an art; if you have precise requirements for some reason, you might need to experiment and test to get things just the way you want them.

Requiring AC Power

If you're setting up a task to run on a portable computer, consider whether you want the task to begin running while the computer is running on battery power. If you do not, select Start The Task Only If The Computer Is On AC Power, in the Power section of the Conditions tab. A second check box below this one lets you decide whether the task, once begun, should cease if the computer switches to battery power.

Waking the Computer to Run a Task

If it's essential that your task run at some particular time, whether or not the computer is asleep, be sure to select Wake The Computer To Run This Task, on the Conditions tab. Once aroused, the computer will then perform whatever duties you've assigned, returning to sleep on completion in accordance with whatever power plan is in effect.

If you do not want to disturb your computer's rest, you might want to stipulate that the task run as soon as possible after the machine awakes. You can do that by selecting Run Task As Soon As Possible After A Scheduled Start Is Missed, on the Settings tab of the New Task dialog box.

Requiring a Network Connection

If your task requires access to network resources, be sure to select Start Only If The Following Network Connection Is Available, on the Conditions tab. Then use the drop-down list directly below this check box to specify which network connection is required. You might want to use this option in conjunction with Run Task As Soon As Possible After A Scheduled Start Is Missed, a check box on the Settings tab.

Running a Task on Demand

One of the small but handy new features in the Windows Vista Task Scheduler is the ability for scheduled tasks to be run on demand, as well as in response to various time or event triggers. You can turn this feature off for a task by clearing the Allow Task To Be Run On Demand check box, on the Settings tab. But unless you're concerned that another user with access to your system might run a task against your wishes, it's hard to imagine why you would want to disallow on-demand execution.

To run a task on demand, assuming you have not disallowed it, locate the task's folder in the Console Tree, right-click the task in the Task Scheduler's upper window, and choose Run from the shortcut menu.

Scheduling Tasks with the Schtasks Command

The Task Scheduler provides a friendly and versatile method of creating and managing scheduled tasks. In some instances, however, you might find it easier to manage scheduled tasks from a command prompt. For these occasions. Windows Vista provides the Schtasks command, a replacement for the venerable At command that was included with earlier versions of the Windows NT platform. With Schtasks, you can create, modify, delete, end, view, and run scheduled tasks—and, of course, you can incorporate the command in batch files and scripts.

Tasks created via Schtasks appear in the top-level folder (Task Scheduler Library) in the Task Scheduler snap-in, and you can edit, run, or delete them from there as well as from the command prompt.

Schtasks is a rather complex command with lots of command-line switches and other parameters, but it has only six main variants:

- **Schtasks /Create** This variant, which you use to create a new scheduled task, is the most complex because of all the available triggering options, conditions, and settings. For details, type **Schtasks /create /?** at the command prompt.

- **Schtasks /Change** This variant allows you to modify an existing task. Among other things, you can change the program that the task runs, the user account under which the task runs, or the password associated with that user account. For details, type **Schtasks /change /?** at the command prompt.

- **Schtasks /Delete** This variant deletes an existing task, or, optionally, all tasks on a computer.

- **Schtasks /End** This variant stops a program that was started by a scheduled task.

- **Schtasks /Query** This variant displays, with optional verbosity, all scheduled tasks on the local or a remote computer. You can use arguments to restrict the display to particular tasks or tasks running in particular security contexts. For details, type **Schtasks /Query /?** at the command prompt.

- **Schtasks /Run** This variant runs a specified task on demand.

A few examples should give you an idea of the power of the Schtasks command. Suppose, for example, you want to take a break every four hours at 20 minutes past the hour to play a hand of Solitaire. The following command sets you up:

```
Schtasks /create /tn "Solitaire break" /tr "%programfiles%\microsoft games\solitaire\
solitaire.exe /sc hourly /mo 4 /st 00:20:00
```

In this example, the /Tn switch speicifes the name of the task, /Tr specifies the path to the executable program, /Sc specifies the schedule type /Mo specifies the interval, and /St specifies the starting time.

The following example creates a task that runs a script on the last Friday of each calendar quarter. (The script isn't included with Windows; it's just an example.)

```
Schtasks /create /tn "Quarterly wrap-up" /tr c:\apps\qtrwrap.vbs /sc monthly /mo last
/d fri /m mar,jun,sep,dec
```

By default, tasks scheduled via the Schtasks command run under the user account that's currently logged on. To make them run under a different account, use the /Ru switch followed by the account name you want to use; you'll also need to know the log-on password for that account. To use the built-in System account, append /ru "System" to the command. No password is required for the System account, but because only administrators can use Schtasks, this doesn't present a problem.

Automating Command Sequences with Batch Programs

A *batch program* (also commonly called a *batch file*) is a text file that contains a sequence of commands to be executed. You define the sequence of commands, name the sequence, and then execute the commands by entering the name at a command prompt. Any action you can take by typing a command at a command prompt can be encapsulated in a batch program.

When you type the name of your batch program at the command prompt (or when you specify it as a task to be executed by Task Scheduler and the appropriate trigger occurs), the command interpreter opens the file and starts reading the statements. It reads the first line, executes the command, and then goes on to the next line. On the surface, this seems to operate just as if you were typing each line yourself at the command prompt. In fact, however, the batch program can be more complicated, because the language includes replaceable parameters, conditional and branching statements, the ability to call subroutines, and so on. Batch programs can also respond to values returned by programs and to the values of environment variables.

Batch programming is a venerable art, having been with us since the earliest days of MS-DOS (long before Windows was so much as a twinkle in Microsoft's eye). These days there are more powerful scripting tools at your disposal. Nevertheless, if you have already invested some time and energy in learning the language of batch programming, that investment can continue to serve you in Windows Vista; your batch programs will run as well as they ever have, and you can execute them on or in response to events, by means of Task Scheduler.

If you are interested in acquiring or refreshing batch-programming skills now, you can take advantage of numerous free resources on the internet. Two good places to start are *http://www.vista-io.com/3001* and *http://www.vista-io.com/3002*.

> ### Recording Keyboard and Mouse Actions as Macros
>
> As an alternative to learning a programming language, you might be able to meet your automation needs with a simple macro recorder—a program that records keystrokes and mouse actions and then plays them back on demand. A number of macro recorder programs are available at little or no cost on the internet. You might want to try the following:
>
> - Aldo's Macro Recorder (*http://www.vista-io.com/3003*)
> - EZ Macros (*http://www.vista-io.com/3004*)
> - Macro Magic (*http://www.vista-io.com/3005*)
>
> A search for "macro" or "macro recorder" on any search engine or shareware download site is likely to turn up dozens of programs in this category.

Automating Tasks with Windows Script Host

Microsoft Windows Script Host (WSH) provides a way to perform more sophisticated tasks than the simple jobs that batch programs are able to handle. You can control virtually any component of Windows and of many Windows-based programs with WSH scripts.

To run a script, you can type a script name at a command prompt or double-click the script's icon in Windows Explorer. WSH has two nearly equivalent programs—Wscript.exe and Cscript.exe—that, with the help of a language interpreter dynamic-link library such as Vbscript.dll, execute scripts written in VBScript or another scripting language. (Cscript.exe is a command-line program; Wscript.exe is its GUI counterpart.)

With WSH, the files can be written in several different languages, including VBScript (a scripting language similar to Microsoft Visual Basic) and JScript (a form of JavaScript).

All the objects are available to any language, and in most situations, you can choose the language with which you are most comfortable. WSH doesn't care what language you use, provided the appropriate interpreter DLL is available. VBScript and JScript interpreters come with Windows Vista; interpreters for Perl, KiXtart (Kix), Python, Rexx, and other languages are available elsewhere.

Because WSH scripts can access ActiveX controls, they provide great flexibility. Several objects are provided with WSH that allow you basic control of Windows and your computer. By using ActiveX, you can control many of the programs on your computer. For example, you can create a script to display a chart in Microsoft Excel.

As an introduction, here's the WSH "Hello World" script. It's as short as it can get in any programming language:

```
Wscript.Echo "Hello World"
```

Using a plain-text editor such as Notepad, put this line in a file with a .vbs file name extension (Hello.vbs, for example), and you have a working WSH script. Simply double-click the file's icon in Windows Explorer to run your script.

Finding Scripting Resources

One of the biggest hurdles to learning to use WSH is finding the information you need. The language, whether it is VBScript or Jscript, is separate from the objects you use in your scripts, and each piece has separate documentation. You must find the reference guide for both the scripting language you choose and the objects you use. An excellent resource from Microsoft is the Windows Script section of the Microsoft Developer Network (MSDN) Library (*http://www.vista-io.com/3006*). You can find documentation of VBScript at *http://www.vista-io.com/3007*. For a wealth of third-party information about scripting and batch programming, visit Rob van der Woude's Scripting Pages website, at *http://www.vista-io.com/3008*.

Scripting and Security

Much has been made about the security risks posed by Windows Script Host. The power and flexibility afforded by scripts can be used by forces of evil as easily as they can be used to make your life simpler. Indeed, the infamous I Love You and Anna Kournikova e-mail worms were powered by VBScript attachments. Luckily, you can make some simple changes that reduce the chance that you'll accidentally run a nefarious script.

As a first line of defense, be sure that the file name extension is always displayed for script files. (This would have tipped off many people who opened an e-mail attachment named Anna Kournikova.jpg.vbs. Because the extension is not displayed by default, many hopeful fans expected to see a picture of the tennis star.) As a second defensive measure, you can change the default association for script files from Windows Script Host to Notepad. This causes script files to open harmlessly in the text editor if you inadvertently double-click them.

To make the extension visible, follow these steps:

1. Open a Windows Explorer window. (Any folder will do.)

2. If the menu bar is not visible, press Alt to make it so.

3. Choose Tools, Folder Options, and click the View tab.

4. In Advanced Settings, select Hide Extensions For Known File Types.

5. Click OK.

To change the default action associated with script files:

1. Choose Control Panel, Programs.

2. Choose Make A File Type Always Open In A Specific Program (under Default Programs).

3. In the Extensions list, select .JS and then click Change Program.

4. In the Open With dialog box, specify Notepad (you might need to click Browse to find Notepad).

5. Repeat steps 3 and 4 for the JSE, VBE, VBS, and WSF file types.

6. Click Close.

Changing a script file's association from Windows Script Host to Notepad protects you against accidental script execution at the cost of making intentional execution more difficult. To run a script, you can right-click it in Windows Explorer and choose Open With, Microsoft Windows Based Script Host. Alternatively, you can type **wscript.exe** or **cscript.exe** at a command prompt and follow either executable with the full name of the script file, complete with its path. (If you want to set up a scheduled task to execute a script, you must take this approach.)

Using the Script File Format

For WSH scripts, you can use VBScript in files with the .vbs extension and JScript in files with the .js extension. Windows Script Host adds another level of tags that provide more flexibility and power. In fact, WSH files, which use the .wsf extension, are actually Extensible Markup Language (XML) files that use tags, as shown in the following example (Hello.wsf):

```
<?XML version="1.0"?>
<package>
<job id="job1">
<?job debug="true"?>
<script language="VBScript" src="MyScript.vbs"/>
```

```
<script language="VBScript">
<![CDATA[
  WScript.Echo "Hello World"
]]>
</script>
</job>
</package>
```

Table 30-1 describes the function of each of these tags, plus a few others.

Table 30-1. Useful XML Tags

Tag	Description
<?XML version="1.0"?>	Marks your code as compliant with XML 1.0. This tag is optional now but might be required by future XML tools.
<package></package>	Encloses multiple jobs in a single file. The <package> tag is optional if you have only one pair of <job> tags.
<job id="job1"> </job>	Identifies jobs in a file. When you have multiple jobs in a file, you can run any one with this syntax: Cscript //Job:MyFirst-Job MyScripts.wsf
<?job debug="true"?>	Allows use of the script debugger. You can add error="true" to this tag to allow error messages for syntax or run-time errors.
<script language="VBScript" src="MyScript.vbs"/>	Includes, or merges, another file into the current one when the script runs. This tag allows you to easily reuse code.
<script language="VBScript"> </script>	Encloses a script. In a single job, you might have several scripts—even in different scripting languages.
<![CDATA[ ]]>	Indicates that the parser should treat your code as character data and not interpret the characters in it. Use this tag if you use the XML tag.
<object>	Defines objects that can be referenced by the script.
<reference>	Provides a reference to an external type library, allowing you to use defined constants from that type library.
<resource>	Isolates text or numeric data that should not be hard-coded in a script.

Finding Resources for Windows PowerShell

Windows PowerShell, described by Microsoft as "next-generation Microsoft command-line shell automation and scripting technology," was still under construction as this book went to press. A wealth of information about Windows PowerShell was already available, however, at http://www.vista-io.com/3009. You can read introductory documentation there, peruse a quick-start command reference, browse sample scripts, watch webcasts, and read an interview with Jeffrey Snover, the product's software architect. You'll also find a PowerShell blog at http://www.vista-io.com/3010.

Advanced Security Management

Previous chapters show some of the security-related changes within Windows Vista. This chapter looks a little deeper at security topics, beginning with Windows Firewall. We'll look at how to examine the rules currently running within Windows Firewall as well as how to define your own custom rules.

We also explore user rights. You'll see exactly what differentiates administrators from standard users when it comes to performing certain tasks. Finally, we look at auditing—a way of keeping tabs on exactly who is doing what on your computer.

What's in Your Edition?

Windows Firewall With Advanced Security is an essential component of Windows security and is included in all editions of Windows Vista. Although user rights are implemented identically in all Windows Vista editions, the console for viewing and modifying them is available only in the Business, Enterprise, and Ultimate editions. When it comes to auditing, the Home Basic and Home Premium editions have preconfigured (and unchangeable) audit settings, whereas the other editions allow granular control over exactly what you audit.

Protecting a System with Windows Firewall

In Chapter 10 we explain the basics of Windows Firewall, including how to enable and disable the firewall and how to create exceptions. In that chapter, we discuss only the Windows Firewall application in Control Panel. In this section we examine two other methods for working with Windows Firewall: the Windows Firewall With Advanced Security console and the Netsh command-line utility.

To open Windows Firewall With Advanced Security, type **wf.msc** at a command prompt. Alternatively, in the Start menu Search box, begin typing **firewall**; when Windows Firewall With Advanced Security appears, click it. Either action opens Windows Firewall With Advanced Security, as shown in Figure 31-1 on the next page.

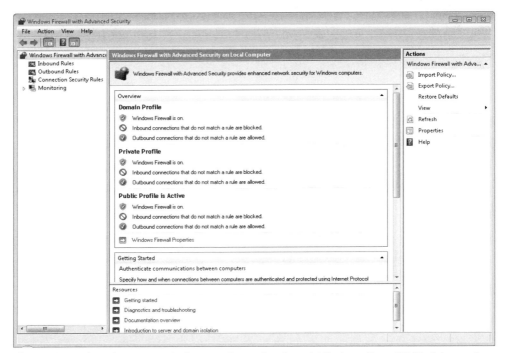

Figure 31-1 When the top item in the console tree is selected, Windows Firewall With Advanced Security displays a summary of firewall settings, and includes links to additional information.

Windows Firewall With Advanced Security is a snap-in for Microsoft Management Console (MMC) and is also saved as an MMC console named Wf.msc. For details about using MMC snap-ins and consoles, see Appendix C, "Using and Customizing Microsoft Management Console."

Viewing Active Rules and Security

A firewall *rule* defines how a given network packet is handled by the Windows Firewall. A rule combines things like the port on which the packet was received, the protocol, the direction (that is, inbound to or outbound from your computer), and other aspects of the packet along with the action to take when a packet that matches those criteria is received. An *exception*, such as those listed in the standard Windows Firewall application, comprises one or more rules.

With Windows Vista, the combinations of programs, protocols, directions, networks, ports, and actions that you can configure and turn into rules are virtually limitless. Then when you consider that you can apply these rules differently depending on the network location type (Domain, Public, or Private), the configuration possibilities are even more complex.

> **For more information about network locations, see "Understanding Location Types,"**
> **Chapter 12.**

The active rules under which Windows Firewall is currently operating can be viewed through Windows Firewall With Advanced Security. Figure 31-2 shows the default view of Inbound Rules in Windows Firewall With Advanced Security.

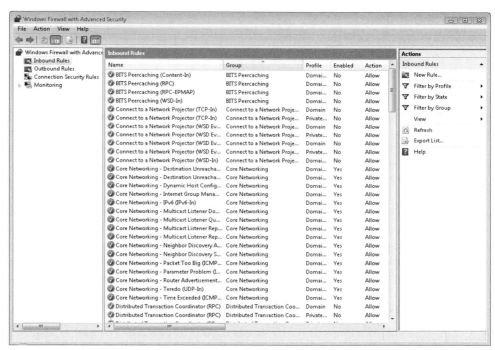

Figure 31-2 Active (enabled) rules are identified by a green icon in the leftmost column; a gray icon identifies a rule that has been defined, but is not currently enabled.

The display includes several columns that, depending on screen resolution, might not be visible unless you scroll to the right. In Figure 31-2 you see the rule name, the group to which it belongs, its profile, whether or not the rule is enabled, and its action. Scrolling to the right reveals several other specifics about the rule, such as the name of the program the rule affects, the local and remote addresses, the local and remote ports, the protocol, and the names of users and computers to which the rule applies.

The default view shows rules from all profiles (Domain, Private, and Public), all states (Enabled and Disabled), and all groups (too many to list here). It's often helpful to view a subset of the rules, such as only the rules that are currently active. To do so, apply a filter. Follow these steps to apply a filter so that you see only the currently enabled rules:

1. In the console tree of Windows Firewall With Advanced Security, select Inbound Rules.

2. In the Action pane, click Filter By State and select Filter By Enabled.

> **Note**
>
> Notice that, with a filter in place, a small arrow appears next to the Filter By State link in the Action pane; in addition, a Clear All Filters link appears. If you're wondering why you're not seeing the rules that you believe should be available, make sure there's no filter applied!

INSIDE OUT   See all active rules

To view all active rules—inbound and outbound—in the console tree select Monitoring\Firewall. You can reach the same page by clicking View Active Firewall Rules on the Monitoring overview page.

As described in Chapters 10 and 12, Windows Firewall has three different profiles—Domain, Private, and Public—with the appropriate one to use determined by the network location. You can see which profile your computer is currently using by selecting Monitoring in the console tree, as shown in Figure 31-3.

Creating a Rule

Windows Firewall With Advanced Security employs a wizard to assist in creating new rules. We'll demonstrate with a simple example to allow certain Internet Control Message Protocol (ICMP) traffic—something you can't do with the basic Windows Firewall application. Although our example nearly duplicates an existing rule named File And Printer Sharing (Echo Request - ICMPv4-In), you'll get an idea of how the wizard works. By the time you need to create a rule—perhaps using port and protocol information provided in the instructions for a program you use—you and the wizard will be old friends.

The TCP and UDP protocols are used to transmit data. But internet communication also relies on ICMP to communicate status, control, and error information between computers. In addition, widely used troubleshooting tools such as Ping and Tracert use ICMP to establish network connectivity. Because ICMP carries no data, it normally can't be used to break into your machine and steal information. However, hackers do use ICMP messages for scanning networks, redirecting traffic, and carrying out Denial of Service (DoS) attacks.

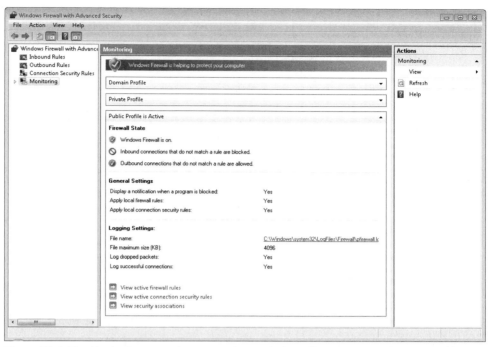

Figure 31-3 The Monitoring page shows at a glance which profile is active—in this case, Public.

By default, Windows Firewall blocks many types of outgoing and incoming ICMP message types. By creating a rule using Windows Firewall With Advanced Security, you can allow certain types of ICMP packets. Follow these steps to enable ICMP Echo Requests, Type 8, into your computer through Windows Firewall:

1. In the console tree of Windows Firewall With Advanced Security, click Inbound Rules.

2. In the Action pane, click New Rule. This opens the New Inbound Rule wizard.

3. Click Custom, as shown on the next page, to indicate that you'd like to create a custom rule and click Next.

4. Select All Programs and click Next. Doing so indicates that this rule should apply to all programs on this computer. Note that you could also select a specific program or service to which this rule should apply.

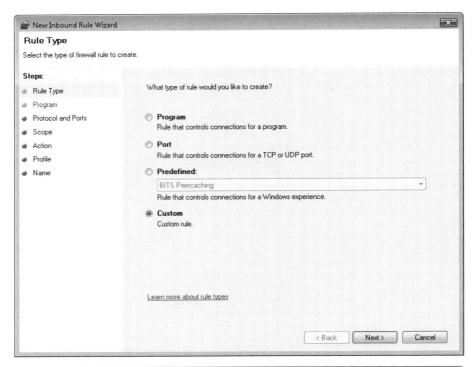

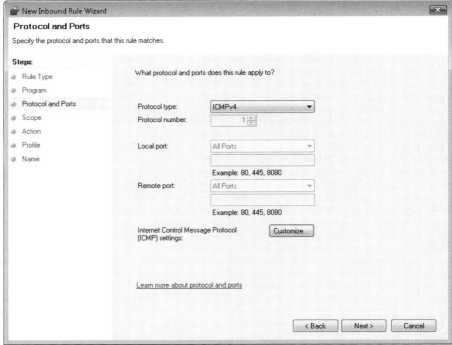

5. On the Protocols And Ports page, select ICMPv4 as the Protocol Type and then click Customize.

6. In the Customize ICMP Settings dialog box, select Specific ICMP Types, select Echo Request, and then click OK. Click Next to continue.

7. The Scope page appears, where you can specify the IP addresses to which the rule will apply. (The Customize button leads to a dialog box wherein you can specify which types of interface—local area network, remote access, or wireless—the rule will affect.) Leave these settings as-is and click Next.

8. On the Action page, you specify what you'd like to happen when a packet matching this rule is received. In this example, you'd like to allow the packet, so the default is acceptable. Click Next to continue.

9. On the Profile page you specify which profiles (Domain, Public, or Private) this rule applies to. Leave them all selected and click Next.

10. On the Name page, you give the rule a name. Choose something short but descriptive; for our example, type **IPv4 ICMP Echo Request**. Click Finish to complete the wizard.

The new rule now appears in the list of Inbound Rules in Windows Firewall With Advanced Security.

Configuring Complex Rules

Windows Vista includes collections of related firewall rules; in Windows Firewall With Advanced Security, each collection is called a group. Each group allows or blocks certain types of network traffic. Tagging rules with a group name makes them much easier to find than identifying them only by port or program name; in addition, you can quickly find all the rules that pertain to a particular firewall exception. For example, one group of rules (which happens to be a group of one) allows the Remote Desktop Protocol (RDP) to come into the computer. This saves you from having to know that RDP operates on TCP port 3389 in order to configure a rule for it.

Examining the rule for Remote Desktop reveals several details about its configuration that are interesting and some that might warrant a change in order to secure it even more. In the Inbound Rules list, find the Remote Desktop (TCP-In) rule; the easiest way is to click Filter By Group and select Remote Desktop. Double-click the rule to open its properties dialog box.

On the General tab of the Remote Desktop (TCP-In) Properties dialog box, shown in Figure 31-4, you can see that the rule is enabled.

Figure 31-4 As the note at the top of the General page explains, some settings in predefined rules like this one cannot be modified; to make changes, you must create a new rule.

The Programs And Services tab shows which program or service (or both) the rule applies to; for this particular rule, it doesn't provide much detail of interest. The Users And Computers tab lets you specify which authorized computers and authorized users are affected by the rule; these settings can be made only for IPsec connections.

Because this rule is predefined, the Protocols And Ports tab, shown in Figure 31-5, doesn't allow any settings modifications but can be used to view the protocol and port settings to which this rule applies.

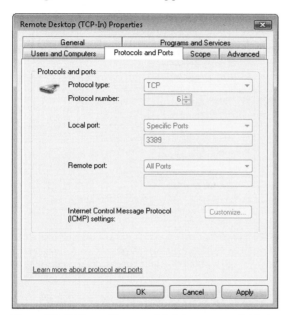

Figure 31-5 The settings on this tab are unavailable because it's a predefined rule.

The Advanced tab, shown in Figure 31-6 on the next page, enables you to set the profile or profiles to which this rule will apply along with setting of the interface types for the rule.

Figure 31-6 The Advanced tab can be used to specify the profile and interfaces to which the rule applies.

If you wanted Remote Desktop connections to be allowed only on local (hard-wired) connections instead of wireless or other interface types, click Customize. Using the dialog box shown in Figure 31-7, you're able to select the interface types to which this rule should apply.

Figure 31-7 The Remote Access option refers to connections through a Virtual Private Network (VPN) or dial-up connection.

Figure 31-8 shows the Scope tab, which contains settings related to the IP addresses from which connections for this rule apply. In the case of Remote Desktop, you might want to only allow connections from certain specific IP addresses or IP ranges—such as your local subnet.

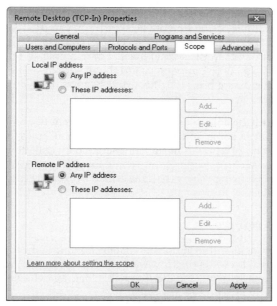

Figure 31-8 Settings related to the IP addresses for the rule are applied on the Scope tab.

Such a configuration can be accomplished through these steps:

1. In the properties dialog box for a rule, click the Scope tab.

2. Under Remote IP Address, select These IP Addresses and click Add. The IP Address dialog box opens.

3. Type the IP address or addresses that will be allowed to connect to this computer—in this example, using Remote Desktop. You can use Classless Inter-Domain Routing (CIDR) notation or enter specific IP addresses. (CIDR notation specifies the number of bits in the subnet mask. For example, to represent a subnet mask of 255.255.255.0, append /24 to the IP address.) The second example shown in the dialog box—192.168.1.0/24—shows how you can include all addresses in a subnet.

Most users will quite happily be able to use the default secure configuration included with Windows Vista. However, some networks require additional rules for exotic protocols or a more advanced configuration than the one included by default with Windows Firewall. For these cases, you can configure quite complex rules using Windows Firewall With Advanced Security using the method described previously in this chapter for enabling ICMP Echo Requests.

Logging Firewall Activity

When Windows Firewall blocks traffic, it doesn't display an (annoying) on-screen alert as some third-party personal firewalls do. However, you can configure Windows Firewall to store a record of its activity in a log file. To enable logging, follow these steps:

1. In the console tree, select Windows Firewall With Advanced Security On Local Computer (the top-level folder). In the Details pane, click Windows Firewall Properties. (Alternatively, right-click the top-level folder and choose Properties.)

2. In the properties dialog box, click the tab for the profile on which you want to collect firewall logs. Under Logging click Customize. The Customize Log Settings dialog box appears.

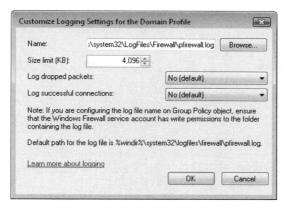

3. Select the kinds of events you want to log—dropped packets, successful connections, or both.

INSIDE OUT   **Log dropped packets only**

You'll get the most useful security information by logging only dropped packets, so that Windows Firewall records each connection that was blocked. Logging successful connections tends to create a large file with information that you probably don't need. A log of dropped packets, however, can lead you to IP addresses that are probing your computer.

4. Specify a file name for the log if you don't want to use the default (%SystemRoot%\System32\LogFiles\Firewall\Pfirewall.log).

5. To keep a log from getting too large, specify a maximum file size.

To read your log, open it in Notepad or another text editor. Figure 31-9 on the next page shows a sample of a Windows Firewall log.

The log uses the W3C Extended Log format, a standard logging format that allows you to analyze data using third-party utilities. To understand what the columns mean, look at the column headers in line 4. (They don't align over the data below, but they're in the correct order.) Table 31-1 on the next page provides a description of each of column.

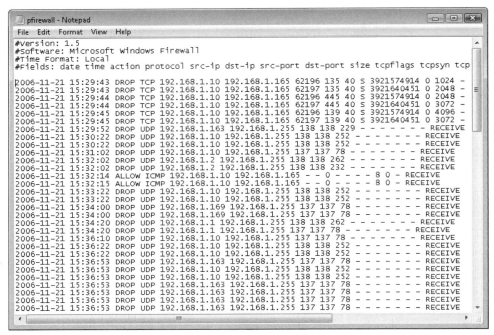

Figure 31-9 A firewall log captures a lot more information than you ever thought you'd need.

Table 31-1. Windows Firewall Log Content

Column	Description
Date	Year-Month-Date of occurrence
Time	Hour:Minute:Second of occurrence
Action	Operation logged by the firewall; possible values are OPEN, CLOSE, DROP, and INFO-EVENTS-LOST
Protocol	Protocol used for the communication; possible values are TCP, UDP, and ICMP
Src-ip	Source IP; IP address of the computer that initiated the communication
Dst-ip	Destination IP; IP address of your computer
Src-port	Source port; the port number of the sending computer
Dst-port	Destination port; port that the sending computer tried to access on your computer
Size	The size of the packet in bytes
TCPFlags	The protocol flags such as SYN, ACK, RST, and so on
TCPSyn	The TCP sequence number, if any, in the packet
TCPAck	The acknowledgement number, if any, in the packet
TCPWin	The Window Size in the packet header

Column	Description
ICMPType	The Type Code of the ICMP header
ICMPCode	The ICMP Code from the header
Info	Any information available about the packet
Path	The direction that the packet is heading

INSIDE OUT   **Use Microsoft Excel to view firewall logs**

Do you have Microsoft Office installed on your computer? If so, skip Notepad and use Microsoft Excel to analyze Windows Firewall log files. After converting the space-delimited text file to Excel columns, you can sort, filter, and search the output. Try using Excel's Filter capability to pick out specific IP addresses or ports from the log; this technique can help zero in on attackers quickly.

Using the Netsh Command to Manage Windows Firewall

If you need to make firewall settings repeatedly—on a single computer as conditions change or, perhaps, on a fleet of computers—you'll find working with Windows Firewall (the Control Panel application) or Windows Firewall With Advanced Security to be a bit cumbersome. The Netsh command, using its Firewall or Advfirewall context, provides an alternative way to view or modify all manner of Windows Firewall settings. For example, you can enable Windows Firewall with this command:

```
netsh firewall set opmode enable
```

The Netsh Firewall context might be considered the basic context, where you can find current firewall settings at a high level. It's roughly comparable to the Windows Firewall application in Control Panel. From the command prompt you can see the basic configuration by typing:

```
netsh firewall show config
```

To see more details about the configuration use the Advfirewall context—the command-line counterpart to Windows Firewall With Advanced Security. The Advfirewall context contains three subcontexts: Consec, Firewall, and Monitor. The Firewall subcontext can be used to show the rule details for specific (or all) rules or set new values for existing rules. You can also add rules on the fly using this subcontext. The Consec subcontext is used to work with connection security rules on the computer. The Monitor subcontext is used to view and set security associations.

To view all of the rules within Windows Firewall from the command line (be prepared for a lot of output) type:

```
netsh advfirewall firewall show rule name=all
```

With dozens of keywords and options, the Netsh Firewall and Netsh Advfirewall commands are quite complex. The best way to learn about the various possibilities is through the help available from the command line. You'll need to do it in several steps, appending another keyword each time. For example, start by entering **netsh firewall ?** at a command prompt. This returns a list of each of the keywords that you can put after *firewall*—Add, Delete, Dump, Help, Reset, Set, and Show—along with a brief description of each. Next you might type **netsh firewall set ?** to learn about each of the Set options. Then you'd type **netsh firewall set opmode ?**—and so on, until you reach a screen that shows the command syntax and explains all the parameters for the command you've entered.

> **Note**
>
> You can make settings for any profile using Netsh, just as you can with Windows Firewall With Advanced Security. In commands where it's relevant, you use the Profile parameter, which you can set to Public, Private, Domain, or All. (If you don't specify a profile, your settings apply to the current profile.)

Testing Your Computer's Network Security

As important as securing your computer is, how do you go about verifying its security from the perspective of a would-be attacker? There are tools available with Windows and others available for download that can help you determine your computer's footprint on the network.

The Netstat command-line tool can be used to show statistics and configuration related to the network settings on the computer. When run with some useful options, you can see the currently active network connections and those that are listening for connections. For example, enter this in a Command Prompt window:

```
netstat -a | more
```

> **Note**
>
> Note the use of the pipe character (|) and the More command. The pipe character sends the output from the Netstat command into the More command, which then paginates the output for easier reading. Without this addition to the command line, the output from Netstat would scroll off of the screen.

Partial output from this command will be similar to this:

```
Active Connections
  Proto  Local Address          Foreign Address         State
  TCP    0.0.0.0:135            Hope-PC:0               LISTENING
  TCP    0.0.0.0:3389           Hope-PC:0               LISTENING
  TCP    0.0.0.0:49152          Hope-PC:0               LISTENING
  TCP    0.0.0.0:49153          Hope-PC:0               LISTENING
  TCP    0.0.0.0:49154          Hope-PC:0               LISTENING
  TCP    0.0.0.0:49155          Hope-PC:0               LISTENING
  TCP    0.0.0.0:49156          Hope-PC:0               LISTENING
  TCP    0.0.0.0:49157          Hope-PC:0               LISTENING
  TCP    192.168.1.165:139      Hope-PC:0               LISTENING
  TCP    192.168.1.165:3389     dhcp-163:1216           ESTABLISHED
  TCP    192.168.1.165:49162    netserver:microsoft-ds  ESTABLISHED
```

From this output, you can see that there several services listening on various TCP ports, as denoted by the State of LISTENING. There are also two established connections, denoted by the ESTABLISHED state. These represent active TCP connections between the local computer and another computer or computers.

This output was generated to include DNS and other name lookups. This is fine in situations where DNS is configured properly for both forward and reverse naming. However, it's usually a good idea to distrust DNS when examining security-related items. This is because DNS names can be spoofed and therefore might provide misleading results. To view the Netstat output without name resolution, use the -N option, as follows:

```
C:\Users\Hope>netstat -an | more
```

```
Active Connections
  Proto  Local Address          Foreign Address         State
  TCP    0.0.0.0:135            0.0.0.0:0               LISTENING
  TCP    0.0.0.0:3389           0.0.0.0:0               LISTENING
  TCP    0.0.0.0:49152          0.0.0.0:0               LISTENING
  TCP    0.0.0.0:49153          0.0.0.0:0               LISTENING
  TCP    0.0.0.0:49154          0.0.0.0:0               LISTENING
  TCP    0.0.0.0:49155          0.0.0.0:0               LISTENING
  TCP    0.0.0.0:49156          0.0.0.0:0               LISTENING
  TCP    0.0.0.0:49157          0.0.0.0:0               LISTENING
  TCP    192.168.1.165:139      0.0.0.0:0               LISTENING
  TCP    192.168.1.165:3389     192.168.1.163:1216      ESTABLISHED
  TCP    192.168.1.165:49162    192.168.1.10:445        ESTABLISHED
```

Notice the difference in output here. No longer is the Foreign Address for the listening connections set to the name of this computer (Hope-PC). Also, the established connections no longer use the reverse DNS names for the IP addresses.

Even with the Netstat output showing that several ports are listening, it's not necessarily clear what ports are tied to which services. Port assignments for the Internet Protocol are managed an assigned by the Internet Assigned Numbers Authority (IANA). IANA maintains a list of well-known port numbers that is useful for finding out which protocols use the various ports on a computer. The list can be found at *http://www.vista-io.com/3101*.

From the IANA port number assignment list, it's possible to find that TCP port 3389 (from the output of the Netstat command) is usually used for MS-WBT Server, also known as Terminal Services or Remote Desktop.

Even with the information from IANA about the ports that are generally used for a given service, there's no guarantee that port 3389 is actually being used for Remote Desktop. It's possible to configure services to listen on ports other than their own default port. Therefore, another option is necessary in order to truly determine what process is listening on a given port in Windows. This command will show the currently active ports along with their Process ID (PID):

```
netstat -aon | more
```

The output will be similar to:

```
Active Connections
  Proto  Local Address         Foreign Address        State         PID
  TCP    0.0.0.0:135           0.0.0.0:0              LISTENING     796
  TCP    0.0.0.0:3389          0.0.0.0:0              LISTENING     1316
  TCP    0.0.0.0:49152         0.0.0.0:0              LISTENING     476
  TCP    0.0.0.0:49153         0.0.0.0:0              LISTENING     964
  TCP    0.0.0.0:49154         0.0.0.0:0              LISTENING     1204
  TCP    0.0.0.0:49155         0.0.0.0:0              LISTENING     1008
  TCP    0.0.0.0:49156         0.0.0.0:0              LISTENING     576
  TCP    0.0.0.0:49157         0.0.0.0:0              LISTENING     564
  TCP    192.168.1.165:139     0.0.0.0:0              LISTENING     4
  TCP    192.168.1.165:3389    192.168.1.163:1216     ESTABLISHED   1316
  TCP    192.168.1.165:49162   192.168.1.10:445       ESTABLISHED   4
  TCP    [::]:135              [::]:0                 LISTENING     796
```

From that output, you can see that PID 1316 is listening for connections on TCP port 3389. Using Windows Task Manager you can see that the TermServices service is using PID 1316, as shown in Figure 31-10.

Chapter 31

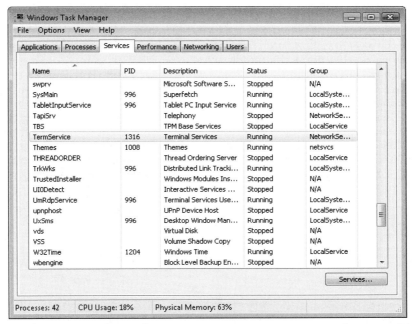

Figure 31-10 Correlating a listening process to a program name can be accomplished using Netstat and Task Manager.

The Netstat command shows which ports are listening along with any active connections at the time that the command is run. However, it's important to realize that even if a port is listening it doesn't necessarily mean that connections will be allowed through Windows Firewall.

To see what ports are actually available from the perspective of a potential attacker, a program such as Nmap (*http://insecure.org/nmap*) must be run from another computer. Nmap and similar programs can query your computer to determine which ports are listening at any given moment. Such output gives you a much better idea of the overall footprint of your computer on the network.

Managing User Rights

Chapter 31

Home Basic ○
Home Premium ○
Business ●
Enterprise ●
Ultimate ●

A *user right* is authorization to perform an operation that affects an entire computer. (A *permission*, by contrast, is authorization to perform an operation on a specific object— such as a file or a printer—on a computer.) For each user right, you can review which user accounts and groups have the user right. This can be helpful if you're having a problem performing a certain function and believe it might be due to the inherent user rights assignments. To review user rights, use the Local Security Policy console, which is available only on computers running the Business, Enterprise, or Ultimate edition of Windows Vista. (At a command prompt, type **secpol.msc** to open Local Security Policy.) Navigate to Security Settings\Local Policies\User Rights Assignment. Then double-click a user right to view or change the list of authorized users and groups, as shown in Figure 31-11.

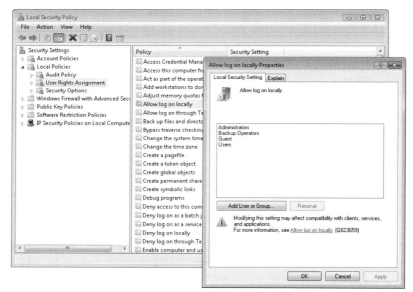

Figure 31-11 To review or change the local setting for a user right, double-click the user right in User Rights Assignment.

> **CAUTION**
>
> It's rarely helpful to change the default user rights assignments that come with Windows. Only for specific problems as directed by Microsoft or a reliable support document such as that in the Microsoft Knowledge Base should the user rights be changed from their default settings.

Some of the user rights—Access This Computer From The Network, Allow Log On Through Terminal Services, Log On As A Batch Job, Log On As A Service, Allow Log On Locally, and their corresponding "Deny" user rights—are known more precisely as *logon rights*. They control how users are allowed to access the computer—whether from the keyboard ("locally") or through a network connection, or whether as a service or as a batch facility (such as Task Scheduler). You can use these logon rights (in particular, Allow Log On Locally and Deny Log On Locally) to control who can log on to your computer. By default, Allow Log On Locally is granted to the local Guest account and members of the Administrators, Backup Operators, and Users groups. If you want to prevent certain users from logging on at the keyboard (but still allow them to connect via the network, for example), create a group, add the unwelcome user accounts to it, and then assign the Deny Log On Locally user right to the new group. Like deny permissions, deny logon rights take precedence over allow logon rights, so if a user is a member of both a group that is allowed to log on and a group that is not (such as the one described in the previous sentence), the user will not be allowed to log on. (Such users are rebuffed with an error message after they type their user name and password on the logon screen.)

For a description of each user right, click the Explain tab in the right's properties dialog box. You can find more detailed information about each right in "Threats and Countermeasures: Security Settings in Windows Server 2003 and Windows XP" (*http://www. vista-io.com/3102*), a white paper from Microsoft that includes a description of each user right along with a discussion of security vulnerabilities exposed by each user right granted and effective countermeasures. Although this document doesn't cover the three new rights added with Windows Vista (Change The Time Zone, Create Symbolic Links, and Increase A Process Working Set), the information is otherwise up to date.

Table 31-2 lists the default rights assigned to the built-in user groups and to the Guest account. Administrator accounts are members of the Administrators group, and standard user accounts are member of the Users group, Chapter 11.

For more information about account types, see "User Accounts and Security Groups."

Table 31-2. Default User Rights of Built-In User Groups in Windows Vista

Group	Default Rights
Administrators	• Access this computer from the network
	• Adjust memory quotas for a process
	• Allow log on locally
	• Allow log on through Terminal Services
	• Back up files and directories
	• Bypass traverse checking
	• Change the system time
	• Change the time zone

Group	Default Rights
Administrators	• Create a pagefile
	• Create global objects
	• Create symbolic links
	• Debug programs
	• Force shutdown from a remote system
	• Impersonate a client after authentication
	• Increase scheduling priority
	• Load and unload device drivers
	• Log on as a batch job
	• Manage auditing and security log
	• Modify firmware environment values
	• Perform volume maintenance tasks
	• Profile single process
	• Profile system performance
	• Remove computer from docking station
	• Restore files and directories
	• Shut down the system
	• Take ownership of files or other objects
Backup Operators	• Access this computer from the network
	• Allow log on locally
	• Back up files and directories
	• Bypass traverse checking
	• Log on as a batch job
	• Restore files and directories
	• Shut down the system
Everyone	• Access this computer from the network
	• Bypass traverse checking
Guest (account)	• Allow logon locally
	• Deny access to this computer from the network*
	• Deny log on locally

Group	Default Rights
Remote Desktop Users	• Allow log on through Terminal Services
Users	• Access this computer from the network
	• Allow log on locally
	• Bypass traverse checking
	• Change the time zone
	• Increase a process working set
	• Log on locally
	• Remove computer from docking station
	• Shut down the system

* The Guest account is removed from the list of accounts with the Deny Access To This Computer From The Network right when network sharing is turned on and password protected sharing is turned off.

Auditing Security Events

Home Basic ○
Home Premium ○
Business ●
Enterprise ●
Ultimate ●

As Microsoft's most secure operating system yet, Windows Vista is designed to prevent unauthorized access to a computer's files, folders, and printers. But if a user inadvertently makes improper settings or if an intruder is especially determined, someone might gain access to resources that should be off limits. Monitoring, or *auditing*, system usage can be a helpful tool in the administration of system security. For example, repeated attempts to log on with the wrong password might be an indication that unauthorized users are trying to gain access to your system. Repeated failure to access a folder might indicate that software has been incorrectly installed or that security for the folder is set up incorrectly.

Windows Vista provides the ability to audit security events by recording attempts to access system resources. In this section, we describe the various auditing tools that you, as a system administrator or resource owner, can use. We examine their purpose and use and explain what information they can supply when used properly.

Enabling Auditing

No events are written to the Security log until you enable auditing, which you do via Local Security Settings. Even if you set up auditing for files, folders, or printers, as explained later in this chapter, those events aren't recorded unless you also enable auditing in Local Security Settings.

> **Note**
>
> To enable auditing, you must be logged on with an account that has the Manage Auditing And Security Log privilege. By default, only members of the Administrators group have this privilege. For information about privileges, see "Setting User Rights."

> **Note**
>
> Like most other settings in Local Security Settings, the audit policy settings can be overridden by domain-level policy settings. If your computer is part of a Windows Server domain, you should use domain-level Group Policy to make audit policy settings instead of using Local Security Settings.

To enable auditing, follow these steps:

1. In Control Panel, open Administrative Tools, Local Security Policy. Alternatively, you can type **secpol.msc** at a command prompt, or simply begin typing **local security** in the Start menu Search box.

2. Expand Local Policies and then click Audit Policy to display the list shown in Figure 31-12.

3. Double-click each policy for which you want to enable auditing, and then select Success, Failure, or both.

Figure 31-12 shows the types of activities you can audit. Some, such as account management and policy change, can provide an audit trail for administrative changes. Others, such as logon events and object access, can help you discover how to better secure your system. Still others, including system events and process tracking, can assist you in locating problems with your system. Table 31-3 provides more details.

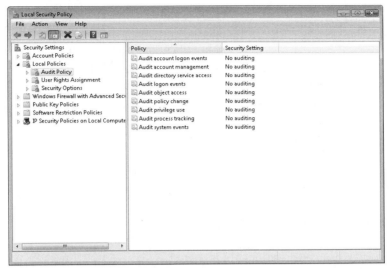

Figure 31-12 You enable auditing using the Local Security Settings console.

Table 31-3. Events That Can Be Audited

Audit Policy	Description
Audit account logon events	Account logon events occur when a user logs on or logs off another computer that uses this computer to validate the account. This happens only on a server running Windows Server, and is therefore not applicable on a computer running Windows Vista.
Audit account management	Account management events occur when a user account or group is created, changed, or deleted; when a user account is renamed, enabled, or disabled; or when a password is set or changed.
Audit directory service access	Directory service access events occur when a user accesses an Active Directory object that has its own system ACL. (This is the same as object access except that it applies only to Active Directory objects in a Windows domain.)
Audit logon events	Logon events occur when a user logs on or logs off a workstation or connects via a network.
Audit object access	Object access events occur when a user accesses a file, folder, printer, registry key, or other object that is set for auditing.
Audit policy change	Policy change events occur when a change is made to user rights assignment policies, audit policies, or trust policies.

Audit Policy	Description
Audit privilege use	Privilege use events occur when a user exercises a user right (other than logon, logoff, and network access rights, which trigger other types of events).
Audit process tracking	Process tracking includes arcane events such as program activation, handle duplication, indirect object access, and process exit. This policy is generally not useful for everyday security concerns.
Audit system events	System events occur when a user restarts or shuts down the computer or when an event occurs that affects system security or the Security log.

Viewing Security Events

Before we examine how to audit events, let's first take a look at Event Viewer—the Microsoft Management Console snap-in that allows you to examine the events that have been recorded. Event Viewer is in Control Panel, Administrative Tools, Event Viewer; or simply type **eventvwr.msc** at a command prompt. If you select the Security log, you'll see a window similar to the one shown in Figure 31-13.

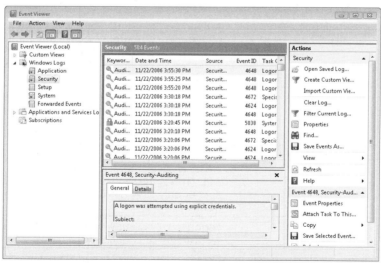

Figure 31-13 The Security log is visible only if you run Event Viewer as administrator.

For more information about Event Viewer, see Chapter 22, "Monitoring System Activities with Event Viewer."

If you want more information about an event in the Security log, double-click the event, or select it and then choose Action, Properties. The Event Properties dialog box appears, similar to the one shown in Figure 31-14.

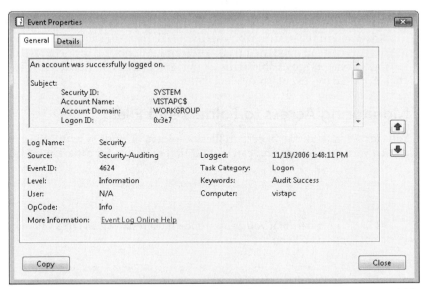

Figure 31-14 This Event Properties dialog box indicates that there was a successful logon.

The security event log can sometimes be filled with extraneous data. It is therefore sometimes helpful to filter the events to just see those that are of interest to you while troubleshooting a particular problem. For example, you could filter the Security log to look for event ID 4625, the ID for logon failure.

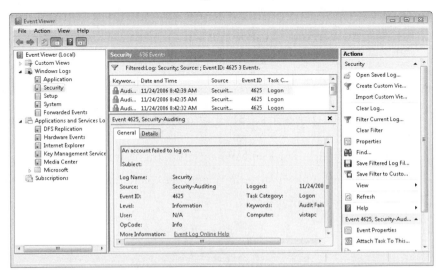

For more information about filtering events, see "Filtering the Log Display."

Monitoring Logon Events

By carefully examining logon events, you might be able to find a pattern in attempts to gain access to the system. You can then take measures to tighten security, such as warning users to change their passwords and monitoring the Security log more closely for specific events. To enable auditing of logon failures, in Local Security Policy double-click Audit Logon Events and select Failure.

Monitoring Access to Folders and Files

You can set up auditing of certain files or folders on your system. Windows Vista can audit a variety of events and can audit different events for different users.

> **Note**
>
> The files and folders that you want to audit must reside on an NTFS volume; FAT volumes do not support auditing.

Avoid auditing too many successful events. Although auditing is a useful technique for monitoring access to your system, you should be careful when auditing busy folders or files—and be particularly careful about auditing successful accesses. Each time a user successfully completes an operation on the file or folder, Windows Vista writes one or more records to the Security log to reflect the access. This slows down your system and adds many events of little value to the log, thereby making it more difficult to find real security breaches. On the other hand, selectively auditing successful file access can be beneficial in some situations. For example, you might want to log all access to a payroll database file, which would allow you to track down who did what (and when) as well as find out if someone without the proper authority accessed the file.

Use the Security tab in the properties dialog box for a file or folder to display its audit settings. You can specify the users and groups whose access to the selected file or folder you want to audit. For each user and group, you can specify which types of access should generate entries in the Security log. You can specify different auditing events for each user and group.

To set up auditing for files and folders, follow these steps:

1. Right-click a file or folder in Windows Explorer and choose Properties.

2. Click the Security tab.

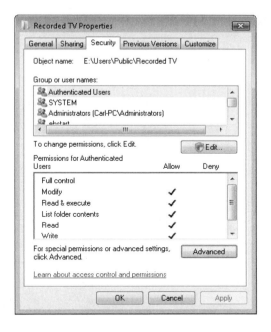

> **Note**
>
> If the selected file or folder is not stored on an NTFS volume, the Security tab doesn't appear, because auditing and other security features are implemented only for NTFS volumes.

3. Click Advanced. The Advanced Security Settings dialog box appears.

4. Click the Auditing tab and, if prompted, click Continue. For each object, you can specify different audit settings for different users.

5. Click Add to add a new user or group, or select an existing user or group and then click Edit to change its audit settings.

6. If you click Add, the Select User Or Group dialog box appears. In this example, the Everyone group is being selected. Click OK.

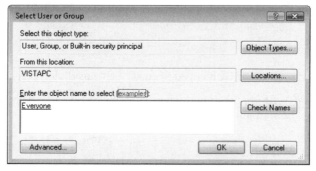

7. Whether editing an existing entry or adding a new one, in the Auditing Entry dialog box, select the types of access you want to audit for the selected user or group (in this case, Everyone).

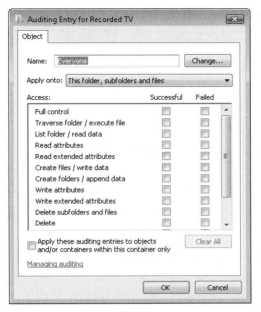

The different types of access you can audit for success or failure are the same types of access for which you can set permissions.

8. If you're making audit settings for a folder, select the scope of objects you want audited from the Apply Onto list.

If you select an event's Successful check box, Windows generates a Security log record (containing, among other information, the time and date) each time the specified user or group successfully attempts the event for the specified file or folder. Similarly, if you select an event's Failed check box, Windows generates a Security log record each time the specified user or group unsuccessfully attempts the event for the specified file or folder.

INSIDE OUT   Change audit settings for more than one file or folder at once

You can change audit settings for multiple files or folders simultaneously. If you select more than one file or folder in Windows Explorer and then click the Security tab in the properties dialog box, the changes you make affect all the selected files or folders. If the existing security settings are not the same for all the items in your selection, a message appears, asking whether you want to reset the audit settings for the entire selection.

Monitoring Other Security Events

Windows Vista can audit several printer events as well as audit different printer events for different users. If you have a color printer that uses expensive ink cartridges, for example, you might want to know who's causing it to run dry so frequently. You can manage all the printer security features through Control Panel's Printers application.

To set up printer security auditing, follow these steps:

1. In Control Panel, open Printers.

2. Right-click the icon for the printer you want to audit, point to Run As Administrator, and click Properties.

3. Click the Security tab.

4. Click Advanced. The Advanced Security Settings dialog box appears.

5. Click the Auditing tab.

    The Auditing tab for a printer object is nearly identical to the one for a file object.

6. Click Add to add a new user or group, or click Edit to change audit settings for an existing user or group. If you click Add, specify the new user or group in the Select User Or Group dialog box that appears and then click OK.

7. In the Auditing Entry dialog box (similar to the one shown here), select the types of access you want to audit.

For a printer, often the most useful information comes from auditing failures rather than successes. Logging printer successes generates a large number of relatively useless log entries. You might want to do this for only a short time to identify users who should not have access to a printer. Printer failures, on the other hand, create few entries and can be used to quickly identify people who attempt to access a printer for which they do not have permission.

When Windows logs a printer event, such as successful printing or a deletion from the print queue, the event record is written to the System log. In contrast, security events, such as attempts to access a printer for which an account does not have permission, result in an event record being written to the Security log.

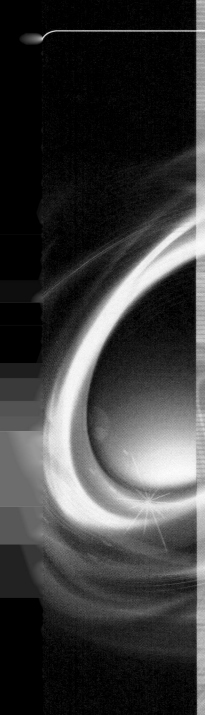

Appendices

APPENDIX A

Windows Vista Editions at a Glance

Home Basic ⬤
Home Premium ⬤
Business ⬤
Enterprise ⬤
Ultimate ⬤

In Chapter 1, we introduced the members of the Windows Vista family, including the specialized ones intended for specific markets. For a brief description of each edition, see "Introducing the Windows Vista Family," page 1xx.

In this appendix, we list in detail which features and capabilities are found in each edition. For the sake of convenience, we've broken a potentially long, confusing listing into a series of tables that breaks out features in groups.

User Experience

The full Aero user experience is available only on premium editions of Windows Vista with hardware that meets the Aero standards. With all editions, the Windows Vista Basic interface is the default choice on systems with underpowered video hardware and is a user-selectable option in all editions.

	Home Basic	Home Premium	Ultimate	Business	Enterprise
Windows Vista Standard interface[1]	●				
Windows Aero interface[1]		●	●	●	●
Windows Vista Basic interface	●	●	●	●	●
Windows Classic and Windows Standard interface options	●	●	●	●	●
Ease of Access Center	●	●	●	●	●
Speech recognition	●	●	●	●	●
Support for multiple languages using the Multi-Lingual User Interface (MUI)			●		●

[1] With appropriate hardware support

Security

The most important security-enhancing features in Windows Vista are available regardless of which edition you install. The Parental Controls feature is found only in consumer-oriented editions, and a few advanced features are included only with business-focused editions.

	Home Basic	Home Premium	Ultimate	Business	Enterprise
User Account Control	●	●	●	●	●
Windows Firewall with Advanced Security	●	●	●	●	●
Windows Defender	●	●	●	●	●
Internet Explorer 7 Protected Mode	●	●	●	●	●
Phishing Filter (Internet Explorer 7 and Windows Mail)	●	●	●	●	●
Parental Controls	●	●	●		
Encrypting File System			●	●	●
Windows BitLocker drive encryption			●		●

Digital Media/Entertainment

The basic tools for playing music and video clips, organizing digital photos, ripping audio CDs to digital files, and creating movie files are found in every Windows Vista edition. Media Center, DVD Maker, and other technologies that are aimed at the living room are reserved for the Home Premium and Ultimate editions.

	Home Basic	Home Premium	Ultimate	Business	Enterprise
Windows Media Player 11	●	●	●	●	●
Share a Media Library with other PCs and devices	●	●	●	●	●
Windows Photo Gallery	●	●	●	●	●
Windows Movie Maker	●	●	●	●	●
Windows Movie Maker HD		●	●		
Windows DVD Maker[1]		●	●		
Themed slide shows		●	●		

	Home Basic	Home Premium	Ultimate	Business	Enterprise
Windows Media Center		●	●		
Live TV recording and playback[1]		●	●		
Support for Media Center Extenders (including Xbox 360)[1]		●	●		
Premium games		●	●	●[2]	●[2]

[1] With appropriate hardware support
[2] Optional; not part of default installation

Hardware

Most mainstream desktop and notebook systems work identically with every edition of Windows Vista. For more advanced hardware configurations, you'll want to choose an edition that specifically supports that hardware.

	Home Basic	Home Premium	Ultimate	Business	Enterprise
Tablet PC and touchscreen support		●	●	●	●
Windows SideShow		●	●	●	●
Support for two physical CPUs			●	●	●
Maximum RAM Supported (32-bit)	4 GB	4 GB	4 GB	4 GB	4 GB
Maximum RAM Supported (64-bit)	8 GB	16 GB	128 GB+	128 GB+	128 GB+
Network Projector		●	●	●	●
Windows Mobility Center (full functionality)		●	●	●	●
Centralized power management through Group Policy			●	●	●

Backup

Every edition of Windows Vista includes the Windows Backup program, but its capabilities vary, depending on edition. Home Basic users can perform interactive backups of data files to local disks or removable media. Home Premium users add the capability to schedule file-based backups. With Ultimate, Business, and Enterprise editions, you can save an image of your system drive using the Complete PC Backup feature and use shadow copies to recover versions of deleted or changed files from days or weeks earlier.

	Home Basic	Home Premium	Ultimate	Business	Enterprise
Back up user files to local disk or DVD	●	●	●	●	●
Scheduled backup of user files		●	●	●	●
Back up user files to a network device		●	●	●	●
Complete PC Backup and Restore			●	●	●
Windows shadow copy (Previous Versions)			●	●	●

Business Applications

Most of the features in this section are specifically intended for business use. Two exceptions, both found in Home Premium as well as the business-focused editions, are the Presentation Settings feature, which allows you to disable screen savers, instant messaging clients, and other distracting interface elements while delivering a presentation, and Windows Meeting Space, an application-sharing tool that replaces the now-obsolete NetMeeting program.

	Home Basic	Home Premium	Ultimate	Business	Enterprise
Presentation Settings		●	●	●	●
Windows Meeting Space	●1	●	●	●	●
Windows Fax and Scan[2]			●	●	●
Small Business Resources			●	●	
Subsystem for UNIX-based applications			●		●
Licensed for use in up to four virtual machines					●

[1] Home Basic users can join a meeting only
[2] With appropriate hardware support

Advanced Networking and Administration

Most of the tools and features listed in this table are designed to meet the needs of network users and administrators in enterprise settings where one or more Windows domain servers are available.

	Home Basic	Home Premium	Ultimate	Business	Enterprise
Remote Desktop (Client)	•	•	•	•	•
Remote Desktop (Host)			•	•	•
Maximum simultaneous SMB connections	5	10	10	10	10
Support for joining a Windows domain			•	•	•
Desktop deployment tools for managed networks			•	•	•
Policy-based quality of service for networking			•	•	•
Internet Information Services 7.0[1]			•	•	•
Windows Rights Management Services (RMS) Client			•	•	•
Control installation of device drivers			•	•	•
Pluggable logon authentication architecture with integrated smart card management			•	•	•
Roaming user profiles			•	•	•
Folder redirection			•	•	•
Group Policy support			•	•	•
Offline files and folder support			•	•	•
Client-side caching			•	•	•

[1] Optional; not part of default installation

Appendix A

APPENDIX B

Working with the Command Prompt

Home Basic   ●
Home Premium   ●
Business   ●
Enterprise   ●
Ultimate   ●

Windows Vista allows you to enter commands, run batch programs, and run applications by typing commands in a Command Prompt window. If you're accustomed to performing administrative tasks at the command line, you don't need to change your ways in Windows Vista. You can open multiple Command Prompt sessions, each session protected from any failures that might occur in other sessions.

What's in Your Edition?

The command prompt works identically in all editions of Windows Vista.

Starting and Ending a Command Prompt Session

To get to the command prompt, do any of the following:

- Type **cmd** in the Start menu Search box, and click the Cmd shortcut when it appears, under Programs, at the top of the menu.

- Press Windows logo key+R and type **cmd** in the Open box.

- Choose Start, All Programs, Accessories, Command Prompt.

- Double-click the Cmd icon in your %SystemRoot%\System32 folder.

- Double-click any shortcut for Cmd.exe.

You can open as many Command Prompt windows as you like. With each additional window, you start another Command Prompt session. For example, you might want to open two Command Prompt windows to see two directories in side-by-side windows. To open another Command Prompt window, type **start** or **start cmd** at the command prompt. (These commands produce the same result. If you don't type a program name after typing **start**, Windows assumes that you want to start Cmd.exe.)

> **Note**
>
> Your activities in a Command Prompt session are subject to the same UAC controls as anything else you do in Windows Vista. At times you might find it convenient to start a Command Prompt session with an Administrator token. To do this, right-click any shortcut for Cmd.exe and choose Run As Administrator from the shortcut menu. If you do this as a standard user, you will be prompted to supply administrative credentials.

When the Command Prompt window is active, you can end a Command Prompt session in any of the following ways:

- Type **exit** at the command prompt.
- Click the Close button.
- Click the Control menu icon and choose Close.
- Double-click the Control menu icon.

If you are running a character-based program in the Command Prompt window, you should use the program's normal exit command to quit the program before attempting to close the window and end the Command Prompt session. Otherwise, it's possible that you'll lose unsaved data. However, if you are sure that the program doesn't have any unsaved information, you can safely and quickly close it using one of the last three methods in the preceding list. If a program is running, a dialog box appears asking whether or not you really want to terminate the program.

INSIDE OUT

By setting a registry value, you can make a particular application, command, batch program, or script run any time Command Prompt starts. For information about this feature, see "Using AutoRun to Execute Commands When Command Prompt Starts."

Starting Command Prompt at a Particular Folder

If you run Cmd.exe from %SystemRoot%\System32, the session begins at that folder. If you run it from the Start menu, it begins in your %UserProfile% folder. To run a Command Prompt session at a different folder, hold down the Shift key while you right-click the folder in Windows Explorer. On the shortcut menu, click Open Command Window Here.

INSIDE OUT **Cmd.exe vs. Command.com**

Cmd.exe is the Windows Vista command processor. Command.com, the 16-bit command processor of MS-DOS days, is still supported, but unless you have a legacy application that requires it, you should use Cmd.exe. You can run external MS-DOS commands, batch programs, and other executables with either processor, but Cmd includes a few internal commands not available in Command.com, and some of the internal commands common to both have additional options in Cmd. Only Cmd understands long file names, and most of the command-line syntax, described later in this appendix, is available only with Cmd.

Starting Command Prompt and Running a Command

The /C and /K command-line arguments allow you to start a Command Prompt session and run a command—an MS-DOS command or a batch program, for example. The difference between the two is the Cmd /C *commandstring* terminates the Command Prompt session as soon as *commandstring* has finished, whereas Cmd /K *commandstring* keeps the Command Prompt session open after *commandstring* has finished. Note the following:

- You must include either /C or /K if you want to specify a command string as an argument to Cmd. If you type **cmd commandstring**, the command processor simply ignores *commandstring*.

- While *commandstring* is executing, you can't interact with the command processor. To run a command and keep the Command Prompt window interface, use the Start command. For example, to run Mybatch.bat and continue issuing MS-DOS commands while the batch program is running, type **cmd /k start mybatch.bat**.

- If you include other command-line arguments along with /C or /K, the /C or /K must be the last argument before *commandstring*.

Note

For more information about using Command Prompt's command-line syntax, see "Using Cmd's Command-Line Syntax."

Appendix B

> ### Cmd.exe and Other Command Prompts
>
> Cmd. Exe, the application whose name is Command Prompt, is only one of several forms of command prompt available in Windows Vista. Others include the Run command (an optional item on the Start menu; press Windows logo key+R to get there), the Address toolbar, the Address bar in Windows Explorer, and even the Address bar in Internet Explorer. In many ways, these command prompts function alike. You can start a Windows-based application from any of them, for example. (If you start from Internet Explorer, you need to include an explicit path specification, and you might need to answer some security prompts.) What's exceptional about Cmd.exe is that it allows you to execute internal MS-DOS commands—that is, commands that are not stored in discrete .exe files.

Using AutoRun to Execute Commands when Command Prompt Starts

Command Prompt's equivalent to the old MS-DOS Autoexec batch mechanism is a feature called AutoRun. By default, Command Prompt executes on startup whatever it finds in the following two registry values:

- The AutoRun value in HKLM\Software\Microsoft\Command Processor

- The AutoRun value in HKCU\Software\Microsoft\Command Processor

The AutoRun value in HKLM affects all user accounts on the current machine. The AutoRun value in HKCU affects only the current user account. If both values are present, both are executed—HKLM before HKCU.

Both AutoRun values are of data type REG_SZ, which means they can contain a single string. (You can enter a multi-string value, but Windows Vista ignores all but the first string.) To execute a sequence of separate Command Prompt statements, therefore, you must use command symbols or store the sequence as a batch program, and then use AutoRun to call the batch program.

To specify an AutoRun value, open a registry editor and navigate to the Command Processor key in either HKLM or HKCU. Create a new string value there, and name it AutoRun. Then specify your command string as the data for AutoRun, exactly as you would type it at the command prompt.

To disable AutoRun commands for a particular Command Prompt session, start Command Prompt with /D. For more about Command Prompt's command-line syntax, see "Using Cmd's Command-Line Syntax."

Using Commands

In most respects, entering commands or running programs at the Windows Vista command prompt is the same as using the command prompt of any other operating system—MS-DOS, OS/2, Unix. If you've used one command prompt, you've used them all. Every operating system has a command to delete files, another to display lists of files, another to copy files, and so on. The names and details might differ, but it's the same cast of characters.

> ## INSIDE OUT   Type /? for help
>
> You can get help on any Command Prompt command by typing its name followed by /?. For example, to see a list and explanation of the command-line switches for the Dir command, type **dir /?**. Alternatively, type the word *help* followed by the command name—for example, **help dir**. For help with network-related commands, precede your help request with **net.** For example, type **net view /?** or **net help view** for information about the Net View command (with the Net commands, **net help *command*** provides more detailed help than **net *command* /?**.) You can also type **help** with no arguments to get a list of the internal commands and system utilities provided with Windows Vista.

Starting Programs

You can start all kinds of programs at the command prompt—programs for Windows Vista, earlier versions of Windows, or MS-DOS—so you don't need to know a program's origin or type to run it. If it's on your disk, simply type its name (and path, if needed) followed by any parameters. It should run with no problem.

If you're starting a character-based program, it runs in the Command Prompt window. When you terminate the application, the command prompt returns. If you start a Windows-based program, it appears in its own window.

In early versions of Windows NT, if you ran a Windows-based program from Command Prompt, the Command Prompt session remained inaccessible until the Windows-based program ended. To continue using Command Prompt after launching a Windows-based program, you had to launch the program with the Start command. That behavior has changed. In Windows Vista (and Windows XP and Windows 2000), the Command Prompt session remains accessible by default. If you prefer the old behavior, launch your program with the Start command, using the /Wait switch:

```
start /wait myprog.exe
```

The /Wait switch is useful only if you need the old behavior for some reason. The Start command has other options that are more useful, however. For instance, for Windows-based programs, you can use /Min or /Max to open a program in a minimized or maximized window. For character-based programs, you can enter (in quotation marks) the title that you want to appear on the program window. Place any parameters or switches that you use with the Start command *before* the name of the program or command you want to start. Anything after the program name is passed to the program as a command-line parameter and is ignored by Start.

INSIDE OUT   **Open Windows Explorer at the current Command Prompt folder**

If you type **start.** (with a period) at a command prompt, a Windows Explorer window opens on the current folder. This amounts to the opposite of Shift+right-clicking a folder in Windows Explorer to open a Command Prompt session at the selected folder.

For more information about the Start command, type **start /?** at the command prompt.

Using Command Extensions

Command extensions are changes or additions to the following internal commands: Del, Erase, Color, Cd, Chdir, Md, Mkdir, Prompt, Pushd, Popd, Set, Setlocal, Endlocal, If, For, Call, Shift, Goto, Start, Assoc, and Ftype. For example, with command extensions enabled, you can use Cd or Chdir to switch to a folder whose name includes space characters, without enclosing the path specification in quotation marks. For details about a particular command's extensions, type the command name followed by /?. (You can also type **help**, followed by the command name.)

Command extensions are available only in Cmd.exe, not in Command.com, and are enabled by default. Set the DWORD value EnableExtensions in HKLM\Software \Microsoft\Command Processor to 0 to disable them for all user accounts. Set Enable-Extensions in HKCU\Software\Microsoft\Command Processor to 0 to disable them for the current user account. Start Command Prompt with /E:off or /E:on to disable or enable command extensions for the current session, regardless of the registry settings.

Using File-Name and Folder-Name Completion

Command Prompt offers an invaluable file-name and folder-name completion feature that can save you the trouble of typing long paths or file names. If you start typing a command string and then press Tab (the default *completion character*), Command Prompt proposes the next file or folder name that's consistent with what you've typed so far. For example, to switch to a folder that starts with the letter Q, you can type **cd q** and press the folder-name completion character as many times as necessary until the folder you want appears.

By default, the completion character for both file names and folder names is the Tab key. You can select a different completion character by modifying the registry values of

HKCU\Software\Microsoft\Command Processor\CompletionChar and HKCU \Software\Microsoft\Command Processor\PathCompletionChar. These DWORD values specify the file and folder completion characters, respectively, for the current user. (To change the settings for all users, modify the same keys in HKLM.) If you decide to experiment with these registry settings, keep in the mind the following: If Completion-Char is defined and PathCompletionChar is either absent or set to the hexadecimal value 0x40, the CompletionChar setting works for both file completion and folder completion. In all cases, the completion characters should be specified as hexadecimal values—for example, 0x9 for Tab, 0x4 for Ctrl+D, 0x6 for Ctrl+F, 0xC for Ctrl+L, and so on.

You can also override the registry settings for an individual Command Prompt session by starting the session with Cmd /F:on or Cmd /F:off. Cmd /F:on starts a Command Prompt session with Ctrl+D as the path-completion character and Ctrl+F as the file-completion character, disabling the completion characters set in the registry. Cmd /F:off starts a Command Prompt session with no completion characters, regardless of your registry settings. Cmd /F:on and Cmd /F:off both disable the Tab key as a completion character.

> **Note**
>
> Command Prompt recognizes wildcards in file and path specifications. Typing **cd pro***, for example, might take you to your Program Files folder (depending, of course, on where you are when you type it.) Because you can include multiple wildcards in a string, you can even create formulations such as cd pro*\com*\mic* to get to Program Files\ Common Files\Microsoft Shared.

Using Cmd's Command-Line Syntax

The complete command-line syntax for Cmd.exe is

```
cmd [/a | /u] [/q] [/d] [/e:on | /e:off] [/f:on | /f:off] [/v:on | .v:off] [[/s] [/c
| /k] commandstring]
```

All arguments are optional.

- **/A | /U** This argument lets you specify the encoding system used for text that's piped to a file or other device. Use /A for ANSI or /U for Unicode. (The default is ANSI.)

- **/Q** The /Q argument starts Command Prompt with echo off. (With echo off, you don't need to include an @Echo Off line to suppress screen output in a batch program. To turn echo back on after starting Command Prompt with /Q, type **echo on** at the command prompt.)

- **/D** The /D argument disables execution of any AutoRun commands specified in the registry. (For more information, see "Using AutoRun to Execute Commands When Command Prompt Starts.")

- **/E:on | /E:off** The /E argument allows you to override the current registry settings that affect command extensions. (See "Using Command Extensions.")

- **/F:on | /F:off** The /F argument allows you to override the current registry settings regarding file-name and folder-name completion. (See "Using File-Name and Folder-Name Completion.")

- **/V:on | /V:off** The /V argument lets you enable or disable delayed variable expansion. With /V:on, for example, the variable *!var!* is expanded only when executed. The default is /V:off. To turn on delayed variable expansion as a default, add the DWORD value DelayedExpansion to HKLM\Software\Microsoft \Command Processor (for all users at the current machine) or HKCU\Software \Microsoft\Command Processor (for the current user account only), and set DelayedExpansion to 1. (Delayed variable expansion is useful in conditional statements and loop constructs in batch programs. For more information, type **help set** at the command prompt.)

- **/S [/C | /K]** *commandstring* The alternative /C and /K arguments allow you to run a command when Command Prompt starts—with /C terminating the session at the command's completion and /K keeping it open. Including /S before /C or /K affects the processing of quotation marks in *commandstring*. For more information, see "Starting Command Prompt and Running a Command."

  If you do not include /S, *and* there are exactly two quotation marks in *commandstring*, *and* there are no "special" characters (&, <, >, (,), @, ^, or |) in *commandstring*, *and* there are one or more white-space characters (spaces, tabs, or linefeeds, for example) between the two quotation marks, *and commandstring* is the name of an executable file, then Command Prompt preserves the two quotation characters.

  If the foregoing conditions are not met and if the first character in *commandstring* is a quotation mark, Command Prompt strips the first and last quotation marks from *commandstring*.

Editing the Command Line

When working at a command prompt, you often enter the same command several times, or enter several similar commands. If you make a mistake when typing a command line, you don't want to retype the whole thing—you just need to fix the part that was wrong. Windows Vista includes a feature that recalls previous commands and allows you to edit them on the current command line. Table B-1 lists these editing keys and what they do.

Table B-1. Command-Line Editing Keys

Key	Function
Up Arrow	Recalls the previous command in the command history
Down Arrow	Recalls the next command in the command history
Page Up	Recalls the earliest command used in the session
Page Down	Recalls the most recent command used
Left Arrow	Moves left one character
Right Arrow	Moves right one character
Ctrl+Left Arrow	Moves left one word
Ctrl+Right Arrow	Moves right one word
Home	Moves to the beginning of the line
End	Moves to the end of the line
Esc	Clears the current command
F7	Displays the command history in a scrollable pop-up box
F8	Displays commands that start with characters currently on the command line
Alt+F7	Clears the command history

The command-line recall feature maintains a history of the commands entered during the Command Prompt session. To display this history, press F7. A window appears that shows the commands you have recently entered. Scroll through the history with the arrow keys to select the command you want. Then press Enter to reuse the selected command, or press the Left Arrow key to place the selected text on the command line without executing the command. (This allows you to edit the command before executing it.)

It's not necessary to display the pop-up window to use the command history. You can scroll through the history within the Command Prompt window with the Up Arrow and Down Arrow keys.

The F8 key provides a useful alternative to the Up Arrow key. The Up Arrow key moves you through the command history to the top of the command buffer and then stops. F8 does the same, except that when you get to the top of the buffer, it cycles back to the bottom. Furthermore, F8 displays only commands in the buffer that begin with whatever you typed before you pressed F8. Type **d** at the command prompt (don't press Enter), and then press F8 a few times. You'll cycle through recently entered commands that start with *d*, such as Dir and Del. Now type **e** (after the *d*), and press F8 a few more times. You'll cycle through Del commands along with any others that start with *de*. You can save a lot of keystrokes using F8 if you know the first letters of the command you're looking for.

Using Wildcards

Windows Vista, like MS-DOS, recognizes two wildcard characters: ? and *. The question mark represents any single character in a file name. The asterisk matches any number of characters.

In MS-DOS, the asterisk works only at the end of the file name or extension. Windows Vista handles the asterisk more flexibly, allowing multiple asterisks in a command string and allowing you to use the character wherever you want.

Using Command Symbols

Old-fashioned programs that take all of their input from a command line and then run unaided can be useful in a multitasking system. You can turn them loose to perform complicated processing in the background while you continue to work with other programs in the foreground. Windows Vista includes features that make command-line programs easier to run and more powerful. These features also allow you to chain programs together so that later ones use the output of their predecessors as input.

In order to work together better, many command-line programs follow a set of conventions that control their interaction:

- By default, programs take all of their input as lines of text typed at the keyboard. But input in the same format also can be redirected from a file or any device capable of sending lines of text.

- By default, programs send all of their output to the screen as lines of text. But output in the same format also can be redirected to a file or another line-oriented device, such as a printer.

Programs are written to set a number called a return value when they terminate, to indicate the results of the program. When programs are written according to these rules, you can use the symbols in Table B-2 to control a program's input and output, and to connect or chain programs together.

Table B-2. Command Symbols

<	Redirects input
>	Redirects output
>>	Appends redirected output to existing data
|	Pipes output
&	Separates multiple commands in a command line
&&	Runs the command after && only if the command before && is successful
||	Runs the command after || only if the command before || fails
^	Treats the next symbol as a character
(and)	Groups commands

The Redirection Symbols

As in MS-DOS and Unix, Command Prompt sessions in Windows Vista allow you to override the default source for input (the keyboard) or the default destination for output (the screen).

Redirecting Output

To redirect output to a file, type the command followed by a greater than sign (>) and the name of the file. For example, to send the output of the Dir command to a file instead of the screen, type the following:

```
dir /b *.bat > batch.lst
```

This command line creates a file called Batch.lst that contains the names of all the .bat files in the current folder.

Using two greater than signs (>>) redirects output and appends it to an existing file. For example:

```
dir /b *.cmd >> batch.lst
```

This command line appends a list of .cmd files to the previously created file containing .bat files. (If you use >> to append to a file that doesn't exist, Windows Vista creates the file.)

Redirecting Input

To redirect input from a file, type the command followed by a less than sign (<) and the name of the file. The Sort and More commands are examples of commands that can accept input from a file. The following example uses Sort to filter the file created with the Dir command above.

```
sort < batch.lst
```

The input file, Batch.lst, contains a list of .bat files followed by a list of .cmd files (assuming you have some of each in the current folder). The output to the screen is the same list of files sorted alphabetically by file name.

Redirecting Input and Output

You can redirect both input and output in a command line. For example, to use Batch.lst as input to the Sort command and send its output to a file named Sorted.lst, type the following:

```
sort < batch.lst > sorted.lst
```

Standard Output and Standard Error

Programs can be written to send their output either to the standard output device or to the standard error device. Sometimes programs are written to send different types of output to each device. You can't always tell which is which because, by default, both devices are the screen.

The Type command illustrates the difference. When used with wildcards (something you can't do with the Type command in MS-DOS or Windows 9x), the Type command sends the name of each matching file to the standard error device and sends the contents of the file to the standard output device. Because they both go to the screen, you see a nice display with each file name followed by its contents.

However, if you try to redirect output to a file like this:

```
type *.bat > std.out
```

the file names still appear on your screen because standard error is still directed to the screen. Only the file contents are redirected to Std.out.

Windows Vista allows you to qualify the redirection symbol by preceding it with a number. Use 1> (or simply >) for standard output and 2> for standard error. For example:

```
type *.bat 2> err.out
```

This time the file contents go to the screen and the names are redirected to Err.out. You can redirect both to separate files with this command line:

```
type *.bat 2> err.out 1> std.out
```

The Pipe Symbol

The pipe symbol (|) is used to send or *pipe* the output of one program to a second program as the second program's input. Piping is commonly used with the More utility, which displays multiple screenfuls of output one screenful at a time. For example:

```
help dir | more
```

This command line uses the output of Help as the input for More. The More command filters out the first screenful of Help output, sends it to the screen as its own output, and then waits for a keypress before sending more filtered output.

The Command Combination Symbols

Windows Vista allows you to enter multiple commands on a single command line. Furthermore, you can make later commands depend on the results of earlier commands. This feature can be particularly useful in batch programs and Doskey macros, but you might also find it convenient at the command prompt.

To simply combine commands without regard to their results, use the & symbol:

```
copy f:file.dat & edit file.dat
```

But what if there is no File.dat on drive F? Then it can't be copied to the current drive, and the Edit command will fail when it can't find the file. Your screen will be littered with error messages. Windows Vista provides to command symbols for better control over situations like this:

- The && symbol causes the second command to run only if the first command succeeds.

- The || symbol causes the second command to run only if the first command fails.

Consider this modified version of the earlier example:

```
copy f:file.dat && edit file.dat
```

With this command line, if the Copy command fails, the Edit command is ignored.

Sometimes you want the opposite effect: Execute the second command only if the first fails:

```
copy f:file.date || copy g:file.dat
```

This command line tries to copy the file from drive F. If that doesn't work, it tries to copy the file from drive G.

The Escape Symbol

Some command symbols are legal characters in file names. This leads to ambiguities. You can resolve such ambiguities by using the caret (^) as an escape to indicate that whatever follows is a character rather than a command symbol.

Consider the following command line:

```
copy f:\cartoons\Tom&Jerry
```

This copies the file F:\Cartoons\Tom to the current folder, and then executes the Jerry command—probably not what you wanted. You might think that because there is no space before or after the & symbol, the system will know that you are referring to the file name Tom&Jerry. Not true. When a command symbol appears on the command line, whatever follows it is assumed to be a command, space or no space. Use the caret as shown below to indicate that you are referring to a file name.

```
copy f:\cartoons\Tom^&Jerry
```

Alternatively, instead of using the ^ symbol, you can enclose a file specification that includes command symbols (or other troublesome characters, such as spaces) within quotation marks to achieve the same effect. For example:

```
dir "f:\cartoons|Tom&Jerry"
```

Pausing or Canceling Commands

You can pause or cancel a command that you enter at the command prompt as the command is running. (Keep this in mind if you accidentally request a directory of all the files—or worse, enter a command to delete all the files—on a huge network server drive!)

To pause the output of a command, press Ctrl+S or the Pause key. To resume output, press any key.

If you have enabled QuickEdit mode for your Command Prompt window (see "Setting Other Options."), simply click in the window to pause command output. To resume output, right-click in the window.

To cancel a command, press Ctrl+C or Ctrl+Break. With either key, your command is canceled, and the command prompt returns. Be aware, though, that any action (such as deleting files) that occurs before you cancel the command is done—and cannot be undone.

Simplifying Command Entry with Doskey Macros

The Doskey utility lets you encapsulate command strings as easy-to-enter macros. For example, by typing the following at the command prompt:

```
doskey 50=mode con:lines=50
```

you create a macro named 50 that executes the command string *mode con:lines=50*. To run a macro, you simply enter its name (in this example, 50) at a command prompt. You can create as many macros as you like with Doskey, but your macros are effective only for the current Command Prompt session. To create a reusable set of Doskey macros, save them in a plain-text file, using an editor such as Notepad. Then load them from the command prompt, using Doskey's /Macrofile switch. For example, if your macros are stored in the file C:\MyMacros.txt, typing

```
doskey /macrofile=c:\mymacros.txt
```

makes those macros available for the current Command Prompt session. If you regularly use the same macro file, consider using the AutoRun feature to load your macros. See "Using AutoRun to Execute Commands When Command Prompt Starts."

Doskey macros can use replaceable parameters, in much the same way batch programs can. The difference between a Doskey parameter and a batch-program parameter is that the former uses a dollar-sign prefix instead of a percentage symbol. Parameters 1 through 9 thus are identified as $1 through $9. For example, the Doskey macro assignment

```
doskey lines=mode con:lines=$1
```

allows you to switch your display by typing lines followed by the number of lines you want.

In Doskey macros, $* represents all the arguments passed, even if there are more than nine.

You can use redirection, piping, and command combination symbols in Doskey macros, but you must insert a caret (^) before each such symbol. For example, the following assignment creates a macro that pipes output through the More filter:

```
doskey mtype=type $* ^| more /e
```

For more information about using Doskey, type **doskey /?** at the command prompt.

Using Environment Variables

Command-prompt operating systems traditionally use environment variables as a means for programs to share information and read global settings. (Windows Vista— and applications written for Windows Vista—use the registry for the same purpose.) To use an environment variable in a command, program, or address, enclose it between percent signs, like this example: %UserName%.

Viewing Environment Variables

The Set command allows you to examine as well as set environment variables. To examine the current environment variables, open a Command Prompt window and type **set** (without any arguments). Windows Vista displays a list of all the current environment variables and their values, as the following example shows:

```
ALLUSERSPROFILE=F:\ProgramData

APPDATA=F:\Users\Craig\AppData\Roaming

CommonProgramFiles=F:\Program Files\Common Files

COMPUTERNAME=Dapple

ComSpec=F:\Windows\system32\cmd.exe

FP_NO_HOST_CHECK=NO

HOMEDRIVE=F:

HOMEPATH=\Users\Craig

LOCALAPPDATA=F:\Users\Craig\AppdData\Local

LOGONSERVER=\\DAPPLE

NUMBER_OF_PROCESSORS=2

OS=Windows_NT

Path=F:\Windows\system32;F:\Windows;F:\WindowsSystem32\Wbem

PATHEXT=.COM;.EXE;.BAT;.CMD;.VBS;.VBE;.JS;.JSE;.WSF;.WSH;.MSC

PROCESSOR_ARCHITECTURE=x86

PROCESSOR_IDENTIFIER=x86 Family 15 Model 4 Stepping 4, GenuineIntel

PROCESSOR_LEVEL=15
```

```
PROCESSOR_REVISION=0404

ProgramData=F:\ProgramData

ProgramFiles=F:\Program Files

PROMPT=$P$G

PUBLIC=F:\Users\Public

SESSIONNAME=Console

SystemDrive=F:

SystemRoot=F:\Windows

TEMP=F:\Users\Craig\AppData\Local\Temp

TMP=F:\Users\Craig\AppData\Local\Temp

USERDOMAIN=DAPPLE

USERNAME=Craig

USERPROFILE=F:\Users\Craig

Windir=F:\Windows
```

Modifying Environment Variables

Command Prompt gets its environment variables from three sources:

- Any variables set in your Autoexec.bat file

- System variables, as recorded in HKLM\SYSTEM\CurrentControlSet\Control\ Session Manager\Environment

- User variables, as recorded in HKCU\Environment

When you log on, Windows Vista scans the Autoexec.bat file in the root folder of your boot drive for environment variables initialized with Set statements. If you don't want Windows Vista to scan your Autoexec.bat file for Set statements, open a registry editor and navigate to HKCU\Software\Microsoft\Windows NT\CurrentVersion\Winlogon. Then change the data associated with the ParseAutoexec value from 1 to 0. System and user variables are both stored in the registry, but you don't need to launch a registry editor to change them. Open System in Control Panel instead. Click Advanced System Settings to get to the System Properties dialog box. Click the Advanced tab and then the Environment Variables button.

Predefined Environment Variables

Many of the environment variables in the preceding example are ones that Windows Vista automatically sets with information about your system. You can use these values in batch programs, Doskey macros, and command lines—and if you're a programmer, in the programs you write. The system-defined environment variables include the following:

- **Information about your place in the network** COMPUTERNAME contains the name of your computer, USERDOMAIN contains the name of the domain you logged on to, and USERNAME contains your logon name.

- **Information about your computer** PROCESSOR_ARCHITECTURE contains the type of processor (such as "x86"), and PROCESSOR_IDENTIFIER, PROCESSOR_LEVEL, and PROCESSOR_REVISION provide specific information about the processor version.

- **Information about Windows Vista** SystemRoot contains the drive and folder in which Windows Vista is installed; SystemDrive contains only the drive letter.

- **Information about your programs** When you type a program name (to start the program) without typing its path, Windows Vista looks first in the current folder. If the program isn't located in the current folder, Windows Vista looks in each folder listed in the Path variable.

- **Information about the command prompt** PROMPT contains codes that define the appearance of the command prompt itself. (For details, type **prompt /?** at the prompt.)

Changes to environment variables made via Control Panel affect your next and subsequent Command Prompt sessions (not the current ones, of course). Changes made via Autoexec.bat are not effective until the next time you log on. In case of conflicting assignments, user variables take precedence over system variables, which take precedence over variables declared in Autoexec.bat. The Path variable, however, is cumulative. That is, changes made in any venue are appended to any changes made elsewhere. (But changes made via Autoexec.bat or HKCU\Environment are not effective until your next logon.)

Within a given Command Prompt session, you can change environment variables by means of Set statements. Such statements affect only the current session and any applications (including additional Command Prompt sessions) spawned from the current session.

Note

The Autoexec.nt file has no effect on the Command Prompt environment. Autoexec.nt affects MS-DOS–based applications only. Command Prompt, although it is the MS-DOS command interpreter, is itself a Windows Vista–based application.

Customizing Command Prompt Windows

You can customize the appearance of a Command Prompt window in several ways. You can change its size, select a font, and even use eye-pleasing colors. And you can save these settings independently for each shortcut that launches a Command Prompt session, so that you can make appropriate settings for different tasks.

To customize a Command Prompt window, you make settings in a properties dialog box that you can reach in any of three ways:

- Right-click a shortcut that opens a Command Prompt window, and choose Properties from the shortcut menu. Changes you make here affect all future Command Prompt sessions launched from this shortcut.

- Click the Control menu icon in a Command Prompt window, and choose Properties from the Control menu. (If Command Prompt is running in full-screen mode, press Alt+Enter to switch to window display.) Changes you make here affect the current session. When you leave the properties dialog box, you'll be given the option of propagating your changes to the shortcut from which this session was launched. If you accept, all future sessions launched from that shortcut will have the new properties.

- Click the Control menu icon in a Command Prompt window, and choose Defaults from the Control menu. Changes here do not affect the current session. Instead, they affect all future sessions, except those launched from a shortcut whose properties you have modified. They also affect future sessions in character-mode, MS-DOS–based applications that do not have a program-information file (PIF) and do not store their own settings.

Setting the Window Size and Position

To change the screen position where a newly launched Command Prompt window appears, open the window's properties dialog box and click the Layout tab (see Figure B-1).

The dialog box maintains two different sizes—the screen buffer size and the window size. The width for both sizes is specified in columns (characters); the height is specified in rows (text lines).

The screen buffer settings control the size of the "virtual screen," which is the maximum extent of the screen. Standard screen sizes are 80 × 25, 80 × 43, or 80 × 50, but you can set your Command Prompt session to any size you want. (Some programs that you launch from a Command Prompt session, however, might work correctly only with standard screen sizes. In such cases, Windows Vista automatically adjusts the screen buffer size to the closest size that the program understands.)

The window size settings control the size of the Command Prompt window on your screen. In most cases, you'll want it the same size as the screen buffer. But if your screen is crowded, you can reduce the window size. If you do, scroll bars are added so that you can scroll to different parts of the virtual screen. The window size settings cannot be larger than the screen buffer size settings.

Figure B-1 Settings on the Layout tab control the number of lines and characters per line that a Command Prompt window can display.

Because you size a window by specifying how many rows and columns of characters it should have, the size of those characters also affects the amount of space the window occupies on your display. For information about changing the character size, see "Selecting a Font."

Setting the Window Size and Position Visually

Rather than guess at the settings for window size and position, you can use the following procedure:

1. Open a Command Prompt window.

2. Drag the window's borders to adjust its size and drag its title bar to adjust its position.

3. Click the Control menu icon and choose Properties.

4. Click the Layout tab. You'll see the settings that reflect the window's current condition.

5. Click OK to apply these settings.

6.   Select Save Properties For Future Windows With Same Title (or Modify Shortcut That Started This Window, if you started the session from a shortcut instead of from the Run command) to retain the settings for future sessions.

Selecting a Font

Unlike most Windows-based applications, applications in a Command Prompt can display only one font at a time. Your choice is relatively limited, as you'll see if you click the Font tab in the Command Prompt window's properties dialog box. Figure B-2 shows the Font tab of the Command Prompt's properties dialog box.

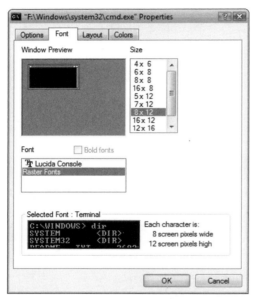

Figure B-2 The small window at the bottom of this dialog box shows an actual-size sample of the selected font; the window at the top shows the relative size and shape of the Command Prompt window if you use the selected font.

You should make a selection in the Font list first because your choice here determines the contents of the Size list. If you select Lucida Console, you'll find point sizes to choose from in the Size list. If you select Raster Fonts, you'll find character widths and height in pixels.

Setting Colors

You can set the color of the text and the background of the Command Prompt window. You can also set the color of the text and the background of pop-up windows that originate from the command prompt, such as the command history.

To set colors, click the Colors tab in the Command Prompt window's properties dialog box, shown in Figure B-3.

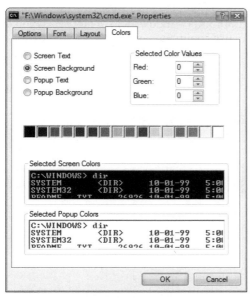

Figure B-3 You can set separate foreground and background colors for the Command Prompt window and pop-up windows, such as the command history window that appears when you press F7.

Setting Other Options

The Options tab in the Command Prompt window's properties dialog box, shown in Figure B-4 on the next page, offers a variety of options that affect how your Command Prompt window operates.

- **Cursor Size** These options control the size of the blinking cursor in a Command Prompt window.

- **Display Options** This setting determines whether your Command Prompt session appears in a window or occupies the entire screen.

- **Command History** These options control the buffer used by Doskey:
  - **Buffer Size** Specifies the number of commands to save in each command history
  - **Number of Buffers** Specifies the number of command history buffers to use. (Certain character-based programs other than Cmd.exe use Doskey's command history. Doskey maintains a separate history for each such program that you start.)

○   **Discard Old Duplicates** If selected, uses the history buffers more efficiently by not saving duplication commands.

● **QuickEdit Mode** This option provides a fast, easy way to copy text from (and paste text into) Command Prompt windows with a mouse. (If you don't select QuickEdit Mode, you can use commands on the Control menu for copying and pasting text.)

● **Insert Mode** This option (on by default) allows you to insert text at the cursor position. To overstrike characters instead, clear the Insert Mode check box.

Figure B-4 You can set cursor size, the size of your command history buffer, and other specifications on the Options tab.

Using and Customizing Microsoft Management Console

Microsoft Management Console (MMC) is an application that hosts tools for administering computers, networks, and other system components. Microsoft Management Console first appeared in Windows 2000, and some consoles included with Windows Vista look identical to their earlier counterparts. Other consoles, however, take advantage of new features added to the Windows Vista version of MMC: the Action pane and support for a richer Details pane.

By itself, MMC performs no administrative services. Rather, it acts as host for one or more modules called *snap-ins*, which do the useful work. MMC simply provides user-interface consistency so that you or the users you support see more or less the same style of application each time you need to carry out some kind of computer management task. A combination of one or more snap-ins can be saved in a file called a Microsoft Common Console Document or, more commonly, an MMC *console*.

Creating snap-ins requires expertise in programming. You don't have to be a programmer, however, to make your own custom MMC consoles. All you need to do is run MMC, start with a blank console, and add one or more of the snap-ins available on your system. Alternatively, you can customize some of the MMC consoles supplied by Microsoft or other vendors simply by adding or removing snap-ins.

Why might you want to customize your MMC consoles? Because neither Microsoft nor any other vendor can anticipate your every need. Perhaps you would like to take some of the functionality from two or more existing MMC consoles and combine them into a single console. (You might, for example, want to combine the Services console with the Event Viewer console, the latter filtered to show only those events generated by services. You might also want to include a link to a website that offers details about services and service-related errors.) Or perhaps you would like to simplify some of the existing consoles by removing snap-ins that you seldom use.

What's in Your Edition?

MMC works identically in all versions of Microsoft Windows Vista. However, certain MMC snap-ins are not included or are not functional in the home editions of Windows Vista, Home Basic and Home Premium; see Table C-2 for details.

You also might find MMC customization worthwhile if you support others in your organization who occasionally need to perform administrative tasks. You can set up consoles that supply only the functionality that your colleagues need, removing or disabling components that might be distracting or confusing. Some of the snap-ins available on your system, for example, are designed to administer remote as well as local computers. If the user you're supporting needs to be able to administer only his or her own machine, you might want to create a custom console for that person that has remote-administration capabilities disabled. Keep in mind, however, that most MMC consoles, as well as MMC itself, require User Account Control (UAC) elevation. Therefore, if you have UAC enabled, the user needs to have access to credentials for an administrator account to gain full functionality.

Running MMC Consoles

MMC consoles have, by default, the extension .msc, and .msc files are associated by default with MMC. Thus you can run any MMC console by double-clicking its file name in a Windows Explorer window or by entering the file name at a command prompt. Windows Vista includes several predefined consoles; the most commonly used ones, described in Table C-1, can be easily found by typing their name in the Start menu Search box.

Table C-1. **Useful Predefined Consoles**

Console Name (File Name)	Description
Computer Management (Compmgmt.msc)	Includes the functionality of the Task Scheduler, Event Viewer, Shared Folders, Reliability and Performance Monitor, Device Manager, Disk Management, Services, and WMI Control snap-ins, providing control over a wide range of computer tasks
Device Manager (Devmgmt.msc)	Uses the Device Manager snap-in to enable administration of all attached hardware devices and their drivers; see Chapter 5, "Setting Up and Troubleshooting Hardware," for more information
Event Viewer (Eventvwr.msc)	Uses the Event Viewer snap-in to display all manner of logged information; see Chapter 22, "Monitoring System Activities with Event Viewer," for details
Local Security Policy (Secpol.msc)	Includes elements of the Group Policy Object Editor snap-in for managing local group policy, Windows Firewall, and other security related settings (available only in Business, Enterprise, and Ultimate editions of Windows Vista)
Print Management (Printmanagement.msc)	Uses the Print Management snap-in for administering multiple printers and print servers; for more information, see "Sharing a Printer," Chapter 14 (available only in Business, Enterprise, and Ultimate editions of Windows Vista)

Console Name (File Name)	Description
Reliability And Performance Monitor (Perfmon.msc)	Uses the Reliability And Performance Monitor snap-in to provide a set of monitoring tools far superior to Performance Monitor in earlier Windows versions; see Chapter 21, "Tuning Up and Monitoring Performance and Reliability," for details
Services (Services.msc)	Uses the Services snap-in to manage services in Windows; for details, see Chapter 25, "Managing Services"
Task Scheduler (Taskschd.msc)	Uses the Task Scheduler snap-in for managing tasks that run automatically; for details, see "Scheduling Tasks to Run Automatically," Chapter 30.
Windows Firewall With Advanced Security (Wf.msc)	Uses the Windows Firewall With Advanced Security snap-in to configure rules and make other firewall settings; for details, see "Protecting a System with Windows Firewall," Chapter 31.

MMC Consoles and UAC

Consoles can be used to manage all sorts of computer components: with a console you can modify hard drive partitions, start and stop services, and install device drivers, for example. In other words, MMC consoles perform the types of tasks that User Account Control is designed to restrict. In the hands of someone malicious (or simply careless) consoles have the power to wreak havoc on your computer.

Therefore, when using an MMC console you're likely to encounter a User Account Control request for permission to continue. If UAC is enabled on your computer, the type of request you get and the restrictions that are imposed depend on what type of account is currently logged on.

- If you're logged on with an administrator account, every attempt to run a console—or even to run MMC with no snap-ins—triggers a UAC consent prompt. You'll have to give your approval or MMC won't run at all; once you do, however, you have full control over MMC and all its snap-ins.

- If you're using a standard account, when you attempt to launch MMC or a console document by double-clicking, Windows does not ask for permission to continue. However, when started in this way, the console is prevented from performing potentially harmful tasks. Unfortunately, there's little consistency in how various snap-ins and consoles handle this situation.

  - Some, like Device Manager (Devmgmt.msc), display a message box informing you that the console will run with limitations. (In effect, it works in a "read-only" mode that allows you to view device information, but not to make changes.) Unfortunately, the message from some consoles is misleading, inaccurate, or both.

Appendix C

○ Other consoles give no obvious indication that they're working in a restricted mode, but they also allow you only to view information without making changes. The Services console (Services.msc), for example, does not let a standard user start or stop services or change a service's startup type.

○ Still other consoles block all use by nonadministrative users. Although the console application runs, all information normally provided by the console is hidden from view.

● You can gain full console functionality while logged on with a standard account by running as an administrator. The easiest way to do that: right-click the console's icon and choose Run As Administrator.

INSIDE OUT   Make MMC work for standard users

To ensure that you don't run into an "access denied" roadblock when performing administrative tasks while logged on with a standard account, always right-click and choose Run As Administrator. On the other hand, if your goal is to create a console that standard users can use to display (but not modify) information, be sure to test it thoroughly while logged on as a standard user to be sure it works the way you expect it to.

For more information about UAC, see "Preventing Unsafe Actions with User Account Control, Chapter 10.

Running a Console in Author Mode

MMC consoles can be run in Author mode or in three varieties of User mode. Author mode gives you full access to MMC's menus and options. In User modes, elements of MMC's functionality are removed.

For more information about the three User modes, see "Restricting User Control of Your Console," later in this chapter.

By default, when you run an MMC console, the console runs in the mode it was last saved in. But you can always run any console in any mode you need to.

To run a console in Author mode, right-click its file in a Windows Explorer window and choose Author from the shortcut menu. Alternatively, you can run a console in Author mode using the following command-line syntax:

```
name.msc /a
```

where *name* is the file name of the console file.

Note

If the console mode was set to Author mode when the console was last saved, the console opens in Author mode without the use of the Author command or /A command-line option.

Running a Console and Specifying a Target Computer

Many of the consoles supplied by Microsoft are set up to operate on the local computer by default, but—provided that you have the appropriate permissions—they can also be used to manage remote computers. To open such a console and specify a target computer, use this command-line syntax:

```
name.msc /computer=computername
```

Be aware that if you use the /Computer switch with a console that has not been set up to allow remote-computer management, you do not get an error message. Instead, you simply get the console applied to the default (typically, the local) computer. In the console tree, you can look at the top-level entry for a snap-in to confirm that you're working with the correct target computer.

Some of the consoles supplied with Windows that are designed to work with remote as well as local computers include a menu command for connecting to a different computer. The Computer Management console (Compmgmt.msc), for example, allows you to switch from one computer to another while the console is running. Others, such as Shared Folders (Fsmgmt.msc), can be used with remote computers, but these consoles manage the local computer unless you specify a different target computer on the command line.

Note

To work with a remote computer, you must be sure that the firewall on the remote computer does not block your connection attempts. Windows Firewall provides predefined exceptions for many commonly used remote management tools, but you must enable the exception on the remote computer before you can connect to it with an MMC console. To enable an exception, in Windows Firewall click Allow A Program Through Windows Firewall. Then select the check box for the feature you want to use, such as Remote Event Log Management, Remote Scheduled Tasks Management, Remote Service Management, and so on. (For more information about firewall exceptions, see "Allowing Connections Through the Firewall," Chapter 10.) In addition, your user account must have administrator privileges on the remote computer.

Using MMC Consoles

Notwithstanding the fact that MMC is intended to provide user-interface consistency across administrative applications, actual MMC consoles can take on quite a variety of appearances. Compare the Event Viewer console (Eventvwr.msc) shown in Figure 22-1 in Chapter 22 with the Disk Management console (Diskmgmt.msc) shown in Figure 28-1 in Chapter 28, for example.

MMC is designed to be extremely flexible. Snap-ins can add elements to the MMC user interface, and console designers can hide or display UI elements as needs dictate. Nevertheless, *most* of the consoles that come with your operating system look somewhat like the one shown in Figure C-1, so we can make a few generalizations about their use.

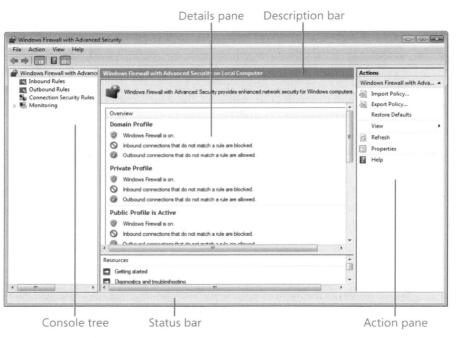

Figure C-1 Most of the MMC consoles that come with Windows Vista include a console tree, a Details pane, and an Action pane.

Console tree, Details pane, and Action pane   The console can be divided vertically into panes. The leftmost pane, whose display is optional, contains the *console tree*, which shows the organization of the console and allows for easy navigation between snap-ins. Outline controls in the console tree function just the way they do in Windows Explorer. The center pane is called the *Details pane*, and it shows information related to the item currently selected in the console tree. The *Action pane*, which (optionally) appears on the right side of the window, lists links to actions that are appropriate for the items selected in the other two panes. If an item is selected in the console tree, tasks relevant to the selected item appear in the top of the Action pane; if an item is selected in the Details pane, relevant task links appear in the bottom of the Action pane. Up arrows and down arrows let you expand or contract a section of the Action pane; clicking a right arrow displays a submenu.

The vertical split bar between the panes can be dragged to the left or right, like its counterpart in Windows Explorer. To display or hide the console tree or the Action pane, use the toolbar buttons (one controls each pane) or the Customize command on the View menu.

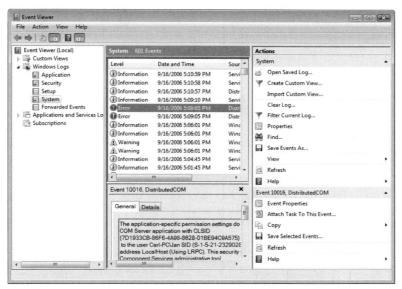

Figure C-2 The top part of the Action pane (under the System heading) shows actions for the item selected in the console tree. The lower part (under the Event 10016 heading) shows actions for the item selected in the Details pane.

Action and View menus The Action menu, if present, provides commands specific to the current selection, providing an alternative to the Action pane. In other words, this is the menu you use to carry out administrative tasks. The View menu, if present, allows you to choose among alternative ways of presenting information. In many MMC consoles, for example, the View menu offers Large Icons, Small Icons, List, and Details commands, similar to the view options in Windows Explorer. The View menu might also include a Customize command. This command presents the Customize View dialog box shown in Figure C-3 on the next page, which allows you, among other things, to hide or display the console tree.

Figure C-3 You can use the Customize View dialog box to control various elements of the MMC console, which are identified in Figure C-1.

Shortcut menus Whether or not an Action menu or Action pane is present, you'll sometimes find that the easiest way to carry out an administrative task is to right-click the relevant item in the console tree or the Details pane and choose an action from the item's shortcut menu. That's because the shortcut menu always includes all the actions available for the selected item. (If you don't immediately find the command you need, look for an All Tasks command; the action you want is probably on the All Tasks submenu.) The shortcut menu also always includes a Help command.

Working with content in the Details pane If the Details pane provides a tabular presentation, like the one shown in Figure C-2, you can manipulate content using the same techniques you use in Windows Explorer. You can sort by clicking column headings, control column width by dragging the borders between column headings (double-click a border to make a column just wide enough for the widest entry), and rearrange columns by dragging headings.

To hide or display particular columns, look for a Add/Remove Columns command on the View menu. Here you can specify which columns you want to see in the Details pane, as well as the order in which you want to see them.

Exporting Details pane data to text or .csv files Many MMC consoles include Action-menu commands for saving data in binary formats. In most consoles that produce tabular displays, however, you can also use the Export List command to generate a tab-delimited or comma-delimited text file, suitable for viewing in a word processing, spreadsheet, or database program. If this command is available, you'll find it on the Action menu or any shortcut menu.

Creating Your Own MMC Consoles

Creating your own MMC console or modifying an existing one involves the following steps (not necessarily in this order):

- Running MMC with no snap-in, or opening an existing MMC console in Author mode

- Displaying the console tree if it's not already visible

- Adding or removing snap-ins, folders, and, if appropriate, extensions (modules that extend the functionality of snap-ins)

- Adding taskpad views (customized pages that appear within the Details pane of a snap-in), if appropriate

- Manipulating windows and other display elements to taste

- Adding items to the Favorites menu, if appropriate

- Naming the console and choosing an icon for it

- Choosing Author mode or one of the three User modes

- Further restricting user options, if appropriate

- Using the File menu to save your .msc file

Running MMC with No Snap-In

To run MMC with no snap-in, simply type **mmc** on a command line. An empty, Author-mode MMC console appears, as shown in Figure C-4 on the next page.

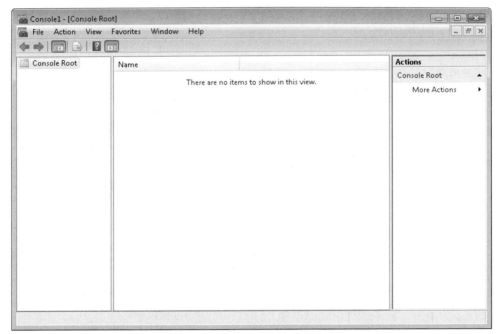

Figure C-4 An empty console document in MMC looks much like an empty document in other applications—mostly white.

MMC is a multiple-document-interface (MDI) application (the Console Root window is a child window), although most of the consoles supplied with Windows do their best to disguise this fact. You can create consoles with multiple child windows, and those windows can be maximized, minimized, restored, resized, moved, cascaded, and tiled, all within the confines of the main MMC window.

Displaying the Console Tree

If the console tree is not visible in the application you're creating or modifying, choose Customize View from the View menu. In the Customize View dialog box (see Figure C-3), select the Console Tree check box. Alternatively, if the standard toolbar is displayed, click the Show/Hide Console Tree button.

Adding Snap-Ins and Extensions

The contents of a console can consist of a single snap-in, or you can craft a hierarchically organized, completely personalized, everything-but-the-kitchen-sink management tool. To add a snap-in to your application:

1. Choose File, Add/Remove Snap-In (or press Ctrl+M) to display the dialog box shown in Figure C-5.

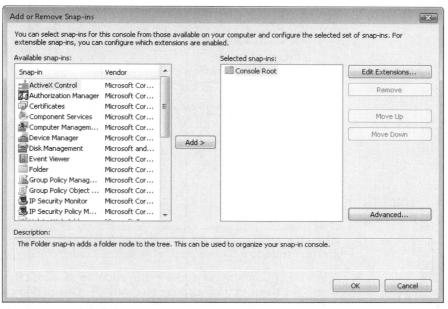

Figure C-5 By default, MMC snap-ins are arranged in a single-level list.

2. If you want a multilevel console tree, click Advanced, select Allow Changing The Parent Snap-In and then click OK.

3. In the Parent Snap-In list, select the parent of the new snap-in. The parent can be Console Root or a folder or snap-in that you've already added. (In a brand new MMC application, your only choice is Console Root.)

4. In the Available Snap-Ins list, select the snap-in you want and click Add.

If the selected snap-in supports remote management, a dialog box similar to the one shown in Figure C-6 on the next page appears.

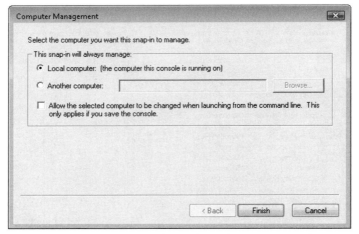

Figure C-6 Some snap-ins can be configured to manage another computer on your network. In this dialog box, specify which computer you want to manage.

5. Select Local Computer to manage the computer on which the console runs, or supply the name of the computer you want to manage. Some snap-ins that allow remote management let you specify the target computer at run time by means of a command-line switch; select the check box to enable this option. For details about the command-line switch, see "Running a Console and Specifying a Target Computer." Then click Finish.

Some snap-ins come with optional extensions. You can think of these as snap-ins for snap-ins—modules that provide additional functionality to the selected snap-in. Some snap-ins comprise many extensions, and you can optionally select which ones you want to enable or disable. Figure C-7 shows the extensions that are part of the Computer Management snap-in.

6. To modify the extensions to a snap-in, select the snap-in in the Selected Snap-Ins list in the Add Or Remove Snap-Ins dialog box, and then click Edit Extensions. Select which extensions you want to use. Click OK.

7. Repeat steps 3 through 6 to add more snap-ins. Click OK when you're finished.

8. If you added one or more folders as containers for other snap-ins, in the console tree, right-click the new folder, choose Rename, and supply a meaningful name.

Table C-2 lists the available snap-ins included with a base installation of Windows Vista.

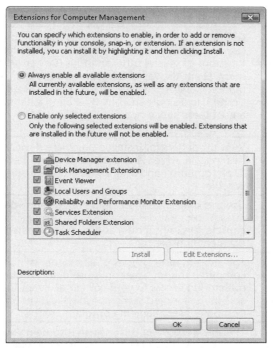

Figure C-7 With some snap-ins, such as Computer Management, you can selectively hide their component extensions.

Table C-2. Available MMC Snap-Ins

Snap-In Name	Description
ActiveX Control	Select this option to add a previously installed ActiveX control as a snap-in, with the Details pane showing the output of the control. The list of available controls includes all installed ActiveX controls, not just those visible within Internet Explorer. Few ActiveX controls are suitable for use in an MMC console, making this option useful mostly to developers.
Authorization Manager	This snap-in allows you to set role-based permissions for Authorization Manager–enabled programs. (These programs rely on a security architecture introduced with Windows 2003 Server, but is also available for Windows 2000 and Windows XP. Such programs rely on the .NET Framework.)
Certificates	Using this snap-in, you can view currently installed security certificates for the current user, a service account, or a computer.
Component Services	This snap-in, also primarily intended for developers, allows you to view and manage settings for programs that use COM+ and DCOM to communicate with the operating system and with each other.

Snap-In Name	Description
Computer Management	Use the assortment of tools in this snap-in to manage system settings, storage, and services. It conveniently incorporates the functions of several other snap-ins (Device Manager, Disk Management, Event Viewer, Local Users and Groups, Reliability and Performance Monitor, Services, Shared Folders, Task Scheduler, and WMI Control) in a single snap-in. By editing extensions, you can disable any of these subcomponents that you don't want to include in your console.
Device Manager	View properties for installed hardware devices and drivers using this snap-in, which is also available in the Device Manager console (Devmgmt.msc) and as one node in the Computer Management console.
Disk Management	Use this snap-in to manage partitions and volumes on local hard disks. You can also gain access to the snap-in via its own saved console (Diskmgmt.msc) and as one node in the Computer Management console.
Event Viewer	This snap-in displays logs of all manner of happenings on your computer; this information is useful for troubleshooting and for monitoring access to your computer. Event Viewer is also available in its standard saved console file (Eventvwr.msc) or from the Computer Management console.
Folder	The sole purpose of this snap-in is to help you organize consoles that contain multiple snap-ins. By using folders to arrange complex consoles, you can simplify their use.
Group Policy Management	This snap-in is used for managing Group Policy on Active Directory networks. With it, you can back up, restore, copy, and import group policy objects across sites, domains, and organizational units. The snap-in is included only in Business, Enterprise, and Ultimate editions of Windows Vista.
Group Policy Object Editor	This is perhaps the most powerful and most misunderstood of all MMC snap-ins. Although Group Policy is most often used to administer Windows domains, you can also use it to control hundreds of settings on a standalone computer running Windows Vista. Group Policy Object Editor is included only in Business, Enterprise, and Ultimate editions of Windows Vista.
IP Security Monitor	If you've enabled Internet Protocol Security (IPsec), you can monitor the status of your secure connections using this snap-in.
IP Security Policy Management	With the help of this snap-in, you can configure IPsec, which enables you to carry on secure communications over standard internet connections. The snap-in provides a series of wizards for creating and configuring policies, although this feature remains complex and confusing.

Snap-In Name	Description
Link To Web Address	This snap-in allows you to display an HTML page in a console. When you add the snap-in, a wizard asks you to specify the path to a page that's stored on your computer or network or the URL to an internet resource. MMC displays the page in the Details pane when you select the link in the console tree.
Local Users And Groups	Manage user accounts and security groups on a single computer using this snap-in, which provides a range of features not accessible through the simplified User Accounts Control Panel option in Windows Vista, as we explain in "Advanced Account Setup Options," page 11xx. Although this snap-in is included in all Windows Vista editions, it's apparently aimed solely at business users; it produces an error message if you try to access the user account database on a computer running Home Basic or Home Premium.
NAP Client Configuration	Use this snap-in to create, configure, and manage client computer health policies for Network Access Protection (NAP), a system for preventing unhealthy computers (such as one that's infected by a virus or doesn't have up-to-date operating system components) from accessing your network. NAP requires server components running on Windows Server "Longhorn."
Print Management	The Print Management snap-in provides a single place to manage your network's printers and print servers, including shared printers on your own computer. For more information, see "Sharing a Printer," Chapter 14. The snap-in is included only in Business, Enterprise, and Ultimate editions of Windows Vista.
Reliability And Performance Monitor	Use this snap-in to display a battery of performance data counters, trace event logs, and performance alerts. For more information about this extremely useful tool, see Chapter 21, "Tuning Up and Monitoring Performance and Reliability."
Reliability Monitor	This snap-in displays graphically an assessment of your system's reliability based on the number of failures and other factors. Reliability Monitor provides a historical record of software installation and removal as well as failures, making it a useful troubleshooting tool. For details, see "Monitoring System Reliability," Chapter 21.
Resultant Set Of Policy	Use this fairly esoteric snap-in to view policies that have been applied to a particular computer and to predict what their effect will be on a specific user. It's useful for identifying conflicts in group policy set at local and domain levels. The snap-in is included only in Business, Enterprise, and Ultimate editions of Windows Vista.
Security Configuration And Analysis	This snap-in allows you to use security template files to apply consistent security policies to computers and users.
Security Templates	Use this snap-in to edit security templates used with the Security Configuration And Analysis snap-in.

Appendix C

Snap-In Name	Description
Services	Using this snap-in, you can start, stop, and configure services running on a local or remote computer. Most users access these tools using the Services console (Services.msc) or the Services And Applications node in the Computer Management console.
Shared Folders	With the help of this snap-in, you can view and manage shared folders, monitor current sessions, and see which network users have opened files on a local or remote computer. For more information, see "Managing Shared Folders," in Chapter 13.
Task Scheduler	This snap-in provides a place to view, create, and manage scheduled tasks. For details, see "Scheduling Tasks to Run Automatically," Chapter 29.
TPM Management	This snap-in configures Trusted Platform Module (TPM) security hardware. TPM hardware, which is incorporated on the motherboard of some computers, provides a method for managing cryptographic keys in a way that makes it virtually impossible for an unauthorized user (or thief) to decrypt information stored on the computer.
Windows Firewall With Advanced Security	This snap-in provides a much richer set of tools for configuring and monitoring Windows Firewall than is available through Control Panel. For information about using this snap-in, see "Blocking Intruders with Windows Firewall," Chapter 10.
WMI Control	Windows Management Instrumentation (WMI) is an essential system service that allows remote and local monitoring of hardware and software. In theory, you can control and configure WMI settings using this snap-in; in practice, no user-configurable options are available on a default installation of Windows.

Adding Taskpad Views

A *taskpad* is a customized page that appears within the Details pane of a snap-in. With it, you can create icons that encapsulate menu commands, command strings, scripts, URLs, and shortcuts to Favorites items. Navigational tabs at the bottom of a taskpad view make it easy for a user to switch between the taskpad view and a normal view of the same data. You can suppress these tabs (by means of the Customize View dialog box) if you don't want to give your console's users this freedom. Figure C-8 shows the beginnings of a taskpad view that provides quick access to commonly used features.

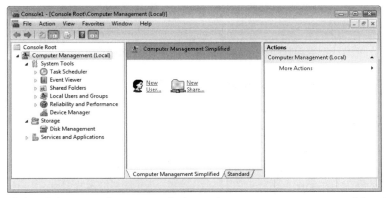

Figure C-8 In one of numerous display options, you can create a consolidated taskpad view that includes icons for performing actions that otherwise would require navigation throughout the console.

To create a taskpad view, start by selecting an item in the console tree to which you want to apply the view. As you'll see, when you create your taskpad view, you have the option of applying it only to the selected console-tree item or to all items at the same outline level.

Next, right-click the selected console-tree entry and choose New Taskpad View from the shortcut menu. The New Taskpad View wizard appears. The sample table at the right side of the wizard's second page makes the options pretty self-explanatory. The default choices work well in most situations.

The default selections in the wizard's third screen apply the new taskpad view to all comparable console-tree items and make the taskpad the default view for those items. Moving on from this screen, you have the opportunity to assign a name and some descriptive text to the new view.

In the wizard's final screen, select Add New Tasks To This Taskpad After The Wizard Closes if you want to create one or more task shortcuts. This selection summons a new wizard that walks you through the process of creating your first shortcut. On the final page of this wizard, select When I Click Finish, Run This Wizard Again if you have additional shortcuts to create.

Managing Windows

With the New Window From Here command on the Action menu, you can create a new child window rooted on the current console-tree selection. You might want to use this command to create multiple-window applications. After you've created your windows, you can use Window menu commands to tile or cascade them.

You can also use the New Window From Here command to remove the Console Root item that appears atop your default console tree:

1. Select the first item below Console Root.

2. Open the Action menu and click New Window From Here (or right-click and choose it from the shortcut menu).

3. Close the original window (the one with Console Root).

Controlling Other Display Elements

The Customize View command on the View menu allows you to hide or display various elements of the MMC visual scene, including taskbars, menus, and the navigational tabs that appear below taskpad views. Note that selections in the Customize View dialog box (see Figure C-3) take effect immediately—you don't need to hit an Apply button or leave the dialog box. Therefore, you can easily try each option and see whether you like it.

INSIDE OUT   **Customize views when the View menu is hidden**

When you clear the Standard Menus check box, the View menu disappears and, along with it, your access to the Customize View dialog box. In other words, once you hide the standard menus, there's apparently no way to get them back or to make other view changes. Don't despair; a back door exists. Click the icon at the left end of the menu bar; the menu that opens includes a Customize View command. (Even this back door is shut if you run the console in User mode and the console author cleared the Allow The User To Customize Views check box in the Options dialog box.)

Using the Favorites Menu

The Favorites menu allows you to store pointers to places within your console tree. If you create a particularly complex MMC console, you might want to consider using Favorites to simplify navigation. To add a console-tree item to your list of favorites, select that item and then choose Add To Favorites from the Favorites menu.

Naming Your Console

To assign a name to your console, choose File, Options. Your entry in the field at the top of the Console tab in the Options dialog box will appear on the title bar of your console, regardless of the file name you apply to its .msc file. If you do not make an entry here, MMC replaces Console1 with the console's eventual file name. Click Change Icon to select an icon for the console. You can select an icon from any DLL or executable file.

> **Note**
> You can rename Console Root (or any other folder in the console tree) by right-clicking it and choosing Rename.

Restricting User Control of Your Console

In the Console Mode list on the Console tab of the Options dialog box (choose File, Options), you can select among MMC's three User modes. In any of these modes, users can't add or remove snap-ins, modify taskpad views, or make other changes to the console. The difference among the modes is how much of the console tree they're able to see and whether they can open new windows.

- **User Mode—Full Access** Users have full access to the console tree and can open new windows, using either the New Window From Here or Window, New Window command. (Changes to the window arrangement can't be saved in User mode, however.)

- **User Mode—Limited Access, Multiple Window** Users have access only to parts of the console tree that are visible. (For example, if you create a hierarchically organized console, open a new window from a node below the console root, and then close the console root window before saving, users will be unable to reach the console root and other nodes at or above the level at which the new window was opened.) Users can open new windows with the New Window From Here command, but the New Window command (which would provide access to the console root) does not appear on the Window menu.

- **User Mode—Limited Access, Single Window** In this most restrictive mode, users have access only to parts of the console tree that are visible. MMC operates in single-window mode, essentially losing its MDI character; users can't open new document windows, nor can they resize the single document window.

If you choose one of the three User modes, the two check boxes at the bottom of the Options dialog box become available. Your choices are as follows:

- **Do Not Save Changes To This Console** With this check box cleared (its default), MMC saves the state of your application automatically when a user closes it. The user's selection in the console tree, for example, is preserved from one use to the next. If you always want your users to see the same thing each time they run the console, select this check box.

- **Allow The User To Customize Views** This check box, selected by default, keeps the Customize View command available, allowing your users, for example, to hide or display the console tree. Clear the check box if you want to deny users access to this option.

Saving a Console

The final step in the process of creating an MMC console is, of course, to save the file. Choose File, Save As, enter a file name in the Save As dialog box, and choose a location (the default location is the Administrative Tools folder in the Start Menu\Programs folder for your profile). Click Save. The resulting console file is saved with the .msc extension.

INSIDE OUT   **Find your saved console**

By default, Administrative Tools doesn't appear anywhere on the Start menu. To further confuse matters, Administrative Tools in Control Panel is merely a collection of shortcuts to various tools, but your saved console does not appear in Control Panel\System And Maintenance\Administrative Tools unless you explicitly place a shortcut there.

If you choose to save your console in Start Menu\Programs\Administrative Tools—the default location—you'll want to customize the Start menu to include it. Right-click the Start button, choose Properties, and click Customize on the Start Menu tab. In the dialog box that appears, select one of the options for displaying Administrative Tools. Alternatively, create a shortcut to your console in a folder of your choice or, more simply, find it by typing its name in the Start menu Search box.

CAUTION

If you want to create a console that can be used with earlier versions of Windows as well as Windows Vista, create it in that version—not in Windows Vista. Although MMC in Windows Vista can use consoles created in MMC versions 1.2 and 2.0 (the versions that came with Windows 2000 and Windows XP, respectively), those earlier versions cannot use consoles created in version 3.0 (the Windows Vista version). In Windows Vista, if you have opened a console that was created using an earlier version and then attempt to save it, MMC asks whether you want to save it in MMC 3.0 format. If you choose Yes, MMC saves the file in a format that can be used only with MMC 3.0. If you choose No, MMC does not save the file in a downlevel format; instead, it doesn't save the file at all. In other words, your only option in Windows Vista is to save an MMC console that works only with Windows Vista.

APPENDIX D

Viewing System Information

Home Basic ●
Home Premium ●
Business ●
Enterprise ●
Ultimate ●

Whether it's for troubleshooting purposes or just out of curiosity, you'll occasionally need to find out more about your computer system: what kind of hardware you have, what software is installed, and so on. This appendix provides an overview of the tools included with Windows Vista for displaying information about your system.

The utilities we describe in this chapter are not the only ones you can use to gather information about your system. Elsewhere in this book, we discuss Task Manager, the Reliability And Performance Monitor, the Services console, and other utilities you can use for troubleshooting and diagnostic purposes. This chapter focuses exclusively on those tools that are related to the interaction between Windows and your system hardware.

What's in Your Edition?

All the tools and utilities described in this appendix are available in all editions of Windows Vista.

Finding Basic Information About Your Computer

For answers to basic questions about your operating system and computer, there's no better place to start than the System Control Panel, shown in Figure D-1 on the next page. No matter where you are in Windows or what your preferred input method is, this display is only a few clicks or keystrokes away. You can open System in any of the following ways:

- Press the Windows logo key+Break.

- Right-click Computer and choose Properties. (This works just about any place that the Computer shortcut appears, including on the Start menu, on the desktop, in the Folders pane of Windows Explorer, and in a Windows Explorer window. It does not work in the Favorite Links pane of Windows Explorer.)

- In Control Panel, open System (in the System And Maintenance category).

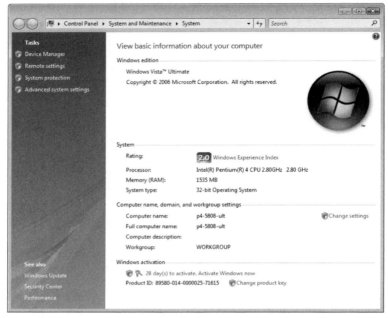

Figure D-1 The System application in Control Panel provides basic details about your computer's configuration.

The System application displays the Windows edition currently running, system details (including processor type, installed memory, and whether the current operating system is a 32-bit or 64-bit version), details about the computer name and domain or workgroup, and the current activation status.

Links scattered around the dialog box lead to additional sources of information. Two in particular are worth noting here:

- Click Device Manager in the Tasks pane along the left side of the dialog box to view detailed information about your installed hardware, including information about drivers, as shown in Figure D-1. You can open Device Manager directly, without first passing through System, by typing **devmgmt.msc** at a command prompt.

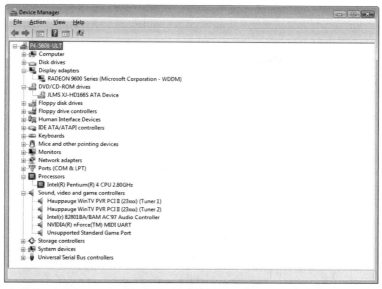

Figure D-2 Device Manager is a Microsoft Management Console (MMC) snap-in that lists installed devices.

For details about how to use the information displayed in Device Manager, see Chapter 5, "Setting Up and Troubleshooting Hardware."

INSIDE OUT   Use Computer Management

The Device Manager snap-in is included in the Computer Management console, along with a number of other useful snap-ins. You can open Computer Management in any of the following ways:

- Right-click Computer and choose Manage.
- In Administrative Tools (on the Start menu or in Control Panel), open Computer Management.
- At a command prompt, type **compmgmt.msc**.

- Click Windows Experience Index to show a numeric breakdown of the five components that make up the base score shown in the System window. Click View And Print Details to display a more detailed (but still not exhaustive) inventory of system components—motherboard and processor, storage, graphics, and network hardware.

Knowing the numeric Experience Index rating for each subsystem is an important first step in improving system performance, as we explain in Chapter 21, "Tuning Up and Monitoring Performance and Reliability."

Digging Deeper with Dedicated System Information Tools

For the most exhaustive inventory of system configuration details in a no-frills text format, Windows offers two tools with similar names, Systeminfo and System Information.

- **Systeminfo** Systeminfo.exe is a command-line utility that displays information about your Windows version, BIOS, processor, memory, network configuration, and a few more esoteric items. Figure D-3 shows sample output.

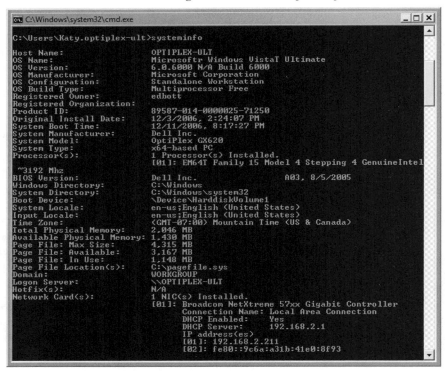

Figure D-3 The command-line utility Systeminfo.exe provides an easy way to gather information on all your network computers in a single database.

To run Systeminfo, open a Command Prompt window, type **systeminfo**, and press Enter. In addition to the list format shown in the figure, Systeminfo offers two formats that are useful if you want to work with the information in another program: Table (fixed-width columns) and CSV (comma-separated values). To use one of these formats, append the /Fo switch to the command, along with the Table or Csv parameter. You'll also need to redirect the output to a file. For example, to store comma-delimited information in a file named Info.csv, enter the following command:

```
systeminfo /fo csv > info.csv
```

The /S switch allows you to get system information about another computer on your network. (If your user name and password don't match that of an account on the target computer, you'll also need to use the /U and /P switches to provide the user name and password of an authorized account.) When you've gathered information about all the computers on your network, you can import the file you created into a spreadsheet or database program for tracking and analysis. The following command appends information about a computer named Badlands to the original file you created.

```
systeminfo /s badlands /fo csv >> info.csv
```

- **System Information**   System Information—often called by the name of its executable, Msinfo32.exe—is a techie's paradise. It provides all manner of information about your system's hardware and software in a no-frills window that includes search capabilities. The following sections discuss System Information in greater detail.

INSIDE OUT   Try a third-party utility

In addition to the tools included with Windows Vista, you can choose from a wide array of third-party utilities that poke around inside your computer to uncover details about installed hardware and software. Two tools that we recommend are the Belarc Advisor (*http://www.vista-io.com/3501*) and Sandra 2007 (*http://www.vista-io.com/3502*).

The system information utilities in Windows Vista identify Intel processors using their technical names, which consist of a family, a model, and a stepping. For help translating those details into the names of specific processors, use the Intel Processor Identification Utility, available at *http://www.vista-io.com/3503*.

Appendix D

Finding and Decoding Information in System Information

System Information displays a wealth of configuration information in a clear display, as shown in Figure D-4 on the next page. You can search for specific information, save information, view information about other computers, and even view a list of changes to your system.

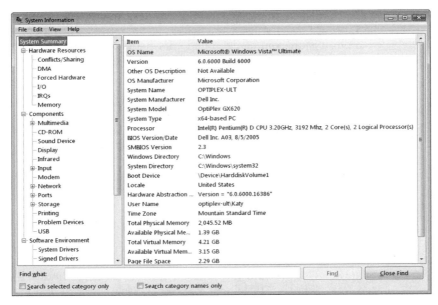

Figure D-4 System Information is for viewing configuration information only; you can't use it to actually configure settings.

To start System Information, use any of the following methods:

- In the Run dialog box, type **msinfo32**.

- In a Command Prompt window, type **start msinfo32**.

- Click Start and choose All Programs, Accessories, System Tools, System Information.

- In the About dialog box of many applications, including Microsoft Office applications, click System Info. (To reach this dialog box in Office 2003 programs, click Help, About. In Office 2007 programs, click the Microsoft Office button, click the Options button at the bottom of the Office menu, click Resources, and finally, click About.)

You navigate through System Information much as you would through Windows Explorer or an MMC console: Click a category in the left pane to view its contents in the right pane. Table D-1 provides a summary of available information in System Information. Because the tool is *extensible*—which means that other programs can provide information about themselves in a format that can be displayed in System Information—you might see additional categories and additional information on your system.

Table D-1. Information Available in Msinfo32.exe

Category	Description
System Summary	Information similar to that provided by Systeminfo.exe: Windows version, computer name, computer make and model, processor, BIOS version and date, memory summary.
Hardware Resources	Information about shared system resources, such as I/O ports and IRQs; device conflicts; DMA channels in use; devices with manually specified resources instead of system-assigned resources; I/O ports in use; IRQs in use; and memory addresses used by devices.
Components	Information about each installed hardware device, including resources used and device descriptions, drivers, and current status.
Software Environment	Information about drivers, environment variables, open print jobs, mapped network connections, running tasks, loaded system-level DLLs, services, Start menu program groups, programs that run at startup, file associations for OLE objects, and reported errors in Windows and Windows applications.
Applications	Application-specific information that can be added to System Information by your installed programs; Office, for example, lists detailed information about everything from file versions to installed fonts to default page layout settings.

To search for specific information, use the Find What box at the bottom of the System Information window. (If the Find bar is not visible, choose Edit, Hide Find.) The Find feature is basic but effective. A couple of things you should know:

- Whenever you type in the Find What box to start a new search, Find begins its search at the top of the search range (the entire namespace unless you select Search Selected Category Only)—not at the current highlight.

- Selecting Search Category Names Only causes the Find feature to look only in the left pane. When this check box is cleared, all text in both panes is searched.

Exporting System Information

You can preserve your configuration information—always helpful when reconstructing a system—in several ways:

- Save the information as an .nfo file. You can subsequently open the file (on the same computer or on a different computer with System Information) to view your saved information. To save information in this format, choose File, Save. Saving this way always saves the entire collection of information.

- Save all or part of the information as a plain text file. To save information as a text file, select the category of interest and choose File, Export. To save all the information as a text file, select System Summary before you save.

- You can print all or part of the information. Select the category of interest, choose File, Print, and be sure that Selection is selected under Page Range. To print everything, select All under Page Range—and be sure to have lots of paper on hand. Depending on your system configuration and the number of installed applications, your report could top 100 pages.

Regardless of how you save your information, System Information refreshes (updates) the information immediately before processing the command.

INSIDE OUT   Save your system information periodically

Saving system configuration information when your computer is working properly can turn out to be very useful when you have problems. Comparing your computer's current configuration with a known, good baseline configuration can help you spot possible problem areas. You can open multiple instances of System Information, so that you could have the current configuration displayed in one window and a baseline configuration displayed in another.

About the Authors

Ed Bott is a best-selling author and award-winning technology journalist who has been covering the personal computer industry since the days when an 8-MHz 80286 was a smokin' machine. Ed's feature stories and columns about Microsoft Windows have appeared regularly in print and on the web for more than 15 years, and he has written books on nearly every version of Microsoft Windows (including *Microsoft Windows XP Inside Out*) and Microsoft Office—so many, in fact, that he's lost count of the exact number. Ed is a three-time winner of the Computer Press Award and a two-time recipient of the Jesse H. Neal award from American Business Press. *Microsoft Windows Security Inside Out for Windows XP and Windows 2000*, which he coauthored with Carl Siechert, earned the Award of Merit from the Society for Technical Communication in 2003. You can read Ed's latest writings at Ed Bott's Windows Expertise (*http://www.edbott.com/weblog*) and Ed Bott's Microsoft Report (*http://blogs.zdnet.com/bott*). Ed and his wife Judy live in New Mexico.

Carl Siechert began his writing career at age eight as editor of the *Mesita Road News*, a neighborhood newsletter that reached a peak worldwide circulation of 43 during its eight-year run. Following several years as an estimator and production manager in a commercial printing business, Carl returned to writing with the formation of Siechert & Wood Professional Documentation, a Pasadena, California firm that specializes in writing and producing product documentation for the personal computer industry. Carl is a coauthor of over a dozen books published by Microsoft Press, including *Field Guide to MS-DOS 6.2*, *Microsoft Windows 2000 Professional Expert Companion*, and *Microsoft Windows XP Networking and Security Inside Out*. In a convergence of new and old technology, Carl's company now operates a popular website for hobby machinists, *http://www.littlemachineshop.com*. Carl hiked the Pacific Crest Trail from Mexico to Canada in 1977 and would rather be hiking right now. He and his wife Jan live in southern California.

Craig Stinson, an industry journalist since 1981, was editor of *Softalk for the IBM Personal Computer,* one of the earliest IBM-PC magazines. Craig is the author of *Running Microsoft Windows 98* and a coauthor of *Microsoft Windows XP Inside Out, Microsoft Excel Inside Out* and *Running Microsoft Windows 2000 Professional*, all published by Microsoft Press. Craig is an amateur musician and has reviewed classical music for various newspapers and trade publications, including *Billboard*, the *Boston Globe*, the *Christian Science Monitor*, and *Musical America*. He lives with his wife and children in Bloomington, Indiana.

The authors have set up a website for readers of this book. At the site, you can find updates, corrections, links to other resources, and more useful tips. In addition, you can discuss Windows Vista with the authors and with other readers. We hope you'll join us at *http://www.vista-io.com*.

Index

Looking for something?
Use the included CD, which contains the full text of this book in searchable format.

Looking for something?
Use the included CD, which contains the full text of this book in searchable format.

Looking for something?
Use the included CD, which contains the full text of this book in searchable format.

Looking for something?
Use the included CD, which contains the full text of this book in searchable format.

Looking for something?
Use the included CD, which contains the full text of this book in searchable format.

Looking for something?
Use the included CD, which contains the full text of this book in searchable format.

Looking for something?
Use the included CD, which contains the full text of this book in searchable format.

Looking for something?
Use the included CD, which contains the full text of this book in searchable format.

Looking for something?
Use the included CD, which contains the full text of this book in searchable format.

Looking for something?

Use the included CD, which contains the full text of this book in searchable format.

Looking for something?
Use the included CD, which contains the full text of this book in searchable format.

Looking for something?
Use the included CD, which contains the full text of this book in searchable format.

Looking for something?
Use the included CD, which contains the full text of this book in searchable format.

Looking for something?
Use the included CD, which contains the full text of this book in searchable format.

Looking for something?
Use the included CD, which contains the full text of this book in searchable format.

Looking for something?
Use the included CD, which contains the full text of this book in searchable format.

Looking for something?
Use the included CD, which contains the full text of this book in searchable format.

Looking for something?
Use the included CD, which contains the full text of this book in searchable format.

Additional Resources for Home and Business

Breakthrough Windows Vista™: Find Your Favorite Features and Discover the Possibilities
Joli Ballew and Sally Slack
ISBN 9780735623620

Jump in for the topics or features that interest you most! This colorful guide brings Windows Vista to life—from setting up your new system; accessing the Windows Vista Sidebar; customizing it for your favorite gadgets; recording live television with Media Center; organizing photos, music, and videos; making movies; and more.

So That's How! 2007 Microsoft® Office System: Timesavers, Breakthroughs, & Everyday Genius
Evan Archilla and Tiffany Songvilay
ISBN 9780735622746

From vanquishing an overstuffed inbox to breezing through complex spreadsheets, discover smarter ways to do everyday things with Microsoft Office. Based on a popular course delivered to more than 70,000 students, this guide delivers the tips and revelations that help you work more effectively with Microsoft Office Outlook®, Excel®, Word, and other programs. Also includes 'webinars' on CD.

Look Both Ways: Help Protect Your Family on the Internet
Linda Criddle
ISBN 9780735623477

You look both ways before crossing the street. Now, learn the new rules of the road—and help protect yourself online with Internet child-safety authority Linda Criddle. Using real-life examples, Linda teaches the simple steps you and your family can take to help avoid Internet dangers—and still enjoy your time online.

The Microsoft Crabby Office Lady Tells It Like It Is: Secrets to Surviving Office Life
Annik Stahl
ISBN 9780735622722

From cubicle to corner office, learn the secrets for getting more done on the job—so you can really enjoy your time off the job! The Crabby Office Lady shares her no-nonsense advice for succeeding at work, as well as tricks for using Microsoft Office programs to help simplify your life. She'll give you the straight scoop—so pay attention!

Microsoft Office Excel 2007: Data Analysis and Business Modeling
Wayne L. Winston
ISBN 9780735623965

Beyond Bullet Points: Using Microsoft Office PowerPoint® 2007 to Create Presentations That Inform, Motivate, and Inspire
Cliff Atkinson
ISBN 9780735623873

Take Back Your Life! Using Microsoft Office Outlook 2007 to Get Organized and Stay Organized
Sally McGhee
ISBN 9780735623439

See more resources at **microsoft.com/mspress**
and **microsoft.com/learning**

Microsoft Press® products are available worldwide wherever quality computer books are sold. For more information, contact your bookseller, computer retailer, software reseller, or local Microsoft Sales Office, or visit our Web site at **microsoft.com/mspress**. To locate a source near you, or to order directly, call 1-800-MSPRESS in the United States. (In Canada, call **1-800-268-2222**.)

What do you think of this book?

We want to hear from you!

Do you have a few minutes to participate in a brief online survey?

Microsoft is interested in hearing your feedback so we can continually improve our books and learning resources for you.

To participate in our survey, please visit:

www.microsoft.com/learning/booksurvey/

...and enter this book's ISBN-10 number (appears above barcode on back cover*).
As a thank-you to survey participants in the United States and Canada, each month we'll randomly select five respondents to win one of five $100 gift certificates from a leading online merchant. At the conclusion of the survey, you can enter the drawing by providing your e-mail address, which will be used for prize notification only.

Thanks in advance for your input. Your opinion counts!

* Where to find the ISBN-10 on back cover

ISBN-13: 000-0-0000-00000-0
ISBN-10: 0-0000-00000-0

00000

0 000000 000000

Example only. Each book has unique ISBN.

***Microsoft**
Press